*To Terri and Kylie*

# Technical Editor

**Eoghan Casey** is founding partner of cmdLabs, author of the foundational book *Digital Evidence and Computer Crime*, and coauthor of *Malware Forensics*. For over a decade, he has dedicated himself to advancing the practice of incident handling and digital forensics. He helps client organizations handle security breaches and analyzes digital evidence in a wide range of investigations, including network intrusions with an international scope. He has testified in civil and criminal cases, and he has submitted expert reports and prepared trial exhibits for computer forensic and cyber-crime cases.

Eoghan has performed thousands of forensic acquisitions and examinations, including e-mail and file servers, mobile devices, backup tapes, database systems, and network logs. He has performed vulnerability assessments; deployed and maintained intrusion detection systems, firewalls, and public key infrastructures; and developed policies, procedures, and educational programs for a variety of organizations. In addition, he conducts research and teaches graduate students at Johns Hopkins University Information Security Institute, is editor of the *Handbook of Digital Forensics and Investigation*, and is Editor-in-Chief of Elsevier's *International Journal of Digital Investigation*.

# Author

**Harlan Carvey** (CISSP), author of the acclaimed *Windows Forensics and Incident Recovery*, is a computer forensics and incident response consultant based out of the Northern VA/Metro DC area. He currently provides emergency incident response and computer forensic analysis services to clients throughout the U.S. His specialties include focusing specifically on the Windows 2000 and later platforms with regard to incident response, Registry and memory analysis, and post mortem computer forensic analysis. Harlan's background includes positions as a consultant performing vulnerability assessments and penetration tests and as a full-time security engineer. He also has supported federal government agencies with incident response and computer forensic services.

# Technical Reviewers

**Troy Larson** is a Senior Forensic Engineer in Microsoft's Network Security team, where he enjoys analyzing Microsoft's newest technologies in a constant race to keep forensics practice current with Microsoft technology. Troy is a frequent speaker on forensics issues involving Windows and Office, and he is currently focused on developing forensic techniques for Vista and Office 2007. Prior to joining Microsoft's forensics team, Troy served tours of duty with Ernst & Young's national forensics practice and Attenex, Inc. Troy is a member of the Washington State Bar and received his undergraduate and law degrees from the University of California at Berkeley.

**Rob Lee** is an information security and forensic consultant providing services to Fortune 500 organizations and the U.S. government. Rob has over 13 years' experience in computer forensics, vulnerability discovery, intrusion detection, and incident response. Rob graduated the U.S. Air Force Academy and served in the U.S. Air Force as a founding member of the 609th Information Warfare Squadron, the first U.S. military operational unit focused on information operations. Later, he was a member of the Air Force Office of Special Investigations, where he conducted computer crime investigations and computer forensics. Prior to his current consultation job, he worked on contracts for a variety of government agencies, where he was the technical lead for a vulnerability discovery team, a contractor lead for a cyber forensics branch, and a leader of a security software development team. Rob is also a fellow and forensic curriculum chair for the SANS Institute. Rob has personally trained more than 8,000 forensic and incident response professionals over nine years. Rob also coauthored the bestselling book, *Know Your Enemy, 2nd Edition*. In addition to working as a security consultant and at the SANS Institute, Rob has just finished his MBA at Georgetown University in Washington, D.C.

**Lance Mueller** (CISSP, GCIH, GREM, EnCE, CFCE, CCE) is the co-owner of BitSec Forensics, Inc., and he conducts computer forensic investigations worldwide. Additionally, Lance teaches computer forensics to local, state, and federal law enforcement officers worldwide. Lance's background includes 15 years in law enforcement, where he was assigned to a computer forensic task force performing computer forensic examinations; he also conducted complex intrusion investigations. Lance continues to serve as a senior consultant to the U.S. Department of State, Bureau of Diplomatic Security Office of Africa, South America, and South East Asia consulting with international law enforcement agencies and government institutions so that they can acquire the skills needed to detect, prevent, and investigate incidents related to cyber terrorism and cyber crime.

# Contents

# Preface

The purpose of this book, as was with the first edition, is to address a need. An issue that many incident responders and computer forensic examiners have seen is that there is an overreliance on what forensic analysis tools purist procedures are telling us, without really understanding where this information is coming from or how it is being created or derived. The "Age of Nintendo Forensics," i.e., of loading an acquired image into a forensic analysis application and pushing a button, is *over*. As analysts and examiners, we can no longer expect to investigate a case in such a manner. Cybercrime has increased in sophistication, and investigators need to understand what artifacts are available on a system, as well as how those artifacts are created and modified. With this level of knowledge, we come to understand that the absence of an artifact is itself an artifact. In addition, more and more presentations and material are available regarding anti-forensics, or techniques used to make forensic analysis more difficult. Not only that, there have been presentations at major conferences that discuss anti-forensic techniques, of using the responder or examiner's training and tools against them. This book is intended to address the need for a more detailed, granular level of understanding. Its purpose is not only to demonstrate what information is available to the investigator on both a live Windows system as well as in an acquired image but also to provide information on how to go about locating additional artifacts that may be of interest, and correlating multiple data sources to build a more complete picture of the incident.

My primary reason for writing this book has been so that I can give back to a community and field of endeavor that has given so much to me. Since I became involved in the information security field over 12 years ago (prior to that, I was in the military and involved in physical and communications security), I've met a lot of great people and done a lot of really interesting things. Over time, people have shared things with me that have been extremely helpful, and some of those things have served as stepping stones into further research. Some of that research has found its way into presentations I've given at various conferences, and from there, others have asked questions and provided insight and answers that have helped push that research forward. The repeated exchange of information and engagement in discussion have moved both the interest and the level of knowledge forward, advancing the field. This is my attempt to give back, and in doing so, expand the field a little bit more.

This book is intended to address the technical aspects of collecting and analyzing data during both live and postmortem investigations of Windows systems. This book does not cover everything that could possibly be addressed. There is still considerable room for research in several areas, and a great deal of information needs to be catalogued. My hope is that this book will awaken the reader to the possibilities and opportunities that exist within Windows systems for a more comprehensive investigation and analysis.

# Intended Audience

This book focuses on a fairly narrow technical area—Windows incident response and forensic analysis—but it's intended for anyone who does, might do, or is thinking about performing forensic analysis of Windows systems. This book will be a useful reference for many, and my hope is that any readers who initially feel that the book is over their heads or beyond their technical reach will use some of the material they find as a starting point and a basis for questions and further study. When I started writing the first edition of this book, it was not intended to be a second or follow-on edition to my first book, *Windows Forensics and Incident Recovery*, published by Addison-Wesley in July, 2004. Rather, my intention was to move away from a more general focus and provide a resource for not only myself but also others working in the computer forensic analysis field. This second edition was written to continue in this vein, particularly in light of the fact that Microsoft keeps developing and releasing new versions of the Windows operating system, each subsequent version with its own unique twists and nuances.

In writing this book, my goal was to provide a resource for forensic analysts, investigators, and incident responders. My hope is to provide not only useful material for those currently performing forensic investigations but also insight to system administrators who have been faced with incident response activities and have been left wondering, "What should I have done?" On that front, my hope is that we can eventually move away from the misconception that wiping the hard drive and reinstalling the operating system from clean media is an acceptable resolution to an incident. Even updating the patches on the system does not address configuration issues, and in many cases, will result in reinfection or the system being compromised all over again.

This book is intended for *anyone* interested in performing incident response and forensic analysis of Windows systems—corporate or government investigators, students or instructors of any of the burgeoning curricula that have sprung up in recent years, law enforcement officers, or corporate consultants (such as myself). My hope is that this book will also serve as a useful reference for those either developing or attending computer forensic programs at colleges and universities.

Throughout this book, the terms *investigator, first responder, examiner,* and *administrator* are used interchangeably. This is due to the fact that in many cases, the same person may be wearing all of these hats. In other cases, the investigator may come into the corporate infrastructure and work very closely with the administrator, even to the point of obtaining an Administrator level account within the domain in order to perform data collection. In some cases, the administrator may escort the investigator or first responder to a compromised system, and the user account may have Administrator privileges on that system. Please don't be confused by the use of the terms, as they are synonymous in most cases.

Reading through this book, you'll likely notice a couple of things. First, there is a heavy reliance on Perl as a scripting language. There's nothing magical about this choice—Perl is simply a very flexible, powerful scripting language that I like to use because I can make changes to the code and run it immediately without having to recompile the program. Speaking of compiling, I should mention that if you're not familiar with Perl and have never used it, you don't have anything to worry about. With only a few exceptions, the Perl scripts presented in the book and provided on the accompanying DVD have been "compiled" into stand-alone Windows executables using Perl2Exe. This will allow you to run the Perl scripts without having to install Perl (the version of Perl used throughout this book is freely available from ActiveState.com) or anything else. Simply extract the necessary files from the location or archive on the DVD and run them. Another useful feature of Perl is that with some care, Perl scripts can be written to be platform independent. Many of the Perl scripts included on the DVD perform data extraction (and to some degree, analysis) from binary files, and where possible, I have tried to make them as platform independent as possible. What this means is that although the Perl script (and the accompanying Windows executable) will run on the Windows platform, the Perl script itself can be run on Linux or even Mac OS X. Many of the Perl scripts on the DVD (although admittedly not all) have been tested and run successfully within the Perl environment on Linux. What this means is that the examiner is not restricted to any particular analysis platform. Some of the scripts will require the installation of additional modules, which can be done via the Perl Package Manager (PPM) application that is part of the ActiveState distribution of Perl, which is available for Windows, Linux, Mac OS X, and a number of other platforms. Another very useful aspect of using Perl is to meet the needs of automation. Many times, I find myself doing the same sorts of things (data extraction, translation of binary data into something human-readable, etc.) over and over again, and like most folks, I'm bound to make mistakes at some point. However, if I can take a task and automate it in Perl, I can write the code once, and not have to be concerned with making a mistake the second, twentieth, or two-hundredth time I perform that same task. It's easy to correct a process if you actually have a process. I find it extremely difficult to correct what I did if I don't know what it was that I did!

Second, you'll notice that the forensic analysis application used throughout this book is ProDiscover Incident Response Edition, from Technology Pathways. Thanks to Chris Brown's generosity, I have worked with ProDiscover since Version 3 (Version 5 was available at the time that the book was being written) and have found the interface to be extremely intuitive and easy to navigate. When it comes to examining images acquired from Windows systems, ProDiscover is an excellent tool to use (albeit not the only one), and it has many useful and powerful features. Chris and Alex Augustin have been extremely responsive to questions and updates, and Ted Augustin (all three of whom are with Technology Pathways) has been an excellent resource when I've met him at conferences and had a chance to speak with him. Not only is ProDiscover itself an excellent analysis platform, but the Incident Response Edition has made great strides into the live response arena, providing an easy and effective means for collecting volatile data. Also, in my opinion, Chris made an excellent decision in choosing Perl as the scripting language for ProDiscover, allowing the investigator to perform functions (e.g., searches, data extraction, a modicum of data analysis, etc.) within the image via Perl "ProScripts." The accompanying DVD contains several ProScripts that I've written and used quite regularly during examinations (please note that although the ProScripts are Perl scripts, they are not "compiled" with Perl2Exe, as the ProScripts must be scripts to be used with ProDiscover).

Another useful and powerful utility that is mentioned in several locations within the book is F-Response. In 2008, Matthew Shannon, through his own efforts, ushered in a new era of incident response and the acquisition of data from live systems. F-Response can be used in three modes, the most powerful of which is the Enterprise Edition (EE). F-Response EE provides a single administrator or consultant with the capability to reach across a data center, across a city, or even between continents to access systems in a read-only mode. Matt has also provided a powerful management console that makes deploying F-Response EE easier than writing this paragraph. Once deployed, F-Response EE provides you with read-only (write operations are buffered and dropped) access not only to the hard drive(s) on the remote system but also to physical memory (or RAM), in a completely tool-agnostic manner. This means that you can use whichever tool you wish to access the resources now available to acquire an image of the hard drive, access physical memory, and so on. You're not restricted to using just one commercial application to do, well, anything.

# Organization of this Book

This book is organized into nine chapters following this preface. Those chapters are:

# Chapter 1: Live Response: Data Collection

This chapter addresses the basic issues of collecting volatile data from live systems. Because of several factors (an increase in sophistication of cybercrime, increases in storage capacity, etc.), live response has gained a great deal of interest, and responders are recognizing the need for live response more and more every day. This increase in interest has not been restricted to consultants such as me, either—law enforcement is beginning to see the need for collecting volatile information from live systems in order to support an investigation. This chapter lists tools and methodologies you can use to collect volatile information and presents the most recent incarnation of the Forensic Server Project.

# Chapter 2: Live Response: Data Analysis

I've separated data collection and data analysis, as I see them as two separate issues. In many cases, the data that you want to collect doesn't change, as you want to get a snapshot of the activity on the system at a point in time. However, how you go about interpreting that data is what may be important to your case. Also, it's not unusual to approach a scene and find that the initial incident report is only a symptom of what is really happening on the system or that it has nothing to do with the real issue at all. During live response, how you analyze the data you've collected, and what you look for, can depend on whether you're investigating a fraud case, an intrusion, or a malware infection. This chapter presents a framework for correlating and analyzing the data collected during live response in order to develop a cohesive picture of activity on the system and make analysis and identification of the root cause a bit easier and more understandable.

# Chapter 3: Windows Memory Analysis

Windows memory analysis is an area of study that has really taken off since its formal introduction to the community during the summer of 2005, and it really grew by leaps and bounds in 2008. In the past, if the contents of physical memory (i.e., RAM) were collected from a live system, they were searched for strings (i.e., potential passwords), IP and e-mail addresses, and then archived. Unfortunately, any information found in this manner had little context. Thanks to research that has been done since the DFRWS 2005 Memory Challenge, methods of obtaining RAM dumps have been investigated, and data within those RAM dumps can be identified and extracted on a much more granular level, even to the point of pulling an executable image out of the dump file. This chapter attempts to provide a snapshot of what tools are available for performing memory collection and analysis, demonstrating what data can be collected (e.g., Registry hives, encrypted passwords, etc.) from memory dumps.

# Chapter 4: Registry Analysis

The Windows Registry maintains a veritable plethora of information regarding the state of the system, and in many cases, the Registry itself can be treated like a log file, as the information that it maintains has a time stamp associated with it in some manner. However, because of the nature of how the data is stored, searches for ASCII or even Unicode strings do not reveal some of the most important and useful pieces of information. This chapter presents the structure of the Registry to the readers so that they'll be able to recognize Registry artifacts in binary data and unallocated space within an acquired image. The chapter then discusses various artifacts (Registry keys and values) at great length, describing their usefulness and value to an investigation, as well as presenting a number of tools for extracting that information from an acquired image. Other important factors discussed in this chapter include differences inherent to various versions of Windows (XP versus Vista, for example), the use of tools such as RegRipper to extract and correlate information from within hive files (including across Windows XP System Restore Points), and how to retrieve deleted Registry keys from unallocated space within hive files.

# Chapter 5: File Analysis

Windows systems maintain a number of log files that many examiners simply are not aware of, and those log files often maintain time-stamp information on the entries that are recorded. In addition, there are a number of files on Windows systems that maintain time-stamp information within the files themselves that can be incorporated into your timeline analysis of an event. Many of these time stamps are maintained by the application and are not immediately obvious. Various files, file formats, and file metadata are discussed in detail, and tools are presented for extracting much of the information that is discussed. Chapter 5 in this edition expands greatly on what was available in the first edition, including illustrating WFPCheck, an application to determine if files "protected" by the operating system were modified or infected (note that this application is illustrated, but is *not* provided on the media that accompanies this book).

# Chapter 6: Executable File Analysis

Executable files represent a special case when it comes to file analysis. For the most part, executable files follow a known and documented structure, as they need to be launched and run on various versions of Windows. However, malware authors have discovered ways to obfuscate the structure in order to make their malware more difficult (albeit not impossible) to analyze. By understanding the format of these files and what they *should* look like, examiners can go further in their investigations in determining which files are legitimate, in addition to what effect the suspicious files have on a Windows system. Using the techniques and information presented in this chapter, the examiner can determine which files are legitimate, as well as what artifacts to attribute to a particular piece of malware.

# Chapter 7: Rootkits and Rootkit Detection

This chapter addresses the topic of rootkits in the hopes of piercing the veil of mystery surrounding this particular type of malware and presenting the administrator, first responder, and forensic analyst (remember, these could all be the same person) with the necessary information to be able to locate and recognize a rootkit. Rootkits are seeing a surge in use, not only in cybercrime but also in "legitimate" commercial applications. An understanding of rootkits and rootkit detection technologies is paramount for anyone working with Windows systems, and this chapter presents a great deal of the information that an investigator will need. Many times, responders will be unable to quickly locate the source of some unusual behavior, and instead of following a thorough, rigorous investigative approach, will chalk it up to "a rootkit." By presenting this information about rootkits and exposing the "rootkit paradox," my hope is that responders and examiners will have the tools they need to determine truly if there is a rootkit or some sort of rootkit functionality involved in their incident.

# Chapter 8: Tying It All Together

It became clear following the release of the first edition of the book that many examiners were taking the information from one chapter, applying it, and then realizing that they were stuck over what to do next. I have seen or heard about this phenomenon from corporate consultants as well as law enforcement examiners. My goal for this chapter is to demonstrate how information from different areas of your examination—the file system, specific files, the Event Logs, and even the Registry—can be correlated and tied together to build a more complete picture, whether you're a law enforcement examiner attempting to disprove the "Trojan defense" or a corporate analyst or consultant attempting to determine if (and when) a system may have been compromised. As such, the chapter reads as a series of case studies or "war stories," I hope that I was able to illustrate, by these examples, how data from various locations within an examination (not just within an acquired image) can be used to corroborate other data and build a thorough examination.

# Chapter 9: Performing Analysis on a Budget

Sometimes, full-blown commercial forensic applications simply are not suitable for use in analysis. They may lack some needed functionality or the functionality you need may be far too cumbersome to get to. As such, the solution should not be to spend thousands of dollars on additional commercial applications when a freely available (or low-cost) tool will be more than sufficient. My goal for this chapter is to demonstrate that forensic analysis is about process, not about tools; remember, the Age of Nintendo forensics is over! Understanding where to look for data, and how to extract and interpret that data, allows an examiner to select the appropriate tool for the job. Many times, freeware tools can provide functionality that commercial tools cannot, and commercial tools can provide validation of findings originally derived from those freeware tools.

# DVD Contents

The DVD that accompanies this book contains a great deal of useful information and tools. All of the tools provided are grouped into the appropriate directory based on the chapter in which they were presented. The DVD also contains all of the tools that were provided in the first edition of the book, even those replaced by other tools. For example, all of the original scripts from Chapter 4 of the first edition are still provided on the DVD, even though they've been replaced by the RegRipper framework. In addition, there is a bonus directory containing several tools that were not specifically discussed in any chapter, but I developed them to meet a need that I had and thought that others might find them useful. This directory also contains a subdirectory titled "WFA_articles," which are a series of PDF documents that I developed to cover specific analysis topics. Each of the documents explains one aspect of analysis in detail; for example, one describes different locations within an image where an analyst might find information about the host system's media access control (MAC) address, while another describes the purpose of each ACMru subkey in detail. My intention in writing these articles was to provide a means for distributing training in specific analysis topics; by providing each topic in a PDF document, users can print and read (and annotate) these documents during travel or place them in a directory and search them when needed.

All of the tools available on the DVD are Perl scripts. However, almost all of the Perl scripts have been "compiled" into stand-alone Windows executables for ease of use. The Perl scripts themselves are, for the most part, platform independent and can be run on Windows, Linux, and even Mac OS X (note that there are some exceptions), and providing Windows executables simply makes them easier for those without Perl installed to use. Several of the chapters also contain ProScripts, which are Perl scripts specifically written to be used with the ProDiscover forensic analysis application from Technology Pathways (the current version available is 5.0). These Perl scripts are launched via ProDiscover and are not "compiled."

In addition, several of the chapter directories contain sample files that the reader can use to gain a familiarity with the tools. It's one thing to have a tool or utility and an explanation of its use, but it's quite another thing to actually use that tool to derive information. Having something immediately available to practice with means that readers can try out the tools anywhere they have a laptop, such as on a plane, and not have to wait until they're able to get copies of those files themselves.

Finally, I have included several movie files on the DVD that I use to explain certain topics. In the past, I wrote an appendix to explain the setup and use of the Forensic Server Project, but I've found that listening to podcasts and watching movies can be much more educational than reading something in a book.

*— Harlan Carvey*

# Author's Acknowledgments

First, I'd like to thank God for the many blessings He's given me in my life, for which I am immensely and eternally grateful. My life has been a continuous chain of His wondrous bounty since I accepted Jesus into my heart and my life.

I'd like to thank the true love and light of my life, Terri, and her beautiful daughter, Kylie, for their continued patience and understanding in supporting me while I wrote this second edition (as if the first one wasn't enough!), and what amounted to my fourth book. I know that I've left them both wondering as I've stared off into space, reasoning and turning over phrases in my mind as I attempted to put them down on "paper." It can't be easy for either of these two wonderful women to be living with a nerd, particularly one who enjoys being a nerd as much as I do.

A huge thank-you goes out to Eoghan Casey for agreeing to be the technical editor for this edition of the book and for putting forth the effort to do such a great job. One of the drawbacks of performing analysis or writing a book is that you often find yourself with your head deep down in the weeds, and when you poke your head up to take a look around, you often find yourself off track. At least, that's how things have gone for me, and Eoghan's done a great job of grounding my efforts with this book. My only regret is that there simply wasn't enough time to fully implement all of Eoghan's suggestions, several of which will be included in any future works.

I'd also like to thank a number of other people for their contributions to this effort. Brett Shavers and his son deserve special thanks for setting up RegRipper.net (and creating a logo for the site), as a showcase for RegRipper and its associated tools. Matt Shannon has been an inspiration to me since we met, not only for his ingenuity in producing F-Response but also for his outlook on life, approach to his business, and the insight and advice he's provided me. Aaron Walters is one of those really smart people who never cease to amaze me. He's one of those people you'd want to clone, just because, like Matt, he's smart and enthusiastic. There are just not enough hours in the day for either of them to do what they want to do. And what they want to do is amazing. Along with Aaron is Brendan "Moyix" Dolan-Gavitt, who is another one of those really smart people I had the pleasure of meeting in 2008.

After writing my first book, I couldn't write another without thanking Jennifer Kolde for everything she so patiently taught me through the painful editing process of *Windows Forensics and Incident Recovery*. I remember sending in an eight-page chapter for Jennifer to review, and by the time I got around to revising it, after many exchanges with Jennifer, all I could think to myself was, "Did I *really* write this? You've *got* to be kidding me!"

A great big thank-you goes to Rob Lee for being a champion, not only for things I've done but also for everything he's contributed to the community through his association with SANS. It was Rob, who in the spring of 2008, hit me with one of those, "hey, wouldn't it be cool if…" ideas that resulted in the *ripXP* tool (discussed in Chapter 4 of this book).

Maggi Grace Holbrook deserves a great big thank-you for all she's done for me—not just in listening, but actually using some of my tools and taking the time to really go out of her way to acknowledge my meager efforts. Early on, shortly after we met, Maggi Grace was kind enough to write a thank-you letter for me on department letterhead. In this community, it's not often that someone even attempts to say "thank you," and Maggi Grace gladly went above and beyond. This doesn't happen very often, but when it does, it is enormously appreciated.

I'd like to thank Jesse Kornblum for his many contributions to the field of computer forensic analysis, from his FRED disk to his hashing tools to the many papers that he's authored. I'd like to thank Cory Altheide, as he was the one who approached me with the idea of tracking artifacts left on Windows systems by the use of USB removable storage devices what seems like oh so many years ago. I'd like to thank Andreas Schuster for his many current and future contributions to the field, remembering his early contributions in the area of Windows memory analysis. Others who have contributed to the field, and hence this book, in one way or another include Lance Mueller, keeper of the *forensickb.com* blog; Don Lewis, Computer Forensic Analyst for the Lakewood, CO, Police Department; Jimmy Weg, Agent in Charge, Computer Crime Unit, Montana Division of Criminal Investigation; and Rich Cummings, CTO of HBGary, Inc., for allowing me to look at some of their tools.

# Chapter 1

# Live Response: Collecting Volatile Data

## Solutions in this chapter:

- **Live Response**
- **What Data to Collect**
- **Nonvolatile Information**
- **Live-Response Methodologies**

☑ **Summary**

☑ **Solutions Fast Track**

☑ **Frequently Asked Questions**

# Introduction

Investigators today are increasingly facing situations in which the traditional, widely accepted computer forensic methodology of unplugging the power to a computer and then acquiring a bit-stream image of the system hard drive via a write blocker is, simply, not a viable option. For instance, it is becoming more common for investigators to encounter servers that are critical to business operations and cannot be shut down. Investigators and incident responders are also seeing instances in which the questions they have (or are asked) cannot be answered using the contents of an imaged hard drive alone. For example, I've spoken with law enforcement officers regarding how best to handle situations involving missing children who were lured from their homes or schools via instant messages (IMs), particularly when faced with the fact that some IM applications do not write chat logs to disk, either at all or in their default configurations.

Questions such as these are not limited to law enforcement. In many cases, the best source of information or evidence is available in computer memory (network connections, contents of the IM client window, memory used by the IM client process, encryption keys and passwords, etc.). In other cases, investigators are asked whether a Trojan or some other form of malware was active on the system and whether sensitive information was copied off the system. Essentially, first responders and investigators are being asked questions regarding what activity was occurring on the system while it was live, and these questions cannot be answered when following the traditional, "purist" approach to digital forensics. Members of information technology (IT) staffs are finding anomalous or troubling traffic in their firewalls and intrusion detection system (IDS) logs, and are shutting off systems from which the traffic is originating before determining which process was responsible for the traffic. Situations such as these require that the investigator perform *live response*—collecting data from a system while it is still running. This in itself raises some issues, which we will address throughout this chapter.

Perhaps more important is that the requirement to perform some kind of live response is no longer something organizations decide to do. Instead, in some ways live response is being mandated by legislation as well as regulatory bodies (the Visa Payment Card Industry, or PCI, comes to mind). When a compromise occurs on a system, these regulatory bodies ask three basic questions:

- Was the system compromised?

- Did the compromised system contain "sensitive" data? (See the appropriate legislation or regulatory guidelines for the definition of "sensitive" data.)

- If the answer to both of the preceding questions is "yes", did the compromise of the system lead to the exposure of that sensitive data?

However, many organizations are simply unprepared for an incident, and as such, the activities of their responders can expose those organizations to greater risk than the incident itself, largely due to the fact that the "shut-the-system-off-and-wipe-it" mentality of many IT organizations does not allow for the collection of the necessary data to answer the inevitable questions. These questions invariably arise when the legal or compliance department of the organization hears about the incident, and then finds out that those questions cannot be answered.

# Live Response

Investigators today face a number of issues where unplugging a system (or several systems) and acquiring an image of the hard drive(s) might not be an option. As the use of e-commerce continues to grow, system downtime is measured in hundreds or thousands of dollars per minute, based on lost transactions. Therefore, taking a system down to acquire a hard-drive image has a serious effect on the bottom line. Also, some companies have service-level agreements (SLAs) guaranteeing "five nines" of uptime—that is, the company guarantees to its customers that the systems will be up and operational 99.999 percent of the time (outside of maintenance windows, of course). Taking a system with a single hard drive offline to perform imaging can take several hours, depending on the configuration of the system.

The Information Superhighway is no longer just a place for joy riders and pranksters. A great deal of serious crime takes place in cyberspace, and criminal activities are becoming increasingly sophisticated. Software programs can get into your computer system and steal your personal information (passwords, personal files, income tax returns, and the like), yet the code for some of these programs is never written to the hard drive; the programs exist only in memory. When the system is shut down, all evidence of the program disappears.

In April 2006, Seagate introduced the first 750GB hard drives. Today, I regularly see external hard drives available in sizes greater than 1.5 terabytes (TB), and I see multiterabyte storage systems on customer networks. Imagine a RAID 5 system with eight 1TB hard drives, topping out at 8 TB of storage. How long would it take you to image those hard drives? With certain configurations, it can take investigators four or more hours to acquire and verify a single 80GB hard drive. And would you need to image the entire system if you were interested in only the activities of a single process and not in the thousands of files resident on the system?

In some cases, we might want to collect some information about the live system before shutting it down, acquiring a bit-stream image of the hard drive or drives, and performing a more traditional computer forensic investigation. The information you would be most interested in is *volatile* in nature, meaning that it ceases to exist when power is removed from the system. This volatile information usually exists in physical memory, or RAM, and consists of such things as information regarding processes, network connections, the contents of the

Clipboard, and so on. This information describes the state of the system at the time you are standing in front of it or sitting at the console or accessing it remotely. As an investigator, you could be faced with a situation in which you must quickly capture and analyze (covered in the next chapter) data to determine the nature and scope of the incident. When power is removed from the system in preparation for imaging the hard drive in the traditional manner, this information simply disappears. However, you also need to keep in mind that any actions you take (e.g., running antivirus scans, searching for files or credit card data, reconfiguring the system, etc.) on a live system are going to leave artifacts of their own, and possibly will overwrite useful or pertinent data. Therefore, collecting and preserving this volatile data should be your first concern.

We do have options available to us—tools and techniques we can use to collect this volatile information from a live system, giving us a better overall picture of the state of the system as well as providing us with a greater scope of information. This is what "live response" entails: accessing a live, running system and collecting volatile (and in some cases, nonvolatile) information.

There is another term you might hear that is often confused with live response: *live acquisition*. Live response deals with collecting volatile information from a system; live acquisition describes acquiring the hard drive while the system is still running and creating an image of that hard drive. In this chapter, we'll start by discussing tools, techniques, and methodologies for performing live response. When we talk about performing live response, we need to understand *what* information we want to collect from the system and *how* we should go about collecting it. In this chapter, we will walk through the *what* and *how* of collecting volatile information from a system; in the next chapter, we will discuss how to analyze this data. Following that, we will examine some solutions for performing a live acquisition. Analysis of the image collected during live acquisition will be covered in the remaining chapters of this book.

Before we start discussing live-response tools and activities, we need to address two important topics: Locard's Exchange Principle and the order of volatility. These concepts are the cornerstones of this chapter and live response in general, and we will discuss them in detail.

# Locard's Exchange Principle

In performing live response, investigators and first responders need to keep a very important principle in mind. When we interact with a live system, whether as the user or as the investigator, changes will occur on that system. On a live system, changes will occur simply due to the passage of time, as processes work, as data is saved and deleted, as network connections time out or are created, and so on. Some changes happen when the system just sits there and runs. Changes also occur as the investigator runs programs on the system to collect information, volatile or otherwise. Running a program causes information to be loaded into physical memory, and in doing so, physical memory used by other, already running processes may be written to the page file. As the investigator collects information and sends it off the system, new network connections will be created. All of these changes can be collectively explained by *Locard's Exchange Principle*. Changes that occur to a system as the system itself apparently sits idle are referred to as "evidence dynamics" and are similar to rain washing away potential evidence at a crime scene.

In the early 20th century, Dr. Edmond Locard's work in the area of forensic science and crime scene reconstruction became known as Locard's Exchange Principle. This principle states, in essence, that when two objects come into contact, material is exchanged or transferred between them. If you watch the popular *CSI* crime show on TV, you'll invariably hear one of the crime scene investigators refer to *possible transfer*. This usually occurs after a scene in which a car hits something or when an investigator examines a body and locates material that seems out of place.

This same principle applies in the digital realm. For example, when two computers communicate via a network, information is exchanged between them. Information about one computer will appear in the process memory and/or log files on the other (see the "Locard and Netcat" sidebar for a really cool demonstration of this concept). When a peripheral such as a removable storage device (a thumb drive, an iPod, or the like) is attached to a Windows computer system, information about the device will remain resident on the computer. When an investigator interacts with a live system, changes will occur to that system as programs are executed and data is copied from the system. These changes might be transient (process memory, network connections) or permanent (log files, Registry entries).

## Tools & Traps...

### Locard and Netcat

You can use simple tools, such as netcat (http://en.wikipedia.org/wiki/Netcat), to demonstrate Locard's Exchange Principle. If you're not familiar with netcat (nc.exe on Windows systems), suffice it to say that netcat is an extremely versatile tool that allows you to read and write information across network connections.

For this example, you will need three tools: netcat (nc.exe), pmdump.exe (www.ntsecurity.nu/toolbox/pmdump/), and strings.exe (http://technet.microsoft.com/en-us/sysinternals/bb897439.aspx) or BinText (available from www.foundstone.com/us/resources/proddesc/bintext.htm). You can run this example using either one or two systems, but it works best when two systems are used. If you're using one system, create two directories, with a copy of netcat in each directory.

**Continued**

Start by launching netcat in listening mode with the following command line:

```
C:\test>nc -L -d -p 8080 -e cmd.exe
```

This command line tells netcat to listen on port 8080, in detached mode, and when a connection is made to launch the command prompt. Once you've typed in the command line and pressed **Enter**, open the Task Manager and note the process identifier (PID) of the process you just created. (Here I am using netcat Version 1.11 NT, which I retrieved from www.vulnwatch.org/netcat. At the time of this writing, the Web site does not appear to be available.)

Now open another command prompt on the same system, or go to your other system and open the command prompt. Type the following command line to connect to the netcat listener you just created:

```
C:\test2>nc <IP address> 8080
```

This command line tells netcat to open in client mode and to connect to the Internet Protocol (IP) address on port 8080, where our listener is waiting. If you're running the test on a single system, use 127.0.0.1 as the IP address.

Once you've connected, you should see the command prompt header that you normally see, showing the version of the operating system and the copyright information. Type a couple of commands at the prompt, such as **dir** or anything else, to simply send information across the connection.

On the system where the netcat listener is running, open another command prompt and use pmdump.exe (discussed later in this chapter) to obtain the contents of memory for the listener process:

```
C:\test>pmdump <PID> netcat1.log
```

This command will obtain the contents of memory used by the process and will put it into the file netcat1.log. You may also dump the process memory of the client side of the connection, if you like. Now that you have the process memory saved in a file, you can exit both processes. Run strings.exe against the memory file from the listener or open the file in BinText and you will see the IP address of the client. Doing the same thing with the client's memory file will display information about the system where the listener was running, demonstrating the concept of Locard's Exchange Principle.

Programs that we use to collect information might have other effects on a live system. For example, a program might need to read several Registry keys, and the paths to those keys will be read into memory. Windows XP systems perform application prefetching, so if the investigator runs a program that the user has already run on the system, the last access and modification times of the prefetch file (as well as the contents of the file itself) for that application will be modified. If the program that the investigator runs hasn't been used before, a new prefetch file will be created in the Prefetch directory (assuming the contents of the Prefetch directory haven't reached their 128 .pf file limit … but more on that later in the book).

Investigators not only need to understand that these changes will occur but also must document those changes and be able to explain the effects their actions had on the system, to a reasonable extent. For example, as an investigator you should be able to determine which .pf files in the XP Prefetch directory are a result of your efforts and which are the result of user activities. The same is true for Registry values. As with the application prefetching capabilities of Windows XP, your actions will have an effect on the system Registry. Specifically, entries may appear in the Registry, and as such the LastWrite times of the Registry keys will be updated. Some of these changes might not be a direct result of your tools or actions, but rather are made by the shell (i.e., Windows Explorer), due simply to the fact that the system is live and running.

By testing and understanding the tools you use, you will be able to document and explain what artifacts found on a system are the result of your efforts and which are the result of actions taken by a user or an attacker.

## TIP

When considering whether to engage in live-response activities it is very important to keep in mind that although your actions do have an effect on the system (processes loaded into memory, files created on the system as a result of your actions, etc.), so does your *inaction*. Think about it. A live system is running, with things going on all the time. Even while a system just sits there, processes are running and actions are occurring on the system. With Windows XP, simply wait 24 hours and a System Restore Point will be created automatically (by default). Wait three days and the system will conduct a limited defragmentation. Also consider the fact that if someone is exfiltrating data from your systems, while you wait and do nothing that person will continue to take more data. So, the question of whether to engage in live response really comes down to (a) do I do nothing, or (b) do I take the correct actions to protect my organization as best I can under the circumstances?

# Order of Volatility

We know that volatile information exists in memory on a live system and that certain types of volatile information can be, well, more volatile than others. That is, some information on a live system has a much shorter shelf life than other information. For instance, network connections time out, sometimes within several minutes, if they aren't used. You can see this by browsing to a specific site or making some other network connection and viewing that connection via netstat.exe. Then shut down the client application you're using and the state of the network connection will change over time before it eventually disappears from the output of netstat.exe. The system time, however, changes much more quickly, while the contents of the Clipboard will remain constant until either they are changed or power is removed from the system. Additionally, some processes, such as services (referred to as *daemons* in the UNIX realm) run for a long time, whereas other processes can be extremely short-lived, performing their tasks quickly before disappearing from memory. This would indicate that we need to collect certain information first so that we can capture it before it changes, whereas other volatile data that happens to be more persistent can be collected later.

A great place to go for this information is the Request for Comments (RFC) document 3227, "Guidelines for Evidence Collection and Archiving" (www.faqs.org/rfcs/rfc3227.html). This RFC, published in February 2002, remains pertinent today, since core guiding principles don't change as technologies change. The RFC specifies such principles for evidence collection as capturing as accurate a picture of the system as possible; keeping detailed notes; noting differences between UTC, local time, and system time; and minimizing changes to data as much as possible. We'll keep these principles in mind throughout our discussion of live response.

**T**IP

RFC 3227 points out that you should note the difference between the system clock and universal coordinated time (UTC), as well as take detailed notes in case you need to explain or justify your actions (the RFC says "testify"), even years later.

Of specific interest in this RFC document is Section 2.1, "Order of Volatility," which lists certain types of volatile information in order, from most to least volatile. Items that are apt to change or expire more quickly due to the passage of time (e.g., processes, network connections, etc.) should be collected first. By contrast, less volatile information, such as the physical configuration of the system, can be collected later. Using these guidelines, we can see what types of information we need to collect from a system, where to look for that information, what tools to use to retrieve it, and even how to get that information off the system, thereby minimizing the impact to the "victim" system while at the same time collecting the information we need to perform our analysis.

# When to Perform Live Response

Perhaps the most prominent question on the minds of investigators and first responders is "When should I consider live response?" In most instances today (e.g., criminal or civil cases, internal corporate investigations), no predefined set of conditions defines conditions for live response. In fact, in many situations, live response and, subsequently, volatile information isn't considered. The decision to perform live response depends on the situation, the environment (taking into consideration the investigator's intent, corporate policies, or applicable laws), and the nature of the issue with which you have been presented.

Let's look at a couple of examples. Say you've been contacted by a system administrator reporting some unusual network traffic. She received an alert from the IDS, and in checking the firewall logs she found some suspicious log entries that seemed to correlate with the IDS alerts. She says some odd traffic seems to be coming from one particular system that sits on the internal network. She already has the IDS alerts and network logs, but you decide to perform a more comprehensive capture of network traffic. In doing so, you realize that you have the network traffic information, but how do you associate it with a particular system? That's pretty easy, right? After all, you have the system's IP address (as either the source or the destination IP address in your network capture), and if you've also captured Ethernet frames, you also have the Media Access Control (MAC) address. But how do you then associate the traffic you see on the network with a particular user and/or process running on the system?

To definitively determine the source of the suspicious traffic (which process is generating it), you'd have to collect information about running processes and network connections from the system prior to shutting it down. Other information collected during live response might reveal that someone is logged in to the system remotely, via a network logon or a backdoor, or that a running process was launched as a Scheduled Task.

What other types of situations might suggest or even require a live response? How about the "Trojan defense," in which illicit activity is attributed to a Trojan or backdoor? In October 2002, Julian Green was found to have several (some reports stated more than 170) illicit images on his system. A forensic examination of his system found that his system had several Trojans that would access illicit sites whenever he launched his Web browser. He was found innocent of all charges.

The following year, Aaron Caffrey claimed that Trojans allowed others to control his computer and launch attacks against other systems, for which he'd been accused. Caffrey's defense argued that although no Trojan had been found on his system during a forensic examination, a Trojan *could* nevertheless have been responsible. His argument was sufficient to get him acquitted.

In cases such as these, hindsight tells us that it would have been beneficial to have some information about running processes and network connections collected at the time the systems were seized, particularly if they were running when the investigator arrived on the scene. This information might have told us whether any unusual processes were running at the time and whether anyone had connected to the system to control it and upload files, direct attacks against other systems, or the like.

Performing live response means you will be collecting information about the state of systems while they are running, which includes information about processes and the files they are accessing, as well as information about network connections originating from and terminating at the system and which processes are using those network connections. In fact, live response is the only way you will be able to obtain this information, as it all disappears when the system is shut off.

As discussed previously, another reason for performing live response is that the system itself cannot be taken down without good (and I mean *really good*) reason. On larger critical systems, such as those used in e-commerce, downtime is measured in lost transactions or hundreds (even thousands) of dollars per minute. As the process of acquiring an image from the hard drives (most systems of this nature use more than one hard drive, in a RAID configuration) can often take considerable time, it's preferable to have some solid facts to justify taking the system offline and out of service, if that is what is necessary. Doing so might not simply be a matter of a system administrator justifying these actions to an IT manager, but one of a CFO justifying them to the board of directors.

Yet another factor to consider is legislation requiring notification. Beginning with California's SB 1386, companies that suffer security breaches in which personally identifiable information (PII) has been compromised must notify their customers who are California residents so that those customers can protect themselves from identity theft. At the time of this writing, other states have begun to follow California's lead, and there is even talk of a federal notification law. This means companies that store and process sensitive information cannot simply remain silent about certain types of security breaches.

The term *sensitive data* really encompasses much more than what is defined in SB 1386; consider also California's CA 1298, which provides a definition for protected health information (PHI). And regulatory bodies such as the PCI Council provide definitions of "sensitive data," as well (PCI covers credit card data). Not only that, but these regulatory bodies mandate the requirement to protect the data in question and even define some steps for doing so; the PCI Data Security Standard (DSS) Version 1.1 has a requirement (12.9) for a Computer Security Incident Response Plan (CSIRP), as well as a requirement (12.9.2) that the plan be tested annually.

In addition, companies storing and processing sensitive data (regardless of the definition followed) are going to want to know definitively whether sensitive information has been compromised during a security breach, due to the fact that the legislative and regulatory mandates require organizations to notify the individuals whose data was exposed. In some cases, companies that are subject to a breach but are not able to definitively determine what specific data was taken may be required to notify their customers of all available data that may have been exposed. And in most cases, alerting customers that their personal information is now in the hands of some unknown individual (or, as could be the case, multiple unknown individuals) may have a significant, detrimental impact on the company. Customers could discontinue service and tell their friends and family in other states what happened. New customers might decide to sign up with a competitor. The loss of current and future revenue will change the face of the company and could lead to bankruptcy. So, why would a company simply suspect that it has been breached and has had sensitive data stolen and dutifully notify its customers? Wouldn't the company first want to know for sure that sensitive personal information about its customers has been compromised? Wouldn't you?

---

### Tools & Traps...

## Live Response and Sensitive Data

This is a trap that many organizations fall into, only they aren't aware of it until after they're in the trap. Frequently, organizations are simply unprepared for an incident, and in a few cases that I've seen, some organizations are prepared but their response processes were created by the IT department in complete isolation from any other department. As a result, malware is detected in an organization through some means, and the IT staff springs into action, locating and cleaning infected systems. At a meeting, someone mentions the work performed by the IT staff, and someone from the legal or compliance department hears about this and says, "These six infected systems were located in the area of the company that handles credit card data ... was any of that data compromised or exposed?"

Let's see; the IT staff identified each system, pulled them off the network, ran antivirus scans, perhaps connected to an isolated segment, and ran a complete Windows Update or simply wiped the drive and reloaded the operating system and as much of the user's data as possible. Was sensitive data on the system? In many cases, we can say "yes". Was the data compromised? At this point, we don't know and can't determine the answer to that question, simply because we have no data to analyze. All of the data we would have had disappeared when the system was shut off. In such cases, the IT department's response has exposed the organization to greater risk than the incident itself, as some regulatory bodies state that unless you can definitively state that sensitive data was *not* exposed, you must assume that it was, and therefore the organization would be obligated to report that all of the data was exposed.

---

Besides the "soft costs" of notification due to a data breach, such as losses due to a drop in customer confidence, consider also the "hard costs," those more quantifiable costs such as the actual costs of notifying customers of the exposure of their sensitive information, fines imposed by regulatory bodies, lawsuits brought on as a result of the exposure of the sensitive data, and so forth. Now, compare these to the "costs" associated with actually taking steps to protect the sensitive data stored and processed by your organization, which includes many of those things mandated by regulatory organizations, such as instituting and annually testing a CSIRP and being able to detect and respond to incidents. Part of this would include the ability to collect the necessary information, through live response, to determine what sensitive data, if any, may have been exposed.

Take, for example, an incident in which an "anonymous" individual on the Internet claims to have stolen sensitive information from an organization. This person claims that he broke into the organization over the Internet and was able to collect customer names, Social Security numbers, addresses, credit card data, and more. The organization's senior management will want to know whether this was, in fact, the case, and if so, how this person was able to do what he claimed he'd done. Investigators will need to perform live response and examine systems for volatile information, such as running processes and network connections. They might also be interested in locating malware that is present in memory but doesn't have any information (e.g., log files) or even so much as an executable image written to disk.

Yet another reason for performing live response is the use of this technique to triage an incident. Incident responders are faced not only with larger storage capacities to deal with, but also larger and more dispersed infrastructures. E-commerce application systems may no longer consist of servers in two or three racks in a single data center, but instead may comprise clusters, with the application cluster in one building and perhaps a database cluster in other building. Corporate connectivity no longer consists of a single network segment in a building; rather, some very simple networks span several blocks in a city or even between cities. As such, incident responders need a means by which they can sift through these systems and perform data reduction, determining and prioritizing affected systems. One way to do this is to use live-response techniques to locate artifacts pertinent to the incident, such as a file (or several files) on a system, a running service or process, a Registry key, and so forth. For example, Chapter 4 addresses the specific topic of Registry artifacts, which may be pertinent in an incident involving data theft in an organization. If the thief were found to have used a removable storage device such as an iPod, the entire infrastructure could be swept to determine every system to which that specific iPod had been connected, and when it had last been disconnected from any system. This single scan would greatly reduce the number of systems possibly affected by or involved in the incident from several thousand (or in some cases, several hundred thousand) to only those to which the thief had actually connected the device.

# What Data to Collect

At this point, we're ready to look at the types of volatile information we can expect to see on a live system, and learn about the tools we could use to collect that information during live response.

When you're performing live response, it's likely that one of the first things you'll want to collect is the contents of physical memory, or RAM. When you take Locard's Exchange Principle into account, it's pretty clear that by collecting the contents of RAM first, you minimize the impact you have on it. From that point on, you know that the other tools you run to collect other volatile information are going to be loaded into memory (as is the tool that you use to collect the contents of RAM), modifying the contents of memory.

We will discuss the topic of collecting and analyzing the contents of RAM in Chapter 3. Here is a list of the specific types of volatile information we'll look at in this chapter:

- System time
- Logged-on user(s)
- Open files
- Network information
- Network connections
- Process information
- Process-to-port mapping
- Process memory
- Network status
- Clipboard contents
- Service/driver information
- Command history
- Mapped drives
- Shares

For each of these types of volatile information, we will look at some tools that we can use to retrieve the information from a Windows system. You will most likely notice that throughout this chapter there is a tendency toward using command-line interface (CLI) tools over those with a graphical user interface (GUI). You might think that this is because CLI tools have a smaller "memory footprint," meaning that they consume less memory, rely on fewer dynamic link libraries (DLLs), and have less of an overall impact on the system. This is partially the case, but keep in mind that the actual "footprint" of any particular tool can be determined only through thorough testing of that tool. To date, I am not aware of any such testing being performed and made public.

> **WARNING**
>
> You should never make assumptions about a tool and its "memory footprint" when run on a system. Without thorough examination and testing (see Chapter 6 for information that pertains to examining executable files), you'll never know the kind of footprint an executable has on a system or the kinds of artifacts it leaves behind following its use.

The primary reason we focus on the use of CLI tools is that they are usually very simple, perform one basic, specific function, and are much easier to automate through the use of batch or script files. CLI tools can be bound together via batch files or scripting languages and their output is usually sent to the console (i.e., STDOUT) and can be redirected to a file or a socket. GUI tools, on the other hand, predominantly require you to save their output to a file, since they pretty much all have a File menu item with Save and Save As entries in the drop-down menu. Most programmers of GUI tools don't necessarily develop them with incident response or forensics in mind. One of our goals is to minimize the impact of our investigative measures on a system (particularly for follow-on imaging and forensic analysis activities), so we want to avoid writing files to the system, in addition to getting the data we need off the system as quickly and efficiently as possible.

Now, this is not to say that GUI tools absolutely cannot be used for live-response activities. If there's a GUI tool that you find absolutely perfect for what you need, then by all means, use it. But consider ahead of time how you're going to get that data off the system.

Regardless of the tools you decide to use, always be sure to check the license agreement before using them. Some tools can be used as you like, but others require a fee for use in a corporate environment. Reading and heeding these agreements in advance can help you avoid major headaches.

## System Time

One of the first pieces of information you want to collect when you're investigating an incident is the system time. This will give a great deal of context to the information collected later in the investigation, and will assist in developing an accurate timeline of events that have occurred on the system.

Figure 1.1 illustrates the most well-known means of displaying the system time.

**Figure 1.1** Displaying the System Date and Time on Windows XP

## Notes from the Underground…

### Getting the System Time

You can get the system time using a simple Perl script, such as:

```
print locatime(time)."\n";
```

This script displays the system time in local format, based on the time zone and daylight saving information that the system has set, but the time can also be displayed in GMT format using a script such as:

```
print gmtime(time)."\n";
```

The systime.pl Perl script located on the media that accompanies this book demonstrates how the system time can be retrieved using the Windows application program interface (API). The systime.exe file is a stand-alone executable compiled from the Perl script using Perl2Exe.

Another method for retrieving this information is to use Windows Management Instrumentation (WMI) to access the *Win32_OperatingSystem* class and display the *LocalDateTime* value.

Not only is the current system time important for the investigator, but the amount of time that the system has been running, or the *uptime*, can also provide a great deal of context to the investigation. For example, noting the amount of time the system has been running compared to the amount of time a process has been running can provide you with an idea of when an exploit or compromise attempt might have been successful (more on retrieving information about processes later in this chapter).

In addition, the investigator should also record the real time, or *wall time*, when recording the system time. Having both allows the investigator to later determine whether the system clock was inaccurate. Information about the "clock skew" provides a better understanding of the actual time at which events recorded in log files occurred. This information can be invaluable when you're trying to combine time stamps from more than one source.

Another piece of time-related information that could be important is the time zone settings for the computer. Windows systems using the NTFS file system store file times in Universal Coordinated Time, or UTC for short, which is analogous to Greenwich Mean Time (GMT) format. Systems using the FAT file system store file times based on the local system time. This is more important to keep in mind during postmortem analysis (discussed later in this book), but it can become extremely important when you're performing live response remotely, particularly across time zones.

## Tools & Traps…

### Tools and Licensing

Throughout this chapter, we're going to be discussing various tools that you can use for data collection from live systems. Some of these tools are native to the system, and others are third-party tools available on the Internet. In most cases, I try to provide links to where you can find those tools, but Web links come and go. One thing you need to be familiar with when using third-party tools are the licenses you agree to when you download the tool for use. Some license agreements state that you can use the tool all you want, unless you are a consultant and are using the tool in your capacity as a consultant. The tools available from Microsoft/Sysinternals have been updated over the past year or so to include a graphical end-user license agreement (EULA) dialog the first time you run the tool. This means that not only do you have to accept the EULA, but if you're running the tool in a batch file on a system on which you've never run that tool, you need to be sure to include the */accepteula* switch in the command line. If you don't, the batch file will hang. Also, when you accept the EULA, through either the dialog or the command-line switch, the tool will create a Registry key to record the fact that you accepted the EULA.

## Logged-on Users

During an investigation, you may want to know which users are logged on to the system. This includes people who are logged on locally (via the console or keyboard) as well as remotely (such as via the *net use* command or via a mapped share). This information allows you to add context to other information you collect from a system, such as the user context of a running process, or the owner or last access times of a file. This information is also useful to correlate against the Security Event Log, particularly if the appropriate auditing (auditing of logon and logoff events, etc.) has been enabled.

## PsLoggedOn

Perhaps the best-known tool for determining logged-on users is psloggedon.exe (http://technet.microsoft.com/en-us/sysinternals/bb897545.aspx). This tool shows the investigator the name of the user logged on locally (at the keyboard) as well as users who are logged on remotely, such as via a mapped share.

As shown in Figure 1.2, psloggedon.exe shows users logged on to the system remotely. To set up this demonstration, I logged in to a Windows 2000 system (Petra) from my Windows XP system and then ran the command on the Windows 2000 system.

**Figure 1.2** Output of psloggedon.exe on Windows 2000

```
Users logged on locally:
        10/13/2006 2:34:30 PM       PETRA\Administrator

Users logged on via resource shares:
        10/13/2006 2:36:26 PM       <null>\ADMINISTRATOR
```

## Net Sessions

The *net sessions* command is native to Windows systems (through the net.exe executable file), and you can use it to see not only the username used to access the system via a remote login session, but also the IP address and the type of client from which it is accessing the system. Figure 1.3 illustrates the output of the *net sessions* command run on a Windows 2003 system.

**Figure 1.3** Output of the *net sessions* Command on Windows 2003

```
Command Prompt                                                      _ □ ×

C:\tools>net sessions
Computer            User name        Client Type        Opens Idle time

\\192.168.1.25      ADMINISTRATOR    Windows 2002 Serv      0 00:02:06
\\192.168.1.28      ADMINISTRATOR    Windows 2002 Serv      0 00:01:49
The command completed successfully.
```

The *net sessions* output illustrated in Figure 1.3 shows two Windows XP systems logged in to a Windows 2003 system using the Administrator account. Neither session has any files open, but neither has been active for very long (as illustrated by the times listed in the "Idle time" column of the output).

# LogonSessions

Logonsessions.exe (http://technet.microsoft.com/en-us/sysinternals/bb896769.aspx) is a CLI tool available from Microsoft that lists all the active logon sessions on a system. Figure 1.4 illustrates a portion of the output of logonsessions.exe on a Windows XP system (the system name is Ender).

**Figure 1.4** Output of logonsessions.exe on Windows XP

```
[6] Logon session 00000000:000478c7:
    User name:      ENDER\Harlan
    Auth package:   NTLM
    Logon type:     Interactive
    Session:        0
    Sid:            S-1-5-21-1606980848-308236825-682003330-1004
    Logon time:     2/6/2006 4:19:42 PM
    Logon server:   ENDER
    DNS Domain:
    UPN:
      304:  C:\WINDOWS\system32\wscntfy.exe
     1372:  C:\WINDOWS\Explorer.EXE
     1828:  C:\Program Files\CyberLink\PowerDVD\DVDLauncher.exe
     1252:  C:\WINDOWS\BCMSMMSG.exe
      892:  C:\Program Files\Synaptics\SynTP\SynTPLpr.exe
      788:  C:\Program Files\Synaptics\SynTP\SynTPEnh.exe
     1000:  C:\WINDOWS\System32\spool\drivers\w32x86\3\hpztsb07.exe
     1016:  C:\Program Files\Viewpoint\Viewpoint Manager\ViewMgr.exe
     1932:  C:\Program Files\QuickTime\qttask.exe
      108:  C:\Program Files\Real\RealPlayer\RealPlay.exe
      552:  C:\Program Files\Mozilla Firefox\firefox.exe
```

Logonsessions.exe provides a great deal more information than the other tools, as illustrated in the output excerpt displayed in Figure 1.4. For example, it lists the authentication package used (it might be important to your investigation that the Kerberos authentication package was used instead of LAN Manager), type of logon, active processes, and so on.

**TIP**

The logonsess.txt file located in the \ch1\dat directory on the media that accompanies this book contains the output of logonsessions.exe from the Windows 2003 system illustrated in Figure 1.3.

Another useful utility you'll find handy is netusers.exe, a free utility from Somarsoft.com. Using the *–local* and *–history* switches with netusers.exe, you can retrieve a brief report of the last time all local users logged on to the system. The last logon time is maintained in the Registry; we'll discuss specifics of this Registry information in Chapter 4. Netusers.exe allows you to retrieve this information from a live system.

Keep in mind, however, that these tools will not show you whether someone is logged on via a backdoor. Backdoors and Trojans such as the infamous SubSeven allow users to "log in" to the Trojan via a raw Transmission Control Protocol (TCP) connection, bypassing the Windows authentication mechanisms. As such, these connections will not show up when you're using tools such as psloggedon.exe. Having the output of these tools, however, can be instrumental in showing that a user you discover later on did not show up in the list. It can also be used to demonstrate hidden functionality, even if the mechanism for that functionality is never found.

## Open Files

If the output of psloggedon.exe shows you that users are logged in to the system remotely, you will also want to see what files they have open, if any. Many times when a person accesses a system remotely, he might be looking for something specific and opening files. A user in a corporate environment could have a share available and allow other users to view images, download songs, and so on. Poorly protected Windows systems, such as Windows 2000 systems that are connected to the Internet with no Administrator password (and no firewall), can be "visited" and files searched for, accessed, and copied. The *net file* command, psfile.exe (http://technet.microsoft.com/en-us/sysinternals/bb896649.aspx), and the openfiles.exe (native to Windows XP Pro and Windows 2003) tools will all show files that are opened on a system via a remote connection.

## Network Information (Cached NetBIOS Name Table)

Sometimes when intruders gain remote access to a system, they want to know what other systems are available on the network and can be "seen" (in the network-centric sense) by the system they've compromised. I've seen this happen often in investigations, in a variety of ways; sometimes batch files have been created on the system and executed, and other times the intruder has launched *net view* commands via SQL injection (by using a browser to send commands to the system through the Web and database servers). When connections are made to other systems using NetBIOS communications (the same as are used for logins, connecting to shares, and the like), the systems will maintain a list of other systems they've "seen." By viewing the contents of the cached name table, you might be able to determine other systems that have been affected.

Let's look at an example. My home "network" consists of one laptop and several VMware sessions that appear as stand-alone systems on a virtual network. To demonstrate the caching of NetBIOS names, I started my Windows 2000 VMware session and logged in to view the IP address that was assigned via Dynamic Host Configuration Protocol (DHCP). I then went back to the host operating system (Windows XP Pro SP2), and in a command prompt I typed **nbtstat −A 192.168.1.22** to view the "remote" system's name table. I then typed **nbtstat −c** to view the cached NetBIOS names on the host operating system. Figure 1.5 shows what I saw.

**Figure 1.5** NetBIOS Name Table Cache

```
Wireless Network Connection:
Node IpAddress: [192.168.1.8] Scope Id: []

            NetBIOS Remote Cache Name Table

      Name              Type        Host Address      Life [sec]
    ---------------------------------------------------------------
    PETRA          <20>  UNIQUE         192.168.1.22          440
```

At this point, you might be thinking "So what? Why is this important?" Well, if I were an attacker and had gained access to one system, I might be interested in gaining access to other systems as well. To do so, I would need to see what systems are on the network and what vulnerabilities they have. Essentially, I'd be looking for easy targets. Now, if I were to start scanning for vulnerabilities, I might alert someone to what was going on. Also, to scan for vulnerabilities, I would need to copy my tools to the system I had already compromised, and that could alert someone to my activities. However, I can use nbtstat.exe to locate potentially vulnerable systems. For example, Figure 1.6 shows the output of the command I ran to populate the NetBIOS name cache.

**Figure 1.6** Output of *nbtstat −A 192.168.1.22*

```
Wireless Network Connection:
Node IpAddress: [192.168.1.8] Scope Id: []

          NetBIOS Remote Machine Name Table

      Name              Type         Status
    ---------------------------------------------------
    PETRA          <00>  UNIQUE      Registered
    PETRA          <20>  UNIQUE      Registered
    WORKGROUP      <00>  GROUP       Registered
    PETRA          <03>  UNIQUE      Registered
    WORKGROUP      <1E>  GROUP       Registered
    INet~Services  <1C>  GROUP       Registered
    IS~PETRA.......<00>  UNIQUE      Registered
    WORKGROUP      <1D>  UNIQUE      Registered
    ..__MSBROWSE__.<01>  GROUP       Registered
    ADMINISTRATOR  <03>  UNIQUE      Registered

    MAC Address = 00-0C-29-EC-6B-96
```

From the output of the *nbtstat* command displayed in Figure 1.6, we can see that the administrator is logged in, and we can see that the system is running the Internet Information Server (IIS) Web server. Penetration testers and attackers alike will use the information in the NetBIOS (http://en.wikipedia.org/wiki/NetBIOS) name table on any system they are able to compromise, to locate other vulnerable systems. Microsoft Knowledge Base articles 163409 (http://support.microsoft.com/kb/q163409) and 119495 (http://support.microsoft.com/kb/119495/EN-US) provide a great deal of information regarding the information available in the name table.

# Network Connections

As soon as possible after an incident is reported, the investigator should collect information regarding network connections to and from the affected system. This information can expire over time, and if too much time passes, it will be lost. An investigator might approach a system and, after an initial look, determine that the attacker is still logged in to and accessing the system. Or she could find that a worm or an Internet Relay Chat (IRC) bot (malicious software that, once installed on a system, makes an outbound connection to an IRC server to await commands) is communicating out from the system, searching for other systems to infect, updating itself, or logging in to a command and control server. This information can provide important clues and add context to other information that the investigator has collected. Not every system will have a firewall installed and even fewer will have a firewall configured to log successful connections into and out of the system. Nor will every system have an application such as Port Reporter (http://support.microsoft.com/kb/837243) installed to record and log network connection information. The investigator must be prepared to react quickly and collect the information she needs in an efficient, timely manner.

I've been involved in several cases where I have been provided with image files acquired from a system, and the client has asked, "Was sensitive data copied from the system?" Without at least some network-based information, the answer will invariably be "There's no way to tell." I have also been in numerous situations where having some information about network connections would greatly reduce what I have to look for, particularly when what alerted the client to the incident in the first place really had nothing to do with the compromise we ended up discovering. In one particular situation, a timeline analysis of the system image showed that the intruder was accessing the system via a backdoor at the same time that two different administrators were accessing the system to remediate two separate issues. Having information about network connections going to and from the system would have been extremely helpful in locating the core intrusion.

## Netstat

Netstat is perhaps the most well-known tool for collecting information regarding network connections on a Windows system. This CLI tool is straightforward and easy to use and provides a simple view of TCP and User Datagram Protocol (UDP) connections and their state, network traffic statistics, and the like. Netstat.exe is a native tool, meaning that it is provided as part of the operating system distribution.

The most common way to run netstat is with the *–ano* switches, which tell the program to display the TCP and UDP network connections, the listening ports, and the identifiers of the processes (the PIDs) using those network connections. Figure 1.7 illustrates the output of the *netstat –ano* command.

**Figure 1.7** Excerpt from the Output of
the *netstat –ano* Command on Windows XP

```
C:\>netstat -ano

Active Connections

  Proto  Local Address          Foreign Address        State           PID
  TCP    0.0.0.0:135            0.0.0.0:0              LISTENING       1344
  TCP    0.0.0.0:445            0.0.0.0:0              LISTENING       4
  TCP    127.0.0.1:1026         0.0.0.0:0              LISTENING       1992
  TCP    127.0.0.1:1031         127.0.0.1:1032         ESTABLISHED     2536
  TCP    127.0.0.1:1032         127.0.0.1:1031         ESTABLISHED     2536
  TCP    192.168.1.25:139       0.0.0.0:0              LISTENING       4
  TCP    192.168.1.25:1310      216.239.51.104:80      ESTABLISHED     2536
  TCP    192.168.1.25:1323      209.18.34.78:80        ESTABLISHED     2536
  TCP    192.168.1.25:1326      209.18.34.41:80        ESTABLISHED     2536
  TCP    192.168.1.25:1327      209.18.34.41:80        ESTABLISHED     2536
  TCP    192.168.37.1:139       0.0.0.0:0              LISTENING       4
  TCP    192.168.206.1:139      0.0.0.0:0              LISTENING       4
```

**TIP**

Under normal circumstances, Windows 2000 does not respond to the –o switch when running netstat.exe. However, Microsoft Knowledge Base article 907980 provides access to a hotfix that allows the version of netstat.exe on Windows 2000 to list the PID for the process that "owns" the network connection listed in the output.

The output of the *netstat –ano* command illustrated in Figure 1.7 shows the active network connections, the state of each connection, and, on the far right, the PIDs of the processes using the ports. What you're looking for in the output of netstat are any unusual connections. For example, it is not unusual on many user systems to see connections going out from a high client port to a remote system, connecting on port 80. The PID of the process using this connection will usually map back to a Web browser. However, the investigator can be easily fooled. I have investigated cases where the tool wget.exe was used to connect to remote systems on port 80 and download malware and hacker utilities. By themselves and without further scrutiny, these connections would look to the investigator (and to an IDS) like legitimate Web-surfing traffic.

**TIP**

Microsoft Knowledge Base article 137984 (http://support.microsoft.com/kb/ 137984) is older but provides descriptions of the states listed in the output of netstat.exe.

Using netstat with the −r switch will display the routing table and show you whether any persistent routes are enabled on the system. This could provide some very useful information to an investigator or even simply to an administrator troubleshooting a system. I've seen systems that have been set up to transfer files to another location as part of a business process, and the only way that process would work was if a persistent route was enabled on the system, since the persistent route redirected certain traffic out over a virtual private network (VPN) connection rather than through the normal routes out of the infrastructure. In troubleshooting an issue that really wasn't making much sense to me, I ran across a persistent route and told one of the system engineers about it. This information jogged his memory a bit, and we were able to track down and resolve the issue.

# Process Information

An investigator will *always* want to know what processes are running on a potentially compromised system. Note the word *always*. When viewing the running processes in the Task Manager, you can see some information about each process. However, during an investigation you will want to collect much more information that's not visible in the Task Manager. You will want:

- The full path to the executable image (.exe file)
- The command line used to launch the process, if any
- The amount of time that the process has been running
- The security/user context in which the process is running
- Which modules the process has loaded
- The memory contents of the process

The Task Manager view provides some of this information, but it does not provide everything. For instance, some malware installs itself under the name svchost.exe, which is the name of a legitimate process on Windows systems (see the "Svchost" sidebar). The executable image for this process is located in the system32 directory and is protected by Windows File Protection (WFP; see the "Windows File Protection" sidebar for more information). This means that as long as WFP is running and hasn't been tampered with, attempts to replace or modify a protected file will cause the new file to be automatically replaced by a "known good" copy from the cache and an Event Log entry to be generated.

Why is this important? If you're looking at the list of processes in the Task Manager, how are you going to tell which process is "suspicious"? An easy way to find suspicious processes is to view the full path to the executable image file (svchost.exe running from something other than C:\Windows\system32 is going to be suspicious) and/or the command line used to launch the process, as inetinfo.exe launched with the arguments *−L −d −p 80 −e cmd.exe* should be suspicious to most administrators and investigators; this command line indicates the use of netcat as a backdoor. Many bits of malware disguise themselves by using names of legitimate files. For example, the W32/Nachi worm places a copy of a Trivial File Transfer Protocol (TFTP) utility in the C:\Windows\system32\Wins directory and names it svchost. exe. When this program is running, there is no way in the Task Manager to really distinguish it from the legitimate version of svchost.exe.

## Are You Owned?

### Windows File Protection

Windows File Protection, or WFP, was added to Windows in Windows 2000 and is present in Windows XP and 2003 as well. In a nutshell, WFP "protects" critical system files from being modified or deleted accidentally. Assuming that the system hasn't been compromised to the point where WFP can be subverted, if an attempt is made to modify or delete a protected file the system will "wake up" and automatically replace that file with a known good copy from cache. An event ID of 64001 (http://support.microsoft.com/default.aspx?scid=kb;en-us;236995) is then generated and written to the Event Log.

Microsoft Knowledge Base article 222193 (http://support.microsoft.com/kb/222193/EN-US), titled "Description of the Windows File Protection feature," provides a more in-depth explanation of the feature along with various Registry keys associated with WFP.

Chapter 5 provides a more detailed discussion of WFP, a common method used to subvert it, and a means to detect whether the method has been used.

Now let's take a look at some tools you can use to view more detailed information about processes.

# Tlist

Tlist.exe, included as part of the Microsoft Debugging Tools (www.microsoft.com/whdc/ devtools/debugging/default.mspx), displays a good deal of information about running processes. For example, the *–v* switch will display the session identifier, PID, process name, associated services, and command line used to launch the process for the investigator, as follows:

```
0    344     svchost.exe      Svcs:    LmHosts,SSDPSRV,WebClient
        Command Line: C:\WINDOWS\System32\svchost.exe -k LocalService
```

Other switches will show this information in isolation. The *–c* switch will show just the command line used to launch each process, whereas the *–s* switch will show the associated services (or the window title, if no services are associated with the process). The *–t* switch will display the task tree, listing each process below its parent process, as follows:

```
System (4)
  smss.exe (628)
    csrss.exe (772)
    winlogon.exe (1056)
      services.exe (1100)
        svchost.exe (1296)
        svchost.exe (1344)
        svchost.exe (1688)
          wscntfy.exe (1184)
```

Tlist.exe also allows you to search for all processes that have a specific module loaded, using the *–m* switch. For example, wsock32.dll provides networking functionality and is described as the Windows Socket 32-Bit DLL. To list all the processes that have this module loaded, type the following command:

```
D:\tools>tlist -m wsock32.dll
```

This command returns the PID and name for each process, such as:

```
WSOCK32.dll - 1688 svchost.exe
wsock32.dll - 344 svchost.exe
WSOCK32.dll - 1992 alg.exe
WSOCK32.dll - 1956 explorer.exe      Program Manager
wsock32.dll - 452 ViewMgr.exe        AXTimer
WSOCK32.dll - 480 realplay.exe
```

# Tasklist

Tasklist.exe, a native utility included with Windows XP Pro and Windows 2003 installations (it is noticeably absent from Windows XP Home), is a replacement for tlist.exe. The differences in the two tools are subtle and mostly concern the name and the implementation of the switches. Tasklist.exe does provide options for output formatting, with choices among table, comma-separated value (CSV), and list formats. The /v (or *verbose*) switch provides the most information about the listed processes, including the image name (but not the full path), PID, name and number of the session for the process, status of the process, username of the context in which the process runs, and title of the window, if the process has a GUI. The investigator can also use the /svc switch to list the service information for each process.

# PsList

Pslist.exe (http://technet.microsoft.com/en-us/sysinternals/bb896682.aspx) displays basic information about running processes on a system, including the amount of time each process has been running (in both kernel and user modes). The −x switch displays details about the threads and memory used by each process. Pslist.exe launched with the −t switch will display a task tree in much the same manner as tlist.exe. Pslist.exe can also show detailed information about threads or memory used by a process. However, it does not provide information about a process in regard to the path to the executable image, the command line used to launch the process, or the user context in which the process runs.

# ListDLLs

Listdlls.exe (http://technet.microsoft.com/en-us/sysinternals/bb896656.aspx) shows the modules or DLLs a process is using. Listdlls.exe will show the full path to the image of the loaded module as well as whether the version of the DLL loaded in memory is different from that of the on-disk image. This information can be extremely important to an investigator because each program loads or "imports" certain DLLs. These DLLs provide the actual code that is used, so application developers don't have to rewrite common functions each time they write a new application. Each DLL makes certain functions available, listing them in their export table, and programs access these functions by listing the DLL and the functions in their import tables. This allows you to "see" (using an appropriate tool) which DLLs the program loads or accesses. However, some programs can load additional DLLs that are not part of the import table; for example, the Internet Explorer browser can load toolbars and browser helper objects for which the code is listed in DLLs. Spyware, Trojans, and even rootkits use a technique called *DLL injection* to load themselves into the memory space of a running process so that they will be running and executing but won't show up in a process listing because they are actually part of another process. This is different from a child process (as illustrated in the output of tlist.exe run with the −t switch) because the executing malware does not have its own PID.

Part of the output displayed by listdlls.exe includes the command line used to launch each process, excerpted as follows:

```
svchost.exe pid: 1292
Command line: C:\WINDOWS\system32\svchost -k DcomLaunch
```

Using listdlls.exe (with the −d dllname switch), you can also list the processes that have loaded a specific DLL, in a manner similar to tlist.exe. This can be extremely useful if you've identified a specific DLL and want to see whether any other processes have loaded it.

# Handle

Handle.exe (http://technet.microsoft.com/en-us/sysinternals/bb896655.aspx) shows the various handles that processes have open on a system. This applies not only to open file handles (for files and directories), but also to ports, Registry keys, and threads. This information can be useful for determining which resources a process accesses while it is running. Figure 1.8 illustrates an excerpt of the output from running handle.exe, without any switches, on a Windows XP SP2 system.

**Figure 1.8** Excerpt of Output of handle.exe

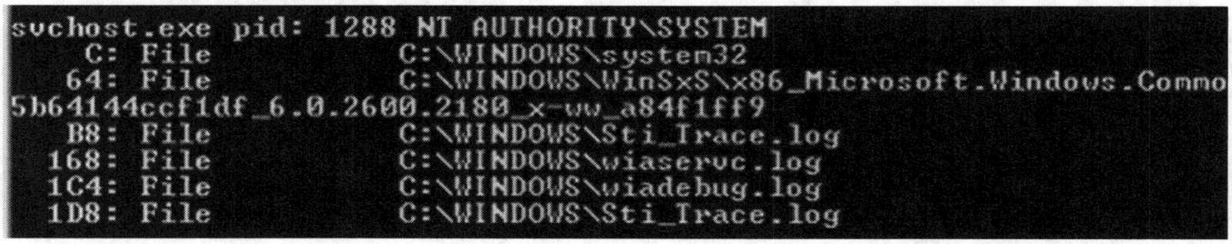

Figure 1.8 illustrates some of the handles opened by svchost.exe—in this case, several log files in the Windows directory. While I was writing this chapter, for example, one of the handles opened by winword.exe included the full path to the Microsoft Word document.

Handle.exe has several switches that could be of use, such as −a to show all handles and −u to show the owning username for each handle.

## Tools & Traps...

### Processes and WMI

The Perl script proc.pl, located in the \ch2\code directory on the accompanying media, illustrates how Perl can be used to implement WMI and retrieve process information via the *Win32_Process* class. Both the script and the stand-alone executable named proc.exe (compiled from the Perl script using Perl2Exe, also available on the accompanying media) display the PID and name of the process, the user context of the process, the PID of the parent process, the command line of the process (if available), the path to the executable image to the process (if available), and the service information for the process.

You can run both the script and the executable locally or against a remote system. Simply type the name of the executable to run it on a local system. The syntax to run the executable against a remote system is as follows:

```
C:\tools>proc <system> <user> <password>
```

An example of this would appear as follows:

```
C:\tools>proc WebSvr Administrator password
```

An excerpt of the output of proc.exe follows:

```
PID          : 668
Name         : spoolsv.exe
User         : NT AUTHORITY\SYSTEM
Parent PID   : 1100 [services.exe]
CmdLine      : C:\WINDOWS\system32\spoolsv.exe
Exe          : C:\WINDOWS\system32\spoolsv.exe
Services     : Spooler
```

You can easily modify the script to display its output in another format, such as CSV, which is suitable for opening and analyzing in a spreadsheet.

The procmon.pl Perl script (and the accompanying executable, procmon.exe) located in the same directory is an interesting demonstration of the use of WMI to monitor the creation of processes on the local system. Simply launch procmon.exe

**Continued**

from the command prompt, and while it is running it will report on the PID, user context, and executable path (and command line) of the new process, as illustrated in the following:

```
PID       USER          PROCESS
----      ----------    -------------------------------------------------
3208      Harlan        C:\WINDOWS\system32\cmd.exe
                        ("C:\WINDOWS\system32\cmd.exe")
1768      Harlan        C:\WINDOWS\system32\ping.exe (ping 192.168.1.1)
3100      Harlan        C:\WINDOWS\system32\sol.exe (sol)
```

Tools such as procmon.exe are extremely useful in that they can be used to augment auditing of process creation as well as provide insight into processes created during the installation of applications and malware.

It should be clear by now that no single tool or utility displays all the information you might want to know about processes that you find during an investigation. You might want to run only one tool for a quick overview (tlist.exe or tasklist.exe would be good candidates), or you might want to run more than one tool; for example, you could run pslist.exe with the −x switch and the listdlls.exe utility. Depending on the level of detail you need for your investigation, you might want to run handle.exe as well. The level of granularity of information that you want to obtain will depend on your investigation. We will discuss this topic in more detail later in this chapter as well as in Chapter 3, when we address issues of correlating and analyzing data.

## Tools & Traps…

### Svchost

Svchost is a process that appears often on Windows 2000, XP, and 2003 systems. It appears several times in the Task Manager, as many as two times (or more) on a default Windows 2000 system installation (with no other applications installed), five times on a Windows XP system, and seven times on a Windows 2003 system. Each instance of svchost.exe is running one or more services, as seen when you use *tasklist /svc* on Windows XP Pro and 2003 systems and *tlist −s* on Windows 2000 systems.

**Continued**

Microsoft Knowledge Base article Q314056 (http://support.microsoft.com/default. aspx?scid=kb;en-us;314056) provides more information regarding svchost.exe on Windows XP systems, and Knowledge Base article Q250320 (http://support.microsoft. com/default.aspx?scid=kb;en-us;250320) provides similar information with regard to Windows 2000.

In a nutshell, svchost.exe provides a generic process for running services from DLLs. Each instance of svchost can run one or more services. On startup, svchost reads the Registry key to obtain the groupings of services it should run:

```
HKEY_LOCAL_MACHINE\Software\Microsoft\Windows NT\CurrentVersion\Svchost
```

Note the space in "Windows NT". This is very important, as by default, there is no Software\Microsoft\WindowsNT key.

Several Trojans and backdoors try to copy themselves to the victim system using the filename svchost.exe. Backdoor.XTS and Backdoor.Litmus are examples of malware that attempt to hide themselves as svchost.exe, most likely due to the fact that administrators and investigators should not be surprised to see multiple copies of svchost listed in the Task Manager. On Windows systems, copying the bogus svchost.exe to the system32 directory proves to be just a plain bad idea, since the file is protected by WFP on Windows 2000, XP, and 2003.

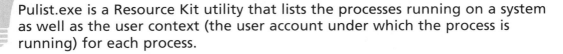

**TIP**

Pulist.exe is a Resource Kit utility that lists the processes running on a system as well as the user context (the user account under which the process is running) for each process.

# Process-to-Port Mapping

When a network connection is open on a system, some process must be responsible for and must be using that connection. That is, every network connection and open port is associated with a process. Several tools are available to the investigator to retrieve this process-to-port mapping.

## Netstat

On Windows XP and Windows 2003, the netstat.exe program offers the −*o* switch to display the PID for the process responsible for the network connection. Once you've collected this information (refer back to the *netstat –ano* command), you will need to correlate it with the output of a tool such as tlist.exe or tasklist.exe to determine the name (and additional information) of the process using the connection.

As of Service Pack 2, Windows XP has an additional *–b* option that will "display the executable involved in creating each connection or listening port." This switch is also included in netstat.exe in Windows 2003 SP1 and can provide more information about the process using a particular port. In some cases, the output will also show some of the modules (DLLs) used by the process. Figure 1.9 illustrates an excerpt from the output of the command run on a Windows XP SP2 system.

**Figure 1.9** Excerpt of Output from
*netstat –anob* from a Windows XP SP2 System

```
TCP     192.168.1.8:1036      205.188.69.61:5190      ESTABLISHED      1976
[AOLSoftware.exe]

TCP     192.168.1.8:1038      64.12.189.249:443       ESTABLISHED      1976
[AOLSoftware.exe]

TCP     192.168.1.8:1039      64.12.25.220:5190       ESTABLISHED      3624
[aim6.exe]

TCP     192.168.1.8:2702      199.45.62.18:80         TIME_WAIT        0
TCP     192.168.1.8:2703      199.45.62.18:80         TIME_WAIT        0
TCP     192.168.1.8:2706      213.200.97.206:80       TIME_WAIT        0
TCP     192.168.1.8:2707      213.200.109.28:80       TIME_WAIT        0
TCP     192.168.1.8:2709      213.200.109.28:80       TIME_WAIT        0
UDP     0.0.0.0:1182          *:*                                      1752
C:\WINDOWS\system32\mswsock.dll
c:\windows\system32\WS2_32.dll
c:\windows\system32\DNSAPI.dll
c:\windows\system32\dnsrslvr.dll
C:\WINDOWS\system32\RPCRT4.dll
[svchost.exe]
```

# Fport

Fport.exe has long been one of the tools of choice for obtaining the process-to-port mapping from a Windows system. The output of the tool is easy to understand; however, you must run the tool from within an Administrator account to obtain its information. This can be an issue if you're responding to a situation in which the user's logged-in account is a user account and does not have Administrator privileges.

# Tcpvcon

Tcpvcon.exe is available from Microsoft (originally part of the Sysinternals.com tools) and is one of the best tools for retrieving the process-to-port mapping information from a Windows system. By default, tcpvcon.exe will show only information regarding TCP connections, and prints the information in the console in a tabular listing format, as illustrated here:

```
[TCP] C:\Program Files\Mozilla Firefox\firefox.exe
      PID:    3476
      State:  ESTABLISHED
      Local:  wintermute.adelphia.net:5918
      Remote: yahoo.com: http
[TCP] C:\Program Files\Mozilla Firefox\firefox.exe
      PID:    3476
      State:  ESTABLISHED
      Local:  wintermute.adelphia.net:5919
      Remote: yahoo.com:http
```

Using the −a and −c switches, you can tell tcpvcon.exe to display information about *all* connections (both TCP and UDP) in a CSV (.csv) format, which is easy to parse (with Perl, of course!) or open in Excel. Using the −n switch, you can tell tcpvcon.exe to not resolve IP addresses to names, so the output appears a bit more quickly. This output is very easy to parse using any number of tools.

**TIP**

In general, you will want to obtain the IP address of the remote system(s) to specifically identify the system(s). However, in some cases you may also want to document the domain name of the remote system since some intruders or malware authors use dynamic domain name system (DNS) servers and the name may be more useful over time than the IP address.

**TIP**

If the system you're responding to is a Windows 2000 system that does not have installed the hotfix I mentioned earlier in the chapter so that netstat. exe is capable of listing the PID for each network connection, an excellent alternative is to use tcpvcon.exe.

As each network connection entry is placed on a line by itself, the output is easy to parse using automation tools (to be addressed in Chapter 2).

Keep in mind that tools such as tcpvcon.exe make use of APIs in DLLs native to the system to extract their information. That being said, you may also opt to use a port scanning tool such as Nmap (www.nmap.org) to remotely gather information on open ports from a potentially compromised system. In doing so, you could find a number of ports open in listening mode, awaiting connections; authentication services, Web servers, and File Transfer Protocol (FTP) servers do this, but so do backdoors. If you scan a system and find certain ports open but neither netstat nor any other tool that shows network connections or process-to-port mappings shows the same port open, you definitely have a mystery on your hands. At that point, you should double-check your scan results and ensure that you scanned the correct system. (Hey, it happens!) If the issue persists, you could have a rootkit on your hands. (See Chapter 7 for more information regarding rootkits.)

**TIP**

Comparing a network traffic capture or port scan to the output of netstat. exe or tcpvcon.exe is an excellent way to validate your findings. During one of my recent engagements, the customer had collected information from network traffic captures and perimeter device logs, and then mapped that information back to specific systems. Using the output of netstat.exe, they were able to validate that they had the correct systems, as they could see indications of the source and destination IP addresses and ports quite clearly. This also validated the fact that the systems were not infected with rootkits, which tend to try to hide such things as processes, files, network connections, and Registry keys.

# Process Memory

A live system will have any number of running processes, and any one of those processes could be suspicious or malicious in nature. When a process is executed on a system, it is most often given the same name as the file where the executable image resides, and on Windows systems in particular a file can be named just about anything. The bad guys simply aren't so helpful as to name their malicious code something that is easily recognizable, such as badstuff.exe. More often than not, they will rename the file to something less conspicuous, or they could try to disguise the intent of the program by using the name of a program usually found on Windows systems (see the "Svchost" sidebar).

Once you've used the tools we've discussed and found what you determine to be a suspicious process, you might decide that you want more information about what that process is doing. You can get this information by dumping the memory the process is using. You can use several tools to accomplish this task. As stated previously, you can find a detailed discussion of collecting the contents of RAM (as well as the memory used by specific processes) in Chapter 3.

# Network Status

Getting information about the status of the network interface cards (NICs) connected to a system can be extremely important to an investigation. For instance, today many laptops come with built-in wireless NICs, so you might not know just by looking at the desktop whether the system is connected to a wireless access point, and if so, what IP address it is using. Knowing the status of the NICs prior to a system being acquired can provide insight into a follow-on investigation.

## Ipconfig

Ipconfig.exe is a utility native to Windows systems that the investigator can use to display information about NICs and their status. The most useful switch for investigators is /all, which is used to display the network configuration of the NICs on the system. This information includes the state of the NIC, whether DHCP is enabled, the IP address of the NIC, and more.

You might find this information useful during an investigation, because you might have network traffic logs to examine, and the IP address of the system could have been modified at some point. Also, many Web-based e-mail services (such as Yahoo! Mail) record the IP address of the system from which an e-mail was drafted in the header of the e-mail. I took part in one particular investigation in which a former employee was sending annoying (not harassing) e-mails to our company. Looking at the e-mail headers, we were able to determine from where he was sending the e-mails. Several of them had been sent from a local copy shop and others from a local public library. With the gracious help of administrators from the copy shop and the county, we were able to narrow the locations even further; in the case of the public library, we were able to pinpoint the branch of the library and the fact that the system he was using was on the second floor (one of the administrators had asked a library staff member to enter the *ipconfig /all* command on several systems until he located the IP address in question). Needless to say, the former employee was shocked when confronted with this information and stopped sending the e-mails. Had he not been fired and had he been sending the e-mails from his work system via Yahoo! Mail, we would have been able to determine his location as well.

# PromiscDetect and Promqry

Sometimes compromised systems will have a "sniffer" installed to capture network traffic, such as login credentials to other systems, or to develop a picture of what other systems are on the network and what services they are running. Some malware payloads include this capability, or it can be a follow-on download installed by an attacker. For the NIC to capture network traffic in this manner, it has to be placed in "promiscuous" mode. This isn't something an administrator or investigator will see, because there is nothing obvious to indicate that the NIC is in promiscuous mode. There's no System Tray icon or Control Panel setting that clearly indicates to the investigator that the system is being used to "sniff" traffic.

Tools are available to tell you whether the NIC is in promiscuous mode. One such tool is promiscdetect.exe (www.ntsecurity.nu/toolbox/promiscdetect/). The other is promqry.exe (available from Microsoft, at a really long URL), written by Tim Rains. The primary difference between the two tools is that promqry.exe can be run against remote systems, allowing an administrator to scan systems within the domain for systems that might be sniffing the network.

## Tools & Traps…

### Promiscuous Mode

The Perl script ndis.pl (located in the \ch2\code directory on the media accompanying this book) implements WMI code to determine the settings for a NIC. Specifically, it was designed to be used to determine whether a NIC is in promiscuous mode and is capable of sniffing packets from the network.

The file ndis.exe in the same directory is a stand-alone executable version of this script, provided for use by those who do not have Perl installed on a Windows system.

Figure 1.10 illustrates an excerpt of the output returned from ndis.exe.

The output displayed in Figure 1.10 was generated by launching the Wireshark (formerly known as Ethereal; www.wireshark.org) sniffer application on the wireless NIC and then running ndis.exe. The highlighted portion of the output clearly shows that the wireless NIC is in promiscuous mode.

Both the Perl script and the associated executable file are intended to be run only on the local system. However, minor modifications to the code will allow the script (or the executable, after the script is modified and recompiled) to be run against remote systems, in the same manner as promqry.exe.

**Figure 1.10** Excerpt from the Output of ndis.exe on Windows XP

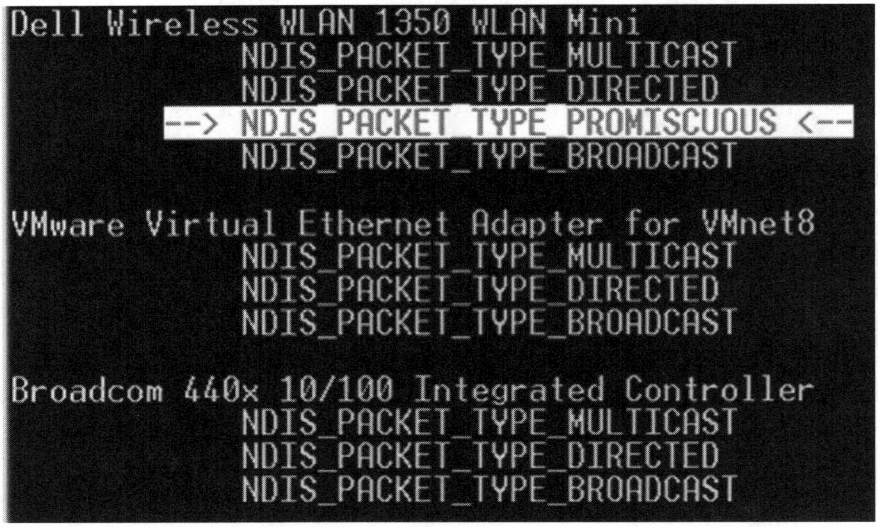

```
Dell Wireless WLAN 1350 WLAN Mini
            NDIS_PACKET_TYPE_MULTICAST
            NDIS_PACKET_TYPE_DIRECTED
    --> NDIS_PACKET_TYPE_PROMISCUOUS <--
            NDIS_PACKET_TYPE_BROADCAST

VMware Virtual Ethernet Adapter for VMnet8
            NDIS_PACKET_TYPE_MULTICAST
            NDIS_PACKET_TYPE_DIRECTED
            NDIS_PACKET_TYPE_BROADCAST

Broadcom 440x 10/100 Integrated Controller
            NDIS_PACKET_TYPE_MULTICAST
            NDIS_PACKET_TYPE_DIRECTED
            NDIS_PACKET_TYPE_BROADCAST
```

Another very important use for tools such as this is to determine what the active network interfaces might be on a live system. My old Toshiba Tecra 8100 systems require a PCIMCIA card to be able to connect to a wireless network, whereas many of the "newer" systems I've dealt with come with wireless networking capability built right into the system. You never see anything sticking out of the laptop case itself, nor do you see any blinking lights, as you do with the RJ-45 Ethernet connection. It's just there. So, when Dave comes into a meeting and sits down behind his laptop, is he just taking notes or is he also surfing the Web and sending e-mail? Wireless access is becoming increasingly ubiquitous, not only because so many locations now have it available, but also because it's being built right into our laptops.

This wireless access may be an entryway into your organization, or even a route that someone uses to get information out of your infrastructure. I once dealt with an issue in which a public relations person in our company decided that she needed to take her personal laptop into meetings so that she could have access to the Internet. But she decided this without contacting anyone from IT, or even me (I was the security administrator). When she fired up her laptop, she found our wireless access points, which had Wireless Encryption Protocol (WEP) keys and MAC address filtering enabled. Because she hadn't contacted us and she was in a meeting and needed the access 10 minutes ago, she decided to connect to an open wireless access point that her system detected—one that was used by a company next door to us and that was wide open, with no security measures in place. Once she made that connection, she created an entry point into our infrastructure that bypassed all the protection mechanisms we had in place, including firewalls and antivirus software. At that point, it was hard to tell which situation was more damaging—her connection being used as a conduit to infect our infrastructure or the legal ramifications should the other company's infrastructure suffer a security breach and any logging mechanisms showing her connection during that time.

During an investigation, it is generally a good idea to collect information about the active network interfaces on the system you are examining. This adds context not only to the volatile data you are collecting, but also to a postmortem analysis, which we will discuss later in this book.

## Clipboard Contents

The Clipboard is simply an area of memory where data can be stored for later use. Most Windows applications provide this functionality through the Edit option on the menu bar. Clicking **Edit** reveals a drop-down menu with choices such as Cut, Copy, and Paste. Microsoft Word 2003 includes an Office Clipboard option.

The Clipboard is most often used to facilitate moving data in some fashion—between documents or between application windows on the desktop. The user selects text or other data, chooses **Copy**, and then chooses **Paste** to insert that data somewhere else. The Cut functionality removes the data from the document the user is working on, and that data goes into the Clipboard.

What many folks don't realize is that they could turn their computer on some Monday morning, work on a file, and copy some information to their Clipboard. Let's say they're editing a document containing sensitive information, and personal information about a customer needs to be added to that document. The user locates, highlights, and copies the information to the Clipboard, then pastes it into the document. As long as the computer is left on, the user doesn't log out, and nothing is added to the Clipboard to replace what was put there, the data remains on the Clipboard.

Try it sometime. Walk up to your computer, open a Notepad or Word document, and simply use the **Control + V** key combination to paste whatever is currently in the Clipboard into a document. Try this on other computers. You might be surprised by what you see. How often do you find URLs, bits of IM conversations, passwords, or entire sections of text from documents still available on the Clipboard? The Clipboard isn't visible on the system, but it's there, and it has been an issue—so much so that there's a Microsoft Knowledge Base article titled "How to Prevent Web Sites from Obtaining Access to the Contents of Your Windows Clipboard" (http://support.microsoft.com/default. aspx?scid=KB;EN-US;Q224993&) that applies to Internet Explorer versions 4 through 6.

Data found in the Clipboard can be useful in a variety of cases, such as information or intellectual property theft, fraud, or harassment. Sometimes such information can provide you with clues; at other times you might find images or entire sections of documents on the Clipboard.

Pclip.exe (available from http://unxutils.sourceforge.net) is a CLI utility that can be used to retrieve the contents of the Clipboard. CLI utilities such as pclip.exe make it easy to automate information collection through batch files and scripts.

**Tools & Traps…**

### Clipboard Contents

Perl provides a simple interface to an API for accessing the contents of the Clipboard. The following script prints the contents of the Clipboard as a string:

```
use strict;
use Win32::Clipboard;
print "Clipboard contents = ".Win32::Clipboard()->Get()."\n";
```

To make more extensive use of Win32::Clipboard, consult the documentation for the module.

## Service/Driver Information

Services and drivers are started automatically when the system starts, based on entries in the Registry. Most users don't even see these services running as processes on the system because there are really no obvious indications, as there are with processes (e.g., you can see processes running in the Task Manager). Yet these services are running nonetheless. Not all services are necessarily installed by the user or even by the system administrator. Some malware installs itself as a service or even as a system driver.

**Tools & Traps…**

### Service Information

The Perl script svc.pl, located in the \ch2\code directory on the accompanying media, uses WMI (accessing the *Win32_Service* class) to retrieve information about services from either a local or a remote system. The file svc.exe is a stand-alone Windows executable generated by compiling the Perl script with Perl2Exe.

**Continued**

Both the Perl script and the executable will display the following information about services:

- Name of the service
- DisplayName for the service
- StartName (the context used to launch the service)
- Description string for the service
- PID for the service (this can be used to map the service to the process information)
- Path to the executable image for the service
- Start mode for the service
- Current state of the service
- Service status
- The type of the service (kernel driver, share process, etc.)
- Tag ID, a unique value used to order service startup within a load order group

Figure 1.11 illustrates an example of the information displayed by this utility. Both the Perl script and the executable can be modified to output this information in various formats, including CSVs to make parsing the information easier or to ease analysis by making the output suitable for opening in a spreadsheet.

**Figure 1.11** Excerpt from the Output of svc.exe on Windows XP

```
Name    : UMWdf
Display : Windows User Mode Driver Framework
Start   : NT AUTHORITY\LocalService
Desc    : Enables Windows user mode drivers.
PID     : 1660
Path    : C:\WINDOWS\system32\wdfmgr.exe
Mode    : Auto
State   : Running
Status  : OK
Type    : Own Process
TagID   : 0
```

# Command History

Let's say you approach a system during an investigation and see one or more command prompts open on the screen. Depending on the situation, valuable clues could be hidden in the commands typed by the user, such as *ftp* or *ping*. To see these previously typed commands, you can run the scroll bar for the command prompt up (if multiple commands are issued via the command prompt, the display will extend above the visible portion of the command prompt window), but that goes only so far. If the user typed the *cls* command to clear the screen, you won't be able to use the scroll bar to see any of the commands that had been entered. Instead, you need to use the *doskey /history* command, which will show the history of the commands typed into that prompt, as illustrated in the following:

```
D:\tools>doskey /history
move proc.exe d:\awl2\ch2\code
perl2exe -small d:\awl2\ch2\code\proc.pl
move proc.exe d:\awl2\ch2\code
y
cd \awl2\ch2\code
proc
cd \perl2exe
perl2exe -small d:\awl2\ch2\code\procmon.pl
procmon
move procmon.exe d:\awl2\ch2\code
cd d:\awl2\ch2\code
procmon
cd \tools
openports -fport
openports -netstat
cls
doskey /history
cd \tools
dir prom*
promqry
dir prom*
promqry
```

I'll give you an example of when I've used this command. I was teaching an incident-response course on the West Coast, and during a lunch break I "compromised" the students' systems. One step I specifically took on several of the computers was to open a command prompt and type several commands, then type *cls* to clear the screen. When the students returned, I noticed one particular individual in the back of the room who immediately closed (not minimized, but closed) the command prompt that he found open on his screen. As intended, the "clues" I left behind in the command prompt provided context to the rest of the "compromise," as students who hadn't closed their command prompts discovered. However, I'll admit that I've never had the opportunity to use this command outside a training environment. In all instances when I've been confronted with a live system, the user hasn't used a command prompt. However, this doesn't mean it won't happen to you.

## Mapped Drives

During the course of an investigation, you might want to know what drives or shares the system you are examining has mapped to. These mappings could have been created by the user, and they might be an indication of malicious intent (this could be the case if the user has guessed an Administrator password and is accessing systems across the enterprise). Further, there might be no persistent information within the file system or Registry for these connections to mapped shares on other systems, though the volatile information regarding drive mappings can be correlated to network connection information that you've already retrieved.

Figure 1.12 illustrates the output of the program di.exe (*di* stands for *drive info*), which you can find on the accompanying media.

**Figure 1.12** Output of di.exe

```
D:\awl2\ch2\code>di
Drive     Type        File System  Path                      Free Space
-----     -----       -----------  -----                     ----------
C:\       Fixed       NTFS                                   1.15   GB
D:\       Fixed       NTFS                                   8.18   GB
E:\       Fixed       NTFS                                   5.19   GB
F:\       CD-ROM                                             0.00
G:\       Removable   FAT32                                  974.45 MB
Z:\       Network     NTFS         \\192.168.1.71\c$         2.96   GB
```

The output of di.exe displayed in Figure 1.12 is the result of the program being run on a Windows XP Home system with one drive mapped to a small Windows 2003 server, specifically to the *C$* share on that server.

Notice that the output of di.exe also shows a removable drive assigned the drive letter G:\. This is a USB-connected thumb drive, the artifacts of which we will discuss in Chapter 4.

## Shares

Besides resources used by the system you are investigating, you will also want to get information regarding resources the system is making available. Information for shares available on a system is maintained in the HKEY_LOCAL_MACHINE\System\CurrentControlSet\ Services\lanmanserver\Shares key, but can also be retrieved from a live system using CLI tools such as share.exe, which is available on the accompanying media. (The Perl source code for the program is also available.)

An excerpt of the output of share.exe follows:

```
Name       -> SharedDocs
Type       -> Disk Drive
Path       -> C:\DOCUMENTS AND SETTINGS\ALL USERS\DOCUMENTS
Status     -> OK
```

**TIP**

Throughout this chapter so far, we've discussed using WMI through Perl. I've presented a number of examples, and made the code available to you on the accompanying media. Microsoft also provides access to WMI through the native CLI tool, wmic.exe (http://support.microsoft.com/kb/290216/en-us). Wmic. exe can be extremely useful for collecting a wide range of information from remote systems across the enterprise. In March 2006, Ed Skoudis published a SANS Handler's Diary entry (http://isc.sans.org/diary.html?storyid=1229) that gave a number of very cool and very useful command-line options for using wmic.exe.

# Nonvolatile Information

During live response, you might not want to restrict yourself to collecting only volatile information. The situation could dictate that the investigator needs to collect information that would normally be considered persistent even if the system were rebooted, such as the contents of Registry keys or files. The investigator could decide that information needs to be extracted from the Registry or that information about (or from) files needs to be collected, either for additional analysis or because an attacker could be actively logged in to the system. In such cases, the investigator may decide that to track the attacker (or botnet), she wants to leave the system live and online, but she also wants to preserve certain information from being modified or deleted.

Once a system has been started, there could have been modifications, such as drives mapped to or from the system, services started, or applications installed. These modifications might not be persistent across a reboot, and therefore might need to be recorded and documented by the investigator.

# Registry Settings

Several Registry values and settings could impact your follow-on forensic analysis and examination. Although these settings are nonvolatile themselves, they could have an effect on how you choose to proceed in the conduct of your investigation or even whether you continue with your investigation at all.

There are several tools for collecting information from the Registry. My favorite (if you haven't guessed by now) is to write a Perl script that provides the various functionality for retrieving specific values or all values and subkeys of a particular key. Reg.exe is a command-line tool for accessing and managing the Registry that is part of the Windows 2000 Support Tools and is native to Windows XP and 2003.

## ClearPageFileAtShutdown

This particular Registry value tells the operating system to clear the page file when the system is shut down. Because Windows uses a virtual memory architecture, some memory used by processes will be paged out to the page file. When the system is shut down, the information within the page file remains on the hard drive and can contain information such as decrypted passwords, portions of IM conversations, and other strings and bits of information that might provide you with important leads in your investigation. Although most examiners understand that the page file is an amorphous blob of data, largely without context (i.e., locating an interesting string in the page file doesn't provide you with important context information, such as which process that string was associated with), advances in Windows memory analysis (for more information on this topic, see Chapter 3) have determined ways to expand the information available in a dump of Windows physical memory by incorporating the page file into the analysis. If this file is cleared during shutdown, this potentially valuable information will be more difficult to obtain, if not completely lost.

Microsoft has Knowledge Base articles for this Registry value that apply to both Windows 2000 (http://support.microsoft.com/kb/182086/EN-US) and Windows XP (http://support.microsoft.com/kb/314834/EN-US/).

## DisableLastAccess

Windows file systems have the ability to disable updating of the last access times on files. According to Microsoft, this was meant as a performance enhancement, particularly on high-volume file servers. On normal workstations and the sorts of desktops and laptops most folks are using (home computers, employee desktops, etc.) this setting doesn't provide any noticeable improvement in performance. On Windows 2003, you would set the following value to 1:

```
HKEY_LOCAL_MACHINE\System\CurrentControlSet\Control\FileSystem\
NtfsDisableLastAccessUpdate
```

According to performance-tuning guideline documents from Microsoft for Windows 2003, this value does not exist by default and must be created.

**W**ARNING

Microsoft Knowledge Base article 555041 (http://support.microsoft.com/kb/555041) refers to this value as *DisableLastAccess*, but Microsoft Knowledge Base article 849372 (http://support.microsoft.com/kb/894372) refers to the value as *NtfsDisableLastAccessUpdate*. Knowledge Base article 150355 refers to the *NtfsDisableLastAccess* value on Windows NT 3.51 and 4.0.

On Windows XP and 2003 systems, you can query or enable this setting via the *fsutil* command. For example, to query the setting, use this command:

```
C:\>fsutil behavior query disablelastaccess
```

If this Registry value has been set, particularly sometime prior to you conducting your examination of the system, it is likely that you won't find anything useful with regard to file last-access times. This means you will need to explore other avenues of analysis, such as described in Chapter 4.

**W**ARNING

The *NtfsDisableLastAccessUpdate* functionality is *enabled* by default on Vista. Keep this in mind when you're performing incident-response and computer forensic investigations. As of this writing, information is still being developed for forensic investigators with regard to this issue.

# Autoruns

Several areas of the Registry (and the file system) are referred to as *autostart locations* because they provide a facility to automatically start applications, usually without any direct interaction from the user. Some of these locations will automatically start applications when the system boots, others when a user logs in, and still others when the user takes a specific action. In instances where an application is started when the user performs a certain action, the user will be unaware that he is launching another application.

Okay, I know this stuff is in the Registry, and that fact in itself might make this seem like a daunting or impossible task, but the good news is that a finite number of locations serve this purpose. The number might be large, but it is finite. Rather than listing them here, I'm going to leave a more in-depth review of Registry analysis for later in the book. However, if you decide you need to collect this information as part of your first-response activities, there are two ways to go about it. The first is to use a tool such as reg.exe (mentioned previously) to collect data from specific keys and values. The second way is to use a tool such as Autoruns (http://technet.microsoft.com/en-us/sysinternals/bb963902.aspx) to do it for you. The authors of Autoruns (Mark Russinovich and Bryce Cogswell, now Microsoft employees) do a great job of maintaining the list of areas checked by the tool. In some cases, I've found new additions to the tool before I've seen those autostart locations in widespread use in malware. Autoruns comes in GUI and CLI versions, both with the same functionality. For example, you can use the −*m* switch in the CLI version to hide signed Microsoft entries (entries for executable files that have been signed by the vendor) or the −*v* switch to verify digital signatures.

Autoruns also does a great job of checking areas within the file system, such as Scheduled Tasks. Sometimes administrators will use Scheduled Tasks to provide themselves with elevated (i.e., SYSTEM level) privileges to perform such tasks as view portions of the Registry that are normally off-limits even to administrators. An attacker who gains Administrator-level access to the system could do something similar to further extend his presence on the system.

Another area of the Registry that can provide valuable information in an investigation is the Protected Storage area (see the "Protected Storage" sidebar). The information held in Protected Storage is maintained in an encrypted format in the Registry. If you acquire an image of the system, tools such as AccessData's Forensic ToolKit will decrypt and recover the information. However, sometimes it is simpler to collect this information as part of live-response activities, particularly if time is of the essence and the information is pertinent to the case.

## Notes from the Underground...

### Protected Storage

Protected Storage is an area of memory where sensitive information for the user is maintained. When the system is turned off, this information is stored in encrypted format in the Registry, and when the user logs in, the information is placed into memory. Windows places information such as passwords and AutoComplete data for Web forms in Protected Storage for later use.

**Continued**

You can view the contents of Protected Storage on a live system by using tools such as pstoreview.exe (www.ntsecurity.nu/toolbox/pstoreview) or the Protected Storage Explorer (www.codeproject.com/KB/cpp/psexplorer.aspx).

Information within Protected Storage can be useful in cases involving access to Web sites and the use of passwords for services such as Hotmail and MSN.

Information in Protected Storage is also useful to bad guys. I've seen systems infected with IRCbots (malicious software that, once installed, connects to an IRC channel awaiting commands; the channel operator can issue one command that is then executed by thousands of bots) that will send information from Protected Storage to the bad guy, on command. On February 19, 2006, Brian Krebs published an article (www.washingtonpost.com/wp-dyn/content/article/2006/02/14/AR2006021401342.html) in the *Washington Post Magazine* about a hacker who wrote bot software and controlled thousands of systems. In that article, Brian wrote that the hacker could type a single command (*pstore*) and retrieve the Protected Storage information from all the infected systems, which contained username and password combinations for PayPal, eBay, Bank of America, and Citibank accounts, as well as for military and federal government e-mail accounts.

The information held by the Protected Storage Service is available through the AutoComplete functionality built into the Internet Explorer Web browser. The AutoComplete Settings, shown in Figure 1.13, are available by clicking **Tools** in the Internet Explorer menu bar and then choosing **Internet Options | Content**, and then clicking the **AutoComplete** button.

With AutoComplete enabled, the users of these infected systems have used Internet Explorer to access their online shopping and banking accounts, making them available to an attacker such as the hacker in Brian's article.

**Figure 1.13** AutoComplete Settings Dialog Box on Internet Explorer 6.0

Tools such as PassView (www.nirsoft.net/utils/pspv.html) and the Protected Storage Explorer (www.forensicideas.com/tools.html) allow you to view the Protected Storage information in a nice GUI format, and pstoreview.exe (www.ntsecurity.nu/toolbox/pstoreview) is a CLI tool that will provide the same information to STDOUT. You might need to collect this information in the course of an investigation, particularly if the issue you're dealing with involves users accessing Web sites that require passwords. You can extract this information from an acquired image, but doing so requires special tools to address the decryption, tools that can be expensive. There may be live-response situations (e.g., data theft or exfiltration, missing persons, etc.) where you will want to collect this information from a system quickly, rather than waiting until an image has been acquired and the data taken to a lab for extraction and analysis.

# Event Logs

Event Logs are essentially files within the file system, but they can change. In fact, depending on how they're configured and what events are being audited, they can change quite rapidly.

Depending on how the audit policies are configured on the "victim" system and how you're accessing it as the first responder, entries can be generated within the Event Logs. For example, if you decide to run commands against the system from a remote location (i.e., the system is in another building or another city, and you cannot get to it quickly but you want to preserve some modicum of data) and the proper audit configuration is in place, the Security Event Log will contain entries for each time you log in. If enough of these entries are generated, you could end up losing valuable information that pertains to your investigation. Tools such as psloglist.exe and dumpevt.exe can be used to retrieve the event records, or the .evt files themselves may be copied off the system (this depends on the level of access and permissions of the account being used). A detailed discussion of the analysis of Windows Event Log files will be provided in Chapter 5.

At this point, you may be thinking "Okay, given all these tools and utilities, I have an incident on my hands. What data do I need to collect to resolve the issue?" The stock answer is "It depends." I know that's probably not the answer you wanted to hear, but let me see if, in explaining that response, we can build an understanding of why that *is* the response.

The volatile data that is the most useful to your investigation depends on the type of incident you're faced with. For example, an incident involving a remote intrusion or a Trojan backdoor will generally mean that the process, network connection, and process-to-port-mapping information (and perhaps even the contents of certain Registry keys) will be the most valuable to you. However, if an employee in a corporate environment is suspected of having stolen company-proprietary data or violating the corporate acceptable use policy (AUP), information about storage devices connected to his system, Web browsing history, contents of the Clipboard, and so on could be more valuable to your investigation.

The key to all this is to know what information is available to your investigation, how you can retrieve that information, and how you can use it. As you start to consider different types of incidents and the information you need to resolve them, you will start to see an overlap between the various tools you use and the data you're interested in for your investigation. Although you might not develop a "one size fits all" batch file that runs all the commands you will want to use for every investigation, you could decide that having several smaller batch files (or configuration files for the Forensic Server Project, which is described later in the chapter) is a better approach. That way, you can collect only the information you need for each situation.

# Devices and Other Information

You could choose to collect other types of information from a system that might not be volatile in nature, but you want to record it for documentation purposes. For example, perhaps you want to know something about the hard drive installed in the system. Di.pl is a Perl script that implements WMI to list the various disk drives attached to the system as well as partition information. Ldi.pl implements WMI to collect information about logical drives (C:\, D:\, etc.), including local fixed drives, removable storage devices, and remote shares. Sr.pl lists information about System Restore Points on Windows XP systems (you can find more information about System Restore Points in Chapters 4 and 5).

DevCon, available from Microsoft, can be used to document devices that are attached to a Windows system. A CLI replacement for the Device Manager, DevCon can show available device classes as well as the status of connected devices.

# A Word about Picking Your Tools

In this chapter as well as other chapters in this book, we mention various tools that you can use to perform certain tasks. This book is not intended as a be-all and end-all list of tools; that's simply not possible. Instead, what I'm trying to do is make you aware of *where* you need to look and show you ways in which you can collect the data you need for your investigations. Sometimes it's simply a matter of knowing that the information is there.

When we're collecting data from live systems, we will most often have to interact with the operating system itself, using the available API. Different tools can use different API calls to collect the same information.

It's always a good idea to know how your tools collect information. What API calls does the executable use? What DLLs does it access? How is the data displayed, and how does that data compare to other tools of a similar nature?

Test your tools to determine the effects they have on a live system. Do they leave any artifacts on the system? If so, what are they? Be sure to document these artifacts because this documentation allows you to identify (and document) steps that you take to mitigate the effects of using, and justify the use of, these tools. For example, Windows XP performs application prefetching, meaning that when you run an application, some information about that application (e.g., code pages) is stored in a .pf file located in the %WINDIR%\Prefetch directory. This directory has a limit of 128 .pf files. If you're performing incident-response activities and there are fewer than 128 .pf files in this directory, one of the effects of the tools you run on the system will be that .pf files for those tools will be added to the Prefetch directory. Under most circumstances, this might not be an issue. However, let's say your methodology includes using nc.exe (netcat). If someone had already used nc.exe on the system, your use of any file by that name would have the effect of overwriting the existing .pf file for nc.exe, potentially destroying evidence (e.g., modifying MAC times or data in the file, such as the path to the executable image).

Performing your own tool testing and validation might seem like an arduous task. After all, who wants to run through a tool-testing process for every single tool? Well, you might have to, because few sites provide this sort of information for their tools; most weren't originally written to be used for incident response or computer forensics. However, once you have your framework (tools, process, etc.) in place, it's really not that hard, and there are some simple things you can do to document and test the tools you use. Documenting and testing your tools is very similar to testing or analyzing a suspected malware program, a topic covered in detail in Chapter 6.

The basic steps of documenting your tools consist of static and dynamic testing. Static testing includes documenting unique identifying information about the tool, such as:

- Where you got it (URL)
- The file size
- Cryptographic hashes for the file, using known algorithms
- Retrieving information from the file, such as portable executable (PE) headers, file version information, import/export tables, etc.

This information is easy to retrieve using command-line tools and scripting languages such as Perl, and the entire collection process (as well as archiving the information in a database, spreadsheet, or flat file) is easy to automate.

## Tools & Traps…

### Native Tools

Most folks I talk to are averse to using native tools on Windows systems, particularly those that are resident on the systems themselves, with the idea being that if the system is compromised, and compromised deeply enough, how can you trust the output of the tools? This is an excellent point, but you can use this to your advantage in your analysis.

**Continued**

Incident responders tend to prefer to run their tools from a CD or DVD, which is immutable media, meaning that if there's a virus on the system you're responding to, the virus can't infect your tools. Another approach taken from the Linux world is the idea of "static binaries," which are executable files that do not rely on any of the libraries (in the Windows world, DLLs) on the victim system. This is not the easiest thing to do with respect to Windows PE files, although there are techniques you can use to simulate this effect. One of these techniques involves accessing the import table of the PE file and modifying the name of the DLL accessed, changing the name of that DLL within the file system, and then copying those files to your CD. The problem with this approach is that you don't know how deep to go within the recursive nature of the DLLs. If you look at the import header of an executable file (Chapter 6 covers the structure of PE files in detail), you'll likely see several DLLs and their functions referenced. If you go to that DLL, you will see the functions exported within the export table, but you will also very likely see that the DLL imports functions from another DLL. As you can see, keeping track of all this just so that the tool you want to use doesn't access any libraries on the victim system can quickly become unmanageable, and you run the risk of actually damaging the system you're trying to rescue.

Another perspective is to use the tools you've decided to use and rely on the native DLLs to provide the necessary functionality through their exported API. This way, you can perform a modicum of differential analysis; that is, by using two disparate techniques to look at the same information. For example, one way to determine whether ports are open on a system is to run a port scan against the system. A technique to see what ports are being used and what network traffic is emanating from a system is to collect network traffic captures. Neither of these techniques relies on the operating system or the code on the system itself. To perform differential analysis, you need to compare the output of the command *netstat –ano* to either the results of the port scan or the information from the collected network traffic capture. If as a result of either of those techniques information appears that is not available or visible in the output of netstat.exe, you may have an issue with executables or the operating system itself being subverted. Chapter 7 provides another example of how to use differential analysis to determine whether a user-mode rootkit is running on a system.

Dynamic testing involves running the tools while using monitoring programs to document the changes that take place on the system. Snapshot comparison tools such as InControl5 are extremely useful for this job, as are monitoring tools such as RegMon and FileMon, both of which were originally available from Sysinternals.com but are now available from Microsoft. RegMon and FileMon let you see not only the Registry keys and files that are accessed by the process, but also those that are created or modified. You might also consider using such tools as Wireshark to monitor inbound and outbound traffic from the test system while you're testing your tools, particularly if your static analysis of a tool reveals that it imports networking functions from other DLLs.

# Live-Response Methodologies

When you're performing live response, the actual methodology or procedure you use to retrieve the data from the systems can vary, depending on a number of factors. As a consultant and an emergency responder, I've found that it's best to have a complete understanding of what's available and what can go into your toolkit (considering issues regarding purchasing software, licensing, and other fees and restrictions) and then decide what works based on the situation.

There are two basic methodologies for performing live response on a Windows system: local and remote.

# Local Response Methodology

Performing live response locally means you are sitting at the console of the system, entering commands at the keyboard, and saving information locally, either directly to the hard drive or to a removable (thumb drive, USB-connected external drive) or network resource (network share) that appears as a local resource. This is done very often in situations where the responder has immediate physical access to the system and her tools on a CD or thumb drive. Collecting information locally from several systems can often be much quicker than locating a network connection or accessing a wireless network. With the appropriate amount of external storage and the right level of access, the first responder can quickly and efficiently collect the necessary information. To further optimize her activities, the first responder might have all her tools written to a CD and managed via a batch file or some sort of script that allows for a limited range of flexibility (e.g., the USB-connected storage device is mapped to different drive letters, the Windows installation is on a D:\ drive, etc.).

The simplest way to implement the local methodology is with a batch file. I tend to like batch files and Perl scripts because instead of typing the same commands over and over (and making mistakes over and over), I can write the commands once and have them run automatically. An example of a simple batch file that you can use during live response looks like this:

```
tlist.exe -c > %1\tlist-c.log
tlist.exe -t > %1\tlist-t.log
tlist.exe -s > %1\tlist-s.log
tcpvcon.exe -can > %1\tcpvcon-can.log
netstat.exe -ano > %1\netstat-ano.log
```

There you go; three utilities and five simple commands. Save this file as local.bat and include it on the CD, along with copies of the associated tools. You may also want to add to the CD trusted copies of the command processor (cmd.exe) for each operating system. Before you launch the batch file, take a look at the system and see what network drives are available, or insert a USB thumb drive into the system and see what drive letter it receives (say, F:\), then run the batch file like so (the D:\ drive is the CD-ROM drive):

```
D:\>local.bat F:
```

Once the batch file completes, you'll have five files on your thumb drive. Of course, you can add a variety of commands to the batch file, depending on the breadth of data you want to retrieve from a system.

Several freely available examples of toolkits were designed to be used in a local response fashion; among them are the Incident Response Collection Report (IRCR; up to Version 2.3 at the time of this writing and available at http://tools.phantombyte.com/) and the Windows Forensic Toolchest (WFT, available from www.foolmoon.net/security/wft/index.html and created by Monty McDougal). Although they differ in their implementation and output, the base functionality of both toolkits is substantially the same: Run external executable files controlled by a Windows batch file, and save the output locally. WFT does a great job of saving the raw data and allowing the responder to send the output of the commands to HTML reports.

Another approach to developing a local response methodology is to encapsulate as much as possible into a single application using the Windows API, which is what tools such as Nigilant32 from Agile Risk Management LLC (www.agilerm.net, which has been incorporated into F-Response at www.f-response.com) attempt to achieve. Nigilant32 uses the same Windows API calls used by external utilities to collect volatile information from a system (see Figure 1.14) and has the added capabilities of performing file system checks and dumping the contents of physical memory (RAM).

## Figure 1.14 Nigilant32 GUI

The interesting thing about the batch file-style toolkits is that a lot of folks have them. When I'm at a customer location or a conference, many times I'll talk to folks who are interested in comparing their approach to others'. Some have included tools that I listed in Chapter 5 of my first book, *Windows Forensics and Incident Recovery*, or they've read about other tools and incorporated them into their toolkits. Oddly enough, when it really comes down to it, there is a great deal of overlap between these toolkits. The batch file-style toolkits employ executables that use the same (or similar) Windows API calls as other tools such as Nigilant32.

Many of the tools we've discussed here (WFT, Nigilant32, and even many of the CLI tools) are also available as part of the Helix distribution put together by Drew Fahey and available through the e-Fense Web site (www.e-fense.com/helix/). Helix includes a bootable Linux side of the CD, as well as a Windows live-response side, and has been found by many to be extremely useful.

# Remote Response Methodology

The remote response methodology generally consists of a series of commands executed against a system from across the network. This methodology is very useful in situations with many systems, because the process of logging in to the system and running commands is easy to automate. In security circles, we call this being *scalable*. Some tools run extremely well when used in combination with psexec.exe from Sysinternals.com, and additional information can be easily collected via the use of WMI. Regardless of the approach you take, keep in mind that (a) you're going to need login credentials for each system, and (b) each time you log in to run a command and collect the output, you're going to add an entry to the Security Event Log (provided the appropriate level of auditing has been enabled). Keeping that in mind, we see that the order of volatility has shifted somewhat, so I recommend that the first command you use is the one to collect the contents of the Security Event Log.

You can use a Windows batch file as the basis of implementing this methodology. Taking three arguments at the command line (the name or IP of the system and the username/password login credentials), you can easily script a series of commands to collect the necessary information. You will need to execute some commands using psexec.exe, which will copy the executable to the remote system, run it, and allow you to collect the output from standard output (STDOUT), or redirect the output to a file, just as though you were running the same command locally. Other commands will take a UNC path (the name of the system prefaced with \\) and the login credentials as arguments, so you will not need to use psexec.exe. Finally, you can implement WMI via VBScript or Perl to collect data. Microsoft provides a script repository (www.microsoft.com/technet/scriptcenter/default. mspx) with numerous examples of WMI code implemented in various languages to include Perl, making designing a custom toolkit something of a cut-and-paste procedure.

Implementing our local methodology batch file for the remote methodology is fairly trivial:

```
psexec.exe \\%1 -u %2 -p %3 -c tlist.exe -c > tlist-c.log
psexec.exe \\%1 -u %2 -p %3 -c tlist.exe -t > tlist-t.log
psexec.exe \\%1 -u %2 -p %3 -c tlist.exe -s > tlist-s.log
psexec.exe \\%1 -u %2 -p %3 -c tcpvcon -can > tcpvcon-can.log
psexec.exe \\%1 -u %2 -p %3 c:\windows\system32\netstat.exe -ano >
%1\netstat-ano.log
```

This batch file (remote.bat) sits on the responder's system and is launched as follows:

```
C:\forensics\case007>remote.bat 192.168.0.7 Administrator password
```

Once the batch file has completed, the responder has the output of the commands in five files, ready for analysis, on her system.

If you're interested in using WMI to collect information remotely but you aren't a big VBScript programmer, you might want to take a look at wmic.exe, the native CLI implementation for WMI. Ed Skoudis wrote an excellent beginner's tutorial (http://isc.sans.org/diary.php?storyid=1622) on the use of wmic.exe for the SANS Internet Storm Center, which included examples such as collecting a list of installed patches from remote systems. Pretty much anything available to you as a Win32 class via WMI can be queried with wmic. exe. For example, to display the processes running locally on your system, you can use the following command:

```
C:\>wmic PROCESS GET ProcessId,Name,ExecutablePath
```

This is a pretty simple and straightforward command, and when it's executed, you can see the output right there in the console. You can also redirect the output to a file, and you can even choose from among various formats, such as CSVs (for opening in Excel or parsing with Perl) or even an HTML table. Using additional switches such as */Node:*, */User:*, and */Password:*, you can include several wmic.exe commands in a batch file and collect an even wider range of data from remote systems. Further, administrators can use these commands to compile hardware and software inventory lists, determine systems that need to be updated with patches, and more. WMI is a powerful interface into managed Windows systems in and of itself, and wmic.exe provides easy access for automating commands.

With the right error handling and recovery as well as activity logging in the code, this can be a highly effective and scalable way to quickly collect information from a number of systems, all managed from and stored in a central location. ProDiscover Incident Response (IR) from Technology Pathways (www.techpathways.com) is a commercial tool that implements this methodology. The responder can install an agent from a central location, query the agent for available information, and then delete the agent. Thanks to ProDiscover's Perl-based ProScript API, the responder can automate the entire process. This approach minimizes the number of logins that will appear in the Security Event Log as well as the amount of software that needs to be installed on the remote system. ProDiscover IR has the added capabilities of retrieving the contents of physical memory (as of this writing, from Windows 2000, XP, and 2003 systems, but not from Windows 2003 SP1 and later) as well as performing a live acquisition of the hard drive via the network.

Another tool that must be mentioned is F-Response (www.f-response.com), designed and developed by Matt Shannon (Matt started with Nigilant32 from www.agilerm.net). Although F-Response is not the same sort of tool as ProDiscover IR or other agent-based or remote access live-response tools available today, it has, without a doubt, changed the face of incident response as we know it. The short description of F-Response is that it provides you with remote, *read-only* access to a remote system's hard drive. There are three editions of F-Response (Field Kit, Consultant, and Enterprise) and they all basically work in the same way; after installing and configuring the agent on the remote system, you can access that remote drive as a read-only local drive on your workstation. This works over the local network, between buildings (across the street or in another part of the city), to a remote data center … anywhere you have TCP/IP network connectivity. The F-Response agent is available to run on Linux, Mac OS X, and Windows systems, and on Windows systems (as of Version 2.03) the system's physical memory will appear on your local system as a virtual drive. In essence, F-Response provides you with a tool-agnostic (you can use any tool you wish to acquire an image of the remote drive) mechanism for performing response activities. Although F-Response *does not* allow you to, say, run tlist.exe and get a process listing from the remote system, it does provide you with the means to easily acquire the contents of RAM, a topic that we will thoroughly discuss in Chapter 3. The media that accompanies this book contains a PDF document that describes, in detail, how to install F-Response Enterprise Edition (EE) remotely; as it turns out, this is also a stealthy method of deploying F-Response EE. This document is also available at the F-Response Web site for registered users of the F-Response product.

The limitation of the remote response methodology is that the responder must be able to access and, in some instances, log in to the systems via the network. If the Windows-style login (via NetBIOS) has been restricted in some way (NetBIOS not installed, firewalls/routers blocking the protocols, or similar), this methodology will not work.

# The Hybrid Approach (a.k.a. Using the FSP)

I know I said there are two basic approaches to response methodologies, and that's true. There is, however, a third approach that is really just a hybrid of the local and remote methodologies, so for the sake of simplicity, we'll just call it the *hybrid methodology* (the truth is that I couldn't think of a fancy name for it). This methodology is most often used in situations where the responder cannot log in to the systems remotely but wants to collect all information from a number of systems and store that data in a central location. The responder (or an assistant) will go to the system with a CD or thumb drive (ideally, one with a write-protect switch that is enabled), access the system, and run the tools to collect information. As the tools are executed, each one will send its output over the network to the central "forensic server." In this way, no remote logins are executed, trusted tools are run from a nonmodifiable source, and very little is written to the hard drive of the victim system. With the right approach and planning, the responder can minimize his interaction with the system, reducing the number of choices he needs to make with regard to input commands and arguments as well as reducing the chance for mistakes.

**W**ARNING

As we know from Locard's Exchange Principle, there will be an exchange of "material." References to the commands run will appear in the Registry, and on XP systems files will be added to the Prefetch directory. It is not possible to perform live response without leaving some artifacts; the key is to understand how to minimize those artifacts, and to thoroughly document your response actions.

Perhaps the simplest way to implement the hybrid methodology is with a batch file. You've already seen various tools and utilities that you have at your disposal for collecting a variety of information. In most of the cases we've looked at, as with the local methodology, we've used CLI tools and redirected their output to a file. So, how do you get the information you've collected off the system? One way to do that is to use netcat, described as the "TCP/IP Swiss army knife" because of the vast array of things you can do with it. For our purposes, we won't go into an exhaustive description of netcat; we'll use it to transmit information from one system to another. First, we need to set up a "listener" on our forensic server, and we do that with the following command line:

```
D:\forensics>nc -L -p 80 > case007.txt
```

This command line tells netcat (nc.exe) to listen (really hard ... keep the listener open after the connection has been closed) on port 80, and anything that comes in on that port gets sent (redirected, actually) to the file named case007.txt. With this setup, we can easily modify our batch file so that instead of writing the output of our commands to files, we send it through netcat to the "listener" on the forensic server:

```
tlist.exe -c | nc %1 %2 -w 5
tlist.exe -t | nc %1 %2 -w 5
tlist.exe -s | nc %1 %2 -w 5
tcpvcon -can | nc %1 %2 -w 5
netstat.exe -ano | nc %1 %2 -w 5
```

Save this file as hybrid.bat, and then launch it from the command line, like so (D:\ is still the CD-ROM drive):

```
D:\>remote.bat 192.168.1.10 80
```

Once we run this batch file, we'll have all our data safely off the victim system and on our forensic server for safekeeping and analysis.

> **TIP**
>
> If you prefer not to pass this sort of information over the network "in the clear," an encrypted version of netcat, called cryptcat, is available on SourceForge at http://sourceforge.net/projects/cryptcat/.

Several freeware tools implement this hybrid methodology. One is the Forensic Server Project (FSP), released in my first book (*Windows Forensics and Incident Recovery*, published by Addison-Wesley) in July 2004 and improved upon quite a bit through the release of the first edition of my second book, titled *Windows Forensic Analysis*. The FSP is open source, written in Perl and freely available. The idea for the FSP arose from the use of netcat, whereby the responder would run a tool from a CD loaded in the CD drive of the victim system and then pipe the output of the command through netcat. Instead of displaying the output of the command on the screen (STDOUT), netcat would be responsible for sending the information to a waiting listener on the server, where the output of the command would be stored (and not written to the victim system's hard drive). This worked well in some situations, but as the number of commands grew and the commands began to have a range of argument options, this methodology became a bit cumbersome. As more commands had to be typed, there was a greater chance for mistakes, and sometimes even a batch file to automate everything just wasn't the answer. So, I decided to create the Forensic Server Project, a framework for automating (as much as possible) the collection, storage, and management of live-response data.

The FSP consists of two components: a server and a client. The server component is known as the FSP (really, I couldn't come up with anything witty or smart to call it, and "Back Orifice" was already taken). You copy the files for the FSP to your forensic workstation (I use a laptop when I'm on-site), and when they're run, the FSP will sit and listen for connections. The FSP handles simple case management tasks, logging, storage, and the like for the case (or cases) that you're working on. When a connection is received from the client component, the FSP will react accordingly to the various "verbs" or commands that are passed to it.

The current iteration of the client component is called the First Responder Utility, or FRU. The FRU is very client-specific, because this is what is run on the victim system, from either a CD or a USB thumb drive. The FRU is really a very simple framework in itself in that it uses third-party utilities, such as the tools we've discussed in this chapter, to collect information from the victim system. When one of these commands is run, the FRU captures the output of the command (which you normally see at the console, in a command prompt window) and sends it out to the FSP, which will store the information sent to it and log the activity. The FRU is also capable of collecting specific Registry values or all values in a specific Registry key. Once all the commands have been run and all data collected, the FRU will "tell" the FSP that it can close the log file, which the FSP will do.

The FRU is controlled by an initialization (i.e., .ini) file, which is a similar format to the old Windows 3.1 INI files and consists of four sections. The first section, [Configuration], has some default settings for the FRU to connect to the FSP—specifically, the server and port to connect to. This is useful in smaller environments or in larger environments where the incident response data collection will be delegated to regional offices. However, these settings can be overridden at the command line.

The next section is the [Commands] section, which lists the external third-party tools to be executed to collect information. Actually, these can be any Windows PE file that sends its output to STDOUT (i.e., the console). I have written a number of small tools, in Perl, and then "compiled" them into stand-alone executables so that they can be run on systems that do not have Perl installed. Many of them are useful in collecting valuable information from systems and can be launched via the FRU's INI files. The format of this section is different from the other sections and is very important. The format of each line looks like the following:

```
<index>=<command line>::<filename>
```

The index is the order in which you want the command run; for example, you might want to run one command before any others, so the index allows you to order the commands. The command line is the name of the tool you're going to run plus all the command-line options you'd want to include, just as though you were running the command from the command prompt on the system itself. These first two sections are separated by an equals sign (=) and are followed by a double colon (::). In most cases, the final sections of one of these lines would be separated by semicolons, but several tools (psloglist.exe from Sysinternals.com) have options that include the possibility of using a semicolon, so I had to choose something that likely would not be used in the command line as a separator. Finally, the last element is the name of the file to be generated, most often the name of the tool, with the .dat extension. When the output is sent to the FSP server, it will be written to a file within the designated directory, with the filename prepended with the name of the system being investigated. This way, data can be collected from multiple systems using the same running instance of the FSP.

One important comment about tools used with the FRU: Because the system you, as the investigator, are interacting with is live and running, you should change the name of the third-party tools you are using. One good idea is to prepend the filenames with something unique, such as *f_* or *fru_*. This is in part due to the fact that your interaction with the system will be recorded in some way (more on this in Chapter 4) and due to the prefetch capability of Windows XP (more about that in Chapter 5). Remember Locard's Exchange Principle? Well, it's a good idea to make sure the artifacts you leave behind on a system are distinguishable from all the other artifacts.

An example taken from an FRU INI file looks like the following:

```
6=tcpvcon.exe -can::tcpvcon-can.dat
```

Another client is available for copying files off the victim system, if the investigator decides this is something she wants to do. Figure 1.15 illustrates the GUI for the file copy client, or FCLI.

**Figure 1.15** File Copy Client GUI

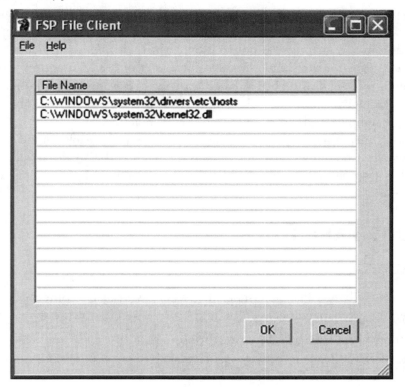

To use the FCLI, the investigator simply launches it and selects **File**, then **Config** to enter the IP address and port of the FSP server. Then she selects **File | Open** and chooses the files she wants to copy. Once she's selected all the files she wants to copy, she simply clicks the **OK** button. The FCLI will first collect the MAC times of the file and other meta-data, and then compute the MD5 and SHA-1 hashes for the file. This information is sent to the FSP. Then the FCLI copies the binary contents of the file to the server. Once the file has completed the copy operation, the FSP server will compute hashes for the copied file and verify those against the hashes received from the FCLI prior to the copy operation. All the actions occur automatically, without any interaction from the investigator, and they're all logged by the FSP.

The media that accompanies this book includes several movie files that illustrate how to set up and use the FSP, along with instructions on where to get the necessary player.

# Summary

In this chapter, we took a look at live response, specifically collecting volatile (and some nonvolatile) information from live Windows systems. As we discussed, live systems contain a lot of data that we can use to enhance our understanding of an incident; we just need to collect that data before we remove power from the system so that we can acquire an image of the hard drive. We also discussed how changes to the computing landscape are increasingly presenting us with situations where our only viable option is to collect volatile data.

My intention in this chapter was not to provide you with *the* "best practice" approach to collecting volatile data, for the simple fact that there isn't one. My intention was to provide you with enough information such that based on your needs and the conditions of the situation you're facing, you can not only employ your own "best practices," but when the situation changes, employ and justify the use of better practices.

All Perl scripts mentioned and described in this chapter are available on the accompanying media, along with a stand-alone executable "compiled" with Perl2Exe. ProScripts for Technology Pathways' ProDiscover product are also available on the accompanying media but are provided as Perl scripts only.

# Solutions Fast Track

## Live Response

- ☑ Locard's Exchange Principle states that when two objects come into contact, material is exchanged between them. This rule pertains to the digital realm as well.

- ☑ Anything an investigator does on a live system, *even nothing*, will have an effect on the system and leave an artifact. Artifacts will be created on the system as it runs with no interaction from a user.

- ☑ The absence of an artifact where one is expected is itself an artifact.

- ☑ The order of volatility illustrates to us that some data has a much shorter "lifespan" or "shelf life" than other data.

- ☑ When we're performing incident response, the most volatile data should be collected first.

- ☑ The need to perform live response should be thoroughly understood and documented.

- ☑ Without the appropriate attention being given to performing live response, an organization may be exposed to greater risk by the incident response activities than was posed by the incident itself.

- ☑ Corporate security policies may state that live response is the first step in an investigation. Responders must take care to follow documented processes, and document their actions.

# What Data to Collect

☑ A great deal of data that can give an investigator insight into her case is available on the system while it is powered up and running, and some of that data is available for only a limited time.

☑ Many times, the volatile data you collect from a system will depend on the type of investigation or incident you're presented with.

☑ When collecting volatile data, you need to keep both the order of volatility from RFC 3227 and Locard's Exchange Principle in mind.

☑ The key to collecting volatile data and using that data to support an investigation is thorough documentation.

# Nonvolatile Information

☑ Nonvolatile information (such as system settings) can affect your investigation, so you might need to collect that data as part of your live response.

☑ Some of the nonvolatile data you collect could affect your decision to proceed further in live response, just as it could affect your decision to perform a follow-on, postmortem investigation.

☑ The nonvolatile information you choose to collect during live response depends on factors such as your network infrastructure, security and incident response policies, or system configurations.

# Live-Response Methodologies

☑ There are three basic live-response methodologies: local, remote, and a hybrid of the two. Knowing the options you have available and having implementations of those options will increase your flexibility for collecting information.

☑ The methodology you use will depend on factors such as the network infrastructure, your deployment options, and perhaps even the political structure of your organization. However, you do have multiple options available.

☑ When choosing your response methodology, be aware of the fact that your actions will leave artifacts on the system. Your actions will be a direct stimulus on the system that will cause changes to occur in the state of the system, since Registry keys may be added (see Chapter 4 regarding USB-connected removable storage devices), files may be added or modified, and executable images will be loaded into memory. However, these changes are, to a degree, quantifiable, and you should thoroughly document your methodology and actions.

# Frequently Asked Questions

**Q:** When should I perform live response?

**A:** There are no hard and fast rules stating when you should perform live response. However, as more and more regulatory bodies (consider SEC rules, HIPAA, FISMA, Visa PCI, and others) specify security measures and mechanisms that are to be used as well as the questions that need to be addressed and answered (was personal sensitive information accessed?), live response becomes even more important.

**Q:** I was involved with a case in which, after all was said and done, the "Trojan defense" was used. How would live response have helped or prepared us to address this issue?

**A:** By collecting information about processes running on the system, network connections, and other areas where you would have found Trojan or backdoor artifacts, you would have been able to rule out whether such things were running while the system was live. Your postmortem investigation would include an examination of the file system, including scheduled tasks and the like, to determine the likelihood that a Trojan was installed, but collecting volatile data from a live system would provide you with the necessary information to determine whether a Trojan was running at the time you were in front of the system.

**Q:** I'm not doing live response now. Why should I start?

**A:** Often an organization will opt for the "wipe-and-reload" mentality, in which the administrator will wipe the hard drive of a system thought to be compromised, then reload the operating system from clean media, reinstall the applications, and load the data back onto the system from backups. This is thought to be the least expensive approach. However, this approach does nothing to determine *how* the incident occurred in the first place. Some might say, "I reinstalled the operating system and updated all patches," and that's great, but not all incidents occur for want of a patch or hotfix. Sometimes it's as simple as a weak or nonexistent password on a user account or application (such as the *sa* password on SQL Server) or a poorly configured service. No amount of patching will fix these sorts of issues. Without determining how an incident occurred and addressing the issue, the incident is likely to occur again and in fairly short order after the bright, new, clean system is reconnected to the network. In addition, as I showed throughout this chapter, a great deal of valuable information is available when the system is still running—information such as physical memory, running processes, network connections, and the contents of the Clipboard—that could have a significant impact on your investigation.

# Chapter 2

## Live Response: Data Analysis

### Solution in this chapter:

- Data Analysis

☑ Summary

☑ Solutions Fast Track

☑ Frequently Asked Questions

# Introduction

Now that you've collected volatile data from a system, the question becomes "How do I 'hear' what it has to say?" or "How do I figure out what the data is telling me?" Once you've collected a process listing, how do you determine which process, if any, is malware? How do you tell whether someone has compromised the system and is currently accessing it? Finally, how can you use the volatile data you've collected to build a better picture of activity on the system, particularly as you acquire an image and perform postmortem analysis?

The purpose of this chapter is to address these sorts of questions. What you're looking for—what artifacts you will be digging for in the volatile data you've collected—depends heavily on the issue you are attempting to address. How do you dig through reams of data to find what you're looking for? In this chapter, I do not think for a moment that I will be able to answer all of your questions; rather, my hope is to provide enough data and examples so that when something occurs that I have not covered, you will have a process by which you can determine the answer on your own. Perhaps by the time you reach the end of this chapter, you will have a better understanding of why you collect volatile data, and what it can tell you.

# Data Analysis

A number of sources of information tell you what data you should collect from a live system to troubleshoot an errant application or assess an incident. Take a look on the Web at sites such as the e-Evidence Info site (www.e-evidence.info), which is updated monthly with new links to conference presentations, papers, and articles that discuss a wide range of topics, to include volatile data collection. Although many of these resources refer to data *collection*, few actually address the issue of data correlation and *analysis*. We will be addressing these issues in this chapter.

To begin, you need to look to the output of the tools, to the data you've collected, to see what sort of snapshot of data is available to you. When you use tools such as those discussed in Chapter 1, you are getting a snapshot of the state of a system at a point in time. Many times, you can quickly locate an indicator of the issue within the output from a single tool. For example, you may see something unusual in the Task Manager graphical user interface (GUI) or in the output of tlist.exe (such as an unusual executable image file path or command line). For an investigator who is familiar with Windows systems and what default or "normal" processes look like from this perspective, these indicators may be fairly obvious and may jump out immediately.

**TIP**

Microsoft provides some information regarding default processes on Windows 2000 systems in Knowledge Base article Q263201 (http://support.microsoft.com/kb/263201/en-us).

However, many investigators and even system administrators are not familiar enough with Windows systems to recognize default or "normal" processes at a glance. This is especially true when you consider that the Windows version (e.g., Windows 2000, XP, 2003, or Vista) has a great deal to do with what is "normal." For example, default processes on Windows 2000 are different from those on Windows XP, and that is just for a clean, default installation, without additional applications added. Also consider that different hardware configurations often require additional drivers and applications. The list of variations can go on, but the important point to keep in mind is that what constitutes a "normal" or legitimate process can depend on a lot of different factors, so you need to have a process for examining your available data and determining the source of the issue you're investigating. This is important, as having a process means you have steps that you can follow, and if something needs to be added or modified, you can do so easily. Without a process, how do you determine what went wrong, and what you can do to improve it? If you don't know what you did, how do you fix it?

Perhaps the best way to get started is to dive right in. When correlating and analyzing volatile data, it helps to have an idea of what you're looking for. One of the biggest issues that some information technology (IT) administrators and responders face when an incident occurs is tracking down the source of the incident based on the information they have available. One example is when an alert appears in the network-based intrusion detection system (NIDS) or an odd entry appears in the firewall logs. Many times, this may be the result of malware (e.g., worm) infection. Usually, the alert or log entry will contain information such as the source Internet Protocol (IP) address and port, as well as the destination IP address and port. The source IP address identifies the system from which the traffic originated, and as you saw in Chapter 1, if you have the source port of the network traffic, you can use that information to determine the application that sent the traffic, and identify the malware.

**W**ARNING

Keep in mind that for traffic to appear on the network, some process some-place has to have generated it. However, some processes are short-lived (e.g., a downloader that grabs and installs another file, such as a Trojan, and then terminates), and attempting to locate a process based on traffic seen in firewall logs four hours ago (and not once since then) can be frustrating. If the traffic appears on a regular basis, be sure to check all possibilities. This includes examining the source IP address of the traffic to locate the system transmitting it, and even installing a network "sniffer" to capture and examine the network traffic to determine whether it is "spoofed."

Another important point is that malware authors will often attempt to hide the presence of their applications on a system by using a familiar name, or a name similar to a legitimate file that an administrator may recognize. If the investigator searches the Web for the name, the search will return information indicating that the file is innocuous or is a legitimate file used by the operating system.

**W**ARNING

While responding to a worm outbreak on a corporate network, I determined that part of the infection was installed on the system as a Windows service that ran from an executable image file named alg.exe. Searching for infor-mation on this filename, the administrators had determined that this was a legitimate application called the "Application Layer Gateway Service." This service appears in the Registry under the CurrentControlSet\Services key, in the ALG subkey, and points to %SystemRoot%\system32\alg.exe as its executable image file. However, the service I found was located within the "Application Layer Gateway Service" subkey (first hint: the subkey name is incorrect) and pointed to %SystemRoot%\alg.exe. Be very careful when searching for filenames, as even the best of us can be tripped up by the information that is returned via such a search. I've seen seasoned malware analysts make the mistake of determining the nature of a file using nothing more than the filename.

To make all of this a little clearer, let's take a look at some examples.

# Example 1

A scenario that is seen time and time again is one in which the administrator or helpdesk is informed of unusual or suspicious activity on a system. It may be unusual activity reported by a user, or a server administrator finding some unusual files on a Web server, and when she attempts to delete them she's informed that they cannot be deleted as they are in use by another process.

In such incidents, the first responder will be faced with a system that cannot be taken down for a detailed postmortem investigation (due to time and/or business constraints), and a quick (albeit thorough) response is required. Very often, this can be accomplished through live response, in which information regarding the current state of the system is quickly collected and analyzed, with an understanding that enough information must be collected to provide as complete a picture of the system state as possible. When information is collected from a live system, although the process of collecting that information can be replicated the information itself generally cannot be duplicated, as a live system is always in a state of change.

Whenever something happens on a system, it is the result of some process that is running on that system. Although this statement may appear to be "intuitively obvious to the most casual observer" (a statement one of my graduate school professors used to offer up several times during a class, most often in the presence of a sixth-order differential equation), often this fact is missed during the stress and pressure of responding to an incident. However, the simple truth is that for something to happen on a system, a process or thread of execution must be involved in some way.

**TIP**

In his "Exploiting the Rootkit Paradox with Windows Memory Analysis" paper, Jesse Kornblum points out that rootkits, like most malware, need to run or execute. Understanding this is the key to live response.

So, how does a responder go about locating a suspicious process on a system? The answer is through live-response data collection and analysis. And believe me, I have been in the position where a client presents me with a hard drive from a system (or an acquired image of a hard drive) and asks me to tell them what processes were running on the system. The fact of the matter is that to show what was happening on a live system, you *must* have information collected from that system while it was running. Using tools discussed in Chapter 1, you can collect information about the state of the system at a point in time, capturing a snapshot of that state. As the information that you're collecting exists in volatile memory, once you shut the system down, that information no longer exists.

In this scenario, I have a Windows 2000 system that has been behaving oddly. The system is an intranet Web server running Internet Information Server (IIS) Version 5.0, and users who have attempted to access pages on the server have reported that they are unable to retrieve any information at all, and are seeing only blank pages in their browser. This is odd, as one would expect to see an error message, perhaps. So, I start up an instance of the Forensic Server (i.e., the Forensic Server Project [FSP] from Chapter 1) on my forensic workstation (IP address 192.168.1.6) using the following command line:

```
C:\fsp>fspc -c cases -n testcase1 -i "H. Carvey" -v
```

I then pick up my First Responder CD, which contains my tools and a copy of the First Responder Utility (i.e., fruc.exe, also from Chapter 1), and search for the affected system. In such incidents, I initially take a minimalist approach; I like to minimize my impact on the system (remember Locard's Exchange Principle) and optimize my efforts and response time. To that end, over time I have developed a minimal set of state information that I would need to extract from a live system to get a view that is comprehensive enough for me to locate potentially suspicious activity.

---

**TIP**

The media that accompanies this book contains desktop capture videos that demonstrate the use of the components of the FSP.

---

I have also identified a set of tools that I can use to extract that information (the fruc.ini file used with the First Responder Utility [FRU] in this scenario is included in the ch2\samples directory on the media that accompanies this book). The [Commands] section of the fruc.ini file contains the following entries:

```
1=psloggedon.exe::psloggedon.dat
2=netusers.exe -l -h::netusers-lh.dat
3=tlist.exe -c::tlist-c.dat
4=tlist.exe -s::tlist-s.dat
5=tlist.exe -t::tlist-t.dat
6=handle.exe -a -u::handle-au.dat
7=listdlls.exe::listdlls.dat
8=tcpvcon.exe -can::tcpvcon-can.dat
9=autorunsc.exe -l -d -s -t -w::autorunsc-ldstw.dat
10=svc.exe::svc.dat
11=auditpol.exe::auditpol.dat
```

Each command is run in order, and from this list you can see commands for collecting information about logged-on users (both local and remote) as well as logon history, autostart locations, processes, network connections and open ports, services, and the audit policy on the system. This set of commands will not only provide a comprehensive view of the state of the system at a snapshot in time, but also collect data that may help direct analysis and follow-on investigative efforts.

### TIP

As you saw in Chapter 1, you can run the FRU against multiple configuration (i.e., INI) files. In issues involving a potential violation of corporate acceptable use policies (employees misusing IT systems), you may want to have additional INI files that collect the contents of the Clipboard, perhaps Protected Storage information, for instance.

Approaching the affected Windows 2000 system, I place the FRU CD into the CD-ROM drive, launch a command prompt, and type in the following command:

```
E:\>fruc -s 192.168.1.6 -p 7070 -f fruc.ini -v
```

### NOTE

Whenever you're performing live incident response, I highly recommend that you collect the complete contents of physical memory (a.k.a. RAM) before performing any other activities. This allows you to acquire the contents of RAM in as pristine a state as possible, and prior to introducing additional changes to the system state. Although this goes beyond the scope of this chapter, it is a great segue into Chapter 3.

Within seconds, all of the volatile data that I want to collect from the system is extracted and safely stored on my forensic workstation for analysis.

### TIP

You can find the data I collected during this scenario in the ch2\samples directory on the media accompanying this book, in the archive named testcase1.zip.

Once back at the forensic workstation, I see that, as expected, the testcase1 directory contains 16 files. One of the benefits of the FSP is that it is self-documenting; the fruc.ini file contains the list of tools and command lines used to launch those tools when collecting volatile data. As this file and the tools themselves are on a CD, they cannot be modified, so as long as I maintain that CD, I will have immutable information about what tools (the version of each tool, etc.) I ran on the system, and the options used to run those tools. One of the files in the testcase1 directory is the case.log file, which maintains a list of the data sent to the server by the FRU and the MD5 and SHA-1 hashes for the files to which the data was saved. Also, I see the case.hash file, which contains the MD5 and SHA-1 hashes of the case. log file after it was closed.

The information that I'm interested in is contained in the other 14 files within the case directory. One of the first things I generally do to start my analysis is to see whether any unusual processes jump out at me. To do that, I will most often start with the output of the *tlist –c* command, as this will show the command line used to launch each active (and visible) process on the system. For example, one of the processes that is immediately visible is the FRUC process itself (thus demonstrating the importance of capturing the physical memory dump first):

```
1000 FRUC.EXE
     Command Line: fruc -s 192.168.1.6 -p 7070 -f fruc.ini -v
```

Scrolling through the rest of the file, I see a lot of "normal" processes; that is, processes that I am used to seeing running on a Windows system. I then run across the process for the IIS Web server that I know to be running on this system:

```
736 inetinfo.exe
     Command Line: C:\WINNT\system32\inetsrv\inetinfo.exe
```

Scrolling further, I run across a process that immediately jumps out at me as unusual and suspicious:

```
816 inetinfo.exe
     Command Line: inetinfo.exe -L -d -p 80 -e c:\winnt\system32\cmd.exe
```

Most IIS Web servers have only one instance of inetinfo.exe running, and this system has two. Not only that, but the "normal" version of inetinfo.exe runs from the system32\inetsrv directory by default, just as we see with the instance of inetinfo.exe with process identifier (PID) 736. However, the instance of inetinfo.exe with PID 816 appears to be running from the system32 directory; in addition, the command line used to launch this process looks suspiciously like the command line used to launch netcat! 

Needing more information on this, and noting that the command line for PID 816 appears to have bound the process to port 80 (which would account for the unusual behavior reported by users), I then open the file containing the output of the eighth command run from the fruc.ini file (i.e., *tcpvcon.exe –can*) to take a look:

```
TCP, C:\WINNT\system32\inetsrv\inetinfo.exe,736,,127.0.0.1:443,*.*
TCP, C:\WINNT\system32\inetsrv\inetinfo.exe,736,,127.0.0.1:21,*.*
TCP, C:\WINNT\system32\inetsrv\inetinfo.exe,736,,127.0.0.1:25,*.*
TCP, C:\WINNT\system32\inetsrv\inetinfo.exe,736,,127.0.0.1:1026,*.*
TCP, C:\WINNT\system32\inetsrv\inetinfo.exe,816,,127.0.0.1:80,*.*
```

Normally, I would expect to see PID 736 bound to port 80, but in this instance, PID 816 is bound to that port instead.

As you can see, I've identified PID 816 as a suspicious process, and it appears that this process would account for the unusual activity that was reported. Checking the output of the other commands, I don't see any unusual services running, or any references to the process in autostart locations. The output of the handle.exe utility shows that the process is running under the Administrator account, but no files appear to be open. Also, the output of the *tcpvcon.exe –can* command shows that there are no current connections to port 80 on that system. At this point, I've identified the issue, and now need to determine how this bit of software got on the system and how it ended up running as a process.

# Example 2

Another popular scenario seen in network environments is unusual traffic that originates from a system appearing in intrusion detection system (IDS) or firewall logs. Most times, an administrator sees something unusual or suspicious, such as traffic leaving the network that is not what is normally seen. Examples of this often include IRCbot and worm infections. Generally, an IRCbot will infect a system, perhaps as the result of the user surfing to a Web page that contains some code that exploits a vulnerability in the Web browser. The first thing that generally happens is that an initial downloader application is deposited on the system, which then reaches out to another Web site to download and install the actual IRCbot code itself. From there, the IRCbot accesses a channel on an Internet Relay Chat (IRC) server and awaits commands from the botmaster.

---

## WARNING

IRCbots have been a huge issue for quite a while, as entire armies of bots, or "botnets," have been found to be involved in a number of cybercrimes. In the February 19, 2006 issue of the *Washington Post Magazine*, Brian Krebs presented the story of botmaster 0x80 to the world. His story clearly showed the ease with which botnets are developed and how they can be used. Just a few months later, Robert Lemos's SecurityFocus article (www.securityfocus. com/news/11390) warned us that IRCbots seem to be moving from a client/ server framework to a peer-to-peer framework, making them much harder to shut down. You can find the article at www.washingtonpost.com/wp-dyn/ content/article/2006/02/14/AR2006021401342.html.

In the case of worm infections, once a worm infects a system, it will try to reach out and infect other systems. Worms generally do this by scanning IP addresses, looking for the same vulnerability (many worms today attempt to use several different vulnerabilities to infect systems) that they used to infect the current host. Some worms are pretty virulent in their scanning; the SQL Slammer worm (www.cert.org/advisories/CA-2003-04.html) ran amok on the Internet in January 2003, generating so much traffic that servers and even ATM cash machines across the Internet were subject to massive denial of service (DoS) attacks.

The mention of DoS attacks brings another important aspect of this scenario to mind. Sometimes IT administrators are informed by an external party that they may have infected systems. In such cases, usually the owner of a system that is being scanned by a worm or is under a DoS attack will see the originating IP address of the traffic in captures of the traffic, do some research regarding the owner of that IP address (usually it's a range and not a single IP address that is assigned to someone), and then attempt to contact them. That's right, even in the year 2009 it isn't unusual for someone to knock on your door to tell you that you have infected systems.

Regardless of how the administrator is notified, the issue of response remains the same. One of the difficulties of such issues is that armed with an IP address and a port number (both of which were taken from the headers of captured network traffic) the administrator must then determine the nature of the incident. Generally, the steps to do that are to determine the physical location of the system, and then to collect and analyze information from that system.

This scenario starts and progresses in much the same manner as the previous scenario, in that I launch the FSP on my forensic workstation, go to the target system with my FRUC CD, and collect volatile data from the system.

**TIP**

You can find the data I collected during this scenario in the ch2\samples directory on the accompanying media, in the archive named testcase2.zip.

Once back at the forensic workstation, I open the output of the *tlist.exe −t* command (which prints the Task Tree showing each process listed, indented beneath its parent process) and PID 980 stands out as odd to me:

```
System Process (0)
System (8)
  SMSS.EXE (140)
    CSRSS.EXE (164)
    WINLOGON.EXE (160) NetDDE Agent
      SERVICES.EXE (212)
        svchost.exe (404)
        spoolsv.exe (428)
        svchost.exe (480)
        regsvc.exe (532)
        mstask.exe (556) SYSTEM AGENT COM WINDOW
        snmp.exe (628)
        VMwareService.e (684)
        WinMgmt.exe (600)
        svchost.exe (720)
          wuauclt.exe (1080)
        inetinfo.exe (736)
        svchost.exe (1192)
      LSASS.EXE (224)
explorer.exe (520) Program Manager
  VMwareTray.exe (1232)
  VMwareUser.exe (1256)
  WZQKPICK.EXE (1268) About WinZip Quick Pick
  CMD.EXE (812) Command Prompt - svchost 192.168.1.28 80
    svchost.exe (980)
```

To see why this process appears odd, it is important to understand that on a default installation of Windows 2000, usually only two copies of svchost.exe are running.

**TIP**

Microsoft Knowledge Base article Q250320 (http://support.microsoft.com/ ?kbid=250320) provides a description of svchost.exe on Windows 2000 (Knowledge Base article Q314056 [http://support.microsoft.com/kb/314056/ EN-US/] provides a description of svchost.exe on Windows XP). The example

> output of the *tlist –s* command not only shows two copies of svchost.exe running, but also references the Registry key that lists the groupings illustrated in the article. Also see Microsoft Knowledge Base article Q263201 (http://support.microsoft.com/?kbid=263201) for a list of default processes found on Windows 2000 systems.

The output of the *tlist –t* command shows an additional copy of svchost.exe, and one that appears to be running from a command prompt window, rather than from services.exe, as with the other instances of svchost.exe.

Checking the output of the *tlist –c* command to view the command-line options used to launch PID 980, I see:

```
980 svchost.exe
   Command Line: svchost 192.168.1.28 80
```

The output of the *tcpvcon.exe –can* command shows me that PID 980 is using a client port:

```
TCP,C:\WINNT\system\svchost.exe,980,ESTABLISHED, 192.168.1.22:1103,
192.168.1.28:80
```

Had it been run and had the *–o* switch been available on the Windows 2000 system, the output of the *netstat.exe –ano* command would have also shown me that PID 980 has an active network connection to a remote system on port 80:

```
TCP     192.168.1.22:1103     192.168.1.28:80     ESTABLISHED     980
```

At this point, based on the information I have, I may want to monitor network traffic by placing a network sniffer or a system with a sniffer installed (such as Wireshark, found at www.wireshark.org) on the network to begin capturing traffic to see what data is being transmitted between the two systems. From the other volatile data that was collected, PID 980 does not appear to have any files open (per the output of the handle.exe tool), and there do not seem to be any additional, unusual processes.

When you are looking at processes on a system, it helps to know a little bit about how processes are created in relation to each other. For example, as illustrated in the output of the *tlist –t* command earlier (taken from a Windows 2000 system), most system processes originate from the process named "System" (PID 8 on Windows 2000, PID 4 on XP), whereas most user processes originate from explorer.exe, which is the shell, or as listed by tlist.exe, the "Program Manager." Generally (and I use this word carefully, as there may be exceptions), we see that the System process is the "parent" process for the services.exe process, which in turn is the parent process for, well, many services. Services.exe is the parent process for the svchost.exe processes, for instance. On the user side, a command prompt (cmd.exe) will appear as a child process to the explorer.exe process, and any command run from within the command prompt, such as *tlist –t*, will appear as a child process to cmd.exe.

So, how is this important to live response? Take a look at the output from the *tlist –t* command again. You'll see an instance of svchost.exe (PID 980) running as a child process to cmd.exe, which is itself a child process to explorer.exe … not at all where we would expect to see svchost.exe!

Now, let's take this a step further. What if the running svchost.exe (PID 980) had been installed as a service? Although we would not have noticed this in the output of *tlist –t*, we would have seen something odd in the output of *tlist –c*, which shows us the command line used to launch each process. The rogue svchost.exe would most likely have had to have originated from within a directory other than the system32 directory, thanks to Windows File Protection (WFP). WFP is a mechanism used, starting with Windows 2000, in which certain system (and other very important) files are "protected," in that attempts to modify the files will cause WFP to "wake up" and automatically replace the modified file with a fresh copy from its cache (leaving evidence of this activity in the Event Log). Windows 2000 had some issues in which WFP could easily be subverted, but those have been fixed. So, assuming that WFP hasn't been subverted in some manner, we would expect to see the rogue svchost.exe running from another directory, perhaps Windows\System or Temp, alerting us to the culprit.

## Warning

WFP can be subverted on all Windows systems, in some cases rather easily. Apparently, an undocumented application program interface (API) function is available through sfc_os.dll, exported at ordinal 5, and has been given the name *SfcFileException*; this is discussed at the Bitsum Technologies site (www.bitsum.com/aboutwfp.asp), in addition to other locations across the Internet. However, the notable exception is Microsoft.com. According to descriptions of this API function, properly calling it will disable WFP for one minute, enough time for a "protected" file to be modified or replaced. As WFP does not poll the protected files, once WFP is enabled again, there is nothing to notify it that the file has been changed. Under normal circumstances, when the operating system generates a file change event, WFP "wakes up," checks to see whether the change event occurred for a protected file, and if so, replaces the file with a "known good" copy from the cache and generates an Event Log record. With WFP disabled for one minute via the *SfcFileException* API, there is nothing to detect or alert to the fact that the file was changed. We will discuss this in greater detail in Chapter 5, where I will also demonstrate an analysis tool to provide indications of this sort of activity during postmortem analysis.

# Example 3

Microsoft's psexec.exe (http://technet.microsoft.com/en-us/sysinternals/bb897553.aspx) is a great tool to demonstrate how you might go about looking for "unusual" or "suspicious" processes on systems. Many times, an intruder will gain access to a system through some means and take advantage of the fact that he has Administrator-level privileges, and escalate those privileges to the System level. This is done, in part, to (a) prevent an administrator from noticing that the bad guy is on the system or has a process running, and (b) prevent the administrator from being able to simply stop the "bad" process from running.

So, the first thing we'll do is download a copy of psexec.exe from the Microsoft/Sysinternals site, and then run it with the following command line:

```
C:\tools>psexec -s cmd
```

At this point, we still have a command prompt, but it's running with System-level privileges. Now, to add some data to observe, launch Solitaire by typing **sol** at the command prompt. You'll notice that you won't see the application pop up on your desktop, but you will get the command prompt back without any errors.

Now, open another command prompt, and run **tlist.exe −t**. The output should look similar to the following (output trimmed for the sake of brevity):

```
D:\tools>tlist -t
System Process (0)
System (4)
  smss.exe (968)
    csrss.exe (1032)
    winlogon.exe (1060)
      services.exe (1104)
        svchost.exe (1360)
        svchost.exe (1704)
          wscntfy.exe (316)
        svchost.exe (1968)
        svchost.exe (352)
        spoolsv.exe (872)
        scardsvr.exe (932)
        alg.exe (1768)
        PSEXESVC.EXE (1560)
          cmd.exe (3664)
            sol.exe (3832)
      lsass.exe (1116)
```

```
explorer.exe (372) Program Manager
  DLACTRLW.EXE (780)
  cmd.exe (2748) Command Prompt - tlist -t
    tlist.exe (2196)
  cmd.exe (2684) \\WINTERMUTE: cmd
    psexec.exe (3448)
```

Notice that beneath the explorer.exe process, you see command prompts running for both tlist.exe and psexec.exe (processes with PIDs of 2748 and 2684, respectively). However, you also see PSEXESVC.EXE running above explorer.exe in the process listing tree view. This is because the process is running with System-level privileges. Beneath the PSEXESVC.EXE process, indented to indicate that it is a child process of PSEXESVC.EXE, is yet another command prompt (process with PID 3664), and beneath *that* process is the Solitaire child process. Processes running as services (such as sol.exe) do not run in interactive mode, as they would if they were run normally by a user.

I used this example to illustrate what can happen when the principle of least privilege isn't followed when creating user accounts. Too often, some sort of downloader gets on a user's system, either through the user accessing a malicious Web site or through some other means, such as an e-mail attachment. The downloader then does its job of grabbing other malware, and because the user account is running on the system with Administrator privileges, the malware then has the ability to do everything the user can, such as create Scheduled Tasks or install Windows services. With its privileges escalated beyond the reach of the Administrator account, the malware now has unfettered access to all system resources. In addition, the malware is no longer interacting with the desktop, which means a number of artifacts will no longer be available (see Chapter 4).

# Agile Analysis

Perhaps one of the most often stated reasons for not performing live response at all is an inability to locate the source of the issue in the plethora of data that has been collected. Many of the tools available for collecting volatile (and nonvolatile) data during live response collect a great deal of data, so much so that it may appear to be overwhelming to the investigator. In the example cases in this chapter, I didn't have to collect a great deal of data to pin down the source of the issue. The data collection tools I used in the example cases take two simple facts into account: that malware needs to run to have any effect on a system, and that malware needs to be persistent to have any continuing effect on a system (i.e., malware authors ideally want their software to survive reboots and users logging in). We also use these basic precepts in our analysis to cull through the available data and locate the source of the issues. To perform rapid, agile analysis, we need to look to automation and data reduction techniques.

Although the example cases were simple and straightforward, they do illustrate a point. The methodology used to locate the suspicious process in each case is not too different from the methodology used to investigate the russiantopz (www.securityfocus.com/infocus/1618) bot in 2002. In fact, it's akin to differential analysis (i.e., looking for the differences between two states). However, a big caveat to keep in mind, particularly if you're performing live response as a law enforcement officer or consultant, is that in most cases, an original baseline of the system from prior to the incident will not be available, and you must rely on an understanding of the workings of the underlying operating system and applications for your "baseline." For instance, in the first example case, had there been only one instance of inetinfo.exe in the process information, and had I not known whether the infected system was running a Web server, I could have correlated what I knew (i.e., inetinfo.exe process running) to the output of the svc.exe tool, which in this instance appears as follows:

```
736,W3SVC,World Wide Web Publishing Service
,C:\WINNT\system32\inetsrv\inetinfo.exe,Running,Auto,Share Process,#
```

This correlation could be automated through the use of scripting tools, and if a legitimate service (such as shown earlier) is found to correlate to a legitimate process (inetinfo.exe with PID 736), we've just performed data reduction.

---

**NOTE**

The svc.exe tool used in the example cases collects information about services on the system, and displays the results in comma-separated value (.csv) format so that the results can be easily parsed, or opened in Excel for analysis. The column headers are the PID, service name, service display name, path to the executable image, service state, service start mode, service type, and whether (#) or not (*) the service has a description string. Many times, malware authors will fail to provide a description string for their service; a lack of this string would be a reason to investigate the service further.

---

A rule of thumb that a knowledgeable investigator should keep in mind while analyzing volatile data is that the existence of an inetinfo.exe process without the corresponding presence of a running W3SVC "World Wide Web Publishing" service may indicate the presence of malware, or at least of a process that merits additional attention.

However, the investigator must also keep in mind that the inetinfo.exe process also supports the Microsoft File Transfer Protocol (FTP) service and the Simple Mail Transfer Protocol (SMTP) e-mail server, as illustrated in the output of the *tlist −s* command:

```
736 inetinfo.exe    Svcs: IISADMIN,MSFTPSVC,SMTPSVC,W3SVC
```

Simply put, a running inetinfo.exe process without the corresponding services also running could point to an issue. Again, this check can also be automated. For example, if the output of the FRUC tools were parsed and entered into a database, SQL statements could be used to extract and correlate information.

---

**T**ɪᴘ

During his presentation at the BlackHat DC 2007 conference, Kevin Mandia stated that a good number of the incidents his company responded to over the previous year illustrated a move by malware authors to maintain persistence in their software by having it install itself as a Windows service. My experience has shown this to be the case, as well. In fact, in a number of engagements, I have seen malware get on a system and create a service that then "shovels" a shell (i.e., command-line connection) off the system and off the network infrastructure to a remote system. When the "bad guy" connects on the other end, he then has System-level, albeit command-line, access to the compromised system.

---

This shows that with some knowledge and work, issues can be addressed in a quick and thorough manner, through the use of automation and data reduction. Automation is important, as incidents are generally characterized by stress and pressure, which just happen to be the conditions under which we're most likely to make mistakes. Automation allows us to codify a process and be able to follow that same process over and over again. If we understand the artifacts and bits of volatile data that will provide us with a fairly complete picture of the state of the system, we can quickly collect and correlate the information, and determine the nature and scope of the incident. This leads to a more agile response, moving quickly, albeit in a thorough manner using a documented process. From here, additional volatile data can be collected, if necessary. Using this minimalist approach upfront reduces the amount of data that needs to parsed and correlated, and leads to an overall better response.

With respect to analysis and automation, the "rules of thumb" used by an investigator to locate suspicious processes within the collected volatile data are largely based on experience and an understanding of the underlying operating system and applications.

**TIP**

Several years ago, a friend of mine would send me volatile data that he'd collected during various incidents. He used a series of tools and a batch file to collect his volatile data, and long after the case had been completed he would send me the raw data files, asking me to find out what was "wrong." With no access to the state and nature of the original system, I had to look for clues in the data he sent me. This is a great way to develop skills and even some of the necessary correlation tools.

Some of these rules can be codified into procedures and even scripts to make the analysis and data reduction process more efficient. One example of this is the svchost.exe process. Some malware authors make use of the fact that usually several copies of svchost.exe are running on Windows systems (my experience shows two copies running on Windows 2000, five on Windows XP SP2, and seven on Windows 2003) and use that name for their malware. We know the legitimate svchost.exe process follows a couple of simple rules, one of which is that the process always originates from an executable image located in the system32 directory. Therefore, we can write a Perl script that will run through the output of the *tlist −c* command and immediately flag any copies of an svchost.exe process that is *not* running from the system32 directory.

This is a variation on the artificial ignorance method of analysis in which you perform data reduction by removing everything you know to be "good," and what's left is most likely the stuff you need to look at. (*Artificial ignorance* is a term coined by Marcus Ranum, who can be found at www.ranum.com.) I've used this approach quite effectively in a corporate environment, not only during incident response activities but also while performing scans of the network for spyware and other issues. What I did was create a Perl script that would reach out to the primary domain controller and get a list of all the workstations it "saw" on the network. Then, I'd connect to each workstation using domain administrator credentials, extract the contents of the Run key (see Chapter 4 for more information on this Registry key) from each system, and save that information in a file on my system. The first time I ran this script, I had quite a few pages of data to sort through. So, I began investigating some of the things I found, and determined that many of them were legitimate applications and drivers. As such, I created a list of "known good" entries, and then when I scanned systems I would check the information I retrieved against this list, and write the information to my log file only if it *wasn't* on the list. In fairly short order, I reduced my log file to about half a page.

This is one approach you can use to quickly analyze the volatile data you've collected. However, the key to agile analysis and a rapid response it to reduce the amount of data you actually need to investigate. This may mean putting the data you have collected into a more manageable form, or it may mean weeding out artifacts that you know to be "good," thereby reducing the amount of data you need to actually investigate.

# Expanding the Scope

What happens when things get a little more complicated than the scenarios we've looked at? We see security experts in the media all the time, saying that cybercrime is becoming increasingly sophisticated (and it is). So, how do we deal with more complicated incidents? After all, not all processes involved in an incident may be as long-lived as the ones illustrated in my example scenarios. For instance, a downloader may be on a system through a Web browser vulnerability, and once it has downloaded its designated target software, it has completed its purpose and is no longer active. Therefore, information about that process, to include network connections used by the process, will no longer be available.

Not too long ago, I dealt with an incident involving an encrypted executable that was not identified by more than two dozen antivirus scanning engines. We also had considerable trouble addressing the issue, as there was no running process with the same name as the mysterious file on any of the affected systems that we looked at. Dynamic analysis (see Chapter 6) of the malware showed that the malware injected itself into the Internet Explorer process space and terminated. This bit of information accounted for the fact that we were not able to find a running process using the same name as the mysterious file, and that all of our investigative efforts were leading us back to Internet Explorer (iexplore.exe) as the culprit. We confirmed our findings by including the fact that on all of the systems from which we'd collected volatile data, not one had Internet Explorer running on the desktop. So, here was the iexplore.exe process, live and running, spewing traffic out onto the network and to the Internet, but there was no browser window open on the desktop.

The interesting thing about this particular engagement wasn't so much the code injection technique used, or the fact that the mysterious executable file we'd found appeared to be unidentifiable by multiple antivirus engines. Rather, I thought the most interesting aspect of all this was that the issue was surprisingly close to a proof of concept worm called "Setiri" that was presented by a couple of SensePost (www.sensepost.com/research_conferences.html) researchers at the BlackHat conference in Las Vegas in 2002. Setiri operated by accessing Internet Explorer as a Component Object Model (COM) server, and generating traffic through Internet Explorer. Interestingly enough, Dave Roth wrote a Perl script (www.roth.net/perl/scripts) called IEEvents.pl that, with some minor modifications, will launch Internet Explorer invisibly (i.e., no visible window on the desktop) and retrieve Web pages and such.

What's the point of all this? Well, I just wanted to point out how sophisticated some incidents can be. Getting a backdoor on a system through a downloader, which itself is first dropped on a system via a Web browser vulnerability, isn't particularly sophisticated (although it is just as effective) in the face of having code injected into a process's memory space.

Another technique malware authors use to get their code running (and to keep it running) can be found in spyware circles, such as browser helper objects (you can find more information on BHOs in Chapter 4). For example, two BHOs found on a system are the Adobe PDF Reader Link Helper and the DriveLetterAccess helper objects. You can find these in the Internet Explorer process space by using listdlls.exe:

```
C:\Program Files\Adobe\Acrobat 7.0\ActiveX\AcroIEHelper.dll
C:\WINDOWS\System32\DLA\DLASHX_W.DLL
```

Keep in mind that as versions of software change, so may their paths within the file system. For example, with Adobe Reader Version 8, the path for the Adobe PDF Reader Link Helper is C:\Program Files\Common Files\Adobe\Acrobat\ActiveX\AcroIEHelper.dll.

If someone compromises a Windows system from the network, you may expect to find artifacts of a login (in the Security Event Log, or in an update of the last login time for that user), open files on the system, and even processes that have been launched by that user. If the attacker is not using the Microsoft login mechanisms (Remote Desktop, "net use" command, etc.), and is instead accessing the system via a backdoor, you can expect to see the running process, open handles, network connections, and so forth.

With some understanding of the nature of the incident, you can effectively target live-response activities to address the issue, not only from a data collection perspective but also from a data correlation and analysis perspective.

# Reaction

Many times, the question that comes up immediately following the confirmation of an incident is "What do we do now?" I hate to say it, but that really depends on your infrastructure. For instance, in the example cases in this chapter, you saw "incidents" in which the offending process was running under the Administrator account. Now, this was a result of the setup for the case, but it is not unusual when responding to an incident to find a process running within the Administrator or even the System user context. Much of the prevailing wisdom in cases such as this is that you can no longer trust anything the system is telling you (i.e., you cannot trust that the output of the tools you're using to collect information is giving you an accurate view of the system) and that the only acceptable reaction is to wipe the system clean and start over, reinstalling the operating system from clean media (i.e., the original installation media) and reloading all data from backups.

To me, this seems like an awful lot of trouble to go through, particularly when it's likely that you're going to have to do it all over again fairly soon. You're probably thinking to yourself, "What??" Well, let's say you locate a suspicious process, and using tools such as pslist. exe you see that the process hasn't been running for very long in relation to the overall uptime of the system itself. This tells you that the process started sometime after the system was booted. For example, as I'm sitting here writing this chapter, my system has been running for more than eight hours. I can see this in the "Elapsed Time" column, on the far right in the output of pslist.exe, as illustrated here:

```
smss       1024    11     3     21     168     0:00:00.062     8:28:38.109
csrss      1072    13    13    555    1776     0:00:26.203     8:28:36.546
```

However, I have other processes that were started well after the system was booted:

```
uedit32     940     8     1     88    4888     0:00:03.703     4:07:25.296
cmd        3232     8     1     32    2008     0:00:00.046     3:26:46.640
```

Although the Media Access Control (MAC) times on files written to the hard drive can be modified to mislead an investigator, the amount of time a process has been running is harder to fake. With this information, the investigator can develop a timeline of when the incident may have occurred, and determine the overall extent of the incident (similar to the approach used in the example cases earlier). The goal is to determine the root cause of the incident so that whatever issue led to the compromise can be rectified, and subsequently corrected on other systems, as well. If this is not done, putting a cleanly loaded system back on the network will likely result in the system being compromised all over again. If systems need to be patched, patches can be rolled out. However, if the root cause of the incident is really a weak Administrator password, no amount of patching will correct that issue. The same is true with application configuration vulnerabilities, such as exploited by network worms.

Now, let's consider another case, in which the suspicious process is found to be a service, and the output of pslist.exe shows us that the process has been running for about the same amount of time as the system itself. Well, as there do not appear to be any Windows APIs that allow an attacker to modify the LastWrite times on Registry keys (MAC times on files can be easily modified through the use of publicly documented APIs), an investigator can extract that information from a live system and determine when the service was installed on the system. A knowledgeable investigator knows that to install a Windows service, the user context must be that of an Administrator, so checking user logins and user activity on the system may lead to the root cause of the incident.

Again, it is important to determine the root cause of an incident so that the situation can be fixed, not only on the compromised system but on other systems as well.

**W**ARNING

Microsoft Knowledge Base article Q328691 (http://support.microsoft.com/default.aspx?scid=kb;en-us;328691), "MIRC Trojan-related attack detection and repair," contains this statement in the Attack Vectors section: "Analysis to date indicates that the attackers appear to have gained entry to the systems by using weak or blank administrator passwords. Microsoft has no evidence to suggest that any heretofore unknown security vulnerabilities have been used in the attacks." Simply reinstalling the operating system, applications, and data on affected systems would lead to their compromise all over again, as long as the same configuration settings were used. In corporate environments, communal Administrator accounts with easy-to-remember (i.e., weak) passwords are used, and a reinstalled system would most likely use the same account name and password as it did prior to the incident.

Determining that root cause may seem like an impossible task, but with the right knowledge and right skill sets, and a copy of this book in your hand, that job should be much easier!

# Prevention

One thing that IT departments can do to make the job of responding to incidents easier (keeping in mind that first responders are usually members of the IT staff) is to go beyond simply installing the operating system and applications, and make use of system hardening guides and configuration management procedures. For example, by limiting the running services and processes on a server to only those that are necessary for the operation of the system itself, you limit the attack surface of the system. Then, for the services you do run, configure them as securely as possible. If you have an IIS Web server running, that system may be a Web server, but is it also an FTP server? If you don't need the FTP server running, disable it, remove it, or don't even install it in the first place. Then, configure your Web server to use only the necessary script mappings (IIS Web servers with the .ida script mapping removed were not susceptible to the Code Red worm in 2001), and you may even want to install the UrlScan tool (http://technet.microsoft.com/en-us/security/cc242650.aspx).

**TIP**

The UrlScan tool, available from Microsoft, supports IIS Version 6.0, and Nazim's IIS Security Blog (http://blogs.iis.net/nazim/default.aspx) mentions that UrlScan 3.0 is available for us in protecting the IIS Web server against some of the more recent SQL injection attacks.

This same sort of minimalist approach applies to setting up users on a system, as well. Only the necessary users should have the appropriate level of access to a system. If a user does not need access to a system, either to log in from the console or to access the system remotely from the network, he should not have an account on that system. I have responded to several instances in which old user accounts with weak passwords were left on systems and intruders were able to gain access to the systems through those accounts. In another instance, a compromised system showed logins via a user's account during times that it was known that the person who was assigned that account was on an airplane 33,000 feet over the Midwestern United States. However, that user rarely used his account to access the system in question, and the account was left unattended.

By reducing the attack surface of a system, you can make it difficult (maybe even *really* difficult) for someone to gain access to that system, to either compromise data on the system or use that system as a steppingstone from which to launch further attacks. The attacker may then either generate a great deal of "noise" on a system, in the form of log entries and error messages, making the attempts more "visible" to administrators, or simply give up because compromising the system wasn't an "easy win." Either way, I'd rather deal with a couple of megabytes' worth of log files showing failed attempts (as when the Nimda worm was prevalent; see www.cert.org/advisories/CA-2001-26.html) than a system that was compromised repeatedly due to a lack of any sort of hardening or monitoring. At least if some steps have been taken to limit the attack surface and the level to which the system can be compromised, an investigator will have more data to work with, in log files and other forms of data.

# Summary

Once you've collected volatile data during live response, the next step is to analyze that data and provide an effective and timely response. Many times, investigators may be overwhelmed with the sheer volume of volatile data they need to go through, and this can be more overwhelming if they're unsure what they're looking for. Starting with some idea of the nature of the incident, the investigator can begin to reduce the amount of data by looking for and parsing out "known good" processes, network connections, active users, and so forth. She can also automate some of the data correlation, further reducing the overall amount of data, and reducing the number of mistakes that may be made.

All of these things will lead to timely, accurate, and effective response to incidents.

# Solutions Fast Track

## Data Analysis

☑ Live response is generally characterized by stress, pressure, and confusion. Investigators can use data reduction and automation techniques to provide effective response.

☑ Once data has been collected and analyzed, the final response to the incident can be based upon nontechnical factors, such as the business or political infrastructure of the environment.

☑ Performing a root-cause analysis when faced with an incident can go a long way toward saving both time and money down the road.

☑ Taking a minimalist approach to system configuration can often serve to hamper or even inhibit an incident altogether. At the very least, making a system more difficult to compromise will generate "noise" and possibly even alerts during the attempts.

# Frequently Asked Questions

**Q:** What is the difference between a "process" and a "service"?

**A:** From the perspective of live response, there isn't a great deal of difference between the two, except in how each is started or launched, and the user context under which each runs. Windows services are actually processes, and can be started automatically when the system starts. When a process is started as a service, it most often runs with System-level privileges, whereas processes started automatically via a user's Registry hive will run in that user's context.

**Q:** I'm seeing some intermittent and unusual traffic in my firewall logs. The traffic seems to be originating from a system on my network and going out to an unusual system. When I see the traffic, I go to the system and collect volatile data, but I don't see any active network connections, or any active processes using the source port I found in the traffic. I then see the traffic again six hours later. What can I do?

**A:** In the fruc.ini file used in the example cases in this chapter, I used autorunsc.exe from Microsoft/Sysinternals to collection information about autostart locations. Be sure to check for scheduled tasks, as well as any unusual processes that may be launching a child process to generate the traffic.

**Q:** I have an incident that I'm trying to investigate, but I can't seem to find any indication of the incident on the system.

**A:** Many times, what appears to be "unusual" or "suspicious" behavior on a Windows system is borne from a lack of familiarity with the system rather than an actual incident. I have seen responders question the existence of certain files and directories (Prefetch, etc.) for no other reason than the fact that they aren't familiar with the system. In fact, I remember one case where an administrator deleted all the files with .pf extensions that he found in the C:\Windows\Prefetch directory (see Chapter 5). A couple of days later, many of those files had mysteriously returned, and he felt the system had been compromised by a Trojan or backdoor.

# Chapter 3

# Windows Memory Analysis

## Solutions in this chapter:

- **Collecting Process Memory**
- **Dumping Physical Memory**
- **Analyzing a Physical Memory Dump**

☑ **Summary**

☑ **Solutions Fast Track**

☑ **Frequently Asked Questions**

# Introduction

In Chapter 1, we discussed collecting volatile data from a live, running Windows system. From the order of volatility listed in RFC 3227, we saw that one of the first items of volatile data that should be collected during live-response activities is the contents of physical memory, commonly referred to as RAM. Although the specifics of collecting particular parts of volatile memory, such as network connections or running processes, have been known for some time and discussed pretty extensively, the issue of collecting, parsing, and analyzing the entire contents of physical memory is a relatively new endeavor, even today. This field of research has really opened up in the past several years, beginning in summer 2005, at least from a public perspective.

The most important question that needs to be answered at this point is "Why?" Why would you want to collect the contents of RAM? How is doing this useful, how is it important, and what would you miss if you didn't collect and analyze the contents of RAM? Until now, some investigators have collected the contents of RAM in the hope of finding something they wouldn't find on the hard drive during a postmortem analysis—specifically, passwords. Programs will prompt the user for a password, and if the dialog box has disappeared from view, the most likely place to find that password is in memory. Malware analysts will look to memory in dealing with encrypted or obfuscated malware, because when the malware is launched, it will be decrypted in memory. More and more, malware is obfuscated in such a way that static, offline analysis is extremely difficult at best. However, if the malware were allowed to execute, it would exist in memory in a decrypted state, making it easier to analyze what the malware does. Finally, rootkits will hide processes, files, Registry keys, and even network connections from view by the tools we usually use to enumerate these items, but by analyzing the contents of RAM we can find what's been hidden. We can also find information about processes that have since exited.

In 2008, Greg Hoglund (perhaps best known for writing the first viable rootkit for Windows systems and rootkit.com, but also as the CEO of HBGary, Inc.) wrote a short paper titled "The Value of Physical Memory Analysis for Incident Response" (www.hbgary.com/resources.html). In that paper, Greg describes what can be extracted from the contents of physical memory, and perhaps most importantly, the value of that information with respect to addressing issues in incident response and computer forensic analysis.

# A Brief History

In the past, the "analysis" of physical memory dumps has consisted of running strings or *grep* against the "image" file, looking for passwords, Internet Protocol (IP) addresses, e-mail addresses, or other strings that could give the analyst an investigative lead. The drawback of this method of "analysis" is that it is difficult to tie the information you find to a distinct process. Was the IP address that was discovered part of the case, or was it actually used by some other process? How about that word that looks like a password? Is it the password an attacker uses to access a Trojan on the system, or is it part of an instant messaging (IM) conversation?

Being able to perform some kind of analysis of a dump of physical memory has been high on the wish lists of many within the forensic community for some time. Others (such as myself) have recognized the need for easily accessible tools and frameworks for retrieving physical memory dumps and analyzing their contents.

In summer 2005, the Digital Forensic Research Workshop (DFRWS; www.dfrws.org) issued a "memory analysis challenge" in order "to motivate discourse, research, and tool development" in this area. Anyone was invited to download the two files containing dumps of physical memory (the dumps were obtained using a modified copy of dd.exe available on the Helix 1.6 distribution) and answer questions based on the scenario provided at the Web site. Chris Betz and the duo of George M. Garner, Jr., and Robert-Jan Mora were selected as the joint winners of the challenge, providing excellent write-ups illustrating their methodologies and displaying the results of the tools they developed. Unfortunately, these tools were not made publicly available.

In the year following the challenge, others continued this research or conducted their own, following their own avenues. Andreas Schuster (http://computer.forensikblog.de/en/topics/windows/memory_analysis) began releasing portions of his research on the English version of his blog, together with the format of the EProcess and EThread structures from various versions of Windows, including Windows 2000 and XP. Joe Stewart posted a Perl script called pmodump.pl as part of the Truman Project (www.secureworks.com/research/tools/truman.html), which allows you to extract the memory used by a process from a dump of memory (important for malware analysis). Mariusz Burdach released information regarding memory analysis (initially for Linux systems but then later specifically for Windows systems) to include a presentation at the BlackHat Federal 2006 conference. Jesse Kornblum has offered several insights in the area of memory analysis to include determining the original operating system from the contents of the memory dump. During summer 2006, Tim Vidas, (http://nucia.unomaha.edu/tvidas/), a senior research fellow at Nebraska University, released procloc.pl, a Perl script to locate processes in RAM dumps as well as crash dumps.

Since then, the field of study with respect to collecting and analyzing memory dumps has grown by leaps and bounds, and in many instances the key figures have risen to the top. Perhaps the most notable individual in the field of memory analysis is Aaron Walters, co-creator of the FATKit (http://4tphi.net/fatkit/) and the Volatility Framework (https://www.volatilesystems.com/default/volatility). Although tools have been released to allow for collecting the contents of physical memory from Windows XP and Vista systems (addressed in detail in this chapter), Aaron and his co-developer, Nick L. Petroni Jr., have focused primarily on providing a framework for analysis of memory dumps. Aaron and Nick have been assisted by Brendan Dolan-Gavitt (you can find Brendan's blog at http://moyix.blog-spot.com/, and his graduate research page is www.cc.gatech.edu/~brendan/) and others who have made significant contributions to the area of memory analysis and specifically to the Volatility Framework. Matthieu Suiche (www.msuiche.net/) has contributed a program for dumping the contents of physical memory, and has also published information and tools for parsing Windows hibernation files (which have been incorporated into the Volatility Framework). Andreas Schuster (http://computer.forensikblog.de/en/) has continued his contributions to parsing of Windows memory dumps, including the release of a PTFinder (discussed later in this chapter) for Vista in November 2008, which is included as part of the PTFinder collection of Perl scripts.

In addition to free, open source tools for parsing Windows memory dumps, the security company Mandiant (the company Web site is www.mandiant.com, and the company blog is http://blog.mandiant.com/) released its Memoryze memory collection and parsing tool, along with the Audit Viewer tool for better presentation of the results of Memoryze. In addition, the folks at HBGary (www.hbgary.com/) have released their own memory analysis application called Responder, which comes in Professional and Field editions. The HBGary Web site includes a wealth of information about the tools, including videos demonstrating how to use them.

# Collecting Process Memory

During an investigation, you might be interested in only particular processes rather than a list of all processes, and you'd like more than just the contents of process memory available in a RAM dump file. For example, you might have quickly identified processes of interest that required no additional extensive investigation. There are ways to collect all the memory used by a process—not just what is in physical memory, but also what is in virtual memory or the page file.

To do this, a couple of tools are available. One is pmdump.exe (www.ntsecurity.nu/toolbox/pmdump/), written by Arne Vidstrom and available from NTSecurity.nu. However, as the NTSecurity.nu Web site states, pmdump.exe allows you to dump the contents of process memory *without* stopping the process. As we discussed earlier, this allows the process to continue and the contents of memory to change while being written to a file, thereby creating a "smear" of process memory. Also, pmdump.exe does not create an output file that can be analyzed with the Microsoft Debugging Tools.

Tobias Klein has come up with another method for dumping the contents of process memory in the form of a free (albeit not open source) tool called Process Dumper (available in both Linux and Windows versions from www.trapkit.de/research/forensic/pd/index. html). Process Dumper (pd.exe) dumps the entire process space along with additional metadata and the process environment to the console (STDOUT) so that the output can be redirected to a file or a socket (via netcat or other tools; see Chapter 1 for a discussion of some of those tools). A review of the documentation that Tobias makes available for pd.exe provides no indication that the process is debugged, halted, or frozen prior to the dumping process. Tobias also provides the Memory Parser graphical user interface (GUI) utility for parsing the metadata and memory contents collected by the Process Dumper. These tools appear to be an extension of Tobias's work toward extracting RSA private keys and certificates from process memory (www.trapkit.de/research/sslkeyfinder/index.html).

---

### Tip

Jeff Bryner wrote pdgmail (you can find the pdgmail tool at www.jeffbryner.com/code/pdgmail), a Python-based tool that uses the output of Tobias's Process Dumper program to search for Gmail artifacts (e.g., contacts, last access records, account names, etc.). Jeff posted to the SANS Forensic blog (http://sansforensics.wordpress.com) regarding pdgmail, stating that he had not tested it on the Windows platform. Jeff subsequently released pdymail for extracting Yahoo! mail remnants (http://jeffbryner.com/code/pdymail) from process memory, as well. In this section of the chapter, we discuss dumping the contents of process memory, whereas later in the chapter we discuss how an analyst can dump the contents of process memory for a full dump of physical memory. You can use either method to retrieve data for use with pdgmail or pdymail.

---

Another tool that is available and recommended by a number of sources is userdump.exe, available from Microsoft. Userdump.exe will allow you to dump any process on the fly, without attaching a debugger and without terminating the process once the dump has been completed. Also, the dump file generated by userdump.exe can be read by the Microsoft Debugging Tools. However, userdump.exe requires that a driver be installed for it to work, and depending on the situation, this might not be something you'd want to do.

Based on conversations with Robert Hensing, formerly of the Microsoft PSS Security team, the preferred method of dumping memory used by a process is to use the adplus.vbs script that ships with the debugging tools, as this methodology attaches a debugger to the process and suspends the process to dump it. *Adplus* stands for *Autodumplus* and was originally written by Robert (the documentation for the script states that versions 1 through 5 were written by Robert, and as of Version 6, Israel Burman has taken over). The help file (debugger.chm) for the MS Debugging Tools contains a great deal of information about the script as well as the cdb.exe debugging tool, which it uses to dump the processes you designate. The MS Debugging Tools do not require that an additional driver be installed, and they can be run from a CD. This means the tools (adplus.vbs and cdb.exe, as well as supporting dynamic link libraries, or DLLs) can be written to a CD (adplus.vbs uses the Windows scripting host Version 5.6, also known as cscript.exe, which comes installed on most systems) and used to dump processes to a shared drive or to a USB-connected storage device. Once the dumps have been completed, you can use the freely available MS Debugging Tools to analyze the dump files. In addition, you can use other tools, such as BinText, to extract ASCII, Unicode, and resource strings from the dump file. Also, after dumping the process, you can use still other tools (such as those discussed in Chapter 1) to collect additional information about the process from the running system, which may provide a quicker view into the details of the process itself. Handle.exe (which is available from http://technet.microsoft.com/en-us/sysinternals/bb896655.aspx and requires that you have Administrator rights on the system when running it) will provide you with a list of handles (to files, directories, etc.) that have been opened by the process, and listdlls.exe (Version 2.25 at the time of this writing, available from http://technet.microsoft.com/en-us/sysinternals/bb896656.aspx) will show you the full path to and the version numbers of the various modules loaded by a process.

Extensive help is available for using adplus.vbs, not only in the MS Debugging Tools help file but also in Microsoft Knowledge Base article 286350 (http://support.microsoft.com/kb/286350). You can use adplus.vbs to hang the process while it is being dumped (i.e., halt it, dump it, and then resume the process) or to crash the process (halt the process, dump it, and then terminate). To run adplus.vbs in hang mode against a process, you would use the following command line:

```
D:\debug>cscript adplus.vbs -quiet -hang -p <PID>
```

This command will create a series of files within the debug directory within a subdirectory prefaced with the name *Hang_mode_* that includes the date and time of the dump. (You can change the location where the output is written using the −*o* switch.) You will see an adplus.vbs report file, the dump file for the process (multiple processes can be designated using multiple −*p* entries), a process list (generated by default using tlist.exe; you can turn this off using the −*noTList* switch), and a text file showing all the loaded modules (DLLs) used by the process.

Although all the information collected about processes using adplus.vbs can be extremely useful during an investigation, you can use this tool only on processes that are visible via the application program interface (API). If a process is not visible (say, if it's hidden by a rootkit), you cannot use these tools to collect information about the process.

You can use the *volatility memdmp* command (we discuss the Volatility Framework later in the chapter) to dump the addressable memory for a process from a Windows XP memory dump, as follows:

```
D:\Volatility>python volatility memdmp -f d:\hacking\xp-laptop1.img -p 4012
```

This command results in a 4012.dmp file that is 118,300,672 bytes in size.

# Dumping Physical Memory

So, how do you go about collecting the full contents of physical memory, rather than just dumping a process? Several methods are available, each with strengths and weaknesses. The goal of this chapter is to provide an understanding of the various options available as well as the technical aspects associated with each option. This way, as a first responder or investigator, you'll make educated choices regarding which option is most suitable, taking the business needs of the client (or victim) into account along with infrastructure concerns.

## DD

*DD* (http://en.wikipedia.org/wiki/Dd_(Unix)) is the short name given to a powerful tool from the UNIX world which has a variety of uses, not the least of which is to copy files or even entire hard drives. DD has long been considered a standard for producing forensic images, and most major forensic imaging/acquisition tools as well as analysis tools support the dd format. GMG Systems Inc. produced a modified version of dd that runs on Windows systems and can be used to dump the contents of physical memory from Windows 2000 and XP systems. This version of dd was part of the Forensic Acquisition Utilities, but is no longer available. This utility was able to collect the contents of physical memory by accessing the \*Device\PhysicalMemory* object from user mode. The following command line could be used to capture the contents of RAM in the file ram.img on a network share or a USB thumb drive attached to the system:

```
D:\tools>dd if=\\.\PhysicalMemory of=F:\ram.img bs=4096 conv=noerror
```

In the preceding command line, the block size (*bs* value) is set to 4 kilobytes (KB) or 4096 bytes, as this is the default size for pages in memory. Therefore, the command tells dd.exe to grab one page at a time. This version of dd.exe also allows compression and the generation of cryptographic hashes for the content. Due to the volatile nature of RAM (i.e., it continues to change throughout the process of dumping it), however, it is not advisable to hash it until it is written from the disk, simply because there is no advantage in doing so. If the user images memory twice, even with little delay, the contents of RAM and thus the subsequent hashes will be different. In this case, it is only worthwhile to employ a cryptographic hash to address the integrity of the collected memory dump.

---

**W**ARNING

The version of dd.exe from George M. Garner, Jr., discussed earlier, is no longer available or supported, but there may be responders out there who still have a copy of the tool on a CD or hard drive someplace (I do!). Discussion of and reference to the tool is provided here for completeness, as well as to recognize George's contributions to the field of memory acquisition and analysis.

---

# Nigilant32

Other tools use a process similar to dd.exe to capture the contents of RAM. Nigilant32 (www.agilerm.net/publications_4.html), from Matt Shannon of Agile Risk Management, uses a graphical interface to allow the responder to acquire the contents of physical memory. Figure 3.1 illustrates a portion of the Nigilant32 GUI, showing the option for imaging physical memory.

**Figure 3.1** Portion of the Nigilant32 GUI

Nigilant32 has the advantage of a GUI, which may be a friendlier tool for some responders to use. You can deploy Nigilant32 on a CD or USB thumb drive along with other tools, and use it to quickly collect the contents of physical memory (primarily from Windows XP systems). As with dd.exe and other tools, Nigilant32 requires local access to the system from which the responder wishes to dump memory. You also can deploy Nigilant32 prior to an actual incident occurring, and responders can either run the tool locally and dump physical memory to a thumb drive or network share, or access the system remotely (via applications such as VNC or Remote Desktop Client) and perform the memory dump.

# ProDiscover

ProDiscover IR (Version 4.8 was used in writing this book, and Version 5.0 was released in summer 2008) also allows the investigator to collect the contents of physical memory (as well as system BIOS) via a remote server applet that can be distributed to a system via removable storage media (CD, thumb drive, etc.) or via the network. Figure 3.2 illustrates the user interface for this capability.

**Figure 3.2** Excerpt of the Capture Image Dialog Box from ProDiscover IR

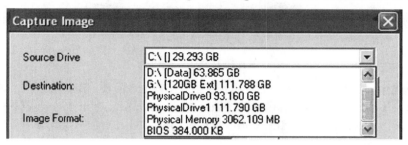

# KnTDD

The problem with using tools such as dd.exe or Nigilant32, however, is that as of Windows 2003 SP1, access to the \Device\PhysicalMemory object has been restricted from user mode (http://technet.microsoft.com/en-us/library/cc787565.aspx). That is, only kernel drivers are allowed to access this object. As such, tools such as dd.exe, Nigilant32, and ProDiscover (as previously mentioned, the Incident Response edition of ProDiscover includes a servlet that will allow an analyst to access physical memory on a remote Windows XP system) will not allow you to collect the contents of physical memory from Windows 2003 SP1 and later systems, including Vista. To address this issue, George M. Garner, Jr. (a.k.a. GMG Systems) produced a new utility called KnTDD, which is part of the KnTTools set of utilities. According to the licensing for KnTTools, the utilities are available for private sale to law enforcement personnel and bona fide security professionals. KnTDD includes the following capabilities:

- Able to acquire the contents of physical memory using multiple methods, including via the \Device\PhysicalMemory object

- Runs on Microsoft operating systems from Windows 2000 through Vista, including AMD64 versions of the operating systems

- Able to convert a raw memory "image" to Microsoft crash dump format so that the resultant data can be analyzed using the Microsoft Debugging Tools

- Able to acquire to a local removable (USB, FireWire) storage device as well as via the network using Transmission Control Protocol/Internet Protocol (TCP/IP)

- Designed specifically for forensic use, with audit logging and cryptographic integrity checks

The KnTTools Enterprise Edition includes the following capabilities:

- Bulk encryption of output using X.509 certifications, AES–256 (default), and downgrading to 3DES on Windows 2000

- Memory acquisition using a KnTDDSvc service

- A remote deployment module that is able to deploy the KnTDDSvc service by either "pushing" it to a remote admin share or "pulling" it from a Web server over Secure Sockets Layer (SSL), with cryptographic verification of the binaries before they are executed

One of the aspects of using dd.exe, and tools like it, that you need to keep in mind is Locard's Exchange Principle. To use these tools to collect the contents of RAM, they must be loaded into RAM as a running process. This means memory space is consumed and other processes may have pages written out to the page file.

Another aspect of these tools to keep in mind is that they do not freeze the state of the system, as occurs when a crash dump is generated. This means that while the tool is reading through the contents of RAM, as the thirtieth "page" is being read the eleventh page could change as the process using that page continues to run. The amount of time it ultimately takes to complete the dump depends on factors such as processor speed and rates of bus and disk I/O. The question then becomes, are these changes that occur in the limited amount of time enough to affect the results of your analysis?

Under most incident response conditions, tools such as dd.exe might be the best method for retrieving the contents of physical memory, particularly from Windows 2000 and XP systems. Such tools do not require that the system be taken down, nor do they restrict how and to where the contents of physical memory are written (e.g., using netcat, you can write the contents of RAM out over a socket to another system rather than to the local hard drive). Tools have been developed and made freely available (discussed later in this chapter) to parse the contents of these RAM dumps to extract information about processes, network connections, and the like. Further, development of the KnTTools and other similar tools allows for continued support of this methodology beyond Windows 2003 SP1.

**NOTE**

The primary issue with using a methodology such as the Forensic Acquisition Utilities or KnTTools is that the system is still running when the contents of physical memory are retrieved. This means that not only are memory pages consumed simply by using the utilities (i.e., executable images are read and loaded into memory), but as the tool enumerates through memory, pages that have already been read can change. That is, the state of the system and its memory are not frozen in time, as would be the case with acquiring a forensic image of a hard drive via traditional "forensic" methodologies. Interacting with a live system, however, may be the only manner with which certain information can be retrieved. Keeping Locard's Exchange Principle in mind, responders must thoroughly and clearly document their actions when performing live response. Issues such as the need for live response, as well as the "footprint" of live-response tools, have been (and will likely continue to be) the subject of discussion for some time.

# MDD

The early part of 2008 saw the release of several new tools for collecting the contents of physical memory from Windows systems, particularly Windows 2003 SP1 and Vista. Fortunately, these tools work equally well on Windows XP systems, making them more universal than previously available tools (e.g., dd.exe, Nigilant32, etc.). Perhaps the most notable was mdd.exe which was released to the public by ManTech International (www.mantech.com/msma/MDD.asp). Mdd.exe is a straightforward and simple command-line interface (CLI) tool, allowing a responder to dump the contents of physical memory with a simple command line:

```
E:\response>mdd.exe -o F:\system1\memory.dmp
```

The preceding command line illustrates an example of mdd.exe run from a CD (E:\), sending the output file (via the *-o* switch) to a USB external hard drive (F:\). You can also run mdd.exe from a batch file, as I described in Chapter 1, using a command line such as:

```
mdd.exe -o %1\mdd-o.img
```

Alternatively, you can use the available variables from a live Windows environment to segregate your collected volatile data by prepending the name of the system from which you're collecting data:

```
mdd.exe -o %1\%ComputerName%-mdd-o.img
```

Once mdd.exe completes the memory dump, it displays an MD5 checksum for the resultant dump file:

```
took 108 seconds to write
MD5 is: 6fe975ee3ab878211d3be3279e948649
```

The analyst can save this information and use it to ensure the integrity of the memory dump file later.

Not only is mdd.exe simple to use and deploy, but also the output of the tool is what is referred to as a raw, dd-style memory dump file, similar to what is achieved using other tools (dd.exe, VMware, etc.). However, prior to using mdd.exe, you should be aware that, according to the ManTech International Web site for the tool, mdd.exe is unable to collect more than 4 GB of RAM. On systems with 8 GB or more of RAM, some users have reported system crashes, so take this into account when considering whether to collect the contents of RAM from a system.

---

**TIP**

If you intend to collect the contents of RAM from a live Windows system as part of your response methodology using a batch file, I recommend that you collect the contents of RAM first. This will provide you with as "clean" a dump as possible, particularly if you've included other third-party (tlist.exe, tcpvcon.exe) and native Windows tools (netstat.exe) in your batch file.

---

# Win32dd

Matthieu Suiche released his own tool for dumping the contents of physical memory, called win32dd (http://win32dd.msuiche.net/). Win32dd is described as a "free kernel land and 100% open-source tool"; this means that like mdd.exe, win32dd.exe is free, but unlike ManTech's tool, win32dd.exe is open source. Win32dd.exe has some additional features, including the ability to create a WinDbg-compatible "crash dump" (similar to a Windows crash dump) which you can then analyze using the Microsoft Debugging Tools (www.microsoft.com/whdc/DevTools/Debugging/default.mspx). As with mdd.exe and other CLI tools, win32dd.exe can be included in batch files.

Version 1.2.1.20090106 of win32dd.exe was available at the time this chapter was being written. You can view the syntax information available for win32dd.exe using the following command:

```
D:\tools\win32dd>win32dd -h

   Win32dd - v1.2.1.20090106 - Kernel land physical memory acquisition
   Copyright (c) 2007 - 2009, Matthieu Suiche <http://www.msuiche.net>
   Copyright (c) 2008 - 2009, MoonSols <http://www.moonsols.com>
Usage:
   win32dd [option] [output path]

Option:
   -r   Create a raw memory dump/snapshot. (default)
   -l   Level for the mapping (with -r option only).
     l 0   Open \\Device\\PhysicalMemory device (default).
     l 1   Use Kernel API MmMapIoSpace()
```

```
 -d   Create a Microsoft full memory dump file (WinDbg compliant).
 -t   Type of MSFT dump file (with -d option only).
   t 0   Original MmPhysicalMemoryBlock, like BSOD. (default).
   t 1   MmPhysicalMemoryBlock (with PFN 0).

 -h   Display this help.
Sample:
Usage: win32dd -d physmem.dmp
Usage: win32dd -l 1 -r C:\dump\physmem.bin
```

As you can see, win32dd.exe has a number of options available for dumping the contents of physical memory. To create a raw, dd-style memory dump file, you can use the following command line:

```
D:\tools\win32dd>win32dd -l 0 -r d:\tools\memtest\win32dd-l0-xp.img
```

Including the command-line options (such as *−l 0*) in the name of the output file serves as a modicum of additional documentation for the analyst, to identify the command-line switches used. As with other CLI tools, including such a command in a batch file is simple and straightforward (besides being self-documenting).

# Memoryze

The consulting company Mandiant released its own memory collection and analysis tool, called Memoryze (www.mandiant.com/software/memoryze.htm). Memoryze finds its origins in the Mandiant Intelligent Response (MIR) product, and has been made freely available from the Mandiant Web site, along with examples of how to run the tool. Once you've downloaded the Memoryze Microsoft installer (MSI) file to your system and installed it, you can run Memoryze to collect a memory dump via the memorydd.bat batch file by typing the following command:

```
D:\Mandiant\memorydd.bat
```

This will create a memory dump file in a directory structure within the current directory; running the command as is on my system created the directory structure Audits\WINTERMUTE\20090103003442\, and within that final directory it created several XML files and a memory image file. Running the batch file with the *−output* switch will let you configure the location for the dump file.

Also, when run on a live system, Memoryze reportedly "makes use of the page file(s)," incorporating memory contents from the page file into the collection process. This allows for more complete collection of data, as memory contents that have been swapped out to the page file are now available during the analysis process. In addition, Memoryze Version 1.3.0 (announced February 9, 2009) is capable of dumping memory that is accessible via F-Response, which we'll discuss later in this chapter.

# Winen

Guidance Software also released its own tool for collecting the contents of physical memory, called winen.exe. Like some of the other tools, winen.exe is a CLI tool, but unlike the other tools, the memory dump is not collected in raw, dd-style format; instead, it is collected in the same proprietary imaging format used by the EnCase image acquisition tool, commonly referred to as Expert Witness Format (or EWF, for short). Most available analysis tools require that the memory dump be in a raw, dd-style format, so memory dumps collected using winen.exe must be converted to a raw format prior to being parsed. As Lance Mueller points out in his blog (www.forensickb.com/2008/06/new-version-of-encase-includes-stand.html), you can run winen.exe by simply providing various options at the console (i.e., typing **winen** at the command prompt and then providing responses to the queries) or by providing the path to a configuration file with the necessary information via the −*f* switch. Winen.exe has a total of six required options, the settings for which can be provided via the command line or in a configuration file: the path to the output file(s), the compression level, the examiner's name, the evidence name, the case number, and the evidence number. An example configuration file is included in the home directory when you download and install EnCase.

Richard McQuown provides additional information about the use of winen.exe in his ForensicZone blog (http://forensiczone.blogspot.com/2008/06/winenexe-ram-imaging-tool-included-in.html), as well as a link to a user manual file for winen.exe (you must have access to the EnCase User Forum and be logged in to obtain the PDF document at https://support.guidancesoftware.com/forum/downloads.php?do=file&id=478).

You can then convert the resultant memory dump to a raw format by opening the memory dump file in FTK Imager and choosing **Create Disk Image** from the menu (http://windowsir.blogspot.com/2008/06/memory-collection-and-analysis-part-ii.html), or by opening the memory dump in EnCase and choosing **Copy/UnErase** from the EnCase menu.

Guidance also has a version of winen.exe for 64-bit versions of the Windows operating system, called winen64.exe. As with the 32-bit version of the tool, winen64.exe allows a responder to dump the contents of physical memory in an EWF format dump file.

# Fastdump

Consulting company HBGary released a copy of its tool for collecting the contents of physical memory, called fastdump (www.hbgary.com/download_fastdump.html). Although fastdump.exe (Version 1.2 is available at the time of this writing) is free, as with Nigilant32 and some of the other available tools it is not able to collect memory contents from Windows 2003 SP1 and later systems, including Vista. You can use this tool only to collect the contents of physical memory from Windows XP and Windows 2003 (no service packs installed) systems.

To address this issue, HBGary also released a commercial version of the tool, called FastDump Pro (fdpro.exe), which is available from the same Web page as fastdump.exe, albeit for a fee. The commercial version supports all versions of Windows, including 32- and 64-bit versions, and will also reportedly dump memory from systems with more than 4 GB of RAM.

Besides being able to dump more than 4 GB of physical memory, FastDump Pro has some other differences from and advantages over other tools. Typing **fdpro** at the command prompt displays the syntax information for the tool:

```
D:\HBGary\bin\FastDump>fdpro
-= FDPro v1.3.0.377 by HBGary, Inc =-
***** Usage Help *****


General Usage: fdpro output_dumpfile_path [options] [modifiers]

FDPro supports dumping .bin and .hpak format files

To dump physical memory only to literal .bin format:
        fdpro mymemdump.bin [options] [modifiers]
To dump physical memory to an .hpak formatted file:
        fdpro mysysdump.hpak [options] [modifiers]

*** Valid .bin [options] Are: ***
-probe [all|smart|pid|help]     Pre-Dump Memory Probing

*** Valid .bin [modifiers] Are: ***
-nodriver                       Use old-style memory acquisition (XP/2k only)
-driver                         Force driver based memory acquisition

*** Valid .hpak [options] Are: ***
-probe [all|smart|pid|help]     Pre-Dump Memory Probing
-hpak [list|extract]            HPAK archive management

*** Valid .hpak [modifiers] Are: ***
-nodriver                       Use old-style memory acquisition (XP/2k only)
-driver                         Force driver based memory acquisition
-compress                       Create archive compressed
-nocompress                     Create archive uncompressed
```

As you can see, fdpro.exe has essentially two modes in which it can be used. The first mode is to dump the contents of physical memory in the usual raw, dd-style format, using either the driver to access physical memory on versions of Windows that require it (i.e., Windows 2003 SP1, Vista, and later), or the *−nodriver* switch to perform "old-style memory acquisition."

Fdpro.exe also has an .hpak-style format, which is described as follows:

> "HPAK is an HBGary proprietary format which is capable of several key features, namely the ability to store and archive the RAM and Pagefile in a single archive. HPAK format also supports compression using the gzip format. This is useful during instances where space on the collecting device/system is limited."

One of the limitations of most of the available tools for dumping physical memory is that they allow access only to physical memory, and do not incorporate the page file. Not only does fdpro.exe provide access to a wide range of Windows operating systems (including 64-bit versions) and memory capacities (i.e., greater than 4 GB), but also (as with Mandiant's Memoryze tool) the tool will incorporate the page file in the collection process, which then allows that data to be incorporated into the analysis process, as well (we will discuss the HBGary Responder product later in this chapter). As you will see later in this chapter, contents of memory that have been swapped out to the page file may contain information pertinent to your response and analysis.

## WARNING

It is important to point out that proprietary formats for data collection often lead to the requirement to use one particular tool for data analysis. Memory dumped using winen.exe, for example, must be converted to a raw format prior to being analyzed using other tools (although EnScripts are available to perform some limited parsing of the dump file). The same holds true with HBGary's .hpak format, as well; at this point, only HBGary's Responder product can be used to analyze an .hpak format memory dump. This is something you must keep in mind when deciding which tool to use.

# F-Response

Finally, 2008 heralded the coming of a new age in incident response with Matt Shannon's release of F-Response. F-Response is an acquisition-tool-agnostic framework that uses the iSCSI protocol to provide raw access to disks over the network. Matt designed and wrote F-Response so that the access is read-only; write operations to the remote disk are buffered and silently dropped. The three editions of F-Response (Field Kit, Consultant, and Enterprise) are all deployed differently, but all allow you to "see" drives on remote systems (e.g., in another room, on another floor, or even in another building) as mounted drives on your own system. F-Response is acquisition-tool-agnostic in the sense that once you're connected to the remote system and can "see" the drive, you can use any tool you want (dd.exe, ProDiscover, FTK Imager, etc.) to acquire an image of that drive. You can deploy F-Response on Mac OS X, Linux, and Windows systems, and on Windows systems it has the added benefit of providing remote, read-only access to physical memory. At the SANS Forensic Summit in October 2008, during his presentation with Aaron Walters, Matt announced the release of F-Response 2.03, which provides remote, real-time, read-only access to a Windows system's physical memory, for all versions of Windows, including XP and Vista. Once the connection to the remote system is set up, a responder can then use tools such as dd.exe or FTK Imager to acquire a copy of physical memory.

F-Response's capability (Version 2.06 beta was used in this example) for obtaining a copy of physical memory from a remote Windows system has tremendous implications for incident response, particularly when deploying the Enterprise Edition (see the "F-Response Enterprise Edition (EE)" sidebar for more information on deploying this capability in an enterprise environment). Matt has several videos linked to the F-Response blog (www.f-response.com/index.php?option=com_content&task=blogsection&id=4& Itemid=9) that demonstrate uses and aspects of the F-Response tool, such as illustrating how to acquire specific data, for example, by accessing a live Microsoft Exchange server.

At the SANS Forensic Summit in October 2008, Matt announced that F-Response would provide remote, read-only access to drives on Windows systems and to physical memory. Upon a successful connection, remote drives appear on the responder's system with the familiar drive icon, as Figure 3.3 illustrates.

**Figure 3.3** Remote Windows System Drive Connected to As F:\

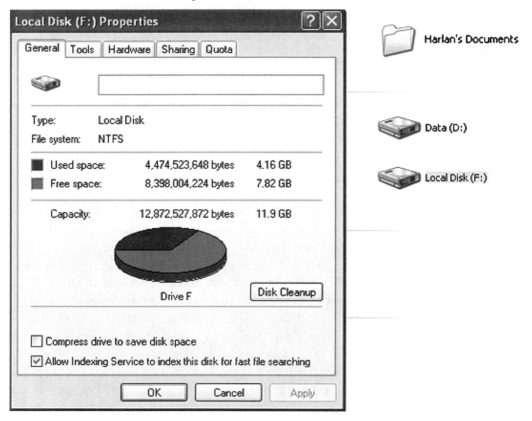

**Continued**

You also can install the agent in a stealthy manner, using tools such as psexec.exe (http://technet.microsoft.com/en-us/sysinternals/bb897553.aspx) or xcmd.exe (http://feldkir.ch/xcmd.htm). The PDF document "Remote (Stealth) Deployment of F-Response EE on Windows Systems," located in the ch3 directory on the media that accompanies this book, clearly illustrates the necessary steps for deploying F-Response EE remotely (or in a stealthy manner) over the network.

In spring 2009, Matt Shannon released the F-Response Enterprise Management Console, or FEMC. The FEMC is a GUI-based tool that completely removes all of the effort required to manually deploy the Enterprise Edition. Clicking through the user interface, a responder (or consultant) can locate systems in the domain (or workgroup) on which to install F-Response EE, as Figure 3.4 illustrates.

**Figure 3.4** FEMC User Interface Populated with Systems

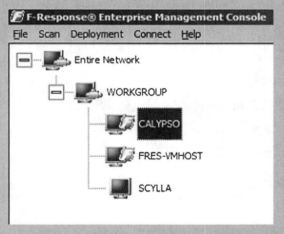

Once systems have been located and selected, deploying and starting the F-Response service is nothing more than a couple of mouse clicks away, as illustrated in part in Figure 3.5. This is the case whether you want to install it on one system or on a dozen systems.

**Continued**

**Figure 3.5** Logging in to F-Response EE via the FEMC User Interface

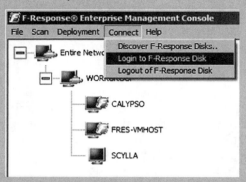

All the responder needs to do is select the systems onto which she wishes to deploy F-Response, and then with a couple of mouse clicks deploy the agent automatically. Even the configuration of the .ini file is handled automatically through the user interface, as Figure 3.6 illustrates.

**Figure 3.6** Configuring F-Response EE via the FEMC User Interface

**Continued**

Information entered into the Domain/Network Credentials section of the Configuration dialog shown in Figure 3.6 is available throughout the duration of the session, but is *not* saved or preserved in any way when the FEMC is closed.

Working with the FEMC, it actually took me more effort to play BrickBreaker on my BlackBerry than it does to deploy F-Response EE across several systems, connect to each, and then completely uninstall the agent. The FEMC pushes the functionality of an extremely powerful and valuable tool forward by a quantum leap (not to take anything away from Scott Bakula...).

As physical memory (RAM) does not contain a partition table, the responder's system will not recognize the connection to the remote system's physical memory as a drive. However, the connection can be seen through the Disk Management Microsoft Management Console (MMC), as Figure 3.7 shows.

**Figure 3.7** F-Response EE Connection to Remote RAM Seen via Disk Management MMC

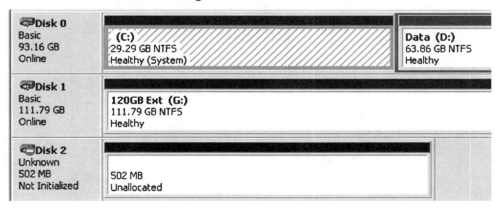

Once the connection to the remote system's RAM has been verified, you can use tools such as FTK Imager to perform a memory dump. Figure 3.8 illustrates selecting the remote system's RAM via FTK Imager.

**Figure 3.8** Selecting a Remote System's RAM via FTK Imager

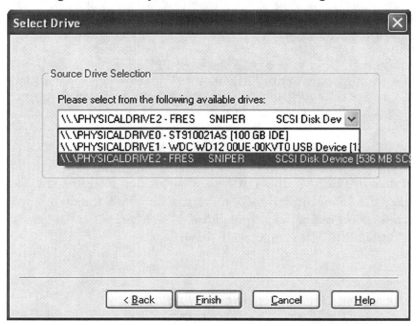

Figure 3.9 illustrates the selected RAM from Figure 3.8 as it appears in the FTK Imager Evidence Tree.

**Figure 3.9** Selected RAM in FTK Imager Evidence Tree

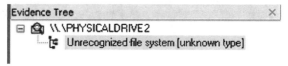

The RAM from the remote system can now be acquired using FTK Imager. Other tools can also be used; F-Response is a tool-agnostic framework, as it does not require that you use a specific tool. A responder can use EnCase, X-Ways Forensics, or even versions of dd.exe to dump RAM from the remote system. Again, the connection is read-only, and as illustrated in Figures 3.8 and 3.9, the remote system's RAM appears on the responder's system as a \\.\*PhysicalDrive* object (i.e., \\.\*PhysicalDrive2* or \\.\*PhysicalDrive3*).

> **NOTE**
>
> At the SANS Forensic Summit in October 2008, Aaron Walters and Matt Shannon gave a presentation that incorporated the use of F-Response and the Volatility Framework in something called "Voltage" (http://volatilesystems.blogspot.com/2008/10/voltage-giving-investigators-power-to.html). Although not available at the time of this writing, Voltage is described as providing an unprecedented level of real-time, read-only, remote access, automation, and visualization to temporally relevant information that has not been available to date. For all the fancy words, Voltage provides a responder with the capability to quickly reach out to remote systems, identify systems that may have malware installed and running, and then collect a sample of physical memory, all without modifying the artifacts on the remote system.

# Section Summary

John Sawyer posted to the SANS Forensics blog (http://sansforensics.wordpress.com/2008/12/13/windows-physical-memory-finding-the-right-tool-for-the-job/) on December 13, 2008, listing some of the various tools available for collecting (as well as analyzing) memory dumps from Windows systems, along with brief descriptions of each of them. In addition to John's blog post, other posts (to blogs and discussion lists) have made comments and addressed concerns about the availability and use of the various tools for dumping memory from Windows systems. In many ways, this chapter serves as an initial step into this realm of tools, as I do not doubt that between the time I submit this chapter to the publisher and the time the finished book is available the tools will have changed. This very thing happened between the time I submitted this chapter for technical review and the time I received the tech editor's comments—in the ensuing time, HBGary had released FastDump Pro and announced its availability to the public. I firmly believe that the landscape of memory dumping (and analysis) tools will change, doing so in relatively short order.

So far in this section you've seen some of the tools available for dumping the contents of physical memory from Windows systems, but little else. In an effort to provide more of a side-by-side comparison of some of these tools, I ran some of my own limited testing. Using the command lines (in the case of Memoryze, the memorydd.bat file) for each tool discussed previously in this chapter that might be run from a CD or USB thumb drive, I ran each of them (with the exception of winen.exe) on a Dell Latitude D820 system with 4 GB of RAM installed, running Windows XP Service Pack 3. My testing process was to simply boot the system, run one of the tools, and once the tool had completed its dump of memory, reboot the system to run the next tool. In doing so, I saved the memory dumps so that I could see the sizes of each of them in relation to the dumps produced by other tools; my final results appear as follows, listed by the size in bytes and the output filename:

```
3,210,854,400  win32dd-10-xp.img
3,210,854,400  win32dd-11-xp.img
3,210,854,400  mdd-xp-2.img
3,210,854,400  mdd-xp.img
3,211,329,536  dd_xp.img
3,211,329,536  nigilant_xp.img
3,211,333,632  fdpro-xp.bin
3,211,334,904  fdpro-xp.hpak
3,211,329,536  memory.1e1d2b07.img (Memoryze)
```

As you can see, I included the name of the tool and some additional identifying information from the command line in the name of the output dump file. Also, it's clear that there are some variations in the sizes of the resultant dumps, likely due to the process each tool used. As expected, the exception to this is the .hpak format dump file produced by FastDump Pro, as the *−page* switch had been used to incorporate the page file in the dump process. The file size would likely have been significantly larger had there been greater activity on the system, and had the system been allowed to run longer.

It should be clear at this point that the tool you should use to collect the contents of physical memory really depends on a number of factors, including the version of Windows (not only Windows XP versus Vista, but also 32- versus 64-bit), the amount of physical memory installed in the system, and your analysis tools.

---

**W**ARNING

As with using any tools that you've downloaded from the Internet, be sure that you've tested the tools and you've read and that you understand the license agreement regarding their use. Some tools, although extremely powerful and useful, cannot be used by consultants. Also, you need to be aware of the artifacts left by various tools. As discussed in Chapter 1, many of the tools available from Microsoft (formerly Sysinternals) create Registry entries when run. Winen.exe does something similar, in that it will write its driver (winen_.sys) to the same directory from which the file is run, and will create a Services subkey within the Registry. The key here, as with all live-response activities, is not to avoid using a tool because it leaves "footprints" or artifacts of its use, but rather to understand this fact and incorporate that understanding into your methodology and documentation.

---

# Alternative Approaches for Dumping Physical Memory

The software we've discussed so far aren't the only means by which the contents of physical memory can be dumped from a live system; several alternative methods have been put forth in the past. Some of those methods use native functionality inherent to the operating system (i.e., crash dumps) or to virtualization platforms (i.e., VMware). As we'll see, other alternative methods for dumping physical memory from a system take a more physical approach.

## Hardware Devices

In February 2004, the *Digital Investigation Journal* published a paper by Brian Carrier and Joe Grand titled "A Hardware-Based Memory Acquisition Procedure for Digital Investigations." In the paper, Brian and Joe presented the concept for a hardware expansion card dubbed Tribble (possibly a reference to that memorable *Star Trek* episode) that could be used to retrieve the contents of physical memory to an external storage device. This would allow an investigator to retrieve the volatile memory from the system without introducing any new code or relying on potentially untrusted code to perform the extraction. In the paper, the authors stated that they had built a proof-of-concept Tribble device, designed as a Payment Card Industry (PCI) expansion card that could be plugged into a PC bus. Other hardware devices are available that allow you to capture the contents of physical memory and are largely intended for debugging hardware systems. These devices may also be used for forensics.

As illustrated in the DFRWS 2005 Memory Challenge (referred to earlier in this chapter), one of the limitations of a software-based approach to retrieving volatile memory is that the program the investigator is using has to be loaded into memory. Subsequently, particularly on Windows systems, the program may (depending on its design) rely on untrusted code or libraries (DLLs) that the attacker has subverted. Let's examine the pros and cons of such a device:

Hardware devices such as Tribble are unobtrusive and easily accessible. Dumping the contents of physical memory in this manner introduces no new or additional software to the system, minimizing the chances of data being obscured in some manner. However, the primary limitation of using the hardware-based approach is that the hardware needs to be installed prior to the incident. At this point, the Tribble devices are not widely available. Other hardware devices *are* available and intended for hardware debugging, but they must still be installed prior to an incident to be of use.

## FireWire

Due to technical specifics of FireWire devices and protocols, there is a possibility that with the right software, an investigator can collect the contents of physical memory from a system. FireWire devices use direct memory access (DMA), meaning they can access system memory without having to go through the CPU. These devices can read from and/or write to memory at much faster rates than systems that do not use DMA. The investigator would need a controller device that contains the appropriate software and is capable of writing a command into a specific area of the FireWire device's memory space. Memory mapping is performed in hardware without going through the host operating system, allowing for high-speed low-latency data transfers.

Adam Boileau (see www.storm.net.nz/projects/16) came up with a way to extract physical memory from a system using Linux and Python. The software used for this collection method runs on Linux and relies on support for the /dev/raw1394 device as well as Adam's pythonraw1394 library, the libraw1394 library, and Swig (software that makes C/C++ header files accessible to other languages by generating wrapper code). In his demonstrations, Adam even included the use of a tool that will collect the contents of RAM from a Windows system with the screen locked, then parse out the password, after which Adam logs in to the system.

Jon Evans, an officer with the Gwent police department in the United Kingdom, has installed Adam's tools and successfully collected the contents of physical memory from Windows systems as well as from various versions of Linux. As part of his master's thesis, Jon wrote an overview on how to install, set up, and use Adam's tools on several different Linux platforms, including Knoppix v.5.01, Gentoo Linux 2.6.17, and BackTrack, from Remote-exploit.org. Once all the necessary packages (including Adam's tools) have been downloaded and installed, Jon walks through the process of identifying FireWire ports and tricking the target Windows system into "thinking" the Linux system is an iPod by using the Linux *romtool* command to load a data file containing the Control Status Register (CSR) for an iPod (the CSR file is provided with Adam's tools). Here are the pros and cons of this approach:

Many systems available today have FireWire/IEEE 1394 interfaces built right into the motherboards, increasing the potential accessibility of physical memory using this method. However, Arne Vidstrom has pointed out some technical issues (see http://ntsecurity.nu/onmymind/2006/2006-09-02.html) regarding the way dumping the contents of physical memory over FireWire can result in a hang or in parts of memory being missed. George M. Garner, Jr., noted in an e-mail exchange on a mailing list in October 2006 that in limited testing, there were notable differences in important offsets between a RAM dump collected using the FireWire technique and one collected using George's own software. This difference could only be explained as an error in the collection method. Furthermore, this method has caused Blue Screens of Death (BSoDs, discussed further in a moment) on some target Windows systems, possibly due to the nature of the FireWire hardware on the system.

# Crash Dumps

We've all seen crash dumps at one point or another; in most cases they manifest themselves as an infamous Blue Screen of Death (a.k.a. BSoD, with more descriptive information available at http://en.wikipedia.org/wiki/Blue_Screen_of_Death). In most cases they're an annoyance, if not indicative of a much larger issue. However, if you want to obtain a pristine, untainted copy of the content of RAM from a Windows system, perhaps the only way to do that is to generate a full crash dump. This is because when a crash dump occurs, the system state is frozen and the contents of RAM (along with about 4 Kb of header information) are written to the disk. This preserves the state of the system and ensures that no alterations are made to the system, beginning at the time the crash dump was initiated.

This information can be extremely valuable to an investigator. First, the contents of the crash dump are a snapshot of the system, frozen in time. I have been involved in several investigations during which crash dumps have been found and used to determine root causes, such as avenues of infection or compromise. Second, Microsoft provides tools for analyzing crash dumps—not only in the Microsoft Debugging Tools (www.microsoft.com/whdc/devtools/debugging/default.mspx) but also in the Kernel Memory Space Analyzer (a tool with a ridiculously long URL, so it's best to do a search for it), which is based on the Debugging Tools.

Sounds like a good deal, doesn't it? After all, other than having a 1GB file written to the hard drive, possibly overwriting evidence (and not really minimizing the impact of your investigation on the system), there are no limitations to this approach, right? Under some circumstances, this is true … or you might be willing to accept that condition, depending on the circumstances. However, there are still a couple of stumbling blocks. First, not all systems generate full crash dumps by default. Second, by default, Windows systems do not generate crash dumps on command.

The first issue is relatively simple to deal with, according to Microsoft Knowledge Base article Q254649 (http://support.microsoft.com/kb/254649). This article lists the three types of crash dumps: small (64 KB), kernel, and complete crash dumps. We're looking for the complete crash dump because it contains the complete contents of RAM. The article also states that Windows 2000 Pro and Windows XP (both Pro and Home) will generate small crash dumps, and Windows 2003 (all versions) will generate full crash dumps. My experience with Windows Vista RC1 is that it will generate small crash dumps, by default.

**NOTE**

Microsoft Knowledge Base article 235496 (http://support.microsoft.com/kb/235496) specifies the Registry entries that contain configuration information for Windows systems with respect to the memory.dmp file that is the result of a crash dump. The default location for the memory.dmp file is %SystemRoot%\memory.dmp, but the administrator can specify another location via the *DumpFile* Registry value.

Along the same lines, Microsoft Knowledge Base article Q274598 (http://support. microsoft.com/kb/274598) states that complete crash dumps are not available on systems with more than 2 GB of RAM. According to the article, this is largely due to the space requirements (i.e., for systems with complete crash dumps enabled, the page file must be as large as the contents of RAM + 1 MB) as well as the time it will take to complete the crash dump process.

Microsoft Knowledge Base article Q307973 (http://support.microsoft.com/kb/307973) describes how to set the full range of system failure and recovery options. These settings are more for system administrators and information technology (IT) managers who are setting up and configuring systems before an incident occurs, but the Registry key settings can provide some significant clues for an investigator. For example, if the system was configured (by default or otherwise) to generate a complete crash dump and the administrator reported seeing the BSoD, the investigator should expect to see a complete crash dump file on the system.

---

**NOTE**

Investigators must be extremely careful when working with crash dump files, particularly from systems that process but do not necessarily store sensitive data. In some cases, crash dumps have occurred on systems that processed information such as credit card numbers, Social Security numbers, or the like, and these crash dumps have been found to contain that sensitive information. Even though the programmers specifically wrote the application so that no sensitive personal information was saved locally on the system, a crash dump wrote the contents of memory to the hard drive.

---

So, let's say the system failure and recovery configuration options on a system are set ahead of time (as part of the configuration policies for the systems) to perform a full crash dump. How does the investigator "encourage" a system to perform a crash dump on command, when it's needed? It turns out that there's a Registry key (see Knowledge Base article Q244139, available at http://support.microsoft.com/kb/244139) that can be set to cause a crash dump when the right Ctrl key is held down and the Scroll Lock key is pressed *twice*. However, once this key is set, the system must be rebooted for the setting to take effect. Let's look at the pros and cons of this technique:

Dumping memory via a crash dump is perhaps the only technically accurate (albeit not "forensically sound") method for creating an image of the contents of RAM. This is because when the *KeBugCheck* API function is called, the entire system is halted and the contents of RAM are written to the page file, after which they are written to a file on the system hard drive (overwriting data). Further, Microsoft provides debugging tools as well as the Kernel Memory Space Analyzer (which consists of an engine, plug-ins, and user interface) for analyzing crash dump files. Some Windows systems do not generate full crash dumps by default (e.g., Vista RC1; I had an issue with a driver when I first installed Vista RC1 and I would get BSoDs whenever I attempted to shut down the machine, which resulted in mini dump files).

In addition, modifying a system to accept the keystroke sequence to create a crash dump requires a reboot and must be done ahead of time to be used effectively for incident response. Even if this configuration change has been made, the crash dump process will still create a file equal in size to physical memory on the hard drive. To do so, as stated in Knowledge Base article Q274598, the page file must be configured to be equal to at least the size of physical memory plus 1 MB. This is an additional step that must be corrected to use this method of capturing the contents of physical memory; it's one that is not often followed.

---

**TIP**

A support article available at the Citrix Web site (http://support.citrix.com/article/CTX107717&parentCategoryID=617) provides a methodology for using livekd.exe (http://technet.microsoft.com/en-us/sysinternals/bb897415.aspx) and the Microsoft Debugging Tools to generate a full kernel dump of physical memory. Once livekd.exe is launched, the command *.dump /f <filepath>* is used to generate the dump file. The support article does include the caveat that RAM dumps generated in this manner can be inconsistent because the dump can take a considerable amount of time and the system is live and continues to run during the memory dump.

---

# Virtualization

VMware is a popular virtualization product (VMware Workstation 5.5.2 was used extensively in this book) that, for one thing, allows the creation of pseudo-networks utilizing the hardware of a single system. This capability has many benefits. For example, you can set up a guest operating system and create a snapshot of that system once you have it configured to your needs. From there, you can perform all manner of testing, including installing and monitoring malware, and you will always be able to revert to the snapshot, beginning anew. I have even seen active production systems run from VMware sessions.

When you're running a VMware session, you can suspend that session, freezing it temporarily. Figure 3.10 illustrates the menu items for suspending a VMware session.

**Figure 3.10** Menu Items for Suspending a Session in VMware Workstation 6.5

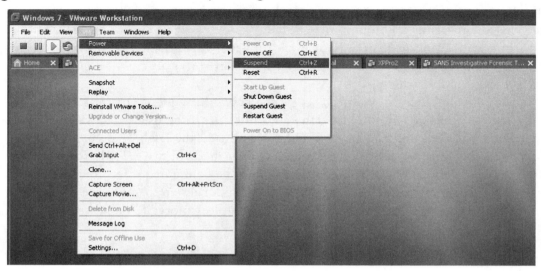

When a VMware session is suspended, the contents of physical memory are contained in a file with the .vmem extension. The format of this file is very similar to that of raw, dd–style memory, and in fact, it can be parsed and analyzed with the same tools discussed previously in the chapter.

VMware isn't the only virtualization product available. Others include VirtualPC from Microsoft, as well as the freeware Bochs (http://bochs.sourceforge.net/). None of these virtualization products have been tested to determine whether they can generate dumps of physical memory; however, if this is an option available to you, suspending a VMware session to obtain a dump of physical memory is quick and easy and minimizes your interaction with and impact on the system.

**TIP**

In May 2006, Brett Shavers wrote an excellent article for the ForensicFocus Web site, titled "VMware as a forensic tool" (available at www.forensicfocus. com/vmware-forensic-tool). Brett followed that article in 2008 with the paper "Virtual Forensics: A Discussion of Virtual Machines Related to Forensics Analysis" (www.forensicfocus.com/downloads/virtual-machines-forensics-analysis.pdf), which is by far the best treatment of the topic that I've been able to find anywhere.

# Hibernation File

When a Windows (Windows 2000 or later) system "hibernates," the Power Manager saves the compressed contents of physical memory to a file called hiberfil.sys in the root directory of the system volume. This file is large enough to hold the uncompressed contents of physical memory, but compression is used to minimize disk I/O and to improve resume-from-hibernation performance. During the boot process, if a valid hiberfil.sys file is located, the NT Loader (NTLDR) will load the file's contents into physical memory and transfer control to code within the kernel that handles resuming system operation after a hibernation (loading drivers, etc.). This functionality is most often found on laptop systems. Here are the pros and cons:

Analyzing the contents of a hibernation file could give you a clue as to what was happening on the system at some point in the past. Matthieu Suiche decoded the hibernation file format and presented his findings at the BlackHat USA 2008 conference (www.blackhat.com/presentations/bh-usa-08/Suiche/BH_US_08_Suiche_Windows_hibernation.pdf). This presentation followed his earlier write-up on the subject from February 2008 titled "Sandman Project" (http://sandman.msuiche.net/docs/SandMan_Project.pdf), and his previous work from 2007 with Nicolas Ruff. The Sandman tool is available from www.msuiche.net/category/sandman/, and the functionality is incorporated into the Volatility Framework (discussed later in this chapter).

Something else to consider about hibernation files is that this functionality may be the only option available for capturing the full contents of physical memory. Some of the available tools for collecting the contents of physical memory may have "issues" (more specifically, they may have caused systems with more than 4 GB of physical memory—including 64-bit systems—to crash) or may not be available or feasible for use in some environments. Using powercfg.exe to enable hibernation mode (if it is not already enabled) and then using some other mechanism or tool to force the system to hibernate may be the only option for obtaining a memory dump. You can force a system with hibernation enabled to hibernate using Microsoft's psshutdown.exe (http://technet.microsoft.com/en-us/sysinternals/bb897541.aspx) utility with the −h option, or by creating a batch file that contains the line:

```
%windir%\System32\rundll32.exe powrprof.dll,SetSuspendState Hibernate
```

The hibernation file is compressed and in most cases will not contain the *current* contents of memory. Thanks to the work performed by Matthieu and Nicolas, the hibernation file can be accessed in the same manner as a live memory dump, so I can't really think of any "cons" to using it. In addition to dumping memory from a live system, having a hibernation file available will give you memory contents from a previous point in time against which to compare your memory dump.

# Analyzing a Physical Memory Dump

Now that you have seen ways to acquire the contents of RAM from a system (both local and remote methods), what can you do with the memory dump? For the most part, prior to summer 2005, the standard operating procedure for most folks who had bothered to collect a memory dump (usually via the version of dd.exe available with George M. Garner, Jr.'s Forensic Acquisition Utilities) was to run strings.exe against it, or run *grep* searches (for e-mail addresses, IP addresses, etc.), or both. Although this would result in investigative leads (finding what appeared to be a password geographically "close" to a username might give an investigator a clue or something to examine further) that would often lead to something definitive, it does not provide overall context to the information that is discovered. For example, is that string that was located part of a word processing or text document, or was it copied to the system Clipboard? What process was using the memory where that string or IP address was located?

With the DFRWS 2005 Memory Challenge as a catalyst, steps have been taken in an attempt to add context to the information found in RAM. By locating specific processes (or other objects maintained in memory) and the memory pages used by those processes, investigators can gain greater insight into the information they discover as well as perform significant data reduction by filtering out "known good" processes and data and focusing on the data that appears "unusual." Several individuals have written tools that can be used to parse through RAM dumps and retrieve detailed information about processes and other structures.

In 2007, Aaron Walters released the Volatility Framework (https://www.volatilesystems.com/), an open source, Python-based framework for parsing memory dumps from (at the time of this writing) Windows XP systems. During summer 2008, Aaron held the first Open Memory Forensics Workshop (https://www.volatilesystems.com/default/omfw) just prior to the DFRWS 2008 conference, during which researchers, analysts, and practitioners could rub elbows and discuss issues surrounding memory acquisition and analysis. Version 1.3 of the Volatility Framework was available at the conference, and was even used during the DFRWS Forensic Rodeo exercise.

Throughout the rest of this chapter, we will look at these tools for performing analysis of memory dumps. We will initially use the memory dumps from the DFRWS 2005 Memory Challenge as exemplars, for examples and demonstrations of tools and techniques for parsing Windows 2000 memory dumps. You're probably asking yourself, why even bother with that? Windows 2000 is the new MS-DOS, right? Well, that's probably not far from the truth, but the dumps do provide an excellent basis for examples because they have already been examined in great detail. Also, they're freely available for download and examination.

# Determining the Operating System of a Dump File

Have you ever been handed an image of a system, and when you asked what the operating system is/was, you simply got "Windows" in response? Shakespeare doesn't cut it here, my friends, because a rose by any other name might *not* smell as sweet. When you're working with an image of a system, the version of Windows that you're confronted with *matters*, and depending on the issue you're dealing with, it could matter a lot. The same is true when you're dealing with a RAM dump file; in fact, it could be even more so. As I've already stated, the structures that are used to define threads and processes in memory vary not only between major versions of the operating system but also within the same version with different service packs installed.

So, when someone hands you a RAM dump and says "Windows," you'd probably want to know how to figure that out, wouldn't you? After all, you don't want to waste a lot of time running the dump file through every known tool until one of them starts producing valid hits on processes, right? Through personal correspondence (that's a fancy term for "e-mail") awhile ago, Andreas Schuster suggested to me that the Windows kernel might possibly be loaded into the same location in memory every time Windows boots. Now, that location is likely to, and does, change for every version of Windows, but so far it seems to be consistent for each version. The easiest way to find this location is to run LiveKD as we did earlier in this chapter, but note in particular the information that's displayed as it starts up (shown here on a Windows XP SP2 system):

```
Windows XP Kernel Version 2600 (Service Pack 2) MP (2 procs) Free x86
compatible
Product: WinNt, suite: TerminalServer SingleUserTS
Built by: 2600.xpsp.050329-1536
Kernel base = 0x804d7000 PsLoadedModuleList = 0x8055c700
```

We're most interested in the information that I've boldfaced—the address of the kernel base. We subtract 0x80000000 from that address and then go to the resultant physical location within the dump file. If the first two bytes located at that address are *MZ*, we could have a full-blown Windows portable executable (PE) file at that location, and we *might* have the kernel. From this point, we can use code similar to what's in lspi.pl to parse apart the PE header and locate the various sections within the PE file. Because the Windows kernel is a legitimate Microsoft application file, we can be sure that there is a resource section within the file that contains a *VS_VERSION_INFO* section. Following information provided by Microsoft regarding the various structures that make up this section, we can then parse through it looking for the file description string.

On the accompanying DVD, you'll find a file called osid.pl that does just that. Osid.pl began life as kern.pl and found its way into Rick McQuown's PTFinderFE utility. Rick asked me via e-mail one day whether there was a way to shorten and clarify the output, so I made some modifications to the file (changed the output, added some switches, etc.) and renamed it.

In its simplest form, you can run osid.pl from the command line, passing in the path to the image file as the sole argument:

```
C:\Perl\memory>osid.pl d:\hacking\xp-laptop1.img
```

Alternatively, you can designate a specific file using the –*f* switch:

```
C:\Perl\memory>osid.pl -f d:\hacking\xp-laptop1.img
```

Both of these commands will give you the same output; in this case, the RAM dump was collected from a Windows XP SP2 system, so the script returns *XPSP2*. If this isn't quite enough information and you'd like to see more, you can add the –*v* switch (for *verbose*), and the script will return the following for the xp-laptop1.img file:

```
OS        : XPSP2
Product : Microsoft« Windows« Operating System ver 5.1.2600.2622
```

As you can see, the strings within the *VS_VERSION_INFO* structure that refer to the product name and product version get concatenated to produce the additional output. If we run the script with both the –*v* and the –*f* switches against the first RAM dump file from the DFRWS 2005 Memory Challenge, we get:

```
OS        : 2000
Product : Microsoft(R) Windows (R) 2000 Operating System ver 5.00.2195.1620
```

Running this script against other memory dumps mentioned previously in this chapter illustrates how well it works across various versions of Windows. For example, when run against the memory dump used in the Memoryze example, we see the following:

```
C:\Perl\memory>osid.pl -f d:\hacking\boomer-win2003.img -v
OS        : 2003
Product : Microsoft« Windows« Operating System ver 5.2.3790.0
```

Running the script against another Windows 2003 memory dump gives us slightly different results:

```
C:\Perl\memory>osid.pl -f d:\hacking\win2k3sp1_physmem.img -v
OS        : 2003SP1
Product : Microsoft« Windows« Operating System ver 5.2.3790.1830
```

This script also works equally well against VMware .vmem files. I ran the script against a .vmem file from a Windows 2000 VMware session and received the following output:

```
OS      : 2000
Product : Microsoft(R) Windows (R) 2000 Operating System ver 5.00.2195.7071
```

I think that more than anything else, this demonstrates the utility of scripts or tools such as this, as it provides an analyst with the ability to more completely document the various items to be analyzed, particularly when such things may not have been completely documented during the response activities when data was initially collected.

<br>

**TIP**

Most analysis tools, discussed later in this chapter, are capable of performing the same function as was just discussed. For example, you can use the Volatility *ident* command to identify the operating system of a memory dump.

# Process Basics

Throughout this chapter, we will focus primarily on parsing information regarding processes from a memory dump. This is due, in part, to the fact that the majority of the publicly available research and tools focus on processes as a source of forensic information. That is not to say that other objects within memory should be excluded, but rather that most researchers seem to be focusing on processes. We will discuss another means of retrieving information from a RAM dump later in the chapter, but for now, we will focus our efforts on processes. To that end, we need to have a pretty good idea of what a process "looks like" in memory. The following section focuses on processes in Windows 2000 memory, but most of the concepts remain the same for all versions of Windows. The biggest difference is in the actual structure of the process itself, and going into the details of the process structures on all versions of Windows is beyond the scope of this book.

## EProcess Structure

Each process on a Windows system is represented as an executive process, or EProcess, block. This EProcess block is a data structure in which various attributes of the process, as well as pointers to a number of other attributes and data structures (threads, the process environment block) relating to the process, are maintained. Because the data structure is a sequence of bytes, with each sequence having a specific meaning and purpose, these structures can be read and analyzed by an investigator. However, the one thing to keep in mind is that the only thing consistent between versions of the Windows operating system regarding these structures is that they aren't consistent. You heard right: The size and even the values of the structures change not only between operating system versions (e.g., Windows 2000 to XP) but also between service packs of the same version of the operating system (Windows XP to XP SP2).

Andreas Schuster has done a great job of documenting the EProcess block structures in his blog (http://computer.forensikblog.de/en/topics/windows/memory_analysis). However, it is relatively easy to view the contents of the EProcess structure (or any other structure available on Windows). First, download and install the Microsoft Debugging Tools and the correct symbols for your operating system and Service Pack. Then download livekd.exe from Sysinternals.com (when you type **sysinternals.com** into the address bar of your browser, you will be automatically redirected to the Microsoft site, because by now, Mark Russinovich has long since been in the employ of Microsoft), and for convenience copy it into the same directory as the Debugging Tools. Once you've done this, open a command prompt, change to the directory where you installed the Debugging Tools, and type the following command:

```
D:\debug>livekd -w
```

This command will open WinDbg, the GUI interface to the debugger tools. To see what the entire contents of an EProcess block "looks like" (with all the substructures that make up the EProcess structure broken out), type **dt −a −b −v _EPROCESS** into the command window and press **Enter**. The −*a* flag shows each array element on a new line, with its index, and the −*b* switch displays blocks recursively. The −*v* flag creates more verbose output, telling you the overall size of each structure, for example. In some cases, it can be helpful to include the −*r* flag for recursive output. The following illustrates a short excerpt from the results of this command, run on a Windows 2000 system:

```
kd> dt -a -b -v _EPROCESS
struct _EPROCESS, 94 elements, 0x290 bytes
   +0x000 Pcb                    : struct _KPROCESS, 26 elements, 0x6c bytes
     +0x000 Header               : struct _DISPATCHER_HEADER, 6 elements, 0x10 bytes
         +0x000 Type             : UChar
         +0x001 Absolute         : UChar
         +0x002 Size             : UChar
         +0x003 Inserted         : UChar
         +0x004 SignalState      : Int4B
         +0x008 WaitListHead     : struct _LIST_ENTRY, 2 elements, 0x8 bytes
            +0x000 Flink         : Ptr32 to
            +0x004 Blink         : Ptr32 to
       +0x010 ProfileListHead    : struct _LIST_ENTRY, 2 elements, 0x8 bytes
         +0x000 Flink            : Ptr32 to
         +0x004 Blink            : Ptr32 to
     +0x018 DirectoryTableBase   : (2 elements)Uint4B
```

The entire output is much longer (according to the header, the entire structure is 0x290 bytes long), but don't worry, we will address important (from a forensic/investigative aspect) elements of the structure as we progress through this chapter.

---

**NOTE**

The Windows kernel keeps track of active processes by way of a doubly linked list; this means that each process "points to" both the process after it and the process before it, in a circular list. The operating system enumerates a list of active processes by walking *PsActiveProcessList* and developing a list of known active processes. Within the EProcess structure is a *LIST_ENTRY* item named *ActiveProcessLinks*. This entry has two values, *flink* and *blink*, which are pointers to the next and previous processes, respectively. Many memory analysis tools will do the same thing (i.e., walk the list of active processes) in a memory dump file, whereas others will perform a brute force enumeration of process objects (e.g., lsproc.pl and Volatility), enumerating even exited processes. This is very important, as some rootkits (see Chapter 7) hide processes by unlinking their processes from this doubly linked list.

---

An important element of a process that the EProcess structure points to is the *process environment block*, or PEB. This structure contains a great deal of information, but the elements that are important to us, as forensic investigators, are:

■ A pointer to the loader data (referred to as *PPEB_LDR_DATA*) structure that includes pointers or references to modules (DLLs) used by the process

■ A pointer to the image base address, where we can expect to find the beginning of the executable image file

■ A pointer to the process parameters structure, which itself maintains the DLL path, the path to the executable image, and the command line used to launch the process

Extracting this information from a dump file can prove to be extremely useful to an investigator, as you will see throughout the rest of this chapter.

# Process Creation Mechanism

Now that you know a little bit about the various structures involved with processes, it would be helpful to know something about how the operating system uses those structures, particularly when it comes to creating an actual process.

A number of steps are followed when a process is created. These steps can be broken down into six stages (taken from *Windows Internals*, 4th Edition, Chapter 6, by Russinovich and Solomon):

1.  The image (.exe) file to be executed is opened. During this stage, the appropriate subsystem (POSIX, MS-DOS, Win 16, etc.) is identified. Also, the Image File Execution Options Registry key (see Chapter 4) is checked to see whether there is a Debugger value, and if there is, the process starts over.

2.  The EProcess object is created. The kernel process block (KProcess), the process environment block, and the initial address space are also set up.

3.  The initial thread is created.

4.  The Windows subsystem is notified of the creation of the new process and thread, along with the ID of the process's creator and a flag to identify whether the process belongs to a Windows process.

5.  Execution of the initial thread starts. At this point, the process environment has been set up and resources have been allocated for the process's thread(s) to use.

6.  The initialization of the address space is completed, in the context of the new process and thread.

At this point, the process now consumes space in memory in accordance with the EProcess structure (which includes the KProcess structure) and the PEB structure. The process has at least one thread and may begin consuming additional memory resources as the process itself executes. At this point, if the process or memory as a whole is halted and dumped, there will at least be something to analyze.

# Parsing Memory Dump Contents

The tools described in the DFRWS 2005 Memory Challenge used a methodology for parsing memory contents of locating and enumerating the active process list, using specific values/offsets (derived from system files) to identify the beginning of the list and then walking through the doubly linked list until all the active processes had been identified. The location of the offset for the beginning of the active process list was derived from one of the important system files, ntoskrnl.exe.

Andreas Schuster took a different approach in his Perl script, called ptfinder.pl. His idea was to take a brute force approach to the problem—identifying specific characteristics of processes in memory and then enumerating the EProcess blocks as well as other information about the processes based on those characteristics. Andreas began his approach by enumerating the structure of the *DISPATCHER_HEADER*, which is located at offset 0 for each EProcess block (actually, it's within the structure known as the KProcess block). Using LiveKD, we see that the enumerated structure from a Windows 2000 system has the following elements:

```
+0x000 Header        : struct _DISPATCHER_HEADER, 6 elements, 0x10 bytes
+0x000 Type          : UChar
+0x001 Absolute      : UChar
+0x002 Size          : UChar
+0x003 Inserted      : UChar
+0x004 SignalState   : Int4B
```

In a nutshell, Andreas found that some of the elements for the *DISPATCHER_ HEADER* were consistent in all processes on the system. He examined the *DISPATCHER_ HEADER* elements for processes (and threads) on systems ranging from Windows 2000 up through early betas of Vista and found that the *Type* value remained consistent across each version of the operating system. He also found that the *Size* value remained consistent within various versions of the operating system (e.g., all processes on Windows 2000 or XP had the same *Size* value) but changed between those versions (e.g., for Windows 2000 the *Size* value is 0x1b, but for early versions of Vista it was 0x20).

Using this information as well as the total size of the structure and the way the structure itself could be broken down, Andreas wrote his ptfinder.pl Perl script, which would enumerate processes and threads located in a memory dump. At the DFRWS 2006 conference he also presented a paper, "Searching for processes and threads in Microsoft Windows memory dumps" (www.dfrws.org/2006/proceedings/2-Schuster.pdf ), which addressed not only the data structures that make up processes and threads but also various rules to determine whether what was found was a legitimate structure or just a bunch of bytes in a file.

**NOTE**

In fall 2006, Richard McQuown (http://forensiczone.blogspot.com/) put together a GUI front end for Andreas Schuster's PTFinder tools. The PTFinder tools are Perl scripts and require that the Perl interpreter be installed on a system to run them. (Perl is installed by default on many Linux distributions and is freely available for Windows platforms from ActiveState.com.)

Not only can Richard's tool detect the operating system of the RAM dump (rather than have the user enter it manually) using code I'll discuss later in this chapter, but it can also provide a graphical representation of the output. PTFinderFE has some interesting applications, particularly with regard to visualization.

In spring 2006, I wrote some of my own tools to assist in parsing through Windows RAM dump files. Because the currently available exemplars at the time were the dumps for Windows 2000 systems available from the DFRWS 2005 Memory Challenge, I focused my initial efforts on producing code that worked for that platform. This allowed me to address various issues in code development without getting too wrapped up in the myriad differences between the various versions of the Windows operating system. The result was four separate Perl scripts, each run from the command line. All of these scripts are provided on the accompanying DVD, and we'll discuss them here.

---

**NOTE**

The following tools (lsproc.pl, lspd.pl, lspi.pl, and lspm.pl) are designed to be used solely with Windows 2000 memory dumps. As we've discussed so far, there are significant changes in the EProcess structure format between the various versions of Windows (2000, XP, 2003, Vista, etc.). As such, significant work needs to be done to produce a single application that will allow you to parse memory dumps from all versions.

---

# Lsproc.pl

*LSproc*, short for *list processes*, is similar to Andreas's ptfinder.pl; however, lsproc.pl locates processes but not threads. Lsproc.pl takes a single argument, the path and name to a RAM dump file:

```
c:\perl\memory>lsproc.pl d:\dumps\drfws1-mem.dmp
```

The output of lsproc.pl appears at the console (i.e., STDOUT) in six columns: the word *Proc* (I was anticipating adding threads at a later date), the parent process identifier (PPID), the process identifier (PID), the name of the process, the offset of the process structure within the dump file, and the creation time of the process. Here is an excerpt of the lsproc.pl output:

```
Proc   820    324    helix.exe          0x00306020   Sun   Jun 5   14:09:27   2005
Proc     0      0    Idle               0x0046d160
Proc   600    668    UMGR32.EXE         0x0095f020   Sun   Jun 5   00:55:08   2005
Proc   324   1112    cmd2k.exe          0x00dcc020   Sun   Jun 5   14:14:25   2005
Proc   668    784    dfrws2005.exe(x)   0x00e1fb60   Sun   Jun 5   01:00:53   2005
Proc   156    176    winlogon.exe       0x01045d60   Sun   Jun 5   00:32:44   2005
Proc   156    176    winlogon.exe       0x01048140   Sat   Jun 4   23:36:31   2005
```

| Proc | 144  | 164  | winlogon.exe      | 0x0104ca00 | Fri | Jun 3 | 01:25:54 | 2005 |
|------|------|------|-------------------|------------|-----|-------|----------|------|
| Proc | 156  | 180  | csrss.exe         | 0x01286480 | Sun | Jun 5 | 00:32:43 | 2005 |
| Proc | 144  | 168  | csrss.exe         | 0x01297b40 | Fri | Jun 3 | 01:25:53 | 2005 |
| Proc | 8    | 156  | smss.exe          | 0x012b62c0 | Sun | Jun 5 | 00:32:40 | 2005 |
| Proc | 0    | 8    | System            | 0x0141dc60 |     |       |          |      |
| Proc | 668  | 784  | dfrws2005.exe(x)  | 0x016a9b60 | Sun | Jun 5 | 01:00:53 | 2005 |
| Proc | 1112 | 1152 | dd.exe(x)         | 0x019d1980 | Sun | Jun 5 | 14:14:38 | 2005 |
| Proc | 228  | 592  | dfrws2005.exe     | 0x02138640 | Sun | Jun 5 | 01:00:53 | 2005 |
| Proc | 820  | 1076 | cmd.exe           | 0x02138c40 | Sun | Jun 5 | 00:35:18 | 2005 |
| Proc | 240  | 788  | metasploit.exe(x) | 0x02686cc0 | Sun | Jun 5 | 00:38:37 | 2005 |
| Proc | 820  | 964  | Apoint.exe        | 0x02b84400 | Sun | Jun 5 | 00:33:57 | 2005 |
| Proc | 820  | 972  | HKserv.exe        | 0x02bf86e0 | Sun | Jun 5 | 00:33:57 | 2005 |
| Proc | 820  | 988  | DragDrop.exe      | 0x02c46020 | Sun | Jun 5 | 00:33:57 | 2005 |
| Proc | 820  | 1008 | alogserv.exe      | 0x02e7ea20 | Sun | Jun 5 | 00:33:57 | 2005 |
| Proc | 820  | 972  | HKserv.exe        | 0x02f806e0 | Sun | Jun 5 | 00:33:57 | 2005 |
| Proc | 820  | 1012 | tgcmd.exe         | 0x030826a0 | Sun | Jun 5 | 00:33:58 | 2005 |
| Proc | 176  | 800  | userinit.exe(x)   | 0x03e35020 | Sun | Jun 5 | 00:33:52 | 2005 |
| Proc | 800  | 820  | Explorer.Exe      | 0x03e35ae0 | Sun | Jun 5 | 00:33:53 | 2005 |
| Proc | 820  | 1048 | PcfMgr.exe        | 0x040b4660 | Sun | Jun 5 | 00:34:01 | 2005 |

The first process listed in the lsproc.pl output is helix.exe. According to the information provided at the DFRWS 2005 Memory Challenge Web site, utilities on the Helix Live CD were used to acquire the memory dump.

The preceding listing shows only an excerpt of the lsproc.pl output. A total of 45 processes were located in the memory dump file. You'll notice in the output that several of the processes have *(x)* after the process name. This indicates that the processes have exited.

## NOTE

Looking closely, you'll notice some interesting things about the lsproc.pl output. One is that the csrss.exe process (PID = 168) has a creation date that appears to be a day or two earlier than the other listed processes. Looking even more closely, you'll see something similar for two winlogon.exe processes (PID = 164 and 176). Andreas Schuster noticed these as well, and according to an entry on data persistence in his blog (http://computer.forensikblog.de/en/2006/04/persistance_through_the_boot_process.html), the system boot time for the dump file was determined to be Sunday, January 5, 2005, at approximately 00:32:27. So, where do these processes come from?

As Andreas points out in his blog, without having more definitive information about the state of the test system prior to collecting data for the
Memory Challenge, it is difficult to develop a complete understanding of this
issue. However, the specifications of the test system were known and documented, and it was noted that the system suffered a crash dump during data
collection.

It is entirely possible that the data survived the reboot. There don't seem
to be any specifications that require that when a Windows system shuts
down or suffers a crash dump, the contents of physical memory are zeroed
out or wiped in some manner. It is possible, then, that contents of physical
memory remain in their previous state, and if they are not overwritten when
the system is restarted, the data is still available for analysis. Many BIOS
versions have a feature to overwrite memory during boot as part of a RAM
test, but this feature is usually disabled to speed up the boot process.

This is definitely an area that requires further study. As Andreas states
(http://computer.forensikblog.de/en/2006/04/data_lifetime.html), this area of
study has "a bright future."

# Lspd.pl

Lspd.pl is a Perl script that will allow you to list the details of the process. Like the other
tools we will be discussing, lspd.pl is a command-line Perl script that relies on the output of
lsproc.pl to obtain its information. Specifically, lspd.pl takes two arguments: the full path of
the dump file and the physical offset of the process that you're interested in (the physical
offset of the process within memory is obtained from the lsproc.pl output). Although lsproc.
pl takes some time to parse through the contents of the dump file, lspd.pl is much quicker,
because you're telling it exactly where to go in the file to enumerate its information.

Let's take a look at a specific process. In this case, we'll look at dd.exe, the process with
PID 284. The command line to use lspd.pl to get detailed information about this process is:

```
c:\perl\memory>lspd.pl d:\dumps\dfrws1-mem.dmp 0x0414dd60
```

**NOTE**

The lsproc.pl output just shown is an excerpt of the entire output; I didn't list
the entire output simply because the excerpt illustrates enough information
for me to make my point. However, the process referenced in the lspd.pl
command line (i.e., at offset 0x0414dd60) is not listed in that excerpt, although
it is visible in the full output of lsproc.pl.

Notice that with lspd.pl, we're using two arguments: the name and path to the dump file and the physical offset in the dump file where we found the process with lsproc.pl. We'll take a look at the output of lspd.pl in sections, starting with some useful information pulled directly from the EProcess structure itself:

```
Process Name                    :   dd.exe
PID                             :   284
Parent PID                      :   1112
TFLINK                          :   0xff2401c4
TBLINK                          :   0xff2401c4
FLINK                           :   0x8046b980
BLINK                           :   0xff1190c0
SubSystem                       :   4.0
Exit Status                     :   259
Create Time                     :   Sun Jun 5 14:53:42 2005
Exit Called                     :   0
DTB                             :   0x01d9e000
ObjTable                        :   0xff158708 (0x00eb6708)
PEB                             :   0x7ffdf000 (0x02c2d000)
InheritedAddressSpace           :   0
ReadImageFileExecutionOptions   :   0
BeingDebugged                   :   0
CSDVersion                      :   Service Pack 1
Mutant                          =   0xffffffff
Img Base Addr                   =   0x00400000 (0x00fee000)
PEB_LDR_DATA                    =   0x00131e90 (0x03a1ee90)
Params                          =   0x00020000 (0x03a11000)
```

**NOTE**

Earlier in the chapter, I mentioned that the list of active processes on a live system is maintained in a doubly linked list. The *flink* and *blink* values seen in the preceding lspd.pl output are the values that point to the next and previous processes, respectively. As displayed in the output of lspd.pl, these pointers are to addresses in memory, not physical addresses or offsets within the dump file.

Lspd.pl also follows pointers provided by the EProcess structure to collect other data as well. For example, we can also see the path to the executable image and the command line used to launch the process (bold added for emphasis):

```
Current Directory Path  = E:\Shells\
DllPath                 = E:\Acquisition\FAU;.;C:\WINNT\System32;C:\WINNT\system;
                          C:\WINNT;E:\Acquisition\FAU\;E:\Acquisition\GNU\;
                          E:\Acquisition\CYGWIN\;E:\IR\bin\;E:\IR\WFT;E:\IR\
                          windbg\;E:\IR\Foundstone\;E:\IR\Cygwin;E:\IR\
                          somarsoft\;E:\IR\sysinternals\;E:\IR\ntsecurity\;
                          E:\IR\perl\;E:\Static-Binaries\gnu_utils_win32\;C:\WINNT\
                          system32;C:\WINNT;C:\WINNT\System32\Wbem
ImagePathName           = E:\Acquisition\FAU\dd.exe
Command Line            = ..\Acquisition\FAU\dd.exe if=\\.\PhysicalMemory of=F:\
                          intrusion2005\physicalmemory.dd conv=noerror --md5sum
                          --verifymd5 --md5out=F:\intrusion2005\physicalmemory.dd.
                          md5 --log=F:\intrusion2005\audit.log
Environment Offset      = 0x00000000 (0x00000000)
Window Title            = ..\Acquisition\FAU\dd.exe if=\\.\PhysicalMemory of=F:\
                          intrusion2005\physicalmemory.dd conv=noerror --md5sum
                          --verifymd5 --md5out=F:\intrusion2005\physicalmemory.dd.
                          md5 --log=F:\intrusion2005\audit.log
Desktop Name            = WinSta0\Default
```

Lspd.pl also retrieves a list of the names of various modules (DLLs) used by the process and whatever available handles (file handles, etc.) it can find in memory. For example, lspd.pl found that dd.exe had the following file handle open:

```
Type : File
Name = \intrusion2005\audit.log
```

As you can see from the preceding command line, the file \intrusion\audit.log is located on the F:\ drive and is the output file for the log of activity generated by dd.exe, which explains why it would be listed as an open file handle in use by the process. Using this information as derived from other processes, you can get an understanding of files you should be concerned with during an investigation. In this particular instance, you can assume that the E:\ drive listed in *ImagePathName* is a CD-ROM drive, because Helix can be run from a CD. You can confirm this by checking Registry values in an image of the system in question (a system image is not provided as part of the memory challenge, however). You can also use similar information to find out a little bit more about the F:\ drive. I will cover this information in Chapter 4.

Finally, one other thing that lspd.pl will do is go to the location pointed to by the Image Base *Addr* value (once it has been translated from a virtual address to a physical offset within the memory dump file) and check to see whether a valid executable image is located at that address. This check is very simple; all it does is read the first two bytes starting at the translated address to see whether they're *MZ*. These two bytes are not a definitive check, but PE files (files with .exe, .dll, .ocs, .sys, and similar extensions) start with the initials of Mark Zbikowski, one of the early architects of MS-DOS and Windows NT. The format of the PE file and its header is addressed in greater detail in Chapter 6.

---

**TIP**

If you dumped the contents of physical memory from a Windows 2000 or XP system using winen.exe and you have a licensed EnCase dongle, you can parse process information from a memory dump using EnScripts written by TK_Lane and available through the "EDD and Forensics" blog (http://eddandforensics. blogspot.com/2008/04/windows-memory-analysis.html).

---

# Volatility Framework

Aaron Walters provides some valuable information about the Volatility Framework in his OMFW presentation, available from https://www.volatilesystems.com/volatility/omfw/ Walters_OMFW_2008.pdf.

The readme.txt file that is part of the Volatility distribution (Version 1.3 beta at the time of this writing) provides a great deal of information about how to use Volatility and what types of commands and capabilities are available, as well as examples of how to launch the various commands. Aaron designed Volatility to use some of the commands that are commonly used in incident response activities; for example, to get a list of running processes from a memory dump, Volatility uses *pslist*. Before using Volatility, be sure to read through the readme.txt file to see what type of information can be retrieved from a Windows XP SP2 or SP3 memory dump.

To illustrate what type of information is available from a raw, dd–style memory dump, let's take a look at an example; in this case a 512MB memory dump from a Windows XP SP2 laptop. We can start by getting some basic information about the memory dump using the *ident* command:

```
D:\Volatility>python volatility ident -f d:\hacking\xp-laptop1.img
        Image Name    : d:\hacking\xp-laptop1.img
        Image Type    : Service Pack 2
          VM Type     : nopae
            DTB       : 0x39000
        Datetime      : Sat Jun 25 12:58:47 2005
```

This can be very useful information in documenting our analysis of the memory dump, as in some instances, we may not have access to the *ident* information as part of our documentation. Using the *pslist* command, we can retrieve the active process list from the memory dump in a format similar to what we're used to seeing when running pslist.exe on a live system:

```
D:\Volatility>python volatility pslist -f d:\hacking\xp-laptop1.img
Name              Pid      PPid     Thds     Hnds     Time
System            4        0        61       1140     Thu  Jan 01 00:00:00  1970
smss.exe          448      4        3        21       Sat  Jun 25 16:47:28  2005
csrss.exe         504      448      12       596      Sat  Jun 25 16:47:30  2005
winlogon.exe      528      448      21       508      Sat  Jun 25 16:47:31  2005
services.exe      580      528      18       401      Sat  Jun 25 16:47:31  2005
lsass.exe         592      528      21       374      Sat  Jun 25 16:47:31  2005
svchost.exe       740      580      17       198      Sat  Jun 25 16:47:32  2005
svchost.exe       800      580      10       302      Sat  Jun 25 16:47:33  2005
svchost.exe       840      580      83       1589     Sat  Jun 25 16:47:33  2005
Smc.exe           876      580      22       423      Sat  Jun 25 16:47:33  2005
svchost.exe       984      580      6        90       Sat  Jun 25 16:47:35  2005
svchost.exe       1024     580      15       207      Sat  Jun 25 16:47:35  2005
spoolsv.exe       1224     580      12       136      Sat  Jun 25 16:47:39  2005
ssonsvr.exe       1632     1580     1        24       Sat  Jun 25 16:47:46  2005
explorer.exe      1812     1764     22       553      Sat  Jun 25 16:47:47  2005
Directcd.exe      1936     1812     4        40       Sat  Jun 25 16:47:48  2005
TaskSwitch.exe    1952     1812     1        21       Sat  Jun 25 16:47:48  2005
Fast.exe          1960     1812     1        22       Sat  Jun 25 16:47:48  2005
VPTray.exe        1980     1812     2        89       Sat  Jun 25 16:47:49  2005
atiptaxx.exe      2040     1812     1        51       Sat  Jun 25 16:47:49  2005
jusched.exe       188      1812     1        22       Sat  Jun 25 16:47:49  2005
EM_EXEC.exe       224      112      2        74       Sat  Jun 25 16:47:50  2005
ati2evxx.exe      432      580      4        38       Sat  Jun 25 16:47:55  2005
Crypserv.exe      688      580      3        34       Sat  Jun 25 16:47:55  2005
DefWatch.exe      864      580      3        27       Sat  Jun 25 16:47:55  2005
msdtc.exe         1076     580      14       166      Sat  Jun 25 16:47:55  2005
Rtvscan.exe       1304     580      37       300      Sat  Jun 25 16:47:58  2005
tcpsvcs.exe       1400     580      2        94       Sat  Jun 25 16:47:58  2005
snmp.exe          1424     580      5        192      Sat  Jun 25 16:47:58  2005
svchost.exe       1484     580      6        119      Sat  Jun 25 16:47:59  2005
wdfmgr.exe        1548     580      4        65       Sat  Jun 25 16:47:59  2005
Fast.exe          1700     580      2        32       Sat  Jun 25 16:48:01  2005
mqsvc.exe         1948     580      23       205      Sat  Jun 25 16:48:02  2005
mqtgsvc.exe       2536     580      9        119      Sat  Jun 25 16:48:05  2005
alg.exe           2868     580      6        108      Sat  Jun 25 16:48:11  2005
```

| wuauclt.exe | 2424 | 840 | 4 | 160 | Sat | Jun 25 16:49:21 | 2005 |
|---|---|---|---|---|---|---|---|
| firefox.exe | 2160 | 1812 | 6 | 182 | Sat | Jun 25 16:49:22 | 2005 |
| PluckSvr.exe | 944 | 740 | 9 | 227 | Sat | Jun 25 16:51:00 | 2005 |
| iexplore.exe | 2392 | 1812 | 9 | 365 | Sat | Jun 25 16:51:02 | 2005 |
| PluckTray.exe | 2740 | 944 | 3 | 105 | Sat | Jun 25 16:51:10 | 2005 |
| PluckUpdater.ex | 3076 | 1812 | 0 | -1 | Sat | Jun 25 16:51:15 | 2005 |
| PluckUpdater.ex | 1916 | 944 | 0 | -1 | Sat | Jun 25 16:51:40 | 2005 |
| PluckTray.exe | 3256 | 1812 | 0 | -1 | Sat | Jun 25 16:54:28 | 2005 |
| cmd.exe | 2624 | 1812 | 1 | 29 | Sat | Jun 25 16:57:36 | 2005 |
| wmiprvse.exe | 4080 | 740 | 7 | 0 | Sat | Jun 25 16:57:53 | 2005 |
| PluckTray.exe | 3100 | 1812 | 0 | -1 | Sat | Jun 25 16:57:59 | 2005 |
| dd.exe | 4012 | 2624 | 1 | 22 | Sat | Jun 25 16:58:46 | 2005 |

We can run similar commands to retrieve information about all process objects in the memory dump, including exited processes, using the *psscan* or *psscan2* command. Commands to retrieve information about all objects (network connections, processes, etc.) are slower, as they use a linear scanning method to run completely through the memory dump file, examining all possible objects, rather than using specific offsets provided by the operating system (see the discussion about LiveKD earlier in this chapter).

One of the more useful things most analysts look to when responding to an intrusion or compromise is network connections. You can retrieve a list of active network connections (similar to using the *netstat −ano* command) from a memory dump using the *connections* command, as follows:

```
D:\Volatility>python volatility connections -f d:\hacking\xp-laptop1.img
Local Address         Remote Address         Pid
127.0.0.1:1056        127.0.0.1:1055         2160
127.0.0.1:1055        127.0.0.1:1056         2160
192.168.2.7:1077      64.62.243.144:80       2392
192.168.2.7:1082      205.161.7.134:80       2392
192.168.2.7:1066      199.239.137.200:80     2392
```

Taking this a step further, you can scan the entire memory dump file for indications of network connection objects, specifically looking for network connections that may have been closed at the time the memory dump was acquired:

```
D:\Volatility>python volatility connscan2 -f d:\hacking\xp-laptop1.img
Local Address         Remote Address         Pid
------------------    -------------------    ------
192.168.2.7:1115      207.126.123.29:80      1916
3.0.48.2:17985        66.179.81.245:20084    4287933200
192.168.2.7:1164      66.179.81.247:80       944
192.168.2.7:1082      205.161.7.134:80       2392
```

| | | |
|---|---|---|
| 192.168.2.7:1086 | 199.239.137.200:80 | 1916 |
| 192.168.2.7:1162 | 170.224.8.51:80 | 1916 |
| 127.0.0.1:1055 | 127.0.0.1:1056 | 2160 |
| 192.168.2.7:1116 | 66.161.12.81:80 | 1916 |
| 192.168.2.7:1161 | 66.135.211.87:443 | 1916 |
| 192.168.2.7:1091 | 209.73.26.183:80 | 1916 |
| 192.168.2.7:1151 | 66.150.96.111:80 | 1916 |
| 192.168.2.7:1077 | 64.62.243.144:80 | 2392 |
| 192.168.2.7:1066 | 199.239.137.200:80 | 2392 |
| 192.168.2.7:1157 | 66.151.149.10:80 | 1916 |
| 192.168.2.7:1091 | 209.73.26.183:80 | 1916 |
| 192.168.2.7:1115 | 207.126.123.29:80 | 1916 |
| 192.168.2.7:1155 | 66.35.250.150:80 | 1916 |
| 127.0.0.1:1056 | 127.0.0.1:1055 | 2160 |
| 192.168.2.7:1115 | 207.126.123.29:80 | 1916 |
| 192.168.2.7:1155 | 66.35.250.150:80 | 1916 |

Volatility is a powerful open source framework, allowing others to extend its capabilities by developing additional modules (knowledge of Python programming is a significant requirement). Brendan Dolan-Gavitt (a.k.a. Moyix) created a Volatility module that looks for Windows messages (http://moyix.blogspot.com/2008/09/window-messages-as-forensic-resource.html), which are various events generated by Windows GUI applications and handled by the message queue. As Brendan points out, an application may be poorly written and may not handle its own messages very well; if this is the case, you may be able to find remnants of those messages still visible in the memory dump. This information may be useful during a forensic examination.

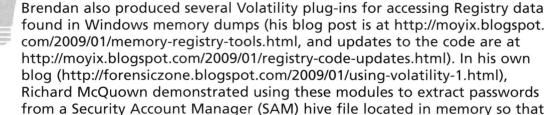

**TIP**

Brendan also produced several Volatility plug-ins for accessing Registry data found in Windows memory dumps (his blog post is at http://moyix.blogspot.com/2009/01/memory-registry-tools.html, and updates to the code are at http://moyix.blogspot.com/2009/01/registry-code-updates.html). In his own blog (http://forensiczone.blogspot.com/2009/01/using-volatility-1.html), Richard McQuown demonstrated using these modules to extract passwords from a Security Account Manager (SAM) hive file located in memory so that he could crack those passwords using his tool of choice.

To use Volatility and Brendan's modules to extract passwords from hive files located in memory, you have to install the PyCrypto modules (available as prebuilt Windows binaries from www.voidspace.org.uk/python/modules.shtml#pycrypto).

In addition, Jesse Kornblum produced two modules: suspicious, which looks for suspicious entries in process command lines, and cryptoscan, which looks for TrueCrypt passphrases. This last module can be extremely beneficial to an analyst, as TrueCrypt (www.truecrypt.org/) is a powerful, albeit free, application that can be used to encrypt volumes and disks.

Volatility works with much more than just simply raw memory dumps. Thanks to the efforts of Matthieu Suiche (www.msuiche.net/), Volatility includes the capability to parse hibernation files, as well. This started out as the Sandman Project, and later became an integral part of the Volatility Framework. In December 2008, Matthieu released a stand-alone, closed source (alpha) version of the hibernation framework shell, called hibrshell (www.msuiche. net/hibrshell/). This version of hibrshell reportedly works with hibernation files from Windows XP, 2003, Vista, and 2008 systems.

## TIP

Regardless of the framework used to analyze it, the hibernation file provides a responder or analyst with several options that were not previously available. First, the hibernation file can be used as historical data, providing information about the system's live, running state at a previous point in time. This can be extremely valuable in malware analysis, as well as to assist in determining a timeline for an intrusion, particularly if the analyst also has a current memory dump to analyze. In circumstances where the previously mentioned tools (e.g., mdd.exe, etc.) cannot be used to dump the contents of physical memory from a system, the responder may be able to force the system to hibernate to create a memory dump that can then be analyzed.

Volatility can also parse crash dump files, as well as convert a raw, dd-style memory dump to crash dump format so that the analyst can use Microsoft's debugger tools.

By now it should be clear that the Volatility Framework provides some extremely powerful capabilities, and just how much information the analyst can retrieve from a memory dump. To help correlate some of the data that can be retrieved using Volatility, Jamie Levy wrote a Perl script called vol2html.pl (http://gleeda.blogspot.com/2008/11/vol2html-perl-script.html). The script takes the output of the Volatility *pslist*, *files*, and *dlllist* commands and correlates them into an HTML report, an example of which you can see at http://venus.cs. qc.edu/~jlevy/code/report/index.html. Similar to the familiar listdlls.exe available from Microsoft (Sysinternals), the Volatility *dlllist* command includes the process command line as part of its output; this command line also appears in the HTML output of vol2html.pl.

Examples of Windows XP memory dump files are available as part of the DFRWS 2008 Forensic Rodeo (www.dfrws.org/2008/rodeo.shtml), as well as from the National Institute of Standards and Technology (www.cfreds.nist.gov/mem/Basic_Memory_Images.html).

Michael Hale Ligh provides two blog posts that describe how he has used the Volatility Framework to great effect, particularly with respect to malware analysis; see "Recovering CoreFlood Binaries with Volatility" (http://mnin.blogspot.com/2008/11/recovering-coreflood-binaries-with.html), and "Locating Hidden Clampi DLLs (VAD-style)" (http://mnin.blogspot.com/2008/11/locating-hidden-clampi-dlls-vad-style.html). Both blog posts provide excellent examples of how the Volatility Framework can maximize an analyst's capabilities.

# Memoryze

Mandiant's Memoryze tool provides the analyst with the ability to parse and analyze memory dumps from several versions of Windows. To install Memoryze, download the MSI file from the Mandiant Web site (mentioned previously in this chapter) and install it. I chose to install it in the D:\Mandiant directory. Then, to install Audit Viewer, download the zipped archive, and be sure that you've downloaded the dependencies (i.e., Python 2.5 or 2.6, wxPython GUI extensions) as described at the Mandiant Web site (if you've already installed and tried Volatility, you already have Python installed). I chose to unzip the Audit Viewer files into the directory D:\Mandiant\AV.

To demonstrate the use of Memoryze and Audit Viewer, we'll start by selecting a memory dump from a Windows 2003 system: boomer-win2003.img. The first thing we'll need to do to analyze this memory dump is to run Memoryze against it to extract various data:

```
D:\mandiant>process.bat -input d:\hacking\boomer-win2003.img -ports true -handles
true -sections true
```

The preceding command tells Memoryze to parse the process information from the memory dump, and get ports, handles, and memory sections (I've purposely opted not to get the strings from each process) for the processes in the active process list. The full range of usage options for process.bat includes the following:

```
Usage: process.bat

-input      name of snapshot. Exclude for live memory.

-pid        PID of the process to inspect. Default: 4294967295 = All

-process    optional name of the process to inspect. Default: Excluded

-handles    true|false inspect all the process handles. Default: false

-sections   true|false inspect all process memory ranges. Default: false

-ports      true|false inspect all the ports of a process. Default: false

-strings    true|false inspect all the strings of a process. Default: false

-output     directory to write the results. Default .\Audits
```

By default, the preceding command line places its resultant XML files in the .\Audit directory. In this case, the full path is D:\mandiant\Audits\WINTERMUTE\20090103134554.

Mandiant's Audit Viewer is a GUI tool that provides the analyst with a graphical interface into the XML files created by using Memoryze to parse memory dumps. To launch Audit Viewer, double-click the **AuditViewer.py** file in the directory where you unzipped the archive downloaded from the Mandiant site. As you've installed the wxPython modules, you will see the Audit Viewer GUI open, at which point you will need to configure the tool by changing the **Memoryze Install Directory** (if necessary), selecting the **Running on image** checkbox, and providing the **Path to image file**, as Figure 3.11 illustrates.

**Figure 3.11** Audit Viewer User Interface Showing Configuration Changes

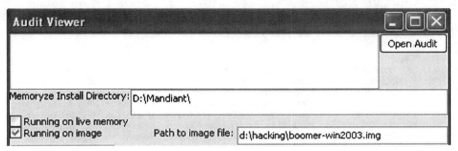

Once you've made the necessary changes, click the **Open Audit** button at the top of the Audit Viewer user interface, and navigate to the directory where the XML audit files were created. Once the directory has been selected, Audit Viewer will parse the available files and populate the Processes tree in the user interface, as shown in Figure 3.12.

**Figure 3.12** Audit Viewer User Interface Showing Processes Tree

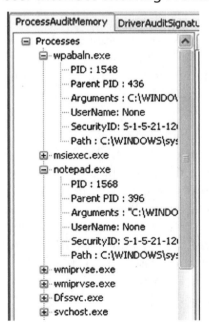

Figure 3.12 also illustrates two processes expanded to show the PID, PPID, arguments (or command line), as well as other information about each process. To dig deeper into each process, double-click the process name in the Processes tree, and then view the contents of the various tabs (Files, Directories, etc.) visible in the Audit Viewer user interface, as Figure 3.13 illustrates.

**Figure 3.13** Audit Viewer User Interface Showing Process Detail Tabs

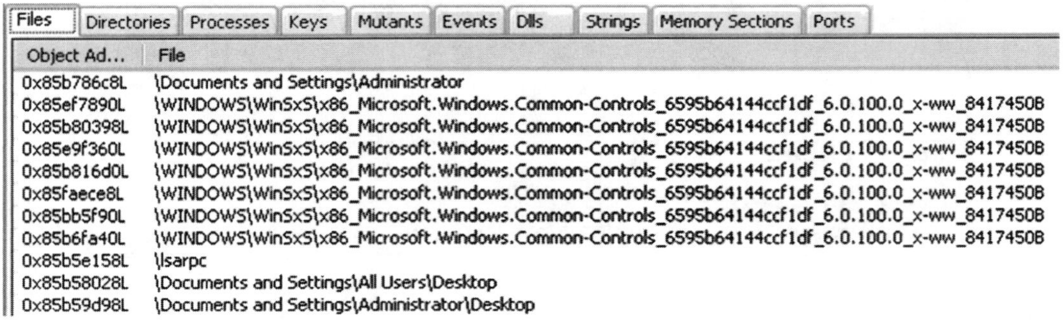

| Files | Directories | Processes | Keys | Mutants | Events | Dlls | Strings | Memory Sections | Ports |
|---|---|---|---|---|---|---|---|---|---|

| Object Ad... | File |
|---|---|
| 0x85b786c8L | \Documents and Settings\Administrator |
| 0x85ef7890L | \WINDOWS\WinSxS\x86_Microsoft.Windows.Common-Controls_6595b64144ccf1df_6.0.100.0_x-ww_8417450B |
| 0x85b80398L | \WINDOWS\WinSxS\x86_Microsoft.Windows.Common-Controls_6595b64144ccf1df_6.0.100.0_x-ww_8417450B |
| 0x85e9f360L | \WINDOWS\WinSxS\x86_Microsoft.Windows.Common-Controls_6595b64144ccf1df_6.0.100.0_x-ww_8417450B |
| 0x85b816d0L | \WINDOWS\WinSxS\x86_Microsoft.Windows.Common-Controls_6595b64144ccf1df_6.0.100.0_x-ww_8417450B |
| 0x85faece8L | \WINDOWS\WinSxS\x86_Microsoft.Windows.Common-Controls_6595b64144ccf1df_6.0.100.0_x-ww_8417450B |
| 0x85bb5f90L | \WINDOWS\WinSxS\x86_Microsoft.Windows.Common-Controls_6595b64144ccf1df_6.0.100.0_x-ww_8417450B |
| 0x85b6fa40L | \WINDOWS\WinSxS\x86_Microsoft.Windows.Common-Controls_6595b64144ccf1df_6.0.100.0_x-ww_8417450B |
| 0x85b5e158L | \lsarpc |
| 0x85b58028L | \Documents and Settings\All Users\Desktop |
| 0x85b59d98L | \Documents and Settings\Administrator\Desktop |

Memoryze and Audit Viewer provide a number of additional options to the analyst. For example, based on your findings in Audit Viewer, you may decide that you'd like to acquire an image of a process executable from the image file. To do so, use the processdd.bat batch file as follows:

```
D:\mandiant\processdd.bat -pid PID -input d:\hacking\boomer-win2003.img
```

You can also use other batch files provided with Memoryze to perform rootkit and hook detection, as well as search for drivers (www.mandiant.com/software/usememoryze.htm). The Mandiant M-union blog (http://blog.mandiant.com/) provides additional examples of how to use Memoryze and Audit Viewer, such as how to integrate the two tools into Guidance Software's EnCase forensic analysis application.

# HBGary Responder

HBGary's Responder product is a commercial GUI memory dump analysis tool that is described on the company Web site (www.hbgary.com) as a "live memory and runtime analysis software suite used to detect, diagnose, and respond to today's advanced computer threats". As with other analysis tools, the Responder products (Professional and Field editions) allow a responder to parse and analyze a memory dump without having to utilize the potentially compromised or infected system's API. Although Responder was written with malware analysis in mind, it is also a fast and capable tool that provides a great deal of functionality with respect to incident response, and is very easy for responders to use to get the information they need quickly.

**NOTE**

An evaluation copy of Responder Professional Edition 1.3.0.377 was used in the examples listed in this section of the chapter. However, the functionality presented and observed in this section is inherent to both the Professional and Field Edition products. We will not conduct a comprehensive review of the Responder Professional product (the Professional product includes binary disassembly, control flow graphing, and reverse engineering capabilities), as doing so is beyond the scope of this book and we are focusing on aspects of the product that most directly pertain to the memory dump analysis pursuant to incident response activities.

All you need to do to begin analyzing a memory dump with Responder Pro is to create a case and then import a physical memory snapshot by selecting **File** from the menu bar, then **Import**, and then **Import a Physical Memory Snapshot**. For this example, we'll use the first Windows 2000 memory dump from the DFRWS 2005 Memory Challenge; however, like Memoryze, Responder works with memory dumps from Windows 2000, all the way up through the latest versions of Windows.

When importing a memory dump "snapshot" file into a Responder case, an option is available to "extract and analyze all suspicious binaries". The rules that the Responder product uses to determine what constitutes "suspicious" are in a text-based file that you can open and review, and to which you can even add or remove comments, reducing false positives; you also can add entries to the file based on experience, thereby increasing the product's effectiveness.

Once the memory dump file has been imported and parsed, Responder will show in the left-hand pane the memory dump file with two folders, Hardware and Operating System, as Figure 3.14 illustrates.

**Figure 3.14** Memory Dump File Imported into a Responder Project

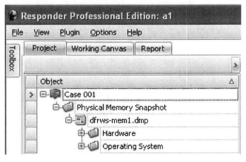

Expanding the folder beneath the Hardware folder will display the Interrupt Table. Expanding the Operating System folder will display a great deal of additional information, including Processes and All Open Network Sockets (in part, what responders may be most interested in), as shown in Figure 3.15.

**Figure 3.15** Expanded Operating System Folder in Responder User Interface

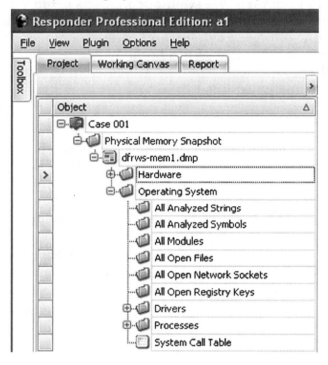

You can then expand the Processes folder to see all of the active processes extracted from the memory dump, or double-click the Processes folder to have the processes and detailed information about each process visible in the right-hand pane of the Responder user interface, as shown in Figure 3.16.

**Figure 3.16** Excerpt of Processes Listed with Details in Responder User Interface

| nc.exe | 592 | 1096 | "c:\winnt\system32\nc.exe" -L -p 3000 -t -e cmd.exe |
| cmd2k.exe | 324 | 1112 | "E:\Shells\cmd2k.exe" /D /T:80 /F:ON /K cmdenv.bat |
| cmd2k.exe | 324 | 1132 | "E:\Shells\cmd2k.exe" /D /T:80 /F:ON /K cmdenv.bat |
| smss.exe | 8 | 156 | \SystemRoot\System32\smss.exe |
| winlogon.exe | 156 | 176 | winlogon.exe |
| csrss.exe | 156 | 180 | C:\WINNT\system32\csrss.exe ObjectDirectory=\Windows SharedSection=1024,3072,51... |
| services.exe | 176 | 228 | C:\WINNT\system32\services.exe |
| lsass.exe | 176 | 240 | |
| dd.exe | 1112 | 284 | ..\Acquisition\FAU\dd.exe if=\\.\PhysicalMemory of=F:\intrusion2005\physicalmemory.dd ... |
| helix.exe | 820 | 324 | E:\helix.exe |

The Responder user interface provides a good deal of information that is immediately useful to you. You can also adjust the columns by selecting them and dragging them to a new location within the same view pane. Also, you can export information (this functionality is not supported in the evaluation version) from the view pane to various formats by clicking the appropriate icon at the top of the view pane, as Figure 3.17 illustrates.

**Figure 3.17** Selecting to Export Data in Responder User Interface

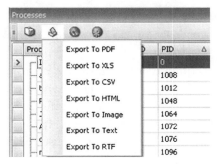

Double-clicking the **All Open Network Sockets** folder will open the Network tab in the right-hand view pane, similar to the output of netstat.exe, as shown in Figure 3.18.

**Figure 3.18** Open Network Sockets from
Memory Dump in Responder User Interface

| Source | | Destination | Type | | Process | |
|---|---|---|---|---|---|---|
| 0.0.0.0:1033 | | 192.168.0.5:4321 | TCP | | lsass.exe (240) | |
| 0.0.0.0:1055 | | 192.168.0.5:4321 | TCP | | lsass.exe (240) | |
| 0.0.0.0:1025 | | 0.0.0.0:0 | TCP | | MSTask.exe (552) | |
| 0.0.0.0:3000 | | 0.0.0.0:0 | TCP | | nc.exe (1096) | |
| 0.0.0.0:1026 | | 0.0.0.0:0 | UDP | | services.exe (228) | |
| 0.0.0.0:135 | | 0.0.0.0:0 | UDP | | svchost.exe (408) | |
| 0.0.0.0:135 | | 0.0.0.0:0 | TCP | | svchost.exe (408) | |
| 0.0.0.0:641 | | 0.0.0.0:0 | TCP | | tgcmd.exe (1012) | |
| 0.0.0.0:653 | | 0.0.0.0:0 | TCP | | tgcmd.exe (1012) | |
| 0.0.0.0:44444 | | 0.0.0.0:0 | TCP | | UMGR32.EXE (668) | |

You can also view the open file handles for all processes by double-clicking the **All Open Files** folder, as Figure 3.19 illustrates.

**Figure 3.19** Partial Listing of Open Files from Responder User Interface

| audit.log | \intrusion2005\audit.log | dd.exe (284) |
| physicalmemory.dd | \intrusion2005\physicalmemory.dd | dd.exe (284) |
| shells | \shells | dd.exe (284) |
| hxdef-rk100sb4d1ba5d | \hxdef-rk100sb4d1ba5d | dfrws2005.exe (592) |
| hxdef-rk100sb4d1ba5d | \hxdef-rk100sb4d1ba5d | dfrws2005.exe (592) |
| ntcontrolpipe9 | \net\ntcontrolpipe9 | dfrws2005.exe (592) |
| svcctl | \svcctl | dfrws2005.exe (592) |

You can view open file handles for a specific process by expanding the tree for each process and selecting **Open Files**. You can do the same for open network sockets and open Registry keys.

In addition to being able to quickly view all of this information, both on a memory dump-wide format as well as on a per-process format, you can parse executable images (.exe and .dll files) for strings, as well as search for specific items within the memory dump using substrings, regular expressions, or exact matches. Having the ability to sort items visible in columns also allows you to identify suspicious processes or modules (i.e., DLLs) much more quickly.

# Parsing Process Memory

We discussed the need for context for evidence earlier in this chapter, and you can achieve this, in part, by extracting the memory used by a process. In the past, investigators have used tools such as strings.exe or *grep* searches to parse through the contents of a RAM dump and look for interesting strings (passwords), IP or e-mail addresses, URLs, and the like. However, when you're parsing through a file that is about half a megabyte in size, there isn't a great deal of context to the information you find. Sometimes an investigator will open the dump file in a hex editor and locate the interesting string, and if she saw what appeared to be a username nearby, she might assume that the string is a password. However, investigating a RAM dump file in this manner does not allow the investigator to correlate that string to a particular process. Remember the example of Locard's Exchange Principle from Chapter 1? Had we collected the contents of physical memory during the example, we would have had no way to definitively say that a particular IP address or other data, such as a directory listing, was tied to a specific event or process. However, if we use the information provided in the process structure within memory and locate all the pages the process used that were still in memory when the contents were dumped, we could then run our searches and determine which process was using that information.

The tool lspm.pl allows you to do this automatically when working with Windows 2000 memory dumps. Lspm.pl takes the same arguments as lspd.pl (the name and path of the dump file, and the physical offset within the file of the process structure) and extracts the available pages from the dump file, writing them to a file within the current working directory. To run lspm.pl against the dd.exe process, use the following command line:

```
c:\perl\memory>lspm.pl d:\dumps\dfrws1-mem.dmp 0x0414dd60
```

The output looks like this:

```
Name : dd.exe -> 0x01d9e000
There are 372 pages (1523712 bytes) to process.
Dumping process memory to dd.dmp…
Done.
```

Now you have a file called dd.dmp that is 1,523,712 bytes in size and contains all the memory pages (372 in total) for that process that were still available when the dump file was created. You can run strings.exe or use BinText (illustrated in Figure 3.20) from Foundstone. com to parse through the file looking for Unicode and ASCII strings, or run *grep* searches for IP or e-mail addresses and credit card or Social Security numbers.

**Figure 3.20** Contents of Process Memory in BinText

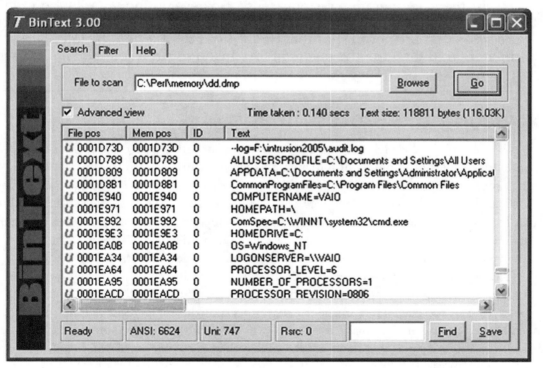

In Figure 3.20, you can see some of the Unicode strings contained in the memory used by the dd.exe process, including the name of the system and the name of the *LogonServer* for the session. All of this information can help further your understanding of the case; an important aspect of this capability is that now you can correlate what you find to a specific process.

Volatility incorporates this same functionality in the *memdmp* command. As mentioned previously in the chapter, you can use the *volatility memdmp* command to dump the addressable memory for a process from a Windows XP memory dump, as follows:

```
D:\Volatility>python volatility memdmp -f d:\hacking\xp-laptop1.img -p 4012
```

**TIP**

You can use Volatility to collect process memory for processes that are hidden by rootkits, even those hidden using direct kernel object manipulation (DKOM) techniques (see Chapter 7). Specifically, DKOM techniques "unlink" the EProcess block for the hidden process from the doubly linked active process list that the operating system "sees." However, using Volatility to examine a Windows XP raw memory dump or hibernation file, you can search for processes that are not part of that doubly linked list (discussed later in the chapter), and then use the *memdmp* command to retrieve the memory used by the process from the memory dump file.

# Extracting the Process Image

As you saw earlier in this chapter, when a process is launched the executable file is read into memory. One of the pieces of information that you can get from the process details (via lspd.pl) is the offset within a Windows 2000 memory dump file to the Image Base Address. As you saw, lspd.pl will do a quick check to see whether an executable image can be found at that location. One of the things you can do to develop this information further is to parse the PE file header (the contents of which we will cover in detail in Chapter 6) and see whether you can extract the entire contents of the executable image from the Windows 2000 memory dump file. Lspi.pl lets you do this automatically.

Lspi.pl is a Perl script that takes the same arguments as lspd.pl and lspm.pl and locates the beginning of the executable image for that process. If the Image Base Address offset does indeed lead to an executable image file, lspi.pl will parse the values contained in the PE header to locate the pages that make up the rest of the executable image file.

Okay, so you can run lspi.pl against the dd.exe process (with the PID of 284) using the following command line:

```
c:\perl\memory>lspi.pl d:\dumps\dfrws1-mem.dmp 0x0414dd60
```

The output of the command appears as follows:

```
Process Name        : dd.exe
PID                 : 284
DTB                 : 0x01d9e000
PEB                 : 0x7ffdf000 (0x02c2d000)
ImgBaseAddr         : 0x00400000 (0x00fee000)
e_lfanew = 0xe8
NT Header = 0x4550
Reading the Image File Header
Sections = 4
Opt Header Size = 0x000000e0 (224 bytes)
Characteristics:
      IMAGE_FILE_EXECUTABLE_IMAGE
      IMAGE_FILE_LOCAL_SYMS_STRIPPED
      IMAGE_FILE_RELOCS_STRIPPED
      IMAGE_FILE_LINE_NUMS_STRIPPED
      IMAGE_FILE_32BIT_MACHINE
Machine = IMAGE_FILE_MACHINE_I860
Reading the Image Optional Header
Opt Header Magic = 0x10b
Subsystem           : IMAGE_SUBSYSTEM_WINDOWS_CUI
Entry Pt Addr       : 0x00006bda
Image Base          : 0x00400000
File Align          : 0x00001000
Reading the Image Data Directory information
Data Directory      RVA            Size
--------------      ----------     ----------
ResourceTable       0x0000d000     0x00000430
DebugTable          0x00000000     0x00000000
BaseRelocTable      0x00000000     0x00000000
DelayImportDesc     0x0000af7c     0x000000a0
TLSTable            0x00000000     0x00000000
GlobalPtrReg        0x00000000     0x00000000
ArchSpecific        0x00000000     0x00000000
CLIHeader           0x00000000     0x00000000
LoadConfigTable     0x00000000     0x00000000
ExceptionTable      0x00000000     0x00000000
ImportTable         0x0000b25c     0x000000a0
unused              0x00000000     0x00000000
```

```
BoundImportTable       0x00000000       0x00000000
ExportTable            0x00000000       0x00000000
CertificateTable       0x00000000       0x00000000
IAT                    0x00007000       0x00000210
Reading Image Section Header Information
Name        Virt Sz         Virt Addr       rData Ofs       rData Sz        Char
----        -------         ---------       ---------       --------        ----
.text       0x00005ee0      0x00001000      0x00001000      0x00006000      0x60000020
.data       0x000002fc      0x0000c000      0x0000c000      0x00001000      0xc0000040
.rsrc       0x00000430      0x0000d000      0x0000d000      0x00001000      0x40000040
.rdata      0x00004cfa      0x00007000      0x00007000      0x00005000      0x40000040
Reassembling image file into dd.exe.img
Bytes written = 57344
New file size = 57344
```

As you can see, the output of lspi.pl is pretty verbose, and much of the information displayed might not be readily useful to (or understood by) an investigator unless that investigator is interested in malware analysis. Again, we will discuss this information in detail in Chapter 6. For now, the important elements are the table that follows the words "Reading Image Section Header Information" and the name of the file to which the executable image was reassembled. The section header information provides you with a road map for reassembling the executable image because it lets you know where to find the pages that make up that image file. Lspi.pl uses this road map and attempts to reassemble the executable image into a file. If it's successful, it writes the file out to the file based on the name of the process, with .img appended (to prevent accidental execution of the file). Lspi.pl will not reassemble the file if any of the memory pages have been marked as invalid and are no longer located in memory (e.g., they have been paged out to the swap file, pagefile.sys). Instead, lspi.pl will report that it could not reassemble the complete file because some pages (even just one) were not available in memory.

Now, the file you extract from the memory dump will not be exactly the same as the original executable file. This is because some of the file's sections are writeable, and those sections will change as the process is executing. As the process executes, various elements of the executable code (addresses, variables, etc.) will change according to the environment and the stage of execution. However, there are a couple of ways you can determine the nature of a file and get some information about its purpose. One of those ways is to see whether the file has any file version information compiled into it, as is done with most files created by legitimate software companies. As you saw from the section headers of the image file, there is a section named .rsrc, which is the name often used for a resource section of a PE file. This section can contain a variety of resources, such as dialogs and version strings, and is organized like a file system of sorts. Using BinText, you can look for the Unicode string *VS_VERSION_INFO* and see whether any identifying information is available in the executable image file. Figure 3.21 illustrates some of the strings found in the dd.exe.img file using BinText.

**Figure 3.21** Version Strings Found in dd.exe.img with BinText

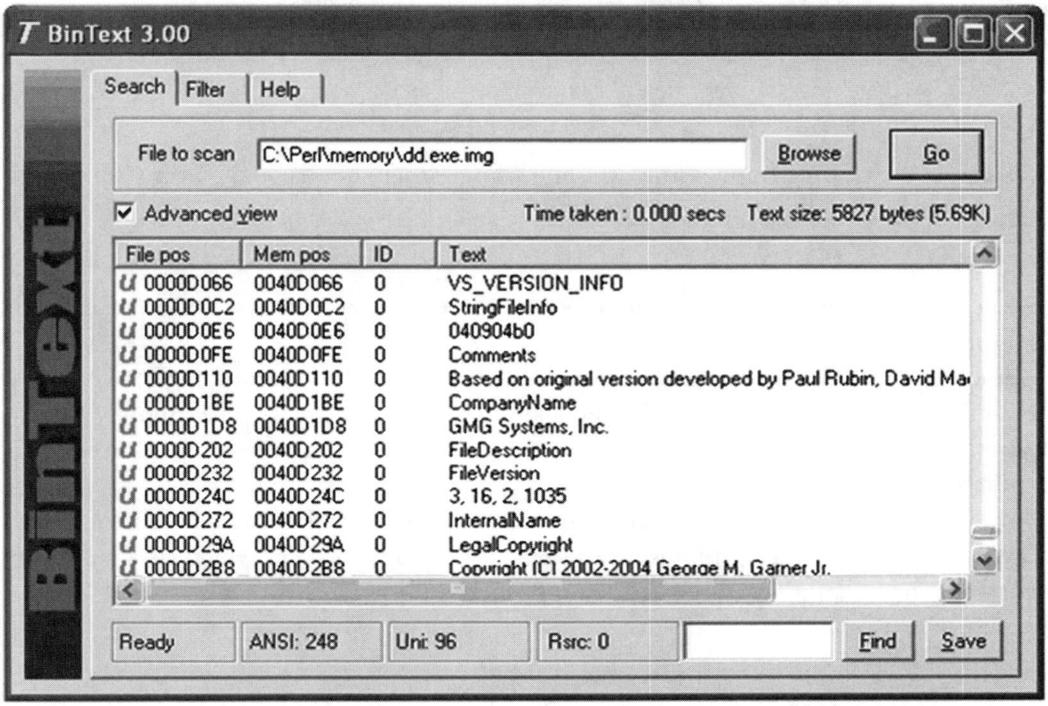

Another method of determining the nature of the file is to use file hashing. You're probably thinking, "Hey, wait a minute! You just said the file created by lspi.pl isn't exactly the same as the original file, so how can we use hashing?" Well, you're right … up to a point. We can't use MD5 hashes for comparison, because as we know, altering even a single bit—flipping a 1 to a 0—will cause an entirely different hash to be computed. So, what can we do?

In summer 2006, Jesse Kornblum released a tool called ssdeep (http://ssdeep.sourceforge. net) that implements something called *context-triggered piecewise hashing*, or *fuzzy hashing*. For a detailed understanding of what this entails, be sure to read Jesse's DFRWS 2006 paper (http://dfrws.org/2006/proceedings/12-Kornblum.pdf) on the subject. In a nutshell, Jesse implemented an algorithm that will tell you a weighted percentage of the identical sequences of bits the files have in common, based on their hashes, and computed by ssdeep. Because we know that in this case, George Garner's version of dd.exe was used to dump the contents of RAM from a Windows 2000 system for the DFRWS 2005 Memory Challenge, we can compare the dd.exe.img file to the original dd.exe file that we just happen to have available.

First, we start by using ssdeep.exe to compute a hash for our image file:

```
D:\tools>ssdeep c:\perl\memory\dd.exe.img > dd.sdp
```

We've now generated the hash and saved the information to the dd.sdp file. Using other switches available for ssdeep.exe, we can quickly compare the .img file to the original executable image:

```
D:\tools>ssdeep -v -m dd.sdp d:\tools\dd\old\dd.exe
d:\tools\dd\old\dd.exe matches c:\perl\memory\dd.exe.img (97)
```

We can also do this in one command line using either the −d or the −p switch:

```
D:\tools\> ssdeep -d c:\perl\memory\dd.exe.img d:\tools\dd\old\dd.exe
C:\perl\memory\dd.exe.img matches d:\tools\dd\old\dd.exe (97)
```

We see that the image file generated by lspi.pl has a 97 percent likelihood of matching the original dd.exe file.

Remember, for a hash comparison to work properly, we need something to which we can compare the files created by lspi.pl. Ssdeep.exe is a relatively new, albeit extremely powerful, tool, and it will likely be awhile before hash sets either are generated using ssdeep.exe or incorporate hashes calculated using ssdeep.exe.

We can use the Volatility Framework to attempt to extract the executable image from a Windows XP memory dump file using the *procdump* command. The *procdump* command syntax (from the Volatility readme.txt file) appears as follows:

```
procdump
--------

For each process in the given image, extract an executable sample.
If -t and -b are not specified, Volatility will attempt to infer
reasonable values.
Options:
  -f        <Image>     Image file to load
  -b        <base>      Hexadecimal physical offset of valid Directory Table Base
  -t        <type>      Image type (pae, nopae, auto)
  -o        <offset>    Hexadecimal physical offset of EPROCESS object
  -p        <pid>       Pid of process
  -m        <mode>      Strategy to use when extracting executable sample.
                        Use "disk" to save using disk-based section sizes or "mem"
                        for memory based sections (default": "mem").
```

Continuing with the Volatility example from earlier in this chapter, we can extract the executable image file for the dd.exe process (PID 4012 in the xp-laptop1.img memory dump file) using this command:

```
D:\Volatility>python volatility procdump -f d:\hacking\xp-laptop1.img -p 4012
****************************************************************************
Dumping dd.exe, pid: 4012 output: executable.4012.exe
D:\Volatility>dir exe*.exe
```

```
Volume in drive D is Data

Volume Serial Number is 8049-F885

Directory of D:\Volatility

01/01/2009 12:45 PM     57,344 executable.4012.exe

1 File(s)             57,344 bytes
```

Although not as verbose as the lspi.pl Perl script for Windows 2000 memory dumps, the *volatility procdump* command extracts the executable image file for the process. This can be extremely useful during malware analysis, as a good deal of the current malware is obfuscated (encrypted, compressed, or both) while on disk, making static analysis (see Chapter 6) difficult. Also, some malware may be memory-resident only, never actually being written to the hard drive; being able to extract an executable image file from a memory dump may be the only way to get a copy of the file for analysis.

**TIP**

Responders may often be confronted with systems that employ some sort of encryption of either a specific volume or the entire disk. I've acquired a number of these systems, and when I have to conduct that acquisition with the intention of performing analysis (as opposed to simply acquiring an image), I've opted to perform a live acquisition of the hard drive. In May 2007, Brian Kaplan wrote a thesis paper titled "RAM is Key: Extracting Disk Encryption Keys from Volatile Memory." Along with that paper, Brian also released a proof of concept tool for extracting Pretty Good Privacy (PGP) Whole Disk Encryption (WDE) keys from a memory dump. The paper and proof of concept tool are available from www.andrew.cmu.edu/user/bfkaplan/#KeyExtraction.

# Memory Dump Analysis and the Page File

So far, we've looked at parsing and analyzing the contents of a RAM dump in isolation—that is, without the benefit of any additional information. This means tools such as lspm.pl that rely solely on the contents of the RAM dump will provide an incomplete memory dump, because memory pages that have been swapped out to the page file (pagefile.sys on Windows systems) will not be incorporated in the resultant memory dump. To overcome this deficiency, in spring 2006 Nicholas Paul Maclean published his thesis work, "Acquisition and Analysis of Windows Memory" (at the time of this writing, I could not locate an active link to the thesis), which explains the inner workings of the Windows memory management system and provides an open source tool called vtop (written in Python) to reconstruct the virtual address space of a process.

In early 2007, Jesse Kornblum's "Buffalo" paper was published in the *Journal of Digital Investigation* (the full title of the paper is "Using Every Part of the Buffalo in Windows Memory Analysis"), and the publisher of the *Journal* allowed Jesse to post a copy of this paper on his Web site.

In this paper, Jesse demonstrates the nuances of page address translation and how the page file can be incorporated into the memory analysis process to establish a more complete (and accurate) view of the information that is available.

## Pool Allocations

When the Windows memory manager allocates memory, it generally does so in 4 KB (4096 bytes) pages. However, allocating an entire 4 KB page for, say, a sentence copied to the Clipboard would be a waste of memory. So, the memory manager allocates several pages ahead of time, keeping an available *pool* of memory. Andreas Schuster has done extensive research in this area, and even though Microsoft provides a list of pool headers used to designate commonly used pools, documentation for any meaningful analysis of these pools is simply not available. Many of the commonly used pool headers are listed in the pooltag.txt (www.microsoft.com/whdc/driver/tips/PoolMem.mspx) file provided with the Microsoft Debugging Tools, and Microsoft provides a Knowledge Base article that describes how to locate pool tags/headers used by third-party applications (http://support.microsoft.com/default.aspx?scid=kb;en-us;298102). Andreas used a similar method to determine the format of memory pools used to preserve information about network connections in Windows 2000 memory dumps (http://computer.forensikblog.de/en/2006/07/finding_network_socket_activity_in_pools.html); he searched for the pool header in the tcpip.sys driver on a Windows 2000 system and was able to determine the format of network connection information within the memory pool.

The downside to searching for memory pool allocations is that although the pool headers do not seem to change between versions of Windows, the format of the data resident within the memory pool changes, and there is no available documentation regarding the format of these memory pools.

# Summary

By now it should be clear that you have several options for collecting physical or process memory from a system during incident response. In Chapter 1, we examined a number of tools for collecting various portions of volatile memory during live response (processes, network connections, and the like), keeping in mind that there's always the potential for the Windows API (on which the tools rely) being compromised by an attacker. This is true in any case where live response is being performed, and therefore we might decide to use multiple disparate means of collecting volatile information. A rootkit can hide the existence of a process from most tools that enumerate the list of active processes (tlist.exe, pslist.exe), but dumping the contents of RAM will allow the investigator to list active and exited processes as well as processes hidden using kernel-mode rootkits (more about rootkits in Chapter 7).

# Solutions Fast Track

## Collecting Process Memory

☑ A responder may be presented with a situation in which it is not necessary to collect the entire contents of physical memory; rather, the contents of memory used by a single process would be sufficient.

☑ Collecting the memory contents of a single process is an option that is available only for processes that are seen in the active process list by both the operating system and the investigator's utilities. Processes hidden via some means (see Chapter 7) might not be visible, and the investigator will not be able to provide the process identifier to the tools he is using to collect the memory used by the process.

☑ Dumping process memory allows the investigator to collect not only the memory used by the process that can be found in RAM, but also the memory located in the page file.

☑ Once process memory has been collected, additional information about the process, such as open handles and loaded modules, can then be collected.

## Dumping Physical Memory

☑ Several methodologies are available for dumping the contents of physical memory. The responder should be aware of the available options as well as their pros and cons so that she can make an intelligent choice as to which methodology should be used.

☑ Dumping the contents of physical memory from a live system can present issues with consistency because the system is still live and processing information while the memory dump is being generated.

☑ When dumping the contents of physical memory, both the responder and the analyst must keep Locard's Exchange Principle in mind.

## Analyzing a Physical Memory Dump

☑ Depending on the means used to collect the contents of physical memory, various tools are available to extract useful information from the memory dump. The use of strings.exe, BinText, and *grep* with various regular expressions has been popular, and research conducted beginning in spring 2005 reveals how to extract specific processes.

☑ Dumps of physical memory contain useful information and objects such as processes, the contents of the Clipboard, and network connections.

☑ Continuing research in this area has demonstrated how the page file can be used in conjunction with a RAM dump to develop a more complete set of information.

# Frequently Asked Questions

**Q:** Why should I dump the contents of RAM from a live system? What use does this have, and what potentially useful or important information will be available to me?

**A:** As we discussed in Chapter 1, a significant amount of information available on a live system can be extremely important to an investigation. This volatile information exists in memory, or RAM, while the system is running. We can use various third-party tools (discussed in Chapter 1) to collect this information, but it might be important to collect the entire contents of memory so that we not only have a complete record of information available, but also can "see" things that might not be "visible" via traditional means (e.g., things hidden by a rootkit; see Chapter 7 for more information regarding rootkits). You might also find information regarding exited processes as well as process remnants left over after the system was rebooted.

**Q:** Once I've dumped the contents of RAM, what can I then do to analyze them?

**A:** Investigators have historically used standard file-based search tools to "analyze" RAM dumps. Strings.exe and *grep* searches have been used to locate passwords, e-mail addresses, URLs, and the like within RAM dumps. Tools now exist to parse RAM dumps for processes, process details (command lines, handles), threads, and other objects as well as extract executable images, which is extremely beneficial to malware analysis (see Chapter 6 for more information on this topic) as well as more traditional computer forensic examinations.

**Q:** I have an issue in which a person is missing. On examination of a computer system in his home, I found an active instant messaging (IM) application window open on the desktop. When I scrolled back through the window and reviewed the conversation, it became clear to me that useful information could be available from that process. What can I do?

**A:** If the issue you're faced with is primarily one that centers around a single visible process, dumping the entire contents of physical memory might not be necessary. One useful approach would be to dump the contents of process memory, then use other tools to extract specific information about the process, such as loaded modules, the command line used to launch the process, or open handles. Once all the information is collected, the next step could be to save the contents of the IM conversation. After all pertinent information has been collected, searching the contents of process memory for remnants of a previous conversation or other data might provide you with useful clues.

# Chapter 4

# Registry Analysis

## Solutions in this chapter:

- **Inside the Registry**
- **Registry Analysis**

☑ **Summary**

☑ **Solutions Fast Track**

☑ **Frequently Asked Questions**

# Introduction

To most administrators and forensic analysts, the Registry probably looks like the entrance to a dark, forbidding cave on the landscape of the Windows operating system. Others might see the Registry as a dark door at the end of a long hallway, with the words "Abandon hope, all ye who enter here" scrawled on it. The truth is that the Registry is a veritable gold mine of information for both the administrator and the forensic investigator. In many cases, software used by attackers will create a footprint within the Registry, leaving the investigator clues about the incident. Knowing where to look within the Registry, and how to interpret what you find, will go a long way toward giving you valuable insight into activity that occurred on the system.

The purpose of this chapter is to provide you with a deeper understanding of the Registry and the wealth of information it holds. Besides configuration information, the Windows Registry holds information regarding recently accessed files and considerable information about user activities. All of this can be extremely valuable, depending on the nature of the case you're working on and the questions you need to answer. Most of the Registry analysis that I'll address in this chapter will be postmortem—in other words, after you've acquired an image of the system. However, in some instances I will describe analysis from a live system as well as provide examples of what the keys and values look like on a live system. There are a few minor considerations to keep in mind when you're performing live versus postmortem analysis; I will point those out when I discuss the subject.

Throughout this chapter, we will discuss various Registry keys and values that can be of interest during an investigation. However, you should not consider this chapter to be a comprehensive listing of all possible Registry values that might be of interest. Although Registry keys associated directly with the operating system could be fairly stagnant once the system has been installed, they can change as Service Packs and patches are installed, as well as across versions of the Windows operating system itself. Also, a great many applications are available, all with their own unique Registry entries, and they can also change between application versions. Think of this chapter as a guide and a reference listing, but also keep in mind that it is by no means complete. My goal in this chapter is to describe the format of Registry files, how the Registry can be examined, and some important keys within the Registry and how to analyze them. By the time you reach the end of this chapter, you should understand what the Registry holds and be adept at retrieving and analyzing information from within the Registry.

# Inside the Registry

So, what *is* the Registry? If you remember back to DOS and early versions of Windows (3.1, 3.11, etc.), configuration information (drivers, settings) for the system was largely managed by several files—specifically, autoexec.bat, config.sys, win.ini (on Windows), and system.ini. Various settings within these files determined what programs were loaded and how the system looked and responded to user input.

Later versions of Windows replaced these files with the Registry, a central hierarchical database (http://support.microsoft.com/kb/256986) that maintains configuration settings for applications, hardware devices, and users. This "database" (I'm using the term loosely) replaces the text-based configuration files used by the previous versions of Microsoft operating systems.

For the most part, administrators directly interact with the Registry through some inter-mediary application, the most common of which are the graphical user interface (GUI) Registry editors that ship with Windows—regedit.exe or regedt32.exe. In many cases, the extent of a user's or Administrator's interaction with the Registry is through an installation program (software applications, patches), which does not permit the user to directly interact with specific keys and values within the Registry. Windows XP and 2003 distributions include reg.exe, a command-line interface (CLI) tool that can be used from the command prompt or in scripts. For more information on the GUI Registry editing utilities, see the "RegEdit and RegEdt32" sidebar.

---

## Tools & Traps...

### RegEdit and RegEdt32

Interestingly, the two Registry editing utilities provided with Windows operating systems are not equivalent on all versions of Windows (http://support.microsoft.com/kb/141377).

For example, on Windows NT and 2000, you would use regedit.exe primarily for its search capabilities but not to modify access control lists (ACLs) on Registry keys. Regedit.exe has an added limitation of not "understanding" the *REG_EXPAND_SZ* (a variable-length string) or *REG_MULTI_SZ* (a multiple-string) data type. If values with either of these data types are edited, the data is saved as a *REG_SZ* (a fixed-length string) data type and the functionality of the key is lost. Regedt32.exe, on the other hand, does not allow you to import or export hive (.reg) files.

On Windows XP and 2003, regedit.exe allows you to do all of these things, and regedt32.exe is nothing more than a small program that runs regedit.exe.

---

When the administrator opens regedit.exe, he sees a treelike structure with five root folders, or "hives," in the navigation area of the GUI, as Figure 4.1 illustrates. This folderlike structure allows the administrator to navigate easily through the Registry, much like a file system.

**Figure 4.1** Regedit.exe View Showing Five Root Hives

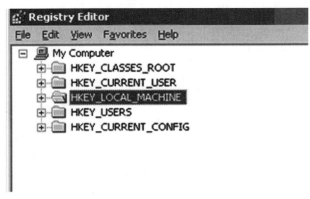

Each of these hives plays an important role in the function of the system. The HKEY_
USERS hive contains all the actively loaded user profiles for that system. HKEY_CURRENT_
USER is the active, loaded user profile for the currently logged-on user. The HKEY_LOCAL_
MACHINE hive contains a vast array of configuration information for the system, including
hardware settings and software settings. The HKEY_CURRENT_CONFIG hive contains
the hardware profile the system uses at startup. Finally, the HKEY_CLASSES_ROOT hive
contains configuration information relating to which application is used to open various files
on the system. This hive is subclassed to both HKEY_CURRENT_USER\Software\Classes
(user-specific settings) and HKEY_LOCAL_MACHINE\Software\Classes (systemwide settings).

All of this is good and fine, but it helps to know where the hives come from and where
they exist on the hard drive within the file system. The contents of much of the Registry
visible in the Registry Editor are available in several files, as listed in Table 4.1.

**Table 4.1** Registry Paths and Corresponding Files

| Registry Path | File Path |
| --- | --- |
| HKEY_LOCAL_MACHINE\System | %WINDIR%\system32\config\System |
| HKEY_LOCAL_MACHINE\SAM | %WINDIR%\system32\config\Sam |
| HKEY_LOCAL_MACHINE\Security | %WINDIR%\system32\config\Security |
| HKEY_LOCAL_MACHINE\Software | %WINDIR%\system32\config\Software |
| HKEY_LOCAL_MACHINE\Hardware | Volatile hive |
| HKEY_LOCAL_MACHINE\System\Clone | Volatile hive |
| HKEY_USERS\*User SID* | User profile (NTUSER.DAT); "Documents and Settings\*User* (changed to "Users\*User*" on Vista) |
| HKEY_USERS\Default | %WINDIR%\system32\config\default |

**TIP**

Vista and Windows 7 include additional Registry hive files, specifically the Components hive file (found in the system32\config directory) and the usrclass.dat file, which is located in the C:\Users\username\AppData\Local\ Microsoft\Windows directory. We will discuss these hives, particularly the usrclass.dat hive, later in this chapter.

You'll notice that several of the Registry paths are volatile and do not exist in files on the hard drive. These hives are created during system startup and are not available when the system shuts down. This is important to remember when you're performing postmortem forensic analysis as well as live response on a running system. If data in volatile hives is important to troubleshooting a system or conducting incident response activities, you should consider either exporting the entire volatile hive to a .reg file via regedit.exe, or employing some other mechanism to collect specific data from the volatile hive before shutting the system down.

In addition to the different sections or hives, the Registry supports several different data types for the various values that it contains. Table 4.2 lists the various data types and their descriptions.

**Table 4.2** Registry Data Types and Descriptions

| Data Type | Description |
|---|---|
| REG_BINARY | Raw binary data |
| REG_DWORD | Data represented as a 32-bit (4-byte) integer |
| REG_SZ | A fixed-length text string |
| REG_EXPAND_SZ | A variable-length data string |
| REG_MULTI_SZ | Multiple strings, separated by a space, comma, or other delimiter |
| REG_NONE | No data type |
| REG_QWORD | Data represented by a 64-bit (8-byte) integer |
| REG_LINK | A Unicode string naming a symbolic link |
| REG_RESOURCE_LIST | A series of nested arrays designed to store a resource list |
| REG_RESOURCE_ REQUIREMENTS_LIST | A series of nested arrays designed to store a device driver's list of possible hardware resources |
| REG_FULL_RESOURCE_ DESCRIPTOR | A series of nested arrays designed to store a resource list used by a physical hardware device |

As you can see, a variety of data types are found in the Registry. There don't seem to be any rules or consistency between values found in different keys; values that serve similar purposes may have different data types, allowing their data to be formatted and stored differently. This can become an issue when you're performing text searches for data within the Registry. Where one application might store a list of recently accessed documents as ASCII text strings, another might store a similar list as Unicode strings in a binary data type, in which case an ASCII text search would miss that data. In fact, a Microsoft Knowledge Base article (http://support.microsoft.com/kb/161678) specifically states that you can use the Find tool in RegEdit only to find ASCII string data and not *DWORD* or binary data.

# Registry Structure within a Hive File

Now that you've seen where the Registry hive files are located, let's take a look inside those files and see the structure of the Registry itself, at a much lower level. You're probably wondering at this point why we would want to do this. Well, by understanding the basic components of the Registry, we might be able to glean some extra information through keyword searches of other locations and sources, such as the page file, physical memory, or even unallocated space. If we know what to look for or what we're looking at, we might be able to extract an extra bit of information. Also, by knowing more about the information that is available within the Registry, we will have a better understanding of what is possible and what to look for.

Mark Russinovich wrote an excellent article for *Windows NT Magazine* called "Inside the Registry" (http://technet.microsoft.com/en-us/library/cc750583.aspx), which describes the different components, or cells, of the Registry. This same information is covered in *Windows Internals*, which Mark co-wrote with David Solomon.

Each type of cell has a specific structure and contains specific types of information. The various types of cells are:

- **Key cell** This cell contains Registry key information and includes offsets to other cells as well as the *LastWrite* time for the key (signature: *kn*).

- **Value cell** This cell holds a value and its data (signature: *kv*).

- **Subkey list cell** This is a cell made up of a series of indexes (or offsets) pointing to key cells; these are all subkeys to the parent key cell.

- **Value list cell** This is a cell made up of a series of indexes (or offsets) pointing to value cells; these are all of the values of a common key cell.

- **Security descriptor cell** This is a cell that contains security descriptor information for a key cell (signature: *ks*).

Figure 4.2 illustrates the various types of cells (with the exception of the security descriptor cell) as they appear in the Registry Editor.

**Figure 4.2** Excerpt of Windows Registry Showing Keys, Values, and Data

Figure 4.3 illustrates an excerpt of a Registry file opened in a hex editor. The figure shows the signatures for a key cell as well as for a value cell. Note that due to endian issues, the signature for a key cell (i.e., *kn*) appears as *nk* and for a value cell (i.e., *kv*) appears as *vk*.

**Figure 4.3** Excerpt of a Raw Registry
File Showing Key and Value Cell Signatures

```
                    M.Q...".ÿÿ nk   ◄─── Key cell
                    Ú.¿¹»„Ä.......ᴮᴵ..
                    ........ÿÿÿÿÿÿÿÿ
                    ....Àç......ÿÿÿÿ
                    .......&.......
                    h³..&...{DE5DBCD
                    C-104A-4cbc-A4D5
Value cell      ▶  QC2104A142C5}".
                    èÿÿ vk  .....hç..
                    ......8ʷØÿÿÿA.c.
                    c.S.t.o.r.e. .C.
```

As mentioned earlier, these signatures can provide us with extremely valuable information during an investigation. Using these signatures, we can potentially carve Registry key and value information out of the unallocated clusters of an acquired image or even out of RAM dumps. (See Chapter 3 for more information on RAM dumps.)

**TIP**

Understanding the binary structure of Registry keys and values can be extremely useful during an investigation. Most investigations that involve some degree of Registry analysis will focus on the Registry files themselves, using tools presented in this chapter. However, in examining unallocated space or the contents of a RAM dump, you could locate the signatures such as those illustrated in Figure 4.3. Knowing the format of the Registry key and value structures allows you to, if necessary, extract and parse the data into something understandable. You might find a Registry key in memory, for example, and be able to extract the *LastWrite* time. Understanding the structure of Registry keys and values provides context to information retrieved from a memory dump or from unallocated space within an acquired image, as well as allows you to parse deleted keys from within the "unallocated" space within hive files themselves. We will address the topic of locating Registry keys within the unallocated space of hive files later in this chapter.

The best reference for the actual programmatic binary structure of the various cells within Registry hive files isn't available from the vendor; oddly enough, it's available from a guy who wrote a Linux utility. Peter Nordahl–Hagen created the Offline Registry and Password Editor (http://home.eunet.no/pnordahl/ntpasswd/), a utility that allows you to boot a Windows system (assuming you have physical access to the system) to a Linux disk and edit the Registry to include changing passwords. Peter provides the source for his utility, and if you choose to download it, you'll be most interested in the file named ntreg.h. This is a C header file that defines the structures for the different types of cells that make up the Registry.

**TIP**

Tim Morgan wrote an excellent paper describing the structure of the Windows Registry, describing the various cell types and how they are interconnected. Tim makes the paper available at the Sentinelchicken.com Web site (www.sentinelchicken.com/data/TheWindowsNTRegistryFileFormat.pdf).

From Peter's source code, we can see that the key cell is 76 bytes long, plus a variable-length name. Therefore, if we locate the signature for a key cell (as illustrated in Figure 4.3) in a RAM dump or in unallocated clusters, we might very well have the contents of a key cell. From there, we can parse the next 74 bytes (the signature is two bytes long—in little endian hex format, 0x6B6E) and see such things as the name of the key and its *LastWrite* time.

For example, say you have some unallocated clusters or a RAM dump from a system and you've located a key cell. Given a variable called $*offset* that is the offset within the file to the key cell you've located, Perl code to parse that key cell and extract data from it looks like this:

```perl
seek(FH,$offset,0);
read(FH,$data,76);
my %nk;
my (@recs)           = unpack("vvV17vv",$record);
$nk{id}              = $recs[0];
$nk{type}            = $recs[1];
$nk{time1}           = $recs[2];
$nk{time2}           = $recs[3];
$nk{time3}           = $recs[4];
$nk{no_subkeys}      = $recs[6];
$nk{ofs_lf}          = $recs[8];
$nk{no_values}       = $recs[10];
$nk{ofs_vallist}     = $recs[11];
$nk{ofs_sk}          = $recs[12];
$nk{ofs_classname}   = $recs[13];
$nk{len_name}        = $recs[19];
$nk{len_classname}   = $recs[20];
# Get the name
seek(FH,$offset + 76,0);
read(FH,$data,$nk{len_name});
```

In this code, *FH* is a Perl file handle to the file containing the data we're examining, and $*data* is a scalar variable meant to hold the contents of what we've just read from the file. This code provides a simple, straightforward method for parsing essential information from a key cell: the key cell identifier value (i.e., $*nk{id}*), as Figure 4.3 illustrated. Also within Figure 4.3, the hexadecimal representation of the key's *LastWrite* time is visible in the first half of the line immediately below the *nk* identifier. The preceding code reads in the binary data and parses it into the various components based on the data structure for a key cell.

We can see values that give us the *LastWrite* time as well as the numbers of subkeys and values associated with the key cell. We can also get offsets to additional data structures, such as lists of other key cells (i.e., the subkeys), as well as to the value list (i.e., values for this key).

> **TIP**
>
> The *$offset* value is important when working with Registry keys, particularly those within Registry hive files. The 4-byte (*DWORD*) value immediately preceding the key signature found at *$offset* is the size of the key. When read as an unsigned long value, in many instances this value will be a negative number. Researchers have found that a negative size value indicates that the key itself is in use; a positive size value indicates that the key has been deleted. We will discuss this at greater length later in the chapter.

The value cells are only 18 bytes long with a variable-length name and variable-length data. The data type is stored in a 4-byte (*DWORD*) value located within the value cell itself. Using the same technique as with the key cell, we can parse information about the value cell from whatever source we're looking at and see the actual values. Perl code to parse the value cell looks like this:

```perl
seek(FH,$offset,0);
my $bytes      = read(FH,$data,20);
my (@recs)     = unpack("vvVVVvv",$data);
$vk{id}        = $recs[0];
$vk{len_name}  = $recs[1];
$vk{len_data}  = $recs[2];
$vk{ofs_data}  = $recs[3];
$vk{val_type}  = $recs[4];
$vk{flag}      = $recs[5];
if ($vk{len_name} == 0) {
$vk{valname} = "Default";
}
else {
seek(FH,$offset + 20,0);
    read(FH,$data,$vk{len_name});
    $vk{valname} = $data;
}
```

As with the key cell, the value cell identifier (i.e., $vk\{id\}$) was illustrated in Figure 4.3.

Although we can parse Registry value data from various sources, there could be insufficient information to add context to what we discover, such as which Registry key the value originally belonged to, when it was created, or how it was used. Remember, Registry keys have a time stamp associated with them (i.e., the *LastWrite* time); Registry values do not. Extracting information about keys and values from RAM dumps or unallocated space might be of limited value, depending on the needs of the investigation.

Awhile ago, I wrote a Perl script that I call the Offline Registry Parser, or regp.pl, for short, based on the structures that Peter provided. It incorporates the Perl code you just saw. The script enables you to parse a raw Registry file, extracting the key and value cell information and printing the information to the console in ASCII format. The output can be redirected to a file for archiving, searching, or comparing with other files. There are several advantages to using this script, and code like it. First, it provides an open source example for how to parse through the raw Registry files; someone with an understanding of Perl programming can easily extend the capabilities of the script, such as recording the output in a spreadsheet or database for easier processing. Second, the script relies on only basic Perl functionality; it does not use any fancy platform–specific modules, nor does it rely on the Microsoft application program interface (API). This means you can run the script on any system that supports Perl, including Linux. If an investigator is using The Sleuth Kit (www.sleuthkit.org) or PyFlag (www.pyflag. net/cgi-bin/moin.cgi) on a Linux system as an analysis platform, she is not prevented from parsing, viewing, and analyzing the contents of the Registry files. Although this doesn't add any new functionality to any of the available forensic analysis tools, it does provide options for data reduction and faster, more efficient processing. Right about the time I was considering extending this script into something more functional and flexible, James MacFarlane released his Parse::Win32Registry Perl module, which provides object–oriented access to Registry hive files, including for Windows 98 and ME systems. As with regp.pl, James' module code is based in part on Peter's descriptions of the various components of the Registry.

**T**IP

Both PlainSight (www.plainsight.info/) and the SANS Investigative Forensic Toolkit (SIFT) Workstation (available from http://forensics.sans.org/community/downloads/) are Linux-based and include RegRipper (www.regripper.net), a Perl-based tool for parsing Registry hive file data during postmortem analysis. RegRipper is based on the Parse::Win32Registry module from James MacFarlane, and installs easily on Windows, Linux, and Mac OS X.

The reg.pl Perl script (as well as a stand–alone Windows executable "compiled" from the script using Perl2Exe) is available on the media that accompanies this book.

Another interesting file Peter provides in the source code for his utility is sam.h. This file provides some very valuable information regarding structures within the SAM portion of the Registry. We will discuss these structures and how you can use them later in this chapter, in the "Finding Users" section.

# The Registry As a Log File

The key cells within the Registry constitute the keys or folders you see when you open the Registry Editor. This is the only one of the structures that contains a time value, called the *LastWrite* time. The *LastWrite* time is a 64-bit *FILETIME* object, which is analogous to the last modification time on a file (see the "Registry Key LastWrite Time" sidebar for more information). Not only does this information provide a time frame reference for certain user activities on the system, but in several cases it will also tell you when a specific value was added to a key or was modified.

## Notes from the Underground…

### Registry Key LastWrite Time

Registry keys have several properties associated with them, one of which is the *LastWrite* time, which is similar to the last modification time associated with files and directories. The *LastWrite* time is stored as a *FILETIME* object (or structure) that represents the number of 100-nanosecond intervals since January 1, 1601 (based on the Gregorian calendar). To convert this 64-bit value into something legible, you must translate (http://msdn.microsoft.com/en-us/library/ms724280.aspx) it to a *SYSTEMTIME* structure. Translating the *FILETIME* structure directly to a *SYSTEMTIME* structure using the *FileTimeToSystemTime()* API will allow you to display the date in UTC format, which is loosely defined as Greenwich Mean Time (GMT). To translate these values into something that accurately represents the current system time, you must first pass the *FILETIME* structure through the *FileTimeToLocalFileTime()* API. This API takes into account daylight saving time and the time zone information of the local system. The *FILETIME* object can be read into Perl as two 32-bit numbers and then translated into a 32-bit UNIX time value (http://en.wikipedia.org/wiki/Unix_time), and displayed using built-in Perl functions.

One particular instance where I've found this to be useful is during postmortem intrusion investigations. I like to open the Registry Viewer in ProDiscover and locate the area where Registry keys specific to Windows services are maintained. From there, I will sort the first level of keys based on their *LastWrite* times, and invariably I've been able to easily locate services that were installed during the intrusion, such as remote access backdoors or even rootkits.

**TIP**

We'll discuss rootkits in greater detail in Chapter 7. However, the W32/Opanki. worm!MS06-040, as identified by Network Associates, serves as a useful example (http://vil.nai.com/vil/Content/v_140546.htm) for our discussion here. The worm installs a rootkit component, creating two Windows services (in addition to a number of other artifacts). Because most compromises occur sometime after the operating system is installed, sorting the Services keys based on their *LastWrite* times will often quickly reveal the issue. This is a useful technique for locating any of the myriad bits of malware that create Windows Services when they infect a system.

In addition to the *LastWrite* times, the Registry maintains time-stamp information in some of the data associated with specific values. We will discuss some of these values later in this chapter, but for now, it's enough to know that there are Registry keys whose values contain eight bytes of binary data that comprise a *FILETIME* object.

**WARNING**

The one thing that is consistent about the Windows Registry is its lack of consistency. I know you're probably reading this and thinking that maybe I've been up too late, or that I've had too much coffee. Well, if you've ever just spent time browsing through the Registry, you know what I mean. Some values in the Registry contain binary data, which, when parsed or translated, can be read as a 64-bit *FILETIME* object. Two examples of this are within some UserAssist key values and the *ShutdownTime* value. However, in other instances a time-stamp value is maintained as a 32-bit UNIX time.

So, why do I refer to the Registry as a log file? It's because log files generally have some sort of action or event associated with a time, and in many cases, this is true for the Registry. Although the Registry can hold literally thousands of entries, not all of them are of interest during an investigation. You will be interested in specific keys during different types of investigations, and if you understand how the system creates, modifies, and uses those keys and values, you will begin to see how the Registry actually records the occurrence of different events, along with an associated time stamp.

# Monitoring Changes to the Registry

There is really no single, consolidated resource of Registry keys that will be useful in any particular situation. A spreadsheet containing many of the keys that I and others find useful during various types of investigations is included in the ch4 directory on the accompanying media. However, this is not a be-all and end-all solution, because there simply isn't one. In some cases, Registry keys that are created during installation or are modified during use may change between versions of a particular application. Shortly after this book goes to print, is published, and is ready for purchase, you can be sure that a new application will be available that records configuration and setting information in the Registry.

So, how do you go about determining Registry keys and values that are important to you? One way is to snapshot the Registry, perform an atomic action (i.e., do just one thing), snapshot the Registry again, and compare the two snapshots for differences. One particular tool that is useful for this task is InControl5, referred to by *PC Magazine* (distributor of the application) as "Inctrl5".

**W**ARNING

Inctrl5 is available from www.pcmag.com/article2/0,4149,9882,00.asp; however, it is not a free download. The publisher charges a small fee to download the tool, and the license agreement specifically forbids redistributing the software.

InControl5 is a great utility for doing all kinds of analysis. I generally tend to run InControl5 in two-phase mode, where I open the application, have it snapshot my system, do whatever I'm going to do (install a peer-to-peer [P2P] file-sharing application or some bit of malware), and then open InControl5 again and have it complete the process. The HTML output is usually enough for my purposes, and I can clearly see the Registry keys (and files) that were added, modified, or deleted during the process.

Another way to discover useful or important keys is to use RegMon from Microsoft (RegMon is available from http://technet.microsoft.com/en-us/sysinternals/bb896652.aspx, but is also included as part of Microsoft's Process Explorer utility) to monitor the Registry in real time. When I was trying to determine where user information was kept within the Registry, I found that by running RegMon while executing the *net user* command I could determine which keys and values were accessed when retrieving user information, as Figure 4.4 illustrates.

**Figure 4.4** Excerpt of RegMon Output

```
lsass.exe:1052    QueryValue    HKLM\SAM\SAM\C
lsass.exe:1052    QueryValue    HKLM\SAM\SAM\Domains\Account\V
lsass.exe:1052    OpenKey       HKLM\SAM\SAM\DOMAINS\Account\Users\Names
lsass.exe:1052    Enumerate...  HKLM\SAM\SAM\DOMAINS\Account\Users\Names
lsass.exe:1052    OpenKey       HKLM\SAM\SAM\DOMAINS\Account\Users\Names\Administrator
lsass.exe:1052    QueryValue    HKLM\SAM\SAM\DOMAINS\Account\Users\Names\Administrator\(Default)
lsass.exe:1052    CloseKey      HKLM\SAM\SAM\DOMAINS\Account\Users\Names\Administrator
lsass.exe:1052    Enumerate...  HKLM\SAM\SAM\DOMAINS\Account\Users\Names
lsass.exe:1052    OpenKey       HKLM\SAM\SAM\DOMAINS\Account\Users\Names\Guest
lsass.exe:1052    QueryValue    HKLM\SAM\SAM\DOMAINS\Account\Users\Names\Guest\(Default)
lsass.exe:1052    CloseKey      HKLM\SAM\SAM\DOMAINS\Account\Users\Names\Guest
lsass.exe:1052    Enumerate...  HKLM\SAM\SAM\DOMAINS\Account\Users\Names
```

Figure 4.4 shows an excerpt of the RegMon output used to monitor the *net user* command. I started the capture, ran the command, and then halted the capture and searched all the output for *SAM*. That way, I was able to see that although I had used net.exe to request the information, net.exe passed off the request to lsass.exe, which accessed the Registry to obtain the information regarding usernames on the system.

Test Drive...

## Monitoring the Registry

Here's something you can try. Download a copy of RegMon to your system, open it, and then halt the capture (click the magnifying glass icon so that it has a red *X* over it). Then open a command prompt and type **net accounts**, but do not press Enter. Go back to RegMon and start the capture, and then go back to the command prompt and immediately press **Enter**. As soon as you see the account policies appear in the command prompt, go back to RegMon and stop the capture. To make things easier, filter on lsass.exe and see which Registry keys were accessed to provide the information you see in the command prompt. Now when you're performing a postmortem investigation you'll know which keys to look in for information pertaining to the account policies.

Throughout the rest of the chapter, you'll see several references to using InControl5 as well as RegMon. It would be a good idea to have copies of them on hand (due to the terms of the licenses for each tool, they cannot be distributed on the media accompanying this book), particularly if you want to follow along and try out some of the different techniques mentioned.

# Registry Analysis

Now that you know the structure of the Registry, let's take a look at retrieving and analyzing information from within the Registry. Much of this information will be available to you during live response (with the exception of the keys you cannot access due to permissions), and all of it (with the exception of the volatile portions of the Registry) will be available during a postmortem investigation.

ProDiscover provides a simple interface (actually, an API) for accessing the Registry during postmortem analysis. When a case is loaded into ProDiscover, all you need to do is right-click the **Windows** directory in the Content View and choose **Add to Registry Viewer**. ProDiscover then locates the necessary files to populate the Registry Viewer, as Figure 4.5 shows.

**Figure 4.5** Registry Viewer in ProDiscover IR

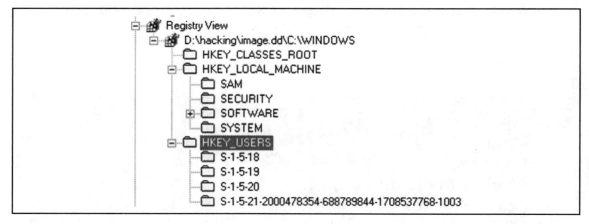

ProDiscover's scripting language, ProScript, is based on Perl and provides an excellent facility for extracting information from the Registry in an automated fashion. The ProScript. pm module facilitates an API for writing Perl scripts that interact almost completely with ProDiscover; just about anything you can do through the ProDiscover user interface you can also do with a ProScript. With respect to the Windows Registry and postmortem forensic analysis, you can use ProScripts to completely automate a great deal of tedious data collection and formatting. Throughout this chapter, I'll describe ProScripts for performing various tasks such as extracting and analyzing information from within the Registry during postmortem analysis. You can find each ProScript in the ch4\code\Proscripts directory on the media that accompanies this book.

# RegRipper

In the first edition of this book, I included a number of Perl scripts that could be used to extract specific data from Registry hive files (all of these scripts have been moved to the ch4\code\ old directory on the media that accompanies this book). As I continued to perform incident response and forensic analysis, I found that I kept looking for the same Registry keys, while at the same time adding additional keys to my quickly growing list of Registry artifacts. I began to see that I needed a means of recording a great deal of information; for example, it was one thing to extract a particular value from a Registry key, but including reference information (e.g., Microsoft Knowledge Base articles, etc.) provided a bit more depth to the information, particularly when adding that information to reports. I then thought that I could develop a framework that made it easy to add all of these facets when new Registry keys and values were found to be pertinent to an examination so that I could provide that framework to others for their own use. Also, the framework had to be powerful, but easy enough to use that someone could easily learn to update and extend it. Plugin-based tools such as Nessus (www.nessus.org) seemed to work well, so I wrote a GUI and began developing what I would come to call RegRipper. Figure 4.6 illustrates the GUI for RegRipper Version 2.02.

**Figure 4.6** RegRipper v.2.02 GUI

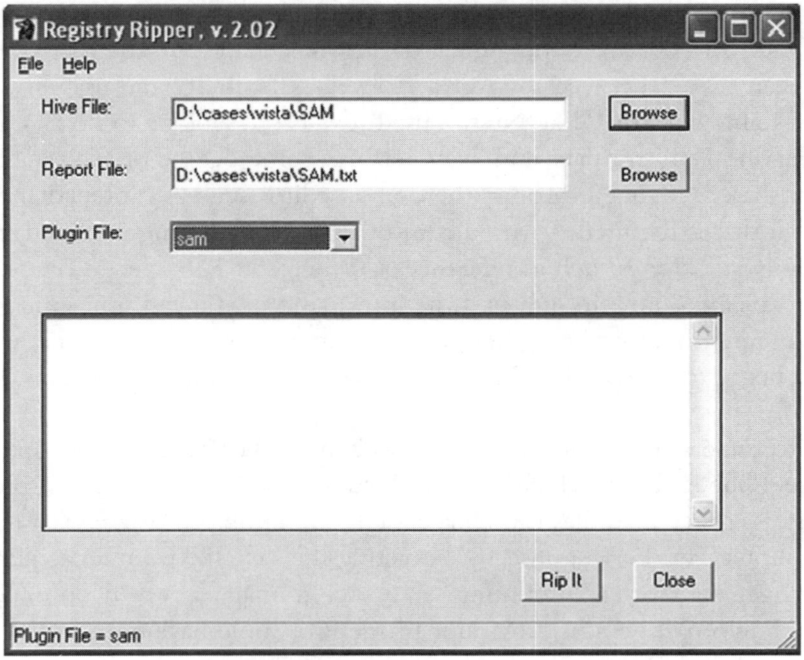

A complete, up-to-date copy of RegRipper v2.02 is available in the ch4\RegRipper directory on the media that accompanies this book.

RegRipper is written in Perl, so you can access the source code to see what it does. The GUI is based on the Win32::GUI module (which means the GUI will run only on Windows systems), and RegRipper uses James MacFarlane's Parse::Win32Registry module to do most of the "heavy lifting" with respect to accessing Registry hive files. However, I also provide RegRipper and the other tools associated with it as executables "compiled" with Perl2Exe (found at www.indigostar.com/perl2exe.htm; other tools such as PerlApp from ActiveState, or PAR, the Perl Archiver, can be used to achieve similar results) so that you can run them on your Windows system without having to install Perl.

To run on other platforms, such as Linux, RegRipper (rr.exe) would need to be run under Wine (www.winehq.org/), with minor modifications to the Perl code to address path separator issues. CLI versions of RegRipper tools can be run from Linux or Mac OS X. Future releases of these tools will include greater care and attention toward cross-platform compatibility.

The basic idea behind RegRipper is pretty simple. I began thinking that I didn't want to keep a list of all of the possible Registry keys I would want to examine under myriad different circumstances. I found myself keeping lists of keys and values, and references to how the keys were modified or why they were important under different circumstances, and I even had little notes about how to correlate the information from multiple Registry keys to build a more complete picture of activity. I began to write specific bits of code to do very specific tasks, and that code made up a great deal of this chapter in the first edition of this book. But I began to see the need for a greater level of flexibility and usability. My thought was to create a framework that, like Nessus, used text-based plugins to do all of the heavy lifting for extracting Registry data, and even perform some degree of analysis. Because the plugins are text-based, anyone can open them in an editor such as Notepad and read or modify them; all that is required is a modicum of Perl programming knowledge. I found that I could easily add things such as references to Microsoft Knowledge Base articles, short "analysis tips" explaining how to interpret the information extracted, and similar information. With enough different plugins being used as code samples, my hope was that eventually analysts would begin to extend the plugins, and even write their own plugins. That's exactly what happened.

You need to understand a couple of concepts behind RegRipper (these apply to other tools in the RegRipper family, which we will discuss shortly) to run the tool properly and effectively. First, Registry hive files can be accessed in a number of ways: via a remote system's hard drive "mounted" via F-Response, by extracting the hive file from an acquired image (using FTK Imager, etc.), or by "mounting" an acquired image as a read-only file system via applications such as Smart Mount or Mount Image Pro. Some have even added RegRipper tools to Guidance Software's EnCase forensic analysis application as an external viewer.

## Warning

You should *not* run RegRipper against the Registry hive files on your live system. Running RegRipper and selecting any of the hive files on your live system is not how the tool was intended to be used. Also, several users have run RegRipper against hive files extracted from the systemprofile or Default Users directory and not found any useful information; in many cases, these files are placeholders and are full of zeros.

As mentioned earlier, you can run RegRipper against live systems if you need to, but you need to have the remote system's hard drive mounted on your analysis system as a read-only drive letter via F-Response to do so. Chapter 3 mentions a PDF document that is on the media that accompanies this book that describes the detailed steps for installing (and removing) F-Response Enterprise Edition remotely over a network.

RegRipper acts as a framework or a facility for running plugins against Registry hive files. Plugins are text-based Perl scripts maintained in the /plugins/ subdirectory within the directory where RegRipper is kept. Plugins have a .pl extension and contain all of the actual code instructions for accessing, extracting, and displaying Registry hive file data.

RegRipper can also parse lists of plugins from plugins files. A plugins file is simply a text file that contains a list of plugins. Whereas a plugin has a .pl extension a plugins file has no extension. Within the plugins file, each plugin the analyst wants to run is listed in the order in which it is to be run, with no extension. For example, the appinitdlls.pl plugin was written to be run against a Software hive file in order to extract the data from the *AppInit_DLLs* Registry value. Within the RegRipper distribution, in the /plugins/ directory, you will also see a file named "software". This file contains a list of plugins that you can run against a Software hive file to extract a wide range of information. Within the software file, you will see appinitdlls listed with no extension; when you select this file in the RegRipper user interface or via the command line, the tool will run all of the listed plugins against the selected hive file.

So, rather than running one plugin against a hive file at a time, you can put together your own list of plugins in a plugins file, put them in the order in which you want them to run, and even create your own examination-specific hive files. The RegRipper distribution ships with several default plugins files based on the names of the hive files for which they are intended; the plugins themselves contain similar information. However, neither RegRipper nor the plugins check to see whether they are being run against the correct hive file type; if an analyst chooses to run a plugin intended for a System hive file against the SAM hive file, he should not be surprised when he doesn't find any useful information.

RegRipper ships as both rr.pl and rr.exe, which is the RegRipper Perl script "compiled" with Perl2Exe so that you do not have to install Perl to run it. To launch RegRipper, simply double-click the **rr.exe** file. The GUI illustrated in Figure 4.6 opens, and from there you can browse to select the hive file you'd like to parse, select the location of your output report file, and then select the plugins file you'd like to run against the hive file from the drop-down box (RegRipper populates this list automatically when it's started). Clicking the **Rip It** button launches the plugins within the selected plugins file, one at a time, against the selected hive file.

Another interesting aspect of RegRipper is that it automatically generates a log of its activity, recording specific events that are included in the plugins. When you select the location of the report file, RegRipper will automatically create its log file using the same filename (with a different extension), in the same directory as the report file. At the least, the log file will contain the path to the hive file examined, the name and version of each plugin run (in order), and the time at which each plugin was run. RegRipper is very fast, so the times in the log file will be very close together; however, this log file serves as thorough documentation that you can add to your case notes.

The RegRipper distribution is available on the media accompanying this book, as well as at the RegRipper.net Web site set up and maintained by Brett Shavers. The RegRipper.net forums and download page serve as a great way to request, test, and distribute new plugins, which several people have done; some have posted their plugins to the site, and others have e-mailed their work directly to me. Jason Koppe even wrote a RegRipper plugin generator (http://nssadoc.blogspot.com/2008/10/regripper-regview-and-bluetooth.html) to facilitate the creation of simple RegRipper plugins.

# Rip

While working with RegRipper, I found that in some instances I just wanted to do a quick check, maybe just run one plugin against a hive file. For example, when analyzing Windows Event Logs, one of the first things I do is extract the audit policy from the Security hive file. I may not want to do this by opening a GUI, but would rather just quickly see the information at the console so that I can perform my analysis and then paste that information into my case notes. So, I wrote a CLI version of RegRipper, called "rip," or rip.pl. Like RegRipper, rip.pl is also provided as a Windows executable file so that you don't have to have Perl installed on your system to use it. Rip is based on the same framework used by RegRipper; it uses the same plugins.

The syntax information for rip.pl/.exe appears as follows:

```
C:\Perl\forensics\rr>rip -h
Rip v.20080419 - CLI RegRipper tool
Rip [-r Reg hive file] [-f plugin file] [-p plugin module] [-l] [-h]
Parse Windows Registry files, using either a single module, or a plugins file.
```

```
All plugins must be located in the "plugins" directory; default plugins file
used if no other filename given is "plugins\plugins".

  -r Reg hive file....Registry hive file to parse
  -g ................Guess the hive file (experimental)
  -f [plugin file]....use the plugin file (default: plugins\plugins)
  -p plugin module...use only this module
  -l ................list all plugins
  -c ................Output list in CSV format (use with -l)
  -h ................Help (print this information)
Ex: C:\>rr -r c:\case\system -f system
    C:\>rr -r c:\case\NTUSER.DAT -p userassist
    C:\>rr -l -c
All output goes to STDOUT; use redirection (ie, > or >>) to output to a file.
```

As you can see, rip.pl has a great deal of utility. I added the ability to list the available plugins just so that I could keep track of what was available, and then I added the ability to list the plugins in a comma-separated value (.csv) format so that I could open the list in Excel and sort it based on things such as the date of the plugin, or the hive file for which the plugin is intended. This capability is accessible via rip.pl's −l and −c switches. The −l switch tells rip.pl to parse through the plugins directory (again, hardcoded to /plugins) and list all of the plugins. By itself, the −l switch lists the various plugins alphabetically, with each one numbered, as illustrated in the following output excerpt:

```
9. auditpol v.20080327 [Security]
  - Get audit policy from the Security hive file

10. autoendtasks v.20081128 [NTUSER.DAT]
  - Automatically end a non-responsive task

11. autorun v.20081212 [NTUSER.DAT]
  - Gets autorun settings

12. banner v.20081119 [Software]
  - Get HKLM\SOFTWARE.. Logon Banner Values

13. bho v.20080418 [Software]
  - Gets Browser Helper Objects from Software hive

14. bitbucket v.20080418 [Software]
  - Get HKLM\..\BitBucket keys\values
```

As you can see, each plugin is listed in alphabetical order, along with the version of the plugin (which is the date in YYYYMMDD format), the hive against which the plugin is intended to be run, and the contents of the short description field within the plugin itself.

Adding the *–c* switch prints the same listing of plugins, only without the numbers and in a comma-separated value (.csv) format. You can filter the plugins at the command line using the *find* command (e.g., *C:\Perl>rip.pl –l –c | find "Software"*) to locate specific plugins, or you can redirect the output to a file (e.g., *C:\Perl>rip.pl –l –c > plugins.csv*) and open and sort the list in Excel. I should point out that the banner.pl plugin was written by a member of law enforcement to meet her needs during analysis; she was nice enough to provide me with a copy of the plugin for distribution with RegRipper.

Another useful, albeit experimental, bit of code that I added was the ability to guess what type of hive file (System, SAM, Software, NTUSER.DAT, Security) against which the tool was being run. I made the switch accessible through the command line, but my intention is to incorporate that directly into the code and make it transparent to the user, as this functionality will likely be included in future versions of RegRipper.

As a tool, rip.pl is extremely flexible and powerful. The most basic and direct way to use rip.pl is to run a single plugin against a hive file:

```
C:\Perl>rip.pl -r d:\case1\Security -p auditpol
Plugins Dir = C:\Perl\forensics\rr\plugins/
Launching auditpol v.20080327
auditpol
Policy\PolAdtEv
LastWrite Time Fri Sep 9 01:11:43 2005 (UTC)
Auditing is enabled.
        Audit System Events        = S/F
        Audit Logon Events         = S/F
        Audit Object Access        = N
        Audit Privilege Use        = N
        Audit Process Tracking     = N
        Audit Policy Change        = S/F
        Audit Account Management   = S/F
        Audit Dir Service Access   = N
        Audit Account Logon Events = S/F
```

In this example, I ran the auditpol plugin against a Security hive file, which (as you can see) allowed me to view the audit policy from that system. The plugin prints some information about the actions and the parsed key that may be useful to the analyst (such as the key *LastWrite* time), and then prints out the audit policy itself. Microsoft Knowledge Base article 246120 (http://support.microsoft.com/kb/246120) provides information on how to translate the binary data in the Registry value into something that is easy for an analyst to read and understand; the auditpol.pl plugin takes care of that translation.

Versions of the Windows operating system beyond XP do have their differences, but when it comes to the Registry hive files neither the structure of the files nor the actual content has changed significantly. As an example, I ran the winver.pl plugin against Software hive files from both a Vista system and a Windows 7 (beta at the time of this writing) system, and saw the following results (emphasis added):

```
C:\Perl\forensics\rr>rip.pl -p winver -r d:\cases\vista\software
Plugins Dir = C:\Perl\forensics\rr\plugins/
Launching winver v.20081210
ProductName  = Windows Vista (TM) Home Premium
CSDVersion   = Service Pack 1
InstallDate = Fri Aug 31 15:21:10 2007

C:\Perl\forensics\rr>rip.pl -p winver -r d:\cases\win7\software
Plugins Dir = C:\Perl\forensics\rr\plugins/
Launching winver v.20081210
ProductName = Windows 7 Ultimate
InstallDate = Fri Dec 12 20:52:50 2008
```

As far as the actual contents of the Registry hive files on the various versions of the Windows operating system are concerned, there are differences in what's stored in the Registry, and how it's stored; I will address these differences throughout the chapter.

Using the rip.pl –f switch, you can run an entire plugin file against a hive file, rather than just one plugin at a time. Or, as rip.pl (and the associated rip.exe) is a CLI tool, you can create batch files that run only specific plugins against hive files. For example, auditpol.bat is provided as part of the RegRipper distribution and contains the following:

```
@echo off
REM Batch file to automate running of auditpol.pl plugin file
REM in order to enumerate the audit policy from the Security hive
REM file.
REM
REM Usage: auditpol <path_to_Security_hive_file>
REM
REM copyright 2008 H. Carvey, keydet89@yahoo.com
```

**rip.exe -r %1 -p auditpol**

As you can see, the batch file is just a standard, everyday DOS batch file that includes comments for readability (and as a means of documentation). The actual code is run in the boldface line at the bottom of the listing.

Running the plugin against a hive file exported from an acquired image using FTK Imager or ProDiscover isn't the only way to use these tools. Mounting an acquired image as a read-only file system using Smart Mount or ImDisk (see Chapter 5 for descriptions of these tools and their use), you can use rip.pl (or batch files using rip.pl or rip.exe) as follows (image mounted read-only as H:\):

```
C:\Perl>auditpol h:\windows\system32\config\security
Launching auditpol v.20080327
auditpol
Policy\PolAdtEv
LastWrite Time Wed Jan 30 05:31:12 2008 (UTC)

Auditing is enabled.
        Audit System Events        = S/F
        Audit Logon Events         = S/F
        Audit Object Access        = N
        Audit Privilege Use        = N
        Audit Process Tracking     = N
        Audit Policy Change        = S/F
        Audit Account Management   = S/F
        Audit Dir Service Access   = N
        Audit Account Logon Events = S/F
```

As you can see, RegRipper, and in particular, rip.pl, are very versatile and flexible tools. Rather than opening a Registry hive file in a viewer (such as RegEdit), tools such as these provide the analyst with an automated means for extracting (and in many cases translating) specific data from Registry hive files. In this way, a more complete and thorough examination can be performed, in a much quicker fashion, reducing mistakes and allowing the analyst to focus on analysis.

As mentioned in the introduction to this chapter, we'll be taking a look at a number of pertinent Registry keys and values found in the various hives that may be of interest to examiners. In doing so, we'll take a look at a number of plugins used by the RegRipper tools (RegRipper, the rip.pl CLI tool, as well as ripxp.pl, described in the next section and demonstrated later in the chapter). However, we will not cover all of the plugins, nor will we be able to discuss all of the available Registry keys.

# RipXP

The family of RegRipper tools also includes another useful tool that is a variation of rip.pl, called ripxp.pl. I chose the name because this is a CLI tool based on rip.pl that is specific to Windows XP. Windows XP maintains System Restore Points (see Chapter 5 for more detailed discussions of XP System Restore Points) which contain portions of Registry hive files. To run ripxp.pl, you need to identify the path to the hive file you're interested in parsing, the path to the Restore Points directory, and then which plugin you want to run.

**NOTE**

Ripxp.pl is *not* provided on the media that accompanies this book. At the time of this writing, this tool is far too raw to be released for public consumption. I demonstrated the use of the tool at the SANS Forensic Summit in Las Vegas in October 2008, and provided an evaluation copy of the tool to a friend, who had great success with it. Part of the reason for this is that you need to follow some very specific steps to run ripxp.pl, so not only do additional training materials need to be developed, but additional work also needs to be done to make the tool more functional and "forgiving."

Ripxp.pl will "guess" the type of the hive file and then determine whether the plugin can be run against the hive file. It will run the plugin against the hive file, and then navigate to the Restore Points directory, locate each restore point, identify and display the creation date of the restore point, and then run the plugin against the specific hive file. It does all of this automatically.

The capability of tools such as ripxp.pl to provide historical data from within Windows XP System Restore Points has been extremely useful. As with most of the tools I've developed, the need for such functionality arose either from my own needs or from someone else saying, "Hey, wouldn't it be really cool if you could…". In fact, the credit for the idea of ripxp.pl goes to Rob Lee, because in spring 2008, he said just that: "Wouldn't it be cool if you could automatically run a tool like RegRipper against the XP System Restore Points?" I thought, yeah, it would be. I will demonstrate the use of ripxp.pl later in this chapter.

# System Information

When working with an acquired image of a Windows system during postmortem analysis, there is a great deal of basic information about the system that you might be interested in. Much of this information is relatively easy to obtain during live response; for example, in many cases you can determine the version of the operating system (such as Windows 2000, XP, 2003, or Vista) by simply looking at the shell. Or you can right-click **My Computer** and choose **Properties** to see a lot of basic information, such as the version of the operating system, the Service Pack level, and the name of the computer. This information is also available in the Registry, where it is easily accessed during postmortem analysis. More importantly, information about the system itself is maintained primarily in the System and Software hive files (there is some in the Security hive file), and information about users is maintained in the SAM hive file. Information specific to users and their activity is maintained in the user's NTUSER.DAT file. In this section of the chapter, we'll focus primarily on the System, Software, and Security hive files.

If you remember, the *CurrentControlSet* is a volatile portion of the Registry, and you won't find it in an acquired image. The "Finding the CurrentControlSet" sidebar illustrates ways in which you can determine which *ControlSet* was marked as "current" on the live system. Once you determine which *ControlSet* was current, you want to focus your examination on keys within that particular *ControlSet*.

## Forensic Feats ...

### Finding the CurrentControlSet

Most times when you access an acquired image, you'll be interested to know which of the two *ControlSet*s visible in the Registry Viewer (in ProDiscover) the operating system used as the *CurrentControlSet*. To do so, navigate to the HKEY_LOCAL_MACHINE\ System\Select key and you'll find several values, as illustrated in Figure 4.7.

The RegRipper distribution ships with a template file that you can use to quickly begin creating a plugin; this template includes code for determining the current control set from a System hive file. In addition, you can use any of the plugins within the /plugins directory that access the System hive as a basis for your own plugins.

**Figure 4.7** Locating the *CurrentControlSet* in an Image

| | | | |
|---|---|---|---|
| ☐ ab | (Default) | REG_SZ | (value not set) |
| ☐ | Current | REG_DWORD | 0x00000001 (1) |
| ☐ | Default | REG_DWORD | 0x00000001 (1) |
| ☐ | Failed | REG_DWORD | 0x00000000 (0) |
| ☐ | LastKnownGood | REG_DWORD | 0x00000002 (2) |

As shown in Figure 4.7, the *ControlSet* that the operating system used as the *CurrentControlSet* while it was active is numbered 1. Within the Registry Viewer are two *ControlSet*s: *ControlSet001* and *ControlSet002*. (In some cases, you'll find different numbers, including *ControlSet03* and *ControlSet04*; however, you will generally see only two *ControlSet*s.)

# ComputerName

You can use much of the information available in the System and Software hives to determine basic information identifying the system. These hive files contain a great deal of information that you can use to perform basic system identification (i.e., the system name, the time zone the system was configured to use, and information about attached devices and available shares), as well as to guide your analysis, such as the system's audit configuration, as demonstrated earlier.

You can find the computer's name in the following key, in the *ComputerName* value:

```
SYSTEM\CurrentControlSet\Control\ComputerName\ActiveComputerName
```

The compname.pl plugin returns the following information:

```
C:\Perl\forensics\rr>rip.pl -p compname -r d:\cases\system
Plugins Dir = C:\Perl\forensics\rr\plugins/
Launching compname v.20080324
ComputerName = PETER

C:\Perl\forensics\rr>rip.pl -p compname -r d:\cases\win7\system
Plugins Dir = C:\Perl\forensics\rr\plugins/
Launching compname v.20080324
ComputerName = TUXDISTRO-PC
```

You can find the time at which the system was last shut down in the following key:

```
SYSTEM\ControlSet00x\Control\Windows
```

The *ShutdownTime* value beneath this key is a *FILETIME* object and can be correlated with other times on the system, such as Event Log entries (discussed in Chapter 6) and the like to assist in developing a timeline of activity and system use.

The following key could also be of value during an investigation:

```
SOFTWARE\Microsoft\Windows NT\CurrentVersion
```

This key holds several values that provide information about the system. The *ProductName*, *CurrentBuildNumber*, and *CSDVersion* values will tell you which operating system and version (including the Service Pack) you're working with. The *RegisteredOrganization* and *RegisteredOwner* values, although not always filled in, can be used to further identify the system. The *ProductId* and *InstallDate* values can also be of use. The winnt_cv.pl plugin extracts all of the values and their data from the key:

```
C:\Perl\forensics\rr>rip.pl -p winnt_cv -r d:\cases\vista\software
Plugins Dir = C:\Perl\forensics\rr\plugins/
Launching winnt_cv v.20080609
WinNT_CV
Microsoft\Windows NT\CurrentVersion
LastWrite Time Fri Dec 12 18:26:31 2008 (UTC)

RegisteredOrganization :
CurrentVersion     : 6.0
CurrentBuildNumber : 6001
CurrentBuild       : 6001
```

```
CSDBuildNumber : 1616
SoftwareType   : System
RegisteredOwner: Harlan
SystemRoot     : C:\Windows
PathName       : C:\Windows
EditionID      : HomePremium
CSDVersion     : Service Pack 1
CurrentType    : Multiprocessor Free
ProductId      : 89578-OEM-7332157-00204
BuildLab       : 6001.vistasp1_gdr.080917-1612
InstallDate    : Fri Aug 31 15:21:10 2007 (UTC)
ProductName    : Windows Vista (TM) Home Premium
BuildGUID      : 4c600e9b-ab0a-4f8e-ac60-b42c6428d3e9
BuildLabEx     : 6001.18145.x86fre.vistasp1_gdr.080917-1612
```

The winnt_cv.pl plugin is written to sort and display the various value data based on the length of the data itself. All of this information provides basic identification of the system being examined, and you can use it to document the system, as well as to guide follow-on analysis.

# TimeZoneInformation

You can find information about the time zone settings in the following key:

SYSTEM\CurrentControlSet\Control\TimeZoneInformation

This information can be extremely important for establishing a timeline of activity on the system. Throughout the rest of this chapter, we'll discuss various scripts that you can use to retrieve information from the Registry; in other chapters we will discuss files, Event Log entries, and the like. Many of the available tools will extract information regarding times and dates in UTC/GMT time, and you can use the *ActiveTimeBias* (listed in minutes) value from the TimeZoneInformation key to translate or normalize the times to other sources from the system, such as entries in log files. RegRipper's timezone.pl plugin displays the information for you.

# Network Interfaces

Information about network interfaces, or network interface cards (NICs), is maintained in both the Software and System hive files. Within the Software hive file, the following Registry key contains information about network cards:

Microsoft\Windows NT\CurrentVersion\NetworkCards

Within the System hive, information about network interfaces is maintained in the following Registry key:

```
ControlSet00n\Services\Tcpip\Parameters\Interfaces
```

Both RegRipper and rip.pl can use the networkcards.pl and nic_mst2.pl plugins to retrieve network interface information from the respective hive files. For example, from a Vista system the networkcards.pl plugin retrieves the following information:

```
C:\Perl\forensics\rr>rip.pl -r d:\cases\vista\software -p networkcards
Launching networkcards v.20080325
NetworkCards
Microsoft\Windows NT\CurrentVersion\NetworkCards

Broadcom 440x 10/100 Integrated Controller [Fri Aug 31 15:19:33 2007]
Intel(R) PRO/Wireless 3945ABG Network Connection [Fri Aug 31 15:19:37 2007]
```

From the same Vista system, the nic_mst2.pl plugin retrieves the following:

```
C:\Perl\forensics\rr>rip.pl -r d:\cases\vista\system -p nic_mst2
Launching nic_mst2 v.20080324
Network key
ControlSet001\Control\Network\{4D36E972-E325-11CE-BFC1-08002BE10318}

ControlSet001\Services\Tcpip\Parameters\Interfaces
LastWrite time Sun Dec 28 04:44:51 2008 (UTC)

Interface {EE564486-60AE-4868-BB0B-E1A906CC2B44}
Name: Local Area Connection
Control\Network key LastWrite time Tue Sep 11 14:33:17 2007 (UTC)
Services\Tcpip key LastWrite time Sun Dec 28 04:44:51 2008 (UTC)
        DhcpDomain      = us.dell.com
        DhcpIPAddress   = 10.12.138.119
        DhcpSubnetMask  = 255.255.248.0
        DhcpNameServer  = 143.166.95.37 143.166.99.14
        DhcpServer      = 143.166.165.254
Interface {D2B6079F-D864-4E0A-A852-4EB72B87E87B}
Name: Wireless Network Connection
Control\Network key LastWrite time Tue Sep 11 14:33:17 2007 (UTC)
Services\Tcpip key LastWrite time Mon Jan 12 12:46:24 2009 (UTC)
        DhcpDomain      =
        DhcpIPAddress   = 192.168.2.102
        DhcpSubnetMask  = 255.255.255.0
        DhcpNameServer  = 192.168.0.1
        DhcpServer      = 192.168.2.1
```

The preceding information can be extremely useful in not only identifying a system, but also correlating a Windows system to other data, such as network device log files or network packet captures.

# MAC Address

As you can see, considerable information about a Windows system's networking setup (i.e., network interfaces and their configurations) is maintained in the Registry. However, the system's Media Access Control (MAC) address, which is the address hardcoded or "burned" into a NIC, is not usually maintained as part of that configuration information. When the Windows operating system needs to determine the MAC address, it will first check a Registry key, and if it cannot find an address it will query the NIC itself. Windows looks for the *NetworkAddress* value in the following key:

```
HKLM\SYSTEM\ControlSet00x\Control\Class\{4D36E972-E325-11CE-BFC1-
08002bE10318}\000n
```

In this Registry key, "000*n*" is the number of the adapter. Again, the MAC address is not maintained within this key by default; those who write tools which allow users to change or "spoof" their MAC address (sometimes for nefarious purposes), such as the Technitium MAC Address Changer (http://tmac.technitium.com/tmac/index.html), are aware of this.

Another location where you *may* find that MAC address (and I emphasized "may" here because I have not found this to be consistent behavior) is in the following key:

```
HKLM\SOFTWARE\Microsoft\Windows Genuine Advantage
```

I have, upon occasion, found a value within this key, named *MAC*, that contained one or more MAC addresses listed as strings (as opposed to binary data that needed to be parsed and translated). For example, on one of my systems, the *MAC* value is visible in the preceding key, and contains the following data (this was copied and pasted out of the Registry):

```
00-15-C5-1B-97-12;00-16-CE-74-2C-B3;00-50-56-C0-00-01;00-50-56-C0-00-08;
```

Each MAC address listed corresponds to values that I can clearly see in the output of the *ipconfig /all* command; those beginning with "00-50-56-C0" correspond to interfaces for my VMware application installation.

The macaddr.pl plugin included with the RegRipper distribution on the accompanying media is something of a hybrid plugin, in that rather than being specific to a single hive file (e.g., either the Software or the System hive file), it includes code that allows it to determine which hive file (Software or System) it is being run against, and then it queries the appropriate Registry key for the necessary information. If the appropriate value is located beneath the aforementioned keys in the respective hive files, the macaddr.pl plugin will extract the information. Interestingly, during testing of Vista, Vista 64-bit, and Windows 7 systems, some of the keys in the System hive files will have the *NetworkAddress* value, albeit with no data.

Locating MAC address information within an image may assist an analyst in a number of ways. Windows shortcut (*.lnk) files may have MAC addresses embedded in them (see Chapter 5), or an analyst may also have network traffic capture data to work with and may need to uniquely identify a system based on the MAC addresses found in the collected data. At the very least, the MAC address information can help to uniquely identify a system, even if Dynamic Host Configuration Protocol (DHCP) is used to assign a different Internet Protocol (IP) address, and the user changes the system name.

# Shares

Many times, Windows systems will have shares available so that users can access the system remotely. In most instances, this is true for file servers, but it may also be true for user workstations, laptops, and so forth. By default, Windows 2000, XP, 2003, and Vista systems will create hidden administrative shares on a system, as well. There is the IPC$ (interprocess communications) share, ADMIN$, shares that refer to the root of the hard drive(s) on the system (C$, D$, etc.), among others. If a user creates an additional share, such as via the *net share* command, that share will appear in the following key (unless otherwise specified, all Registry keys in this section are located in the HKEY_LOCAL_MACHINE hive):

```
SYSTEM\CurrentControlSet\Services\lanmanserver\Shares
```

You can use the shares.pl plugin to retrieve information about available shares from a System hive file, as illustrated here:

```
C:\Perl\forensics\rr>rip.pl -p shares -r d:\cases\local\system
Plugins Dir = C:\Perl\forensics\rr\plugins/
Launching shares v.20090112
  print$
    Path=C:\WINDOWS\system32\spool\drivers
    Remark=Printer Drivers
    Type=0

  SharedDocs
    Path=C:\DOCUMENTS AND SETTINGS\ALL USERS\DOCUMENTS
    Remark=
    Type=0

  Printer2
    Path=hp deskjet 5550 series,LocalsplOnly
    Remark=hp deskjet 5550 series
    Type=1
```

As you can see, the plugin retrieves information about the share, including the name, the path for the share, any remarks, and the type of share. According to the *Win32_Share*

Windows Management Instrumentation (WMI) class (http://msdn.microsoft.com/en-us/library/aa394435(VS.85).aspx), *Type=0* means the share is for a disk drive and *Type=1* means the share is for a print queue.

Now, by default, you might not see any shares listed under the Shares key. This simply means the user hasn't created any new shares. However, Windows systems will create certain administrative shares automatically. If the user or administrator took steps to *disable* the creation of those hidden administrative shares, you'll want to look beneath the following key:

```
SYSTEM\CurrentControlSet\Services\lanmanserver\parameters
```

If you see a value named *AutoShareServer* (http://support.microsoft.com/kb/288164) beneath this key and the data is 0, this indicates that the system has been modified specifically to prevent the creation of the hidden administrative shares. The shares.pl plugin checks for the presence of the *AutoShareServer* value.

---

> **W**ARNING
>
> Different versions of the Windows operating system can spell some subkeys differently. For example, on Windows XP, the Lanmanserver subkey is spelled "lanmanserver", whereas on Vista it's spelled "LanmanServer". On Windows XP, the Parameters subkey (beneath the Lanmanserver key) is spelled "parameters", and on Vista it's spelled "Parameters". The shares.pl plugin includes code that compensates for this disparity.

---

# Audit Policy and Event Logs

On Windows 2000, XP, and 2003 systems, the system's audit policy (http://support.microsoft.com/kb/246120) is maintained in the Security hive, beneath the Policy\PolAdtEv key. The *(Default)* value is a *REG_NONE* data type and contains binary information into which the audit policy is encoded. The audit policy extracted from a sample image using the Offline Registry Parser shows:

```
\SECURITY\Policy\PolAdtEv
LastWrite time: Fri Sep 9 01:11:43 2005
--> Default;REG_NONE;01 17 f5 77 03 00 00 00 03 00 00 00 00 00 00 00 00 00 00
00 00 00 00 03 00 00 00 03 00 00 00 00 00 00 00 03 00 00 00 09 00 00 00
```

The first *DWORD* (four bytes) of the binary data (actually, the first byte) lets you know whether auditing was enabled. In this case, the value is 01, so auditing was enabled (00 indicates that it was disabled). Windows 2000 and XP systems have nine event types that can be audited, and each of those areas is represented by a *DWORD* value in the sequence of bytes. The final *DWORD* value is not used.

**W**ARNING

The information in this section applies only to Windows 2000, XP, and 2003. The audit and logging mechanisms for the Windows operating systems were changed with the advent of Vista, to include a greater number of logs and a different log format (XML, rather than binary).

To decipher this information, we need to understand a bit about the format. Map the following template over the data retrieved from the PolAdtEv key:

```
0Z XX XX XX AA 00 00 00 BB 00 00 00 CC 00 00 00 DD 00 00 00 EE 00 00 00
FF 00 00 00 GG 00 00 00 HH 00 00 00 II 00 00 00 XX 00 00 00
```

The value for $Z$ determines whether auditing is enabled (1 for enabled, 0 for disabled). The rest of the values correspond to the following listing (we don't care about the $X$ values):

```
AA      Audit System Events
BB      Audit Logon Events
CC      Audit Object Access
DD      Audit Privilege Use
EE      Audit Process Tracking
FF      Audit Policy Change
GG      Audit Account Management
HH      Audit Directory Service Access
II      Audit Account Logon Events
```

For each lettered pair, 00 means there is no auditing, 01 means success events are audited, 02 means failure events are audited, and 03 means both success and failure events are audited.

We can see that both success and failure auditing was enabled on the sample image for System events, Logon events, Policy Change events, Account Management events, and Account Logon events.

This information can be useful during an examination of Windows 2000, XP, and 2003 systems, because it will tell us what sorts of events we should expect to see in the Event Log. (We'll discuss Event Log analysis in Chapter 5.) The auditpol.pl RegRipper plugin will extract and interpret the data from the Security hive file, as illustrated here:

```
C:\Perl\forensics\rr>rip.pl -p auditpol -r d:\cases\local\security
Plugins Dir = C:\Perl\forensics\rr\plugins/
Launching auditpol v.20080327
auditpol
Policy\PolAdtEv
LastWrite Time Mon Aug 7 16:14:22 2006 (UTC)
**Auditing is NOT enabled.
```

```
C:\Perl\forensics\rr>rip.pl -p auditpol -r d:\cases\security
Plugins Dir = C:\Perl\forensics\rr\plugins/
Launching auditpol v.20080327
auditpol
Policy\PolAdtEv
LastWrite Time Fri Sep 9 01:11:43 2005 (UTC)

Auditing is enabled.
      Audit System Events           = S/F
      Audit Logon Events            = S/F
      Audit Object Access           = N
      Audit Privilege Use           = N
      Audit Process Tracking        = N
      Audit Policy Change           = S/F
      Audit Account Management       = S/F
      Audit Dir Service Access      = N
      Audit Account Logon Events    = S/F
```

As you can see, in one instance, the auditpol.pl plugin indicated that auditing was not enabled, and in the other, that auditing was enabled and what the various settings are for the different events (N = no auditing, S = auditing of successful events, F = auditing of failure events, and S/F = auditing for both successful and failure events).

Information about the Event Log files themselves is maintained in the HKLM\System\ControlSet00x\Services\EventLog key. This is true on all Windows systems, including Windows 2000, XP, 2003, Vista, and Windows 7; however, the difference for each is how many subkeys are found beneath the EventLog key on each version of Windows, as the number of subkeys equates to the number of different Event Logs that are available. For example, on Windows XP systems, you will most often find Application, System, Security, and possibly even Internet Explorer (if the system has been upgraded to Internet Explorer Version 7) subkeys. In the case of Windows 2003, you may also find a domain name system (DNS) Server Event Log, and I have seen instances of Event Logs for specific applications. In most instances (particularly with the default Microsoft Event Logs), you will find values that pertain to the name and location of the Event Log file, its maximum size, and how many days Event Log entries are to be retained (although Microsoft Knowledge Base article 102998, http://support.microsoft.com/kb/102998, is older, the information still pertains). The eventlog.pl plugin extracts this information, processes some of the various settings into something a bit more readable, and displays it as illustrated here:

```
C:\Perl\forensics\rr>rip.pl -p eventlog -r d:\cases\local\system
Launching eventlog v.20090112

Application \ Fri Dec 12 12:06:13 2008Z
   File = %SystemRoot%\system32\config\AppEvent.Evt
```

```
    DisplayNameFile        = %SystemRoot%\system32\els.dll

    MaxSize                = 512.00KB

    Retention              = 7.00 days

    AutoBackupLogFiles     = 0

Internet Explorer \ Fri Aug 29 00:36:11 2008Z

Security \ Fri Aug 29 00:36:11 2008Z

    File                   = %SystemRoot%\System32\config\SecEvent.Evt

    DisplayNameFile        = %SystemRoot%\System32\els.dll

    MaxSize                = 512.00KB

    Retention              = 7.00 days

System \ Mon Oct 6 23:15:13 2008Z

    File                   = %SystemRoot%\system32\config\SysEvent.Evt

    DisplayNameFile        = %SystemRoot%\system32\els.dll

    MaxSize                = 512.00KB

    Retention              = 7.00 days
```

As you can see, the eventlog.pl plugin extracts considerable information about the Event Log settings. Each Event Log name is displayed along with the key's *LastWrite* time, indicating the last time the contents of the key were changed. Maximum file sizes and retention times (listed in the Registry as seconds, but displayed by the plugin as days), in addition to the file path to the log file itself, are displayed. As you can see from the preceding Application Event Log entry, the *AutoBackupLogFiles* value (the value is described in Microsoft Knowledge Base article 312571, http://support.microsoft.com/kb/312571/) is displayed, if it is available. Another value specific to the Security Event Log is the *WarningLevel* value (described in Microsoft Knowledge Base article 945463, http://support.microsoft.com/kb/945463), which will cause the Security Event Log to generate an event with ID 523 when it reaches the designated capacity. The eventlog.pl plugin will also display this value, if it is available.

---

**TIP**

Around the same time I was writing the eventlog.pl plugin, Don Weber of Cutaway Security (www.cutawaysecurity.com/) wrote his own plugin called eventlogs.pl, and posted it to the RegRipper.net forum.

Also, as part of the Windows 2000 Resource Kit, Microsoft released an Event Log management Perl script named eventlog.pl, which is described in Microsoft Knowledge Base article 318763 (http://support.microsoft.com/kb/318763). This script is intended to be run on a live system, and allows an administrator to get a lot of the same information as is available from the RegRipper eventlog.pl plugin—in particular, the properties of the Event Logs.

---

# Wireless SSIDs

On live systems (most often laptops), Windows will maintain a list of service set identifiers (SSIDs) to which it has connected. If the wireless connections are managed by the Wireless Zero Configuration Service (WZCSVC), this list is maintained in the following Registry key:

```
SOFTWARE\Microsoft\WZCSVC\Parameters\Interfaces\{GUID}
```

The *GUID* in this case is the globally unique identifier (GUID) for the wireless interface. Beneath this key, you might see the value *ActiveSettings* and then several other values called *Static#000x*, where *x* is an integer, starting at 0. These values are all binary, and the SSIDs for any wireless access points that have been accessed will be included within the binary data. Within the binary data, at offset 0x10, is a *DWORD* value that contains the length of the SSID. The SSID name immediately follows this *DWORD* value for the number of bytes/characters listed. Figure 4.8 illustrates the binary contents of the *ActiveSettings* value, taken from a live system. Note that the SSID has been highlighted.

**Figure 4.8** *ActiveSettings* Value from a Live System, Showing the SSID

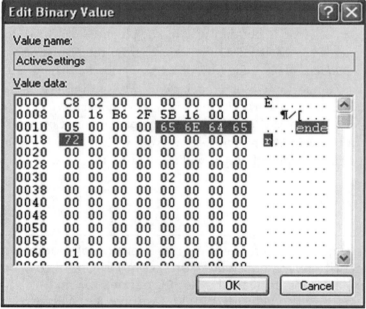

Now and again, a question appears on a public listserv regarding determining SSIDs to which the system has been connected. This can be useful in situations where unauthorized access is an issue or in a case where it's important to trace the IP address that the individual

was using. As such, the ssid.pl plugin will extract the data from the Software hive, including both the SSID of the wireless access point connected to, as well as the date of the last connection to that SSID, as illustrated here:

```
C:\Perl\forensics\rr>rip.pl -p ssid -r d:\cases\test\software
Plugins Dir = C:\Perl\forensics\rr\plugins/
Launching ssid v.20080327
SSID
Microsoft\WZCSVC\Parameters\Interfaces
NIC: 11a/b/g Wireless LAN Mini PCI Express Adapter
   Static#0000 SSID : tmobile [Wed Oct 3 16:44:25 2007]
   Static#0001 SSID : ender [Mon Oct 8 10:12:46 2007]
```

From this information, we can see that the system (in this case, a laptop) last connected to a wireless access point with the "tmobile" SSID (usually offered through Starbucks, among other locations) in October 2007, and to the "ender" SSID in the same month. This information can be extremely valuable in establishing a timeline of activity on the system, particularly when correlated with other data. However, keep in mind that the time-based information from this plugin (and the others, as well) is presented in Universal Coordinated Time, or UTC format, and may need to be corrected for the appropriate time zone.

## Autostart Locations

Autostart locations within the Registry are locations that allow applications to be launched without any interaction from the user and very often unbeknownst to the user as he does... *something* on the system. These locations were originally provided for the user's convenience. Some applications, such as touch pad drivers and applications on laptops, as well as antivirus and firewall applications, are most useful when they're started automatically. In other cases, users like to have applications such as instant messaging (IM) clients started automatically when they log in to their systems, as a matter of convenience.

In 2004, members of the Microsoft Research Center's CyberSecurity and Systems Management Research group presented a paper, "Gatekeeper: Monitoring Auto-Start Extensibility Points for System Management," at a USENIX conference. In that paper, the authors refer to the autostart locations as *auto-start extensibility points*, or ASEPs. The paper categorizes the ASEPs in a different manner than I have and provides a graph showing that perhaps the most popular ASEP used by spyware (at the time the data was compiled) was to install as a browser helper object (BHO). A BHO is essentially a dynamic link library (DLL) that Internet Explorer loads automatically when it starts, and from there it can monitor the user's activities. See the "BHOs" case study for an example of how you can use this autostart/ASEP.

## Are You Owned?

### Case Study: BHOs

I was the security admin at a financial services firm when I ran into an interesting use of BHOs. My employer provided credit monitoring and identity theft protection services to its customers, allowing for a variety of levels of monitoring of their credit, from quarterly reports to nearly-instant pages and/or e-mails whenever a query appeared. And like most businesses, my employer had competition. At one point, I got a call from folks on the business development side of the house with a potential security issue. Several users had gone to the company Web site, and when they loaded the main Web page each instance of our company's name was highlighted, and clicking it took the user to a competitor's Web site!

It turned out that a BHO had been installed on the user's system (it was happening to several people and our business development staff had figured out how to get "infected" as well) and would monitor the user's browsing activity. Various companies would subscribe to this adware/BHO provider, and whenever their competitor's names appeared in a Web page, the BHO would automatically turn the name into a hyperlink to their subscriber's Web site. So, let's say Consumer Electronics Company A signed up with the adware provider. When the adware had infected a user's system, every time a Web page was loaded that had the names of A's competitors, those names would be made into hyperlinks to A's Web site.

Fortunately, Microsoft is kind enough to provide Knowledge Base article 298931 (http://support.microsoft.com/kb/298931) to tell users how to disable BHOs. The Knowledge Base article provides links to more detailed information regarding BHOs, which are listed beneath the Registry key HKLM\SOFTWARE\Microsoft\Windows\CurrentVersion\Explorer\Browser Helper Objects. RegRipper's bho.pl plugin extracts and displays this information for you.

Note that this key is in the HKEY_LOCAL_MACHINE hive, which means that browser loads the BHOs whenever it is opened, regardless of the user.

The bho.pl Perl script located on the accompanying media (in the ch4\code\old directory) allows you to view the BHOs that have been installed on a live system.

One school of thought seems to be that most users and administrators aren't all that familiar with autostart locations within the Registry and believe that only a very few keys (in particular, the ubiquitous Run and RunOnce keys) can be used for such purposes. This manner of thinking is supported, in part, by documentation and applications provided by the operating system vendor. For example, on a live Windows XP system, a command called *MSConfig* launches the System Configuration utility (http://support.microsoft.com/

kb/310560). You can run this command by clicking the **Start** button on the Task Bar, choosing **Run**, and typing **msconfig** into the text box, then pressing **Enter**. Figure 4.9 illustrates the System Configuration utility opened to show the contents of the Startup tab.

**Figure 4.9** System Configuration Utility Startup Tab

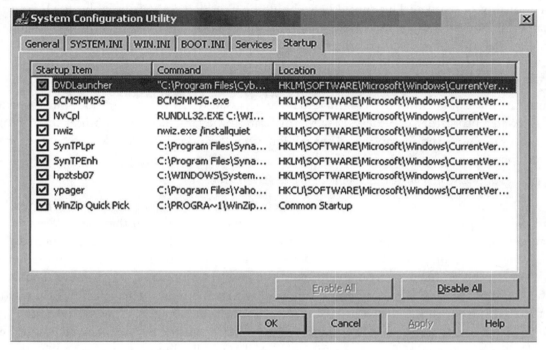

Run this command on your XP system and take a closer look at the Location column. You'll see that the Registry keys examined are the Run key from both the HKEY_CURRENT_ USER and HKEY_LOCAL_MACHINE hives. Unfortunately, these seem to be the only keys examined. There is a WMI class named *Win32_StartupCommand* that will allow a programmer to automatically retrieve the contents of these keys, but as with the System Configuration utility, it checks only a very limited number of startup locations within the Registry.

Another school of thought is that the sheer number of autostart locations within the Registry is so large that examining these locations is best left to professionals and/or software created by professionals, such as commercial antivirus and antispyware utilities.

The truth is somewhere in between. Yes, there are a number of autostart locations within the Registry, but for the most part, they are finite and limited. In the following sections, I'll break down these locations into three areas and describe some of the Registry keys that are accessed when the system boots, those accessed when a user logs in, and those accessed when a user performs some activity on the system. Then we'll look at ways to enumerate the entries in these locations. However, the listed keys should not be considered all-inclusive or representative of a complete and comprehensive list of all keys. The media that accompanies this book includes a spreadsheet named regref.xls that contains several worksheets. Each worksheet includes various Registry keys that fall into that worksheet's category, as well as a brief description of the key and, where applicable, a credible reference that describes the functionality of that key. This spreadsheet should be considered a starting point for Registry analysis, but because there are a great many applications out there and new versions being produced all the time, it should not be considered complete.

# System Boot

Autostart locations within the Registry that are accessed when the system boots are favorites of malware authors because they allow the malware to be launched with no user interaction whatsoever—not even logging in to the system. One location is the Windows Services, or more specifically:

```
HKEY_LOCAL_MACHINE\System\CurrentControlSet\Services
```

When the system starts, the value for the current *ControlSet* to be used is determined, and the settings for that *ControlSet* are used. The services listed within that *ControlSet* are scanned, and services that are set to start automatically (*Start* value is 0x02) are launched.

When performing an intrusion analysis, often all you have to go on is an acquired image of a system and an incident report (and often the incident report isn't much more than "we saw this occur on this date"). When you're faced with something such as this, an easy way to get started is to open the image in ProDiscover, populate the Registry Viewer, locate the *ControlSet* marked *Current*, and then sort the subkeys beneath the Services key based on their *LastWrite* times. Many of these *LastWrite* times will generally line up in accordance with the last time the system was booted, as many of the Services keys are modified, rather than simply read, during the boot process. However, in several cases I've used this technique to locate services and drivers installed by the attacker, including rootkits and a driver called rdriv.sys (which is a rootkit driver file used by some Trojans and Internet Relay Chat, or IRC, bots). In some cases I've located these services, and neither the names of the services nor the *LastWrite* times correlated to the incident report I had received. Essentially, I'd found an intrusion separate from the one I was investigating!

You can find other interesting artifacts using this same technique. For example, I've located npf.sys, the driver installed with the WinPcap utilities that allow you to perform packet sniffing on your system. This driver is installed by tools such as Wireshark and the sniffer tools available with the WinPcap utilities—but they might also be installed by an attacker.

RegRipper can use two plugins, svc.pl and svc2.pl, to parse the information available in the Services key. In both cases, the information is extracted and sorted based on each subkey's *LastWrite* time. The svc.pl plugin presents a short, quick view of the information, whereas svc2.pl presents more detailed information (including the service or drive display name, path, service/driver type, etc.) in a comma-separated value (.csv) format. When run with rip.pl, the svc2.pl plugin output can be redirected to a file and opened in Excel for quick analysis.

In some cases, an incident responder may need to access Services key information on live systems. For instance, there is malware that uses Windows Services as its persistence mechanism, and installs as a DLL that is run under the svchost.exe process (Microsoft Knowledge Base article 314056, http://support.microsoft.com/kb/314056, provides a description of the svchost.exe process on Windows XP Professional). As malware that uses this persistence mechanism is not easily visible (e.g., the Conficker worm writes a random entry, making it even harder to find), I wrote a CLI tool to run on live systems, called regscan. pl (this tool is stand-alone and is *not* part of RegRipper; it is available on the media that accompanies this book in the ch4\code\Regscan directory) which parses through the Services key and lists basic information about each service, including the *LastWrite* time of the key, the *ImagePath* value (if available), and the *Parameters\ServiceDll* value (if available). This information is pipe-delimited and sent to STDOUT, for ease of use. A responder can run regscan.pl (or the "compiled" executable) on a local system, or provide an IP address or system name to which she has Administrator access and extract the same data. Locating malware installed using this method is as simple as typing the following command:

```
C:\Perl\regscan>regscan.pl | find "svchost.exe -k netsvcs"
```

This command extracts all of the Services information from the local system, but performs data reduction by piping the output through the *find* command to display only the entries that are launched via the svchost.exe process. An excerpt of the output appears as follows:

```
Wed Jan 14 01:16:37 2009Z|BITS|%SystemRoot%\system32\svchost.exe -k
netsvcs|C:\WINDOWS\system32\qmgr.dll
Wed Jan 14 01:16:37 2009Z|Browser|%SystemRoot%\system32\svchost.exe -k
netsvcs|%SystemRoot%\System32\browser.dll
Wed Jan 14 01:16:37 2009Z|CryptSvc|%SystemRoot%\system32\svchost.exe -k
netsvcs|%SystemRoot%\System32\cryptsvc.dll
Wed Jan 14 01:16:37 2009Z|Dhcp|%SystemRoot%\system32\svchost.exe -k
netsvcs|%SystemRoot%\System32\dhcpcsvc.dll
```

The pipes ("|") between each segment of the output make it easy to parse and analyze, and allow the output for each key to be on one line so that other tools such as the *find* command can be used to reduce the amount of visible data that a responder needs to deal with. The data is listed by each service's *LastWrite* time, so if the responder has an approximate date or time window for the incident, she can narrow down the data even further.

# User Login

According to Microsoft documentation, the startup process for a system is not considered complete until a user logs in. When a user logs in to a system, certain Registry keys are accessed and parsed so that listed applications can be run. Those keys are (in order):

1. HKLM\Software\Microsoft\Windows\CurrentVersion\Runonce

2. HKLM\Software\Microsoft\Windows\CurrentVersion\Policies\Explorer\Run

3. HKLM\Software\Microsoft\Windows\CurrentVersion\Run

4. HKCU\Software\Microsoft\Windows NT\CurrentVersion\Windows\Run

5. HKCU\Software\Microsoft\Windows\CurrentVersion\Run

6. HKCU\Software\Microsoft\Windows\CurrentVersion\RunOnce

For the sake of brevity, *HKLM* refers to the HKEY_LOCAL_MACHINE hive, and *HKCU* refers to the HKEY_CURRENT_USER hive.

Each time a new user logs in to the system, keys 1, 3, 5, and 6 are parsed, and the programs listed are run (http://support.microsoft.com/kb/137367). By default, these Run keys are ignored if the system is started in Safe Mode. However, on Windows XP and 2003 systems, if you preface the *RunOnce* values (keys 1 and 6) with an asterisk (*), you can force the associated program to be run even if the system is started in Safe Mode (http://support. microsoft.com/kb/314866). Further, on Windows XP, keys 1, 3, 5, and 6 are provided for legacy programs and backward compatibility so that programs written for earlier versions of Windows (or prior to Windows XP being released) can still be used.

# User Activity

Autostart Registry locations that fall under this category are those that are accessed when the user performs an action, such as opening an application like Internet Explorer or Outlook. If you run RegMon on a system and just move the mouse or open an application (or do nothing whatsoever), you'll see that there are quite a number of accesses to the Registry, even when there is apparently nothing going on with regard to the user interacting with the system. As with other autostart locations, malware (virus, Trojan, worm, etc.) authors find these Registry keys extremely useful in maintaining the persistence of their products, ensuring that they're up and running.

One such notable location is:

```
HKEY_LOCAL_MACHINE\Software\Classes\Exefile\Shell\Open\command
```

This Registry key as well as the keys for other classes of files (batfile, comfile, etc.) control what happens when that class of file is opened. For example, in Windows Explorer, right-click any file and a context menu will appear with the word *Open* at the top of the menu, in bold. The boldfaced action is, in most cases, what happens when that file is double-clicked.

When you double-click a file, Windows will scan the Registry for that file class and then determine what actions to take, based on the Registry settings for the file class. Malware such as the SirCam (http://support.microsoft.com/kb/311446) and Pretty Park (http://support.microsoft.com/kb/310585) worms have used this Registry location to maintain persistence on an infected system.

For example, let's say you want to play Solitaire on your system. You go to the command prompt and type the command:

```
C:\>dir /s sol.exe
```

The output of this command tells you where the executable for Solitaire is located within the file system. (On my Windows XP Home system, sol.exe is located in the C:\Windows\system32 directory.) Just out of curiosity, you wonder what happens when you double-click the file icon for Solitaire, so you type the following command:

```
C:\>ftype exefile
```

The output of the command shows you *exefile="%1" %\**. This basically tells the system to launch the file with the first argument (the filename) and any successive arguments. However, additions can be made to the *shell\open\command* Registry entry so that other files are launched whenever a particular class of file is opened. Entries in this key (and others similar to it, as described in a moment) should contain simply *'%1' %\** and nothing else, by default. Any other data in this value should be considered suspicious and investigated immediately.

Another entry to check for similar information is:

```
HKEY_CLASSES_ROOT\Exefile\Shell\Open\Command
```

This functionality does not apply to just the Exefile entry beneath HKEY_CLASSES_ROOT. Some malware will modify other entries of the same type to ensure its persistence on the system. For example, some backdoors modify entries to the following key:

```
HKEY_CLASSES_ROOT\Word.Document.x\shell\open\command
```

In this case, *x* is the version number (8, 9, etc.) for Word. This tells the system that whenever the Open command for Microsoft Word documents is run through the shell (Windows Explorer), such as when the user double-clicks a document, the malware will be executed.

Another location that can be used in a similar fashion is the following key:

```
HKEY_LOCAL_MACHINE\Software\Microsoft\Command Processor\AutoRun
```

You can find an excellent reference for the AutoRun key at http://technet.microsoft.com/en-us/library/bb490880.aspx.

This Registry value lists commands that are run whenever the command processor (cmd.exe) is run. For example, it will run an application whenever a command prompt is opened. The value is empty by default. Entries can also be made in the same value within the HKEY_CURRENT_USER hive, and if there is an entry there, it takes precedence over the entry in the HKEY_LOCAL_MACHINE hive.

To illustrate how simple this is, open RegEdit and navigate to the Command Processor key. On my Windows XP Pro SP2 system, that value is visible, but there is no data associated with it. Right-click the value and choose **Modify**, and then press **Enter**. Figure 4.10 illustrates an example of data that can be added to the Registry value.

**Figure 4.10** Adding Data to the Command Processor\AutoRun Value

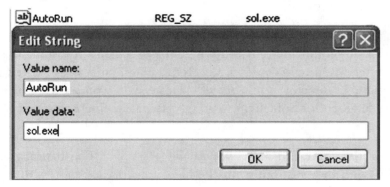

Once you've changed the value, click **OK**. Then click **Start | Run**, type **cmd**, and press **Enter**. The command prompt will open, as will the application that you chose. In Figure 4.10, I chose an application with a nice GUI interface so that when I ran the command prompt, it would be obvious that something else was opened as well. A number of other actions can be performed, such as silently installing a user or service or starting a Trojan backdoor that doesn't have a GUI.

Speaking of GUIs, there's a little-known Registry key that can be used to load a DLL into memory whenever a GUI application is started. This key is:

```
HKLM\Software\Microsoft\Windows NT\CurrentVersion\Windows\AppInit_DLLs
```

Microsoft Knowledge Base article 197571 (http://support.microsoft.com/kb/197571) indicates that the DLLs listed in this value are loaded into memory using the *LoadLibrary()* function during the *DLL_PROCESS_ATTACH* process of user32.dll; this is where instructions for various GUI elements, such as windows and dialog boxes, are stored.

In 2000, J. D. Glaser (formerly with Foundstone, now running NT OBJECTives) gave presentations at BlackHat and USENIX conferences regarding tracking down the compromise of a server and finding an entry in the AppInit_DLLs key.

The AppInit_DLLs key is extremely effective as a hiding place for malware. The CoolWebSearch spyware is known to use this key, for example. Why is this key so effective? When I have taught hands-on incident response training, one of the first exercises I would run is a simple "infection" exercise that is meant to look at the attendees' process rather than determine who can find the "infection" first. I've taught the course to new and experienced Windows administrators as well as experienced UNIX and Linux admins who also have responsibilities for Windows systems. Invariably, across the board, 100 percent of the time, the first step that every attendee takes is to open a GUI tool on the desktop. It could be the Event Viewer; it could be the Task Manager; or even Windows Explorer. However, their first instinct is to always reach for a GUI application.

Windows operating systems provide the ability to alert external functions when certain events occur on the system, such as when a user logs on or off or when the screensaver starts. These notifications are handled by the following Registry key:

`HKLM\Software\Microsoft\Windows NT\CurrentVersion\Winlogon\Notify\`

Entries beneath this key point to DLLs that receive notifications of certain events. Googling for *Winlogon\Notify* will give you a long list of links to malware that uses this key's functionality. When you're performing forensic analysis of a system, it would be a good idea to sort the subkeys beneath *Notify* based on their *LastWrite* times and pay particular attention to any entries that are near the date of the suspected incident, as well as any entries that list DLLs in the *DLLName* value that have suspicious file version information or no file version information at all. (Chapter 6 covers the topic of getting file version information from an executable file.)

Beneath the WinLogon key (listed previously) is a value named *TaskMan* that might be of interest to investigators because it allows the user to choose an application to replace the Task Manager. This value doesn't exist by default but can be added. In fact, installing Process Explorer from Sysinternals allows you to choose Process Explorer to replace the usual Task Manager. If the *TaskMan* value exists beneath the WinLogon key, you should consider this "suspicious" under most normal circumstances and thoroughly investigate the application listed in the data.

There is an interesting Registry key that allows a user (usually an application developer or someone debugging applications) to specify a debugger to be launched when an application is run. The Registry key is:

`HKLM\SOFTWARE\Microsoft\Windows NT\CurrentVersion\Image File Execution Options`

Microsoft provides several Knowledge Base articles that discuss using this key to debug Common Gateway Interface (CGI) applications (http://support.microsoft.com/kb/238788) as well as to turn off the Windows Update feature under Windows XP (http://support. microsoft.com/kb/892894). Creating a subkey for the application you want to block, for example, and adding the *Debugger* value with the *ntsd --* (*ntsd* followed by a space and two dashes) data will cause the debugger to attach to the process and then exit immediately. However, Dana Epp identified (http://silverstr.ufies.org/blog/archives/000809.html) a method of using this key as an "attack vector," or perhaps more appropriately, as a method of persistence for malware. To see this in action, first add a subkey to the Image File Execution Options key that is the name of the executable you want to circumvent (e.g., notepad.exe). You don't need to provide a path, just the name of the executable. Then add to the key a string value called *Debugger* and point it to the command prompt, as Figure 4.11 illustrates.

**Figure 4.11** Adding the Debugger Value to the Image File Execution Options Key

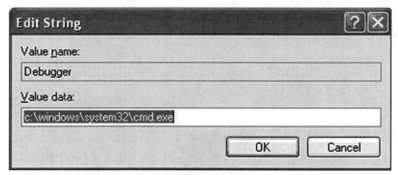

Click **OK** and then choose **Start | Run** and type **notepad**. You'll see the command prompt open instead of Notepad. No reboot is required for the change to take effect.

At this point, I could highlight some interesting ways to take advantage of this sort of thing, such as pointing the *Debugger* value to a Trojan'ed copy of notepad.exe that not only opens Notepad but also launches a backdoor or an IRCbot or a worm of some kind. However, enough examples of malware are currently available that establish a foothold in this Registry key to make it clear that this is definitely a key worth examining. In fact, I've actually seen this method of persistence used by malware during a number of examinations, including intrusion cases. Simply navigate through all the subkeys and examine the executable pointed to by the *Debugger* value (if there is one; not all subkeys will have a *Debugger* value), or use the imagefile.pl plugin to run this search within a Software hive file automatically.

## Enumerating Autostart Registry Locations

One of the best tools currently available for retrieving information from a great number of autostart locations on a live system is Autoruns, from Microsoft (Version 9.39 is available at the time of this writing from http://technet.microsoft.com/en-us/sysinternals/bb963902. aspx). This is an updated tool that comes in both GUI and CLI versions. Figure 4.12 shows the GUI version of Autoruns.

**Figure 4.12** Autoruns (GUI)

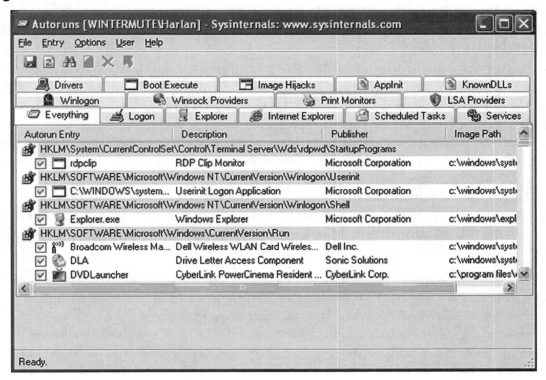

As shown in Figure 4.12, Autoruns will retrieve entries from a number of Registry keys and display what it finds. Autoruns will also retrieve the description and publisher from the executable file pointed to by each Registry value and listed in the Image Path column (shown only partially). This information provides a quick indicator to the investigator as to whether anything that could be suspicious is running in one of these locations and should be investigated.

Other tools exist for enumerating the contents of autostart Registry locations. One in particular is the Visual Basic script called Silent Runners, which you can find at www. silentrunners.org. The Web site includes a complete list of launch points enumerated by the script, which was first made available to users via NTBugTraq (www.ntbugtraq.com) on May 12, 2004. The script is intended to run on most versions of Windows, including Windows 98, which is outside the scope of this book. Keep this in mind when running the script, because several of the locations enumerated (in the Registry and within the file system) apply only to those versions of Windows. These locations are pointed out in the listing of launch points.

For postmortem investigations, analysts require tools that allow not only viewing but also enumeration of a Registry that has been reconstructed from the component files with a system image. ProDiscover's ProScript capability allows the analyst to use Perl scripts similar to those written for live systems to search the Registry on an image during postmortem analysis. Tools such as Autoruns are kept up to date and provide the most comprehensive lists of Registry keys that have some sort of autostart functionality.

# AutoRun Functionality

In addition to autostart locations within the Registry, Windows systems also provide something referred to as "AutoRun" or "AutoPlay" capability. You are probably most familiar with this when you put a music CD into your CD-ROM drive, and once you hear the drive spin up, the appropriate application (such as Windows Media Player or RealPlayer) will automatically start and the first track of the CD will play. Another example of AutoRun capability is when you put a software installation CD into the CD-ROM drive and the installation routine automatically starts.

The way this capability works is that on designated drive types, Windows will look for an autorun.inf file in the root of the drive, and if it finds one, it will parse and execute the *load=* or *run=* lines within the file. Microsoft has long stated that this behavior is controlled or regulated by the following Registry key:

```
HKLM\Software\Microsoft\Windows\CurrentVersion\Policies\Explorer\
```

Within this key, the *NoDriveTypeAutoRun* value allows you to disable the AutoPlay functionality on specific drive types. The value is a bitmapped value, meaning that each bit within a byte corresponds to a specific drive type, and a "1" at any position disables the AutoPlay functionality on the corresponding drive type. Therefore, a value of 0x95 (149 in decimal notation) disables AutoPlay functionality on removable and network drives, and a value of 0xFF disables the functionality on all drive types.

> **WARNING**
>
> You can find the *NoDriveTypeAutoRun* value in either the HKLM or HKCU hive. According to Microsoft, if the value exists in the HKLM hive, the value in the HKCU hive is ignored.

On September 11, 2008, Microsoft first published Knowledge Base article 953252 (http://support.microsoft.com/kb/953252), which stated that for Windows 2000, XP, 2003, and Vista (Windows 2008 was not affected), for the *NoDriveTypeAutoRun* capability to actually be effective users had to install an additional patch which would add the *HonorAutorunSetting* value to the \Policies\Explorer key within the HKLM hive, setting it to 0x1. The Knowledge Base article contains a complete treatment of both the *NoDriveTypeAutoRun* and *HonorAutorunSetting* values. This was an important issue around the time the Knowledge Base article was published, as variants of the Sality (and later, Conficker) malware would propagate, in part, by writing the malware and an autorun.inf file referring to the malware to the root of every drive found on an infected system. In fact, some variants of Sality were found to infect removable storage devices that were connected to the system long after it was initially infected.

**Tools & Traps…**

## CD-ROMs

In addition to the *NoDriveTypeAutoRun* value, you can enable the AutoPlay capability for CD-ROM drives by setting the *Autorun* value in the HKLM\System\CurrentControlSet\Services\CDRom key to 1 (you can disable it by setting it to 0). According to Microsoft Knowledge Base article 319287 (http://support.microsoft.com/kb/319287), the real function of the *Autorun* value is to enable or disable media change notifications. If the *NoDriveTypeAutoRun* value is set to 0xb5, the AutoPlay capability will also be disabled for CD-ROMs. For details on these settings, as well as additional information, see Microsoft Knowledge Base article 330135 (http://support.microsoft.com/kb/330135).

# NtfsDisableLastAccessUpdate

Most analysts are aware that Windows systems (as with many operating systems) maintain time stamps on files referred to as "MAC time" (I'll address this topic in more detail in Chapter 5). What many may not realize is that Windows systems can be configured, through a single Registry value, to not update the file time-stamp data when the file is accessed. You can use the *NtfsDisableLastAccessUpdate* Registry value to disable this functionality, as a means of increasing the performance of high-volume file servers, as described in Microsoft Knowledge Base article 894372 (http://support.microsoft.com/kb/894372). However, this value is enabled by default on Windows Vista and Windows 7 systems, as illustrated in the output of the disablelastaccess.pl RegRipper plugin shown here:

```
C:\Perl\forensics\rr>rip.pl -r d:\cases\vista\system -p disablelastaccess
Launching disablelastaccess v.20090118
DisableLastAccess
ControlSet001\Control\FileSystem
NtfsDisableLastAccessUpdate = 1
C:\Perl\forensics\rr>rip.pl -r d:\cases\win7\system -p disablelastaccess
Launching disablelastaccess v.20090118
NtfsDisableLastAccessUpdate
ControlSet001\Control\FileSystem
NtfsDisableLastAccessUpdate = 1
```

This can be an important factor to take into account, particularly when performing analysis of Windows Vista and Windows 7 systems, as a lack of file last access time stamps may appear to be a significant obstacle during an examination. This value is not enabled by default on Windows XP and 2003 systems, so its existence, in addition to a value of 1, can be very telling during an examination. Even with this value set, however, as you'll see later in this chapter, there are a number of locations in the Registry where you can find indications of access to files, as well as the type of access.

## NukeOnDelete

When users delete files on a Windows XP or 2003 system, in most instances the default behavior is that the Explorer shell will send that file to the Recycle Bin. Users can bypass the Recycle Bin by holding down the Shift key when deleting the file, or by adding the *NukeOnDelete* value that can be found in the following Registry key in the Software hive file:

```
Microsoft\Windows\CurrentVersion\Explorer\BitBucket
```

Adding the *NukeOnDelete* value and setting it to 1 effectively disables the Recycle Bin, as deleted files will bypass the Recycle Bin. Therefore, if during an examination you find that there are no files in the Recycle Bin, be sure to check this Registry value to see whether perhaps it has been added and set to 1.

As I mentioned previously, although the binary structure of the Registry has remained the same from Windows NT through Windows 7 beta, keys and values have been found to change between versions of the operating system. For example, the location of the *NukeOnDelete* value just discussed applies to Windows XP and 2003, and changed with the advent of Windows Vista. On Windows XP and 2003 systems, the BitBucket key is located in the Software hive file, so the setting applied to all users on the system. On Vista and Windows 7, the BitBucket key moved into the user's hive file (NTUSER.DAT) in the following path:

```
Software\Microsoft\Windows\CurrentVersion\Explorer\BitBucket\Volume\{GUID}
```

Whereas Windows XP and 2003 maintained the *NukeOnDelete* value on a systemwide basis, Vista and Windows 7 provide the functionality on a per-user, per-volume basis.

# USB Removable Storage Devices

One of the more popular topics when I've presented at conferences has been how to track USB removable storage devices across Windows systems. When I first presented on this topic, there was a lot of the "Hey, I didn't know you could do that" kind of interest. Since then, I've answered or witnessed a continual stream of questions regarding this topic.

When a USB removable storage device, such as a thumb drive, is connected to a Windows system, footprints or artifacts are left in the Registry. (Artifacts are left in the setupapi.log file as well.) When the device is plugged in, the Plug and Play (PnP) Manager receives the event and queries the device descriptor in the firmware (this information is *not* located within the memory area of the device) for information about the device, such as the manufacturer. The PnP Manager then uses this information to locate the appropriate driver for the device (based on the contents of .inf files) and, if necessary, loads that driver.

(This information is recorded in the setupapi.log file.) Once the device has been identified, a Registry key will be created beneath the following key:

```
HKEY_LOCAL_MACHINE\System\CurrentControlSet\Enum\USBSTOR
```

Beneath this key, you will see subkeys that look like this:

```
Disk&Ven_###&Prod_###&Rev_###
```

This subkey represents the device class identifier, because it identifies a specific class of device. The fields represented by ### are filled in by the PnP Manager based on information found in the device descriptor. For example, I have a 1GB Geek Squad thumb drive that I purchased from Best Buy; the class ID for the device looks like this:

```
Disk&Ven_Best_Buy&Prod_Geek_Squad_U3&Rev_6.15
```

You can use UVCView to view the contents of the device descriptor. Figure 4.13 illustrates a portion of the device descriptor for the Geek Squad thumb drive mentioned previously.

**Figure 4.13** Portion of a Device Descriptor via UVCView

```
iManufacturer:                         0x01
        English (United States)    "Best Buy"
iProduct:                              0x02
        English (United States)    "Geek Squad U3"
iSerialNumber:                         0x03
        English (United States)    "0C90195032E36889"
```

As you can see in Figure 4.13, the iManufacturer and iProduct information from the device descriptor is mapped to the device class ID.

**NOTE**

Microsoft used to provide the UVCView utility as a free download, but has since moved it to the Windows Driver Kit (WDK), per http://msdn.microsoft.com/en-us/library/aa469207.aspx. UVCView is an application that allows an analyst to view the device descriptor information from a USB device; this information is *not* part of the memory area of a USB thumb drive, for example, and is therefore not retrieved when an image is acquired from such a device.

Once the device class ID has been created, a unique instance identifier needs to be created for the specific device. Notice that in Figure 4.13 there's a value called *iSerialNumber*. This is a unique instance identifier for the device, similar to the MAC address of a NIC. This value is used as the unique instance ID for the device so that multiple devices of the same class (e.g., two 1GB Geek Squad thumb drives) can be uniquely identified on the system. From the USB FAQ: Intermediate (www.microsoft.com/whdc/connect/usb/usbfaq_intermed.mspx):

> "If the device has a serial number, Microsoft requires that the serial number uniquely identify each instance of the same device. For example, if two device descriptors have identical values for the *idVendor*, *idProduct*, and *bcdDevice* fields, the *iSerialNumber* field will distinguish one from the other."

Figure 4.14 illustrates a device class ID and subordinate unique instance ID as it appears in RegEdit.

**Figure 4.14** Portion of RegEdit Showing Device Class ID and Unique Instance ID

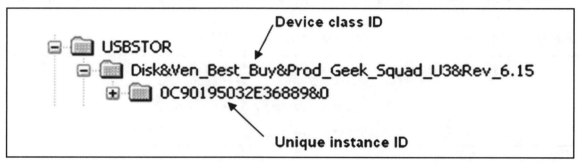

Although a unique serial number is required for devices that manufacturers want to qualify for the Windows Logo program (www.microsoft.com/whdc/archive/usbfaq.mspx#ERCAC), not all devices include a serial number. For devices that do not have a serial number, the PnP Manager will create a unique instance ID for that device, which will look similar to the following:

`6&26c97b61&0`

Notice that the second character is an ampersand (&). If you see a unique instance ID beneath the USBSTOR key that looks like this, you know the device that was plugged into the system does not have a serial number in its device descriptor.

So, if the unique instance ID does not have an & as the second character, you might be able to identify the unique device that was connected to the system. In cases involving multiple systems and storage media, investigators should be sure to include the use of UVCView in their methodology so that the devices can later be tied to the system, not only through Registry artifacts in the USBSTOR key but also in the MountedDevices key as well as in Shortcuts and other references to files located on the system.

Once the unique instance identifier key has been created, the key is then populated with several values, including a *FriendlyName*. The value of interest to investigators will be the *ParentIdPrefix* value. Microsoft does not provide any information regarding how this value is created or whether this value is unique across Windows systems. However, the *ParentIdPrefix* value can be used to correlate additional information from within the Registry.

For example, using both the unique instance identifier and the *ParentIdPrefix*, you can determine the last time the USB device was connected to the Windows system. On a live system, you need to navigate to the following key:

```
HKEY_LOCAL_MACHINE\SYSTEM\CurrentControlSet\Control\DeviceClasses
```

You'll see a number of subkeys beneath this key, all of which are GUIDs. The specific device classes that we're interested in are {53f56307-b6bf-11d0-94f2-00a0c91efb8b} and {53f5630d-b6bf-11d0-94f2-00a0c91efb8b}. These two classes are defined in the ntddstor.h header file (you can see an example of the header file at www.reactos.org/generated/doxygen/d1/d09/ntddstor_8h.html) as being the GUIDs for the disk and volume device interfaces, respectively. Navigating to the disk device GUID, we see a number of subkeys with some really long names; referring back to the device illustrated in Figure 4.13, we see a subkey with the following name:

```
USBSTOR#Disk&Ven_Best_Buy&Prod_Geek_Squad_U3&Rev_6.15#0C90195032E36889&0
#{53f56307-b6bf-11d0-94f2-00a0c91efb8b}
```

For the purpose of this example, I've highlighted the unique instance identifier (in this case, the serial number of the device) to illustrate where within the key name the ID is located. The *LastWrite* time of this key corresponds to the last time the disk device was connected to the system. This is because when a device is connected to a Windows system, a subkey named "Control" is created; when the device is disconnected from the system, the Control subkey is deleted. Both of these actions cause the *LastWrite* time of the DeviceClasses key for the specific device to be modified.

We can also conduct the same correlation with the volume device interface GUID, using the *ParentIdPrefix* for the device, as follows:

```
##?#STORAGE#RemovableMedia#7&326659cd&0&RM#{53f5630d-b6bf-11d0-94f2-00a0c91efb8b}
```

Again, I've highlighted the *ParentIdPrefix* within the device subkey to illustrate where it can be found. The *LastWrite* time of this key corresponds to the last time the volume was connected to the system. As with the disk device GUID, a Control subkey is created beneath the volume device GUID, and then deleted when the volume (i.e., the device) is disconnected, causing the key's *LastWrite* time to be updated accordingly.

We will cover more information regarding use of the *ParentIdPrefix* to correlate information from the Registry in the "Mounted Devices" section later in this chapter.

RegRipper includes several plugins to extract USB removable storage data from the System hive file. The first is the usbstor.pl plugin that parses the contents of the USBSTOR key, listing each of the device classes' keys, and all of the unique instances of devices within those keys, as illustrated here:

```
CdRom&Ven_SanDisk&Prod_U3_Cruzer_Micro&Rev_3.27 [Fri Aug 29 00:36:11 2008]
    S/N: 0000161511737EFB&1 [Fri Aug 29 00:36:11 2008]
      FriendlyName : SanDisk U3 Cruzer Micro USB Device

Disk&Ven_Best_Buy&Prod_Geek_Squad_U3&Rev_6.15 [Fri Aug 29 00:36:11 2008]
    S/N: 0C90195032E36889&0 [Fri Dec 5 14:02:08 2008]
      FriendlyName : Best Buy Geek Squad U3 USB Device
      ParentIdPrefix: 7&326659cd&0

Disk&Ven_Generic&Prod_STORAGE_DEVICE&Rev_0026 [Fri Aug 29 00:36:11 2008]
    S/N: 0000082509&0 [Fri Aug 29 00:36:11 2008]
      FriendlyName : Generic STORAGE DEVICE USB Device
      ParentIdPrefix: 7&2a5b4c66&0

Disk&Ven_Hitachi&Prod_Easy_Device&Rev_ [Fri Aug 29 00:36:11 2008]
    S/N: 200718900AEA&0 [Fri Aug 29 00:36:11 2008]
      FriendlyName : Hitachi Easy Device USB Device
    S/N: 200718900CDC&0 [Fri Aug 29 00:36:11 2008]
      FriendlyName : Hitachi Easy Device USB Device

Disk&Ven_Maxtor&Prod_OneTouch&Rev_0121 [Fri Aug 29 00:36:11 2008]
    S/N: 2HAA06KR____&0 [Fri Aug 29 00:36:11 2008]
      FriendlyName : Maxtor OneTouch USB Device
    S/N: 2HAA07XG____&0 [Fri Aug 29 00:36:11 2008]
      FriendlyName : Maxtor OneTouch USB Device
```

In the preceding excerpt of output from the usbstor.pl plugin, we see a number of devices listed, the first of which is a U3 device (we will discuss these devices in detail in the next section). We also see two Maxtor OneTouch devices listed, and we can surmise that because neither of these has a *ParentIdPrefix* value listed, they are external hard drives rather than thumb drives (and in fact, they are). The devclass.pl plugin retrieves the data we described previously from the DeviceClasses key, for both the disk and volume GUID keys; an excerpt of the output from the disk GUID key is shown here:

```
Wed Dec 17 13:18:41 2008 (UTC)

Disk&Ven_SanDisk&Prod_U3_Cruzer_Micro&Rev_3.27,0000161511737EFB&0
Wed Dec 17 13:16:36 2008 (UTC)

Disk&Ven_USB_2.0&Prod_USB_Flash_Drive&Rev_0.00,3de63180700745&0
Fri Dec 5 14:02:11 2008 (UTC)

Disk&Ven_Best_Buy&Prod_Geek_Squad_U3&Rev_6.15,0C90195032E36889&0
```

Notice that in the output from the devclass.pl plugin the various devices are listed sorted by the *LastWrite* times of their respective keys. Again, when a device is connected to a Windows system, the device keys beneath the DeviceClasses keys have a Control subkey added, and when the device is disconnected, the Control subkey is removed. These actions cause the *LastWrite* time for the device key itself to be modified.

Another plugin that I wrote due to a request is the usbstor2.pl plugin. Like all other plugins, this plugin can be run as part of RegRipper, but it was intended to run with rip.pl as part of a batch file. I received a request from an analyst who said he had acquired images from 30 systems, and his task was to correlate USB removable storage devices across all 30 systems, looking for a pattern of usage of the devices. To facilitate that, I wrote the usbstor2. pl plugin, which extracts the same information as the usbstor.pl plugin, plus additional information, and presents it in a comma-separated value (.csv) format. Here is an excerpt of the output of usbstor2.pl:

```
WINTERMUTE,CdRom&Ven_SanDisk&Prod_U3_Cruzer_Micro&Rev_3.27,0000161511737EFB&1,
1219970171,SanDisk U3 Cruzer Micro USB Device

WINTERMUTE,Disk&Ven_&Prod_USB_DISK&Rev_1.13,0738015025AC&0,1219970171,
USB DISK USB Device,7&2713a8a1&0

WINTERMUTE,Disk&Ven_Best_Buy&Prod_Geek_Squad_U3&Rev_6.15,0C90195032E36889&0,
1228485728,Best Buy Geek Squad U3 USB Device,7&326659cd&0
```

As you can see, the output lists the system name, the device class identifier, the unique instance identifier (or serial number), the key *LastWrite* time in 32-bit UNIX time format, and the friendly name of the device. The last value is the *ParentIdPrefix* value, if there is one. So, I suggested to my friend that he run the usbstor2.pl plugin via rip.pl, and output each iteration of the command to a single file using redirection:

```
C:\Perl>rip.pl -p usbstor2.pl -r path\system >> devices.csv
```

Once the plugin had been run across all of the System hive files, he could open the devices.csv file in Excel and sort based on the various devices, or system names, or however he chose to look at the data. Had he worked with a Registry viewing application, even one built into a forensic analysis application, it might have taken him days to accomplish what he was able to do in minutes with rip.pl.

# USB Device Issues

USB removable storage devices have long been known (particularly by security professionals) to pose a threat to security, especially within the corporate infrastructure. Since the days of the floppy disk (even back as far as when these things really were floppy!), the amount of storage capacity has increased as the size of the device (the "form factor") has decreased. As I write this, thumb drives with 2GB and 4GB capacity are available on the shelves of many local stores, all at reasonable prices. Want to steal a file from an organization? How about an entire database? And they call these things "thumb" drives; remove the plastic casing and strip the device down to just the circuit board, and you've got a "thumbnail" drive that is quite literally the size of a thumbnail.

To make matters worse, these devices are ubiquitous. It used to be that anyone who had a 64MB thumb drive was probably some kind of über-admin. Now just about everyone has these things and uses them for storing pictures, presentations, and more. How about iPods and MP3 players? We see them in the gym, in the office, on the bus; they're everywhere. In fact, we're *used* to seeing them, so seeing one on a desk, plugged into a laptop, isn't unusual at all. Right now, you can purchase an 8GB iPod Nano for around $200. If someone plugs one of these into a laptop that's connected to a corporate local area network (LAN), who's to know whether the user is listening to music or downloading financial forecasts, compensation plans, contract bids, and other confidential information to the storage device?

Another issue has to do with the AutoPlay functionality mentioned previously in the chapter. When a CD or DVD is placed in the drive on a Windows system, the new media is detected, and if an autorun.inf file is located in the root of the drive, it is parsed and the *run=* and *load=* lines are executed. This is all part of the enhanced user experience Windows offers. By default, AutoRun functionality is not enabled for removable storage devices such as thumb drives; however, it *is* enabled by default for what the system believes to be CD-ROMs, which is what part of the U3 device appears to be, due to how it's formatted. Instructions are available on the Internet that show you how to create your own data and programs to be written over the existing U3 partition, making this an extremely dangerous mechanism for gaining access to systems.

The company U3 provides a utility to give users more mobility with their applications. This utility creates a small partition at the beginning of a thumb drive and marks it as a CDFS (CD file system) partition so that Windows systems recognize the partition as a CD rather than a removable storage device. The utilities (browser and the like) are then run from the CDFS partition, and the rest of the device is used for storage. However, this means that even though AutoRun functionality is disabled (by default) for removable storage devices, it is *enabled* (by default) for the CDFS partition.

When I connected a U3-enabled thumb drive to my Windows XP system, I found that two separate device class ID entries were created for the same device:

```
CdRom&Ven_Best_Buy&Prod_Geek_Squad_U3&Rev_6.15
```

and

```
Disk&Ven_Best_Buy&Prod_Geek_Squad_U3&Rev_6.15
```

Both of these device class IDs had the same unique instance ID subkey beneath them. When you're performing postmortem forensic analysis, this is definitely something to look for because it might identify an infection vector or method of compromise. Where this comes into play is that an attacker can create a custom ISO image to install into the CDFS partition and then remove all indication of the U3 utilities or logo on the device. If someone plugs that device into a system, the AutoRun functionality for the CDFS partition will kick in, and anything the attacker can conceive of (installing Trojan backdoors, collecting Protected Storage info and other passwords) will be executed automatically.

See the "USBDumper" sidebar for additional information regarding threats posed by removable storage devices. Although not specifically associated with Registry analysis, these threats do pose interesting issues for security professionals.

Tools & Traps…

## USBDumper

A utility called USBDumper exposes another security risk associated with USB removable storage devices, but with a different twist (http://wiki.hak5.org/wiki/USB_Hacksaw). USBDumper is installed on a Windows system, and whenever a USB removable thumb drive is connected to the system, the contents of the device are silently copied off the device. There has also been talk of a utility that silently acquires an image of a thumb drive when it's connected to a system so that not only can all the currently active files be retrieved, but deleted files can be as well. Both of these issues were mentioned in Bruce Schneier's "Schneier on Security" blog on August 25, 2006.

# Mounted Devices

The MountedDevices key stores information about the various devices and volumes mounted to the NTFS file system. The complete path to the key is:

```
HKEY_LOCAL_MACHINE\System\MountedDevices
```

For example, when a USB removable storage device is connected to a Windows system, it is assigned a drive letter; that drive letter shows up in the MountedDevices key. If the device is assigned the drive letter F:\, the value in the MountedDevices key will appear as \DosDevices\F:. We can map the entry from the USBSTOR key to the MountedDevices key using the *ParentIdPrefix* value found within the unique instance ID key for the device. The *ParentIdPrefix* value for the USB device discussed in the previous section has the data *7&326659cd&0*. Note that this is *not* the unique instance ID and is therefore not the serial number we discussed earlier.

Once we have the data from the *ParentIdPrefix* Registry value, we then locate the drive letter that was assigned to it by locating the *DosDevices* entry within the MountedDevices key that contains the *ParentIdPrefix* within its data. On a live system, we can do this easily by right-clicking each Registry value and choosing **Modify**; when the **Edit Binary Value** dialog opens, we can view the contents of the data to see whether the *ParentIdPrefix* value is there. The *ParentIdPrefix* value is stored in the Registry as a string, but the *DosDevices* values within the MountedDevices Registry key are stored as binary data types, so some translation is necessary. Figure 4.15 illustrates the Edit Binary Value dialog box for the \ *DosDevices\F:* entry.

**Figure 4.15** Data for the MountedDevices \\*DosDevices\F:* Value

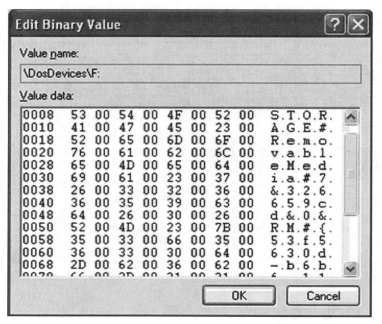

We can clearly see the *ParentIdPrefix* value of *7&326659cd&0* in Figure 4.15. Using the *ParentIdPrefix* value to map between the USBSTOR and MountedDevices Registry keys, we can locate the driver letter assigned to the device. As we continue our postmortem forensic investigation, we might find references in other locations in the Registry or in Shortcut files that point to the F:\ drive. We can then correlate the *LastWrite* times of the unique instance ID key, the MountedDevices key, and the MAC times on files to develop a timeline.

**W**ARNING

When performing correlation between the USBSTOR and MountedDevices keys using a device's *ParentIdPrefix* value, be sure to keep in mind that several devices might have been connected to the system in a serial fashion, and mapped to the same drive letter. I have several different USB thumb drives from different manufacturers and of different sizes, and whenever I connect them to my laptop one at a time they all get mapped to the F:\ drive. When performing this type of correlation, it is important to keep this in mind, particularly when analyzing a Windows XP or 2003 system. As you'll see later in this chapter, Windows Vista and Windows 7 systems offer some additional avenues of analysis as far as mapping a device to a drive letter is concerned.

Looking at the MountedDevices key, you might notice that there are \DosDevices entries (in particular, \DosDevices\C:) whose data is only 12 bytes (three DWORDs) long. Figure 4.16 illustrates an example of this.

**Figure 4.16** Data for MountedDevices \DosDevices\C: and D: Values

| | | |
|---|---|---|
| \DosDevices\C: | REG_... | 16 23 ab 41 00 7e 00 00 00 00 00 00 |
| \DosDevices\D: | REG_... | 16 23 ab 41 00 5e c6 52 07 00 00 00 |

The binary values shown in Figure 4.16 consist of the drive signature (also known as a *volume ID*) for the hard drive (first *DWORD*) and the partition offset (second and third *DWORD*s). A drive's signature is located at offset 0x1b8 (440 in decimal) within the Master Boot Record (MBR) of the hard drive.

For the \DosDevices\C: value shown in Figure 4.16 the second and third *DWORD*s together translate to the hex value 0x7e00, which is 32256 in decimal. Each sector on the hard drive is 512 bytes in size; 32256/512 = 63, so the C:\ partition starts at sector 63.

In looking at the entry for \DosDevices\D: in Figure 4.15, we see that the binary data indicates that the D:\ drive has the same drive signature as the C:\ drive, but a different partition offset. This is because the D:\ drive is another partition on the same physical disk as the C:\ drive. Using the information about the partition offsets, we can compute the C:\ partition to be a little more than 29 GB in size.

To show how to find this information during a forensic investigation, I opened ProDiscover and then opened a sample case. I located the \DosDevices\C: entry in the MountedDevices key in the Registry Viewer and saw that the drive signature was 5D EC 5D EC in hex. I then clicked the cluster view for the case (which starts at 0). Figure 4.17 illustrates an excerpt from ProDiscover, showing a portion of the MBR.

**Figure 4.17** Excerpt from ProDiscover
Cluster View Showing Drive Signature (5D EC 5D EC)

```
00000180   00 00 00 00 00 00 00 00   00 00 00 00 00 00 00 00   ................|
00000190   00 00 00 00 00 00 00 00   00 00 00 00 00 00 00 00   ................
000001A0   00 00 00 00 00 00 00 00   00 00 00 00 00 00 00 00   ................
000001B0   00 00 00 00 00 2C 44 63   5D EC 5D EC 00 00 80 01   .....,Dc]ï]ï..€.
000001C0   01 00 07 FE BF 4F 3F 00   00 00 11 1E 91 00 00 00   ...þ¿O?.....'...
000001D0   00 00 00 00 00 00 00 00   00 00 00 00 00 00 00 00   ................
000001E0   00 00 00 00 00 00 00 00   00 00 00 00 00 00 00 00   ................
000001F0   00 00 00 00 00 00 00 00   00 00 00 00 00 00 55 AA   ..............Uª
```

As Figure 4.17 shows, the drive signature we got from the MountedDevices key is clearly visible at offset 0x1B8.

Why is this important? After all, if we've acquired an image of the hard drive, we should already have and be able to verify the drive signature from both the Registry and the MBR. However, where this information becomes useful to us is if there are external hard drives associated with the case. In my "day job" as an incident responder and forensic engineer, I use external hard drives for storing things such as client data, drive images, and log files. I do this because once the case is complete and the final report has been accepted, I can easily wipe the external drive. If I maintained all of this data on my laptop's hard drive, I would have to wipe the drive and reinstall the operating system and all my applications and data, including PGP keys and the like. Also, as I'm writing this book, all the files associated with the book are maintained on a 120GB Western Digital USB-connected hard drive. This device appears in the USBSTOR key with the following device class ID:

```
Disk&Ven_WDC_WD12&Prod_00UE-00KVT0&Rev_0000
```

As one might expect, this device has a serial number (which I can verify with UVCView), as indicated by the unique instance ID I see in my Registry. However, within the unique instance ID Registry key, there is *no value named ParentIdPrefix*. When the device is plugged into my laptop, it appears as the G:\ drive, and the appropriate information, including the drive signature, is stored in the MountedDevices key. Had this been a case I was investigating, I could then uniquely tie the external hard drive to the system, even though there is no *ParentIdPrefix* value for the external drive.

Values within the MountedDevices key that begin with "\??\Volume" can be tied to a specific user, by navigating to the following key within the user's NTUSER.DAT file:

```
Software\Microsoft\Windows\CurrentVersion\Explorer\MountPoints2
```

Several different types of subkeys are beneath this key, but the ones we're interested in at this point are those that look like GUIDs; for example, "{d37df1d3-265b-11db-a216-0015c51b9712}". Beneath the MountedDevices key, you should expect to see a corresponding *\??\Volume {d37df1d3-265b-11db-a216-0015c51b9712}* value, as well. The RegRipper mp2.pl plugin parses the subkeys beneath the user's MountPoints2 key and lists the entries according to the type of mount point, as illustrated here (emphasis added):

```
C:\Perl\forensics\rr>rip.pl -p mp2 -r d:\cases\NTUSER.DAT
Launching mp2 v.20090115
MountPoints2
Software\Microsoft\Windows\CurrentVersion\Explorer\MountPoints2
LastWrite Time Mon Sep 26 23:32:34 2005 (UTC)

  Drives:
    A Mon Sep 26 22:50:40 2005 (UTC)
    D Mon Sep 26 22:50:40 2005 (UTC)
    C Mon Sep 26 22:50:40 2005 (UTC)
```

```
Remote Drives:
  ##192.168.1.22#c$ Mon Sep 26 23:26:00 2005 (UTC)
  ##192.168.1.71#c$ Mon Sep 26 23:32:34 2005 (UTC)
Volumes:
  {2490fb15-f08b-11d8-958e-806d6172696f} Mon Sep 26 22:50:58 2005 (UTC)
  {2490fb13-f08b-11d8-958e-806d6172696f} Mon Sep 26 23:37:22 2005 (UTC)
  {082b2da3-6b36-11d9-95d0-000c29960ded} Mon Sep 26 23:14:02 2005 (UTC)
  {2490fb12-f08b-11d8-958e-806d6172696f} Mon Sep 26 22:50:58 2005 (UTC)
Analysis Tip: Correlate the Volume entries to those found in the
MountedDevices entries that begin with "\??\Volume".
```

The GUIDs listed under "Volumes:" can then be correlated to the values listed in the MountedDevices key. For example, the RegRipper mountdev2.pl plugin was run against the System hive file extracted from the same system image as the NTUSER.DAT file used earlier, and the following information was displayed (emphasis added):

```
Device: \??\STORAGE#RemovableMedia#7&2713a8a1&0&RM#{53f5630d-b6bf-11d0
-94f2-00a0c91efb8b}
  \??\Volume{082b2da3-6b36-11d9-95d0-000c29960ded}
  \DosDevices\E:
```

In this case, the removable storage device with the listed *ParentIdPrefix* value had been mounted as the E:\ drive, and had been accessible to the user from whose profile the NTUSER.DAT file was retrieved. Now, intuitively this makes sense on systems used predominantly by one user; however, on systems with multiple user profiles, it may be important for an analyst to determine which user had access to a removable storage medium.

## Tools & Traps…

### Data Exfiltration

I've received a number of questions both via e-mail and from customers, asking about data exfiltration. In the vast majority of cases, someone has a system (or an image acquired from a system) and wants to know what data was copied off that system, possibly onto a removable storage device. The fact of the matter is that there are a number of means by which a user can copy data off a system, such as by attaching files to Web-based e-mails, using the built-in File Transfer Protocol (FTP) client, and so forth. When you're looking for indications or "evidence" that files were copied from

**Continued**

the system to removable media (e.g., a thumb drive, iPod, etc.), the simple fact is that at this time, there are no apparent artifacts of this process, and you would need to acquire and analyze both pieces of media (i.e., the system that was the source, and the removable media that was the target). Artifacts of a copy operation, such as using the *copy* command or drag-and-drop, are not recorded in the Registry, or within the file system, as far as I and others have been able to determine.

One caveat to this is that if a user copies data to a thumb drive and then double-clicks the file that was copied to the thumb drive (say, to verify that it was copied correctly), a Windows shortcut (.lnk) file will be generated in the user's Recent Documents folder for that file. Although this will provide a great deal of useful information (e.g., time stamps, a file path, etc.), the only information that may indicate that the file was copied from the system to the thumb drive may be the file's MAC times, which are embedded within the shortcut file itself. Still, no available artifacts clearly indicate that the file was copied from the system to the thumb drive.

# Portable Devices

In spring 2008, Rob Lee (of SANS fame) contacted me to tell me he'd found that Windows Vista maintains a history of portable devices within the Software hive file. Although the Microsoft Web site contains a great deal of information with respect to portable device standards, it offers very little information (if any at all) with respect to the following Registry key:

```
HKLM\Software\Microsoft\Windows Portable Devices\Devices
```

Beneath this key, there may be a number of subkeys whose names appear to be formatted in a similar manner as those beneath the USBSTOR key mentioned previously in this chapter. In fact, some of the subkey names may include the word *USBSTOR*. Within these subkeys, you may find a *FriendlyName* Registry value that appears to be what you'd see in the My Computer applet when you attach a removable storage device. The port_dev.pl RegRipper plugin extracts and displays the information from the Devices key, as illustrated here:

```
C:\Perl\forensics\rr>rip.pl -r d:\cases\vista\software -p port_dev
Launching port_dev v.20090118
RemovDev
Microsoft\Windows Portable Devices\Devices
LastWrite Time Mon Jan 12 12:44:46 2009 (UTC)

Device   :
LastWrite : Fri Sep 19 01:49:23 2008 (UTC)
SN       :
Drive    : Canon EOS DIGITAL REBEL XTi
```

```
Device      :
LastWrite : Fri Dec 12 03:22:09 2008 (UTC)
SN          :
Drive       : Apple iPod

Device      : DISK&VEN_APPLE&PROD_IPOD&REV_1.62
LastWrite : Fri Sep 21 01:42:42 2007 (UTC)
SN          : 000A270018A0E610&0
Drive       : IPOD (F:)

Device      : DISK&VEN_BEST_BUY&PROD_GEEK_SQUAD_U3&REV_6.15
LastWrite : Thu Feb 7 13:26:19 2008 (UTC)
SN          : 0C90195032E36889&0
Drive       : GEEKSQUAD (F:)

Device      : DISK&VEN_CASIO&PROD_DIGITAL_CAMERA&REV_1.00
LastWrite : Sat Jun 28 18:38:28 2008 (UTC)
SN          : 1100101211329640&0
Drive       : Removable Disk (F:)

Device      : DISK&VEN_CASIO&PROD_DIGITAL_CAMERA&REV_1.00
LastWrite : Sat Dec 15 01:17:56 2007 (UTC)
SN          : 6&14BB4B7C&0
Drive       : Removable Disk (F:)
```

As you can see, a number of devices have been connected to this Vista system (the output shown is only an excerpt of what is available), to include iPods, digital cameras, and a Geek Squad thumb drive. Also, a serial number (if available) is displayed, as is the *FriendlyName* value, listed in the output along with *Drive:*. Of the four devices listed, you can see that they were all mapped to the F:\ drive. I have found on several XP systems that when connecting multiple USB removable storage devices to the systems one at a time in a serial fashion, they all get mapped to the same drive letter. On XP and Windows 2003 systems, this can be a serious shortcoming when attempting to map a removable storage device to the drive letter assigned when it was plugged into the system, as you saw previously in this chapter during our discussion of the MountedDevices key. However, with Vista (and Windows 7, it seems), at least a partial history of drive letter assignments appears to be maintained in the Software hive.

# Finding Users

Information about users is maintained in the Registry, in the SAM hive file. Under normal circumstances, this hive is not accessible, even to administrators, not without taking special steps to manually edit the access permissions on the hive. There's a good reason for this: Although much of the Registry can be "messed with," there are areas of the Registry where minor changes can leave the system potentially unusable. The SAM file is one of those areas.

Much of the useful information in the SAM hive is encoded in binary format, and fortunately, Peter Nordahl-Hagen's sam.h C header file is extremely helpful in deciphering the structures and revealing something understandable.

You can use the userdump.pl ProScript (v.0.31, 20060522 provided in the ch4\code\ ProScripts directory on the media that accompanies this book) to extract user and group membership information from the Registry Viewer in a ProDiscover project, once the Registry Viewer has been populated. To run the ProScript, click the **Run ProScript** button on the menu bar and select the location of the ProScript from the **Run ProScript** dialog box. (Optionally, you can enter any arguments for a ProScript as well.) Select the **user-dump.pl** ProScript, and once the execution of the script has completed, the information parsed from the SAM hive will be visible in the results window, where it can be selected, copied, and pasted into a file or report.

Running the userdump.pl ProScript against a sample case that I have available, we can view excerpts from the results to see the breadth of information returned by the script. For example, the ProScript parses information about user accounts on the system, including the username, comment, account creation date, number of logins, and user flags (which provide information about the account). The ProScript will also display the last login time, if it is nonzero.

```
Username : Administrator
Comment  : Built-in account for administering the computer/domain
Acct Creation Date  : Thu Aug 19 17:17:29 2004
RID                 : 500
Logins              : 0
Flags               :
                    Password does not expire
                    Normal user account
Username            : Mr. Evil
Acct Creation Date  : Thu Aug 19 23:03:54 2004
RID                 : 1003
Logins              : 15
Flags               :
                    Password does not expire
                    Normal user account
```

This user information is maintained in the *F* value located in the following path:

```
SAM\SAM\Domains\Account\Users\{RID}
```

The {*RID*}, or Relative Identifier, is the portion of a Security Identifier (SID) that identifies a user or group in relation to the authority that issued the SID. Besides providing quite a bit of information about how SIDs are created, Microsoft also provides a list of

RIDs (http://support.microsoft.com/kb/157234) for well-known users and groups as well as well-known aliases (seen in the SAM\SAM\Domains\Builtin\Aliases key).

The *F* value within the key is a binary data type and must be parsed appropriately (see the sam.h file, part of the source code for Peter's utility) to extract all the information. Some important dates are available in the contents of the binary data for the *F* value—specifically, several time/date stamps represented as 64-bit *FILETIME* objects. Those values and their locations are as follows:

- Bytes 8–15 represent the last login date for the account.

- Bytes 24–31 represent the date that the password was last reset (if the password hasn't been reset or changed, this date will correlate to the account creation date).

- Bytes 32–39 represent the account expiration date.

- Bytes 40–47 represent the date of the last failed login attempt (because the account name has to be correct for the date to be changed on a specific account, this date can also be referred to as the date of the last incorrect password usage).

Tools such as AccessData's Registry Viewer will decode this information for you automatically, as Figure 4.18 illustrates.

**Figure 4.18** Portion of AccessData's
Registry Viewer Showing Decode of a User's *F* Value

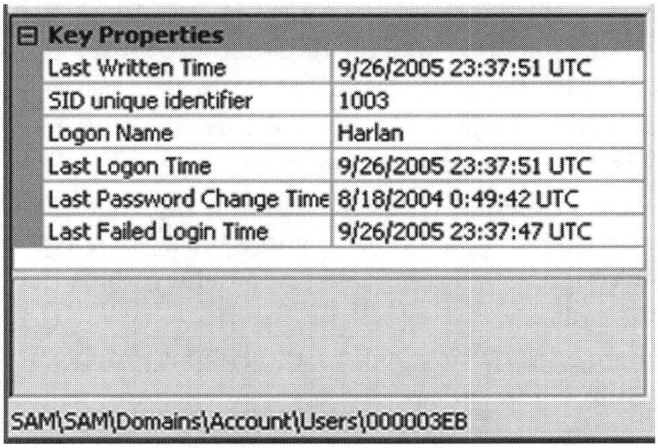

| □ **Key Properties** | |
|---|---|
| Last Written Time | 9/26/2005 23:37:51 UTC |
| SID unique identifier | 1003 |
| Logon Name | Harlan |
| Last Logon Time | 9/26/2005 23:37:51 UTC |
| Last Password Change Time | 8/18/2004 0:49:42 UTC |
| Last Failed Login Time | 9/26/2005 23:37:47 UTC |

SAM\SAM\Domains\Account\Users\000003EB

AccessData's Registry Viewer is available for download (www.accessdata.com/downloads. html) and will run in demo mode if you do not have an AccessData dongle. To use the Registry Viewer to decode these values, you must first extract the raw Registry file (in this case, the SAM file) from the image, copying it to another location.

The Perl module Parse::Win32Registry (available from http://search.cpan.org/ ~jmacfarla/) provides a freely available, cross-platform method for parsing the contents of raw Registry files that have similarly been extracted from an acquired image (or have been made available via some other means). To install Version 0.41 (as of this writing) of this module on Windows systems, simply use ActiveState's Perl Package Manager (ppm) utility as follows:

```
C:\Perl>ppm install parse-win32registry
```

The samparse.pl plugin (the stand-alone sam_parse.pl Perl script is located in the ch4\code\old directory on the accompanying media) uses this module to extract and display much of the same information available from the Registry Viewer, plus some additional information:

```
Username        : Harlan [1003]
Full Name       :
User Comment    :
Last Login Date : Mon Sep 26 23:37:51 2005 Z
Pwd Reset Date  : Wed Aug 18 00:49:42 2004 Z
Pwd Fail Date   : Mon Sep 26 23:37:47 2005 Z
Login Count     : 35
  --> Password does not expire
  --> Normal user account
```

The samparse.pl plugin not only displays the time stamps available from the user information in the SAM file, but also parses the user flags and the number of times the user has logged in to the system.

Because the Parse::Win32Registry module does not rely on Windows APIs, Perl scripts that use the module will be platform-independent. This means analysts and investigators are not restricted to a Windows platform when they want to parse the contents of raw Registry files. As long as the files are available (i.e., extracted from an image file, etc.), code written using the module can be run on Linux, Windows, or even Mac OS X systems that support Perl.

Each of these keys also has a *V* value that is also a binary data type and can be parsed to get the user's account settings, such as full name, comment, path to the login script (if any), and encrypted password hashes.

The samparse.pl plugin also retrieves information about groups on the system, including the group name, the group comment, and the users assigned to the group:

```
Group Name    : Administrators [2]
LastWrite     : Wed Aug 18 00:46:24 2004 Z
Group Comment : Administrators have complete and unrestricted access to the
computer/domain
Users :
  S-1-5-21-839522115-1801674531-2147200963-500
  S-1-5-21-839522115-1801674531-2147200963-1003
```

Information about group membership is maintained in the SAM\SAM\Domains\ Builtin\Aliases key. Each RID subkey beneath the Aliases key has a *C* value that is a binary data type and needs to be parsed to determine which users are members of the group. The best road map I found for parsing this binary data is available from Andreas Schuster's blog (http://computer.forensikblog.de/en/2006/02/list_members_of_a_windows_group.html). This information was incorporated into the userdump.pl ProScript.

Information about users and group membership is extremely valuable in understanding the context of an examination, specifically which users had access to the system and what level of access they had (via group membership). Much of this information is easily extracted during live response using available tools. With a bit more information about the various structures maintained within the Registry, you can extract similar information from a postmortem image.

# Tracking User Activity

You can use a number of Registry keys to track user activity. This type of Registry key is different from the autostart/user activity Registry keys, which are keys accessed when a user performs a specific action. You can find these Registry keys in the NTUSER.DAT file for the user and they are updated (i.e., entries are added) when a user performs specific actions. When this happens, the key's *LastWrite* time is updated, which brings us back to the concept of the Registry as a log file. Also, there are keys that track user activity and add or modify time-stamp information associated with the Registry values (e.g., *UserAssist* subkeys); this time-stamp information is maintained in the value data.

The HKEY_CURRENT_USER hive contains the most information about user activities in locations referred to as most recently used, or MRU, lists. This name comes from the fact that, as you'll see, these keys maintain a list of files or commands as well as a value referred to as the *MRUlist*. Each value within the key is designated by an identifier, such as a lowercase letter, and the *MRUlist* value displays the order in which they were accessed.

## The UserAssist Keys

Quite a lot has been written about the UserAssist keys, most of which has appeared in the form of questions. The specific keys we're interested in are located beneath the following key path in the user's NTUSER.DAT file:

```
Software\Microsoft\Windows\CurrentVersion\Explorer\UserAssist\{GUID}\Count
```

The *GUID* is a globally unique identifier; in this case, two such keys are beneath the UserAssist key: 5E6AB780-7743-11CF-A12B-00AA004AE837 and 75048700-EF1F-11D0-9888-006097DEACF9. Within the HKEY_CLASSES_ROOT hive, the GUID 5E6AB780-7743-11CF-A12B-00AA004AE837 points to the Internet Toolbar (such as %SystemRoot%\system32\browseui.dll), and the GUID 75048700-EF1F-11D0-9888-006097DEACF9 points to the ActiveDesktop (such as %SystemRoot%\system32\

SHELL32.dll). The importance of this will become apparent after you discover what's in these keys and why it's useful.

Beneath each Count key are several values; in fact, there might be many, many values. When I first began researching these keys (most often referred to as UserAssist keys rather than Count keys), I found sites on the Internet that reported upward of 18,000 or more entries beneath one key and 400 or so beneath the other. That system was a Windows 2000 system that had been running for about five years when the post was made to the Web site. What's so special about these keys? In a nutshell, they log user activity, to a degree. Yes, that's right, you read it correctly. To a degree, these keys actually record user activity like a log file.

However, if you navigate to these keys in RegEdit, you won't see that at all. You'll see something like HRZR_HVGBBYONE, which makes absolutely no sense. That's because the value names beneath these two keys are ROT-13 "encrypted." *ROT-13* refers to a Caesarian cipher in which each letter is replaced with the letter 13 spaces farther down in the alphabet. Using a simple substitution (in Perl, tr/N-ZA-Mn-za-m/A-Za-z/), we can then see that HRZR_HVGBBYONE is really UEME_UITOOLBAR. Okay, that's a little more readable, but we're really no closer to an answer at this point, are we?

The value names beneath both keys are ROT-13-encrypted and can be easily decrypted. In fact, the Perl script uassist.pl (included on the accompanying media) illustrates how simple this translation is to accomplish on a live system. The real treasure within these keys is in the data associated with each value. In many cases, the decrypted value name points to an application or an executable. In those cases, the data is often 16 bytes (four *DWORD*s) long and includes not only a run count (the number of times that application or executable has been run), but also a last run time (an 8-byte *FILETIME* object). The run count is stored in the second *DWORD* and starts at 5; therefore, a run count of 6 means the application was launched once. The *FILETIME* object is in the third and fourth *DWORD*s.

When you decrypt the value names, you'll see that many of them are preceded by *UEME_*, and then *RUNPATH*, *RUNPIDL*, *RUNCPL*, and so on. These tags can be relatively easy to sort out:

- **RUNPATH** Refers to an absolute path within the file system; it occurs when you double-click an icon for an executable in Windows Explorer or type the name of the application in the **Start | Run** box.

- **RUNCPL** Refers to launching a Control Panel applet.

- **RUNPIDL** A *PIDL*, or pointer to an ID list, part of the internal Explorer namespace and used to refer to an object. In the case of the UserAssist keys, these are most often shortcuts or LNK files, as when you choose **Start | Documents** and select a file.

For example, the system I'm writing this book on is a Dell Latitude D820, purchased in the beginning of August 2006. Whenever I purchase a new system, I reformat the hard drive and install the operating system all over again. For Dell systems, this means I have to download and install several drivers (Dell makes it very easy to locate the necessary drivers). When I ran the uassist.pl script on my system, I saw the following entry:

```
UEME_RUNPATH:F:\D820\D820_A02_bios.EXE
        Mon Aug 7 16:35:39 2006 -- (1)
```

The script returns the *FILETIME* object in a local time, so we can see that the application D820_A02_bios.exe was executed one time, on August 7. Other entries include:

```
UEME_RUNCPL:"C:\WINDOWS\system32\desk.cpl",Display
        Thu Aug 24 21:27:45 2006 -- (1)
UEME_RUNCPL:"C:\WINDOWS\system32\powercfg.cpl",Power Options
        Thu Aug 24 21:27:07 2006 -- (1)
```

Here we can see that the Display and Power Options Control Panel applets were both executed on August 24, and that was the only time each was launched. Just for fun, on October 4, at about 10:55 P.M., I opened the Display applet in the Control Panel and then reran the Perl script to find that the date had been changed to Wed Oct 4 22:55:59 2006.

So, essentially, these keys record the number of times certain applications have been launched and the last time that action was taken. This information can be very helpful when you're working on a case. For example, seeing something such as UEME_RUNCPL:timedate.cpl might indicate that the user accessed the Date and Time Control Panel applet; possibly to alter the system time.

The userassist.pl will assist you in collecting information from NTUSER.DAT files during an investigation. The plugin uses the Parse::Win32Registry module to access the raw NTUSER.DAT file (which you've extracted from your acquired image) and locate the UserAssist key that contains the GUID that points to ActiveDesktop. It gets the *LastWrite* time for the key and then parses through the key, extracting and "decrypting" value names. The output from the script, which follows, is sorted based on the time stamps found in the data for each of the values:

```
LastWrite time = Mon Sep 26 23:33:06 2005 (UTC)
Mon Sep 26 23:33:06 2005 (UTC)
    UEME_RUNPATH
    UEME_RUNPATH:C:\WINDOWS\system32\notepad.exe
Mon Sep 26 23:26:43 2005 (UTC)
    UEME_RUNPATH:Z:\WINNT\system32\sol.exe
Mon Sep 26 23:22:30 2005 (UTC)
    UEME_UISCUT
    UEME_RUNPATH:Downloads.lnk
Mon Sep 26 23:16:26 2005 (UTC)
    UEME_RUNPATH:C:\Program Files\Morpheus\Morpheus.exe
Mon Sep 26 23:16:25 2005 (UTC)
    UEME_RUNPATH:Morpheus.lnk
```

```
Mon Sep 26 23:15:04 2005 (UTC)
    UEME_RUNPATH:C:\Program Files\Internet Explorer\iexplore.exe
Mon Sep 26 23:04:08 2005 (UTC)
    UEME_RUNPATH:d:\bintext.exe
```

One question I get time and again when I illustrate these tools running against Registry hive files from Windows XP and 2003 systems is "Yeah, but does it work on Vista?" Well, yes, it does. Here's an excerpt of the output from a user's hive file from a Vista system:

```
Sun Dec 28 02:19:10 2008 (UTC)
    UEME_RUNPATH:C:\Program Files\Zango\bin\10.3.75.0\ZangoUninstaller.exe (2)
Sun Dec 28 02:15:32 2008 (UTC)
    UEME_RUNPIDL:%csidl23%\LimeWire\LimeWire 4.18.3.lnk (1)
Tue Dec 23 01:43:50 2008 (UTC)
    UEME_RUNPIDL:%csidl23%\AIM\AIM 6.lnk (1)
Tue Dec 23 01:43:24 2008 (UTC)
    UEME_RUNPATH:C:\Program Files\AIM\aim.exe (21)
    UEME_RUNPIDL:C:\Users\Public\Desktop\AIM.lnk (2)
Thu Dec 18 23:07:27 2008 (UTC)
    UEME_RUNPATH:C:\Program Files\Microsoft Works\WksWP.exe (80)
    UEME_RUNPIDL:%csidl23%\Microsoft Works\Microsoft Works
Word Processor.lnk (47)
Wed Dec 17 23:14:58 2008 (UTC)
    UEME_RUNPATH:C:\Users\user \Music\LimeWire\LimeWire.exe (4)
Wed Dec 17 23:14:57 2008 (UTC)
    UEME_RUNPIDL:C:\Users\user\Desktop\LimeWire 4.18.3.lnk (4)
Wed Dec 17 01:54:05 2008 (UTC)
    UEME_RUNPIDL:%csidl23%\Adobe Photoshop Elements 6.0.lnk (1)
Tue Dec 16 02:21:28 2008 (UTC)
    UEME_RUNPIDL:%csidl23%\iTunes\iTunes.lnk (15)
```

One of the benefits of parsing the contents of the UserAssist key is that it not only shows what actions the user took through the shell (e.g., double-clicking icons, launching an application through the Start menu, or accessing Control Panel applets), but also shows when these actions occurred.

The Parse::Win32Registry Perl module allows easy access to the binary contents of the Registry hive files. Some aspects of the Registry changed between various releases of the operating system; however, the binary structure does not appear to have changed. The UserAssist key structure and values have remained the same from Windows 2000 through Vista, but a brief look at the Windows 7 Beta in January 2009 indicated to me that there were changes that need to be addressed. Although the binary format of the Registry hive files has not changed, the contents of the UserAssist keys have, and will require analysis and additional coding to be added to RegRipper plugins.

Uassist.pl, a ProScript for use with ProDiscover, is available on the media that accompanies this book, in the ch4\code\Proscripts directory. You can run this ProScript (Version 0.11, 20060522) against the Registry once the Registry Viewer has been populated. The script parses through the UserAssist Registry key entries for all users and extracts the information in a readable format, decrypting the value names and parsing the run count and last run times from the data, where applicable. Once this is done, the script sorts all the values with time stamps so that the information can be used for timeline analysis. This version of the ProScript sends its results to the command window in ProDiscover, where the investigator can then select, copy, and paste those results into a file or report.

## Are You Owned?

### Case Study: Defragged?

I dealt with an incident in which an employee for my client might have known he was under suspicion, and while he was allowed access to his system he might have deleted a number of files. The suspicious filenames were located as deleted files, but the content simply wasn't there. There was the additional suspicion that he'd not only deleted the files, but also defragmented the hard drive. The information in the UserAssist key showed that the employee had run the Add/Remove Programs Control Panel applet. Information in the Prefetch directory (more on that in Chapter 5) showed that the defrag utility had been run, but there was nothing in the UserAssist key to indicate that the employee had done so. This activity was determined to be part of the limited defrag that Windows XP runs every three days.

**TIP**

If you've installed or are examining an image of a system on which the user had installed Internet Explorer Version 7, you will find a third subkey beneath the UserAssist Registry key.

# MUICache

In addition to the UserAssist key values, there's another way to see what software may have been run under a user account on the system. The MUICache key is located in the following path:

```
Software\Microsoft\Windows\ShellNoRoam\MUICache
```

Unlike the UserAssist key, the values within the MUICache key do not have time and date data associated with them. In fact, the values in the MUICache key have descriptive comments associated with them. Although some of the values, such as those that start with "@," seem to be default entries for software that may already be installed on the system, others seem to be created when software is run on the system.

The muicache.pl RegRipper plugin extracts data from the MUICache key within the NTUSER.DAT hive file, and skips over the values that start with "@" and displays the remaining values as illustrated here:

```
C:\Perl\forensics\rr>rip.pl -r d:\cases\NTUSER.DAT -p muicache
Launching muicache v.20080324
MUICache
Software\Microsoft\Windows\ShellNoRoam\MUICache
LastWrite Time Mon Sep 26 23:34:11 2005 (UTC)
    C:\Program Files\VMware\VMware Tools\VMwareTray.exe (VMwareTray)
    C:\Program Files\VMware\VMware Tools\VMwareUser.exe (VMwareUser)
    C:\Program Files\WinZip\WZQKPICK.EXE (WinZip Executable)
    C:\PROGRA~1\MOZILL~1\FIREFOX.EXE (Firefox)
    C:\Program Files\Internet Explorer\iexplore.exe (Internet Explorer)
    C:\WINDOWS\system32\notepad.exe (Notepad)
    C:\WINDOWS\system32\cmd.exe (Windows Command Processor)
    C:\WINDOWS\regedit.exe (Registry Editor)
    C:\WINDOWS\notepad.exe (Notepad)
    C:\WINDOWS\Explorer.EXE (Windows Explorer)
    C:\PROGRA~1\WINZIP\winzip32.exe (WinZip)
    C:\WINDOWS\system32\zipfldr.dll (Compressed (zipped) Folders)
    C:\WINDOWS\System32\shimgvw.dll (Windows Picture and Fax Viewer)
    C:\WINDOWS\system32\mspaint.exe (Paint)
    C:\Program Files\Windows NT\Accessories\WORDPAD.EXE (WordPad)
    C:\WINDOWS\system32\shell32.dll (Windows Shell Common Dll)
    C:\Program Files\Windows Media Player\wmplayer.exe (Windows Media Player)
    d:\bintext.exe (bintext)
    C:\WINDOWS\system32\SNDVOL32.EXE (Volume Control)
    C:\Program Files\Morpheus\Morpheus.exe (Morpheus)
```

```
     C:\Program Files\Windows Media Player\setup_wm.exe (Microsoft Windows Media
Configuration Utility)
     C:\WINDOWS\inf\unregmp2.exe (Microsoft Windows Media Player Setup Utility)
     Z:\WINNT\system32\sol.exe (Solitaire Game Applet)
     D:\ShellExe.exe (ShellExe launches documents from autorun files!)
     D:\PDServer.exe (PDServer, Win32 Application)
```

As you can see, a variety of value names and data is visible. Again, little (i.e., no) documentation, particularly from the vendor, describes how values are added to this key, or any circumstances under which values may be removed from the key. However, it appears that for a value to be created in the MUICache key, the software program or application needs to be run on the system by the user; therefore, the contents of this key would give an analyst an indication of user activity, even if the user deleted the application, or (as indicated by the preceding plugin output) ran the application from separate media.

Diane Barrett of the University of Advancing Technology has done work in the area of virtualization artifacts; that is, looking for indications of the use of virtualization technologies that have been used on systems. In one particular presentation, Diane revealed that the use of virtualization applications such as MokaFive (you can find additional information at www. mokafive.com/, as well as at http://en.wikipedia.org/wiki/Moka5) and MojoPac (www. mojopac.com/) can be seen in the MUICache key. In some cases, these types of applications may be used to keep the user's activities private, in that the applications on the host are not used, and the applications (Web browser, etc.) are specifically configured or designed to not maintain a cache or history of activity. Interestingly, MojoPac reportedly maintains its own Registry, so in cases involving this virtualization environment, you'd want to look for a MojoPac device to acquire and analyze, as well. Also, keep in mind that other virtualization environments, such as the free Portable Virtual Privacy Machine from MetroPipe (www. metropipe.net/pvpm.php), exist and may be in use.

# MRU Lists

Many applications maintain an MRU list, which is a list of files that have been most recently accessed. Within the running application, these filenames generally appear at the bottom of the drop-down menu when you select **File** on the menu bar.

Perhaps the most well-known (and all-inclusive) MRU list Registry key is the RecentDocs key:

```
\Software\Microsoft\Windows\CurrentVersion\Explorer\RecentDocs
```

This key can contain quite a number of values, all of which are binary data types. We are interested in the values that have numbers as names, which contain the names of the files accessed (in Unicode), and the value named *MRUListEx*, which records the order in which the files were accessed (as *DWORD*s). For example, on my system, the first *DWORD* (i.e., 4-byte value) in the *MRUListEx* value data is 0x26, or 38 in decimal. The value with the name "38" points to a directory that I opened. Given that adding a value and its associated data to the key, as well as modifying the *MRUListEx* value, constituted modifying the key, the *LastWrite* time of the RecentDocs key will tell us when that file was accessed.

Again, to be clear, the values beneath the RecentDocs key (and its subkeys) have numbers as names; however, these names alone do not correspond to the order in which the files referenced in the data were last accessed. This information is maintained in the *MRUListEx* value data.

---

**TIP**

In most cases, MRU keys contain some way of determining when the most recent activity took place. With the RecentDocs key, the *MRUListEx* value contains the ordered list of those activities. Other keys have different ways of maintaining this information, depending upon the specific key. However, the *LastWrite* time of the key corresponds to the time that the most recent activity occurred. For analysis purposes, this provides additional information that can be used to develop a timeline of activity on the system.

---

The RecentDocs key also has a number of subkeys, each one being the extension of a file that was opened (.doc, .txt, .html, etc.). The values within these subkeys are maintained in the same way as in the RecentDocs key: The value names are numbered, and their data contains the name of the file accessed as a binary data type (in Unicode). Another value called *MRUListEx* is also a binary data type and maintains the order in which the files were accessed, most recent first, as *DWORD*s. The recentdocs.pl plugin parses the RecentDocs key contents, as well as the contents of each subkey, and lists the values in *MRUListEx* order, as illustrated in the plugin output excerpt that follows:

```
Software\Microsoft\Windows\CurrentVersion\Explorer\RecentDocs\.MOV
LastWrite Time Mon Oct 27 00:23:40 2008 (UTC)
MRUListEx = 4,1,3,7,9,2,8,0,6,5
    4 = CIMG1801.MOV
    1 = CIMG1800.MOV
    3 = CIMG2597.MOV
    7 = CIMG2596.MOV
    9 = CIMG2595.MOV
    2 = CIMG2594.MOV
    8 = CIMG2593.MOV
    0 = CIMG2592.MOV
    6 = CIMG2591.MOV
    5 = CIMG2589.MOV
```

```
Software\Microsoft\Windows\CurrentVersion\Explorer\RecentDocs\.mp3
LastWrite Time Fri Jul 11 19:45:05 2008 (UTC)
MRUListEx = 1,0,4,9,8,7,6,5,3,2
    1 = full_9c0a82e420f4e17f240aa142f209935e.mp3
    0 = full_7702b626e3e56525356e08ef5bde6d9e.mp3
    4 = djsona.mp3
    9 = full_27fb554b26316c4b20cd8e6a013a6214.mp3
    8 = 03-britney_spears-radar.mp3
    7 = Britney_Spears-_Radar.mp3
    6 = full_bac9c7b07c84213659d8a8b9098d8379.mp3
    5 = heizman.mp3
    3 = full_025d9af06f9e17201f60f248207f905b.mp3
    2 = Christina_Aguilera_-_Can't_Hold_Us_Down.mp3
```

As you can see, the plugin displays the RecentDocs subkey name, the *LastWrite* time for the key, the contents of the *MRUListEx* value (with the final, terminating 0xffffffff value removed), and then value names in *MRUListEx* order. From this example, we can see that the user viewed a MOV movie file Monday, October 27, and listened to a particular MP3 file Friday, July 11.

You can find another popular *MRUList* in the RunMRU key:

```
\Software\Microsoft\Windows\CurrentVersion\Explorer\RunMRU
```

This key maintains a list of all the values typed into the Run box on the Start menu. Figure 4.19 illustrates what the contents of this key might look like.

**Figure 4.19** Excerpt from RunMRU Key

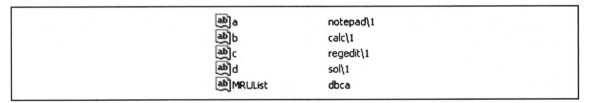

The RunMRU *MRUList* value is maintained in clear text and is more easily readable than the RecentDocs *MRUListEx* value. As with the RecentDocs key, however, the most recently typed items are listed first within the *MRUList* value.

Entries are added to this key when a user clicks the **Start** button, chooses **Run**, and types a command, name of a file, or the like. The runmru.pl plugin displays the information within the RunMRU key as shown here:

```
C:\Perl\forensics\rr>rip.pl -p runmru -r d:\cases\lenovo\NTUSER.DAT
Launching runmru v.20080324
RunMru
```

```
Software\Microsoft\Windows\CurrentVersion\Explorer\RunMRU
LastWrite Time Thu Jan 31 21:43:17 2008 (UTC)
MRUList = edchbgfa
a     \\Server\1
b     \\Server\Share\1
c     calc\1
d     notepad\1
e     regedit\1
f     conf\1
g     services.msc\1
h     cmd\1
```

The *MRUList* value within the RunMRU key tells us that the most recent item to be typed into the Run box is item "e", which, in this case, is "regedit". The RunMRU key value names, much like the values beneath the RecentDocs key, do not correspond to the order in which the various items were typed into the Run box; rather, the *MRUList* value maintains that information. In the preceding example, the "h" value (i.e., "cmd") was not the most recent item typed into the Run box; "regedit" was the most recent item the user typed into the Run box.

During investigations centered around user or employee activity, I have found entries in the RunMRU key that show accesses to remote systems (such as those listed in the preceding example), as well as to applications and files on removable storage media.

Another key similar to the RunMRU key is the TypedURLs key:

```
\Software\Microsoft\Internet Explorer\TypedURLs
```

Similar to the RunMRU key, the TypedURLs key maintains a list of the URLs the user types into the Address bar in Internet Explorer. However, the value names within the TypedURLs key are ordered with the most recently typed URL having the lowest number; consequently, this key doesn't have an *MRUList* or *MRUListEx* value. The typedurls.pl plugin displays the information from within this key as follows:

```
C:\Perl\forensics\rr>rip.pl -p typedurls -r d:\cases\lenovo\NTUSER.DAT
Launching typedurls v.20080324
TypedURLs
Software\Microsoft\Internet Explorer\TypedURLs
LastWrite Time Mon Feb 4 23:02:44 2008 (UTC)
    url1 -> http://mail.yahoo.com/
    url2 -> http://groups.yahoo.com/
    url3 -> http://www.forensicfocus.com/
    url4 -> http://www.orbitz.com/
    url5 -> http://www.facebook.com/
    url6 -> http://www.google.com/
```

```
url7 -> http://www.blogger.com/
url8 -> http://news.yahoo.com/
```

This information can be combined with Temporary Internet files to show which Web sites were visited by clicking a link and those that the user typed in by hand.

You can find yet another location for MRU lists in the following key:

```
\Software\Microsoft\Windows\CurrentVersion\Explorer\ComDlg32\OpenSaveMRU
```

This key (a good reference is available at http://support.microsoft.com/kb/322948) maintains MRU lists of files opened via the Open and SaveAs dialogs within the Windows shell. Similar to the RecentDocs key, the OpenSaveMRU key also maintains subkeys of specific file extensions that have been opened or saved. Like the RunMRU key, however, the data within these keys consists of string data types and is easily read. The contents of this key can be very useful in several ways. First, some file extensions do not appear frequently during normal system use, so the subkey beneath the OpenSaveMRU key for that file extension may have only one entry, named *a*. In this case, the data for the *MRUList* value will have only *a* listed, as shown in Figure 4.20. The *LastWrite* time for the key will tell you when that file was opened or saved.

**Figure 4.20** Excerpt from a Subkey of the OpenSaveMRU Key

| | | |
|---|---|---|
| ab a | REG_SZ | G:\book2\memory\pe_image.h.htm |
| ab MRUList | REG_SZ | a |

Opening an image acquired from a Windows XP system in ProDiscover, I navigated to the OpenSaveMRU key for the user. The *LastWrite* time for the exe subkey is listed as August 17, 2004, at 11:18 A.M. Figure 4.21 illustrates the contents of the exe subkey.

**Figure 4.21** Excerpt from the exe
Subkey of the OpenSaveMRU Key (via ProDiscover)

| a | REG_SZ | C:\Documents and Settings\Mr. Evil\Desktop\lalsetup250.exe |
|---|---|---|
| MRUList | REG_SZ | cdba |
| b | REG_SZ | C:\Documents and Settings\Mr. Evil\Desktop\netstumblerinstaller_0_4_0.exe |
| c | REG_SZ | C:\Documents and Settings\Mr. Evil\Desktop\ethereal-setup-0.10.6.exe |
| d | REG_SZ | C:\Documents and Settings\Mr. Evil\Desktop\WinPcap_3_01_a.exe |

Figure 4.21 shows that the most recent file accessed was the Ethereal setup utility (Ethereal is a suite of network traffic capture and analysis tools, now called Wireshark), used to install the application. This information can then be correlated with the contents of the

UserAssist key (using the uassist.pl ProScript, Version 0.11, 20060522). When the ProScript is run against a test image, we see the following:

```
--> Fri Aug 27 15:34:54 2004
    --> UEME_RUNPATH:C:\Program Files\Ethereal\ethereal.exe
--> Fri Aug 27 15:33:02 2004
    --> UEME_RUNPATH:C:\Program Files\Cain\Cain.exe
--> Fri Aug 27 15:28:36 2004
    --> UEME_RUNPATH:C:\Documents and Settings\Mr. Evil\Desktop\
ethereal-setup-0.10.6.exe
--> Fri Aug 27 15:15:08 2004
    --> UEME_RUNPATH:C:\Documents and Settings\Mr. Evil\Desktop\
WinPcap_3_01_a.exe
--> Fri Aug 27 15:14:44 2004
    --> UEME_RUNCPL
    --> UEME_RUNCPL:"C:\WINDOWS\System32\appwiz.cpl",Add or Remove Programs
--> Fri Aug 27 15:12:35 2004
    --> UEME_RUNPATH:C:\Program Files\Network Stumbler\NetStumbler.exe
--> Fri Aug 27 15:12:11 2004
    --> UEME_RUNPATH:C:\Documents and Settings\Mr. Evil\Desktop\
netstumblerinstaller_0_4_0.exe
```

As you can see, our user was quite busy on August 27, 2004. (The ProScript extracts raw *FILETIME* data and translates it into UTC time, which is roughly equivalent to GMT time. The ProDiscover application shows all times relative to the examiner's system and TimeZoneInformation settings.) The TimeZoneInformation Registry key shows that when the system was running, it was set for the Central time zone, with automatic adjustments for daylight saving time enabled. The ActiveTimeBias is 300 minutes (five hours), and ActiveTimeBias on my system (with ProDiscover open) is 240 minutes (four hours). From this information, we see that about 10 minutes after saving the Ethereal setup application to his system the "suspect" installed that application.

Another way this information can be useful is to show the use of external storage devices. Not only will the *LastWrite* time of the subkey provide the date and time the device was connected to the system, but also the information can be correlated to the contents of the MountedDevices key to provide additional information about the device.

Yet another MRU list can be found beneath the following key:

```
Software\Microsoft\Windows\CurrentVersion\Explorer\FileExts
```

The subkeys beneath this key correspond to extensions for files that have been opened on the system. Beneath the file extension subkeys, you will find subkeys called OpenWithProgIDs and OpenWithList. These Registry entries tell the system what application to use to open a file with that extension when the user double-clicks the file. This may be important during an examination as a user may have installed and then uninstalled an application that would open files with a particular extension. When the application is removed, information may still remain in the FileExts key. The fileexts.pl RegRipper plugin parses and displays this information.

## Search Assistant

When a user clicks the **Start** button in Windows XP and chooses **Search**, then chooses **For Files and Folders**, the search terms entered into the dialog box are stored in the following Registry key:

```
Software\Microsoft\Search Assistant\ACMru
```

The ACMru key will generally have some combination of four subkeys: 5001, 5603, 5604, and 5647. The 5001 subkey contains the MRU list for the Internet Search Assistant, the 5603 subkey contains the MRU list for the Windows XP files and folders search, and the 5604 subkey contains the MRU list that corresponds to the "word or phrase in a file" dialog box. The 5647 subkey maintains the MRU list for the computers entered via the "for computers or people" selection in the Search Results dialog. The value names within the subkeys are three-digit numbers. The smallest number (i.e., 000) represents the most recent search, and the *LastWrite* time associated with the key will give you the time and date that the search was launched. The acmru.pl plugin displays the information within this key, as illustrated here:

```
C:\Perl\forensics\rr>rip.pl -p acmru -r d:\cases\NTUSER.DAT
Launching acmru v.20080324
ACMru - Search Assistant
Software\Microsoft\Search Assistant\ACMru
LastWrite Time Mon Sep 26 23:02:08 2005 (UTC)
5603 [Mon Sep 26 23:32:56 2005 (UTC)]
    000 -> port*
    001 -> sol.exe
    002 -> hacker*
    003 -> hack*
    004 -> lad*
5604 [Mon Sep 26 23:33:30 2005 (UTC)]
    000 -> disk
    001 -> ha*
```

Knowing the purpose of the various subkeys and the way they are populated will give you insight into the user's activities on the system. This can be useful during investigations that concern what a user was doing and when. In the preceding example, the user searched for various terms such as *port\** and *sol.exe*, looking for filenames, and searched for *disk* as a keyword within files. In one examination of a system compromise in which the intruder had accessed systems via Terminal Services, we saw that he searched for the term *bank\**.

Search information for "legacy" systems, such as Windows 2000, is maintained in different Registry keys and might be found on the system if it was upgraded from Windows 2000 to XP. The key in question is:

```
Software\Microsoft\Internet Explorer\Explorer Bars\{C4EE31F3-4768-11D2-
BE5C-00A0C9A83DA1}
```

According to the contents of the HKEY_CLASSES_ROOT\CLSID key, that GUID refers to the File Search Explorer Band, contained in shell32.dll. Two subkeys beneath this key, FilesNamedMRU and ContainingTextMRU, correlate to the 5603 and 5604 subkeys (respectively) found on Windows XP systems.

# Connecting to Other Systems

When a user uses the Map Network Drive Wizard (right-click the **My Computer** icon and choose **Map Network Drive**) to connect to a remote system, an MRU list is created beneath the following key:

```
Software\Microsoft\Windows\CurrentVersion\Explorer\Map Network Drive MRU
```

Each entry is given a letter as the value name, and the *MRUList* value illustrates the order in which the user connected to each drive or share.

Whether the user uses the Map Network Drive Wizard or the *net use* command, the volumes the user added to the system will appear in the following key:

```
Software\Microsoft\Windows\CurrentVersion\Explorer\MountPoints2
```

As mentioned earlier, the MountPoints2 subkeys that appear as GUIDs can be mapped to the \??\Volume entries in the MountedDevices key. These GUIDs can also be mapped to the CPC\Volume subkey beneath the MountPoints2 key.

I've used the *net use* command on my system to perform testing, and when I connect to the C$ share on another system, I see subkeys such as ##192.168.1.22#c$ and ##192.168.1.71#c$.

These IP addresses (I have a flat test network that is not a domain, so the computer names are essentially the IP addresses) also appear in the following Registry key:

```
Software\Microsoft\Windows\CurrentVersion\Explorer\ComputerDescriptions
```

This key maintains descriptions of computers that are seen by the network browser. For systems that were part of a domain, it is normal to see several computer names listed in this key. However, for stand-alone systems, such as home users and other systems that are not part of a domain, you likely won't see values listed for this key. On my home system, only systems that I have explicitly connected to using the *net use* command appear in this key. I use my work system to connect to my employer's intranet via a virtual private network (VPN), and several systems that I have connected to appear in the ComputerDescriptions key. One in particular has the description Samba 2.2.7a, indicating that it is a Linux system running Samba. Because this key is found in the NTUSER.DAT file, there could be different entries for different users on the same system.

# CD Burning

When dealing with an incident in which a user may have removed data from a system, there are a number of avenues to consider. Did the user copy the file to a USB removable storage device (e.g., thumb drive, iPod, etc.), or did the user send that data out as an attachment to a Web-based (Yahoo!, Gmail) e-mail? Another means of data extraction to consider is XP's built-in ability to burn CDs. Although many systems come with CD and DVD burning software installed or available (e.g., my Dell systems and my Lenovo ThinkPad came with Sonic/Roxio products installed), Windows XP and Vista have the built-in capability to burn CDs. For Windows XP, this capability is described in Microsoft Knowledge Base article 279157 (http://support.microsoft.com/kb/279157). When the user inserts a blank CD-R or CD-RW into the system, a dialog box will open, offering him the opportunity to **Open writable CD folder using Windows Explorer**. With that folder open, he can drag files and directories to the folder, which are copied to a special staging area until he is ready to select **Write these files to CD**. When the user is ready to write the files to CD, a monolithic disk image file named "Cd burning stash file.bin" is created in the staging area. That special staging area is in the following directory on XP systems (by default):

```
%USERPROFILE%\Local Settings\Application Data\Microsoft\CD Burning
```

On Vista systems, the default staging area is:

```
%USERPROFILE%\AppData\Local\Microsoft\Windows\Burn\Burn
```

The staging area location is listed and maintained in the user's NTUSER.DAT hive file in the following key:

```
Software\Microsoft\Windows\CurrentVersion\Explorer\Shell Folders
```

The shellfolders.pl RegRipper plugin extracts and lists all of the value names and their data from this key. Users can change the location of the CD Burning directory by editing the Registry value and providing another location. If the directory path was changed, this may indicate to the analyst that a corporate policy was in place, or that the user has some degree of technical proficiency. This may also indicate that the analyst will need to look for the .bin file artifacts in another directory.

**TIP**

According to Microsoft Knowledge Base article 326982 (http://support. microsoft.com/kb/326982), users cannot copy files to a CD-R/CD-RW drive on Windows 2003 systems because, by default, the IMAPI CD-Burning COM Service is disabled. This is because Windows 2003 is considered a server operating system, and the ability to burn CD-Rs is not considered critical. However, analysts should check all Windows systems, not only for the values within the Shell Folders key but also for the status of the IMAPI CD-Burning COM Service within the Services key, when attempting to determine whether the user could have used this functionality to exfiltrate data from the system.

# IM and P2P

IM and P2P file-sharing applications are immensely popular—a popularity that seems to cross all generations. Where people once wrote letters that took time to write and to get to the recipient, a quick e-mail can be sent and will be waiting for that person the next time he logs on. Or you can be half a world away and receive a notification the instant your friend logs in to her IM application. Or, using P2P file sharing, you can find any number of useful (or perhaps not so useful) files—music, movies, images, and more. The popularity of these applications has spawned a proliferation of various frameworks and client applications. Yahoo!, AOL, and Microsoft all have their own IM client applications, each with its own functionality and unique forensic "footprints" on a system. To top it off, you can use various third-party applications to replace those clients or even combine them into a single interface. For example, Trillian (trillian.cc) allows users to combine other IM "identities" into a single application, so they only have to log in to a single interface to access multiple IM networks. Meebo.com provides a similar, Web-based interface.

The same type of proliferation is true for P2P networks, as well. Each has its own unique challenges when it comes to forensic analysis. For example, how does an investigator identify with whom a suspect was chatting (on IM) if the application does not log conversations by default? Or how does an investigator determine whether a saved conversation was the result of the user specifically saving the conversation or the result of a third-party add-on for logging conversations? Regarding P2P, how does an investigator determine which search terms a suspect used, which files were retrieved from the sharing network, and from where the files originated?

The variation of clients for both IM and P2P is so great that they would require their own book to fully address the forensic analysis of each. When you consider that like other applications, IM and P2P clients will change between versions, including new functionality and creating new Registry keys and files, the issue of cataloguing the forensic artifacts of these applications becomes even more daunting. For example, when I was using older versions of the AOL Instant Messaging (AIM) client, there was a specific set of Registry keys within the user's profile that you could go to and see the user's encrypted password. This was the result of the user choosing to automatically log in to the AIM network without having to retype his password. If, as part of your investigation, you found it necessary to gather information about this user's activities on AIM, you could use that encrypted password to set up a similar profile on another system, then log in as that user. I decided to try out the new AIM Triton client awhile ago, and it works great, although it takes a little getting used to. One of the major interface changes was that instead of a different client window being opened for each conversation, each window is now tabbed in a single window. From a forensic perspective, however, I now open RegEdit and there are no entries for AOL or AIM beneath the HKEY_CURRENT_USER\Software hive.

To make matters worse, no effort has been made to publicly catalogue these artifacts. Over the years, forensic investigators and law enforcement have encountered situations requiring that they analyze IM and P2P artifacts, yet there haven't been any attempts to develop a database or online Wiki for these items. This is an area of research that needs to be developed.

**TIP**

Other Registry keys can be used to track user activity. For example, the ShellNoRoam\BagMRU (http://support.microsoft.com/kb/813711) key maintains information about the user's view settings and customizations for folders. This means the user has to have shell access (i.e., Windows Explorer, by default, via either the keyboard or a remote desktop application) to make these customizations. The Explorer\Streams (http://support.microsoft.com/kb/235994) and StreamMRU keys maintain information about the size and location of a window when it's closed. This indicates that the user took specific actions to modify the size and/or location of the window on the desktop, which also indicates specific user interaction with the Windows Explorer shell.

# Windows XP System Restore Points

Windows XP includes something called System Restore, which maintains a series of restore points so that should your system become unusable or start performing oddly, you can roll back the system to a previous configuration, when it was working properly. I'll readily admit to having had to do this several times myself. Every now and then I'll do ("do" usually means "install") something that ends up causing my system to start having fits. Or the installation might simply be a coincidence. Having the ability to "roll back" to a day when

I know the system was working properly is great. I'm sure that many other users have found the same to be true.

This is an extremely useful utility for users as well as for forensic investigators. After all, here's a facility that operates in the background without the user's knowledge, silently creating backups of critical system configuration information. Restore points are created based on certain triggers, such as when applications or unsigned drivers are installed, or during AutoUpdate installations. Restore points can be created manually and the System Restore service also creates restore points once a day by default.

To better understand how useful System Restore Points can be for forensic analysis, you need to understand a bit about how System Restore works: what gets backed up, what doesn't get backed up, and what Registry keys control how System Restore behaves.

System Restore restores the following items:

- Registry
- Local (not roaming) profiles
- COM+ database
- Windows File Protection DLL cache
- WMI database
- Internet Information Server (IIS) Metabase
- Files with extensions listed in the *<include>* portion of the Monitored File Extensions list in the System Restore section of the Platform SDK

System Restore *does not* restore the following:

- DRM settings
- SAM hive
- WPA settings (Windows authentication information is not restored)
- Specific directories/files listed in the Monitored File Extensions list in the System Restore section of the Platform SDK
- Any file with an extension not listed as *<included>* in the Monitored File Extensions list in the System Restore section of the Platform SDK
- User-created data stored in the user profile
- Contents of redirected folders

It is important to note that although the System Restore service does not *restore* the SAM hive, it does back it up—at least part of it, anyway. Checking the contents of the restore points, you will see copies of the SAM hive backed up, along with other Registry files.

For the purposes of this chapter, we are most interested in the System Restore Points because they contain backups of certain Registry files, such as NTUSER.DAT, SYSTEM, SOFTWARE, and SAM. Figure 4.22 illustrates the contents of the snapshot directory of a restore point, as shown in ProDiscover.

**Figure 4.22** Excerpt from ProDiscover
Showing a Restore Point Snapshot Directory

| Select | File Name | File Exten... | Size |
|---|---|---|---|
| | Repository | | |
| | ComDb | Dat | 22512 bytes |
| | domain | txt | 36 bytes |
| | _REGISTRY_MACHINE_SAM | | 24576 bytes |
| | _REGISTRY_MACHINE_SECURITY | | 45056 bytes |
| | _REGISTRY_MACHINE_SOFTWARE | | 9134080 bytes |
| | _REGISTRY_MACHINE_SYSTEM | | 4558848 bytes |
| | _REGISTRY_USER_ | DEFAULT | 241664 bytes |
| | _REGISTRY_USER_NTUSER_S-1-5-18 | | 241664 bytes |
| | _REGISTRY_USER_NTUSER_S-1-5-19 | | 229376 bytes |
| | _REGISTRY_USER_NTUSER_S-1-5-20 | | 229376 bytes |
| | _REGISTRY_USER_NTUSER_S-1-5-21... | | 679936 bytes |
| | _REGISTRY_USER_USRCLASS_S-1-5-... | | 8192 bytes |
| | _REGISTRY_USER_USRCLASS_S-1-5-... | | 8192 bytes |
| | _REGISTRY_USER_USRCLASS_S-1-5-... | | 16384 bytes |

As you can see, from a Registry analysis perspective the System Restore backs up quite a bit of very useful information. The Registry files that are backed up to the restore points are only a percentage of the size of those found in the system32\config directory, but they can still provide an investigator with valuable insight into the configuration of the system at points in the past.

We will address the files that the System Restore service backs up in Chapter 5. In this chapter, we'll focus our attention on the Registry files.

Our analysis techniques, particularly using tools such as the Offline Registry Parser, are just as effective with the Registry files located in the restore points as they are with the raw Registry files that we find in the system32\config directory. In fact, many of the keys and values we discussed in this chapter are also found in the restore point backups of the Registry files. This allows the investigator to take a peek into the past and see some of the configuration settings and installed software on the system at that time.

Some caveats about System Restore are in order, though. By default, System Restore requires that 200 MB of disk space be available on the system. If this space requirement is not met, the System Restore service will go dormant until that space becomes available. This fact could be important during an investigation if you don't see the restore points you would expect to see on the system. Some investigators might suspect that someone was able to access the System Volume Information directory and intentionally delete the restore points when in fact they had not been created.

Another thing to be aware of when working with restore points is that the SYSTEM\ControlSet00x\Control\BackupRestore key also plays a role in determining what is and what isn't backed up or restored by the System Restore service. This key has three subkeys (AsrKeysNotToRestore, FilesNotToBackup, and KeysNotToRestore) that are fairly self-explanatory. Beneath each subkey you'll see a list of Registry keys or files (in the case of the files, you'll see extensions listed with wildcards, meaning all files with that extension). These values and their data may also have an effect on what the investigator sees or has access to during a postmortem investigation.

System Restore configuration information (http://support.microsoft.com/kb/295659) is maintained in the following Registry key:

```
HKEY_LOCAL_MACHINE\SOFTWARE\Microsoft\Windows NT\CurrentVersion\SystemRestore
```

Several important values are beneath this key. The *RPGlobalInterval* value specifies how often restore points are created. The default value is 86400, which tells XP to create a restore point each calendar day (60 sec × 60 sec/hr × 24 hrs/day = 86400, or one calendar day). If the *DisableSR* value is set to 1, the System Restore functionality was disabled. By default, this value is set to 0. The *RPLifeInterval* value specifies how long restore points will be retained (7776000 seconds = 90 days).

A simple way to access information about System Restore on a *live* Windows XP system is via the *SystemRestore* (http://msdn.microsoft.com/en-us/library/aa378951.aspx) and *SystemRestoreConfig* (http://msdn.microsoft.com/en-us/library/aa378955.aspx) WMI classes. The sr.pl Perl script on the accompanying DVD provides an example of how these classes can be used. The Perl script will retrieve the System Restore configuration settings (essentially, Registry values) that are accessible via the *SystemRestoreConfig* WMI class and display information about each restore point (i.e., the sequence number, the creation date, and the string describing why the restore point was created). The information available via the *SystemRestore* class can be retrieved from files within the restore points (i.e., the rp.log file) and will be addressed in Chapter 5.

Knowing this, how are the Registry files within the restore points useful from an investigative standpoint? The Registry hive files maintained in the restore points contain much of the same information as what is on the live system itself. If you don't have a system image available and want to see what these files look like, download a copy of psexec.exe from Microsoft to a Windows XP system, then type the command **psexec –s cmd**. This opens a command prompt running as SYSTEM, which is required in order to access the

System Volume Information directory due to NTFS permissions. Change directories to the System Volume Information directory by typing:

```
cd \sys*
```

From there, proceed to the subdirectory that holds the restore points:

```
cd _restore*
```

At this point, if you request a directory listing, you should see several restore points, listed as directory names that start with *RP*. If you *cd* to one of these directories and then again to the snapshot subdirectory, you'll see the Registry files. From here, you can copy any of these files to another directory for analysis. One way to view the information in the Registry hive files is to open RegEdit and select the **HKEY_USERS** hive. Click **File | Load Hive**, and then navigate to one of the hive files you copied out of the restore point. When asked, give the hive a name, such as **test hive** or **test system** (if you're using the System file). Figure 4.23 illustrates a System hive loaded in this manner.

**Figure 4.23** System Hive from Restore Point Loaded in RegEdit

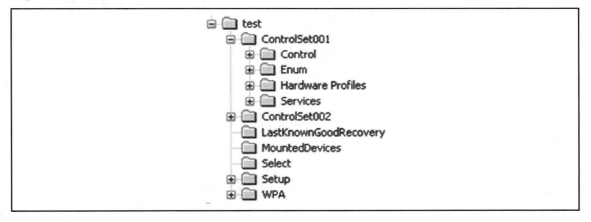

From here, you can view the contents of keys and even run tools against the Registry to extract the values and data, just as you would against a live system. You can also export values from within the hive.

Another way to do this is to use one of the RegRipper tools mentioned earlier in the chapter, called ripxp.pl. This is a specific version of rip.pl written to work with Windows XP restore points found within acquired images. Ripxp.pl works by examining a specific hive file, running one plugin against it (at this time, ripxp.pl runs only one plugin at a time, as running several plugins listed in a plugins file could lead to simply too much information being displayed), and then accessing the restore points and running the same plugin against the corresponding hive file located in those restore points. It does all of this automatically to reduce the potential for mistakes, and to increase the efficiency of the analyst.

To run ripxp.pl, some setup is required. First, mount your acquired image as a read-only file system, using any of the freeware (VDKWin or ImDisk) or commercial (Smart Mount or Mount Image Pro) utilities available for doing this; see Chapter 5 for more information about these tools. In this example, I mounted an acquired image on my test system as H:\. Next, open a command prompt and type the command **psexec –s cmd** as described earlier; again, this is required to access the restore point files within the System Volume Information directory.

At this point, it may be a good idea to open another command prompt, using the psexec.exe command already employed, and then navigate to the Restore Point directory within the mounted image, using the commands listed previously in this chapter. At this point, the output of the *dir* command on my test image looks as follows (some of the lines will wrap):

```
H:\System Volume Information\_restore{506D8C9A-F73D-497E-AAD1
FD40F23F5B51}>dir
Volume in drive H has no label.
Volume Serial Number is B0A6-5D8E

Directory of H:\System Volume Information\_restore{506D8C9A-F73D-497E-
AAD1-FD40F23F5B51}

01/30/2008   09:51 AM               130 drivetable.txt
01/30/2008   11:33 PM    <DIR>          RP0
01/30/2008   11:43 PM    <DIR>          RP1
01/30/2008   09:09 AM    <DIR>          RP2
01/30/2008   09:47 AM    <DIR>          RP3
01/30/2008   09:51 AM                24 _driver.cfg
01/30/2008   11:33 PM            22,712 _filelst.cfg
               3 File(s)         22,866 bytes
               4 Dir(s)     380,102,656 bytes free
```

So, it appears that we have three restore points within the mounted image. Now, go back to the first command prompt that we opened and navigate to the directory where you stored ripxp.pl and the plugins directory. Typing just **ripxp.pl** (or **ripxp**, if you're using the "compiled" version running on Windows) will show you the syntax for the CLI tool. We will start by running a simple query for the computer name, using the compname.pl plugin. The command you will need to enter appears as follows:

```
C:\Perl\forensics\rr>ripxp.pl -d "H:\System Volume Information\_restore
{506D8C9A-F73D-497E-AAD1-FD40F23F5B51}"
-r H:\Windows\system32\config\System -p compname
```

As you can see, it's probably a good idea to paste the complete path to the Restore Point directory from one command prompt window to another, or into a Notepad document for later use. The command is quite long, even with only three elements. As the path to the Restore Point directory contains spaces, we have to enclose the path in quotes.

What's really interesting is the output of the command, which appears as follows:

```
RipXP v.20081001
Launched Tue Jan 13 01:18:44 2009 Z

H:\Windows\system32\config\System

ComputerName = ACME-N6A1H8ZLJ1
-----------------------------------------
Restore Point Info
Description   : System Checkpoint
Type          : System Checkpoint
Creation Time : Thu Jan 31 04:33:11 2008

H:\System Volume Information\_restore{506D8C9A-F73D-497E-AAD1-FD40F23F5B51}\RP1\
snapshot\_REGISTRY_MACHINE_SYSTEM

ComputerName = ACME-N6A1H8ZLJ1
-----------------------------------------
Restore Point Info
Description   : Installed VMware Tools
Type          : Application Install
Creation Time : Thu Jan 31 04:43:38 2008

H:\System Volume Information\_restore{506D8C9A-F73D-497E-AAD1-FD40F23F5B51}\
RP2\snapshot\_REGISTRY_MACHINE_SYSTEM

ComputerName = ACME-N6A1H8ZLJ1
-----------------------------------------
Restore Point Info
Description   : Installed WinZip 11.1
Type          : Application Install
Creation Time : Wed Jan 30 14:09:49 2008

H:\System Volume Information\_restore{506D8C9A-F73D-497E-AAD1-FD40F23F5B51}\RP3\
snapshot\_REGISTRY_MACHINE_SYSTEM

ComputerName = ACME-N6A1H8ZLJ1
```

As discussed, ripxp.pl starts by running the selected plugin (compname.pl) against the selected hive file (i.e., the System hive, located in the default directory). It then accesses each restore point, parses the rp.log file (more information on the format of that file is available in Chapter 5), displays the information about the restore point (i.e., reason and date for creation), and then runs the plugin against the appropriate hive file (ripxp.pl contains code that allows it to identify the specific type of hive file).

You can run ripxp.pl against more than just a System hive file. For example, you can use the following command to run the userassist.pl plugin against an NTUSER.DAT file, as well as all corresponding NTUSER.DAT files in the restore points:

```
C:\Perl\forensics\rr>ripxp.pl -d "H:\System Volume Information\_restore{506D8C9A-
F73D-497E-AAD1-FD40F23F5B51}"
-r "H:\Documents and Settings\username\NTUSER.DAT" -p userassist
```

Or you can use a command such as the following to run the auditpol.pl plugin against all of the Security hive files, both in the system32\config directory and in the restore points:

```
C:\Perl\forensics\rr>ripxp.pl -d "H:\System Volume Information\_restore{506D8C9A-
F73D-497E-AAD1-FD40F23F5B51}"
-r H:\Windows\system32\config\Security -p auditpol
```

By now, it should be clear that you can retrieve a great deal of historical data from Windows XP System Restore Points. As an example of why you might want to use a tool such as ripxp.pl, say you are investigating a case and you suspect that a software program was deleted from the system. Setting up your analysis system as described earlier and using ripxp.pl, you may be able to use the compname.pl plugin to determine when a system's name was changed, or use the muicache.pl plugin to determine when an executable may have first been run on a system. Ripxp.pl is an extremely powerful tool that uses all of the same plugins used by RegRipper and rip.pl, and can be used to view historical data from the system, and possibly even to observe changes that occurred over time. Say, for example, that you suspect the user disabled auditing or hibernation during a specific period of time, or deleted some critical entries from his NTUSER.DAT hive file. You may be able to quickly and easily get a view into that data, adding additional insight to your examination.

# Redirection

When an analyst encounters 64-bit versions of the Windows operating system, one thing that needs to be kept in mind is that the operating system employs something called "redirection." This means on 64-bit versions of Windows, Registry data specific to 32-bit applications is maintained in a separate location in the Software hive file. Per Microsoft Knowledge Base article 305097 (http://support.microsoft.com/kb/305097), 32-bit application data is written to the following key path:

```
HKLM\Software\WOW6432Node
```

Although Registry hive files from 64-bit versions of Windows do not appear to differ at all from those of 32-bit versions of Windows on a purely binary level, differences in Registry keys, such as in the case of redirection, can cause issues with analysts looking for specific keys, or using tools such as RegRipper, and not taking this node into account.

# Virtualization

With the advent of Windows Vista, Microsoft introduced virtualization in the Registry. Prior to Vista, if an administrator installed an application that required elevated privileges to run and a regular user tried to run the application, it would fail. With Vista, Microsoft opted to employ a virtualization mechanism that allows Registry write operations that would potentially have a global impact (i.e., written to the Software hive) to be written to a per-user location. This prevents any potentially hazardous write operations to the Registry (typically the creation or modification of keys or values) from having a global impact on the system. For example, if an application attempts to write to the HKLM\Software\\*App* key, it will automatically be redirected to the following key:

```
HKEY_USERS\{User SID}_Classes\VirtualStore\Machine\Software\
```

This key, in turn, does not exist in the user's NTUSER.DAT hive file, but instead, the following file is mapped to that key when the user logs in:

```
%UserProfile%\AppData\Local\Microsoft\Windows\usrclass.dat
```

According to Mark Russinovich's TechNet article regarding Vista User Access Control (http://technet.microsoft.com/en-us/magazine/2007.06.uac.aspx), "only keys that are commonly modified by legacy applications … are virtualized." Modifications to the virtualized keys (keys such as Software\Classes, Software\Microsoft\Windows, and Software\Microsoft\Windows NT are exempted from virtualization) are redirected to the user's usrclass.dat file. This file is a valid hive file on a binary level, and can be opened by most Registry Viewers, as well as accessed via the Parse::Win32Registry Perl module. At the time of this writing, however, no RegRipper plugins that are part of the distribution were specifically designed to retrieve information from this hive file.

# Deleted Registry Keys

At the beginning of this chapter, we discussed the need for understanding the structure of Registry keys, as an examiner can find indications of keys in unallocated space, the page file, a memory dump, and so on. Knowing the structure of the keys will allow you to parse the data you find into something readable, providing context to what you've found. Another place you can locate Registry keys that aren't seen by RegEdit or other analysis tools is with the hive files themselves, in what's referred to as "unallocated space" within the hive file.

As you saw earlier in the chapter in Figure 4.3, Registry keys can be identified by the signature *nk*. In spring 2008, Jolanta Thomassen (JT) determined that the four bytes, or *DWORD*s, immediately preceding the key signature, when read as an unsigned long value (using Perl's *unpack()* function, you'll read it as *L* rather than the *V* used in many instances to *unpack() DWORD* values) will, for most valid Registry keys, be a negative number. This is true for Registry keys visible through such tools as RegEdit and others. JT also found signatures for apparently valid keys for which the preceding *DWORD* value was positive; her research revealed that these were, in fact, deleted keys, which were resident within the hive file itself.

JT's research was part of her graduate studies at the University of Liverpool. I had the opportunity to meet JT at the DFRWS 2008 conference held in Baltimore in August 2008. I also met Tim Morgan there, who was performing his own research into deleted keys in Registry hive files, completely independent of JT's work. You can find Tim's paper, titled "Recovering Deleted Data from the Windows Registry," and his presentation slides at the DFRWS 2008 conference site (www.dfrws.org/2008/program.shtml).

JT released working Perl code that will parse a hive file (extracted from an acquired image, or accessible via an image mounted as a read-only file system, or accessible via Matt Shannon's F-Response product), extracting and displaying information about deleted Registry keys and values, as well as slack space within the hive file. JT's Perl script, regslack. pl, is included in the ch4\code\jt directory on the media that accompanies this book, along with a "compiled" Windows PE version of the tool.

To run regslack.pl, simply type the following at the command prompt:

```
C:\perl\jt>regslack.pl d:\cases\SAM > sam.txt
```

Regslack.pl doesn't require any additional Perl modules, so it can be run as a Perl script using nothing more than the basic Perl installation from ActiveState.com. The preceding command redirects the output of the script from the console to a file named sam.txt. I recommend that you do something like this because the script has a considerable amount of information that it sends to the console, so capturing that information in a file makes it easier to view, as well as preserves it for later review. An excerpt of the sam.txt file, illustrating a recovered Registry key from the SAM file, is shown here:

```
SAM\SAM\Domains\Account\Users\000003F7
Offset: 0x4ed8 [Thu Sep 13 12:31:00 2007]
Number of values: 2
Offset: 0x5a30 -->REG_BINARY; F;
02 00 01 00 00 00 00 00 84 56 8d 99 7a 69 c8 01 .........V..zi..
00 00 00 00 00 00 00 00 04 d4 d7 ad 73 51 c8 01 ................sQ..
00 00 00 00 00 00 00 00 34 e9 55 e2 81 53 c8 01 ........4.U..S..
f8 03 00 00 01 02 00 00 10 02 00 00 00 00 00 00 ................
00 00 c7 01 01 00 00 00 00 00 ff ff eb 06 91 7c ..............|
Offset: 0x4330 -->REG_BINARY; V;
```

In this case, regslack.pl located a deleted Registry key that pertains to a user, as well as the contents of both the *F* and *V* values (the *V* value name is displayed, but for the sake of brevity, the entire binary contents of the value data are not displayed). The preceding output shows the name of the key with the full path recovered, the offset at which the key was found, as well as the *LastWrite* time of the key. In addition to the value names and data, the offsets to the values themselves are also displayed, allowing for visual verification. Regslack.pl also displays slack space from within the hive file.

Extracting this type of data as part of an examination can be extremely revealing. As you've seen throughout this chapter, a number of keys and values within the Registry can provide clues to the presence of malware, user activities, and so on. Intruders may delete Registry keys to attempt to cover their tracks, and users may try to hide indicators of unauthorized activity. However, in some instances, even if the Registry keys themselves are deleted, you may be able to recover those keys from within the hive file itself.

# Summary

Knowing how to navigate the Registry for specific information can prove to be an extremely valuable skill for administrators, consultants, and forensic analysts. The Registry will gladly spill forth its secrets to those who know where to look and how to interpret the information they find. Digging into the depths of the Registry is not unlike Indiana Jones tracking down ancient secrets in the shifting sands of time.

You can find a comprehensive (for obvious reasons, I am extremely hesitant to use the word *complete*) list of autostart locations and user MRU lists within the Registry in the regref.xls spreadsheet included on the accompanying media. This list should be considered a starting point, albeit a comprehensive one, for the reader. The Registry keys listed were retrieved from online lists, applications such as Autoruns, reports of malware on antivirus Web sites, and through personal experimentation.

This chapter should not be considered a complete reference of all the various Registry keys that might be of importance to a specific case. Registry keys with similar functionality differ in name and location between applications and, in some cases, between versions of the same application. No book can be considered a complete authoritative reference resource for Registry keys of interest; it would be far too large and expensive and then almost immediately out of date as soon as it was published. The purpose of this chapter is to illustrate what information is available and how to go about finding additional information.

# DVD Contents

The media that accompanies this book includes a directory specifically for this chapter. That directory includes several subdirectories, one that contains the code presented in this chapter, in particular the RegRipper distribution (including rip.pl and all of the plugins, and as stated, ripxp.pl is not included). The media also includes all Perl scripts from the first edition of the book (in the "old" subdirectory), as well as the ProScripts (Perl scripts specifically written to be used with the ProDiscover forensic analysis application) discussed in the chapter. The "spreadsheet" subdirectory includes a copy of the Registry reference spreadsheet that I compiled a bit ago. This spreadsheet lists several Registry keys and values of interest to forensic analysts as well as a brief description of their purpose and, where applicable, references. The spreadsheet is split up into different worksheets, each covering a specific area of functionality.

There is also a "samples" subdirectory that includes several Registry files from real systems—not only those found in the system32\config directory, but also those from restore points. I encourage you to look at these files, open them in a hex editor, and use any of the tools included in the code subdirectory for this chapter so that you can develop a familiarity with the tools as well as with the raw Registry files themselves.

# Solutions Fast Track

## Inside the Registry

☑ The Windows Registry is a binary, hierarchical database of configuration information that not only controls various operating system and application configuration settings, but also maintains information about various aspects of the user's interaction with the system.

☑ By understanding the format of the various Registry structures (i.e., keys and values) you can then parse and view portions of the Registry found in memory and unallocated space.

☑ Some portions of the Registry are volatile, created when the system is started, and will not be found in an acquired image of a system.

☑ Registry keys (and some values) have time stamps associated with them that can be used in timeline analysis. For this reason, the Registry can be considered a log file of sorts.

☑ There is no apparent standard for the way information is maintained in the Registry. Some MRU keys, for example, maintain their value data as binary types, others as ASCII strings (making searches for ASCII strings somewhat easy). Other Registry keys have their value names obfuscated with ROT-13 "encryption" or their value data maintained in such a way as to hamper string searches. You need to understand the structure of the specific key and value to parse the data stored in that location.

☑ Tools are available to track accesses and modifications to the Registry on a live system; this information can be used to locate Registry keys of interest as well as determine artifacts left by applications and user activity.

## Registry Analysis

☑ A number of locations within the Registry contain information pertinent to most investigations. Other locations contain information pertinent to specific types of investigations, such as intrusions, fraud, or abuse of acceptable use policies.

☑ Some specific Registry keys and values can be of importance to an investigation, but often it is the correlation of several Registry keys and values that can provide the most complete picture.

☑ Windows XP System Restore Points maintain portions of the Registry that can be useful during an investigation. For example, examining the contents of the preserved SAM file, an investigator might be able to determine when a user's group membership changed (e.g., going from the User to the Administrators group), if that is pertinent to the investigation. You might also be able to tell what applications were installed on the system in the recent past.

# Frequently Asked Questions

**Q:** How do I determine whether there are any browser helper objects (BHOs) installed and what they are?

**A:** BHOs are maintained in the HKEY_LOCAL_MACHINE hive, which means they affect all users on the system. The BHOs are listed under the Software\Microsoft\ Windows\CurrentVersion\Explorer\Browser Helper Objects key. Beneath this key, each BHO will be listed as a GUID-named subkey. From there, go to the Software\Classes\ CLSID key in the HKEY_LOCAL_MACHINE hive and locate each GUID. Once you locate the key with the same GUID as the BHO, check the *Default* value of that key for the name of the BHO. To get the DLL for the BHO, check the *Default* value of the InProcServer subkey. The Perl script bho.pl that is included on the accompanying DVD can be used to retrieve BHOs from a local system.

**Q:** During a search of a system, I found a Registry key in the user's hive (Software\ Microsoft\Windows\CurrentVersion\Internet Settings\ZoneMap\Domains) that had a number of subkeys with the domains of Web sites. What is this key, and what do the subkeys represent?

**A:** You can add these entries to Internet Explorer by going to **Tools | Internet Options | Restricted Sites** and clicking the **Sites** button. However, look closely at the sites listed, because some malware will add sites to this key so that the user cannot access those Web sites. Although entries within this key might indicate Administrator activity or Group Policies, they could also indicate a malware infection.

**Q:** During an investigation, it became clear, based on information from a Windows XP system (installed software, etc.), that the user had Local Administrator rights on the system. In discussing this with the IT director, it was revealed that all users are provided with only User-level access to their systems. How can I track down when the user was added to the Administrators group on the system?

**A:** This sort of information about users is maintained in the SAM file. The *LastWrite* time on the Registry key that maintains group membership information could provide you with some clues. In addition, there could be enough historical data in the Windows XP System Restore Points for you to locate the last time the user's RID was associated with the User group and not the Administrators group.

# Chapter 5

# File Analysis

## Solutions in this chapter:

- **Log Files**
- **File Metadata**
- **Alternative Methods of Analysis**

☑ **Summary**

☑ **Solutions Fast Track**

☑ **Frequently Asked Questions**

# Introduction

Windows systems maintain quite a number of files that are useful from a forensic perspective. In fact, many investigators might not realize the wealth of data they can find within some of the files that Windows systems use to track various activity and functions. Knowing multiple locations where information is maintained within the system allows an investigator to corroborate information that is found in other areas and reduce the amount of uncertainty in their analysis. In this chapter, we'll discuss some of the various files, including log files, you can find on Windows systems as well as information about files in general, along with other specific files that could be of value to an investigator. We will discuss a number of apparently different aspects that are tied together by the fact that they all reside within files or the file system, whether in a human-readable ASCII format or in a cryptic binary format.

# Log Files

Windows systems maintain log files for a number of events and actions that may be relevant to an analyst. Besides application log files, which maintain logs of events with respect to specific applications, the Windows operating system also maintains a number of logs. In this chapter, we'll examine the log files most relevant to analysis, the most notable of which is perhaps the Windows Event Log.

## Event Logs

The Event Logs are perhaps the most well-known logs on Windows systems, the rough equivalent of syslog on Linux systems. The Event Logs record a variety of day-to-day events that occur on Windows systems and are configurable (as discussed in Chapter 4) to record a range of additional events. These events are split into categories that are implemented through the various Event Logs themselves, such as Security, System, and Application Event Logs. The Event Logs can provide a good deal of information that's useful for troubleshooting issues as well as for understanding events during forensic analysis.

## Tip

On most Windows systems, you can use the Resource Kit tool auditpol.exe to query and set the audit policy. On Windows XP SP2 and 2003 SP1, auditusr. exe allows for per-user audit policies. For example, logon auditing can be set for all users, but more detailed auditing can be enabled for a specific user. Changes made with auditusr.exe modify the HKEY_LOCAL_MACHINE\SYSTEM\ CurrentControlSet\Control\Lsa\Audit\PerUserAuditing\System Registry key. The use of this tool can give the investigator an indication of the types of events she should expect to see in the Event Log as well as an indication of the technical skill level of the user or administrator.

# Understanding Events

On the Windows NT family of operating systems, from Windows 2000 through XP and 2003, the Event Logs consist of a binary structure, with a header and a series of event records stored in the file. Based on the way the operating system was designed, when certain events, such as a user logging on or off, occur, a record of these events is generated. Some events are recorded by default; others are recorded based on the audit configuration maintained in the PolAdtEv Registry key, as discussed in Chapter 4. Other aspects of the event log configuration (file size, how long records are retained, etc.) are maintained in the following Registry key:

```
HKEY_LOCAL_MACHINE\SYSTEM\CurrentControlSet\Services\Eventlog\<Event Log>
```

By default, Windows 2000, XP, and 2003 all have Application, Security, and System Event Logs. Systems that are configured as domain controllers will also have File Replication and Directory Service Event Logs, and systems configured as domain name system (DNS) servers will have DNS Event Logs. Other systems may have application-specific Event Log files, as well.

Administrators are most familiar with interacting with the Event Logs through the Event Viewer, which is a graphical user interface (GUI) manager for the Event Logs. When the administrator views an event record on Windows XP, he will see something similar to what appears in Figure 5.1.

**Figure 5.1** Windows XP Event Record Viewed in the Event Viewer

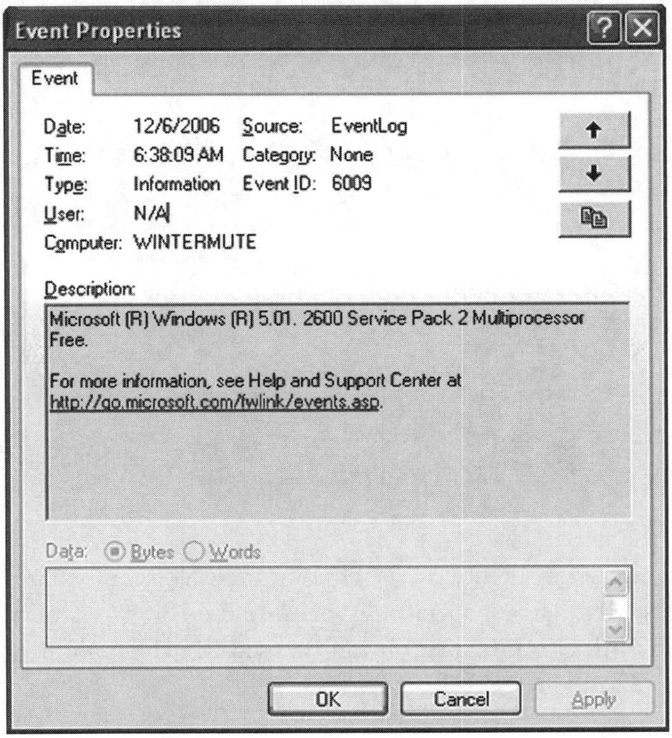

When the Event Viewer opens an event record, it populates the *Description*: field by reading the strings values from the event record, then locating the appropriate message file (dynamic link library, or DLL) on the system. The message files contain message strings that are used to support internationalization on the Windows operating systems, and the strings values from the event records are inserted into the appropriate locations within those strings. This allows for the internationalization of the Event Logs by providing event message strings in the language native to the system (English, German, French, or the like) and simply "filling in the gaps" with the necessary information (system name, date/time stamp, etc.). This shows a tight correlation among the Event Log, the Windows Registry, and many of the DLLs on the system. It also means third-party applications that write to the Event Log will need to include their own message files.

Prior to Windows 2003, logon events would contain only the NetBIOS name of the system from which the logon originated. Beginning with Windows 2003, the Security Event Log records both the workstation name and the Internet Protocol (IP) address of the system, as Figure 5.2 illustrates.

**Figure 5.2** Windows 2003 Event Record Showing IP Address

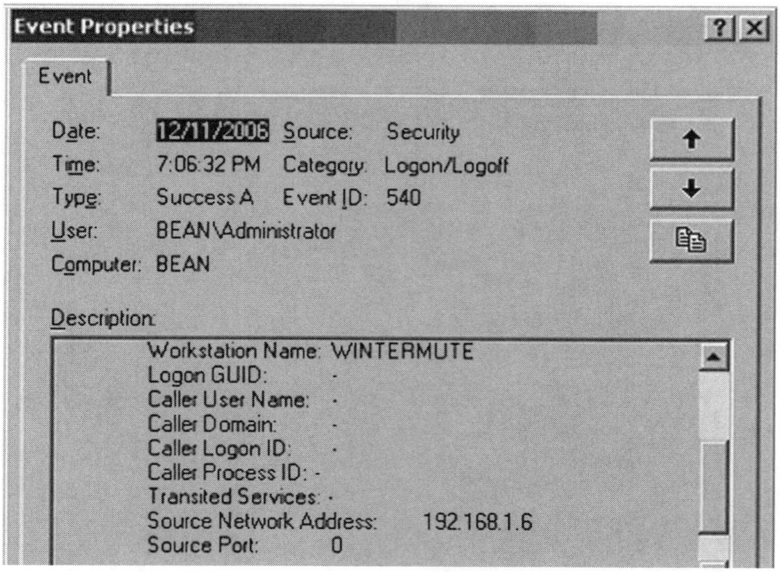

The information shown in Figure 5.2 (such as Source Network Address) can be extremely useful during an investigation, most specifically because the IP address of the remote system is visible in the event record. This information can be used to determine the source of logons and logon attempts.

Even without the DLL message files it is not difficult to tell what the different event records pertain to, because there is other identifying information in the record. In Figure 5.2, for example, we see an event ID, an event source, and other information we can use to sort on when analyzing event records. There is also a date/time stamp that we can use for time-line analysis; actually, there are two date/time stamps in an event record (as we'll discuss later in the chapter). Microsoft provides a good deal of information regarding some of the event records that you are likely to see. For example, if auditing and logging of logon/logoff events are enabled (see Chapter 4 for how to determine this from an acquired image), the investigator should see event IDs 528 (successful logon) and 538 (logoff) in the Security Event Log. If he sees several event records all with event ID 528, he will want to check the logon type, because there are nine different logon type codes. Table 5.1 lists the various security logon type codes for successful logons and what they mean.

**Table 5.1** Event Logon Types

| Logon Type | Title | Description |
| --- | --- | --- |
| 2 | *Interactive* | This logon type indicates that the user logged in at the console |
| 3 | *Network* | A user/computer logged in to this computer from the network, such as via *net use*, accessing a network share, or a successful *net view* directed at a network share. (This has been replaced by Event ID 540) |
| 4 | *Batch* | Reserved for applications that run as batches |
| 5 | *Service* | Service logon |
| 6 | *Proxy* | Not supported |
| 7 | *Unlock* | The user unlocked the workstation |
| 8 | *NetworkClearText* | A user logged on to a network, and the user's credentials were passed in an unencrypted form |
| 9 | *NewCredentials* | A process or thread cloned its current token but specified new credentials for outbound connections |

**Continued**

**Table 5.1 Continued.** Event Logon Types

| Logon Type | Title | Description |
|---|---|---|
| 10 | *RemoteInteractive* | Logon using Terminal Services or a Remote Desktop connection |
| 11 | *CachedInteractive* | A user logged on to the computer with credentials that were stored locally on the computer (domain controller may have been unavailable to verify credentials) |
| 12 | *CachedRemoteInteractive* | Same as *RemoteInteractive*, used internally for auditing purposes |
| 13 | *CachedUnlock* | The logon attempt is to unlock a workstation |

From a more general perspective, Microsoft provides Knowledge Base articles 299475 (http://support.microsoft.com/kb/299475) and 301677 (http://support.microsoft.com/kb/301677) that list Windows 2000 Security Event descriptions. The security events are listed with a brief description as well as placeholders (%1, %2, etc.) where the strings from the event record are inserted.

**TIP**

Event ID 540 (network logon) was introduced in Windows 2000 and means the same thing as, and replaces, event ID 528 type 3 (successful logon from the network). Incident responders operating in an enterprise environment may encounter event records that refer to Kerberos, such as event ID 672. Microsoft Knowledge Base article 301677 (http://support.microsoft.com/kb/301677) provides information about these event IDs for Windows 2000, and Knowledge Base article 274176 (http://support.microsoft.com/kb/274176) describes how to associate an account logon event with a process creation event, such as when a service is started with a user account on Windows XP. The event ID 672 records include a client IP address, which may be useful information during an examination.

With Vista and Windows 2008, the logon events were collapsed back down to a single event ID (4624). Microsoft Knowledge Base article 947226 (http://support.microsoft.com/kb/947226) provides a list of security event IDs for Vista and Windows 2008, and describes a method for obtaining more detailed information about events through the use of wevtutil.exe.

For other event records, many sites provide detailed information regarding event record details, why the events are generated, and so on. For detailed information regarding specific entries in the Application Event Log, you might need to check with the vendor. One of the best sites I've found for gaining an understanding of what's in the event records is EventID.net. Some information is available from the EventID.net site without a subscription, but if you're spending a great deal of time investigating event records of different types, that subscription fee is well worth the additional information and trouble saved in Googling. In many instances, you simply need to provide the event ID in question and you'll be given information about the event, as generated by various sources, as well as links to references. For example, if I search for event ID 6009, I get four different event sources. From there, I can click the details for the one I want (in this case, the event source is *EventLog*) and I get commentary from two authors as well as three links to the Microsoft site that provide detailed information regarding the event ID. In this case, in fairly short order, I see that the event ID is generated when a Windows system is booted (so the time that the event record was generated approximates to the time that the system was booted) and that information about the operating system version is written to the *Description* field of the event.

**T**ɪᴘ

The event ID 6009 record from source *EventLog* can be used to determine or verify the operating system of the host system as well as the system name. The *Computer:* entry will contain the host name, and the *Description* of the event record will contain a string that identifies the version of the Windows operating system.

Besides EventID.net, an excellent source of information on Windows event logging is Eric Fitzgerald's Windows Security Logging and Other Esoterica blog (http://blogs.msdn.com/ericfitz/default.aspx). Eric's blog contains a great deal of very useful information regarding Event Logs, including how they can be used to meet Visa's Payment Card Industry (PCI) compliance standards, as well as auditing tips and tricks. I have found a wealth of information on Eric's blog, such as a description of logon type 0, as well as how to get detailed security event information for Windows Vista and Windows 2008 Security events. Microsoft also has the Events and Errors Message Center: Advanced Search site (www.microsoft.com/technet/support/ee/ee_advanced.aspx) that you can use to gather information about various Event Log entries.

> **TIP**
>
> Remember discussing artifacts of USB removable storage devices in Chapter 4? In Windows 2000, whenever a USB removable storage device was connected to a system the Removable Storage Service generated an event record with ID 134. When the device was removed, it generated an event ID of 135. These events are no longer visible as of Windows XP, and Knowledge Base article 329463 (http://support.microsoft.com/kb/329463/en-us) provides a clue as to the reason. The article notes that once the hotfix is installed:
>
> *"… Netshell no longer listens for Plug and Play device arrival notifications. Therefore, you are not notified about new devices."*
>
> So, you should not expect to see notifications in the Event Log that USB removable storage devices have been inserted or removed.

Also, you might want to drop by Randy Franklin's UltimateWindowsSecurity.com site; he has pages dedicated specifically to the Windows Security Event Log, including an event ID reference sheet and an encyclopedia (www.ultimatewindowssecurity.com/encyclopedia.aspx). With regard to the Security Event Log, this site is well worth a visit and a bookmark.

# Event Log File Format

At times during an investigation you might need to examine the contents of an Event Log .evt file in an understandable format. (The Event Log format discussed in this section pertains to the versions of the Windows operating system from Windows 2000 through 2003, and does not cover Vista.) So, you extract the .evt file from an acquired image, and you figure that you just open the file in the Event Viewer. Or you may try using a tool such as the Event Log Explorer (www.eventlogxp.com/), rather than the native Event Viewer. However, when you attempt to do so, you get an error message telling you that the Event Log is "corrupt." At other times you might be searching through unallocated clusters in an image, looking for some information that could be useful to your case. In either situation, knowing the details of the structure of the Event Log file can be extremely valuable.

The Windows Event Log (for Windows 2000, XP, and 2003) is a binary format with distinct, recognizable features that can assist an investigator in recognizing and interpreting Event Log files or simply event records on a system, either in files or located in unallocated space. Each Event Log consists of a header section and a series of event records, both of which we will discuss in detail. The Event Log is maintained as a circular buffer, so as new event records are added to the file, older event records are cycled out of the file.

# Event Log Header

The Event Log header is contained in the first 48 bytes of a valid Event Log file. If the .evt file has not been corrupted in any way, the header will appear similar to the sample Event Log header in Figure 5.3.

**Figure 5.3** Event Log Header

```
00000000h: 30 00 00 00 4C 66 4C 65 01 00 00 00 01 00 00 00 ; 0...LfLe........
00000010h: 30 00 00 00 F0 A9 00 00 AD 00 00 00 01 00 00 00 ; 0...ö©..-.......
00000020h: 00 00 01 00 09 00 00 00 80 3A 09 00 30 00 00 00 ; ........€:..0...
```

The Event Log header consists of 12 distinct *DWORD* values. Table 5.2 lists nine of those values and provides a brief description of each.

**Table 5.2** Event Log Header Structure

| Offset | Size | Description |
|---|---|---|
| 0 | 4 bytes | Size of the record; for an .evt file header, the size is 0x30 (48) bytes. Event record sizes are 56 bytes |
| 4 | 4 bytes | Magic number (*LfLe*) |
| 16 | 4 bytes | Offset within the .evt file of the oldest event record |
| 20 | 4 bytes | Offset within the .evt file to the next event record to be written |
| 24 | 4 bytes | ID of the next event record |
| 28 | 4 bytes | ID of the oldest event record |
| 32 | 4 bytes | Maximum size of the .evt file (from the Registry) |
| 40 | 4 bytes | Retention time of event records (from the Registry) |
| 44 | 4 bytes | Size of the record (repeat of *DWORD* at offset 0) |

The value of importance in the header is the "magic number," which appears as *LfLe* beginning at the fourth byte (the second *DWORD*) in the header. This value is unique to the Windows Event Log (for Windows 2000, XP, and 2003) and is associated with event records. Microsoft refers to this value as the *ELF_LOG_SIGNATURE*. (A description of the event record structure at the Microsoft site states that this is "a *DWORD* value that is always set to *ELF_LOG_SIGNATURE*.") Notice that the size of the record (for the header, 0x30, or 48 bytes) brackets the header, appearing at both the beginning and the end of the header record. This allows the investigator to either programmatically (using code) or manually (using a hex editor) locate the header (or an event record), whether looking at an Event Log file, unallocated space, or a file of unknown type. The ID numbers for the next event record to be written and the oldest event record can be used to determine the total number of event records that the investigator should expect to see.

---

**NOTE**

When we're working with files, we use the term *magic number* to refer to a specific series of bytes within the file that are unique to that file or file type. These magic numbers are used in performing file signature analysis, a technique used to determine whether a file has the correct file extension based on its magic number. In the case of Event Log files, the magic number is 0x654c664c, or as shown in Figure 5.3, 4C 66 4C 65. Even though this series of bytes translates to the string *LfLe* when the endianness is reversed, it is still referred to as a magic number.

---

The values for the maximum size of the Event Log file and the retention time of event records are taken from the Registry of the system where the Event Logs are maintained.

# Event Record Structure

Event records have some structure values in common with the Event Log header, but event records contain much more information, as illustrated in Figure 5.4. However, the basic header for an event record is somewhat larger than the header of the Event Log itself (as described above), weighing in at 56 bytes. Although the record size provided in the event record (0xF4, or 244 bytes) is larger than 56 bytes, the first 56 bytes of the event record constitute an event record header.

**Figure 5.4** Sample Event Record Structure

```
00000030h: F4 00 00 00 4C 66 4C 65 01 00 00 00 3D E1 20 43 ; ó...LfLe....⌐á C
00000040h: 3D E1 20 43 64 02 00 00 08 00 15 00 06 00 00 00 ; ⌐á Cd...........
00000050h: 00 00 00 00 72 00 00 00 1C 00 00 00 56 00 00 00 ; ....r.......V...
00000060h: 00 00 00 00 EE 00 00 00 53 00 65 00 63 00 75 00 ; ....î...S.e.c.u.
```

As you can see, the Event Log magic number appears in the second *DWORD* value of the event record, just as it does for the header. Table 5.3 provides details of the content of the first 56 bytes of an event record.

**Table 5.3** Event Record Structure

| Offset | Size | Description |
| --- | --- | --- |
| 0 | 4 bytes | Length of the event record, or size of the record in bytes |
| 4 | 4 bytes | Reserved; magic number |
| 8 | 4 bytes | Record number |
| 12 | 4 bytes | Time generated; measured in UNIX time, or the number of seconds elapsed since 00:00:00 1 Jan 1970, in Universal Coordinated Time (UTC) |
| 16 | 4 bytes | Time written; measured in UNIX time, or the number of seconds elapsed since 00:00:00 1 Jan 1970, in UTC |
| 20 | 4 bytes | Event ID, which is specific to the event source and uniquely identifies the event; the event ID is used along with the source name to locate the appropriate description string within the message file for the event source |
| 24 | 2 bytes | Event type (0x01 = Error; 0x10 = Failure; 0x08 = Success; 0x04 = Information; 0x02 = Warning) |
| 26 | 2 bytes | Number of strings |
| 28 | 2 bytes | Event category |
| 30 | 2 bytes | Reserved flags |
| 32 | 4 bytes | Closing record number |
| 36 | 4 bytes | String offset; offset to the description strings within this event record |
| 40 | 4 bytes | Length of the user Security Identifier (SID); size of the user SID in bytes (if 0, no user SID is provided) |
| 44 | 4 bytes | Offset to the user SID within this event record |
| 48 | 4 bytes | Data length; length of the binary data associated with this event record |
| 52 | 4 bytes | Offset to the data |

Table 5.3 illustrates the first 56 bytes of an event record. Keep in mind that the actual length of the record itself is listed in the first and last *DWORD*s of the record. (The size of the record brackets the actual record, just as it does with the file header.) With this information in hand, it is a relatively straightforward process to parse through the contents of an Event Log file, extracting and displaying the event records.

Having the event record structure definition also makes it possible to reassemble partial event records found in unallocated space. Using the magic number as a guide post, an analyst can search through unallocated space; should she locate the magic number, all she has to do is read the preceding *DWORD* for the size of the event record, then extract that number of bytes for the full event record. Even if the entire event record is not available, the first 56 bytes will provide a road map for reconstructing portions of an event record.

## Tools & Traps...

### Reading Event Logs

Once, I was assisting with a case in which an analyst who is extremely familiar with Linux was using PyFlag (www.pyflag.net) as his forensic analysis tool. He decided that he wanted me to open the Event Logs and retrieve available records; he'd tried to do so, but when he copied the .evt files to his Windows desktop system and tried to open the files with Event Viewer, he received a message that the files were corrupted.

I had already been researching the Event Log and event record structure, so I tweaked my Perl script just a bit and parsed through the Event Log files, retrieving all the event records with no problems whatsoever. However, I found a disparity between the information I was receiving from the header of one of the Event Logs and what I was seeing in the output of the event records; no matter how I approached the situation, I always had one more complete event record than the header information was telling me I should have. After investigating this issue for some time, I determined that according to the application program interface (API), a section of the Event Log just preceding the first record was a buffer area left over from when the Event Log was cleared. This buffer area was not read by the API, and if the system had been allowed to continue normally, it would have been flushed out of the circular buffer as new event records were written to the file. However, this buffer contained one complete event record; because the tool I was using did not use the API to retrieve event records but instead read through the file in binary mode, parsing the information it found, the tool didn't recognize this buffer area.

**Continued**

> Although the "lost" event record did not have a significant impact on the case, it did show the usefulness (with regard to forensic analysis) of understanding the format of certain files on Windows systems, and where possible, developing tools that parse through the information in those files in a manner that does not rely on the Windows API. Not only does this provide the investigator with the possibility of discovering "hidden" information, but it also allows the investigator to perform analysis on platforms other than Windows (particularly on Linux); investigators are not restricted to analyzing Windows images on a Windows platform.

The ch5\code\EVT directory on the accompanying DVD contains several Perl scripts that allow you to collect information from Event Log files from Windows 2000, XP, and 2003 systems. Evtstats.pl displays simple statistics collected from an .evt file, as shown here:

```
C:\Perl\forensics\evt2xls>evtstats.pl d:\cases\evt\secevent.evt
Max Size of the Event Log file              = 65536 bytes
Actual Size of the Event Log file           = 65536 bytes
Total number of event records (header info) = 172
Total number of event records (actual count) = 260
Total number of event records (rec_nums)    = 260
Total number of event records (sources)     = 260
Total number of event records (types)       = 260
Total number of event records (IDs)         = 260
```

The script parses the header of the Event Log file and determines the number of records that should exist, then parses through the contents of the Event Log file itself and, using various tags from within each event record, performs an actual count of the number of event records found within the Event Log file.

**TIP**

To install the code within the ch5\code\EVT directory on your system, simply copy all of the files within the directory to your analysis system. If you're going to use the Perl scripts, be sure to have Perl installed and to keep the ReadEvt.pm Perl module within the same directory as the scripts. Alternatively, you can use the executable files, but you will need to keep the DLL in the same directory as the EXE files.

The evtrpt.pl Perl script displays additional statistics about an Event Log file:

```
C:\Perl\forensics\evt2xls>evtrpt.pl d:\cases\evt\secevent.evt
EVT file parsed: d:\cases\evt\secevent.evt (65536 bytes)
```

```
Total number of event records counted: 260
------------------------------------------------------------
Event Source/ID Frequency

Source                              Event ID    Count
----------                          --------    -----
Security                                 513        4
Security                                 514       28
Security                                 515       34
Security                                 518        4
Security                                 520        3
Security                               528,2        7
Security                               528,5       35
Security                               529,2        7
Security                               538,2        5
Security                               538,3        8
Security                               540,3       12
Security                                 551        7
Security                                 576       42
Security                                 612        5
Security                                 615        5
Security                                 680       14
Security                                 806        4
Security                                 848        4
Security                                 849        4
Security                                 850       28
Total: 260
------------------------------

Event Type Frequency
Type              Count
----------        -----
AUDIT_SUCCESS       245
AUDIT_FAILURE        15
Total: 260
------------------------------

Date Range (UTC)
Fri Sep 9 01:11:25 2005 to Tue Sep 27 00:38:58 2005
```

I use evtrpt.pl quite often when I'm conducting Event Log analysis. I usually start by parsing the Security hive file for the audit policy (see Chapter 4) to see what types of events I should expect to see within the Event Log, as well as determining whether auditing is enabled. From there, I tend to run evtrpt.pl against the Event Log file (extracted from the acquired image) to determine the frequency of the different event IDs and sources within the Event Log file, as well as determine the date range of the events within the Event Log. The time field that evtrpt.pl collects is the time at which the event was generated (as opposed to when it was written), and this will let me know whether there are event records within the log file that fall within the time window for the incident in question. This can be very revealing with respect to the various Event Logs, particularly if the Application Event Log contains events generated by the antivirus application.

Another Perl script, lsevt.pl, uses the ReadEvt.pm Perl module to parse through the Event Log file and display event records in a simple listing format, as illustrated here:

```
Record Number        : 251
Source               : Security
Computer Name        : PETER
Event ID             : 528
Event Type           : EVENTLOG_AUDIT_SUCCESS
Time Generated       : Mon Sep 26 23:37:51 2005
Time Written         : Mon Sep 26 23:37:51 2005
SID                  : S-1-5-21-839522115-1801674531-2147200963-1003
Message Str          : Harlan PETER (0x0,0x141B9C) 2 User32    Negotiate PETER
                       {00000000-0000-0000-0000-000000000000}
Record Number        : 252
Source               : Security
Computer Name        : PETER
Event ID             : 576
Event Type           : EVENTLOG_AUDIT_SUCCESS
Time Generated       : Mon Sep 26 23:37:51 2005
Time Written         : Mon Sep 26 23:37:51 2005
SID                  : S-1-5-21-839522115-1801674531-2147200963-1003
Message Str          :(0x0,0x141B9C) SeChangeNotifyPrivilege
                             SeBackupPrivilege
                             SeRestorePrivilege
                             SeDebugPrivilege
```

Lsevt.pl includes parsing of the user's SID (where applicable) into a format that is readable and can be correlated with other data (e.g., from the Registry) during analysis.

Lsevt2.pl provides a bit more flexibility than lsevt.pl in that it allows you to choose to output the format as comma-separated values (CSVs). This way, the investigator can run the script against a Windows Event Log file using the following command line:

```
C:\Perl>lsevt2.pl -f d:\cases\appevent.evt -c > testevt.csv
```

She can then open the resultant testevt.csv file in Excel for sorting, searching, and analysis. Further, lsevt2.pl is a stand–alone script and does not require the use of the ReadEvt.pm Perl module. However, lsevt2.pl does not translate the user's SID into a more recognizable format.

Evt2xls.pl is a Perl script that reads through the Event Log file, extracting all of the event records, parses them, and writes them to a spreadsheet format that is binary–compatible with Microsoft Excel. This allows you to open the spreadsheet and sort on various fields, such as the event source (e.g., to show all Application Popup event records) or event ID. To use evt2xls.pl, you need to specify several options at the command line; for example:

```
C:\perl>evt2xls.pl -e d:\cases\evt\secevent.evt -o d:\cases\secevent.xls
```

The preceding command line uses the *–e* switch to specify an Event Log file to be read, and the *–o* switch specifies the location and name of the output spreadsheet file. Simply typing **evt2xls.pl** at the command line, with no arguments, will display the syntax usage information. For example, the *–r* switch will allow you to specify the location of a report file, similar to what is generated by evtrpt.pl. Also, the *–x* switch allows you to specify a comma–separated list of event IDs that you'd like to skip or leave out of the resultant spreadsheet. This was originally intended for large Event Logs that had more than 65,535 entries, as some versions of Microsoft Excel are limited to that number of rows per worksheet. However, Excel 2007 apparently does not contain this limitation, and other spreadsheet applications, such as the one that is part of OpenOffice (www.openoffice.org/), should have no trouble opening the file. Further, evt2xls.pl uses the Spreadsheet::WriteExcel Perl module to create the spreadsheet, and the Spreadsheet::Read or Spreadsheet::ParseExcel module can be used to extract data from the output spreadsheet.

---

**TIP**

Rob Faber wrote an excellent article titled "Windows log forensics: did you cover your tracks?" for the April 2008 edition of *INSECURE* magazine (Issue 16, available from www.net-security.org/dl/insecure/INSECURE-Mag-16.pdf). In the article, Rob presents some excellent information that can be used in a wide range of examinations. It's well worth printing this issue of *INSECURE* magazine, if not for the entire magazine, then just for Rob's article.

---

All of these Perl scripts parse through the Event Log files in binary mode, bypassing the Windows API altogether. This way, not only can the Event Log files be parsed on a platform other than Windows (Mac OS X, Linux, etc.), but an investigator can still parse the Event Log files even if the Event Viewer gives him error messages that the file is somehow corrupted. Several of the scripts do require the use of the ReadEvt.pm Perl module that is also included on the accompanying DVD.

---

### WARNING

In February 2007, Andreas Schuster blogged about a special condition regarding Event Log records, in which a record is written to the end of the .evt file but wraps around to the beginning of the file so that part of the record follows the header. This record will be incorrectly read by tools (such as the Perl scripts listed in this chapter) that look for the event record magic number, because only part of the record will be identified. Andreas was kind enough to provide an example .evt file so that parsers can be tested (and improved) against this condition (you can find the blog post and sample test file at http://computer.forensikblog.de/en/2007/02/a_common_misconception.html).

---

# Vista Event Logs

A lot about the Windows operating system has changed with the advent of Vista, including the Event Log structure used by the operating system. For example, this service is now referred to as Windows Event Log rather than Event Logging, and it takes on a whole new format for the saved event records. Vista uses an XML format for storing events, and now supports central collection of event records.

Other changes include the fact that although Vista still maintains the three main categories of event log (Application, Security, and System), it now has a wide range of categories under which different events can be logged, as Figure 5.5 illustrates.

**Figure 5.5** Vista Event Viewer

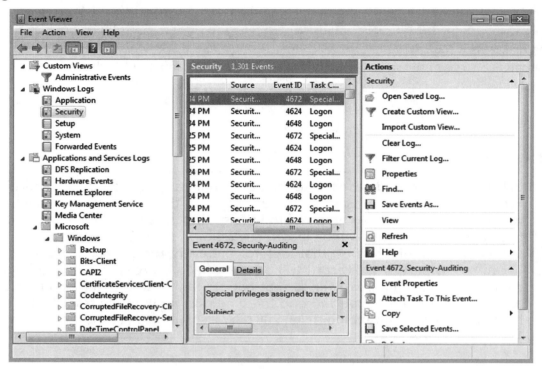

As Figure 5.5 illustrates, there are now more Event Logs, including one for Internet Explorer as well as Hardware Events. (Installing the new Internet Explorer Version 7 also adds an Internet Explorer Event Log to Windows XP and 2003.) Although the log container is created, it is not enabled and seems to be used only for application compatibility testing (http://msdn.microsoft.com/en-us/library/bb250493.aspx); as such, there does not seem to be much value from a forensic analysis perspective.

Also notice on the lower right-hand side of Figure 5.5, under Actions, the item called Attach Task To This Event…. As tools are developed for parsing through Vista Event Logs and as incident responders and forensic analysts use those tools, this item will be of interest.

Andreas Schuster and Eric Fitzgerald have posted some information in their respective blogs about the structure used to store event records. Andreas also provides a blog post that describes some of the data types available in the new Event Logs (http://computer.forensikblog.de/en/2007/08/evtx_data_types.html), as well as a parser to convert Vista Event Logs into plain text (http://computer.forensikblog.de/en/2007/08/evtx_parser.html).

On a live Vista system, you can use the wevtutil.exe command to retrieve information about the Windows Event Log that isn't readily apparent via the Event Viewer user interface. For example, the following command will display a list of the available Event Logs on the system:

```
C:\>wevtutil el
```

From there, you can use the next command to list configuration information about a specific Event Log, including the name and path to the file:

```
C:\>wevtutil gl log name
```

Much of the information displayed by this command is also available in the following Registry key on a Vista system:

```
HKEY_LOCAL_MACHINE\System\ControlSet00x\Services\EventLog\log name
```

This will be useful information for incident responders and forensic analysts alike. Tools and techniques need to be developed that allow incident responders and forensic analysts to extract relevant and pertinent information from the Windows Event Logs on Vista systems.

For ease of analysis when examining Event Logs from both XP and Vista systems, Event Log (.evt) files can be converted to the Windows Event Log (.evtx) format using any of the options listed in the Ask the Performance Team blog on Microsoft's TechNet site (http://blogs.technet.com/askperf/archive/2007/10/12/windows-vista-and-exported-event-log-files.aspx).

# IIS Logs

Microsoft's Internet Information Server (IIS) is a Web server platform that's popular with both users and attackers. It is easy for administrators to install—to the point that sometimes they aren't even aware that they have a Web server running on their system. It is also a very popular target for attackers, and with good reason. Many times there are vulnerabilities to the Web server due to coding or configuration issues that, when left unaddressed, leave not only the Web server software but the entire platform open to exploitation. One of the best ways to uncover attempts to compromise the IIS Web server or details of a successful exploit is to examine the logs generated by the Web server.

The IIS Web server logs are most often maintained in the %WinDir%\System32\LogFiles directory. Each virtual server has its own subdirectory for log files, named for the server itself. In most situations, only one instance of the Web server might be running, so the log subdirectory will be W3SVC1. During an investigation, you might find multiple subdirectories named W3SVC*n*, where *n* is the number of the virtual server. However, the location of the logs is configurable by the administrator and can be modified to point to any location, even a shared drive. By default, the log files are ASCII text format (this is also configurable by the administrator), meaning that they are easily opened and searchable. In many cases, the log files can be quite large, particularly for extremely active Web sites, so opening and searching the file by hand isn't going to be feasible or effective. Searches can be scripted using Perl scripts or *grep* searches, or if you're looking for something specific, the find/search capability found in whichever editor you choose to use might also work.

Speaking of searches, one of the biggest questions investigators face is, how do we cull through voluminous Web server logs to find what might be the proverbial needle in a haystack? On a high-volume server, the log files can be pretty large, and searching through them for relevant data can be an arduous task. Sometimes using a victim's incident report can help an investigator narrow the time frame of when the attack occurred, allowing for a modicum of data reduction. However, this doesn't always work. It is not uncommon for an investigator to find a system that had been compromised weeks or even months before any unusual activity was reported. So, what do you do?

---

**W**ARNING

When analyzing IIS log files, one thing to keep in mind is that the time stamp for the events will most likely be in GMT format (http://support.microsoft. com/kb/194699). When IIS logs in W3C Extended log file format, which is the default, time stamps are logged in GMT format, rather than based on the local time zone format for the system. As a result, the IIS logs will roll over to the next day at midnight GMT (per http://support.microsoft.com/kb/944884), which will also need to be taken into account when performing analysis.

Also, be aware of fields that may be available in the logs on different versions of IIS. For example, IIS 6.0 and 7.0 include a "time-taken" field (http://support. microsoft.com/kb/944884) that may be useful in analysis of the logs.

---

Awhile back—a long while in Internet years, all the way back to 1997—Marcus Ranum developed an outline for what he referred to as "artificial ignorance" (AI). The basic idea is that if you remove all legitimate activity from the Web server logs, what you have left should be "unusual."

---

### Tools & Traps...

### Implementing "AI"

I've used the "artificial ignorance" method for filtering various items, and it has been a very useful technique. I had written a Perl script that would reach out across the enterprise for me (I was working in a small company with between 300 and 400 employees) and collect the contents of specific Registry keys from all the systems that were logged in to the domain. I could run this script during lunch and come back to a

**Continued**

nice log file that was easy to parse and open in Excel. However, it was pretty large, and I wanted to see only those things that required my attention. So, I began examining some of the entries I found, and as I verified that each entry was legitimate, I would add it to a file of "known-good" entries. Then I would collect the contents of the Registry keys and log only those that did not appear in the known-good file. In a short time, I went from several pages of entries to fewer than half a page of items I needed to investigate.

With Web server logs, it is a fairly straightforward process to implement this type of AI. For example, assume that you're investigating a case in which a Web server might have been compromised, and there are a very small number of files on the server—the index.html file and perhaps half a dozen other HTML files that contain supporting information for the main site (about.html, contact.html, links.html, etc.).

IIS Web server logs that are saved in ASCII format (which is the default) have a rather simple format, so it is a fairly easy task to use your favorite scripting language to open the file, read in each log entry, one line at a time, and perform processing. IIS logs will generally have column headers located at the top of the file, or that information might be somewhere else in the file if the Web server was restarted. Using the column headers as a key, you can then parse each entry for relevant information, such as the request verb (*GET*, *HEAD*, or *POST*), the page requested, and the status or response code (you can find a listing of IIS 5.0 and 6.0 status codes at http://support.microsoft.com/kb/318380) that was returned. If you find a page that was requested that is not on your list of known-good pages, you can log the filename, date/time of the request, source IP address of the request, and the like to a separate file for analysis.

# WARNING

I am not providing code for this technique, simply because not all IIS Web logs are of the same format. The information that is logged is configurable by the Web server administrator, so I really cannot provide a "one size fits all" solution. Further, the exact specifications of a search may differ between cases. For example, in one case you might be interested in all pages that were requested that are not part of the Web server; in another case, you might be interested only in requests issued from a specific IP address or address range. In yet another case, you might be interested only in requests that generated specific response codes.

"Artificial ignorance" is one approach to take when searching Web server logs; this technique is very flexible and can be implemented on a wide range of logs and files. Another technique you can use is to look for specific artifacts left behind by specific attacks. This technique can be very useful in cases where more information about the infrastructure, the level of access the attacker obtained, and other specifics are known. Also, if there seems to be a particular vulnerability that was released around the time of the intrusion or there is an increase in reported attempts against a specific exploit, searching for specific artifacts could be an effective technique.

---

**W**ARNING

I used to marvel at how some attacks just grew in popularity, and I figured that it had to do with the success of the attack itself. In some cases, a great deal of very technically detailed and accurate information is available about attacks. For example, a SQL injection cheat sheet that addresses a number of variations on SQL injection attacks is available from http://ferruh.mavituna. com/sql-injection-cheatshee-oku/. From information within this cheat sheet, something very interesting that you may find in logs as a result of a SQL injection attack is the use of the *sp_password* keyword. This keyword is usually used for password changes, and tells the Microsoft SQL Server not to log the command. For an attacker, this is an issue only if logging is enabled on the SQL server; the attack still appears in the Web server logs. However, it is kind of sneaky!

---

For example, if an IIS Web server uses a Microsoft SQL database server as a back end, one attack to look for is SQL injection (http://en.wikipedia.org/wiki/SQL_injection). An attacker may use queries submitted to the Web server to be processed by the back-end database server to extract information, upload files to the server, or extend their reach deep into the network infrastructure. A telltale sign of a SQL injection attack is the existence of *xp_cmdshell* in the log file entries. *Xp_cmdshell* is an extended stored procedure that is part of the Microsoft SQL server that can allow an attacker to run commands on the database server with the same privileges as the server itself (which is usually System-level privileges). In mid- to late 2007, we saw a number of these attacks that were essentially plain-text attacks, in that once indications of the SQL injection were found within the IIS Web server log files (usually by doing a keyword search for *xp_cmdshell*), the analyst could clearly see the attacker's activities. In many cases, the attacker would perform network reconnaissance using tools native to the Microsoft SQL Server system, such as *ipconfig /all*, *nbtstat −c*, *netstat −ano*, variations of the *net* commands to map out other systems on the network or to add user accounts to the system, as well as using ping.exe or other tools to determine network connectivity from the system. Once this was done, the attacker would then download tools to the SQL server using tftp.exe or ftp.exe (after using *echo* commands to create a File Transfer Protocol [FTP] script file). In one particular instance, the attacker broke an executable file into 512-byte chunks, and then wrote each chunk to a database table. Once all of the chunks were loaded into the database, the attacker told the database (again, all of this was being done remotely through the Web server) to extract the chunks, reassemble them into a single file, and then launch that file. Fascinatingly, it worked!

### TIP

It is important to note that during a SQL injection attack, the Web server itself is not actually compromised and directly accessed by the attacker. The attacker issues the specifically constructed queries to the Web server, which then forwards those queries to the database for processing. Another important factor that an analyst should keep in mind when examining Web server log files is that the Web server status or response code does not indicate whether the SQL injection code succeeded.

As the year rolled into spring 2008, the news media published a number of articles that described the use of SQL injection to subvert Web servers by injecting malicious JavaScript files into the Web server pages. Although this highlighted the SQL injection issue, it certainly ignored the arguably more malicious attacks that continued to lead to a complete subversion of the victim's network infrastructure. Analysts started to see more and more pervasive attacks, but there was also a marked increase in the sophistication of the SQL injection attack techniques used, as they were no longer using plain-text, ASCII commands. Keyword searches were not finding any hits on *xp_cmdshell*, even when it was clear that some form of access similar to what could be attained through SQL injection had been achieved. A closer look revealed that attackers were now using *DECLARE* and *CAST* statements to encode their commands in hexadecimal strings, or in sequences of character sets (e.g., the character "%20" is equivalent to a space). Other unique terms, such as *nvarchar*, were also being used in the SQL injection statements. For an example of what such a log file entry would look like, see the blog post "The tao of SQL Injection exploits" (http://dominoyesmaybe.blogspot.com/2008/05/tao-of-sql-injection-exploits.html). As a result of these new adaptations to the attack, new analysis and detection techniques needed to be developed.

By default, the IIS Web server will record its logs in a text-based format. This format consists of a number of fields, the sequence of which will appear in the *#Fields*: line at the top of the log file. One means of analysis that can be used to detect SQL injection attacks regardless of encoding is to parse through the logs, extracting the *cs-uri-stem* field, which is the target Web page, such as default.asp or jobs.asp. Then, for each unique *cs-uri-stem* field, keep track of the lengths of the *cs-uri-query* fields, which show the actual query entered for the target Web page. As SQL injection commands are very often much longer than the normal queries sent to those pages during regular activity, you can easily track down log entries of interest. The *cs-uri-stem* field can also be used to determine which Web pages were vulnerable to SQL injection attacks, based solely on the contents of the logs themselves.

You can search for a number of other issues based on various keywords or phrases. For example, the existence of *vti_auth\author.dll* in the Web server logs can indicate the issue (http://xforce.iss.net/xforce/xfdb/3682) with the permissions on FrontPage extensions that can lead to Web page defacements. Other signatures I have used in the past to look for the Nimda (www.cert.org/advisories/CA-2001-26.html) worm (see the "System Footprint" section in the CERT advisory) included attempts to execute cmd.exe and tftp.exe via URLs submitted to the Web browser.

## Notes from the Field...

### Web Server Logs

A number of engagements have involved Web server log analysis, and in several instances I've seen clear indications of the use of automated Web server scanning applications based on the "footprints" of the application in the logs. When I find these entries, I like to ask the Web server administrator whether the organization is subject to scans based on regulatory compliance requirements. Sometimes the response is "yes," and the dates and IP addresses of the scans can be tied directly to authorized activity, but this is not always the case.

Analysis of IIS (and other Web server) logs can be an expansive subject, one suitable for an entire chapter all on its own. However, as with most log files, the principles of data reduction remain the same: Remove all the entries that you know should be there, accounting for legitimate activity. Or, if you know or at least have an idea of what you're looking for, you can use signatures to look for indications of specific activity.

## Notes from the Field...

### FTP Logs

I was assisting with an investigation in which someone had access to a Windows system via a remote management utility (such as WinVNC or pcAnywhere) and used the installed Microsoft FTP server to transfer files to and from the system. Similarly to the IIS Web server, the FTP server maintains its logs in the LogFiles directory, beneath the MSFTPSVCx subdirectory. There were no indications that the individual did anything to attempt to hide or obfuscate his presence on the system, and we were able to develop a timeline of activity using the FTP logs as an initial reference. Thanks to the default FTP log format, we had not only the date/time stamp of his visits and the username he used, but also the FTP address from which his connections originated. We correlated that information to date/time stamps from activity in the Registry (e.g., UserAssist keys, etc.) and the Event Logs (several event ID 10 entries stated that the FTP connection had timed out due to inactivity) to develop a clearer picture of this individual's activity on the system.

# Log Parser

Now that we've discussed both the Windows Event Logs and the IIS Web server logs, it's a good time to mention a tool that Microsoft produced that has been extremely useful to analysts (even though it does not get a great deal of attention from the vendor). That tool is Log Parser (the URL is quite long and may change, so suffice it to say that the best way to locate a link to the tool is to Google for *log parser*), a powerful tool that allows you to use SQL to search a number of text- or XML-based files, as well as binary files such as Event Logs and the Registry, and output the data into text, SQL, or even syslog format.

To make the tool easier to use, a Visual Log Parser GUI is available from www.codeplex. com/visuallogparser.

Log Parser is such a powerful yet underrated tool that Gabriele Giuseppini and Mark Burnett wrote *Microsoft Log Parser Toolkit*, which is available from Syngress Publishing (as well as on Amazon and at bookstores). Also, a number of resources are available that provide examples of the use of Log Parser at varying levels of complexity, such as the Windows Dev Center (www.windowsdevcenter.com/pub/a/windows/2005/07/12/logparser.html). I have heard of analysts who use Log Parser as a matter of course, as well as those who use it for specific tasks, such as parsing through significant numbers of Event Logs from multiple systems.

# Web Browser History

On the opposite end of the Web server logs is the Internet Explorer Web browsing history. Internet Explorer is installed by default on Windows systems and is the default browser for many users. In some cases, as with corporate users, some corporate intranet Web sites (for submitting timecard information or travel expenses) could be specifically designed for use with Internet Explorer; other browsers (such as Firefox and Opera) are not supported. When Internet Explorer is used to browse the Web, it keeps a history of its activity that the investigator can use to develop an understanding of the user's activity as well as to obtain evidence. The Internet Explorer browser history files are saved in the user's profile directory, beneath the Local Settings\Temporary Internet Files\Content.IE5 subdirectory. Beneath this directory path, the investigator might find several subdirectories with names containing eight random characters. The structure and contents of these directories, including the structure of the index.dat files within each of these directories, has been covered at great length via other resources, so we won't repeat that information here. For live systems, investigators can use the Web Historian tool (Version 1.3 is available from Mandiant.com at the time of this writing) to parse the Internet browser history. When examining an image, the investigator can use tools such as ProDiscover's Internet History Viewer to consolidate the browser history information into something that is easy to view and understand. The index.dat file from each subdirectory (either from a live system or when extracted from an image) can be viewed using tools such as Index Dat Spy (www.stevengould.org/index.php?option=com_content&task=view&id=57&Itemid=220) and Index.dat Analyzer (www.systenance.com/indexdat.php).

---

**TIP**

Often when you're conducting an investigation, there are places you can look for information about what you should expect to see. For example, if the auditing on a system is set to record successful logons and you can see from the Registry when various users last logged on, you should expect to see successful logon event records in the Security Event Log. With regard to Internet browsing history, Internet Explorer has a setting for the number of days it will keep the history of visited URLs. You can find that setting in the user's hive (ntuser.dat file, or the HKEY_CURRENT_USER hive if the user is logged on), in the \Software\Microsoft\Windows\CurrentVersion\Internet Settings\URL History key. The value in question is *DaysToKeep*, and the default setting is 0x014, or 20 in decimal notation. If the data associated with the value is not the default setting, you can assume that the value has been changed, most likely by choosing **Tools** from the Internet Explorer menu bar and selecting **Internet Options**, then looking in the **History** section of the **General** tab. The *LastWrite* time for the Registry key will tell you when the value was changed.

---

Many investigators are familiar with using the Internet browsing history as a way of documenting a user's activities. For example, you could find references to sites from which malicious software tools may be downloaded, MySpace.com, or other sites that the user should not be browsing. As with most aspects of forensic artifacts on a system, what you look for as "evidence" really depends on the nature of your case. However, nothing should be overlooked; small bits of information can provide clues or context to your evidence or to the case as a whole. However, not all users use the Internet Explorer browser, and a number of other browsers are available—namely, Mozilla, Firefox, Opera, and Google's Chrome browser. Freely available tools from NirSoft (www.nirsoft.net/utils/) allow you to view the history, cache, and cookie archives for a number of browsers, as well as (in some cases) retrieve passwords maintained by the browser itself. All of these tools can provide extremely valuable information during an examination.

Other tools available for forensic analysis of browsers include Firefox Forensics (F3) and Google Chrome Forensics, both available (for a fee) from Machor Software (www.machor-software.com/home), and Historian from Gaijin (free, in German, from www.gaijin.at/dlhistorian.php). A number of articles that cover Web browser forensics are also available, such as John McCash's SANS Forensics blog post on Safari forensics (http://sansforensics. wordpress.com/2008/10/22/safari-browser-forensics/), as well as a two-part series of articles on Web browser forensics from Keith Jones and Rohyt Belani at the SecurityFocus Web site (part 1 is at www.securityfocus.com/infocus/1827). Searching Google for *browser forensics* reveals a great deal of information, although some is not as detailed as the articles I've mentioned. However, a great deal of work is being performed and documented in this area, so keep your eyes open.

# Other Log Files

Windows systems maintain a number of other, less well-known log files, during both the initial installation of the operating system and day-to-day operations. Some of these log files are intended to record actions and errors that occur during the setup process. Other log files are generated or appended to only when certain events occur. These log files can be extremely valuable to an investigator who understands not only *that* they exist but also what activities cause their creation or expansion and how to parse and understand the information they contain. In this section, we're going to take a look at several of these log files.

## Setuplog.txt

The setuplog.txt file, located in the Windows directory, is used to record information during the setup process, when Windows is installed. Perhaps the most important thing to an investigator about this file is that it maintains a time stamp on all the actions that are recorded, telling you the date and time the system was installed. This information can help you establish a timeline of activity on the system.

An excerpt of a setuplog.txt file from a Windows XP SP2 system is shown here:

```
08/07/2006 16:14:22.921,d:\xpsprtm\base\ntsetup\syssetup\syssetup.c,6434,
BEGIN_SECTION,Installing Windows NT

08/07/2006 16:14:24.921,d:\xpsprtm\base\ntsetup\syssetup\wizard.c,1568,,
SETUP: Calculating registery size

08/07/2006 16:14:24.921,d:\xpsprtm\base\ntsetup\syssetup\wizard.c,1599,,
SETUP: Calculated time for Win9x migration = 120 seconds

08/07/2006 16:14:24.937,d:\xpsprtm\base\ntsetup\syssetup\syssetup.c,6465,
BEGIN_SECTION,Initialization

08/07/2006 16:14:24.984,d:\xpsprtm\base\ntsetup\syssetup\syssetup.c,6585,
BEGIN_SECTION,Common Initialiazation

08/07/2006 16:14:25.000,d:\xpsprtm\base\ntsetup\syssetup\syssetup.c,1674,
BEGIN_SECTION,Initializing action log

08/07/2006 16:14:25.046,d:\xpsprtm\base\ntsetup\syssetup\log.c,133,,GUI mode
Setup has started.

08/07/2006 16:14:25.078,d:\xpsprtm\base\ntsetup\syssetup\syssetup.c,1679,
END_SECTION,Initializing action log

08/07/2006 16:14:25.093,d:\xpsprtm\base\ntsetup\syssetup\syssetup.c,1764,
BEGIN_SECTION,Creating setup background window
```

**W**ARNING

While writing this book, I made sure to take a look at the various versions of Windows in regard to the setuplog.txt file. On Windows 2000, the file had time stamps, but no dates were included. On Windows XP and 2003, the contents of the file were similar in that each entry had a time stamp with a date. I did not find a setuplog.txt file on Vista.

As you can see from the excerpt of the setuplog.txt file from an XP system, the date and time stamp are included with each entry.

**W**ARNING

If you're analyzing an image from a system and the time stamps that you see in the setuplog.txt file don't seem to make sense (e.g., the timeline doesn't correspond to other information you've collected), the system might have been installed via a ghosted image or restored from backup. Keep in mind that the setuplog.txt file records activity during an installation, so the operating system must be installed on the system for the file to provide useful information.

# Setupact.log

The setupact.log file, located in the Windows directory, maintains a list of actions that occurred during the graphical portion of the setup process. On Windows 2000, XP, and 2003, this file has no time stamps associated with the various actions that are recorded, but the dates that the file was created and last modified will provide the investigator with a clue as to when the operating system was installed. On Vista, this file contains entries that do include time and date stamps on many of the actions that are recorded.

# Setupapi.log

The setupapi.log file (maintained in the Windows directory) maintains a record of device, service pack, and hotfix installations on a Windows system. Logging on Windows XP and later versions of Windows is more extensive than on previous versions, and although Microsoft uses this file primarily for troubleshooting purposes, the information in this file can be extremely useful to an investigator.

Microsoft maintains a document called "Troubleshooting Device Installation with the SetupAPI Log File" that provides a good deal of extremely useful information about the setupapi.log file. For example, the setupapi.log file contains a Windows installation header section that lists the operating system version along with other information. If the setupapi.log file is deleted for any reason, the operating system creates a new file and inserts a new Windows installation header.

Device installations are also recorded in this file, along with time stamps that an investigator can use to track this sort of activity on the system. In Chapter 4, you saw that when a USB removable storage device (thumb drive, iPod, or the like) is attached to a Windows system, changes are recorded in the Registry. When a particular kind of device is first attached to the system, a driver has to be located and loaded to support the device. In instances where multiple copies of the same type of device are attached to a Windows system, only the first device attached will cause the driver to be located. All subsequent devices of the same type that are connected to the system will make updates in the Registry. Take a look at this excerpt from a setupapi.log file:

```
[2006/10/18 14:11:53 1040.8 Driver Install]
#-019 Searching for hardware ID(s): usbstor\disksony____sony_
dsc_____5.00,usbstor\disksony____sony_dsc_____,usbstor\disksony____,usbstor\
sony____sony_dsc_____5,sony____sony_dsc_____5,usbstor\gendisk,gendisk
#-018 Searching for compatible ID(s): usbstor\disk,usbstor\raw
#-198 Command line processed: C:\WINDOWS\system32\services.exe
#I022 Found "GenDisk" in C:\WINDOWS\inf\disk.inf; Device: "Disk drive"; Driver:
"Disk drive"; Provider: "Microsoft"; Mfg: "(Standard disk drives)"; Section name:
"disk_install".
#I023 Actual install section: [disk_install.NT]. Rank: 0x00000006. Effective
driver date: 07/01/2001.
```

```
#-166 Device install function: DIF_SELECTBESTCOMPATDRV.
#I063 Selected driver installs from section [disk_install] in "c:\windows\
inf\disk.inf".
#I320 Class GUID of device remains: {4D36E967-E325-11CE-BFC1-08002BE10318}.
#I060 Set selected driver.
#I058 Selected best compatible driver.
#-166 Device install function: DIF_INSTALLDEVICEFILES.
#I124 Doing copy-only install of "USBSTOR\DISK&VEN_SONY&PROD_SONY_
DSC&REV_5.00\6&1655167&0".
```

From this log file excerpt, we can see that a USB removable storage device manufactured by Sony was first connected to the system on October 18, 2006. Based on what we covered in Chapter 4, we can see from the last log entry in the excerpt that the device had no serial number. However, the date and time stamp from the "Driver Install" section shows us the date that the device was first plugged into the system, which we can use along with the *LastWrite* time of the appropriate Registry key to determine a timeline of when the device was used on the system.

# Netsetup.log

The netsetup.log file is created during system setup; on Windows XP you can find it in the Windows\Debug folder. The file records information about workgroup and domain membership for the system, maintaining time stamps on all the messages it records. The time stamps within the netsetup.log file occur within the same time frame as those within the setuplog.txt file. Additional entries will be added to the file if the workgroup or domain of the system is changed. For example, I installed the Windows XP operating system for my personal laptop on August 7, 2006, as evidenced by the time stamps in the netsetup.log and setuplog.txt files. On November 19, 2006, I modified the workgroup membership (I moved from workgroup WorkGroup to workgroup Home) of the system by enabling file sharing. This information was recorded in the netsetup.log file, along with the appropriate time stamps. Log entries will also be added to the file if the system is added to or removed from a domain.

# Task Scheduler Log

The Task Scheduler service on Windows systems can be accessed through at.exe or the Scheduled Tasks Wizard in the Control Panel. This service allows a user with Administrator privileges to schedule a task to be run at some point in the future or to be run repeatedly at specific times each day, week, or month. This is very beneficial for administering and managing a system or an entire network. This same feature is useful to intruders who want to make a piece of malware run persistently on the compromised system; in fact, a number of examples of malware (e.g., Conficker/Downadup) use this very method as a means of remaining persistent on an infected system. Fortunately, in a file called schedlgu.txt, this service keeps a log of the tasks that have been run. This log file is actually the default name associated with the *LogFile* value located in the following Registry key:

```
HKEY_LOCAL_MACHINE\SOFTWARE\Microsoft\SchedulingAgent
```

On Windows XP, the schedlgu.txt log is located in the Windows directory by default (C:\Windows), whereas on Windows 2003 and Vista, the schedlgu.txt file is located (by default) in the Tasks directory (C:\Windows\Tasks).

**TIP**

Microsoft maintains a great deal of information in Knowledge Base articles. One in particular that relates to Scheduled Tasks is information on how to limit the size of the Scheduled Task log file, in Knowledge Base article 169443 (http://support.microsoft.com/kb/169443).

Note that Administrator-level privileges are required to create a scheduled task; very often, malware infecting systems and using this (and other) persistence mechanisms is successful because ordinary users have Administrator-level privileges.

If the Task Scheduler isn't used by the administrator, the investigator should expect to see entries stating that the Task Scheduler service started and exited on specific dates and times. Because the Task Scheduler service is usually set to start up along with the system, this information can give the investigator a view of when the system was started and shut down.

If a task was scheduled and executed, you will see entries in the schedlgu.txt file that look like the following (excerpted from a Windows XP schedlgu.txt file):

```
"At1.job" (regedit.exe)
  Started 9/26/2006 4:35:00 PM
"At1.job" (regedit.exe)
  Finished 9/26/2006 4:35:04 PM
  Result: The task completed with an exit code of (0).
"Pinball.job" (PINBALL.EXE)
  Started 9/26/2006 4:36:00 PM
"Pinball.job" (PINBALL.EXE)
  Finished 9/26/2006 4:36:07 PM
  Result: The task completed with an exit code of (0).
```

The first job was set up via at.exe, and the second job (pinball.job) was set up via the Scheduled Tasks Wizard. These .job files are kept in the Windows\Tasks directory.

## Notes from the Underground...

### Hiding Scheduled Tasks

There's an effective method for hiding Scheduled Tasks. Create a Scheduled Task via either at.exe or the Scheduled Tasks Wizard. Go to the Control Panel and open the **Scheduled Tasks** applet and see that the task you just created is listed. Now close the applet, open a command prompt, navigate to the **Windows\Tasks** directory, and use **attrib.exe** to set the hidden bit on the .job file. Once you've done this, go back to the **Scheduled Tasks** applet and you won't see the task listed any longer. Of course, the usual caveats apply to the command prompt (you must use the right switch with the *dir* command) and Windows Explorer (by default, it will not show files with the hidden attribute set). However, the task will run when you schedule it to do so.

I actually caught myself with this while writing my first book. I did some writing while on vacation and ran through the preceding procedure with the Solitaire card game. However, I never deleted the file, so when I got home I was working away one weekend and took a break. When I returned to my office, Solitaire was open on my desktop and at first I thought someone had been in my office! Then it struck me as to what happened, and I deleted the .job file.

Unfortunately, the full path to the executable run by the task is not recorded in the log file, but an indication of when a program was run via the Task Scheduler service is provided.

# XP Firewall Logs

Most of us are familiar with the firewall components shipped with Windows XP, perhaps from the news media and issues that were addressed in the release of Windows XP SP2. Most users don't even see or interact with the XP firewall, and it is enabled by default. The firewall can be disabled (some malware attempts to do this) and this may be part of a corporate configuration scheme to ease management of those systems. The firewall can also be manually configured to allow specific applications to have network access.

The Windows XP firewall has a log file in which it records various activities that occur, but by default, no logging occurs. Figure 5.6 illustrates the default settings via the Log Settings dialog for the firewall.

**Figure 5.6** Configure Windows XP Firewall Logging

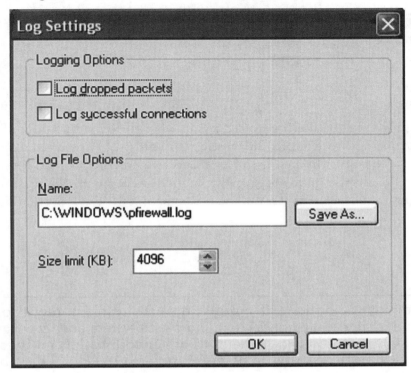

As you can see, the logging options are pretty limited. Logging is not enabled by default, so you might not find the firewall log pfirewall.log on most systems. The lack of a log file does not mean the firewall was not enabled. However, should you find a copy of the log file on the system, the firewall log format is straightforward and easy to understand. An excerpt from an example firewall log appears as follows:

```
#Version: 1.0
#Software: Microsoft Internet Connection Firewall
#Time Format: Local
#Fields: date time action protocol src-ip dst-ip src-port dst-port size tcpflags
tcpsyn tcpack tcpwin icmptype icmpcode info
2003-10-10 10:21:11 DROP ICMP 131.107.0.2 131.107.0.1 - - 60 - - - - 8 0 -
2003-10-10 10:21:16 DROP ICMP 131.107.0.2 131.107.0.1 - - 60 - - - - 8 0 -
```

```
2003-10-10 10:21:21 DROP ICMP 131.107.0.2 131.107.0.1 - - 60 - - - - 8 0 -
2003-10-10 10:21:26 DROP ICMP 131.107.0.2 131.107.0.1 - - 60 - - - - 8 0 -
2003-10-10 10:21:34 DROP TCP 131.107.0.2 131.107.0.1 1045 21 48 S
1226886480 0 16384 - - -
2003-10-10 10:21:37 DROP TCP 131.107.0.2 131.107.0.1 1045 21 48 S
1226886480 0 16384 - - -
2003-10-10 10:21:43 DROP TCP 131.107.0.2 131.107.0.1 1045 21 48 S
1226886480 0 16384 - - -
```

The *Fields* tag in the firewall log header tells us what the various portions of the log entries refer to and how to interpret the information in the log file. We can see from the entries listed in the excerpt from pfirewall.log that several Internet Control Message Protocol (ICMP) packets (perhaps from the ping.exe application) were dropped, as were several attempts to connect to the computer on port 21, which is the default port for FTP servers.

**W**ARNING

Often it might be difficult to interpret the activity in a pfirewall.log file without a more detailed understanding of the system and its environment. For example, when viewing other logs of network-based activity, such as corporate firewall or intrusion detection system (IDS) logs, I have been asked by the administrator what the activity represented. In the case of a single system, attempts to access well-known ports such as port 80 (Web server) or 21 (FTP server) do not necessarily indicate something running on that system, but rather that someone might have been trying to determine whether something was running on that port. This can indicate reconnaissance activity such as port scanning. If the logs show that similar activity was directed at several systems, all around the same time, this would indicate widespread port scanning. The point is that just because a log entry shows activity directed at a specific port, it does not necessarily mean the port was open (that a service was listening on that port) on the system. This is a commonly misunderstood phenomenon, particularly when it comes to widespread scanning activity directed toward ports used by Trojan backdoor applications.

For ease of viewing, a number of freely available utilities will parse this file and make it easier to interpret, even to the point of color coding certain entries. You can Google for various combinations of *XP* and *firewall* and *viewer* to locate one that will meet your needs.

**TIP**

The accompanying DVD includes a subdirectory within the Chapter 5 directory called samples. This subdirectory contains a file named nmap_xp_scan. txt, which contains the command line used to launch an Nmap scan against a Windows XP SP2 system (with the firewall enabled), as well as the results of the scan that were sent to STDOUT. Another file named pfirewall_nmap_ scan.txt contains a portion of the logged packets that were sent to the target system. For ease of viewing, the Nmap scan was launched from 192.168.1.28, and the target system was 192.168.1.6.

## Mrt.log

In addition to security software such as firewalls, Microsoft also deploys solutions to address issues with malware, one of which is the Malicious Software Removal Tool (http://support. microsoft.com/kb/890830), or MRT. Much like the Stinger tool from McAfee (http://vil. nai.com/vil/stinger/), MRT is not designed to detect and protect against all malware threats; rather, MRT is designed to scan for and address very specific threats, which are listed in Knowledge Base article 890830. You should note that every month or so, the tool is updated to address one or two additional threats, although in June 2008, Version 1.42 of the tool addressed a total of eight threats.

The log file for MRT is, oddly enough, mrt.log, located in the %WinDir%\Debug directory. This log file contains information about the version of the tool, when it was installed, and the results of the scan, as illustrated here:

```
Microsoft Windows Malicious Software Removal Tool v2.5, December 2008
Started On Fri Dec 12 06:55:23 2008-
Results Summary:
----------------
No infection found.
Return code: 0
Microsoft Windows Malicious Software Removal Tool Finished On
Fri Dec 12 06:56:52 2008
```

This information can be useful to an examiner, giving her some sense while searching for malware of what the system may have been susceptible to and what threats it may have been protected against.

You may also find a file named mrteng.log in the same directory that contains similar information, albeit without the scan results.

# Dr. Watson Logs

The Dr. Watson tool (http://support.microsoft.com/kb/308538/) has shipped with versions of Windows for quite some time, but generally it doesn't come up in conversation these days. When a program error occurs on a system, the Dr. Watson tool collects information about the system and the program error in a text log file that can then be sent to support personnel for troubleshooting and program resolution. This information can also be useful when you're investigating an issue on a system.

The text log file produced by Dr. Watson is named drwtsn32.log and is maintained in the following directory:

```
C:\Documents and Settings\All Users\Application Data\Microsoft\Dr Watson
```

The configuration information for the Dr. Watson tool is maintained in the following Registry key:

```
HKEY_LOCAL_MACHINE\SOFTWARE\Microsoft\DrWatson
```

This Registry key contains a number of values that are visible in the Dr. Watson GUI, which is visible when you click **Start | Run** and type **drwtsn32**. By default, the log file will maintain information from 10 program exceptions. These values will indicate to the investigator what she should expect to see if any exceptions have occurred on the system.

When an error occurs, the information saved by the Dr. Watson tool is appended to the drwtsn32.log file. Dr. Watson first writes a section that begins with *Application exception occurred*: to the file. This section contains information about the program that caused the error, along with the date and time the error occurred:

```
App: C:\Perl\bin\perl.exe (pid=4040)
When: 8/21/2006 @ 10:17:35.859
```

Notice that the name of the program that caused the error can include the full path to the executable image along with a date/time stamp. As we've seen in previous chapters, this information can be useful to an investigator, particularly in instances in which the program in question is malware or something placed on the system as a result of an intrusion or misuse. Dr. Watson then writes some system information, a list of running processes, a list of modules (DLLs) loaded by the program, and stack dumps to the log file that can be used to troubleshoot the program exception. An investigator can use this information to demonstrate the user that was logged in to the system on a certain date, what processes were running (which could show applications that were installed), and what DLLs were loaded by the program that caused the exception (which might show browser helper objects [BHOs] installed via Internet Explorer, any DLLs that were injected into a process to subvert that process, etc.).

**N**OTE

The Dr. Watson log can be extremely beneficial in demonstrating or corroborating a timeline of activity on a system. In one case, an individual who had accessed a system had uploaded tools to that system and, when attempting to run some of those tools, had generated application exceptions. We found logs of his access to the system, logs showing when he'd uploaded the tools (including the IP address from which his connection originated), Event Log entries showing the application exception pop-up message, and the Dr. Watson log that showed the application that had crashed. In addition to this information, we also had the user context for the application when it crashed as well as a list of other applications that were running at the time of the crash. All of this information helped solidify our view of what applications were already in place prior to this person accessing the system, what application he had added to the system, and when he had used them.

Dr. Watson also produces a crash dump file (user.dmp) that is located in the same directory as the text-based log file. This dump file contains private pages used by the process at the time of the exception and does not contain code pages from executable files (EXE, DLL, or the like). The user.dmp file can be opened in the WinDbg tool, which is part of the Microsoft Debugging Tools. However, the user.dmp file is overwritten with each exception, so you will see only the user.dmp file from the last exception. However, the available user.dmp file may contain extremely useful information, such as passwords, plain-text or unencrypted data, or indications of user activity.

## Cbs.log

Windows Vista and 2008 systems include a Package Manager application used to install and uninstall various packages on the operating systems. The Package Manager maintains its logs in the file %WinDir%\Logs\Cbs\cbs.log. Microsoft provides some excellent information explaining how to analyze the entries in this file (http://support.microsoft.com/kb/928228), and an analyst may find something useful in the file to help explain an issue. For example, the Windows Resource Checker (sfc.exe) logs entries to this file, verifying during a scan that non-configurable system files have not changed. Microsoft Knowledge Base article 928228 provides an example of a "clean" scan, as well as an example of an issue with a corrupted file being found and addressed. The information in this log can potentially be a good source of information for an analyst, illustrating or ruling out issues with corrupted files. According to Microsoft Knowledge Base article 954402 (http://support.microsoft.com/kb/954402), you may also find in the cbs.log file on Windows 2008 systems that some files were not repaired, even though the scan is reported as completing successfully.

# Crash Dump Files

We discussed crash dump files in Chapter 3. I thought it would be a good idea to reference them in this chapter, too, for the sake of completeness.

In Chapter 3, we discussed ways to configure and generate crash dump files, but in most cases I've found that the systems themselves haven't been modified at all. During some incidents or investigations, if you do find a crash dump file, it might be a good idea to see what it holds. You can use tools such as dumpchk.exe (for Windows 2000/2003, see http://support.microsoft.com/kb/156280; for XP, see http://support.microsoft.com/kb/315271) to verify the dump file and ensure that it is valid. You can then load the file into a debugging tool (such as WinDbg) and use commands such as *!process 0 0* to view the list of running processes at the time of the crash or *lm kv* to view a list of loaded kernel mode drivers. Further, you can use tools such as strings.exe, bintext.exe, and *grep* expressions to locate specific information.

# Recycle Bin

Most forensic investigators are aware of the old adage that when a file is deleted, it isn't really gone. This is even truer with the advent of the Recycle Bin on the Windows desktop. The Recycle Bin exists as a metaphor for throwing files away, as though you're crumpling them up and tossing them into a wastebasket. The Recycle Bin also allows us to retrieve and restore files that we've "accidentally" thrown away. We can open the Recycle Bin, select files that we've previously thrown away, and restore them to their previous location.

So, when something is deleted through the shell—that is, when a user selects a file on the desktop or through Windows Explorer and "deletes" it—it isn't really gone. The file is simply moved to the Recycle Bin, which appears by default in the file structure as the Recycler directory at the root of each drive. In many cases, this directory can provide a significant amount of information relevant to an investigation.

To better understand how information in this directory can be used as evidence, let's take a look at what happens when a user deletes a file through the shell. Once each user on a system begins to delete files through the shell (as opposed to using the *del* or *erase* command at the command line), a subdirectory is created for that user within the Recycler directory; that subdirectory is named with the user's SID. For example, from the command prompt, the subdirectory will look something like this:

```
C:\RECYCLER\S-1-5-21-1454471165-630328440-725345543-1003>
```

When you open the Recycle Bin from the desktop, the user's subdirectory is automatically opened for his view. So, if you were to sit down at a user's laptop with a user's account logged in and you opened the Recycle Bin to view the contents, you would see the files that the user had "deleted." If you were to switch accounts and repeat the process, you would automatically see the files deleted within the active user account.

When viewing the Recycler directory via an image, you should expect to see a subdirectory for each active user on the system that has deleted files via the shell, as Figure 5.7 illustrates.

**Figure 5.7** Example of a Recycle Bin Viewed via ProDiscover

Within each subdirectory, you might see a number of files, depending on the user's activity and how often the user has emptied the Recycle Bin. Files sent to the Recycle Bin are maintained according to a specific naming convention (http://support.microsoft.com/kb/136517) which, once you understand that convention, makes it relatively easy to identify certain types of files and which ones might be of interest. When the file is moved to the Recycle Bin, it is renamed using the following convention:

```
D<original drive letter of file><#>.<original extension>
```

The filename starts with the letter *D* and is followed by the letter of the original drive from which the file was deleted, then a zero-based index for the number of the file (i.e., the fifth file deleted will have the number 4). The file maintains the original extension. Further, a record is added to the INFO2 file within the directory, which is a log file of all files that are currently in the Recycle Bin. The index number of the deleted file serves as a reference to the original filename (and path) maintained in the INFO2 file.

Fortunately, Keith Jones (formerly of Foundstone and Mandiant) was able to document the format of the INFO2 file so that this information would be more useful to forensic analysts. The INFO2 file contains records that correspond to each deleted file in the Recycle Bin; each record contains the record number, the drive designator, the time stamp of when the file was moved to the Recycle Bin, the file size, and the file's original name and full path, in both ASCII and Unicode.

The INFO2 file begins with a 16-byte header, of which the final *DWORD* value is the size of each record. This value is 0x320 (little endian), which translates to 800 bytes. The first record begins immediately following the header and is a total of 800 bytes in length.

The first *DWORD* (four bytes) of the record can be disregarded. The file's original full path and name, in ASCII format, is a null-terminated string beginning after the first *DWORD* and taking up the first 260 bytes of the record. Opening an INFO2 file, you'll see that most of the space consumed by the ASCII format of the filename is zeros. These zeros can be stripped out to retrieve only the filename. The rest of the items within the record appear as follows:

- The record number is the *DWORD* located at offset 264 within the record.

- The drive designator is the *DWORD* located at offset 268 within the record. The drive designator is used to determine which drive the file was deleted from; 2 = C:\, 3 = D:\, and so on.

- The time stamp for when the file was moved to the Recycle Bin is the 64-bit *FILETIME* object located at offset 272 within the record.

- The size of the deleted file (in increments of a cluster size) is the *DWORD* located at offset 280 within the record.

The original filename in Unicode format consumes the rest of the record, from offset 284 within the record to the end (516 bytes). Simply stripping out the null bytes will give you the path and name of the file in English ASCII format. (The Unicode format is two bytes wide, and removing the null bytes from the second half of the Unicode format will leave you with just the ASCII format, in English.)

The recbin.pl Perl script located on the accompanying DVD will retrieve the various elements from each record, displaying the record number, the time stamp telling when the file was moved to the Recycle Bin (in UTC format; the time zone settings for the system are not taken into account), and the original name and path of the file. The script takes the path to an INFO2 file as its only argument, and the output can be easily manipulated to provide any structure and format that the investigator requires.

Keith Jones has also provided a tool called Rifiuti (the name means *trash* in Italian) for parsing the contents of an INFO2 file. Rifiuti.exe is freely available from Foundstone.com and will parse the INFO2 file in a format that is easily opened for viewing in spreadsheet format.

## Notes from the Underground…

### Looking Closely in the Recycle Bin

Investigators should also be on the lookout for files that have been added to the Recycler directory but are not stored within one of the user SID subdirectories, as well as files that do not meet the naming convention for files moved to the Recycle Bin. This could indicate malicious activity by a user or by malware, intending to purposely hide a file. Investigators should also be aware that applications such as Norton AntiVirus might use the Recycle Bin; Norton's Recycle Bin Protector will place a file called nprotect.log in the directory. Datalifter, a company that produces forensic analysis tools, has an NProtect Viewer (www.datalifter.com/tutorial/bt/NProtect_Using_NProtect.htm) that will parse the contents of the nprotect.log file. The NProtect Viewer is part of the Datalifter .Net Bonus Tools pack.

One of the things I do when digging into an image is to check the last modification time on the INFO2 file. This will tell me when the last record was added to the INFO2 file, which approximates to the time that the file in question was moved to the Recycle Bin. If the user's subdirectory within the Recycler directory contains only the desktop.ini and INFO2 files and the INFO2 file is small, the last modification time refers to the time at which the user cleared the Recycle Bin (i.e., right-clicked the **Recycle Bin** and chose **Empty Recycle Bin** from the context menu).

## Vista Recycle Bin

Yet another aspect of the Windows operating system that changed with the advent of Vista is the underlying architecture of how the Recycle Bin is implemented. Although this is transparent to the user, the change provides a very useful resource to the forensic analyst, as Mitchell Machor addressed in his paper, "The Forensic Analysis of the Microsoft Windows Vista Recycle Bin" (www.forensicfocus.com/downloads/forensic-analysis-vista-recycle-bin.pdf). As with previous versions of Windows, files deleted by a user are still associated with the user's SID but are now found in the C:\$Recycle.Bin directory. Where Vista continues to handle deleted files differently is that a deleted file is renamed to "$R", followed by a series of six random characters, and then the original file extension. Then, a second file of the same name, with "$I" instead of "$R", is created that contains information similar to what is found in the INFO2 file. However, this "index" file within the Vista Recycle Bin contains only the original filename, the file's original size, and the date and time the file was deleted.

# XP System Restore Points

We discussed the Registry files maintained in Windows XP System Restore Points in Chapter 4. In this chapter, we will address the other log files maintained within those restore points.

## Rp.log Files

Rp.log is the restore point log file located within the restore point (RPxx) directory. This restore point log contains a value indicating the type of the restore point, a descriptive name for the restore point creation event (i.e., application or device driver installation, application uninstall, or the like), and the 64-bit *FILETIME* object indicating when the restore point was created. The restore point type is a 4-byte (*DWORD*) value starting at the fourth byte of the file. The description of the restore point is a null-terminated Unicode string that starts at offset 16 (0x10) within the file, and the creation date/time is the 8-byte (*QWORD*) value located at offset 528 (0x210) within the file.

You can run the Perl script sr.pl (located on the accompanying media; this is the same sr.pl Perl script that we discussed in Chapter 4) on a live system to collect information about restore points. The script implements the *SystemRestore* Windows Management Instrumentation (WMI) class to access the *RestorePointType*, *Description*, and *CreationTime* values for each restore point and display them to the user.

The sysrestore.pl Perl script (located on the accompanying DVD) is a ProScript that you can use with ProDiscover to retrieve information from the rp.log files located in the restore point directories of an image of a Windows XP system (that is open in ProDiscover). The script opens the rp.log file within each directory and retrieves the description of the restore point and the date that the restore point was created.

The description for the restore point can be useful to the investigator, particularly if he's looking for information regarding the installation or removal of an application. System restore points will be created when applications and unsigned drivers are installed, when a Windows AutoUpdate installation is performed, and when a restore operation is performed. Restore points can also be created manually.

When a restore point is created, a description of the event that caused the restore point creation is written to the rp.log file. Many times, you'll see the description *System Checkpoint*, which is the restore point that is created by Windows XP every 24 hours (default setting). The description *Software Distribution Service* refers to Windows Updates being installed. I've also seen descriptions such as *Installed QuickTime*, *Removed ProDiscover 4.8a*, and *Installed Windows Media Player 11* on systems. The description might tell the investigator the date that a particular application was installed or removed.

The creation date of the restore point could also be useful to the investigator in other ways. Not only does it add information to the timeline of activity on the system, but the investigator can also use the creation date to determine whether changes were made to the system time. If successive restore points (successive based on the number of the restore point, such as RP80, RP81, RP82, etc.) have non-sequential creation dates, it could indicate that someone modified the system time.

# Change.log.x Files

Once the restore point has been created, key system and application files continue to be monitored so that the system can be restored to a particular state. File changes are recorded, and if necessary, the entire file is preserved so that the system can be restored. These changes are recorded in the change.log files, which are located in the restore point directories. As changes to the monitored files are detected by the restore point file system driver, the original filename is entered into the change.log file along with a sequence number and other necessary information, such as the type of change that occurred (file deletion, change of file attributes, or change of content). If the monitored file needs to be preserved (as with a file deletion operation), the file is copied to the restore point directory and renamed to the format Axxxxxxx.*ext*, where *x* represents a sequence number and .*ext* is the file's original extension.

When the system is restarted, the first change.log file is appended with a sequence number (the name of the change.log file is changed to change.log.1) and a new change.log file is created. However, you won't find a file named change.log in the restore point directories; rather, you'll find several files named change.log.*x*, where *x* is the number of the change.log file.

Each change.log.*x* file consists of a number of change log records. I was able to locate a Web site that contained detailed information regarding the binary format of these records (to include the 0xABCDEF12 "magic number" for identifying change log records in unallocated space). Using the information on this site, I was able to create a Perl script that parses and interprets the contents of the change.log.*x* files. The lscl.pl (for *LiSt Change Log*) Perl script is located on the accompanying DVD.

---

**TIP**

Fifo.log is another file maintained by (and located in the root of) the System Restore. As the System Restore reaches 90 percent of its capacity, it will delete restore points on a first-in, first-out (FIFO) basis, reducing the capacity to 75 percent of the maximum size (either the default or a user-defined value). The fifo.log file maintains a list of restore points that were "fifoed" or deleted from a monitored drive, as well as the date and time they were deleted. Restore points will also be "fifoed" when they are 90 days old.

---

# Vista Volume Shadow Copy Service

Windows Vista uses a function similar to XP's System Restore Points to maintain copies of important files; the function is called Volume Shadow Copy (http://technet.microsoft.com/en-us/library/cc785914.aspx). Like XP restore points, the volume shadow copies are maintained in the System Volume Information directory and are enabled by default on Vista. Typically, volume shadow copies are created at system boot, but they can also be created at other times. As with the XP restore points, Vista volume shadow copies can contain a wealth of information valuable to forensic analysts. Unlike XP restore points, however, volume shadow copies are apparently accessible only on a live Vista system, via vssadmin. exe. For information on booting an acquired image from a Windows system, please see the "Alternative Methods of Analysis" section of this chapter.

---

**TIP**

Christopher Hargreaves and Howard Chivers authored a paper titled "Potential Impacts of Windows Vista on Digital Investigations" (www.forensicfocus.com/downloads/potential-impact-windows-vista.pdf), an expanded version of which is available in the *Journal of Digital Investigation*. In the article, they describe a similar method of obtaining access to the information stored in volume shadow copies as described in this section. In addition to the method described

> in this section, ShadowExplorer (www.shadowexplorer.com/) can also be used to access information as well as files and folders within volume shadow copies on live Vista systems (and on Windows 2003, if the capability is enabled).

Using vssadmin.exe on a live Vista system, you can use the following command to list the available volume shadow copies:

```
C:\>vssadmin list shadows /for=c:\
```

Once the available volume shadow copies have been listed, you can create a link to any of them using mklink.exe as follows (where *n* is a number of an identified volume shadow copy) to create a symbolic link to the volume shadow copy:

```
C:\>mklink /d C:\Voln \\?\GLOBALROOT\Device\HarddiskVolumeShadowCopyn
```

At this point, the volume shadow copy files are accessible via C:\Vol*n* (e.g., *C:\Vol3* would be a symbolic link to *HarddiskVolumeShadowCopy3*). In addition to this process, Rob Lee mentioned in the SANS Forensic blog (http://sansforensics.wordpress.com/2008/10/10/shadow-forensics/) that dd.exe can be used to acquire an image of a specific shadow. Rob states in his blog post that the following command, run from a USB thumb drive, can be used to acquire an image of a volume shadow copy:

```
F:\>dd.exe if=\\.\HarddiskVolumeShadowCopy4 of=f:\snapshot4.img --localwrt
```

You can find dd.exe at http://gmgsystemsinc.com/fau/.

Given the fact that you apparently can access volume shadow copies only on a live Vista system, you must be careful to ensure that responders are aware of this fact so that the appropriate steps can be taken to preserve data. This may include acquiring images of volume shadow copies from live systems, or it may include obtaining a username and password to access an acquired image that has been booted to access the volume shadow copies.

# Prefetch Files

Beginning with Windows XP, Microsoft operating systems began using something called "prefetching" to improve system performance. XP, Windows 2003, and Vista perform boot prefetching by default, and XP and Vista also perform application prefetching by default.

For boot prefetching, the Cache Manager monitors hard page faults (require that data be read from disk) and soft page faults (require that data in memory be added to a process's working set) during whichever occurs first—the first two minutes of the boot process, the first minute after all Windows services have started, or the first 30 seconds following the start of the user's shell. The fault data is processed along with references to files and directories that are accessed, which ultimately allows all of this data to be accessed from a single file rather than requiring that the data be retrieved from different files and directories scattered across the hard drive. This, in turn, decreases the amount of time required to boot the system.

During application prefetching, the Cache Manager monitors the first 10 seconds after a process is started. Once this data is processed, it is written to a .pf file in the Windows\ Prefetch directory. This file's name is created using the application's name followed by a dash and then by a hexadecimal representation of the hash of the path to the application. Therefore, the same program run from different locations will create different .pf files. For example, on a Windows XP system, two different .pf files will be created when Notepad is run from the C:\Windows directory and from the C:\Windows\system32 directory. (For some reason, Windows XP has a copy of Notepad in each directory.)

Prefetching is controlled by the following Registry key:

```
HKEY_LOCAL_MACHINE\SYSTEM\ControlSet00x\Control\Session Manager\Memory Management\
PrefetchParameters
```

Within this key is a value named *EnablePrefetcher*. The data associated with this value will tell you which form of prefetching the system uses:

- 0: Prefetching is disabled.
- 1: Application prefetching is enabled.
- 2: Boot prefetching is enabled.
- 3: Both application and boot prefetching are enabled.

On Windows XP and Vista, the default value for *EnablePrefetcher* is 3; it is 2 on Windows 2003. One of the interesting things about application prefetching is that Windows XP has a limit of 128 .pf files.

Some information in the .pf files in the Prefetch directory can be extremely useful to an investigator. At offset 144 within the file is a *DWORD* (4-byte) value that corresponds to the number of times the application has been launched. At offset 120 within the file is a 64-bit value that is a *FILETIME* object that corresponds to the last time the application was run. This value is stored in UTC format, which is analogous to GMT time. The prefetch.pl Perl script on the accompanying DVD is a ProScript that will parse the Prefetch directory for .pf files and then extract the run count and last run times from the .pf files. The pref.pl Perl script (a "compiled" executable version of the script is also available on the accompanying DVD) will run through the Prefetch directory on a live system and retrieve the MAC times (more on MAC times in the next section) and the last run time from .pf files, sending its output to the console in a comma-delimited format (suitable for opening in an Excel spreadsheet).

The path to the application that was run is saved in a Unicode string within the .pf file (along with a range of other strings), as Figure 5.8 illustrates.

**Figure 5.8** Example of a File Path in a .pf File

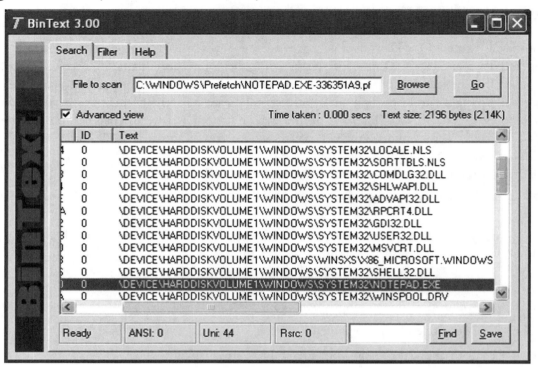

You can correlate the various information from within a .pf file with information from the Registry (refer to Chapter 4) or the Event Log to determine who was logged on to the system, who was running which applications, and so on. One of the benefits of this correlation is that if the user installs an application, runs it, and then deletes the application, traces of that application could be left in the Prefetch directory. When I've spoken to law enforcement officers about issues such as steganography applications used in online crime, all of them have said they don't usually look for steganography unless something indicates that such an application was used. The existence of a .pf file with the name of a particular application can be that indication.

# Vista SuperFetch

Windows Vista incorporates a version of prefetching called SuperFetch, and creates files similar in nature to Windows XP application prefetching. However, offsets within the file are slightly different for various metadata than those for XP application prefetch files. The vista_pref.pl Perl script (and associated "compiled" executables, both available on the media accompanying this book) will extract the last run date from a Vista prefetch file.

# Shortcut Files

Shortcut files can prove useful during an investigation. Think of the way shortcuts (files with .lnk extensions) are created and accessed in normal day-to-day use. A user accesses a document on her hard drive, a removable storage device, or a network share, and a shortcut is created on the system in the Recent folder (the Recent folder is a hidden folder within the user's profile directory). Shortcuts can provide information about files (or network shares) that the user has accessed as well as devices that the user might have had attached to her system at one point. Several commercial forensic analysis tools, such as AccessData's Forensic Toolkit (FTK) and EnCase from Guidance Software, provide the ability to parse the contents of the .lnk files to reveal information embedded within the file. Also, the Windows File Analyzer (WFA) from MiTeC is a freeware tool that will parse information from within an .lnk file. Not long ago, Jesse Hager published a white paper, "The Windows Shortcut File Format," in which he documented the offsets and sizes of the various components of a shortcut file. Nathan Weilbacher wrote an article (www.forensicfocus.com/link-file-evidentiary-value) for the ForensicFocus.com site that referenced Jesse's paper and detailed the evidentiary value of Windows shortcut files.

The Perl script lslnk.pl (found on the accompanying DVD) implements much of Jesse's white paper and allows an investigator to view the internals of Windows shortcut files, displaying information such as the MAC times of the target file, various flag and attribute settings, and local volume information, an example of which is shown here:

```
Shortcut file is on a local volume.
Volume Name = C-DISK
Volume Type = Fixed
Volume SN  = 0x303d30de
```

If the target file is on a network share, lslnk.pl will extract the path to the share, as illustrated here:

```
File is on a network share.
Network Share name = \\192.168.1.22\c$ Z:
```

The lslnk.pl script opens the shortcut file in binary mode, parsing the contents without using the Windows API. You can use the Perl script on any system that supports Perl. Jake Cunningham wrote a similar Perl script that is named lnk-parse.pl and is available on his JAFAT Web site (http://jafat.sourceforge.net/files.html).

# File Metadata

The term *metadata* refers to *data about data*. The most commonly known metadata about files on Windows systems are the file MAC times; in this case, *MAC* stands for *modified*, *accessed*, and *created*. The MAC times are time stamps that refer to the time at which the file was last modified in some way (data was either added to the file or removed from it), last accessed (when the file was last opened), and originally created. How the operating system manages these times depends on the file system used. For example, on the FAT file system, times are stored based on the local time of the computer system, whereas the NTFS file system stores MAC times in UTC format, which is analogous to GMT. When applications such as Windows Explorer display the MAC times, time zone and daylight saving time settings need to be taken into account. Further, MAC time resolution for the FAT file system is 10 milliseconds for the creation time, two seconds for the modification time, and one day for the last access time (the date, really, which isn't terribly granular). For the NTFS file system, the last access time has a resolution of one hour.

---

**W**ARNING

On Windows systems, the *NtfsDisableLastAccessUpdate* Registry value (located in the HKEY_LOCAL_MACHINE\System\CurrentControlSet\Control\FileSystem key) will allow you to disable the updating of last access times within the operating system (a *DWORD* value of 1 disables the functionality). Although this is a recommended setting for high-volume file servers (to optimize performance and increase overall response time), it can make things difficult for a forensic analyst, particularly when determining file access times is an important part of the case. You can set this value via the *fsutil* command on Windows XP and 2003, and it comes set (i.e., updating of last access times is disabled) by default on Vista. This means forensic analysts will need to develop additional analysis techniques and methodologies and rely on other sources of evidence.

---

Another aspect of file and directory MAC times that an investigator might be interested in is the way the time stamps are displayed (http://support.microsoft.com/?kbid=299648) based on various move and copy actions. For the FAT16 file system:

- **Copy myfile.txt from C:\ to C:\subdir** Myfile.txt keeps the same modification date, but the creation date is updated to the current date and time.

- **Move myfile.txt from C:\ to C:\subdir** Myfile.txt keeps the same modification and creation dates.

- **Copy myfile.txt from a FAT16 partition to an NTFS partition** Myfile.txt keeps the same modification date, but the creation date is updated to the current date and time.

- **Move myfile.txt from a FAT16 partition to an NTFS partition** Myfile.txt keeps the same modification and creation dates.

For the NTFS file system:

- **Copy myfile.txt from C:\ to C:\subdir**  Myfile.txt keeps the same modification date, but the creation date is updated to the current date and time.

- **Move myfile.txt from C:\ to C:\subdir**  Myfile.txt keeps the same modification and creation dates.

In a nutshell, regardless of the file system in use, if the file is copied, the creation date for the file is updated to the current date and time; if the file is moved, the creation date stays the same. The modification date is updated when a change is made to the file.

## Notes from the Underground…

### Modifying MAC Times

As useful as file MAC times can be to an investigation, you need to keep in mind that there are people out there who might be actively attempting to hide data on a system by modifying the MAC times of the files. I have demonstrated the use of tools that allow the user to modify the MAC times on a file at conferences, using Perl scripts to access the necessary (and thoroughly documented) Windows APIs to first create a file, then change the creation date to six years in the future and make the modification date two years in the past. That sort of thing can throw off an investigation, and when you see something like that, how are you to trust *any* MAC times?

But that's not all. The Metasploit Project has an Anti-Forensics Project (www. metasploit.org/research/projects/antiforensics/) that includes a tool called timestomp. exe that allows an attacker to modify not only the MAC times of a file but also the "entry modified" date/time stamp, which indicates when file attributes were modified. Hopefully by the time you've reached this point in the book, however, you have come to realize that antiforensic tools are intended to subvert the analyst, rather than a specific forensic analysis application.

The rest of this section addresses metadata embedded within various file formats.

# Word Documents

Metadata contained within Word documents has long been an issue. Word documents are compound documents, based on the object linking and embedding (OLE) technology that defines a "file structure within a file." Besides formatting information, Word documents can contain quite a bit of additional information that is not visible to the user, depending on the user's view of the document. For example, Word documents can maintain not only past revisions but also a list of up to the last 10 authors to edit a file. This has posed an information disclosure risk to individuals and organizations. Perhaps one of the most visible was made public in mid-2003 by Richard M. Smith, in relation to a document released by British Prime Minister Tony Blair (www.computerbytesman.com/privacy/blair.htm). The Blair government had released a dossier of Iraq's security and intelligence organizations as a Word document on the Web in February 2003. A lecturer in politics at Cambridge University recognized portions of the content of this document as having originally been written by a U.S. researcher in Iraq. This caused quite a number of people to look much more closely at the document. In his discussion of the information disclosure issue, the lecturer illustrated information he was able to extract from the Word document, which consists of a list of the last 10 authors to modify the document. This information proved quite embarrassing to Prime Minister Blair's staff.

On his Web site, the lecturer mentions a utility that he wrote to extract this information from Word documents, yet this utility is not provided for others to use. I wrote a Perl script called wmd.pl, included on the accompanying DVD, which parses through the binary header of the Word document to extract some information. The script uses Perl modules (the script does not use the Microsoft Word API, so you can run the Perl script on any system that supports Perl and has the necessary modules, as listed in the *use* pragmas for the script, installed) to retrieve additional information. The output of the script run against the Blair document appears as follows:

```
C:\Perl>wmd.pl g:\book2\ch5\blair.doc
--------------------
Statistics
--------------------
File        = g:\book2\ch5\blair.doc
Size        = 65024 bytes
Magic       = 0xa5ec (Word 8.0)
Version     = 193
LangID      = English (US)
Document was created on Windows.
Magic Created : MS Word 97
Magic Revised : MS Word 97
--------------------
Last Author(s) Info
--------------------
1 : cic22 : C:\DOCUME~1\phamill\LOCALS~1\Temp\AutoRecovery save of Iraq -
security.asd
2 : cic22 : C:\DOCUME~1\phamill\LOCALS~1\Temp\AutoRecovery save of Iraq -
security.asd
```

```
3 : cic22 : C:\DOCUME~1\phamill\LOCALS~1\Temp\AutoRecovery save of Iraq -
security.asd
4 : JPratt : C:\TEMP\Iraq - security.doc
5 : JPratt : A:\Iraq - security.doc
6 : ablackshaw : C:\ABlackshaw\Iraq - security.doc
7 : ablackshaw : C:\ABlackshaw\A;Iraq - security.doc
8 : ablackshaw : A:\Iraq - security.doc
9 : MKhan : C:\TEMP\Iraq - security.doc
10 : MKhan : C:\WINNT\Profiles\mkhan\Desktop\Iraq.doc
-------------------
Summary Information
-------------------
Title       : Iraq- ITS INFRASTRUCTURE OF CONCEALMENT, DECEPTION AND INTIMIDATION
Subject     :
Authress    : default
LastAuth    : MKhan
RevNum      : 4
AppName     : Microsoft Word 8.0
Created     : 03.02.2003, 09:31:00
Last Saved  : 03.02.2003, 11:18:00
Last Printed : 30.01.2003, 21:33:00
----------------------------
Document Summary Information
----------------------------
Organization : default
```

As you can see, some of the information "hidden" in Word documents can be quite revealing and potentially quite embarrassing. In addition to the last 10 authors, the script will reveal the platform (Windows or Mac) that the document was created on, as well as which version of Word was used to create and later revise the document. The script also extracts summary information from the document (discussed further in the "NTFS Alternate Data Streams" section of this chapter).

I have also included another small utility on the accompanying DVD, called oledmp.pl. This utility uses the same Perl modules as wmd.pl but performs a slightly different function. Oledmp.pl will list the OLE streams and trash bins embedded in a Word document as well as the same summary information that wmd.pl extracts, as illustrated in the following sample output:

```
C:\Perl>oledmp.pl blair.doc
ListStreams
Stream     : *CompObj
Stream     : WordDocument
```

```
Stream      : *DocumentSummaryInformation
Stream      : ObjectPool
Stream      : 1Table
Stream      : *SummaryInformation

Trash Bin      Size
BigBlocks      0
SystemSpace    940
SmallBlocks    0
FileEndSpace   1450

Summary Information
subject
lastauth       MKhan
lastprinted    30.01.2003, 21:33:00
appname        Microsoft Word 8.0
created        03.02.2003, 09:31:00
lastsaved      03.02.2003, 11:18:00
revnum         4
title          Iraq- ITS INFRASTRUCTURE OF CONCEALMENT, DECEPTION AND INTIMIDATION
authress       default

1Table
1  cic22          C:\DOCUME~1\phamill\LOCALS~1\Temp\AutoRecovery save of Iraq -
                  security.asd
2  cic22          C:\DOCUME~1\phamill\LOCALS~1\Temp\AutoRecovery save of Iraq -
                  security.asd
3  cic22          C:\DOCUME~1\phamill\LOCALS~1\Temp\AutoRecovery save of Iraq -
                  security.asd
4  JPratt         C:\TEMP\Iraq - security.doc
5  JPratt         A:\Iraq - security.doc
6  ablackshaw     C:\ABlackshaw\Iraq - security.doc
7  ablackshaw     C:\ABlackshaw\A;Iraq - security.doc
8  ablackshaw     A:\Iraq - security.doc
9  MKhan          C:\TEMP\Iraq - security.doc
10 MKhan          C:\WINNT\Profiles\mkhan\Desktop\Iraq.doc
```

The *ListStreams* information displays the names of the various OLE streams that make up the Word document. Microsoft refers to OLE as "a file system within a file," and these stream names refer to the "files" in the document.

**W**ARNING

Sometimes it can be pretty shocking how much information is revealed in Word document metadata. Try a little experiment: Look around a file server at work (with permission, of course) and find some Word documents, such as something that might have been sent to clients, and see what the hidden metadata says about the documents. I tried something similar, only I used Google instead of a corporate file server. Due to the number of responses I received, I restricted my searches to .mil and .gov domains, but I still found more documents than I really knew what to do with.

Interestingly enough, as I was writing my first book, one of the technical reviewers did not want me to know his name and specifically requested that the publisher not share any of the reviewer's information with me. Taking things a step further, this reviewer would complete the review forms in Word documents but save the content as a straight ASCII text document, removing all metadata. I guess he *really* didn't want me to know who he was!

Not only can this metadata pose an information disclosure risk to an individual or organization, but it can also be useful to an investigator who is looking for specific information regarding documents. This can be particularly important during e-discovery cases, especially if searches for keywords or phrases are confined to the visible text of the documents.

For the sake of completeness on this topic, I need to add a couple of things before moving on to the next topic. First, Microsoft provides information to users regarding metadata in Word documents and ways to minimize the available metadata. Second, Word documents are not the only Office files that have an issue with metadata. To address both of these items, Microsoft provides the following Knowledge Base articles:

- 223790: WD97: "How to Minimize Metadata in Microsoft Word Documents"

- 223396: OFF: "How to Minimize Metadata in Microsoft Office Documents"

- 223789: XL: "How to Minimize Metadata in Microsoft Excel Workbooks"

- 223793: PPT97: "How to Minimize Metadata in Microsoft PowerPoint Presentations"

- 290945: "How to Minimize Metadata in Word 2002"

- 825576: "How to Minimize Metadata in Word 2003"

In addition to these Knowledge Base articles, Microsoft also provides the Remove Hidden Data tool (http://support.microsoft.com/kb/834427) as a plug-in to Office 2003 and XP. Authors can use this tool to remove a great deal of metadata from documents.

This is an excellent tool to ensure that the amount of available metadata is minimized, even if your authoring process includes saving the file in a different format, such as PDF.

## Notes from the Underground...

### The Merge Streams Utility

A utility called Merge Streams (www.ntkernel.com/w&p.php?id=23), available from NT Kernel Resources, implements an interesting aspect of Office OLE documents. In a nutshell, it allows you to "merge" an Excel spreadsheet into a Word document. The utility has a simple GUI that allows you to select a Word document and an Excel spreadsheet and merge the two together. Say you have one of each document in a directory. If you run the utility and merge the two documents, you will be left with a Word document that is larger than the original Word document as well as being larger than the original Excel spreadsheet. However, if you were to delete the Excel spreadsheet, change the file extension of the Word document to .xls, and then double-click the file, you would see the Excel spreadsheet opened on the desktop, with no evidence of the original Word document or its contents. Changing the file extension back to .doc allows you to open the Word document with no apparent evidence of the Excel spreadsheet.

When presenting on this subject at conferences, I generally include a demonstration of the tool. Most often I demonstrate it from the aspect of a corporate user trying to smuggle a spreadsheet of financial forecasts or contract information pertinent to an important bid out of an organization. All the "user" has to do is merge the Excel spreadsheet into the Word document (something harmless, such as a letter) and then copy the Word document to a thumb drive. If anyone stops the user on the way out the front door and inspects the contents of the thumb drive, all he will see is the Word document.

When talking to law enforcement officers, however, I take a slightly different approach. Suppose a corporate employee has some illicit images that he'd like to share with his buddies. He copies the images into a Word document, then locates an Excel spreadsheet on the file server that all of them have access to (as well as a legitimate need to access) and merges them. He then renames the Word document to the original name and extension of the spreadsheet and lets his buddies know what he's done. This way, he can distribute the images without leaving any traces.

Detecting the use of a utility such as Merge Streams isn't necessarily an overly difficult task. Using scripts that include functionality similar to oledmp.pl, as mentioned previously in this chapter, you can list the OLE streams that make up the Word document. If you see any stream names (Workbook, Worksheet, or the like) that would indicate the presence of an Excel spreadsheet, the Word document is definitely worth examining.

**TIP**

The oledmp.pl Perl script has been extremely useful in examinations involving Excel spreadsheets and PowerPoint presentations, as well. In one instance, I was performing an examination of a system from which the customer suspected that someone had performed fraud, using account numbers that the employee had access to as part of his day-to-day responsibilities. Using a keyword list created with the help of the customer, I located an Excel spreadsheet on the system, extracted it from the image, and provided it to the customer for review. As part of my report, I was able to include information about where the file had come from (according to the location of the file, it had been an Outlook attachment), when the user had accessed the file (based on data found in the Registry), as well as the fact that the user had edited and then printed the spreadsheet. These last two bits of information were retrieved from the spreadsheet metadata using oledmp.pl.

Cory Althiede recently pointed out to me yet another means of extracting potentially useful information from Microsoft Word (and other OLE) documents. When writing the manuscript for this book, I would highlight/select text from a file, copy it to the Clipboard, paste that text into the document I was working on, and then ensure that it was properly formatted for its purpose. However, when someone drags and drops text into a Microsoft Word document, it becomes an attachment. If you ever have a need to extract those OLE document attachments, Cory pointed out an excellent tool to use, called b2xtranslator (http://b2xtranslator.sourceforge.net/). According to the About section of the Web site, the purpose of this tool is to allow users to transition from the binary document format to the new XML/zip format used in later versions of Microsoft Office (e.g., move from the .doc format to the .docx format). The Documentation page linked from the main Web page provides some very good illustrations of how the tool works conceptually, and shows how various OLE objects embedded within a Word document or Excel spreadsheet can be accessed. If you need to do more than just review the last author or the date that an OLE document was printed, you might consider taking a look at this tool.

# PDF Documents

Portable document format (PDF) files can also contain metadata such as the name of the author, the date the file was created, and the application used to create the PDF file. Often the metadata can show that the PDF file was created on a Mac or that the PDF file was created by converting a Word document to PDF format. As with Word documents, this metadata can pose a risk of information disclosure. However, depending on the situation, this information can also be useful to an investigator, either to assist in e-discovery or to show that a particular application had been installed on the user's system.

On the accompanying DVD, I've included two Perl scripts (pdfmeta.pl and pdfdmp.pl) that I have used to extract metadata from PDF files. The only difference between the two scripts is that they use different Perl modules to interact with PDF files. To be honest, I've had varying amounts of success with the scripts; in some instances, both scripts will successfully retrieve metadata from a PDF file, whereas in other cases, one or the other will fail for some reason. As a test, I used Google to search for some sample PDF files and found two, one from the FTC and another from the IRS. The PDF file from the FTC was called idtheft.pdf, and pdfmeta.pl returned the following information:

```
C:\Perl>pdfmeta.pl d:\pdf\idtheft.pdf
Author          FTC
CreationDate    D:20050513135557Z
Creator         Adobe InDesign CS (3.0)
Keywords        identity theft, id theft, idtheft, credit
ModDate         D:20050513151619-04'00'
Producer        Adobe PDF Library 6.0
Subject         Identity Theft
Title           Take Charge: Fighting Back Against Identity Theft
```

The PDF file downloaded from the IRS site was a copy of the 2006 Form W-4, called fw4.pdf. Pdfmeta.pl returned the following information:

```
C:\Perl>pdfmeta.pl d:\pdf\fw4.pdf
Author          SE:W:CAR:MP
CreationDate    D:20051208083254-05'00'
Creator         OneForm Designer Plus
Keywords        Fillable
ModDate         D:20060721144654-04'00'
Producer        APJavaScript 2.2.1 Windows SPDF_1112 Oct 3 2005
Subject         Employee's Withholding Allowance Certificate
Title           2006 Form W-4
```

Both of these examples are fairly innocuous, but it should be easy to see how the metadata in PDF files can be used in e-discovery or should at least be considered in keyword searches. If you have trouble retrieving metadata with either of the two Perl scripts provided with this book, the old standby is to open the file in Adobe Reader (freely available from Adobe.com) and click **File | Document Properties**. The **Description** tab of the Document Properties dialog box contains all the available metadata. Figure 5.9 illustrates the document properties for idtheft.pdf.

**Figure 5.9** Idtheft.pdf Document Properties

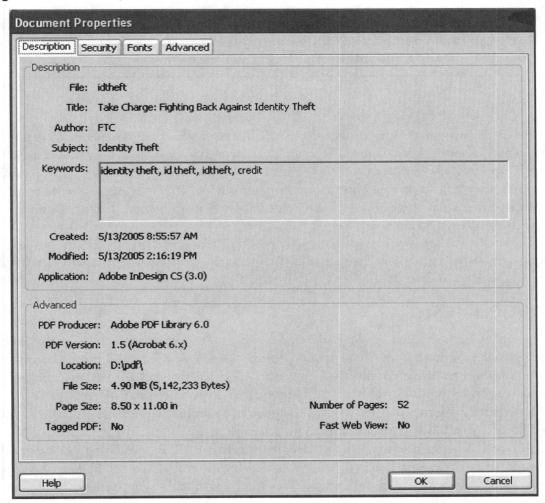

In fall 2008, Didier Stevens developed a Python-based tool called pdf-parser.py (available from http://blog.didierstevens.com/programs/pdf-tools/#pdf-parser; the site also includes a link to a screencast showing the tool in action). According to Didier, this Python script "will parse a PDF document to identify the fundamental elements used in the analyzed file. It will not render a PDF document."

**TIP**

You can download a free Python interpreter from ActiveState.com, the same site that makes a Perl interpreter freely available.

Pdf-parser.py extracts various metadata and contents from a PDF document, to include objects and JavaScript code embedded in the document. For example, Didier posted a blog entry (http://blog.didierstevens.com/2008/11/10/shoulder-surfing-a-malicious-pdf-author/) in which he described parsing information from a malicious PDF document that contained code that exploited a vulnerability to the util.printf JavaScript function (http://cve.mitre.org/cgi-bin/cvename.cgi?name=2008-2992).

Didier also makes available his Python script, ExtractScripts (http://blog.didierstevens.com/programs/extractscripts/), which extracts potentially malicious scripts embedded within HTML files into separate files.

# Image Files

Word processing files aren't the only files that maintain internal metadata. In February 2006, an article about a bot-herder (someone who infects systems with bots and then manages and even rents those networks) in the *Washington Post Magazine* included a JPEG image in the online version of the story. Although the author of the story took pains to keep the bot-herder's identity a secret, the JPEG image included notes from the photographer that stated the location (city and state) where the photo was taken.

The metadata available in a JPEG image depends largely on the application that created or modified it. For example, digital cameras embed Exchangeable Image File Format (EXIF) information in images, which can include the model and manufacturer of the camera (unfortunately, no serial number seems to be either used or stored), and can even store a thumbnail or audio information (EXIF uses the TIFF image file directory format). Applications such as Adobe's Photoshop have their own set of metadata that they add to JPEG files.

Tools such as Exifer (www.friedemann-schmidt.com/software/exifer/), IrfanView (www.irfanview.com), and the Image::MetaData::JPEG Perl module allow you to view, retrieve, and in some cases modify the metadata embedded in JPEG image files. ProDiscover can also display EXIF data found in a JPEG image. Chris Brown (of Technology Pathways) provides a white paper (http://toorcon.techpathways.com/cs/forums/storage/8/11/EXIF.pdf) that describes the EXIF data and, to a small degree, the format of a JPEG file.

# File Signature Analysis

During an investigation, you might come across files with unusual extensions or files with familiar extensions that are in unusual locations. In such cases, you can use *file signature analysis* to determine the nature of these files as well as gain some insight into an attacker's technical abilities. One way to determine the true nature of files, regardless of their extension, is through file signature analysis.

File signature analysis pertains to collecting information from the first 20 bytes of a file and looking for a specific signature or "magic number" that will tell you the type and function of the file. Different file types have different signatures, and these signatures are independent of the file extension. In fact, often the bad guy will change the extension of a file so that when it's viewed in Windows Explorer, the file will appear with an icon that effectively masks the contents and intent of the file. Once, long ago, on a system far, far away, I was analyzing an IRCbot that I dubbed the russiantopz bot (www.securityfocus.com/infocus/1618). This IRCbot deposited a number of files on the infected system and gave those files .drv and .dll extensions, so when an administrator viewed those files, they would appear to be ominous files that most administrators simply do not open. After all, in most cases when an administrator opens a file with one of those extensions in a hex editor, all he sees is a bunch of binary "stuff." During my analysis, I actually opened those files and was able to see that they contained text information, specifically configuration information and actions that the bot would perform when sent a command.

Forensic analysis tools such as ProDiscover allow the investigator to readily perform file signature analysis and easily view the results. When such tools perform the analysis, they get the file's extension and compare the signature associated with that extension to the information contained in the first 20 bytes of the file. For example, Windows portable executable (PE) files will begin with the letters *MZ* (a reference to Mark Zbikowski [http://en.wikipedia.org/wiki/Mark_Zbikowski], a Microsoft architect), which are located at the first two bytes of the PE file. Executable files can have .exe, .dll, .sys, .ocx, or .drv (to name a few) file extensions, as seen in the headersig.txt file used by ProDiscover as its "database" of file extensions and signatures. In short, if a file has an executable extension, you should expect to see a valid executable signature. Files that do not have valid signatures that match their extensions are flagged for further investigation.

Image files such as JPEG and GIF files also have their own signatures. The signature for a JPEG file is JFIF, and the signature for a GIF file is GIF87a or GIF89a. Figure 5.10 illustrates the signature for a PDF document, or %PDF-, followed by the version of the Portable Document Format for the file.

**Figure 5.10** PDF File Signature

```
00000000h: 25 50 44 46 2D 31 2E 35 0D 25 E2 E3 CF D3 0D 0A ; %PDF-1.5.‡âãÏÓ..
```

The sigs.pl Perl script located on the accompanying DVD will allow you to perform file signature analysis on live systems. The script will examine a file, a directory of files, or all the files in a directory structure to determine whether the file signatures match the file extensions. The script uses that headersig.txt file from Technology Pathways as its default "database" of file signatures; however, other listings of the same format can be used. As the script parses through the files, it will determine whether the file signature matches the extension, but it will also alert the investigator if the file extension is not found in its "database." If this is the case, the script will provide the extension and the signature so that the investigator can update her database, if she deems it necessary to do so. By default, the script sends its output to the console in comma-separated value (.csv) format so that it can be redirected to a file and opened in Excel for easy analysis.

# NTFS Alternate Data Streams

An NTFS alternate data stream (ADS) is a feature of the NTFS file system that is neither well known nor understood among members of the system administration community. After all, why would it be? On the surface, ADSes are used "behind the scenes" by several Microsoft applications, so they can't be bad, right?

Let me put it another way. What if I were to tell you that there is a way to create legitimate files on a Windows system, files that can contain data as well as scripts or executable code, and that these files can be created or launched but that there are no native tools within the operating system distribution that will allow you to detect the presence of arbitrary files. That's right. The Windows operating system has all the native tools to create, modify, and manipulate ADSes, but no native tools are available to view the existence of arbitrary ADSes. Well, that's not completely true, because beginning with Vista, the *dir* command now has a switch to let you see ADSes. We'll address this in a moment.

So, what are alternate data streams, where do they come from, and how are they used? ADSes are a feature of the NTFS file system that were introduced beginning with Windows NT 3.1. ADSes were added to the file system to support the Hierarchical File System (HFS) used by the Macintosh. HFS employs resource forks so that the file system can maintain metadata about the file, such as icons, menus, or dialog boxes. This functionality was incorporated into the NTFS file system but was never something that was widely discussed. In fact, for the longest time, there was very little discussion of ADSes and very little information available on the topic, even from Microsoft. Although Microsoft applications and functionality in the shell allow for the creation of specific ADSes, the fact remains that there is very little operational, day-to-day use for ADSes. Bad guys have picked up on this and have used ADSes to hide tools, even as part of rootkits. This is an effective approach because some antivirus utilities either do not scan ADSes or do not do so by default. Therefore, malware that is dropped onto a system in an ADS might not be detected or removed/quarantined by the antivirus application.

## Notes from the Underground…

### Using ADSes

In the late 1990s, as a consultant, I was involved in a number of penetration tests and vulnerability assessments. During a penetration test, if we gained access to a Windows system and had authorization to do so, we'd leave an ADS on the system. This had no effect other than to consume a few bytes, because we left only a text message. However, this was our way of telling the system administrator, "Tag, you're it!" and to provide proof that we'd gotten as far as we said we had. I have spoken to other pen testers who will copy all their tools over to a compromised system into ADSes.

## Creating ADSes

Creating an ADS is relatively simple; heck, some Microsoft applications do it automatically. Any user can do it, as long as the user has the ability to create a file. For example, the simplest way to create an ADS is to type the following command:

```
D:\ads>notepad myfile.txt:ads.txt
```

You'll initially see a dialog box that will ask you whether you want to create a new file. Click **Yes**, add some text to the window, save the file, and then close the Notepad window. At this point, if you type **dir**, you'll see that the file myfile.txt is zero bytes in size, although you just typed a bunch of text into Notepad.

Another way to create an ADS is to use the *echo* command:

```
D:\ads>echo "This is another ADS test file" > myfile.txt:ads2.txt
```

Okay, so you've created two ADSes, and whether you type **dir** or view the contents of the directory in Windows Explorer, you'll see a single file in the directory, and that file will be zero bytes in size.

Yet another way to create an ADS is to use the *type* command to copy another file into an ADS:

```
D:\ads>type c:\windows\system32\sol.exe > myfile.txt:ads3.exe
```

So, now what you've done is copied the contents of the file called sol.exe (which is the Solitaire card game on Windows 2000, XP, and 2003) into an ADS. You can run these same commands on Vista to create ADSes, although for some applications (such as the Solitaire game) the paths to the executable files might be different.

You can add ADSes to directory listings as well, using the following syntax:

```
D:\ads>echo "This is an ADS attached to a directory" > :ads.txt
```

Notice that no specific filename was provided. This causes the ADS to be attached to the directory listing; in this case, D:\ads.

ADSes will also be created in other ways, often without you ever being aware of it. When you right-click a file and choose **Properties**, one of the tabs you see is called Summary (interestingly enough, this tab doesn't seem to be available on Vista). You can enter just about anything in the various text fields, and when you save the information by clicking **OK**, the information is saved in an ADS (unless you're working with an Office document, in which case the information you entered is saved within the structured storage or OLE document itself).

Further, the Attachment Manager (http://support.microsoft.com/kb/883260) which is part of Windows XP SP2 will add an ADS to files downloaded from the Internet or retrieved as file attachments from an e-mail (via Internet Explorer and Outlook, respectively). When you download a file through Internet Explorer, the file will be written to whichever location you choose and an ADS named Zone.Identifier will be appended to the file (assuming that the file system is NTFS, of course; otherwise, per Knowledge Base article 883260, the Attachment Manager will fail silently). The ADS is added to the file so that when the user attempts to execute or open the file, he is presented with a warning dialog box that notifies him that the file might not be safe to open.

## Enumerating ADSes

Now that you've created several ADSes, how do you go about detecting them? As I mentioned before, there are no tools native to Windows systems that allow you to enumerate arbitrary ADSes. You can't see them through Windows Explorer, and the *dir* command is equally useless. Well, that last statement isn't exactly true; Vista has a switch that allows you to enumerate ADSes with *dir* using the */r* switch, as Figure 5.11 illustrates.

**Figure 5.11** Example of Enumerating ADSes on Vista

```
C:\ads>dir /r
 Volume in drive C has no label.
 Volume Serial Number is 98A5-80D5

 Directory of C:\ads

11/20/2006  07:17 PM    <DIR>          .
11/20/2006  07:17 PM    <DIR>          ..
11/20/2006  07:33 PM                 0 myfile.txt
                                    23 myfile.txt:ads.txt:$DATA
                                    34 myfile.txt:ads2.txt:$DATA
                               982,528 myfile.txt:ads3.exe:$DATA
               1 File(s)              0 bytes
               2 Dir(s)  14,823,571,456 bytes free
```

Figure 5.11 shows the results of running the *dir /r* command on Vista after creating several ADSes in a similar manner as we did in the "Creating ADSes" section (in that section, we created ADSes on XP).

With the other Windows operating systems (2000, XP, and 2003), you need to get outside help to enumerate ADSes. My favorite is lads.exe (www.heysoft.de/Frames/f_sw_la_en.htm), written by Frank Heyne. Lads.exe is a command-line interface (CLI) tool that you can run against any directory.

```
D:\tools>lads d:\ads
LADS - Freeware version 4.00
(C) Copyright 1998-2004 Frank Heyne Software (http://www.heysoft.de)
This program lists files with alternate data streams (ADS)
Use LADS on your own risk!
Scanning directory d:\ads\

      size    ADS in file
----------    -------------------------------
         0    d:\ads\myfile.txt:ads.txt
        34    d:\ads\myfile.txt:ads2.txt
   1032192    d:\ads\myfile.txt:ads3.exe
   1032226    bytes in 3 ADS listed
```

Lads.exe is just one of the available tools that allow you to enumerate ADSes on Windows. There are others that are also CLI tools, there are GUI tools, and there are even some that install as shell plug-ins so that you can enumerate ADSes via the Windows Explorer user interface.

ADSes added to a file by adding summary information to the file (mentioned in the previous section) appear somewhat different from the ADSes we've already added. For example, if we add summary information to myfile.txt and then run lads.exe again, we see:

```
      size    ADS in file
----------    -------------------------------
       120    d:\ads\myfile.txt: *DocumentSummaryInformation
       232    d:\ads\myfile.txt: *SummaryInformation
         0    d:\ads\myfile.txt:ads.txt
        34    d:\ads\myfile.txt:ads2.txt
   1032192    d:\ads\myfile.txt:ads3.exe
         0    d:\ads\myfile.txt:{4c8cc155-6c1e-11d1-8e41-00c04fb9386d}
```

From the output of lads.exe, we can see that three additional ADSes have been added to myfile.txt: one that appears as a globally unique identifier or GUID (and is 0 bytes in size) and two others that start with *. These last two are where the information entered into the Properties | Summary tab is saved.

Sometimes you may see an ADS named AFP_AfpInfo or AFP_Resource. If you see an ADS named in this manner, you should check to see whether the File Services for Macintosh service is installed and enabled on your system. If so, the unnamed stream might have been copied from a Macintosh system via the AppleTalk protocol. When this occurs, the data fork for the file is saved to a filename, such as myfile.txt. The resource fork is then saved to myfile. txt:AFP_Resource, and the finder or attribute information is saved to myfile.txt:AFP_AfpInfo.

As previously mentioned, other tools exist for enumerating ADSes. Streams.exe (a Sysinternals tool available from Microsoft), lns.exe (from Arne Vidstrom, at NTSecurity.nu), and sfind.exe (part of the Forensic Toolkit available from Foundstone.com) are CLI tools similar to lads. exe. ADS Detector is a shell (i.e., Windows Explorer) plug-in from CodeProject.com that allows for "visual real-time viewing of a nonencrypted file's alternative data streams." Finally, CrucialADS (from CrucialSecurity.com) and ADS Spy (from SpyWareInfo.com) are GUI-based tools for enumerating ADSes. ADS Spy, illustrated in Figure 5.12, also allows the user to delete selected ADSes.

**Figure 5.12** ADS Spy GUI

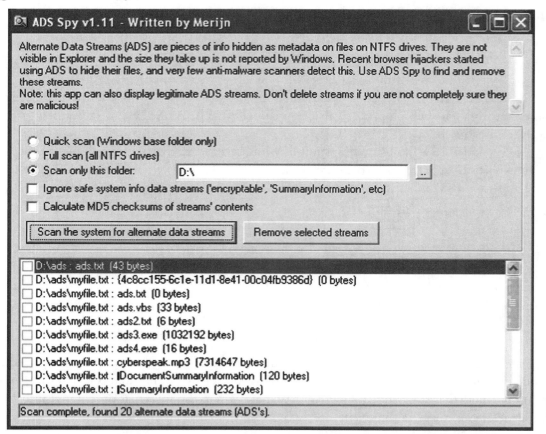

Once you've located an ADS, you can view the contents of the file by opening it in Notepad or by using the *cat* utility, part of the UnxUtils package on SourceForge.net. You can use *cat* to view the contents of an ADS at the console (i.e., *STDOUT*) or by redirecting the output of the command to a separate file.

---

**W**ARNING

In 2000, Benny and Ratter, then of the virus-writing group known as 29A (the hexadecimal representation for 666), released a virus named W2K. Stream that used ADSes. The virus would infect a file, replace it, and then copy the original file into an ADS. For example, if the virus infected notepad. exe, it would replace the executable file and copy the original Notepad into Notepad.exe:STR. This worked only on NTFS-formatted systems. If the file system was formatted as a FAT file system, there was no ADS, and all you were left with was the infected file.

In June 2006, the F-Secure antivirus company blog contained an entry that described the Mailbot.AZ (a.k.a. Rustock.A) kernel-mode rootkit driver (more about rootkits in Chapter 7) that makes detection especially difficult by hiding itself in an ADS. Further, the ADS reportedly cannot be enumerated by tools that detect ADSes, because it is hidden by the rootkit. Very tricky!

---

# Using ADSes

So, you're probably wondering, what can ADSes be used for besides hiding data? As it turns out, they can be used for a number of things. For example, you can put an executable file into an ADS and run it from there. Use the *type* command, just as we did before, to place an executable in an ADS, like so:

```
D:\ads>type c:\windows\system32\sol.exe > myfile.txt:ads4.exe
```

In this case, we've placed the Solitaire game in an ADS. This is a good example to use because when run, it results in a nice GUI that lets us see that things are working properly. To execute the program, type the following command:

```
D:\ads>start .\myfile.txt:ads4.exe
```

As you can see, we're presented with the Solitaire GUI. And this isn't restricted to executables, because scripts (Windows Scripting Host [WSH], Perl, etc.) can be hidden in

ADSes and launched just as easily. The WSH tools (cscript.exe, wscript.exe) will run scripts hidden in ADSes with no trouble, as will Perl; even the IIS Web server will serve up HTML and script files hidden in ADSes (which is a great way to grade "capture the flag" events).

Attempting to execute an ADS on Vista returns a different result, as Figure 5.13 illustrates.

**Figure 5.13** Dialog Box Returned When You Attempt to Execute an ADS on Vista

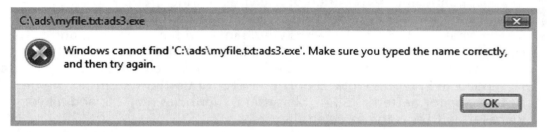

Attempts to launch the ADS (myfile.txt:ads3.exe contains the Vista version of Solitaire) were met with the same result, including variations of the *start* command as well as using Start | Run. However, launching WSH scripts from within an ADS worked without any issues on Vista.

Another interesting use for ADSes is in hiding media. Movies and podcasts can be hidden in ADSes, and then the Windows Media Player can be launched from the command line to open the media:

```
wmplayer d:\ads\myfile.txt:cyberspeak.mp3
```

I listened to an edition of the CyberSpeak podcast this way. Interestingly enough, although the podcast was launched from the command line, the filename appeared in the following Registry key:

```
HKEY_CURRENT_USER\Software\Microsoft\MediaPlayer\Player\RecentFileList
```

The entry was listed in the data associated with the *File0* value, indicating that whenever a new file is added to this list, the filename is added to the top of the list and the older filenames are pushed down the list; the smaller the file number, the more recent the file. As you learned in Chapter 4, getting the *LastWriteTime* from the Registry key will tell you when that file was accessed via the Windows Media Player.

## Warning

When looking at a sample case in ProDiscover, I noticed that there were several ADSes in the Recycle Bin. ProDiscover displays ADSes with a red-colored font so that they stand out and are obvious. I had deleted some files I'd been working with, one of which I downloaded from the Internet. I noticed that the Zone.Identifier ADS was visible for the file (I had downloaded the file via Internet Explorer) but that the record count for the total number of files via the INFO2 file did not reflect the existence of the ADS.

# Removing ADSes

Now that you've seen how ADSes can be created and used, what can you do about removing them? There are several ways to go about this, and the way you choose depends on your needs and preferences.

One way to remove an ADS is to simply delete the file to which the ADS is attached. However, the obvious result is that if the original file was important to you (document, spreadsheet, image file), you lose that data.

To save your original data, you might want to use the *type* command to copy the contents of the original unnamed stream (in our example, myfile.txt) to another filename and then delete the original file. Another option is to copy the file to non–NTFS media. Remember, ADSes are an NTFS feature, so copying the file to a floppy disk (remember those?), thumb drive, or another partition formatted in FAT, FAT32, or some other file system (FTP file to a Linux-system-formatted ext2 and then back again) will effectively remove the ADS.

But what if the ADS you've detected is attached to a directory listing, such as C:\ or C:\windows\system32? You can't just delete the directory, and copying it to and from another file system is going to be a bit cumbersome. So, what do you do? Using the *echo* command, you can reduce the ADS to a harmless text file, regardless of its contents. From our previous example of copying the Solitaire game into an ADS, we can run lads.exe and get information about that ADS:

```
56832 d:\ads\myfile.txt:ads4.exe
```

Okay, so we have an ADS that is 56,832 bytes in size, and we already know this is an executable file. So, type in the following command:

```
D:\ads>echo "deleted ADS" > myfile.txt:ads4.exe
```

Rerunning lads.exe, we see that the file size has changed:

```
16 d:\ads\myfile.txt:ads4.exe
```

So, we've effectively "taken care of" the ADS; although we didn't delete it, we rendered it harmless. You can even write a message to the ADS stating the nature of the ADS you located, your name, and when you deleted it.

Finally, another option is to use the ADS Spy GUI application mentioned previously.

## ADS Summary

At this point, we've covered a lot of information about ADSes, discussing how they are created and how they can be used and removed. This information is important to keep in mind when you're performing either incident response or computer forensic activities. ADSes are unusual enough that commercial forensic analysis tools such as ProDiscover display ADSes in red. However, not all ADSes are malicious in nature; you saw how some applications use ADSes simply as part of how they operate.

One thing investigators should keep in mind is to view the contents of an ADS. Just because an ADS is named using one of the naming schemes employed by known, legitimate applications doesn't mean that what's in the ADS isn't malicious. That is to say, do not simply write off the ADS as benign because it's named AFP_AfpInfo. Bad guys love to hide malware in plain sight by naming it something an administrator or forensic analyst will most likely overlook.

# Alternative Methods of Analysis

Sometimes when you're conducting a postmortem computer forensic analysis (after you've acquired an image) you might need to perform analysis that is simply more cumbersome when you're working with an image. For example, you might decide that you want to scan the system for malware, such as Trojans, backdoors, or spyware. When you're working with an image of the system, you've got what amounts to a single file (or, as is often the case, multiple files that add up to the size of the original hard drive), and you need a way to scan the files within the image. So, rather than pulling all the files out of the image, there are some tools that you can use to convert the image into a format suitable for scanning.

One such tool is available via ProDiscover. Beginning with Version 4.85 of ProDiscover, the tool has the ability to convert an image from either the native ProDiscover format or the *dd* format to an ISO format. ProDiscover also has the ability to create files needed to boot the image in VMware. Figure 5.14 illustrates these new options.

**Figure 5.14** ProDiscover Menu Showing New Tools

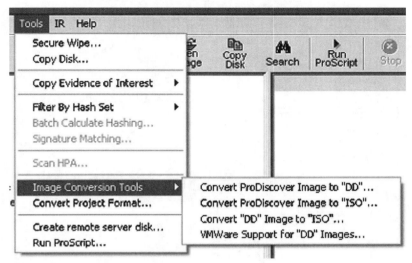

As you can see in Figure 5.14, you can use ProDiscover to convert from the native ProDiscover .eve file format to *dd* format or from either a ProDiscover or *dd* image to an ISO 9660 Joliet specifications image. You can also use ProDiscover to create the necessary files required to boot the image in VMware, which is similar to what the VMware P2V (which stands for "physical to virtual") Assistant tool allows you to do. Using tools such as this, you can boot the system to perform additional analysis, such as antivirus and antispyware scanning, or to simply see what the system "looked like" when it was running. Sometimes this can be very useful when you're investigating a case, because it is so difficult to determine the nature of a running system (given the interactions between various configuration settings, installed software, etc.) during a postmortem analysis.

A technical Webinar available at the Technology Pathways Resource Center Web site (www.techpathways.com/DesktopDefault.aspx?tabindex=8&tabid=14) walks you through the details of how to use the ProDiscover tools to ultimately boot an image in VMware. The Webinar requires the appropriate client software from WebEx.com.

Another tool that is free and extremely easy to use to boot an acquired image in VMware is Live View (http://liveview.sourceforge.net), which is available from CERT. Live View uses an easy-to-understand GUI (as illustrated in Figure 5.15) to walk you through many of the configuration options required to configure an image to be booted in VMware, and it automates the creation of the necessary files.

**Figure 5.15** Live View GUI

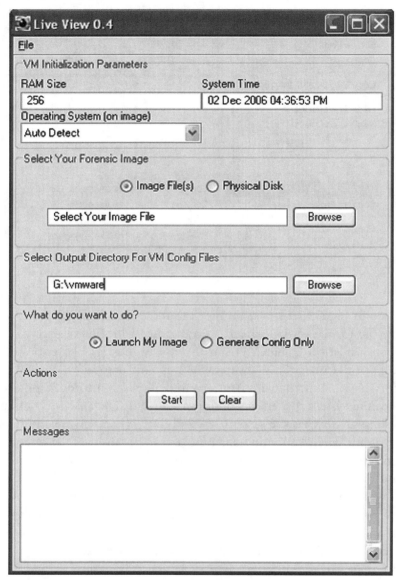

Running Live View is a straightforward and intuitive process. Live View supports most versions of Windows and has limited support for Linux. I've used the tool successfully several times to boot and log in to acquired images.

**NOTE**

Once you get the image to boot, you can do a variety of things. If you're using the VMware Workstation product and have it configured as a bridged network, you can enable the network interface for your newly booted image and scan it just as though you were doing a remote port scan and/or vulnerability scan. You might also want to log in to the running system, so unless the Administrator or user password is blank, you're going to need to get the user's or the organization's information technology (IT) department's cooperation to obtain the password or guess the password using brute force tools or passwords obtained from forensic examination of the system.

Booting an image via Live View is something that an analyst may include as part of her analysis to "see what the user saw." An alternative to using tools such as Live View is to mount the image as a read-only file system.

## Mounting an Image

Another excellent (albeit not free) tool is Mount Image Pro (MIP, available from www.mount-image.com). MIP is a great tool that allows you to mount an image as a read-only drive on your current system. Figure 5.16 illustrates two images mounted as drives F:\ and H:\ via the 30-day evaluation version of Mount Image Pro.

**Figure 5.16** Images Mounted As Drive Letters via Mount Image Pro v2.02

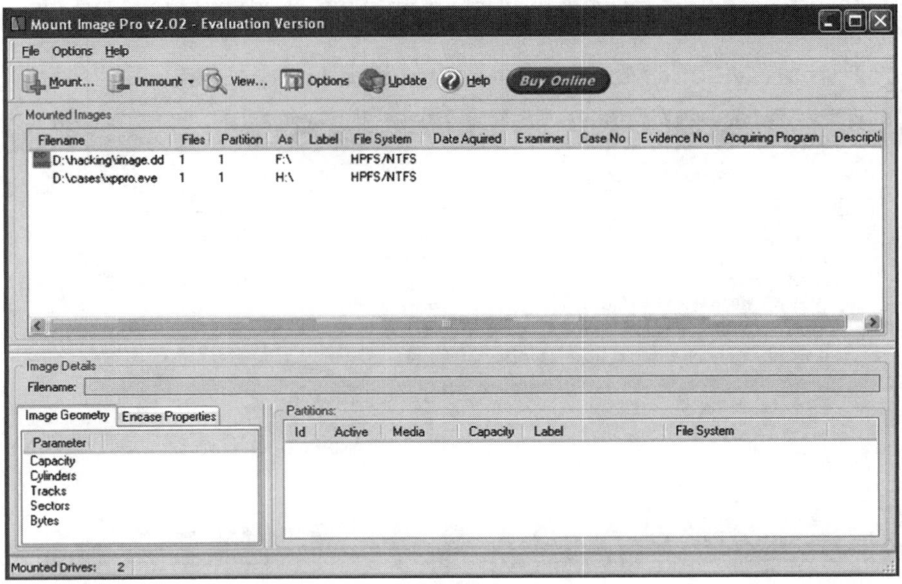

MIP does not boot the image and allow you to access the image as a running system; you will not be able to extract running processes for that system from physical memory. Rather, it mounts the image as a drive letter so that you can access the files within the image just as you would any other drive letter, and it does so in read-only mode so that no changes are made to the image. To verify this, I used md5deep.exe to compute a cryptographic hash for an image of an acquired system that was contained in a single file. I then used MIP to mount the image as a drive letter, and I accessed several files and copied several files from the mounted drive to another partition on my system. Once I had completed several actions, including running several Perl scripts against files in the mounted drive, I dismounted the drive letter and shut the MIP application down completely. I then reran md5deep.exe against the image file and the returned hash was identical to the first hash that I had calculated, verifying that the image is mounted read-only. Creating and verifying cryptographic hashes using a known and accepted algorithm should be part of your standard operating procedure if you're using tools such as Mount Image Pro. (Several freely available tools such as MD5, SHA-1, and SHA-256 implement many of the accepted algorithms.)

Another very powerful tool to use to mount an acquired image as a read-only file system is Smart Mount from ASR Data (www.asrdata.com/SmartMount/). According to ASR Data's Andy Rosen, the author of the tool, Smart Mount offers considerably more functionality (e.g., it runs on Windows and Linux, will mount password-protected .E01 files without the password, etc.) than MIP, and although it is also a commercial product that must be purchased, an evaluation version is also available.

Smart Mount will mount a wide range of image files, including VMware .vmdk files and EnCase Expert Witness Format (EWF) files, as well as raw image files. Figure 5.17 illustrates part of the process of using Smart Mount to mount an acquired image file as a read-only file system (note that the acquired image is available from www.cfreds.nist.gov/Hacking_Case.html).

**Figure 5.17** Smart Mount Mounting an Acquired Image File

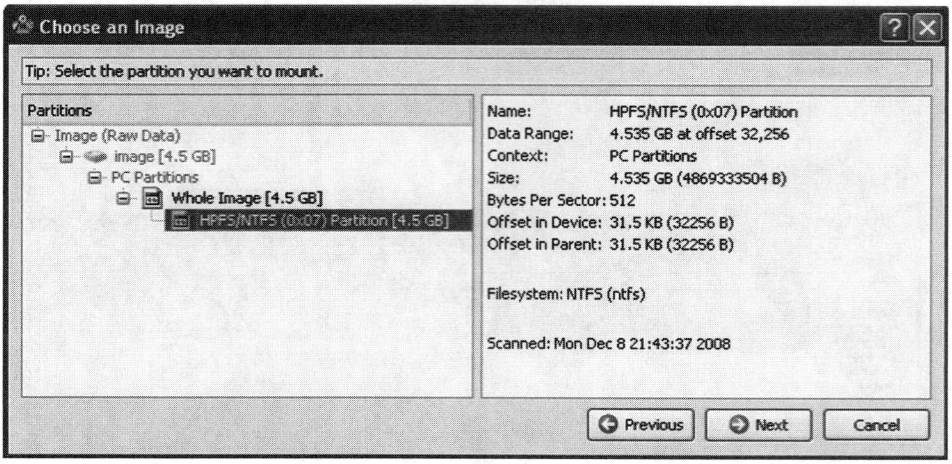

You also can use freely available tools to mount acquired images as file systems, albeit with varying levels of ease of use and functionality. Two such tools are VDK (http://chitchat. at.infoseek.co.jp/vmware/vdk.html) and ImDisk (www.ltr-data.se/opencode.html). VDK installs as a CLI executable file (vdk.exe) and as a driver (vdk.sys). Typing the command **vdk help** at the command line will show you the various options available with VDK, or you can download and install the VDK Win GUI (http://petruska.stardock.net/Software/VMware. html), which is currently available as Version 1.1.1 and allows you to mount image files as virtual, read-only drives. VDK allows you to mount both VMware virtual disks (.vmdk files) as well as raw images as read-only file systems. You can also use vdk.exe to perform a variety of functions; for example, to get information about an acquired image file, such as the partitions within the image file, using the *view* command:

```
D:\vdk\vdk view D:\hacking\image.dd
```

The output of this command looks like the following:

```
Image Name      : image
Disk Capacity   : 9514260 sectors (4645MB)
Number Of Files : 1

  Type     Size        Path
-------   -------    -------------------

  FLAT    9514260    d:\hacking\image.dd

Partitions      :

   #       Start Sector    Length in sectors    Type
  --      ------------    --------------------   ----

   0                 0     9514260 (4645MB)     <disk>
   1                63     9510417 (4643MB)     07h:HPFS/NTFS
```

ImDisk installs as a console application and a Control Panel applet (as Figure 5.18 illustrates), and provides similar functionality as VDK.

**Figure 5.18** ImDisk Control Panel Icon

Figure 5.19 illustrates the ImDisk dialog once the image file has been selected. The next step in the process will mount the selected image file as a read-only virtual disk with the drive letter H:\.

**Figure 5.19** ImDisk Dialog

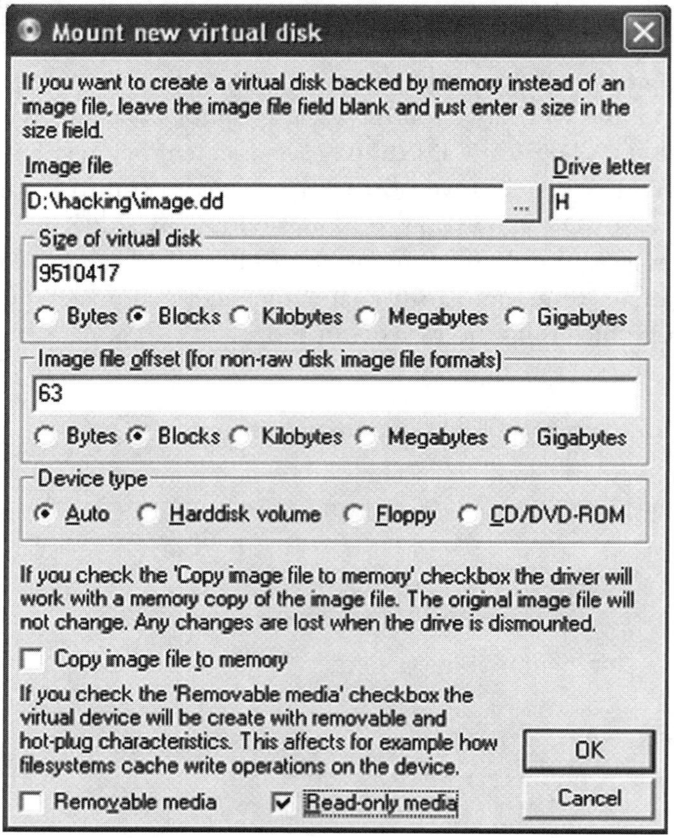

Mounting images as read–only drive letters has a lot of advantages, particularly in the areas of data reduction and analysis. For example, you can run any number of tools, such as antivirus and spyware detectors, file signature analysis, and tools for enumerating NTFS ADSes, against images in an automated fashion. Rather than enumerating through an image and then having to copy files of interest out of the image for more detailed analysis, you can automate many of these methodologies via Perl scripts.

# Discovering Malware

One laborious analysis task that many analysts encounter is locating malware on a system, or within an acquired image. In one instance, I was examining an image of a system on which the user had reported suspicious events. I eventually located malware that was responsible for those events, but using a tool to mount the acquired image as a read–only file system would not only allow me to locate the specific malware much more quickly by scanning for it with an antivirus scanning application, but also allow me to automate scans across several images to locate that malware, or to use multiple tools to scan for malware or spyware. This would have been beneficial to me in one particular case where the initial infection to the system occurred two years prior to the image being acquired. Having the ability to scan files from an acquired image just as though they were files on your live system, but without modifying them in any way, can be extremely valuable to an examiner.

## TIP

When attempting to determine whether an acquired image contains malware, one excellent resource is the log files from the installed antivirus application, if there is one. For example, the mrt.log file mentioned earlier in this chapter may give you some indications of what the system had been protected against. Other antivirus applications maintain log files in other locations within the file system, some depending upon the version of the application. McAfee VirusScan Enterprise Version 8.0i maintains its log files in the C:\ Documents and Settings\All Users\Application Data\Network Associates\ VirusScan directory, whereas another version of the application maintains its onaccessscanlog.txt file in the C:\Documents and Settings\All Users\Application Data\McAfee\DesktopProtection directory. Also be sure to check the Application Event Log for entries written by antivirus applications.

Once you've mounted the acquired image (read-only, of course), you're ready to scan it with your antivirus scanning application of choice. A number of commercial and freeware antivirus solutions are available, and it is generally a good idea to use more than one antivirus scanning application. Claus Valca has a number of portable antivirus scanning applications listed in his Grand Stream Dreams blog (http://grandstreamdreams.blogspot.com/2008/11/ portable-anti-virusmalware-security.html). When using any antivirus or spyware scanning tools (there are just too many options to list here) be sure to configure the tools to not delete or quarantine or otherwise modify any files that are detected. Many scanning tools come with an option to alert only and take no other action, so be sure to check those options.

Because mounting the acquired image can provide read-only access to the files within an image, you can access those files just like regular files on a system, without changing the contents of the files. As such, scripting languages such as Perl will return file handles when you open the files and directories, making restore point and prefetch directory analysis a straightforward process. Perl scripts used on live systems to perform these functions need only be "pointed to" the appropriate locations. RegRipper, discussed at length in Chapter 4, is a tool that operates like this; the analyst can mount the acquired image file as a read-only file system, and then point RegRipper to the appropriate Registry hive files. In the examples used in the "Mounting an Image" section, the analyst would point RegRipper toward H:\ Windows\system32\config, where the Registry hive files are located within that mounted image. Using tools such as RegRipper in this manner will allow you to check autostart locations within the Registry (you can use other tools to check autostart locations within the file system) for possible indications of malware.

> **TIP**
>
> Autostart locations are locations within Windows systems that allow applications to be started with little or no user interaction. As you saw in Chapter 4, the Windows Registry contains many such locations, as does the file system. In Chapter 1, you saw that you can use the Autoruns application available from Microsoft (from the Sysinternals site) or its CLI brother, autorunsc.exe, to quickly check the autostart locations on a live system.

Another example is of a tool I wrote called WFPCheck (WFPCheck is not available on the accompanying media). At the SANS Forensic Summit in October 2008, the consultants from Mandiant mentioned malware that could infect files protected by Windows File Protection (WFP), and those files would remain infected. I had read reports of similar malware previously, and had done research into the issue. I found that there is reportedly an undocumented API call called *SfcFileException* (www.bitsum.com/aboutwfp.asp) that will allegedly suspend WFP for one minute. WFP "listens" for file changes and "wakes up" when a file change event occurs for one of the designated protected files, and does not poll the protected files on a regular basis to determine whether any have been modified in some way. Suspending WFP for one minute is more than enough time to infect a file, and once WFP resumes, there is no way for it to detect that a protected file has been modified.

> **TIP**
>
> The *SfcFileException* API is called by the demonstration tool, WfpDeprotect (www.bitsum.com/wfpdeprotect.php).

As a result of this issue, I decided to write WFPCheck (wfpchk.pl). WFPCheck works by first reading the list of files from the system32\dllcache directory and generating MD5 hashes for each file. Then WFPCheck will search for each file, first within the system32 directory and then within the entire partition (skipping the system32 and system32\dllcache directories). As a file with the same name as one of the protected files is located, WFPCheck generates an MD5 hash for that file and compares it to the hash that it already has on hand. WFPCheck outputs its results to a comma-separated value (.csv) file, and writes a text-based log of its activities to the same directory as the .csv file. Figure 5.20 illustrates WFPCheck being run against a mounted image file.

**Figure 5.20** WFPCheck Being Run against a Mounted Image File

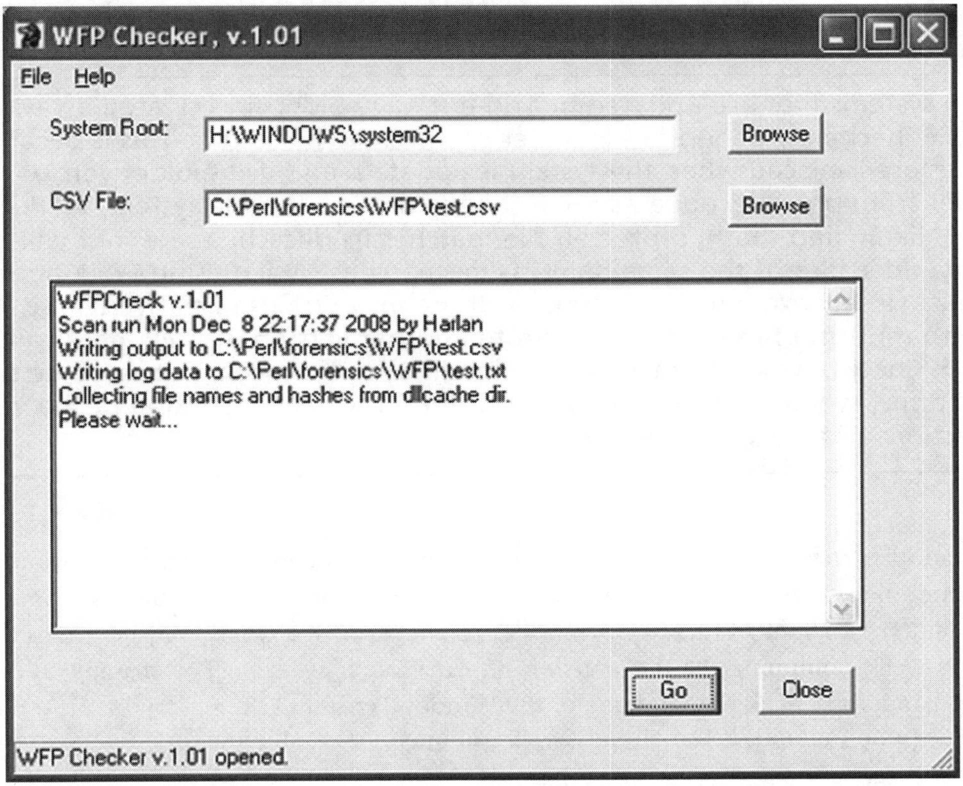

The .csv file from WFPCheck consists of three columns: the filename from the system32\ dllcache directory, the full path to where the file was found (outside the dllcache directory), and the results of the comparison. If WFPCheck finds that the generated hash values match, the result will be "Match" (illustrated in Figure 5.21). If the hashes do not match, the result will be "Mismatch", followed by two sets of colon-separated values; the respective file sizes followed by their respective hashes. These two sets of numbers are themselves separated by a dash.

**Figure 5.21** Excerpt of WFPCheck Output .csv File

| File | Full Path | Result |
|---|---|---|
| 12520437.cpx | H:\WINDOWS\system32\12520437.cpx | Match |
| 12520850.cpx | H:\WINDOWS\system32\12520850.cpx | Match |
| 6to4svc.dll | H:\WINDOWS\system32\6to4svc.dll | Match |
| aaaamon.dll | H:\WINDOWS\system32\aaaamon.dll | Match |
| access.cpl | H:\WINDOWS\system32\access.cpl | Match |
| acctres.dll | H:\WINDOWS\system32\acctres.dll | Match |
| accwiz.exe | H:\WINDOWS\system32\accwiz.exe | Match |

---

**WARNING**

On systems that are updated but do not have older files cleared away, WFPCheck may generate a number of "Mismatch" results. This is because files are replaced when the system is updated, and if the older versions of files from previous updates are left lying around the file system, WFPCheck will likely find that a protected file matches its dllcache mate, but will identify older files of the same name as mismatches. When using WFPCheck, you must closely examine the results, as there may be false positives. To assist with reducing false positives, I wrote another version of WFPCheck called WFPCheckf, which extracts file version information from the resource section of a file, where appropriate (see Chapter 6 for an explanation of the various sections of an executable file).

---

Yet another means for checking for potential malware in an acquired image mounted as a read-only file system is to use sigcheck.exe from Microsoft (http://technet.microsoft.com/en–us/sysinternals/bb897441.aspx). Sigcheck.exe checks to see whether a file is digitally signed, as well as dumping the file's version information, if available. For example, the following command will check the contents of the Windows\system32 directory of a mounted image file (mounted as the H:\ drive) for all unsigned executable files:

```
D:\tools>sigcheck -u -e H:\Windows\system32
```

Although not definitive, you can use this technique as one of several techniques employed to provide a comprehensive analysis of files in an acquired image while searching for malware.

# Timeline Analysis

Timeline analysis is a means of identifying or linking a sequence of events in a manner that is easy for people such as incident responders to visualize and understand. So much of what we do as analysts is associated to time in some way; for example, one of the things I track when I receive a call for assistance is the time when I received that call. During the triage process, I try to determine when the caller first received an indication of an incident, such as when he first noticed something unusual or received notification from an external source. This information very often helps me narrow down what I would be looking for during response as well as during my analysis, and where within the acquired data (images, memory dumps, logs, etc.) I would be looking. All of this has to do with having data that has some sort of time value associated with it, or is "time-stamped" in some manner.

Once a responder becomes engaged in an incident, suddenly the door is open to a significant amount of time-stamped data. Files within an acquired image have MAC times associated with them, indicating when they were last modified or accessed. Log files on the system (Windows Event Logs, IIS Web server logs, FTP service logs, antivirus application log files, etc.) contain entries that have times associated with specific events. As you saw in Chapter 4, not only do Registry keys have time stamps in the form of *LastWrite* times, but in the case of most recently used (MRU) lists, the most recent event is associated with that key's *LastWrite* time. Add to that the various Registry values that contain time values within their data and there is quite a bit of time-stamped data available to the responder to not only get an idea of when the incident may have occurred, but also possibly determine additional artifacts of the incident.

Most often, analysts have begun developing a timeline by collecting time-stamped data and adding it to a spreadsheet. One of the benefits of this sort of timeline development is that adding new events as they are discovered is relatively simple, and as new data is added, the entries can be sorted to put all of the entries in the proper sequence on the timeline. This process is also useful for data reduction (as the analyst adds only the values of interest), but it can be time-consuming and cumbersome. Also, this process is not particularly scalable, as with modern operating systems and other sources of data during an examination, the analyst can quickly be overwhelmed by the sheer number of events that may or may not have any impact on or relevance to the examination.

An automated means for collecting time-stamped information from an acquired image is to use the fls tool available with The Sleuth Kit (TSK, which you can find at www.sleuthkit. org/), which was written by Brian Carrier. The fls tool is run against an acquired image file to list the files and directories in the image, as well as recently deleted files, sending its output to what is referred to as a "body file" (http://wiki.sleuthkit.org/index.php?title=Body_file). The body file can then be parsed by the mactime.pl Perl script to convert the body file to a timeline in a more understandable, text-based format. The Timelines page at the Sleuth Kit Web site (http://wiki.sleuthkit.org/index.php?title=Timelines) provides additional information about this process.

Displaying time-stamped file data from an acquired image using fls.exe is relatively straightforward. Using the following command, the output from the tool is displayed in the console (i.e., STDOUT) in mactime or body file format:

```
D:\tools\tsk>fls -m C: -i raw -f ntfs -l -r d:\cases\xp\xp.001
```

Note that to display only the deleted entries from the acquired image, add the −*d* switch. For more details on the use of fls, refer to the man page for the tool, which you can find at www.sleuthkit.org/sleuthkit/man/fls.html. The output of fls is pipe-separated (and easily parsed), and can be redirected to a file for storage and later analysis. An excerpt of the output of fls appears as follows:

```
0|C:/Program Files/Internet Explorer/Connection Wizard/inetwiz.exe|5091-128-3|r/
rrwxrwxrwx|0|0|20480|1201700419|1057579200|1201700199|1201700199

0|C:/Program Files/Internet Explorer/Connection Wizard/isignup.exe|5092-128-3|r/
rrwxrwxrwx|0|0|16384|1201700420|1057579200|1201700199|1201700199

0|C:/Program Files/Internet Explorer/Connection Wizard/msicw.isp|5107-128-1|r/
rrwxrwxrwx|0|0|158|1201700200|1057579200|1201700200|1201700200

0|C:/Program Files/Internet Explorer/Connection Wizard/msn.isp|5108-128-1|r/
rrwxrwxrwx|0|0|197|1201700200|1057579200|1201700200|1201700200

0|C:/Program Files/Internet Explorer/Connection Wizard/phone.icw|4949-128-3|r/
rrwxrwxrwx|0|0|2921|1201700184|1057579200|1201700184|1201700184
```

This data appears in the body file and can then be parsed by the mactime Perl script to produce timeline information. The times associated with the file are all "normalized" to 32-bit UNIX epoch times, even as the times themselves are maintained by the file system (the image is of a system using the NTFS file system) as 64-bit *FILETIME* objects. Alternatively, you can parse the contents of the body file with Michael Cloppert's Ex-Tip tool (http://sourceforge.net/projects/ex-tip/) and view the output in a slightly different format. We will discuss Ex-Tip at greater length in Chapter 8.

# Summary

Most of us know, or have said, that no two investigations are alike. Each investigation we undertake seems to be different from the last, much like snowflakes. However, some basic concepts can be common across investigations, and knowing where to look for corroborating information can be an important key. Too often we might be tugged or driven by external forces and deadlines, and knowing where to look for information or evidence of activity, beyond what is presented by forensic "analysis" GUIs, can be very important. Many investigations are limited due to time and resources for merely a search for keywords or specific files, whereas a great deal of information could be available if only we knew where to look and what questions to ask. Besides the existence of specific files (illicit images, malware), we can examine a number of undocumented (or poorly documented) file formats to develop a greater understanding of what occurred on the system and when.

Knowing where to look and where evidence should exist based on how the operating system and applications respond to user action are both very important aspects of forensic analysis. Knowing where log files should exist, as well as their format, can provide valuable clues during an investigation—perhaps more so if those artifacts are absent.

A lack of clear documentation of various file formats (as well as the existence of certain files) has been a challenge for forensic investigations. The key to overcoming this challenge is thorough, documented investigation of these file formats and sharing of this information. This includes not only files and file formats from versions of the Windows operating system currently being investigated (Windows 2000, XP, and 2003), but also newer versions such as Vista.

# Solutions Fast Track

## Log Files

☑ A good deal of traditional computer forensic analysis revolves around the existence of files or file fragments. Windows systems maintain a number of files that can be incorporated into this traditional view to provide a greater level of detail of analysis.

☑ Many of the log files maintained by Windows systems include time stamps that can be incorporated into the investigator's timeline analysis of activity on the system.

## File Metadata

☑ The term *metadata* refers to data about data. This amounts to additional data about a file that is separate from the actual contents of the file (i.e., where many analysts perform text searches).

☑ Many applications maintain metadata about a file or document within the file itself.

# Alternative Methods of Analysis

☑ In addition to the traditional means of computer forensic analysis of files, additional methods of analysis are available to the investigator.

☑ Booting an acquired image into a virtual environment can provide the investigator with a useful means for both analysis of the system as well as presentation of collected data to others (such as a jury).

☑ Accessing an image as a read-only file system provides the investigator with the means to quickly scan for viruses, Trojans, and other malware.

# Frequently Asked Questions

**Q:** I was performing a search of Internet browsing activity in an image, and I found that the "Default User" had some browsing history. What does this mean?

**A:** Although we did not discuss Internet browsing history in this chapter (this subject has been thoroughly addressed through other means), this is a question I have received, and in fact, I have seen it myself in investigations. Robert Hensing (a Microsoft employee and all around completely awesome dude) addressed this issue in his blog (http://blogs.tech-net.com/robert_hensing/default.aspx). In a nutshell, the Default User does not have any Temporary Internet files or browsing history by default. If a browsing history is discovered for this account, it indicates someone with SYSTEM-level access making use of the WinInet API functions. I have seen this in cases where an attacker was able to gain SYSTEM-level access and run a tool called wget.exe to download tools to the compromised system. Because the wget.exe file uses the WinInet API, the "browsing history" was evident in the Temporary Internet Files directory for the Default User. Robert provides an excellent example to demonstrate this situation by launching Internet Explorer as a Scheduled Task so that when it runs it does so with SYSTEM credentials. The browsing history will then be populated for the Default User. Analysis can then be performed on the browsing history/index.dat file using the Internet History Viewer in ProDiscover, or Web Historian from Mandiant.com.

**Q:** I've acquired an image of a hard drive, and at first glance, there doesn't seem to be a great deal of data on the system. My understanding is that the user who "owned" this system has been with the organization for several years and has recently left under suspicious circumstances. The installation date maintained in the Registry is for approximately a month ago. What are some approaches I can take from an analysis perspective?

**A:** This question very often appears in the context that while analyzing a system, the investigator believes that the operating system was reinstalled just prior to the image being acquired. This could end up being the case, but before we go down that route, there are places the investigator can look to gather more data about the issue. The date/time stamp for when the operating system is written to the *InstallDate* value in the following Registry key during installation:

```
HKEY_LOCAL_MACHINE\SOFTWARE\Microsoft\Windows NT\CurrentVersion
```

The data associated with the *InstallDate* value is a *DWORD* that represents the number of seconds since 00:00:00, January 1, 1970. Microsoft Knowledge Base article 235162 (http://support.microsoft.com/?id=235162) indicates that this value may be recorded incorrectly. Other places that an investigator can look for information to confirm or corroborate this value are the date/time stamps on entries in the setuplog.txt file, in

*LastWrite* times for the Service Registry keys, and so on. Also be sure to check the *LastWrite* times for the user account Registry keys in the SAM file. Refer to Chapter 4 for more information regarding extracting information from the Registry (UserAssist keys and the like). Other areas the investigator should examine include the Prefetch directory on Windows XP systems and the MAC times on the user profile directories.

**Q:** I've heard talk about a topic called *antiforensics*, where someone makes special efforts and uses special tools to hide evidence from a forensic analyst. What can I do about that?

**A:** Forensic analysts and investigators should never hang a theory or their findings on a single piece of data. Rather, wherever possible, findings should be corroborated by supporting facts. In many cases, attempts to hide data will create their own sets of artifacts; understanding how the operating system behaves and what circumstances and events cause certain artifacts to be created (note that if a value is changed, that's still an "artifact") allows an investigator to see signs of activity. Also keep in mind that the absence of an artifact where there should be one is itself an artifact.

# Chapter 6

# Executable File Analysis

## Solutions in this chapter:

- **Static Analysis**
- **Dynamic Analysis**

☑ **Summary**

☑ **Solutions Fast Track**

☑ **Frequently Asked Questions**

# Introduction

At times during an investigation you may come across a suspicious executable file on which you would like to perform some analysis to get an idea of what it does or what function it performs. Many times, an intruder may leave scripts or configuration files behind, and these files are generally text files that can be opened and viewed. In the case of scripts, some knowledge of programming may be necessary to fully understand the function of the file.

In Chapter 5, we discussed file signature analysis, a method for determining whether a file has the correct file extension based on the file's type. This is one of the simplest means of obfuscation an attacker uses to hide or mask the presence of files on a compromised system; by changing the filename and extension, the attacker can (many times, correctly) assume that if the administrator discovers the file, she won't be very eager to access it and determine its true nature if the file has an extension such as .dll.

In this chapter, we will discuss ways in which you, as the investigator, can attempt to determine the nature of an executable file. I will present tools and techniques you can use to gather information about an executable file, and get clues about its purpose. This discussion will not be simply about malware analysis; rather, I will present techniques for analyzing executable files in general, of which malware may be just one class of executable file. In this chapter, we will discuss several analysis techniques, but we will stop short of any discussion of disassembling the code, or using tools such as IDA Pro (www.hex-rays.com/idapro/). The use of disassembler applications is a separate topic that warrants a book of its own. In this chapter, we will stick to methods and techniques that most administrators and forensic analysts will be able to perform.

Before we begin, however, you may be asking why we are doing this. What's the purpose of analyzing malware files? Isn't that what antivirus vendors do? Well, very recent history has shown that this may not be entirely the case. For example, the end of 2008 and beginning of 2009 saw the proliferation of the Conficker worm (a.k.a. Downadup) through corporate networks, due in large part to a lack of security updates (specifically Microsoft's MS08-067 vulnerability). Organizations employing enterprisewide antivirus solutions found themselves at the mercy of the worm when a new, as-yet-unseen variant was released. However, it was a lack of understanding of the nature of malware in general, as well as the nearly complete reliance on an antivirus solution, which caused the most trouble for corporate infrastructures. First responders being able to perform some modicum of analysis immediately will lead to faster response and recovery times for the organization as a whole, which in turn can further assist the response team in determining the root cause of the infection. Quicker response will also lead directly to a decrease in the potential of access to sensitive data by an intruder (via a Trojan, backdoor, or bot) or by the malware itself, as the analysis of the malware will lead to an understanding of its infection vector (how it got in), its persistence mechanism (how it stays running on systems), and any artifacts it may leave. These artifacts can then be used to locate other infected systems, particularly when the malware variant is not recognized by antivirus applications. This capability can mean the difference between taking decisive, *reasoned*, and *informed* action now and waiting several days for a vendor representative to show up, collect samples, and then roll out an updated signature file.

That being said, let's look at how to analyze executable files.

# Static Analysis

Static analysis consists of collecting information about and from an executable file without actually running or launching the file in any way. When most people open an executable file in Notepad (I've done this many times to illustrate something for a client) or even a hex editor, all they see is a bunch of binary data that appears to be meaningless garbage. Now and again, you may see a word that you recognize, but for the most part that word has no context; it could be anything. Investigators need to keep in mind that executable files have to follow certain rules with regard to their format, as there are specific things we can expect to see in an executable file found on a Windows system. Understanding those rules lets us delve into the apparent gobbledygook (aren't you glad I'm using technical engineering terms as I write this?) of executable files and extract meaningful information.

Before we dig in to an executable file, however, there are a couple of things we need to talk about.

## Locating Files to Analyze

One of the questions I am asked fairly frequently is how do you locate malicious or suspicious files on a system or within an image acquired from a system?

As we discussed in Chapter 3, one way to locate these files requires that you collect a memory dump from the system, parse the memory dump with one of the tools mentioned in the chapter, and locate a process associated with the suspicious activity using Aaron Walters' Volatility tool set. Once you find that process and parse the EProcess block, you will have the path to the executable file image. You can then locate that file within the file system in the system image based on that path.

Another way to locate suspicious files is to examine the contents of the Windows Registry autostart locations, as we discussed in Chapter 4. Should you find a suspicious Registry entry—say, in the Run key—you can then simply locate that file within the system image.

**TIP**

Using remote live-response techniques, as discussed in Chapter 1, you can reach out to remote systems to make the necessary queries to search those Registry autostart locations. Another method for doing this is to deploy

F-Response on the remote system, and once you have the remote drive connected, use a tool such as RegRipper to collect information from the remote system's Registry, just as you would had you extracted the hive files for analysis. You can also automate the data extraction by putting the necessary commands to implement rip.exe, the command-line interface (CLI) version of RegRipper, into a batch file.

Yet another means of locating malicious or suspicious executable files on a system image is to mount the image as a read-only drive letter on your analysis system using Smart Mount (www.asrdata.com/SmartMount) or Mount Image Pro, and then scan that drive letter with an antivirus scanning application. In fact, given that there are many instances where actual malicious files are not found by one antivirus application or another, you may want to scan the drive letter with more than one antivirus scanner.

**T**ɪᴘ

Claus Valca of the Grand Stream Dreams blog (http://grandstreamdreams. blogspot.com/) posts now and again on various antivirus applications that are available for use. Some of the applications he mentions are free but a more fully featured version of the application is available for a fee. However, in many cases, the freely available version provides the ability to scan for malware, which is what we're really interested in here. Some of the antivirus scanning applications that Claus mentions can be configured or were specifically written to be run from a thumb drive, which allows you to download, update, and use the application without having to have them all restricted to a single system. Go to his blog and search for *anti-virus software* and *malware tools* to see a list of the blog articles on those subjects.

However, even with the state of antivirus scanning applications the way they are today, they have one principal drawback: Because these applications are signature-based, all the malware authors need to do is make a small change to their software, and then recompile and redeploy it, and the malware may not be detected. I've seen instances (I've had a few myself) and heard of others who have submitted malware to various sites (such as VirusTotal. com) for review and found the executable file to not be detected or identified by 35 (or more) different antivirus scanning applications. As such, we need to develop different means by which we can identify malicious executable files, on systems or within system images. Another technique beyond those mentioned already would be to perform a deeper version of file signature analysis; that is, rather than simply looking for the letters *MZ* in the first two bytes of a potential executable file and then comparing that to the file extension, hoping to find "exe" or "dll" or another valid extension, we should dig a little deeper. Aside from the initial file signature, does the rest of the file have the appropriate file structure for that type of file? You can also verify that files are digitally signed using Microsoft's sigcheck.exe (http://technet.microsoft.com/en-us/sysinternals/bb897441.aspx), or use WFPCheck, as described in Chapter 5, to attempt to locate files protected by Windows File Protection (WFP) that were replaced or modified.

Regardless of the means you use to locate and identify executable files that may be suspicious or malicious (ideally employing more than one of the aforementioned techniques), you should be sure to thoroughly document what you do, as well as the results of scans or searches.

# Documenting the File

Before analyzing or digging into the executable file in any way, the first thing you should do is document it. However, it's a widely held belief (almost to the point of being an urban legend) that technically oriented folks hate to document anything. Well, this is true, at least in part. I can't tell you the number of times that I've responded to an incident (on-site or remote) and been told by the responders, "We found a file." When asked, "Where did you find the file?" the responders replied with wide-eyed, thousand-yard stares. Where the file was found can be extremely useful in adding context to other information, and helping you figure out what happened.

So, the first thing you need to do is document the full path and location of the file you found; what system it was on, what the complete path to the file was, and who found it and when.

> **WARNING**
>
> One thing that many technical folks do not seem to realize is that on a computer system (not just on Windows) a file can be named just about anything. Monitor any of the public listservs for a period of time and you'll find posts where some-one will say, "I found this file on my system and a Google search tells me that it's harmless..." Searching for information about a file based solely on the name of the file can turn up some interesting or useful information, but that information should not be considered the end of the investigation. I responded to an incident once where the on-site information technology (IT) staff had located several files on an infected system, and then Googled for information about each file. Typing in the name of one of the files they found, they saw that the file was legitimate, provided by Microsoft, and they ended their investigation there. However, by examining the file further using techniques presented in this chapter, I was able to determine that the file was, in fact, the malware to which I was responding.

Depending on how the suspicious file was originally located, you may already have the documentation for the file available. If you responded to a live system, for example, and used one (or more) of the response techniques mentioned in Chapter 1, it is likely that you already have documentation, such as the full path to the file, available. The same is true if you located the file in a system image using ProDiscover or some other forensic analysis tool or technique.

Another aspect of the file that is important to document is the operating system and version on which it was located. The Windows operating systems vary between versions, and even between Service Packs within the same version. The effect that the malware has on a target may depend on, or even vary depending on, the version of Windows on which it was located. For example, the Teddy Bear virus hoax e-mail identified the jdbgmgr.exe file as being malware (it was referred to as the "Teddy Bear" virus because the icon for this file is a teddy bear) and told the reader to immediately delete the file. If this was done on Windows NT 4.0, the file would be deleted. However, on Windows 2000, WFP would have immediately replaced the file. The set of files protected by WFP differs between Windows 2000 and Windows XP. Back in 2000, Benny and Ratter released the W32.Stream proof of concept virus that made use of NTFS alternate data streams (ADSs; see Chapter 5 for a detailed explanation of ADSs). If the virus made its way onto a Windows system with the file system formatted as FAT/FAT32, the virus appeared to behave differently, but only because the FAT file system does not support ADSs.

Besides noting where within the file system the file was found and on which version of Windows during your response procedures, you should also collect additional information about the file, such as the file's MAC times and any references to that file within the file system (e.g., shortcuts in a user's StartUp folder) or Registry, that you may notice during your initial examination.

## WARNING

Investigators need to be very careful when initially approaching a system, particularly one that is still running. Earlier in this book, we discussed Locard's Exchange Principle and the fact that ASCII and Unicode text searches do not always work on searches of the Registry, as some values are stored in binary format. Anything an investigator does on a system will leave artifacts on that system, so if you find an unusual file, limit your searches for extra information about the file as much as possible. Any activities you do engage in should be thoroughly documented.

The more complete your documentation, the better. It is a good idea to make a habit of doing this for every investigation, as it will save you a great deal of heartache in the future. Further, this constitutes a "best practice" approach.

Another step you will need to follow to document the file is to calculate cryptographic hashes for the file. Cryptographic hashes are used in information security and computer forensics to ensure the integrity of a file; that is, that no changes have been made to the file. One popular hash algorithm is the MD5 function, which takes input of arbitrary length and produces a 128-bit output hash which is usually represented in 32 hexadecimal characters. Any changes to the input, even switching a single bit, will result in a different MD5 hash. Although deficiencies in the MD5 algorithm that allow for collisions have been noted (http://en.wikipedia.org/wiki/Md5), the algorithm is still useful for computer forensics. Another popular hash algorithm is SHA-1 (http://en.wikipedia.org/wiki/Sha-1). Organizations such as the National Software Reference Library (NSRL) at NIST use the SHA-1 algorithm when computing cryptographic hashes for the Reference Data Set (RDS) CDs. Reference sets such as this allow investigators a modicum of data reduction by filtering out "known-good" (legitimate) and "known-bad" (known malware) files from the data set.

## TIP

Once you've calculated the MD5 hash of an executable file that you think may be malicious in nature, you can go to the VirusTotal.com Web site and post either the file itself or the MD5 hash for review. If you post the executable file for analysis, the site scans the file with about 35 different antivirus scanning applications. If you submit the MD5 hash, it is compared to the database of hashes maintained at the site. This site is a great resource for those with limited access to more than just one or two scanning applications, or for those who'd like to get 34 second opinions.

Another useful hashing algorithm was implemented by Jesse Kornblum in his tool called ssdeep(which is based on spamsum by Dr. Andrew Tridgell), available from http://ssdeep.sourceforge.net/. Ssdeep.exe computes "context triggered piecewise hashes" (www.dfrws.org/2006/proceedings/12-Kornblum.pdf), which means that instead of computing a cryptographic hash across the entire file start to finish, it computes a hash using a piecewise approach, hashing randomly sized sections (e.g., 4 KB) at a time. Not only does this technique produce a hash that can then later be used to verify the integrity of the original file, but it can also be used to see how similar two files may be. For example, if a Word document is hashed using ssdeep.exe and then modified slightly (adding/removing text, changing formatting, etc.), and then the hash is recomputed, ssdeep.exe will be able to show how similar the files are. You can use this technique with other file types, as well, such as images, videos, and audio files.

Once you've documented information about the file, you can begin gathering information from within the file itself.

# Analysis

One of the first steps of static analysis that most investigators engage in is to scan the suspicious file with antivirus software. This is an excellent way to start, but do not be surprised if the antivirus scan comes up with nothing definitive. New malcode is being released all the time. In fact, one antivirus company released a report in January 2007, looking back over the previous year, in which it identified a total of 207,684 different threats that its antivirus product protected against, and 41,536 new pieces of malcode that its product detected. Scanning the suspicious file may provide you with insight as to the nature of the file, but do not be overly concerned if the response you receive is "no virus detected". Scanning with multiple antivirus engines may provide a more comprehensive view of the file, as well.

The next step that most investigators will take with a suspicious executable file is to run it through strings.exe (http://technet.microsoft.com/en-us/sysinternals/bb897439.aspx), extracting all ASCII and Unicode strings of a specific length. This can be very helpful, in that the investigator may get an idea of the nature of the file from the strings within the file. The latest version of strings.exe (as of this writing) allows you to search for both ASCII and Unicode strings, as well as print the offset of where within the file the string is located. This offset will tell you which section the string appears in, and provides context to the string (we will discuss sections and section headers later in this chapter). You can even run the strings.exe program to search for specific strings in all files, using the example command line listed at the Web site for the application.

> **NOTE**
>
> Back "in the day," I was assisting with an investigation of a file taken from a system that was spewing traffic out onto the Internet from within a corporate infrastructure. The file turned out to be the IE0199 virus (www.f-secure.com/v-descs/antibtc.shtml) that would infect a system and start sending traffic to the Bulgarian telecommunications infrastructure. We found ASCII strings within the file that made up a "manifesto," and fortunately someone on our team had received Russian language training in the U.S. Army and was able to interpret what we'd found. Evidently, the author was upset with the prices charged for Internet access in Bulgaria, and wanted to conduct a denial of service (DoS) attack against the infrastructure.

Another useful utility for searching for strings in a binary file is BinText, which used to be available from Foundstone (owned by McAfee, Inc.). BinText would locate all ASCII, Unicode, and resource strings within a binary file and display them within a nice graphical user interface (GUI), along with the offset with the binary file where the string was found. Figure 6.1 illustrates several of the strings found in notepad.exe.

**Figure 6.1** Notepad.exe Open in BinText

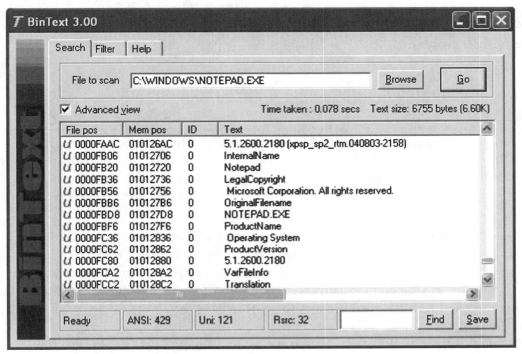

Although the strings found in the file do not paint a complete picture of what the file does, they can give you clues. Further, the strings may be out of context, other than their location. For example, in Figure 6.1, we see that the strings are Unicode (see the "U" on the left of the interface) and that they appear to be part of the file versioning information (more on this later in this chapter). Other strings may not have this same level of context within the file. Another option is that strings that appear odd or unique (in all seriousness, I actually found the string "supercalifragilisticexpialidocious" in a file once; honest) within the file can be used for searches in other files, as well as on the Internet. The results of these searches may provide you with clues to assist in further analysis (either static or dynamic) of the executable file.

A great many Web sites are available on reverse engineering malware or even legitimate applications, and oddly enough, they all point to some of the same core techniques for collecting information from executables, as well as use some of the very same tools. Two of the tools that we'll be using throughout the next sections of this chapter are pedump.exe and peview.exe.

In February 2002, the first of two articles by Matt Pietrek, titled "An In-Depth Look into the Win32 Portable Executable File Format," was published. In these articles, Matt not only described the various aspects of the portable executable (PE) file format in detail, but also provided a CLI tool called pedump.exe (found at www.wheaty.net) that you can use to extract detailed information from the header of a PE file. The information extracted by pedump.exe is sent to STDOUT, so it can be easily viewed at the console or redirected to a file for later analysis.

**TIP**

You can find part 1 of Matt Pietrek's articles at http://msdn.microsoft.com/en-us/magazine/cc301805.aspx. You can find part 2 at http://msdn.microsoft.com/en-us/magazine/cc301808.aspx.

Another useful tool for exploring the internals of Windows PE files is peview.exe (www.magma.ca/~wjr/), from Wayne Radburn. Peview.exe is a GUI tool that allows you to see the various components of the PE header (and the remaining portions, as well) in a nicely laid out format. The most current version of peview.exe available at the time of this writing is Version 0.96, and that version does not include the ability to save what is viewed in the GUI to a file.

Neither of these tools is provided on the accompanying DVD, due to licensing and distribution issues. Besides, going to the Web sites to obtain the tools will ensure that you have the latest available versions. The DVD does, however, contain Perl code for accessing the PE file structures. The Perl script pedmp.pl uses the File::ReadPE Perl module to access the contents of the PE header and to parse the various structures. The Perl script and module are provided for educational and instructional purposes so that you can see what goes on behind the scenes with the other tools. Also, the Perl code is written to be as platform-independent as possible; that is, when byte values are retrieved from the executable file, the Perl *unpack()* function is used with unpack strings that force the values into little-endian order. This way, you can run the scripts on Windows, Linux, and even Mac OS X (which is beneficial for analysis, as it is unlikely that on Linux or Mac OS X you will "accidentally" execute Windows malware and infect the system), so you are not restricted to performing analysis on a single platform.

# The PE Header

At www.microsoft.com/whdc/system/platform/firmware/PECOFF.mspx, Microsoft has thoroughly documented the format of PE files (as well as the Common Object File Format, or COFF, found on VAX/VMS systems), and has made that documentation public. Microsoft has also made most of the structures used within the file headers publicly available, as part of the documentation for the ImageHlp (http://msdn2.microsoft.com/en-gb/library/ms680198.aspx)

API structures. With this and other resources, we can understand the structure of a PE file, delve into its depths, and extract information that may be of use to us during an investigation.

A PE file can be broken down into several areas of interest (I hesitate to say "sections," as we will be using this term for a specific purpose in our discussion). The first, and perhaps most important, part of a PE file (if not the most important, then one of the best bits of geek trivia) is the file signature. For executable files on Windows systems, the file signature consists of the letters *MZ*, found in the first two bytes of the file. As noted earlier in the book, these two letters are the initials of Mark Zbikowski (http://en.wikipedia.org/wiki/ Mark_Zbikowski), the Microsoft architect credited with designing the executable file format. However, as you'll see, it takes much more than those two letters and an ".exe" at the end of the file name to make a file executable.

Mark's initials are the signature for a 64-byte structure called the IMAGE_DOS_ HEADER. The important elements of this structure are the first two bytes (the "magic number" 0x5a4d in little-endian hexadecimal format, or *MZ*) and the last *DWORD* (4-byte) value, which is referred to as *e_lfanew*. This value is defined in the ntimage.h header file as the file address (offset) of the new EXE header; that is, the offset at which we should find the signature for the beginning of the IMAGE_NT_HEADERS structure. The *e_lfanew* value points to the location of the PE header, enabling Windows to properly execute the image file. Figure 6.2 illustrates these values from an executable file opened in a hex editor.

**Figure 6.2** IMAGE_DOS_HEADER Structure Viewed in a Hex Editor

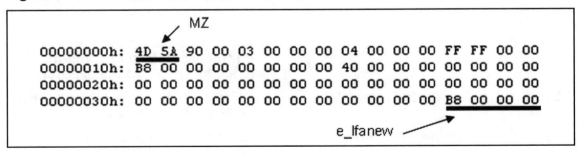

In the example illustrated in Figure 6.2, the IMAGE_NT_HEADERS structure should be located at offset 0xB8 (184 in decimal notation) within the file. The IMAGE_NT_ HEADERS structure consists of a signature and two additional structures, IMAGE_FILE_ HEADER and IMAGE_OPTIONAL_HEADER. The signature for a PE header is, sensibly enough, "PE" followed by two zero values (the signature value is a *DWORD*, or four bytes in length, and appears as "PE\00\00"), and is illustrated in Figure 6.3.

**Figure 6.3** IMAGE_NT_HEADERS Signature Value

```
000000b0h:  00 00 00 00 00 00 00 00 50 45 00 00 4C 01 03 00
000000c0h:  C2 E1 C2 40 00 00 00 00 00 00 00 00 E0 00 0F 01
000000d0h:  0B 01 06 00 00 80 07 00 00 30 00 00 00 00 00 00
```

The IMAGE_FILE_HEADER (http://msdn.microsoft.com/en-gb/library/ms680313. aspx) structure is contained in the 20 bytes immediately following the "PE\00\00" signature, and includes several values that can be useful to investigators. Table 6.1 lists the values and descriptions of the IMAGE_FILE_HEADER structure.

**Table 6.1** IMAGE_FILE_HEADER Structure Values

| Size | Name | Description |
|---|---|---|
| 2 bytes | *Machine* | Designates the architecture type of the computer; the program can be run only on a system that emulates this type |
| 2 bytes | *Number of Sections* | Designates how many sections (IMAGE_SECTION_HEADERS) are included in the PE file |
| 4 bytes | *TimeDateStamp* | The time and date that the linker created the image, in UNIX time format (i.e., number of seconds since midnight, 1 Jan 1970). This normally indicates the system time on the programmer's computer when he compiled the executable |
| 4 bytes | *Pointer to Symbol Table* | Offset to the symbol table (0 if no COFF symbol table exists) |
| 4 bytes | *Number of Symbols* | Number of symbols in the symbol table |
| 2 bytes | *Size of Optional Header* | Size of the IMAGE_OPTIONAL_HEADER structure; determines whether the structure is for a 32-bit or 64-bit architecture |
| 2 bytes | *Characteristics* | Flags designating various characteristics of the file |

Figure 6.4 illustrates the IMAGE_FILE_HEADER of a sample application opened in PEView.

**Figure 6.4** IMAGE_FILE_HEADER Viewed in PEView

| pFile | Data | Description | Value |
|---|---|---|---|
| 000000BC | 014C | Machine | IMAGE_FILE_MACHINE_I386 |
| 000000BE | 0003 | Number of Sections | |
| 000000C0 | 40C2E1C2 | Time Date Stamp | 2004/06/06 Sun 09:20:02 UTC |
| 000000C4 | 00000000 | Pointer to Symbol Table | |
| 000000C8 | 00000000 | Number of Symbols | |
| 000000CC | 00E0 | Size of Optional Header | |
| 000000CE | 010F | Characteristics | |
| | 0001 | | IMAGE_FILE_RELOCS_STRIPPED |
| | 0002 | | IMAGE_FILE_EXECUTABLE_IMAGE |
| | 0004 | | IMAGE_FILE_LINE_NUMS_STRIPPED |
| | 0008 | | IMAGE_FILE_LOCAL_SYMS_STRIPPED |
| | 0100 | | IMAGE_FILE_32BIT_MACHINE |

For forensic investigators, the *TimeDateStamp* value may be of significance when investigating an executable file, as it shows when the linker created the image file (investigators should also be aware that this value can be modified with a hex editor without having any effect on the execution of the file itself). This normally indicates the system time on the programmer's computer when the programmer compiled the executable and may be a clue as to when this program was constructed. When performing analysis of the file, the number of sections that are reported in the IMAGE_FILE_HEADER structure should match the number of sections within the file. Also, if the file extension has been altered, the *Characteristics* value will provide some clues as to the true nature of the file; for instance, within the *Characteristics* value illustrated in Figure 6.4, if the *IMAGE_FILE_DLL* flag is set (i.e., 0x2000), the executable file is a dynamic link library (DLL) and cannot be run directly. One class of files that usually occur as DLLs are browser helper objects, or BHOs (discussed in Chapter 4). These are DLLs that are loaded by Internet Explorer and can provide all manner of functionality. In some instances, these DLLs are legitimate (such as the BHO used to load Adobe's Acrobat Reader when a PDF file is accessed via the browser), but in many cases these BHOs may be spyware or adware. The MSDN page for the IMAGE_FILE_HEADER provides a list of possible constant values that can comprise the *Characteristics* field.

The value that gives the size of the IMAGE_OPTIONAL_HEADER structure (http://msdn.microsoft.com/en-gb/library/ms680339.aspx) is important for file analysis, as it tells you whether the optional header is for a 32-bit or a 64-bit application. This value corresponds to the "magic number" of the IMAGE_OPTIONAL_HEADER structure, which is located in the first two bytes of the structure; a value of 0x10b indicates a 32-bit executable image, a value of 0x20b indicates a 64-bit executable image, and a value of

0x107 indicates a ROM image. In our discussion, we will focus on the IMAGE_OPTIONAL_HEADER32 structure for a 32-bit executable image. Figure 6.5 illustrates the IMAGE_OPTIONAL_HEADER of a sample application viewed in PEView.

**Figure 6.5** IMAGE_OPTIONAL_HEADER Viewed in PEView

| pFile | Data | Description | Value |
|---|---|---|---|
| 00000108 | 0007C000 | Size of Image | |
| 0000010C | 00001000 | Size of Headers | |
| 00000110 | 0007F430 | Checksum | |
| 00000114 | 0002 | Subsystem | IMAGE_SUBSYSTEM_WINDOWS_GUI |
| 00000116 | 0000 | DLL Characteristics | |
| 00000118 | 00100000 | Size of Stack Reserve | |
| 0000011C | 00001000 | Size of Stack Commit | |
| 00000120 | 00100000 | Size of Heap Reserve | |
| 00000124 | 00001000 | Size of Heap Commit | |
| 00000128 | 00000000 | Loader Flags | |
| 0000012C | 00000010 | Number of Data Directories | |

The values visible in Figure 6.5 indicate that the sample application was designed for the Windows GUI subsystem, and a *DLL Characteristics* value of 0000 indicates that the sample application is not a DLL.

As you saw earlier, the size of the IMAGE_OPTIONAL_HEADER structure is stored in the IMAGE_FILE_HEADER structure, which contains several values that may be useful for certain, detailed analyses of executable files. This level of analysis is beyond the scope of this chapter.

However, a value of interest within the IMAGE_OPTIONAL_HEADER is the *Subsystem* value, which tells the operating system which subsystem is required to run the image. Microsoft even provides a Knowledge Base article (90493, http://support.microsoft.com/kb/90493) that describes how (and includes sample code) to determine the subsystem of an application. Note that the MSDN page of the IMAGE_OPTIONAL_HEADER structure provides several more possible values for the *Subsystem* than the Knowledge Base article.

Another value that investigators will be interested in is the *AddressofEntryPoint* value within the IMAGE_OPTIONAL_HEADER. This is a pointer to the entry point function relative to the image base address. For executable files, this is where the code for the application begins. The importance of this value will become apparent later in this chapter.

Immediately following the IMAGE_OPTIONAL_HEADER structure are the IMAGE_DATA_DIRECTORY (http://msdn.microsoft.com/en-us/library/ms680305.aspx) structures. These data directories, illustrated in Figure 6.6, act as a directory structure for information within the PE file, such as the IMPORT NAME and IMPORT ADDRESS tables (listings of DLL functions that are imported into and used by the executable file), the EXPORT table (for DLLs, the location of functions that are exported), the starting address and size of the Debug directory (http://msdn.microsoft.com/en-us/library/ms680305.aspx), if there is one, and the Resource directory, to name a few (of the 16 possible directories). Each data directory is listed as a relative virtual address (RVA) and size value, and in a specific, defined order.

**Figure 6.6** Excerpt of IMAGE_DATA_DIRECTORY Structures Viewed in PEView

| | | | |
|---|---|---|---|
| 00000138 | 00078004 | RVA | IMPORT Table |
| 0000013C | 00000028 | Size | |
| 00000140 | 0007A000 | RVA | RESOURCE Table |
| 00000144 | 0000114C | Size | |
| 00000148 | 00000000 | RVA | EXCEPTION Table |
| 0000014C | 00000000 | Size | |
| 00000150 | 00000000 | Offset | CERTIFICATE Table |
| 00000154 | 00000000 | Size | |

Figure 6.6 shows four of the 16 data directories available in the sample application. The values listed are the locations or offsets within the PE file where the information is located. For instance, the first line in Figure 6.6 shows that the IMPORT table is located at offset 0x138, the value at that location (0x78004), and the name of the value (RVA). From the information visible in Figure 6.6, we can see that the sample application has both an IMPORT table and a RESOURCE table.

**TIP**

An RVA is used within an executable file when an address of a variable (for example) needs to be specified but hardcoded addresses cannot be used. This is because the executable image will not be loaded into the same location in memory on every system. RVAs are used because of the need to be able to specify locations in memory that are independent of the location where the file is loaded. An RVA is essentially an offset in memory, relative to where the file is loaded. The formula for computing the RVA is as follows:

RVA = (Target Address) − (Load Address)

To obtain the actual memory address (a.k.a. the Virtual Address, or VA), simply add the Load Address to the RVA.

The final portion of the PE file that is of interest to us at this point is the IMAGE_ SECTION_HEADER (http://msdn.microsoft.com/en-us/library/ms680341.aspx) structures. The IMAGE_FILE_HEADER structure contains a value that specifies the number of sections that should be in a PE file, and therefore the number of IMAGE_SECTION_HEADER structures that need to be read. The IMAGE_SECTION_HEADER structures are 40 bytes in size, and contain the name of the section (eight characters in length), information about the size of the section both on disk and in memory (you saw reference to this in Chapter 3), and the characteristics of the section (i.e., whether the section can be read, written to, executed, etc.). Figure 6.7 illustrates the structure of an IMAGE_SECTION_HEADER.

**Figure 6.7** IMAGE_SECTION_HEADER Viewed in PEView

| pFile | Data | Description | Value |
|---|---|---|---|
| 000001B0 | 2E 74 65 78 | Name | .text |
| 000001B4 | 74 00 00 00 | | |
| 000001B8 | 000776EC | Virtual Size | |
| 000001BC | 00001000 | RVA | |
| 000001C0 | 00078000 | Size of Raw Data | |
| 000001C4 | 00001000 | Pointer to Raw Data | |
| 000001C8 | 00000000 | Pointer to Relocations | |
| 000001CC | 00000000 | Pointer to Line Numbers | |
| 000001D0 | 0000 | Number of Relocations | |
| 000001D2 | 0000 | Number of Line Numbers | |
| 000001D4 | 60000020 | Characteristics | |
| | 00000020 | | IMAGE_SCN_CNT_CODE |
| | 20000000 | | IMAGE_SCN_MEM_EXECUTE |
| | 40000000 | | IMAGE_SCN_MEM_READ |

**TIP**

One thing to keep in mind when viewing the section names is that there are no hard and fast requirements as to what section names should or can be. The section name is nothing more than a series of characters (up to eight) that can be anything. Rather than ".text", the section name could be "timmy". Changing the name does not affect the functionality of the PE file. In fact, some malware authors will edit and modify the section names, perhaps to throw off inexperienced malware analysts. Most "normal" programs have names such as .code, .data, .rsrc, or .text. System programs may have names such as PAGE, PAGEDATA, and so forth. Although these names are normal, a malware author can easily rename the sections in a malicious program so that they appear innocuous. Some section names can be associated with packers and cryptors directly. For example, any program with a section name beginning with *UPX* has been processed using one of those programs. We will discuss this at greater length later in this chapter.

All of the PE file information is also available via pedump.exe. The section information in Figure 6.7 appears as follows when viewed via pedump.exe:

```
01 .text    VirtSize: 000776EC VirtAddr:         00001000
   raw data offs:    00001000 raw data size:  00078000
   relocation offs:  00000000 relocations:     00000000
   line # offs:      00000000 line #'s:         00000000
   characteristics:  60000020
CODE EXECUTE              READ ALIGN_DEFAULT(16)
```

As you can see, there is no significant difference in the information available via the two tools. The virtual size and address information determines how the executable image file will "look" when in memory, and the "raw data" information applies to the executable image file as it exists on disk. As you saw in Chapter 3, this information also provides you with a road map when extracting the executable image from a memory dump.

## IMPORT Tables

It's very rare these days that an application is written completely from scratch. Most programs are constructed by accessing the Windows application program interface (API) through various functions made available in libraries (DLLs) on the system. Microsoft provides a great number of DLLs that offer access to ready-made functions for creating windows, menus, dialogs, sockets, and just about any widget, object, and construct on the system. There is no need to create any of these completely by hand when creating an application or program.

That being the case, when programs are written and then compiled and linked into executable image files, information about the DLLs and functions accessed by that program needs to be available to the operating system when the application is running. This information is maintained in the IMPORT table and the IMPORT ADDRESS table of the executable file.

**NOTE**

Awhile back, I had the opportunity to work on a project that involved determining whether an executable file had network capabilities. I had done some work examining applications to determine whether they had capabilities of either a network server (listened for connections, like a Trojan backdoor) or client (made connections to servers, like an IRCbot), but with this project the goal was to automate the process. So, we started by examining available DLLs to determine which of them provided networking functionality (i.e., wininet.dll, ws2_32.dll, etc.), and then we determined which functions provided the core functionality in question. Once we had that information, we could automate the process by parsing the PE file structures, locating the IMPORT table and determining which DLLs and functions were used. One thing to keep in mind, however, is that reading the IMPORT table of a malware executable file may not be that easy if the file is obfuscated in some manner.

The pedump.exe tool provides easy access to the IMPORT table information, by locating the import data directory and parsing the structures to determine the DLLs and the functions the application uses. Example output from pedump.exe appears as follows:

Import Table:

...

```
KERNEL32.dll
  OrigFirstThunk:   0000D114 (Unbound IAT)
  TimeDateStamp:    00000000 -> Wed Dec 31 19:00:00 1969
  ForwarderChain:   00000000
  First thunk RVA:  0000B000
  Ordn Name
    448 GetSystemTimeAsFileTime
     77 CreateFileA
    393 GetNumberOfConsoleInputEvents
    643 PeekConsoleInputA
    571 LCMapStringW
    570 LCMapStringA
    443 GetSystemInfo
```

As you can see, the sample application imports several functions from kernel32.dll. Although the DLL actually provides a number of functions that are available for use (see the "EXPORT Table" section later in this chapter), this example executable imports functions such as *GetSystemTimeAsFileTime()* and *CreateFileA()* for use. Microsoft provides a good deal of information regarding many of the available functions, so you can do research online to see what various functions are meant to do. For example, the *GetSystemTimeAsFileTime()* function retrieves the current system time as a 64-bit *FILETIME* object, and the returned value represents the number of 100-nanosecond intervals since 1 Jan 1601, in Universal Coordinated Time (UTC) format.

**TIP**

You can look up Microsoft API functions via MSDN. I keep a link to the Microsoft Advanced Search page on my browser toolbar for quick access. Typing in the name of the function I'm interested, such as *GetSystemTimeAsFileTime*, provides me not only with information about the API function, but also with important ancillary information.

Seeing what functions an application imports gives you a general clue as to what it does (and does not do). For example, if the application does not import any of the DLLs that contain networking code, either as low-level socket functions or higher-level Internet APIs, it is unlikely that the application is a backdoor or that it can be used to transmit information off the system and onto the Internet. This is a useful technique, one that I have used to provide information and answer questions about an application. I was once given an executable image and asked whether it was or had the capability of being a network backdoor. After documenting the file, I took a look at the IMPORT table and saw that none of the imported DLLs provided networking capabilities. I took my analysis a step further by looking at the functions that were imported and found that although several provided mathematic functionality, none provided networking capability.

Another useful tool for viewing the information regarding DLLs and functions required by an application is the Dependency Walker tool, also known as depends.exe, available from the Web site of the same name. Figure 6.8 illustrates an excerpt of the Dependency Walker GUI, with the sample application dcode.exe open in the Dependency Walker.

**Figure 6.8** Excerpt from Dependency Walker GUI

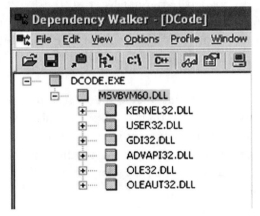

As illustrated in Figure 6.8, the dcode.exe application relies on functions from MSVBVM60.DLL, which in turn relies on functions from six other DLLs (each DLL ships with the most current Windows distributions). Figure 6.9 illustrates a portion of the functions exported by MSVBVM60.DLL, as reported by the Dependency Walker tool.

**Figure 6.9** Functions Exported by MSVBVM60.DLL

| E | Ordinal ^ | Hint | Function | Entry Point |
|---|-----------|------|----------|-------------|
| C | 100 (0x0064) | 60 (0x003C) | ThunRTMain | 0x0000DE3E |
| C | 101 (0x0065) | 73 (0x0049) | VBDllUnRegisterServer | 0x0001BCFC |
| C | 102 (0x0066) | 70 (0x0046) | VBDllCanUnloadNow | 0x0002C692 |
| C | 103 (0x0067) | 72 (0x0048) | VBDllRegisterServer | 0x000A4A8A |
| C | 104 (0x0068) | 71 (0x0047) | VBDllGetClassObject | 0x00028FCA |
| C | 105 (0x0069) | 69 (0x0045) | UserDllMain | 0x0001BBA7 |
| C | 106 (0x006A) | 13 (0x000D) | DllRegisterServer | 0x000D3AD5 |
| C | 107 (0x006B) | 14 (0x000E) | DllUnregisterServer | 0x000D3CB3 |
| C | 108 (0x006C) | 94 (0x005E) | __vbaAryLock | 0x000E24D0 |

The Dependency Walker tool allows you to see not only the DLLs and functions that an executable imports—be it an .exe or a .dll file—but also the functions exported by DLLs. We will discuss the EXPORT table a bit more in the next section.

The Dependency Walker tool also has a useful profiling function, which allows you to set specific parameters for how a module or application will be profiled, and then to launch the application to see which modules (DLLs) will be loaded. This allows you to trace the various DLL function calls and returned values as the application runs. This can be useful in detecting modules that are dynamically loaded but aren't listed in the IMPORT tables of other modules, or for determining why an "application failed to initialize properly" error is reported. However, this falls outside the scope of static analysis, as it requires the file to be run.

# EXPORT Table

As DLLs provide functions that other executable files can import, the DLLs themselves maintain a table of functions available in their (you guessed it) EXPORT table. These are functions that are available for other executable images (DLLs, EXEs, etc.) to import or make use of so that application authors do not need to write their own code for everything they want to do on a system. The DLLs act as libraries or repositories of prewritten code that are available for use on the system.

Pedump.exe will dump the EXPORT table from DLLs. For example, here is a portion of the EXPORT table for ws2_32.dll:

```
exports table:
  Name:            WS2_32.dll
  Characteristics: 00000000
  TimeDateStamp:   41107EDA -> Wed Aug 04 02:14:50 2004
  Version:         0.00
  Ordinal base:    00000001
  # of functions:  000001F4
  # of Names:      00000075
```

```
Entry            Pt Ordn Name
00011028         1  accept
00003E00         2  bind
00009639         3  closesocket
0000406A         4  connect
00010B50         5  getpeername
0000951E         6  getsockname
000046C9         7  getsockopt
00002BC0         8  htonl
00002B66         9  htons
00004519         10 ioctlsocket
00002BF4         11 inet_addr
```

If you have any experience with UNIX and/or Perl socket programming, you will recognize the exported functions as being the core functionality for network-based communications. For example, the *bind()* and *accept()* functions are used by services or daemons that listen for connections (backdoors, etc.), and the *connect()* function is used by client utilities that connect to servers, such as Web browsers and IRCbots.

I should point out that DLLs can import functions from other DLLs, in addition to exporting their own functions. For example, using pedump.exe to view the PE information for ws2_32.dll, we see that the executable imports functions from kernel32.dll, ws2help.dll, ntdll.dll, and others. Some DLLs will import functionality from other DLLs to build on the base functionality provided. Tools such as the Dependency Walker will show you these chained or cascading DLL dependencies in a nice GUI format.

# Resources

Many times, a PE file will have a section named ".rsrc", and will have a Resource data directory listed, as well. This resource section can contain information about things such as dialogs and icons, and other useful bits of information that may help you identify a file, but perhaps the most useful thing during analysis of an executable file is file versioning information.

The Perl script fvi.pl (located on the accompanying media) uses the Win32::File::VersionInfo module to extract file version information from a PE file, if such information is available. Fvi.pl takes a filename (with the full path) as the sole argument, and returns the information it finds as follows:

```
C:\Perl>fvi.pl c:\windows\system32\svchost.exe
Filename          : c:\windows\system32\svchost.exe
Type              : Application
OS                : NT/Win32
Orig Filename     : svchost.exe
File Descriptoin  : Generic Host Process for Win32 Services
```

```
File Version        : 5.1.2600.2180 (xpsp_sp2_rtm.040803-2158)
Internal Name       : svchost.exe
Company Name        : Microsoft Corporation
Copyright           : • Microsoft Corporation. All rights reserved.
Product Name        : Microsoft« Windows« Operating System
Product Version     : 5.1.2600.2180
Trademarks:
```

You need to keep a couple of things in mind when using tools such as this. First, the Win32::File::VersionInfo module is specific to the Windows platform. Second, neither the module nor the Perl script makes any attempts to verify that the file in question is actually a PE file. This means that if fvi.pl fails to return any information, it does not mean the file in question is malware. In fact, many malware authors make sure that such information is not compiled into their tools, whereas others will include faked file version information to throw off investigators. Some even include file versioning information simply to amuse themselves and others.

## Notes from the Underground...

### The Russiantopz Bot

While performing analysis of the russiantopz IRCbot, one of the interesting bits of information I discovered about the bot program (which was named statistics.exe) was that it really wasn't an IRCbot written by anyone from Russia! Looking past the name of the file and delving into the file versioning information, I found that the file was really a copy of the mirc32.exe (www.mirc.com/get.html) IRC client application. The GUI Internet Relay Chat (IRC) client was hidden from the desktop by a file called team-scan.exe, which was really a copy of Adrian Lopez's hidewndw.exe (http://premium. caribe.net/~adrian2/creations.html) utility.

Although the use of file versioning information is not always a conclusive means of analysis, it does provide additional information that will add to the overall picture of your investigation.

## Obfuscation

So far, we've used normal, legitimate executable files to illustrate the various structures of PE files. Although you can use these tools and techniques to identify files, malware authors often put forth effort to disguise or "obfuscate" their files, not only to avoid detection by administrators and investigators but also to hide from antivirus and other security software programs. Many times, the malware authors will use packers and even encryption tools to disguise their software, or they will simply create new versions of their programs.

You can use a variety of utilities to obfuscate executable files, such as binders, packers, and cryptors. We'll take a look at each of these in turn.

## Binders

Binders are utilities that allow the user to bind one application to another, in essence creating a Trojan application. The idea is that the carrier application will entice the user to launch it; examples include games and other executables. When the victim launches the carrier application, he sees the application run, and nothing seems amiss. All the while, however, the Trojan application runs, often behind the scenes, unbeknownst to the victim. One of the first binders available was eLiTeWrap (http://homepage.ntlworld.com/chawmp/elitewrap/), but Silk Rope and SaranWrap (http://packetstormsecurity.org/trojans/bo/index3.html) became popular when the Cult of the Dead Cow released its Back Orifice utility. Looking at write-ups and descriptions of malware available at antivirus sites (as well as others), it would appear that binders are no longer "in vogue" among malware authors, and perhaps are no longer considered "cool." This may be largely due to the fact that binders leave behind signatures that have long been detected by antivirus software.

Although many binders are available under many different names, they all perform the same basic function: to bind one executable to another. ELiTeWrap is perhaps unique in that it allows the user to configure a script of commands to be run or responses to be provided, offering some additional functionality in the bound executables.

---

### WARNING

After downloading ELiTeWrap 1.04 to a Windows XP Pro SP2 system, I tried several different times to produce a working, bound package, and failed each time. I tried using ELiTeWrap in interactive mode, as well as using a script. Each time, I ended up with an output file much smaller than any of the input files, and when I attempted to run the output file, I received a dialog that stated "Error #57 reading package".

---

## Packers

"Packers" is another name for programs that allow users to compress their programs, saving space. Another name for such tools is "compressors." Although this is not much of an issue due to expanding storage capacity, compressing the executable file does allow it to transit the network more quickly and potentially allows it to avoid detection by both host- and network-based antivirus and intrusion protection systems. Packers also make analysis of the executable more difficult. Some legitimate companies pack their programs to make them run faster (less to load from disk into RAM) or to protect trade secrets. Although many packers are available, popular packing programs include ASPack (www.aspack.com) and UPX (http://upx.sourceforge.net).

ASPack works by compressing the executable image, writing a small decompression routine at the end of the file. The executable's entry point is then changed to point to the beginning of the decompression routine, and the original entry point is saved. When the executable is decompressed into memory, the entry point is reset to the original value. One indication that ASPack has been used is the existence of section names such as .adata, .udata, and .aspack (keep in mind, however, that the section names are just that, names, and they can be altered). Tools reportedly are available that will allow you to unpack files packed with ASPack.

UPX is another popular packer, and although you can use it as a packer, you also can use it to decompress files that have been packed with UPX; so, it's an unpacker for itself, as well. One indication that you have a file compressed with UPX is the existence of the section names UPX0 and UPX1, but you should keep in mind that these names can be changed by simply editing the PE file with a hex editor.

These are just a few examples of compression utilities used by malware authors, and there are many, many more out there. Depending on the compression utility used, you may find an application or plug-in that is meant to decompress that algorithm, reversing the process. You may have to spend some time doing research on the Internet to see whether reversing the compression is an option, and whether there is a utility to assist you.

Tools such as ProcDump32 (www.fortunecity.com/millenium/firemansam/962/html/procdump.html) include the ability to unpack common compression algorithms. Figure 6.10 illustrates the Choose Unpacker dialog for ProcDump32 from which the user can select the algorithm used to pack the executable.

**Figure 6.10** Choose Unpacker Dialog from ProcDump32

ProcDump32 also includes other functionality, such as allowing the user to dump a running process to disk, unpack or decrypt a PE file using common algorithms, and edit PE headers. You've already seen other tools that allow you to do this, but ProcDump32 does provide some fairly useful functionality, and should be included as part of your malware analysis toolkit.

## Cryptors

"Cryptors" is a slang term for programs that allow the user to encrypt other programs. Encrypting an executable is another method that malware authors use to attempt to avoid detection by both host- and network-based antivirus and intrusion protection systems. This actually seems to be a pretty popular method for obfuscating malware, and in some cases the encryption algorithm or routine may be known or at least discoverable (based on a signature of some kind), whereas in others it may be completely unknown.

As an example of an obfuscated bit of malware, we'll look at a file that we know has been obfuscated in some way. The Honeynet Project provided interesting "Scan of the Month" (SotM) challenges (http://old.honeynet.org/scans/index.html) for some time, offering a variety of different data and scenarios for folks to try their hand at deciphering. The interesting thing about the SotM challenges is that after a period of time, the submissions are judged and posted, so you get to see how the challenges were solved in detail. Ed Skoudis provides similar challenges at his site, CounterHack.net.

For example, the Honeynet SotM 32 was designed to analyze a malware binary called rada.exe. Figure 6.11 illustrates the icon for the malware binary.

**Figure 6.11** Icon for the rada.exe Malware Binary

RaDa

Using pedump.exe and PEView to look at rada.exe, we see that it has a pretty normal PE header, and that everything seems to translate well. By that I mean the tools can parse the PE header information, and from a parsing perspective it seems to make sense. If it didn't, pointers would be pointing off to strange sections of the file, or off the end of the executable file altogether.

Perhaps the most interesting thing we see is that the file has three sections: JDR0, JDR1, and .rsrc. Now, .rsrc is a section that we're familiar with, but the other two we haven't seen in the PE files we've looked at so far. Another thing that we notice is that the IMPORTS table lists only two DLLs, KERNEL32.DLL and MSVBVM60.DLL, as shown here:

```
Imports Table:
  KERNEL32.DLL
  OrigFirstThunk:      00000000  (Unbound IAT)
  TimeDateStamp:       00000000 -> Wed Dec 31 19:00:00 1969
  ForwarderChain:      00000000
  First thunk RVA:  00010BE0
  Ordn Name
      0 LoadLibraryA
      0 GetProcAddress
      0 ExitProcess
  MSVBVM60.DLL
  OrigFirstThunk:      00000000  (Unbound IAT)
  TimeDateStamp:       00000000 -> Wed Dec 31 19:00:00 1969
  ForwarderChain:      00000000
  First thunk RVA:  00010BF0
  Ordn Name
    618
```

This is odd, because we know this is malware, and any malware that actually does anything is going to import more than two DLLs, and definitely more than just three functions from KERNEL32.DLL.

**TIP**

This is also a great way to spot obfuscated malware quickly. When the IMPORT table shows just KERNEL32.DLL (or maybe that DLL, and one or two others), and only a few imported functions from that DLL include *LoadLibraryA* and *GetProcAddress*, this indicates that the file has been obfuscated in some way.

The other imported module, MSVBVM60.DLL, is a Visual Basic runtime. The output of fvi.pl tells us that the file description from the resource section of that DLL is "Visual Basic Virtual Machine". From this, we can deduce that the malware itself was written using Visual Basic. This deduction is also borne out in the challenge submissions for analyzing this file listed at the Honeynet site.

As rada.exe has a resource section, we can run fvi.pl against it, and in doing so retrieve the following:

```
Filename          : d:\tools\rada.exe
Type              : Application
OS                : Unknown/Win32
Orig Filename     : RaDa
File Descriptoin  :
File Version      : 1.00
Internal Name     : RaDa
Company Name      : Malware
Copyright         :
Product Name      : RaDa
Product Version   : 1.00
Trademarks        :
```

Very interesting, and nice to know that the author is letting us know that, yes, this is malware. Don't expect this to happen often, if at all.

Now that we've seen definite signs that this malware is obfuscated (and yes, we cheated a bit by choosing a program we already knew was obfuscated), we'd like to know how it was obfuscated. Was a packer used? Was compression used, or how about encryption? We can use a handy tool called PEiD (http://peid.has.it/) to examine this file and attempt to determine the obfuscation method. Figure 6.12 illustrates rada.exe loaded into PEiD.

**Figure 6.12** Rada.exe Loaded into PEiD

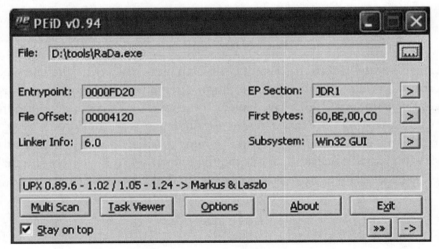

Notice that PEiD detected the obfuscation method as a version of the UPX compression utility. This is interesting, as the section names listed by PEView were JDR0 and JDR1, rather than UPX0 and UPX1. As I mentioned earlier, the UPX0 and UPX1 section names indicate the UPX compression utility. This tells us that if the PEiD information is accurate, the author used an editor to modify those section names.

**TIP**

Everything we've looked at with respect to executable files so far has given us some idea of different aspects of the files we can investigate to identify the nature of the file itself. This is particularly helpful in understanding what our antivirus products are telling us, or what they're not telling us when they are unable to identify the latest variant of some malware. This is where tools such as Yara (http://code.google.com/p/yara-project/) may be helpful. The Yara Project provides a framework to assist malware researchers (as well as responders) in identifying and classifying various aspects of malware files. Yara runs on Windows and Linux, and is also available as a Python module. Don Weber extended the Yara Python module (www.cutawaysecurity.com/blog/archives/422) into something he calls Yara-Scout Sniper or yara-ss, adding some useful capabilities, such as accessing remote systems. You can also use the publicly available PEiD signatures (look for userdb.txt at www.peid.info/BobSoft/Downloads.html) as part of your Yara rules. Something such as this can be extremely helpful in quickly identifying and classifying new variants of malware, particularly when it is maintained and extended as part of a community effort.

PEiD detects common packers, cryptors, and compilers by locating the entry point of the application and analyzing the bytes at that location, attempting to identify the obfuscation method used. The authors of PEiD have collected signatures for many different obfuscation tools and included them with PEiD. They've also included some nifty tools along with PEiD, among them a task viewer for viewing running processes and the modules they use, a dialog for viewing extra information about the file (illustrated in Figure 6.13), a dialog for viewing the PE header, and even a dialog for viewing the disassembled binary.

**Figure 6.13** PEiD Extra Information Dialog with rada.exe Loaded

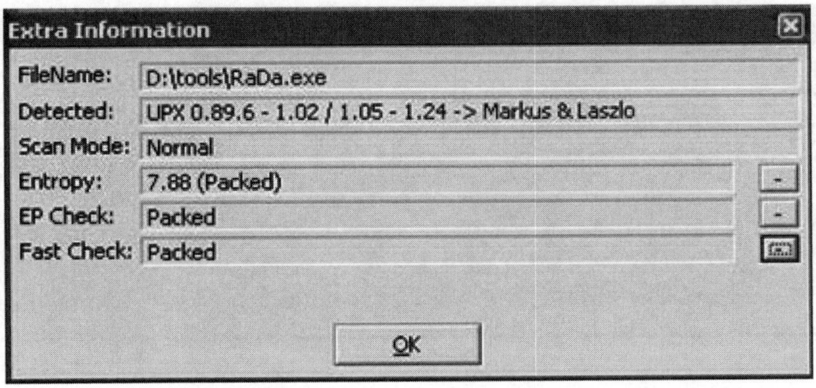

If you take the opportunity to download both PEiD and the rada.exe file, run the disassembler by clicking the button with the right arrow to the right of the First Bytes text field. If you're familiar with assembly language programming (I haven't done it since graduate school when we programmed the Motorola 68000 microprocessor) the things that may grab your immediate attention are the jump instructions and the many, many add instructions that you see listed. If you're curious about the details of the analysis of this binary, take a look at the submissions at the Honeynet site, particularly the one by Chris Eagle. Chris is a well-known instructor and presenter at BlackHat (www.blackhat.com) conferences, as well as a senior lecturer and associate chair for the Department of Computer Science at the Naval Postgraduate School in Monterey, California.

Mandiant's Red Curtain tool (www.mandiant.com/software/redcurtain.htm) takes a lot of the functionality you've seen so far in this chapter, including that of PEiD, one step further. This tool will reportedly look at the contents of the executable file, looking for entropy/randomness, indications of packing or obfuscation, the presence of digital signatures, as well as other characteristics of the executable file, and generate a threat "score." This is intended to indicate to the analyst whether he should investigate the file a bit further. Figure 6.14 illustrates the rada.exe file open in Mandiant's Red Curtain tool.

**Figure 6.14** Rada.exe Loaded in Mandiant's Red Curtain

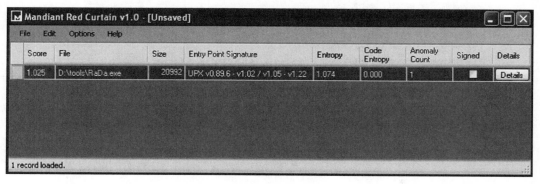

Much of the information presented by Red Curtain is similar to what is available in PEiD. Clicking on the **Details** button on the far right of the Red Curtain interface opens another dialog that illustrates the PE sections (JDRO, JDR1, .rsrc) and their information, as well as the anomaly identified, which in this case is "checksum_is_zero", indicating possible tampering with the file (see the Red Curtain User Manual, accessible from the Help menu option, for more information about the tool and the information presented).

---

**TIP**

If you're interested in delving deeper into the inner workings of malware and executable files in general, it is a good idea to read through the submissions for SotM 32 and 33 at the Honeynet Challenge site. Not only will you see commonalities among all of the analyses, but you will also see information about other tools you can use to go further into your analysis.

---

# Dynamic Analysis

Dynamic analysis involves launching an executable file in a controlled and monitored environment so that you can observe and document its effects on a system. This is an extremely useful analysis mechanism, in that it gives you a more detailed view of what the malware does on and to a system, and especially in what order. This is most useful in cases in which the malware is packed or encrypted, as the executable image must be unpacked or decrypted (or both) in memory prior to being run. So, not only will you see the tracks in the snow and the broken tree limbs, as it were, but using techniques for capturing and parsing the contents of memory (as discussed in Chapter 3) you can actually see the Abominable Snowman, live and in action.

# Testing Environment

If you intend to perform dynamic analysis of malware, one of your considerations will be the testing or host environment. After all, it isn't a good idea to see what a piece of malware does by dropping it onto a production network and letting it run amok. It's bad enough that these things happen by accident; you don't want to actually do this on purpose.

One way to set up your testing environment is to have a system on a separate network, with no electrical connectivity (notice here that I don't say "logical connection" or "VLAN on a switch") to the rest of your network. There has to be that "air gap" there; I strongly recommend that you don't even mess with having a knife switch to separate your malware "cage" from your infrastructure, because we all know that one day, when you're testing something really nasty, someone's going to look up and realize that he forgot to throw the switch and separate the networks. Also, if you're undergoing an audit required by any sort of regulatory body, the last thing you want to have is a way for malware that will potentially steal sensitive personal data to get into a network where sensitive personal data lives. If your lab is accredited or certified by an appropriate agency, you can seriously jeopardize that status by running untrusted programs on a live network. Losing that accreditation will make you very unpopular with what is left of your organization. This applies not only to labs accredited for forensic analysis work, but also to other regulatory agencies, as well.

One of the drawbacks of having a "throwaway" system or two is that you have to reinstall the operating system after each test; how else are you going to ensure that you're collecting clean data and that your results aren't being tainted by another piece of malware? One way to accomplish this is with virtualization.

# Virtualization

If you don't have a throwaway system that you can constantly reinstall and return to a pristine state (who really wants to do that?), virtualization is another option available to you. A number of freeware and commercial virtualization tools are available to you, such as:

- **Bochs** Runs on Windows, Linux, and even Xbox, and is free and open source (http://bochs.sourceforge.net/).

- **Parallels** Runs on the Mac platform as well as Windows and Linux (www.parallels.com).

- **Microsoft Virtual PC** Runs on Windows as the host operating system; can run DOS, Windows, and OS/2 guest operating systems, and is freely available (www.microsoft.com/windows/products/winfamily/virtualpc/default.mspx).

- **Virtual Iron** "Bare metal install" (meaning it is not installed on a host operating system) and can reportedly run Windows and Linux at near-native speeds (www.virtualiron.com/).

- **Win4Lin**  Runs on Linux; allows you to run Windows applications (http://win4lin.net/content/).

- **VMware**  Runs on Windows and Linux, and allows you to host a number of guest operating systems. The VMware Server and VMware Player products are freely available. VMware is considered by many to be the de facto standard for virtualization products, and is discussed in greater detail in the following sections (www.vmware.com).

**TIP**

In January 2009, as I was preparing the manuscript for this book to go to the publisher, an interesting tool called Zero Wine (http://zerowine.sourceforge.net/) caught my eye. Zero Wine is a QEMU-based virtual environment with a Debian Linux guest operating system installed. The guest operating system has Wine installed as well, and when run it starts a Web-based dynamic malware analysis platform. Essentially, you can upload a malware executable image file much as you would to the VirusTotal.com Web site, only with Zero Wine, the malware is executed within the virtual environment and *all* system activity (access to API functions, Registry activity), as well as static analysis parsing is recorded and made available to the analyst.

This is by no means a complete list, of course. The virtualization option you choose depends largely on your needs, environment (i.e., available systems, budget, etc.), and comfort level in working with various host and guest operating systems. If you're unsure as to which option is best for you, take a look at the "Comparison of virtual machines" page (http://en.wikipedia.org/wiki/Comparison_of_virtual_machines) on Wikipedia. This may help you narrow down your choices based on your environment, your budget, and the level of effort required to get a virtualization platform up and running.

The benefit of using a virtual system when analyzing malware is that you can create a "snapshot" of that system and then "infect" it, and perform all of your testing and analysis. Once you've collected all of your data, you can revert back to the snapshot, returning the system to a pristine, prior-to-infection state. In this way, not only can systems be more easily recovered, but multiple versions of similar malware can be tested against the same platform for a more even comparison.

Perhaps the most commonly known virtualization platform is VMware. VMware provides several virtualization products for free, such as VMware Player, which allows you to play virtual machines (although not create them), and VMware Server. In addition, a number of prebuilt virtual machines or appliances are available for download and use. As of this writing, I saw ISA Server and Microsoft SQL Server virtual appliances available for download.

There is a caveat to using VMware, and it applies to other virtualization environments, as well. Not long ago, there were discussions about how software could be used to detect the existence of a virtualization environment. Soon afterward, analysts began seeing malware that would not only detect the presence of a virtualization environment, but also actually behave differently or simply not function at all. On November 19, 2006, Lenny Zeltser posted an ISC handler's diary entry (http://isc.sans.org/diary.php?storyid=1871) that discussed virtual machine detection in malware through the use of commercial tools. This is something you should keep in mind, and consider when performing dynamic malware analysis. Be sure to thoroughly interview any users who witnessed the issue, and determine as many of the potential artifacts as you can before taking your malware sample back to the lab. That way, if you are seeing radically different behavior in the malware when running in a virtual environment, you may have found an example of malware that includes this code.

## Throwaway Systems

If virtualization is simply not an option (due to price, experience, comfort level, etc.) you may opt to go with throwaway systems that can quickly be imaged and rebuilt. Some corporate organizations use tools such as Symantec's Norton Ghost to create images for systems that all have the same hardware. That way, a standard build can be used to set up the systems, making them easier to manage. Other organizations have used a similar approach with training environments, allowing the IT staff to quickly return all systems to a known state. For example, when I was performing vulnerability assessments, I performed an assessment for an organization that had a training environment. They proudly told me that using Norton Ghost, they could completely reload the operating systems on all 68 training workstations with a single diskette.

If this is something you opt to do, you need to make sure the systems are not attached to a corporate or production network in any way. You might think that this goes without saying, but quality assurance and testing networks have been taken down due to a rushed administrator or an improperly configured virtual local area network (VLAN) on a switch. You should ensure that you have more than just a logical gap between your testing platform and any other networks. An actual air gap is best.

Once you've decided on the platform you will use, you can follow the same data collection and analysis processes that you would use in a virtual environment on the throwaway systems; the process really does not differ. On a throwaway system, however, you will need to include some method for capturing the contents of memory on your platform (remember, VMware sessions can simply be suspended), particularly if you are analyzing obfuscated malware.

# Tools

You can use a variety of tools to monitor systems when testing malware. For the most part, you want to have all of your tools in place before you launch your malware sample. Also, you want to be familiar with what your tools are capable of as well as how to use them.

One of the big differences between malware analysis and incident response is that as the person analyzing the malware, you have the opportunity to set up and configure the test system prior to being infected. Although it's true, in theory, that system administrators have this same opportunity, it's fairly rare that you'll find major server systems that have been heavily configured with security and especially incident response in mind.

When testing malware, there are some challenges that you have to be aware of. For example, you do not know what the malware is going to do when launched. I know it sounds simple, but more than once I've talked to people who've not taken this into account. What I mean is that you don't know whether the malware is going to open up and sit there, waiting to be analyzed, or whether it's going to do its job quickly and disappear. I've seen some malware that would open a port awaiting connections (backdoor), other malware that has attempted to connect to systems on the Internet (IRCbots), and malware that has taken only a fraction of a second to inject its code into another running process and then disappear. When doing dynamic analysis, you have the opportunity to repeat the "crime" over and over again to try to see the details. When we perform incident response activities, we're essentially taking snapshots of the scene, using tools to capture state information from the system at discrete moments in time. This is akin to trying to perform surveillance with a Polaroid camera. During dynamic analysis, we want to monitor the scene with live video, where we can capture information over a continual span of time rather than at discrete moments. That way, hopefully we'll be able to capture and analyze what goes on over the entire lifespan of the malware.

So, what tools do we want to use? To start, we want to log any and all network connectivity information, as malware may either attempt to communicate out to a remote system or open a port to listen for connections, or both. One way we can do this is to run a network sniffer such as Wireshark (formerly known as Ethereal, found at www.wireshark.org) on the network. If you're using a stand-alone system you'll want to have the sniffer on another system, and if you're using VMware you'll want to have Wireshark running on the host operating system, while the malware is being executed in one of the guest operating systems. The reason we do this will be apparent in a moment.

Another tool you'll want to install on your system is Port Reporter (http://support.microsoft.com/kb/837243), which is freely available from Microsoft. Port Reporter runs as a service on Windows systems and records Transmission Control Protocol (TCP) and User Datagram Protocol (UDP) port activity. On Windows XP and Windows 2003 systems, Port Reporter will record the network ports that are used, the process or service that uses those ports, the modules loaded by the process, and the user account that runs the process.

Less information is recorded on Windows 2000 systems. Port Reporter has a variety of configuration options, such as where within the file system the log files are created, whether the service starts automatically on system boot or manually (which is the default), and so forth. You can control these options through command-line parameters added to the service launch after installing Port Reporter. Before installing Port Reporter, be sure to read through the Knowledge Base article so that you understand how it works and what information it can provide.

**TIP**

Some malware may stop functioning and simply shut down if it is unable to connect to a system on the Internet, such as a command and control server. One way around this is to take a look at the network traffic being generated by the process and see whether it does a domain name system (DNS) lookup for a specific host name. You can then modify your hosts file (located in the %WinDir%\system32\drivers\etc directory) to point your system to a specific system on your network, rather than one on the Internet. See Microsoft Knowledge Base article 172218 (http://support.microsoft.com/kb/172218) for specific information on how Windows systems resolve TCP/Internet Protocol (IP) host names.

Port Reporter creates three types of log files: an initialization log (i.e., PR-INITIAL-*.log, with the asterisk replacing the date and time in 24-hour format for when the log was created) that records state information about the system when the service starts; a ports log (i.e., PR-PORTS-*.log) that maintains information about network connections and port usage, similar to netstat.exe; and a process ID log (i.e., PR-PIDS-*.log) that maintains process information.

Microsoft also provides a WebCast (http://support.microsoft.com/kb/840832) that introduces the Port Reporter tool and describes its functionality. Microsoft also has the Port Reporter Parser (http://support.microsoft.com/kb/884289) tool available to make parsing the potentially voluminous Port Reporter logs easier and much more practical.

With these monitoring tools in place, you may be wondering, why do I need to run a network sniffer on another system? Why can't I run it on the same dynamic analysis platform with all of my other monitoring tools? Well, the answer has to do with rootkits, which we will discuss in Chapter 7. However, the short answer is that rootkits allow malware to hide its presence on a system by preventing the operating system from "seeing" the process, network connections, and so on. As of this writing, thorough testing has not been performed using various rootkits, so we want to be sure we collect as much information as possible. By running the network sniffer on another platform, separate from the testing platform, we ensure that part of our monitoring process is unaffected by the malware once it has been launched and is active.

**TIP**

It may also be useful during dynamic malware analysis to run a scan of the "infected" system from another system. This scan may show a backdoor that is opened on the system but hidden through some means, such as a rootkit (we'll discuss rootkits in greater detail in Chapter 7). You can use tools such as Nmap (http://nmap.org/) and PortQry (http://support.microsoft.com/kb/832919) to quickly scan the "infected" system and even attempt to determine the nature of the service listening on a specific port. Although issues of TCP/IP connectivity and "port knocking" are beyond the scope of this book, there is always the possibility that certain queries (or combinations of queries) sent to an open port on the "infected" system may cause the process bound to that port to react in some way.

Remember, one of the things we need to understand as forensic examiners is that the absence of an artifact is in itself an artifact. In the context of dynamic malware analysis, this means that if we see network traffic emanating from the testing platform and going out to the Internet (or looking for other systems on the local subnet), but we do not observe any indications of the process or the network traffic being generated via the monitoring tools on the testing platform, we may have a rootkit on our hands.

As a caveat and warning, this is a good opportunity for me to express the need for a thorough and documented dynamic malware analysis process. I have seen malware that does not have rootkit capabilities, but instead injects code into another process's memory space and runs from there. This is something you need to understand, as making the assumption that a rootkit is involved will lead to incorrect reporting, as well as incorrect actions in response to the issue. If you document the process and tools you use, the idea is that someone else will be able to verify your results. After all, using the same tools and the same process and the same malware, someone else should be able to see the same outcome, right? Or that person will be able to look at your process and inquire as to the absence or use of a particular tool, which will allow for a more thorough examination and analysis of the malware.

**TIP**

When performing dynamic malware analysis, you have to plan for as much as you possibly can, but at the same time you should not overburden yourself or load your system down with so many tools that you're spending so much time managing the tools that you've lost track of what you're analyzing. I was working on a customer engagement once when we found an unusual file. The initial indication of the file was in the Registry; when launched, it added a value to the user's Run key, as well as to the RunOnce key. Interestingly enough, it added the value to the RunOnce key by prefacing the name of the file with "*"; this tells the operating system to parse and launch the contents of the key even if the system is started in Safe Mode (pretty tricky!). We had to resort to dynamic analysis, as static analysis quickly revealed that the malware was encrypted, and PEiD was unable to determine the encryption method used. After launching the malware on our platform and analyzing the captured data, we could see where the malware would launch the Web browser invisibly (the browser process was running, but the GUI was not visible on the desktop) and then inject itself into the browser's process space. From this we were able to determine that once the malware had been launched, we should be looking for the browser process for additional information. It also explained why, during volatile data analysis, we were seeing that the browser process was responsible for the unusual network connections, and there was no evidence of the malware process running.

It's also a good idea to enable auditing for Process Tracking events in the Event Log, for both success and failure events. The Event Log can help you keep track of a number of different activities on the system, including the use of user privileges, logons, object access (this setting requires that you also configure access control lists [ACLs] on the objects—files, directories, Registry keys, etc.—that you specifically want monitored), and so forth. Because we're interested in processes during dynamic malware analysis, enabling auditing for Process Tracking for both success and failure events will provide us with some useful data. Using auditpol.exe from the Resource Kit (which we discussed in Chapter 1), we can configure the audit policy of the dynamic analysis platform, as well as confirm that it is set properly prior to testing. For example, use the following command line to ensure that the proper auditing is enabled:

```
C:\tools>auditpol /enable /process:all
```

To confirm that the proper auditing is still enabled prior to testing, simply launch auditpol. exe from the command line with no arguments.

**TIP**

You may also want to enable auditing of System events, but be sure to not enable too much auditing. There is such a thing as having too much data, and this can really slow down your analysis, particularly if the data isn't of much use to you. Some people may feel they want to monitor everything so that they ensure that they don't miss anything, but there's a limit to how much data you can effectively use and analyze. Thoroughly assess what you're planning to do, and set up a standard configuration for your testing platform and stick with it, unless there is a compelling reason to change it. Too much data can be as hazardous to an investigation as too little data.

As mentioned earlier, one way to monitor access to files and Registry keys is to enable object access auditing, set ACLs on all of the objects you're interested in, and once you've executed the malware, attempt to make sense of the contents of the Event Log. Or you could look at two ways to monitor access to files and Registry keys: One is to take before and after snapshots and compare the two, and the other is to use real-time monitoring. When performing dynamic malware analysis, your best bet is to do both, and to do that you'll need some tools. You can go to the Microsoft Web site and download the FileMon and RegMon tools (which let you monitor file system and Registry activity in real time), or you can download Process Monitor. The benefit of using real-time monitoring tools instead of snapshot tools is that not only do you see files and Registry keys that were created or modified, but also you get to see files and Registry keys that may have been searched for but were not located. Further, you get to see a timeline of activity, seeing the order in which the files or Registry keys were accessed. This can be an important part of your analysis of the malware.

**TIP**

FileMon and RegMon are excellent monitoring tools available from Microsoft's Sysinternals Web site (http://technet.microsoft.com/en-us/sysinternals/bb795535.aspx). Although each of these tools is still provided separately, both of them have had their functionality added to the Process Monitor tool, also available from the same site.

We will discuss some of the snapshot-based tools that are available in the next section.

# Process

The process for setting up your testing platform for dynamic analysis of malware is pretty straightforward and simple, and the key is to actually have a process or a checklist. As with volatile data collection or forensic analysis, you don't want to try to perform dynamic analysis from memory every time, as sometimes you're going to be rushed or you're simply going to forget an important step in the process. We're all capable and guilty of this; I've had my share of analysis scenarios where I had to start all over because I forgot to enable one of my tools. I had to go back and completely clean and refresh the now-infected system, and then ensure that my tools were installed and that my system configuration was correct. I'm sure that I don't have to describe how frustrating this can be.

The first thing you want to do is ensure that you've identified, downloaded, and installed all of the tools you're going to need. I've addressed a good number of tools in this chapter, but in the future, there may be other tools that you'll be interested in using. Keep a list of the tools you're using for dynamic analysis and keep it updated. Every now and then, share it with others, and add new tools, remove old ones, and so on.

Once you have all of your tools in place, be sure that you understand how they are used, and ensure that you know and understand the necessary configuration options. Most of the tools will be started manually, and you need to have a checklist of the order in which you're going to start your tools. For example, tools such as Regshot (http://sourceforge.net/projects/regshot/), illustrated in Figure 6.15, and InControl5, illustrated in Figure 6.16, take snapshots of the system for comparison, so you want to launch the first phase (collect the baseline snapshot) first, and then start the real-time monitoring tools.

**Figure 6.15** Regshot GUI

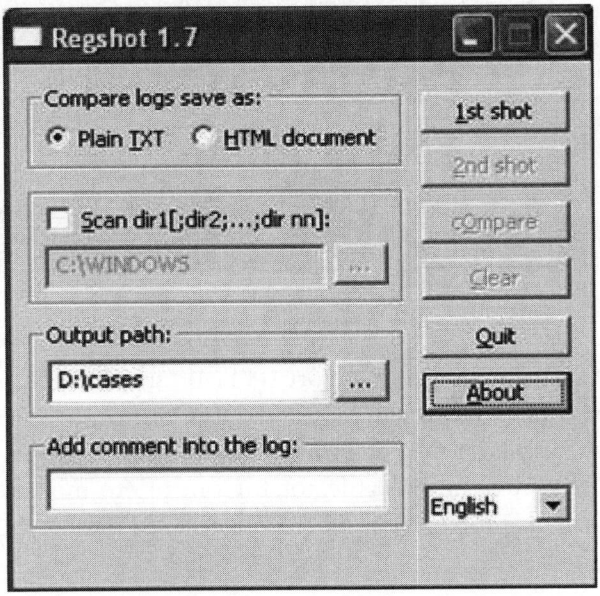

Regshot saves its output in plain text or HTML format. When using snapshot and monitoring tools such as Regshot, you should keep in mind that most tools will be able to monitor changes only within their own user context or below. This means running the tools within an Administrator account will allow you to monitor changes made at that user context and below, but not changes made by SYSTEM-level accounts.

**Figure 6.16** InControl5 GUI

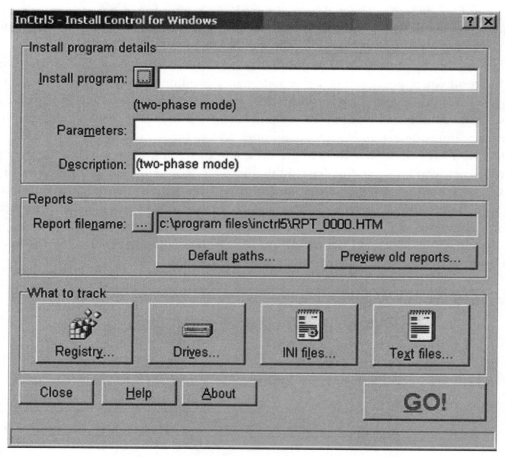

InControl5 provides you with a nice report (HTML, spreadsheet, or text) of files and Registry keys that were added, modified, or deleted. InControl5 will also monitor specific files for changes, as well, although the list of files monitored is fairly limited. You can also select an install program, such as an MSI file, for InControl5 to monitor. However, I haven't seen many Trojans or worms propagate as Microsoft installer files.

Once you've launched your malware and collected the data you need, you want to halt the real-time monitoring tools and then run the second phase of the snapshot tools for comparison. At this point, it's your decision as to whether you want to save the logs from the real-time monitoring tools before or after you run the second phase of the snapshot tools. Your testing platform is for your use, and it's not going to be used as evidence, so it's your decision as to the order of these final steps. Personally, I save the data collected by the real-time monitoring tools first, and then complete the snapshot tools processes. I know I'm going to see the newly created files from the real-time monitoring tools in the output of the snapshot tools, and I know when and how those files were created. Therefore, I can easily separate that data from data generated by the malware.

To take things a step further, it's a good idea to create a separate directory for all of your log files. This makes separating the data during analysis easier, as well as making it easier to collect the data off the system when you've completed the monitoring. In fact, you may even consider adding a USB removable storage device to the system and sending all of your log files to that device.

In short, the process looks something like this:

- Ensure that all monitoring tools are updated/installed; refer to the tool list.

- Ensure that all monitoring tools are configured properly.

- Create a log storage location (local hard drive, USB removable storage, etc.).

- Prepare the malware to be analyzed (copy the malware file to the analysis system, document the location with the file system).

- Launch the baseline phase of the snapshot tools.

- Enable the real-time monitoring tools.

- Launch the malware (document the method of launch; scheduled task, double-click via shell, launch from command prompt, etc.).

- Stop the real-time monitoring tools, and save their data to the specified location.

- Launch the second phase of the snapshot tools; save their data to the specified location.

I know this is pretty simple, but you'd be surprised how much important and useful data gets missed when a process like this *isn't* followed. Hopefully, by starting from a general perspective, you have a process that you can follow, and from there you can drill down and provide the names of the tools you're going to use. These tools may change over time. For example, for quite a while, RegMon and FileMon from Sysinternals.com were the tools of choice for monitoring Registry and file system accesses, respectively, by processes.

Figure 6.17 illustrates the Process Monitor toolbar.

**Figure 6.17** The Process Monitor
Toolbar, Showing the RegMon and FileMon Icons

If you've used RegMon or FileMon in the past, the Process Monitor toolbar illustrated in Figure 6.17 should seem familiar; most of the icons are the same ones and in the same order as the two legacy applications.

When using Process Monitor to capture Registry and file system access information, you need to be aware that *all* accesses are captured and that this can make for quite a bit of data to filter through. For example, click the magnifying glass with the red X through it and just sit and watch, without touching the keyboard or mouse. Events will immediately start appearing in the Process Monitor window, even though you haven't done a thing! Obviously, quite a lot happens on a Windows system every second that you never see. When viewing information collected in Process Monitor, you can click an entry and choose **Exclude | Process Name** to filter out unnecessary processes, and remove extraneous data.

---

**TIP**

Remember the Image File Execution Options Registry key that we discussed in Chapter 4? Process Monitor is great for showing how the Windows system accesses this key. As a test, open a command prompt and type the command **net use**, but do not press Enter. Open Process Monitor and begin capturing Registry access information. Go back to the command prompt and press **Enter**, and once you see the command complete, halt the Process Monitor capture by clicking the **magnifying glass** so that the red X appears. Figure 6.18 illustrates a portion of the information captured, showing how the net.exe process attempts to determine whether there are any Image File Execution Options for the listed DLLs.

---

**Figure 6.18** Excerpt of Process Monitor Capture
Showing Access to the Image File Execution Options Registry Key

```
\Windows NT\CurrentVersion\Image File Execution Options\ntdll.dll      NAME NOT FOUND
\Windows NT\CurrentVersion\Image File Execution Options\kernel32.dll   NAME NOT FOUND
\Windows NT\CurrentVersion\Image File Execution Options\msvcrt.dll     NAME NOT FOUND
\Windows NT\CurrentVersion\Image File Execution Options\RPCRT4.dll     NAME NOT FOUND
\Windows NT\CurrentVersion\Image File Execution Options\ADVAPI32.dll   NAME NOT FOUND
\Windows NT\CurrentVersion\Image File Execution Options\NETAPI32.dll   NAME NOT FOUND
```

You might consider using some other tools, as well. For example, the July 2007 edition of *toolsmith* (written by Russ McRee and available from http://holisticinfosec.org/toolsmith/docs/july2007.pdf), which was titled "Malware Analysis Software Tools," demonstrates SysAnalyzer from iDefense (http://labs.idefense.com/software/malcode.php). SysAnalyzer allows you to monitor the live system runtime state while executing malware during dynamic analysis. SysAnalyzer will monitor various aspects of the system while the malware is executing, so it goes without saying that the system will be infected; however, using a virtual system makes reverting back to a previous, pristine state extremely simple.

One final step to keep in mind is that you may want to dump the contents of physical memory (RAM) using one of the methods discussed in Chapter 3. Not only will you have all of the data from dynamic analysis that will tell you what changes the malware made on the system, but in the case of obfuscated malware, you will also have the option of extracting the executable image from the RAM dump, giving you a view of what the malware really looks like, enhancing your analysis.

**TIP**

This chapter presented a great deal of very useful information to help you understand Windows PE files, including information about their structure. However, in summer 2008, Syngress Publishing published *Malware Forensics: Investigating and Analyzing Malicious Code* and the authors (Cameron Malin, Eoghan Casey, and James Aquilina) should be credited with producing perhaps the most useful and comprehensive guide on this subject available today, addressing both Windows and Linux malware from a number of perspectives. One of the many valuable aspects of the book is the number of freely available tools listed that can be used in a wide range of analysis scenarios.

# Summary

In this chapter, we looked at two methods you can use to gather information about executable files. By understanding the specific structures of an executable file, you know what to look for as well as what looks odd, particularly when specific actions have been taken to attempt to protect the file from analysis. The analysis methods we discussed in this chapter allow you to determine what effects a piece of software (or malware) has on a system, as well as the artifacts it leaves behind that would indicate its presence. Sometimes this is useful to an investigator, as antivirus software may not detect it, or the antivirus vendor's write-up and description do not provide sufficient detail. As a first responder, these artifacts will help you locate other systems within your network infrastructure that may have been compromised. As an investigator, these artifacts will provide you with a more comprehensive view of the infection, as well as what the malware did on the system. In the case of Trojan backdoors and remote access/control software, the artifacts will help you establish a timeline of activities on the system.

Each analysis technique presented has its benefits and drawbacks, and like any tool, each should be thoroughly justified and documented. Static analysis lets you see what kinds of things may be possible with the malware, and it will give you clues as to what you may expect when you perform dynamic analysis. However, static analysis many times provides only a limited view into the malware. Dynamic analysis can also be called "behavioral" analysis, as when you execute the malware in a controlled, monitored environment, you get to see what effects the malware has on the "victim" system, and in what order. However, dynamic analysis has to be used with great care, as you're actually running the malware, and if you're not careful you can end up infecting an entire infrastructure.

Even if you're not going to actually perform any analysis of the malware, be sure to fully document it—where you found it within the file system, any other files that are associated with it, compute cryptographic hashes, and so forth. Malware authors don't always name their applications with something that stands out as bad, such as "syskiller.exe". Many times, the name of the malware is innocuous, or even intended to mislead the investigator, so fully documenting the malware will be extremely important.

# Solutions Fast Track

## Static Analysis

☑ Documenting any suspicious application or file you find during an investigation is the first step in determining what it does to a system and its purpose.

☑ The contents of a suspicious executable may be incomprehensible to most folks, but if you understand the structures used to create executable files, you will begin to see how the binary information within the file can be used during an investigation.

☑ Do not rely on filenames alone when investigating a suspicious file. Even seasoned malware analysts have been known to fall prey to an intruder who takes even a few minutes to attempt to "hide" his malware by giving it an innocuous name.

# Dynamic Analysis

☑ A dynamic analysis process will let you see what effects malware has on a system.

☑ Using a combination of snapshot-based and real-time monitoring tools will show you not only the artifacts left by a malware infection, but also the order (based on time) in which they occur.

☑ When performing dynamic analysis, it is a good idea to use monitoring tools that do not reside on the testing platform so that information can be collected in a manner unaffected by the malware.

☑ Once dynamic malware analysis has been completed, the testing platform can be subject to incident response as well as postmortem computer forensic analysis. This not only allows an analyst to hone her skills, but it will also provide additional verification of malware artifacts.

# Frequently Asked Questions

**Q:** When performing incident response, I found that a file called svchost.exe was responsible for several connections on the system. Is this system infected with malware?

**A:** Well, the question isn't really whether the system is infected, but rather whether svchost.exe is a malicious piece of software. Reasoning through this, the first question I would ask is, what did you do to view the network connections? Specifically, what is the status of the connections? Are they listening, awaiting connections, or have the connections been established to other systems? Second, what ports are involved in the network connections? Are they normally seen in association with svchost.exe? Finally, where within the file system did you find the file? The svchost.exe file is normally found in the system32 directory, and is protected by Windows File Protection (WFP), which runs automatically in the background. If there are no indications that WFP has been compromised, have you computed a cryptographic hash for svchost.exe and compared it to a known-good exemplar? Many times during incident response, a lack of familiarity with the operating system leads the responder down the wrong road to the wrong conclusions.

**Q:** I found a file during an investigation, and when I open it in a hex editor, I can clearly see the "MZ" signature and the PE header. However, I don't see the usual section names, such as ".text", ".idata", and ".rsrc". Why is that?

**A:** PE file section header names are not used by the PE file itself for anything in particular, and can be modified without affecting the rest of the PE file. Although "normal" PE files and some compression tools have signatures of "normal" section header names, these can be easily changed. Section header names act as one small piece of information that you can use to build a "picture" of the file.

**Q:** I've completed both static and dynamic analysis of a suspicious executable file, and I have a pretty good idea of what it does and what artifacts it leaves on a system. Is there any way I can verify this?

**A:** Once you've completed your own analysis, it may be a good idea to use an available antivirus software package to scan the malware. In most cases, an investigator will do this first, but this does not always guarantee a result. Many an incident responder has shown up on-scene to find a worm clearly running amok on a network, even though there are up-to-date antivirus utilities on all affected systems. If you do not get any results from the available utilities, try uploading the file to a site such as www.virustotal.com, which will scan the file with more than two dozen antivirus engines and return a result. If your results are still limited, submit the file for analysis, including all of your documentation, to your antivirus vendor.

**Q:** I am interested in reading more about executable file and malware analysis. Can you recommend any resources?

**A:** The best possible resource at this time is *Malware Forensics: Investigating and Analyzing Malicious Code* (Syngress Publishing), written by James Aquilina, Eoghan Casey, and Cameron Malin. This book covers analysis of malicious binaries on both Windows and Linux systems, and is perhaps the most complete and comprehensive book available on the subject to date. Depending on the amount of time you have to invest in something going further with this subject, a number of additional resources are available on "reverse engineering" executable code. Many of the techniques discussed pertain equally well to malware analysis. Some such sites include REblog (http://malwareanalysis.com/communityserver/blogs/geffner/default.aspx) and OpenRCE (www.openrce.org/articles/).

# Chapter 7

# Rootkits and Rootkit Detection

## Solutions in this chapter:

- **Rootkits**
- **Rootkit Detection**

☑ **Summary**

☑ **Solutions Fast Track**

☑ **Frequently Asked Questions**

# Introduction

At the RSA Conference in February 2005, Mike Danseglio and Kurt Dillard, both from Microsoft, mentioned the word *rootkit*, and the ensuing months saw a flurry of activity as "experts" pontificated about rootkits and software companies produced tools to detect them. Even though rootkits had been around for years, originating in the UNIX world and then migrating over into the Windows realm, this issue was largely misunderstood and in some corners even ignored, in a "head buried in the sand" sort of way. The mention of rootkits at the 2005 conference resulted in a surge of interest in rootkits, and commercial rootkit detection tools were announced soon after. (There had been several freeware tools and methodologies available for some time.) As detection techniques have improved, rootkit authors have devised new ways of subverting the operating system and even the kernel in attempts to remain undetected.

The rootkit threat is significant; there is no question about that. Rootkits can hide the presence of other tools, such as keyloggers, network sniffers, and remote access backdoors, not only from the user but also from the operating system. The insidious nature of rootkits can cause issues when they are actually present as well as when they aren't but incident responders assume that they have been, due to lack of knowledge and training. Assuming (without any hard-core data to back it up) that a rootkit has been installed on a system or infrastructure can lead an investigator or incident manager down an incorrect path with regard to reactions and decisions based on the misleading incident assessment. Considerable resources could be invested in unnecessary activities, or systems could be wiped of all data and reinstalled from clean media, all without determining the root cause, and then become reinfected soon after being put back into service.

# Rootkits

So, just what is a rootkit? A Sophos podcast (www.sophos.com/pressoffice/news/articles/2006/08/rootkit-podcast.html) released on August 24, 2006, includes the statement that as a result of a poll conducted by Sophos, 37 percent of respondents did not know the definition of a rootkit. Wikipedia defines a rootkit (http://en.wikipedia.org/wiki/Rootkit) as "a set of software tools intended to conceal running processes, files, or system data from the operating system." In the first part of their three-part series of articles on rootkits published on SecurityFocus, Jamie Butler, a widely regarded expert in rootkit technologies, and Sherri Sparks define a rootkit as follows (www.securityfocus.com/infocus/1850):

> A program or set of programs that an intruder uses to hide her presence on a computer system and to allow access to the computer system in the future. To accomplish its goal, a rootkit will alter the execution flow of the operating system or manipulate the data set that the operating system relies upon for auditing and bookkeeping.

Another way of looking at it is that a rootkit is a software program that modifies the operating system so that it is capable of hiding itself and other objects from users, administrators, and even the operating system.

Rootkits are used to hide processes, network connections, Registry keys, files, and the like from the operating system and, by extension, the administrator. The term *rootkit* comes from the UNIX world, where such tools were often used to gain and/or maintain "root" (akin to the Administrator on Windows) level access to a system. As similar functionality was developed in malware on Windows, the name made a similar transition along with the tools.

One of the first rootkits developed for Windows was NTRootkit, written by Greg Hoglund and released in 1999. NTRootkit consists of a driver and is still available with source code, as illustrated in Figure 7.1.

**Figure 7.1** NTRootkit 0.44 Archive Showing Source Files

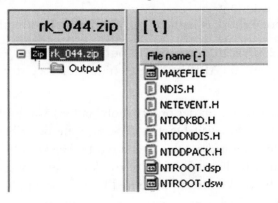

Since then, significant research has gone into the development of rootkits and rootkit technologies. Hoglund and others have conducted classes at the BlackHat Security Conference and other conferences on how to write rootkits, and his Web site, Rootkit.com, has become the preeminent site for Windows rootkit knowledge, development, and information sharing. Over the years, other rootkits have appeared on the scene, and development of new rootkit techniques continues unabated. There is also a great book available on rootkits, the way they are designed, and the way they work: *Rootkits: Subverting the Windows Kernel*. This book was written by Greg Hoglund and Jamie Butler and is available on Amazon.com.

Immediately following the RSA Conference in February 2005, there was an explosion in interest in rootkits and rootkit detection, and as detection techniques became more sophisticated, so did the rootkits. Think of the trend as an ever-escalating battleground, with developments on one side spurring further developments on the other.

There are several different types of rootkits. Early versions of rootkits worked by replacing operating system utilities and applications with Trojan'ed versions so that when the Trojan'ed version of the utility was run, it was programmed not to show specific objects. For example,

Trojan'ing the *netstat* command would first remove the attacker's network connections from the file listing and then display the remaining network connections as they would normally appear.

Later came the DLL injection or "user-mode" rootkits. These rootkits install in the security context of the user currently logged into the system and replace, hook, or patch various operating system calls or DLL functions. To put our *netstat* example in the context of a user-mode rootkit, rather than replacing the *netstat* command itself, a user-mode rootkit will hook Windows API function calls so that the functions themselves do not return a complete listing of all network connections. The *netstat* command then proceeds to display all the information it receives from the function call, not knowing that it has been given incomplete and misleading information. Hooking the listed function calls also hides the network connections from any other programs that use the same API functions. User-mode rootkits that hide files will hook the *FindFirstFile()* and *FindNextFile()* function calls so that no program that uses these function calls, including the shell (i.e., Windows Explorer), will see the files that the rootkit is hiding.

Examples of user-mode rootkits include, but are not limited to, the following:

- AFX Rootkit 2005 is an open source rootkit written in Delphi (by Aphex) that uses DLL injection and API hooking to hide files, Registry keys, processes, and the like.

- Hacker Defender (from Hxdef.org, by holy_father) was perhaps the most popular and widespread rootkit available. The F-Secure site describes Hacker Defender as the most widely deployed rootkit in the world. Hacker Defender also uses port redirection so that traditional means of rootkit detection, such as remote port scans, cannot detect the backdoor implemented by the rootkit. Hacker Defender uses a configuration file, which can be found in the contents of physical memory collected from an infected system. Portions of the configuration file can be found in physical memory; it can't recover the file as a whole. Furthermore, an examination of physical memory sees right through Hacker Defender; the examiner can see all the processes it has been hiding. The examiner has to compare the running processes found during memory analysis to the list presented by the operating system to know which ones were being hidden by the rootkit.

- NTIllusion (www.securiteam.com/securityreviews/5FP0E0AGAC.html) was designed to be able to infect a system, running under the lowest privileges available, subverting processes owned by the current user.

- Vanquish is a Romanian DLL injection rootkit that can hide files, processes, Registry keys, and the like. Vanquish consists of an autoloader (.exe file) and a DLL, which in turn consists of six submodules. Vanquish requires Administrator privileges to install properly and, according to the readme file that accompanies the distribution, does not work when other rootkits are present on the system.

■  Gromozon (www.antirootkit.com/articles/gromozo/The-strange-case-of-Dr-Rootkit-and-Mr-Adware.htm) is a user-mode rootkit that infects a system via a browser helper object (BHO) and uses multiple techniques to maintain persistence on the infected system (hides code in EFS files and NTFS alternate data streams, creates a service, creates a reference in the AppInit_DLLs Registry key, and the like). In addition, the rootkit removes the Debug privilege from user accounts to inhibit rootkit detection tools from functioning properly. The Symantec write-up (https://forums.symantec.com/syment/blog/article?message.uid=305212) on this rootkit describes it as "spaghetti" due to the various methods of persistence that the authors designed into the code.

**TIP**

Many rootkits are available for download online, and in many cases at Rootkit.com.

Much more insidious are the "kernel-mode" rootkits because they subvert the operating system kernel itself. Not only will kernel-mode rootkits intercept low-level API calls but also they will manipulate kernel data structures. One example of a kernel-mode rootkit is FU, developed by Jamie Butler, which uses a technique called *direct kernel object manipulation* (DKOM) to hide on the system. DKOM is the process of manipulating kernel-level data structures without using the Windows APIs. For example, the Windows kernel maintains a doubly linked circular list of all running processes on the system, and FU will remove requested processes from the list. The processes are still there but are not "seen" by the kernel. The scheduling quantum for the system is a thread, not a process, so the FU thread continues to run while the process is invisible to the system. FU uses a driver, named msdirectx.sys by default, to gain access and control the system. The FU program, fu.exe, terminates after it loads the driver into memory.

Kernel-mode rootkits may also subvert other kernel structures. The FUTo (www.uninformed.org/?v=3&a=7) rootkit, released as the successor to the FU rootkit, is discussed at great length in volume 3 of the *Uniformed Journal* (www.uninformed.org, released in January 2006). FUTo extends FU's DKOM capabilities by using assembly language code (rather than API calls) to manipulate the *PspCidTable* variable, which is a pointer to the handle table for process and thread client IDs. This handle table is used to keep track of all process identifiers.

Shadow Walker is a proof-of-concept kernel-mode rootkit that was discussed at the BlackHat 2005 conference. Based on the FU rootkit, Shadow Walker contains an additional driver that manipulates the memory manager to hide the existence of the rootkit files. Shadow Walker does this, in short, by ensuring that all hidden pages are in nonpaged memory and by intercepting all accesses to those pages. When the operating system requests to read those pages, the rootkit returns pages of zeros. When the operating system requests to execute those pages, it returns the malicious code. Remember the scene from the *Star Wars* movie in which Obi-Wan Kenobi told the StormTrooper commander, "These are not the droids you are looking for"? Yeah, just like that.

One caveat to kernel-mode rootkits is that they can also cause the system to "blue screen" if they are not properly written. Microsoft support personnel have helped many customers track down repeated BSoDs (the dreaded Blue Screen of Death), only to find that a kernel-mode rootkit was the issue. As mentioned in Chapter 3, a crash dump or BSoD will cause a crash dump file to be written to the hard drive, and support personnel can use this file to diagnose the issue. Often, this is the way a rootkit (one that is known or perhaps a new variant) is discovered on a system.

Occasionally, the term *rootkit* is used in a somewhat lazy manner. For example, there is an interesting entry in the Symantec Security Response Web log from September 2006 titled "The Poor Man's Rootkit." In that entry, the author describes a bit of malware named Trojan.Zonebac that uses a camouflage technique to "hide" its presence on the system. In short, during installation the Trojan scans the contents of the ubiquitous Run key and selects a commonly used application. It backs up the executable image for the file pointed to by the Registry value and writes itself to the file system using the name of the original file. When the system is started, the Trojan is run automatically, and it then runs the backed-up file as well, so nothing appears amiss. Furthermore, the *LastWrite* time of the Run key is not updated since no actual changes were made to the key.

Although this is indeed a novel and even ingenious method for hiding on a system, it is not a rootkit. In fact, hiding in plain sight by renaming the malware executable image to something innocuous is a common and effective practice. It is not uncommon for this sort of technique to be listed under "hack the admin" or "hack the examiner" rather than "hack the server."

## Warning

Relying on nothing more than the name of a file to diagnose an issue can be misleading and could even cause an investigator to completely miss the true root cause of the incident. Too often, an administrator will find a suspicious file and Google the filename. He'll then find that there is a legitimate Microsoft file by that name and so declare the incident closed. This does not apply only to administrators; I have seen malware analysts do the same thing. However, I have also seen instances in which malware was installed on a system using the name of a legitimate Microsoft file, such as alg.exe or svchost.exe. In most of the cases that I have been involved with, the administrator has found this "legitimacy" and looked no further. No one noticed that the executable images were not located in the system32 directory, for example. The point is that you cannot rely solely on the filename as a means of identifying a file and the effect it might have on a system or infrastructure.

Rootkits have also been used commercially. Not only have several rootkit authors branched out to provide custom rootkits to whomever was willing to pay their fees but also corporations have used rootkits to hide functionality. On October 31, 2005, Mark Russinovich (of SysInternals fame, now with Microsoft) announced on his blog that he'd discovered that Sony Corporation was using a rootkit in an effort to affect digital rights management and protect its property (http://blogs.technet.com/markrussinovich/archive/2005/10/31/sony-rootkits-and-digital-rights-management-gone-too-far.aspx). Among other things, Mark pointed out that not only was the use of this rootkit completely unknown to the person who had purchased the music CD and installed the software on her computer (users were not explicitly warned of the use of the rootkit, nor was it listed in the end-user license agreement) but also an attacker who did find this software installed on a system could take advantage of it and install his own tools, which would then be hidden under Sony's umbrella. Since the discovery of this issue and the ensuing furor, Mark has moved on to be employed by Microsoft. Mark's blog entry is archived at the Virus Bulletin site.

## Notes from the Underground...

### Information Sharing

In his blog entry regarding the Sony rootkit issue (at the Virus Bulletin site), Mark makes the following statement:

*Until a few years ago we made the source code to Regmon available publicly, which led to the use of our hooking functions and support routines in the NTRootkit example that's published on www.rootkit.com. The structure of the code in Aries indicates that it's likely to be derived from NTRootkit code.*

It's interesting to see how different sources are used to further the development of applications, including malware. In this case, the use of the hooking functions has come full circle.

Mark and others explored the use of rootkits by corporations in their software products, and on January 10, 2006, Symantec (www.symantec.com/avcenter/security/Content/2006.01.10.html) released information stating that its Norton Protected Recycle Bin uses rootkit-like functionality as well.

# Rootkit Detection

So now that we've seen a little something about what rootkits are and what they can do, how do we go about detecting the presence of a rootkit on a system? To answer this question, let's look at two detection modes, live and postmortem. In live-detection mode, the basic scenario is that we've got a running system and we're going to attempt to determine whether there is a rootkit on the system. In postmortem detection mode, we're working with an acquired image of the system. One of the benefits of employing both detection modes is that effective rootkit detection really requires a combination of various techniques discussed in other chapters of this book, such as memory analysis, Registry and file system analysis, port scans, and the analysis of network traffic captures. All of these techniques combine to develop as complete a picture as possible to assist you in detecting rootkits.

## Live Detection

Live detection of rootkits can be a tricky issue to deal with, particularly if the investigator is not knowledgeable about rootkit artifacts and what to look for on a system that might be infected with a rootkit. Often this results in a misdiagnosis and misidentification of the incident, and any further response is taken in the wrong direction.

---

**W**ARNING

An important caveat to running any tool that performs malware detection is that you do not want it to automatically delete files or other artifacts; all you want the tool to do is detect the presence of the malware and alert you. Deleting artifacts defeats the purpose of your analysis.

---

In fall 2006, Jesse Kornblum published a very interesting paper in the *International Journal of Digital Evidence* titled "Exploiting the Rootkit Paradox with Windows Memory Analysis" (www.utica.edu/academic/institutes/ecii/publications/articles/EFE2FC4D-0B11-BC08-AD2958256F5E68F1.pdf). In this paper, Jesse identified two basic principles that all rootkits attempt to follow; that is, they want to remain hidden, and they want to run. Essentially, to remain hidden on a system, a rootkit has to minimize its footprint while still interacting with the system in some way. The system itself, specifically the operating system, needs to be able to execute the rootkit, which is trying to remain hidden and persistent across reboots. Therefore, Jesse proposes that if the operating system can find the rootkit, so can an examiner. I might add "a sufficiently knowledgeable examiner" to that statement, but I'm sure that's what Jesse meant to say.

The predominant technique for rootkit detection on a live system is sometimes referred to as *behavioral* or *differential* (or *high/low*) analysis. The basic idea is that by making two different kinds of queries for the same information and looking for differences in the responses, you can detect the presence of a rootkit or of something being hidden by a rootkit. For example, one of the early rootkit detection tools was a Visual Basic script named rkdetect.vbs (which is still available at www.security.nnov.ru/files/rkdetect.zip) that could detect the popular Hacker Defender rootkit by running a remote query to enumerate services using sc.exe, followed by a local query (using psexec.exe and sc.exe), and then looking for anomalies or differences between the two outputs. In my first book, *Windows Forensics and Incident Recovery*, I included a Perl script called rkd.pl that would perform differential analysis against processes, services, and some Registry keys. The script would note differences in output between remote and "local" queries (again, the tools were run locally on a remote system using psexec.exe), but it also included some signature checks—that is, specific checks for specific rootkits. In the book, I demonstrated the use of such tools against the AFX Rootkit 2003.

## NOTE

Lenny Zeltser, an incident handler with the SANS Internet Storm Center (ISC), posted a diary entry (http://isc.sans.org/diary.html?storyid=1487) titled "Behavior Analysis of Rootkit Malware" on July 16, 2006. In that diary entry, Lenny provides screen captures and descriptions of several rootkit detection tools (as well as links to others) being tested against some of the rootkits mentioned previously in this chapter.

Over time, rootkits have evolved, using more sophisticated hiding and stealth techniques, and rootkit detection techniques have had to keep up. Differential analysis is still the best approach to detecting rootkits, but the items queried are even more granular. For example, some tools will scan the file system using commands similar to *dir /s* and *dir /s /ah* and then compare their output to the contents of the Master File Table (MFT). The idea is to perform a high-level query followed by a very low-level query (as low as possible) and note any differences in the output between the two.

Several freeware and commercial rootkit detection tools are available, yet none of them provide details of *how* they operate. This is done so that the rootkit authors do not have an easy means of determining how the detection tools function and can then add techniques to their rootkits to avoid detection by those tools. However, this does not deter the rootkit authors from downloading the tools and determining how they work for themselves.

# RootkitRevealer

RootkitRevealer (http://technet.microsoft.com/en-us/sysinternals/bb897445.aspx, illustrated in Figure 7.2) is a rootkit detection tool that appeared on the scene in spring 2005. (RootkitRevealer was "slashdotted" at http://it.slashdot.org/it/05/02/23/1353258.shtml?tid=172&tid=218—that is, posted to and discussed on the Slashdot.org Web site—on February 23, 2005.) Since the initial release, it has gone through a number of changes to keep up with changes in rootkit techniques. Whenever rootkits are developed that include new techniques to avoid detection, tools such as RootkitRevealer quickly incorporate counter-antidetection techniques.

The author's description of RootkitRevealer specifically states that although the tool is designed to and can detect rootkits that hide files and Registry keys, it does not detect kernel-mode rootkits (such as FU) that modify kernel objects.

---

**W**ARNING

When running any tool, you need to be aware of how it works and what it does; this applies to rootkit detection tools as well as any other tool. I worked an engagement once where the customer's incident response was badly managed and uncoordinated. While some administrators were instructed to do specific tasks, several took it upon themselves to run destructive antivirus scans on systems as well as run RootkitRevealer. To perform its scans, Rootkit-Revealer installed itself as a service, and the executable image had a random name, although the image file itself had random padding (so that the hash of the file was never the same). This was done as an antirootkit detection technique. At one point, an administrator called me to tell me that he had discovered a "massively infected" system that had eight strange services running, and RootkitRevealer had not detected them as rootkits. Well, first of all, if the administrator could "see" the services listed, they probably weren't hidden by a rootkit. Second, all the executable image files had the same icon. Third, all the executable image files were RootkitRevealer. Due to a lack of coordination and knowledge of the tools being used, incident-response activities resulted in what appeared at first glance to be a massive infection.

**Figure 7.2** RootkitRevealer GUI

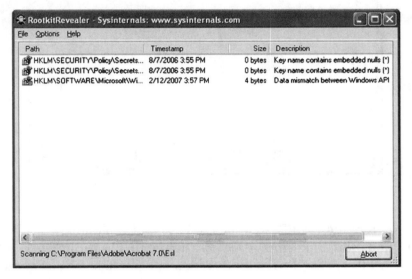

# GMER

GMER (www2.gmer.net/) is a freeware GUI-based rootkit detection application that attempts to detect:

- Hidden processes, files, services, Registry keys, and drivers
- Drivers hooking the system service descriptor table (SSDT), interrupt descriptor table (IDT), or IO request packet (IRP) calls

GMER is also capable of showing NTFS alternate data streams, as illustrated in Figure 7.3.

**Figure 7.3** GMER GUI

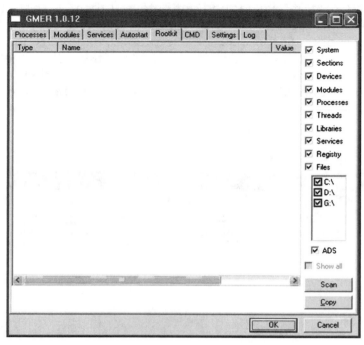

Also available from the GMER Web site is a small CLI application called *catchme* that is capable of detecting user–mode rootkits such as Gromozon, Hacker Defender, AFX, and Vanquish. The GMER site has the rootkit detection tool available for download as well as several videos of rootkits being detected and log files from scans where rootkits were detected. GMER also detects Master Boot Record (MBR) rootkits and allows the inclusion of your preferred antivirus application in the GMER user interface.

# Helios

Helios (www.mielesecurity.com/) is described as an "advanced malware detection system" that uses behavioral analysis and does not employ signatures as a detection mechanism. Although it is described as a malware detection system, Helios is also capable of detecting rootkits. Helios is not open source, but it is free, and (according to the Web site, www.anti-rootkit.com/software/Helios.htm) it does have an API that provides access to the product's core functionality. Helios will not only detect rootkits but also inoculate against rootkit installation. The Helios GUI is illustrated in Figure 7.4.

**TIP**

If you are going to download and use Helios, make sure that you install the .NET Framework 2.0. A link to the necessary file is available on the Helios download page.

**Figure 7.4** Helios GUI

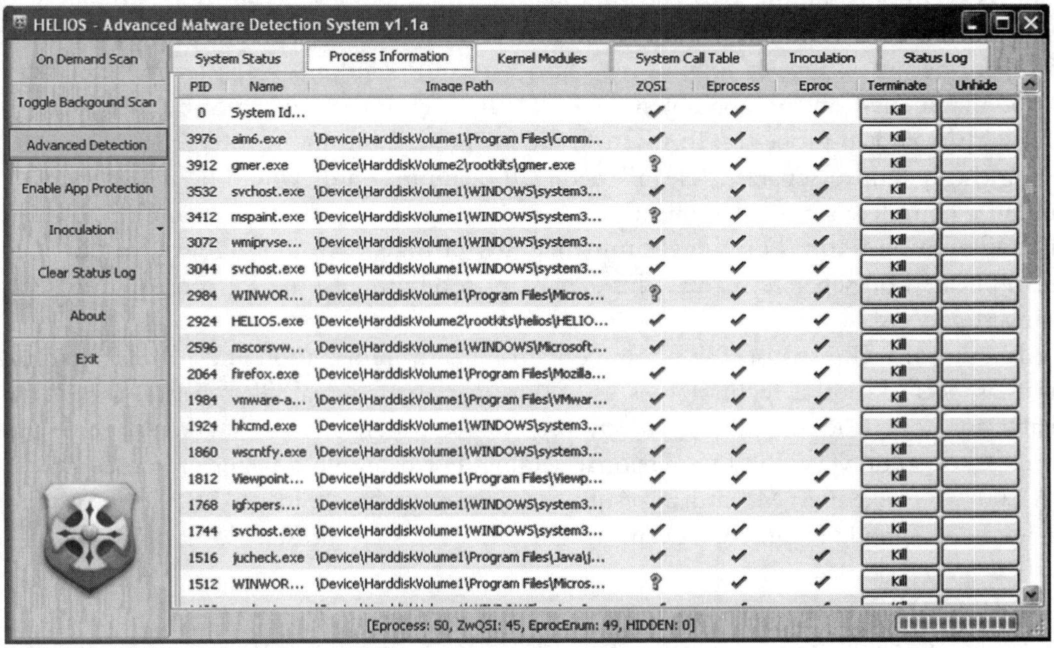

The Helios Web site includes several videos (downloadable or watchable via streaming) that demonstrate the application's use and capabilities.

**TIP**

Many of the freely available rootkit detection applications that are presented in this chapter are easily downloaded and run from a single directory. Deploying these tools during incident-response activities can be as easy as copying them to a USB thumb drive, then enabling the write-protect switch (if your thumb drive has one) and plugging the thumb drive into the system you want to scan. However, you do need to keep in mind any dependencies and requirements, such as Helios requiring the Microsoft .NET Framework 2.0.

# MS Strider GhostBuster

The Microsoft Research Center has devoted significant resources to the study of the detection of rootkits on Windows systems, the result of which is the Strider GhostBuster project (http://research.microsoft.com/rootkit/), a tool that is designed to detect rootkits that hook or subvert Window API functions. GhostBuster uses a technique that is referred to as "cross-view diff" (which amounts to a technique similar to behavioral or differential analysis). By performing one query on an "infected" system and then booting to "clean" media (a bootable Windows CD that is uninfected) and running the same query, you can then perform a "diff" between the two outputs and determine what is hidden. This is particularly useful with regard to files, but because an exact copy of the entire system (including all applications and patches) must be maintained on the bootable CD/DVD, this technique might not be particularly useful with regard to processes. To locate "hidden" processes using this technique (such as booting the system to separate, "clean" media), the administrator would be required to maintain a complete set of all applications as well as operating system and application patches and configuration settings on the clean media. Any change, even the slightest, would need to be replicated on separate media. This is perhaps too cumbersome for most infrastructures and investigations.

Although the GhostBuster site does contain links to information and papers regarding various aspects of rootkit technologies, as of this writing an actual GhostBuster tool is not available for download and use. However, some of the papers at the site are extremely useful and make for some very good professional reading. For example, a paper presented at Usenix LISA 2004, "Gatekeeper: Monitoring Auto-Start Extensibility Points (ASEPs) for Spyware Management," provides some excellent insight into Registry autostart locations.

# ProDiscover

ProDiscover Incident Response (IR) edition, from Technology Pathways (www.techpathways.com), includes functionality to assist the investigator in examining systems for rootkits during incident response activities. Installing the ProDiscover server applet (PDServer.exe) on a system (by either running it from a CD or thumb drive or installing it remotely over the network), the investigator can then connect to the server and perform a variety of actions, some of which are illustrated in Figure 7.5.

**Figure 7.5** ProDiscover Functionality for Rootkit Detection

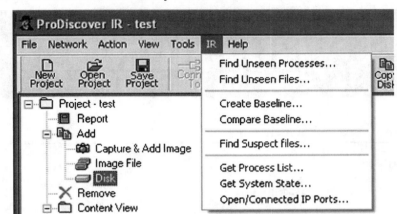

As shown in Figure 7.5, the investigator can attempt to locate unseen processes and files as well as collect some information with regard to the active process list and system state via the menu system in ProDiscover IR. The ProScript API allows a bit more granularity and flexibility in the information that can be collected as well as how it is managed. Attempting to locate unseen processes and files can assist the investigator in locating rootkits on the system.

# F-Secure BlackLight

F-Secure is a Finnish company that produces antivirus software (according to the company's blog, its antivirus product was recently incorporated into the VirusTotal.com scanning site), as well as a rootkit elimination product called BlackLight (www.f-secure.com/blacklight). BlackLight detects objects hidden by rootkit technologies and provides the user with an opportunity to eliminate or remove the offending software.

BlackLight, freely available on a trial basis, comes with both GUI and CLI versions that are available for download from the F-Secure Web site. Figure 7.6 illustrates the BlackLight GUI.

**Figure 7.6** BlackLight GUI

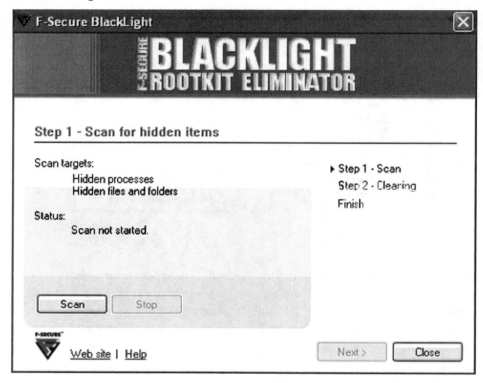

Like many of the other rootkit detection applications, BlackLight ships as an executable and does not include an installation program (i.e., .msi file); once you download the executable for whichever version you choose, you can run the application immediately.

> **W**ARNING
>
> When using tools that can detect rootkits, or any other malware, for that fact, you want to be sure to avoid using tools that will automatically take action for you, such as deleting files or other artifacts. The whole purpose of doing this sort of examination is to locate those artifacts so that you can develop a profile of the rootkit's activity and characteristics, and possibly detect it on other systems. Automatically deleting the files once they're detected will make your job that much tougher because now you have to determine what other actions were automatically taken and what other artifacts may have been deleted.

# Sophos Anti-Rootkit

Sophos is another antivirus vendor that also provides antirootkit software. The Sophos Anti-Rootkit (www.sophos.com/support/knowledgebase/article/17004.html) product is freely available for download and use, and like the F-Secure BlackLight product, it comes in both GUI (illustrated in Figure 7.7) and CLI versions. The Sophos product can be used to scan the infrastructure, in addition to single hosts, for rootkits, as well as remove them. Anti-Rootkit scans the system for hidden processes, Registry keys, and files on the local hard drives.

**Figure 7.7** Sophos Anti-Rootkit GUI

---

**TIP**

The third article in a three-article series by Jamie Butler and Sherri Sparks, "Windows Rootkits of 2005," was published on SecurityFocus.com on January 5, 2006. This article (www.securityfocus.com/infocus/1854), which discusses five rootkit detection techniques and highlights a total of nine rootkits, is well worth reading.

---

# AntiRootkit.com

F-Secure and Sophos aren't the only antivirus companies that provide rootkit detection and/or elimination products. Other vendors include the capability to detect rootkits, either as separate products or as integrated components, in their antivirus products. The McAfee Rootkit Detective product searches for hidden files, processes, and Registry keys or values on a potentially infected system, as does Trend Micro's RootkitBuster product.

Perhaps the best site available for information on rootkit detection techniques and products is AntiRootkit.com. The site provides a blog as well as a list of free and commercial rootkit detection/elimination products (products are listed predominantly for Windows, but there are Linux, BSD, and even a Mac OS X product listed) as well as a list of rootkit prevention products that can be used to prevent or inhibit rootkits from installing in the first place. News and articles referenced on this Web site provide access to even more information.

Additional resources for tools can be found at other Web sites and blogs, such as the following:

- RaDaJo blog Anti-rootkit Windows Tools (http://radajo.blogspot.com/2007/11/anti-rootkit-windows-tools-searching.html)

- GrandStreamDreams blog post Anti-Rootkit Tools Revisited (http://grandstream-dreams.blogspot.com/2008/01/anti-rootkit-tools-roundup-revisited.html)

# Postmortem Detection

Postmortem detection of a rootkit poses its own set of challenges. You're probably thinking, how difficult can this be? After all, you're looking at an image, not a live system … what would you be looking for? Given various techniques available to malware authors, including antiforensics techniques that are discussed and made publicly available (the MetaSploit Project has an entire section of its Web site dedicated to antiforensics techniques), locating the offending malware, even on an image, can be difficult. However, if you understand what you're looking for and where to look for it, you are more likely to be successful in your examination.

One method of postmortem detection of rootkits is to mount the image as a virtual file system on your analysis system using a tool such as SmartMount (www.asrdata.com/SmartMount/) or Mount Image Pro (www.mountimage.com), allowing the files to be read as a file system without engaging the operating system from the image to do so. Both tools can mount the image as read-only so that no changes can be made to the files. From here, you can run any number of antivirus tools against the files in the image. The files within the image appear as just that—files. None of the processes and services from the image are running, so the rootkit will not be engaged, and the kernel of the analysis system is not subverted.

Using SmartMount to access an acquired image as a file directory structure
is great if you want to scan it with antivirus and spyware detection tools,
but the available rootkit detection tools will not be of much use to you.
The reason is that these tools search for things being hidden—files, Registry
keys, processes, and the like—and when an acquired image is mounted as
a drive letter, none of the information is hidden.

Another option available to you is to boot the image into VMware using
LiveView (http://liveview.sourceforge.net) and examine the live system for a
possible rootkit using any of the tools intended for live systems. This assumes,
of course, that you have a username and password so that you can log into
the image once it has booted. In Chapter 6, I mentioned that some malware
uses software to detect the presence of a virtual environment, and if it does
detect that it is running in an environment such as VMware, it can change its
behavior to avoid detection. Of course, some rootkits might do this as well,
and that secondary behavior could cause issues (i.e., prevent components of
the operating system from running correctly or simply cause a BSoD) on the
system. You can also scan the virtual system with a port scanner such as
Nmap and then compare the results of the scan to the output of netstat.exe
or openports.exe. If you find ports that are open using Nmap but you don't
see those ports in the output of netstat.exe, you might have a live rootkit on
the system.

A method that I use to quickly check for the presence of a rootkit in an acquired image
is to access the Registry Viewer within ProDiscover and navigate to the Services key in each
available ControlSet, as illustrated in Figure 7.8.

**Figure 7.8** Excerpt from ProDiscover Registry View

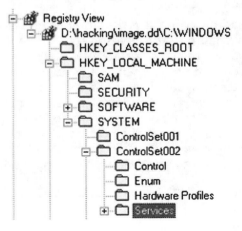

**TIP**

To determine the *ControlSet* that is marked as "current" or loaded as the *CurrentControlSet* when the system is booted, locate the *Current* value in the System\Select key. The data is a *DWORD* Registry type and tells you which of the available *ControlSets* is marked as "current".

Once I've located the key, I then sort the entries in the right-hand pane based on the *LastWrite* time of each key. Most of the entries in this list will correspond to when the system was originally installed. In some cases, several keys might all have the same *LastWrite* time as a result of a software update that affected all of them, often on the same day. However, when a kernel-mode rootkit driver is installed, it will usually stand out with only one or two entries made on one day. This *LastWrite* time doesn't always correspond to the dates provided in an incident report, but in most cases they will stand out like a sore thumb. In addition, they will provide you with a date on which to orient your timeline analysis of activity on the system. Because there does not seem to be any publicly available Windows API for modifying Registry key *LastWrite* times from user-mode applications, you can be sure that the key's *LastWrite* time corresponds to when the rootkit and its driver were installed.

## Tools & Traps…

### Using RegRipper to Look for Rootkits

Another means for performing this same analysis without loading the image file into a project or case file within your favorite forensic analysis application is to use RegRipper (discussed in Chapter 4) or its associated CLI tool, rip.exe (along with the appropriate plugin) to parse through the Services key within a System hive file, and sort the subkeys by *LastWrite* time. You can do this quite easily by mounting the image with SmartMount and using a batch file to launch the appropriate command line. However, if you don't have an image and are instead forced to work with a live system, another option that is available to you is to run RegRipper via F-Response (www.f-response.com). A blogger with the nom de plume of "Hogfly" posted a video on YouTube demonstrating how he used F-Response and RegRipper (http://forensicir. blogspot.com/2008/04/ripping-registry-live.html) to extract data from the Registry of a live system.

An additional means of rootkit detection that hangs someplace between live and postmortem was discussed in Chapter 3. If the investigator dumps the contents of physical memory and quickly analyzes it, the system might still be running, but the analysis will actually occur on a snapshot of RAM. As Jesse pointed out in his "Paradox" paper, a "smart" rootkit will not interfere with the memory dump process because doing so could reveal the presence of the rootkit. After all, a rootkit that causes the operating system to crash dump (resulting in the dreaded BSoD) renders the system unusable to both the administrator/user and the intruder. Refer to Chapter 3 for a list of tools to
collect and analyze the contents of physical memory from Windows systems.

If the rootkit were to cause the system to crash dump, the resulting crash dump file could be analyzed to reveal the existence of the rootkit. By collecting the contents of RAM and searching for EPROCESS blocks (refer to Chapter 3 for information regarding searching RAM dumps for process information), you can compare the processes that have not exited with those visible in the active process list to determine which, if any, were hidden by a rootkit.

# Prevention

We've talked quite a bit about rootkit detection but not about actually preventing rootkits from being installed on Windows systems. The first step to rootkit detection is prevention, performed through system configuration and hardening, vulnerability testing, and so on, all of which is beyond the scope of this book. However, suffice it to say that taking a minimalist approach to system configuration (e.g., not providing a user with Administrator-level access unless he requires it, and then for those instances in which he does require that level of access) can go a long way toward preventing or inhibiting the installation of rootkits. If a rootkit installation is inhibited, the rootkit won't function normally and you'll be able to tell that it's there; in fact, it might be glaringly obvious that a system has been the victim of an attempted rootkit installation due to error messages or simply extremely unusual behavior.

**W**ARNING

Some folks opt not to take a minimalist approach to system configuration. The major issue is users having Administrator-level access to their systems and being allowed to install any software they can find. I once worked on a case in which I found a system that had a total of four remote desktop services running, and I determined that the intruder had used one of them to gain access to the system. At first, I thought that the intruder had installed some of the remote access software, but the system administrator later told me that all four of the applications were legitimate and had been installed by the IT department; each of the remote access applications was a backup for the others. None of the system administrators had the time or skills to manage all the remote access applications, and the intruder was able to use one of them to gain access to the system.

# Summary

Although rootkits have been around for quite a while in both the Linux and Windows worlds, interest in rootkits exploded in February 2005 when the word was mentioned by Microsoft employees at the RSA Conference. Books (Hoglund's *Rootkits: Subverting the Windows Kernel* and even a book called *Rootkits for Dummies* are available on Amazon.com) and training courses (Hoglund has taught rootkit techniques during training sessions at BlackHat conferences) covering rootkit development are available, as are samples of working (albeit in some cases proof-of-concept) rootkits.

Rootkits pose a significant threat to systems and infrastructures, the most serious of which is a lack of education and knowledge on the part of administrators and investigators as to exactly what a rootkit is, what a rootkit is capable of, and how it works. With a stronger understanding of these areas, investigators will be better equipped to address issues of rootkits during both live-response and postmortem investigations.

# Solutions Fast Track

## Rootkits

- ☑ Rootkits are capable of hiding files, Registry keys, processes, network connections, and other objects from the administrator as well as the operating system.

- ☑ The use of rootkits and rootkit technologies in malware and cybercrime is increasing.

- ☑ A better understanding of rootkit function and capabilities will prepare investigators to address the issues of rootkits.

## Rootkit Detection

- ☑ Detecting rootkits on live systems requires the use of differential analysis.

- ☑ Detecting rootkits on an acquired image of a system can be as straightforward as scanning a mounted image (via Mount Image Pro) with antivirus software or even sorting the Services Registry keys based on their *LastWrite* times.

- ☑ Rootkits might be detected on live systems by capturing and parsing the contents of physical memory to locate processes that are active but not part of the active process list.

# Frequently Asked Questions

**Q:** I found some unusual traffic logged in my firewall, with a time stamp from four hours ago. It seems that a system on my network attempted to make a connection out to the Internet on an odd port. I went to the system in question and didn't find any active network connections that would account for that traffic. Do I have a rootkit?

**A:** The short answer is maybe not. Everything that originates from a system, especially network traffic, must have a process or thread that is responsible for generating it. Services will generally run for as long as the system is running, but processes can be short lived. If you do not continue to see similar firewall log entries, it is likely that the process completed and exited, which is why you do not see it on the system.

**Q:** How do I prevent rootkits from getting on a system in the first place?

**A:** Configuration management can go a long way toward preventing or inhibiting rootkit infections. If you take a minimalist approach, such as providing only the minimum services and access necessary for the function of the system, you greatly reduce the attack surface. For example, if users cannot install arbitrary software, they are prevented from installing spyware, rootkits, and the like. Reducing the number of services running on a system reduces the options an attacker has available for gaining access and installing his tools and rootkit.

**Q:** I found a rootkit on one of my servers; now what? I'm told that there's no way of telling what happened and that I should just wipe the hard drive and completely reinstall the operating system from "clean" media and then load the data back on from uninfected backups.

**A:** This is very often the route that most administrators take when they've encountered a rootkit. However, there are several problems with this approach. First, you should conduct a thorough investigation of the system (or hire professionals to do it) since you might be able to tell what occurred (such as theft of data). Next, you need to determine, as much as possible, how the rootkit got on the system in the first place; perform a root-cause analysis. Without this sort of investigation, you're going to put a system right back on the network that might be compromised or infected all over again. Finally, if you're subject to any regulatory oversight (Visa PCI, HIPAA, FISMA, or similar), you might be required (either implicitly or explicitly) to investigate the issue and provide a report, and you need to provide as much information as possible.

# Chapter 8

# Tying It All Together

## Solutions in this chapter:

- **Case Studies**
- **Getting Started**
- **Extending Timeline Analysis**

☑ **Summary**

☑ **Solutions Fast Track**

☑ **Frequently Asked Questions**

# Introduction

Throughout the book so far, we've covered a great deal of very technical information, but in each case that information has been very specific to one particular area—Windows memory, the Registry, files, and so on. However, most of the incident response that a responder is required to do, or computer forensic analysis that an examiner will be required to do, involves more than one of these areas. For example, suspicious network traffic or a suspicious process may lead to a file on the system, which in turn will lead to the persistence mechanism for the malware, which may be a Registry key. Understanding the relationship between these various components and being able to understand and recognize the need to go from one to the other may very well mean the difference between understanding how an incident occurred and not understanding how it occurred.

Forensic examinations should not rely on analysis of the file system alone, particularly when the analyst is examining an image acquired from a Windows system. There is simply too much information available from the Registry, as well as from within various other files such as Windows Event Logs, for an analyst to rely solely on the most basic examination procedures and techniques.

In this chapter, I present scenarios and past examinations—let's call them "case studies"—that have utilized several of the techniques presented thus far in the book in order to achieve their goals. In each case, I'll try to be as technically complete as the situation allows, understanding that many specific details need to be either sanitized or omitted. In some case studies, the information may be drawn from a number of incidents or examinations, but the overall point remains the same—to demonstrate how information from different chapters in this book can lead to and be correlated with other information to build as complete a picture as possible of an incident.

# Case Studies

## Case Study 1: The Document Trail

I received an examination that involved multiple hard drives, each with a single primary user, and each with the Windows XP SP2 operating system installed. The incident background was simply that fraudulent activity had been occurring against accounts maintained by the customer's organization, and their own investigation into the issue led them to the point where they suspected that the fraud may have been the result of the actions of a malicious employee.

The first step was to attempt to determine what I was looking for; to do that, I got in touch with the customer and walked through the particulars of their own investigation into the relevant activity. It appeared that the issue, from their perspective, centered around the accounts themselves, and in particular the numbers used to track the accounts.

Getting information about these account numbers led me fairly quickly to the realization that attempting to look for any numbers matching the structure of the account numbers (using a Perl regular expression) would be difficult and likely lead to a great many false positives. I needed some way to reduce the amount of data I was going to have to review.

The customer agreed to send me a list of the account numbers that they had determined had been affected by the fraud. Using those numbers as a keyword list, I ran a search across each of the acquired images and found hits in only one image, with the user profile for one specific user. In fact, the search hits were focused primarily in one file that, according to an article I located in the Microsoft Knowledge Base, appeared in the directory used by Outlook to store files that are opened from an e-mail attachment. My next step at that point was to extract a copy of that file (a spreadsheet) from the image for analysis. Opening the spreadsheet on my analysis system, I could see the content but I had no idea what it represented, other than it contained account information, and given the hits I had received from the search, the accounts correlated to those against which the suspicious activity had been committed.

Because I had already extracted the Registry hive files from their locations within the image (see Chapter 4), I parsed information from the user's RecentDocs Registry key, as well as the key that listed the Excel spreadsheets that the user had opened. I found a file-name reference to the spreadsheet from the Outlook temporary storage directory (the user's Outlook.pst file was not located on the system) as well as to other spreadsheets, one of which appeared to be located on a file server, possibly in the user's document directory (many organizations have their employees store documents on a file server so that they can be part of a regular backup process). I wasn't able to locate the other spreadsheets that appeared to be referenced and located on the user's system, and none of the results from my search were found in unallocated space, indicating that files containing the search terms hadn't been deleted recently.

My next step was to extract metadata from the Excel spreadsheet. Microsoft Office documents (Word documents, Excel spreadsheets, and even PowerPoint presentations) use a compound storage, "file-system-within-a-file" structure for storing data. As such, a great deal of metadata can be (and is) stored within the document structure and can be extracted for analysis and use. Using the oledmp.pl Perl script found on the media that accompanies this book, I was able to extract the metadata and see that the user in question had opened, edited, and printed the spreadsheet. These metadata fields within the spreadsheet included dates and times that showed when these actions took place, and these dates and times correlated to file system and Registry time stamps as well.

Once I had pulled all of this information together into a comprehensible timeline, I provided it in a report to the customer. Like many analysts, I don't often have visibility into how engagements progress beyond the point of my final report, and this was yet another example of that sort of situation. However, this examination did illustrate how multiple analysis techniques can be employed to really drill down and get a great deal of information about an incident. In this case, a keyword search provided a great deal of data reduction and led to a specific document, whose location within the file system revealed the likely source of document (an Outlook e-mail attachment). Then, Registry analysis illustrated that the user had accessed the document, as well as other documents with similar titles, in addition to the fact that at least one of those documents was located on a file server. Finally, analysis of metadata extracted from the document revealed that whoever had access to the user account had modified and printed the file, and gave the dates of these actions. This provided a great deal of information to the customer to assist them in identifying the source of the fraudulent activity.

# Case Study 2: Intrusion

This case study involved an intrusion into a corporate infrastructure that started with the compromise of an employee's home system. This type of incident is probably more prevalent than one would think. Home user systems, in addition to systems used by regular users (students using laptops, corporate employee desktop and laptop systems, etc.), are very often subject to compromise because they are seen as easy targets; there are a lot of them out there (i.e., a "target-rich environment") and, for the most part, they are poorly managed. Many home users don't realize what data of value is actually on their systems. Home users do online banking and file their tax returns each year from those computer systems. Gamers access online games, and believe it or not, there is actually an economy for selling online gaming characters. So, besides hard drive space, RAM, and processing power being added to a botnet, home computer systems can offer quite a bit of treasure to an intruder.

## Tools & Traps…

### The Value of a System

One of the few things that many people seem to be able to accept or understand is the value that their system—a desktop that they use at home, a laptop that a student uses for schoolwork, and so on—can represent to a "bad guy." Several years ago, I was teaching a Windows 2000 incident response course at the University of Texas at Austin, and one of the young ladies in the class got this strange look on her face. I asked her to share her thoughts with the class, and she blurted out, "Why would anyone want my computer?!"

**Continued**

Think about what your computer, or any computer, can offer to someone. First, what do you use your computer for? Do you do your taxes each year on your computer? Do you do online banking or make online purchases with your computer? Simply loading a keystroke logger on your system will provide the intruder with that information as well. Besides getting access to your personal information, your computer offers resources to the intruder, such as a bot host that can be added to an overall botnet and rented out to others for spam or denial-of-service attacks (DoS).

That being said, in this case, an intruder accessed an employee's home system and installed a keystroke logger (this was later confirmed via separate analysis of the employee's home system). From there, the intruder discovered that the employee logged into the corporate infrastructure via the Windows Remote Desktop Client, and because he had captured the employee's keystrokes, he had the employee's login username and password. From that point, it was a simple matter for him to fire up his own Remote Desktop Client, launch it against the right IP address, and provide his newly discovered credentials … and he was on the corporate network, appearing for all intents and purposes to be the employee.

It turned out that the intruder was easy to track. By accessing the infrastructure via the Remote Desktop Client, the intruder had shell-level access, meaning that his actions caused him to interact with the Windows Explorer shell just like a normal user sitting at the desktop. Due to this, many of the intruder's actions were recorded via the Registry. Also, the intruder had a fairly high level of access due to the fact that the stolen credentials were for a user who managed user accounts. Even so, the intruder activated a dormant domain administrator account—one that had been set up but simply never used. This meant that each time the intruder accessed another system within the corporate infrastructure, a profile for the domain administrator account was created on that system. This made the intruder's movements throughout the infrastructure fairly easy to track, at least initially (i.e., we did not want to make the mistake of assuming that this was all the intruder had done).

Working closely with the on-site IT staff, we created a script that would search all systems within the domain for indications of the user profile in question. We first identified systems on which the profile existed, which gave us an initial count of the systems the intruder had accessed. Acquiring each one, we then began the process of developing a timeline of activity, using the creation date of the profile directory as an indicator of when the intruder first accessed each system and the last modification time of the profile's NTUSER.DAT Registry hive file as an indication of when the intruder last accessed the system. These time windows were later confirmed as we examined the contents of the UserAssist keys.

**TIP**

This is an excellent example of an engagement in which, had the customer maintained Event Logs in a central log repository, a great deal of corroborating information would have been available. Although it wasn't absolutely necessary (the creation date on the NTUSER.DAT files within the user profile gave us the date that the intruder first logged onto each system, and Registry artifacts gave us indications of the intruder's periods of activity), had the audit configuration been set appropriately and the Event Log records collected and archived in a central location, we would have been able to narrow down a complete list of affected systems much quicker.

Once we had mapped the intruder's travels through the network, the next step was to determine what the intruder had done or tried to do on each system. Again, the fact that the intruder was accessing each system through Windows Explorer provided us with a great deal of very valuable information. This particular customer had already spent a great deal of time and effort mapping sensitive data within their infrastructure and had a list of where this sensitive data (as defined by state notification laws such as California's SB-1386, as well as the Visa Payment Card Industry [PCI] Data Security Standard) existed. Again turning to Registry analysis, we focused on the user profile's NTUSER.DAT file, checking the RecentDocs key, as well as lists of recently accessed documents such as Excel spreadsheets and MSWord documents, and any other indications that we could find. We were able to focus our efforts by checking the RecentDocs keys to see what file types had been accessed (i.e., .xls, .doc, .jpg, etc.) and then checking for the most recently used (MRU) lists for the applications normally used to access those files. Interestingly, not many files had been accessed, perhaps due in part to what we found in the ACMru Registry key. It seems that the intruder had conducted searches by clicking **Start | Search | For Files and Folders** and had attempted to identify files with certain keywords. This had likely gone unnoticed by employees because some of the systems were housed in the data center, but the information the intruder was looking for using keywords wasn't something that the organization really maintained. However, it was clear from indications on a few systems that the intruder had looked for and found a spreadsheet containing passwords, and the appropriate steps were taken to address this compromised information.

Again, multiple sources of data were used pursuant to this response and examination. VPN logs were used to confirm access and identify the intruder's IP address, and then file system and MAC time analysis was used to confirm the intruder's movements throughout the network. Finally, Registry analysis provided a clear picture of the intruder's actions, including searches and file accesses. This last bit of analysis proved to be extremely valuable in determining whether or not the intruder had accessed sensitive data; thorough Registry analysis provided us with a strong argument that the intruder had not accessed files that had been previously determined to contain sensitive data.

# Case Study 3: DFRWS 2008 Forensic Rodeo

In August 2008, Cory Altheide and I attended the DFRWS 2008 conference. We had a great time there, and on Tuesday night, Cory participated in the Forensic Rodeo. I didn't so much want to participate as I wanted to observe, to look over other people's shoulders and see how they approached the task at hand. Sitting in my office, usually performing analysis of some kind by myself, I don't often get such an opportunity to not only engage with others about the work we do and the burdens we share but also actually see them in action. Looking back, it's kind of funny to hear myself saying, "… in action," because truth be told, there's about as much action in forensic analysis as there is in watching hair grow. Overall, however, this was a very enlightening experience, with the additional benefit of allowing others to try their hand at this sort of thing. That's right, the forensic rodeo scenario and files can be found at www.dfrws.org/2008/rodeo.shtml.

The Forensic Rodeo challenge involved a memory dump (see Chapter 3) and an image acquired from a thumb drive. The goal of the challenge was to analyze the two pieces of data and answer some of the questions provided by the referees, Eoghan Casey and Dan Kalil. Dr. Michael Cohen won the rodeo, having been judged to have completed more of the provided questions than anyone else. I don't want to provide any tips or inside information with respect to the rodeo data, but I will say that pursuing the rodeo involved memory analysis and data carving (no Registry analysis this time!).

# Case Study 4: Copying Files

A question I see (and get asked) very often is whether it is possible to determine files that had been copied to or from a thumb drive or external storage device. I see this question many times in public listservs, and when I attended the first SANS Forensic Summit in October 2008, I was asked this question from two attendees as well as from one of my own team members who was fielding the question for a customer. Given how ubiquitous USB thumb drives are these days, as well as other removable storage media such as digital cameras, iPods, and so on, this is a very real concern for many organizations with respect to data exfiltration (i.e., theft of data such as intellectual property, etc.). Unfortunately, far too often it is a concern after the fact rather than something that is addressed proactively.

As we saw in Chapters 4 and 5, USB removable storage devices can be tracked across systems. Using analysis techniques from both chapters, we can determine not only when a device was first plugged into a system but also when it was last disconnected from a system. This can be very useful information when it comes to mapping the connection of removable storage devices to a system or across a number of systems. This also gives us something with which to start a timeline.

Now, one of the issues with respect to the original question is that most modern operating systems (and I say "most" simply because I haven't seen them all) do not audit or log the copy or move operations within the file system. However, many folks seem to think that because forensic analysis can recover deleted files, other kinds of magic can be performed as well—magic such as determining who copied a file from one location to another and when they did this. Contrary to popular TV shows such as *CSI*, this simply isn't the case in most instances. If the analyst were to have both pieces of media—the source and the destination drives or volumes for the copy—then he or she could determine by analyzing the files on both pieces of media (and their time stamps) which piece of media was the source and which was the destination. However, in most instances, the analyst does not have both pieces of media.

Having only one piece of media to examine may not allow the analyst to definitively determine files that were copied *from* that media, but the analyst may be able to determine indications of files that may have been copied *to* the media, using information provided in Microsoft Knowledge Base article 299648, titled "Description of NTFS date and time stamps for files and folders" (*http://support.microsoft.com/?kbid=299648*). This Knowledge Base article gives a clear description of how file times are affected by copy or move operations from one media to another. For example, if a file is copied from a FAT partition (most thumb drives are formatted with the FAT file system by default) to an NTFS partition, the last modification date of the file remains unchanged, but the creation date of the file is updated to the current time on the system. The same holds true if the file is copied from an NTFS directory to an NTFS subdirectory. However, if the file is moved (rather than copied), the file's creation date is updated to that of the file in the original location. According to the article, "In all examples, the modified date and time of a file does not change unless a property of the file has changed. The created date and time of the file changes depending on whether the file was copied or moved."

As a caveat, however, the Knowledge Base article does not describe the method used to move the file. For example, consider the following command line "move" commands, in which a file is copied from a FAT-formatted removable storage device (E:\) to an NTFS directory:

```
C:\test>dir /tc E:\Dec03_0004.jpg
Volume in drive E has no label.
Volume Serial Number is 18DA-DF72

Directory of E:\

12/03/2008 09:59 PM 7,250 Dec03_0004.jpg
1 File(s) 7,250 bytes
0 Dir(s) 72,757,248 bytes free
C:\test>move E:\Dec03_0004.jpg
C:\test>dir /tc Dec03_0004.jpg
Volume in drive C has no label.
```

```
Volume Serial Number is B83C-BC0A
Directory of C:\test
12/05/2008 09:36 AM 7,250 Dec03_0004.jpg
1 File(s) 7,250 bytes
0 Dir(s) 11,019,108,352 bytes free
```

As you can see from this example, the create date of the file did not remain the same after the move operation took place, which is contrary to what is stated in Microsoft Knowledge Base article 299648. This clearly illustrates the need for testing and examination of tools and techniques.

This points out several important factors regarding our analysis, the first of which is that if the user copies a file and then modifies the file in some way, we've lost information that may indicate a file that was copied from one location to another; specifically, a file with a modification date older than the creation date might indicate that the file was copied. Consider that statement for a moment—shouldn't a file have to be created first and then, at some point after it was created, modified? By default, MS Word will automatically save a copy of a file you are editing approximately every 10 minutes, so after the first 10 minutes, you would expect to have a creation date 10 minutes older than the modification date (in ideal circumstances, of course). Another factor to consider is that with only a single piece of media to analyze, you may not be able to definitively determine files that had been moved from one location to another simply due to the fact that the file times are updated to that of the original file (assuming the Cut&Paste menu option is used rather than the move command at the CLI).

Finally, although the file times associated with the file system are affected by a copy or move operation, times embedded within the contents of the file (such as OLE content within some versions of MS Office documents, as discussed in Chapter 5) as metadata will not be modified and can therefore be used in some modicum of analysis. Depending on the type of document and the extent of metadata maintained within the document, you may be able to clearly determine that the document originated from another location besides the media being analyzed.

Analyzing an acquired image in an attempt to determine files that may have been copied to the system can involve Registry analysis as well as file system and MAC time analysis. In some instances, depending on the type of document that was copied, file metadata analysis may shed some light on the situation.

# Case Study 5: Network Information

There are times during incident detection or response activities when network operations personnel may have access to firewall logs from egress filtering or to network traffic captures that show traffic (and possibly data) leaving the internal infrastructure. Regardless of the source (logs or traffic captures), someone will have access to data that clearly shows the source

IP address of the traffic (as it originates from inside the network infrastructure), which can be traced to an active system on the internal network, either through tracing the system via a static, unchanging IP address or through DHCP logs. Another piece of information, the source port of the traffic (part of the TCP or UDP header), will help you tie that outbound traffic to a process running on the system.

Before proceeding with this description, an important fact needs to be pointed out and understood: Nothing happens on a computer system without a process executing. More appropriately, threads are the execution quantum on Windows systems, but the fact is that for traffic to be generated from a system, there *has* to be some code executing on the system to generate any network traffic. That being the case, an immediate response to the discovery of the network traffic details (i.e., source IP address and port) would lend itself to a term I heard Aaron Walters use—"temporal proximity." Although it sounds very "Star Trek-y," this term refers to responding immediately and relatively close to the time in which an incident is detected, as opposed to waiting hours or even days to respond. By observing temporal proximity with respect to the incident, a responder would be more likely to collect fresher (and perhaps more complete) data; the output of netstat.exe (or the network connections visible in a memory dump) might still show indications of that output connection and refer the responder to the process from which the traffic originated. For example, on my test system, the command line *netstat –ano* returns the following entry, an excerpt of the output of the command:

```
TCP 192.168.1.5:8352 98.136.112.141:80 ESTABLISHED 3536
```

This excerpt of the output of the netstat command illustrates the source IP address and port used by the process with the PID of 3536, which in this case is firefox.exe. This same information would be clearly visible in a network traffic capture (as described previously), or it may be visible in firewall logs or logs maintained by other network devices. Knowing how to smoothly transition from network-based to host-based data collection and analysis can significantly reduce the amount of time it takes to identify and respond to an incident. In such a situation, device logs can be correlated with network traffic captures and host-based data (i.e., memory dump) to determine the volume and type of data that was leaving the network.

# Case Study 6: SQL Injection

In the latter half of 2007, a number of SQL injection attacks occurred and as the weeks and months passed, they seemed to increase not only in frequency but also in sophistication. SQL injection is a technique that takes advantage of weaknesses in the application layer between a Web server and a database system. An intruder will submit specially crafted queries to the Web server, which will pass those queries on to the database with no validation of the user input, no bounds checking, and so on. In turn, the database will process those commands for the intruder (see Chapter 5).

Tools & Traps...

## SQL Injection

A quick Google search for "SQL injection" reveals a number of links explaining the technique in detail, providing links to presentations and "cheat sheets" for how to perform these attacks, as well as providing videos demonstrating SQL injection attacks. The fact that there is no end of extremely detailed resources available for perpetrating these attacks should be more than enough to convince CIOs and CISOs to commit resources to protecting organizations. This can be accomplished through a thorough infrastructure assessment that takes the storage and processing of sensitive data into account and results in a prioritized approach to protecting the data and the infrastructure.

In early spring 2008, there was a great deal of media attention toward a certain type of SQL injection attack, in which apparently automated software would inject specially crafted links to JavaScript into the database, and those links would then be processed by a user's Web browser as the database provided those links back to the Web server as dynamic Web content. This type of attack received media attention because it was very visible, whereas the attacks that weren't being talked about publicly were those in which the intruder used SQL injection to get deep within the target's infrastructure and, in many cases, remain on the network with extremely high privileges for a considerable period of time.

The basis of the SQL injection attack takes advantage of sound infrastructure design in that the publicly available Web server is positioned in the "demilitarized zone" or DMZ portion of the infrastructure, and the database resides on the internal infrastructure. The intruder's commands would be received by the Web server and passed on to the database server, completely bypassing the firewall (because communication between the Web and database servers is a business requirement). From an incident response perspective, the intruder's commands were clearly visible in the Web server logs in ASCII format, initially with no special encoding. Extracting the logs, a responder could clearly see initial contact, testing of the vulnerability, reconnaissance into the network (intruder-issued commands such as *ipconfig /all* and *net view*), and even branching out to other systems. Invariably at some point the intruder would establish a foothold on systems they had access to by downloading software to those systems. Initially, this would be accomplished through the use of the TFTP client using the UDP protocol to download files to the system. Then there was the creation and execution of FTP scripts (i.e., create the scripts using the "echo" command and then launch them using *ftp −s:filename*) to download archives to the platform. It appeared that in several cases the downloaded archives were self-extracting executables because the Web server logs showed the intruder launching the downloaded.exe file and then either checking for (via *dir*) the resulting files or simply running the commands.

During the course of the incident response, several samples were collected of executable files that were downloaded to systems. At first, these samples were not detected by antivirus scanners or identified when submitted to sites such as VirusTotal.com. As winter passed, incident response activities continued to include SQL injection attacks that were increasing in sophistication. Within a few short months, the search terms used to locate SQL injection attacks in Web server logs were useless because the attackers were using new techniques to encode (hexidecimal encoding or, in some cases, character set encoding) their commands. Therefore, search criteria needed to be updated in order to detect the attacks. One method for doing this is to identify the page being requested and then look for abnormally long requests being submitted to that page. Adding newly discovered keywords to the search criteria helped narrow down false positives, and custom Perl scripts helped quickly decode the queries into human-readable format. Another technique that the attacker used to get executable code onto the system was to break an executable file into 512-byte chunks and submit each chunk in a numbered sequence into database fields (remember, through SQL injection, the attacker is executing commands on the database at the same privilege level as the database, which for MS SQL Server is usually System) and then reassemble and execute the code within the file system of the database server. In instances in which this technique was used, we were able to extract and reassemble the executable code from the Web server logs and then validate that we had a correctly formatted executable file by parsing the PE header (see Chapter 6). If we had similarly named executables in our archive from previous SQL injection attacks, we used Jesse Kornblum's ssdeep.exe (http://ssdeep.sourceforge.net/) to perform fuzzy hash comparison and, in most cases, determined that the files were 98 percent or 99 percent similar. Parsing the PE header to break the executable file down into sections allowed us to identify sections that had changed (through MD5 hash comparison) from previous versions of the files.

When responding to SQL injection attacks, techniques for tracking the attacker within the infrastructure included Registry analysis because the attacker was able at some point to interact with the Windows Explorer shell of the compromised systems. In a few cases, collective (or communal) administrative accounts were compromised (i.e., easily guessed passwords), but in most cases the attacker would create domain administrator-level user accounts (in some cases, the existence of the accounts was corroborated by Event Log entries showing the account creation) and then used those accounts to access other systems within the infrastructure. File system analysis illustrated the creation of user profiles on the systems and provided an initial timeline for the use of those accounts, whereas Registry analysis provided indications of the attacker's activities on those systems, as well as the use of persistence mechanisms employed by the attacker for malware added to compromised systems. Because the Web server is not compromised during a SQL injection attack, the Web server logs provided a clear picture of the attacker's initial activities (in some cases, reconnaissance probes reached back weeks or months) in gaining access to the infrastructure. File or malware analysis provided indications that similar (more advanced) tools were being used as time went by.

# Case Study 7: The App Did It

Not long ago, I was performing some incident response that might have had to do with some malicious activity. As is very often the case as a corporate consultant, my initial call with respect to the incident came from the customer, and one common factor among most of my customers is that they are not experienced incident responders. In this case, the issue involved repeated domain name lookups for "suspicious" domains—suspicious in the sense that at least one of the domains appeared to be in China. The customer had Googled the domain name and found that it was associated with an application vulnerability identified in spring 2008. With that, and little else, they called us.

Upon arriving on-site, I found that a specific system had been identified as being the origination point of at least some of the suspicious DNS traffic. This system apparently had been configured with a static IP address (as opposed to using DHCP), so it was relatively easy for the customer to track down and obtain from their employee. Unfortunately, the only steps taken were to shut down the system and remove it from the network; neither the contents of physical memory nor other volatile data were collected from the system prior to shutting it down. Another wrinkle that was thrown into all of this was that when the employee had been informed that there was suspicious traffic originating from his system and that the system would have to be examined, he had reportedly stated that he was going to "securely delete stuff" from the system. At this point, the goals of my examination were twofold: (1) determine if the employee had, in fact, installed and used a secure deletion utility and (2) determine the source of the suspicious DNS lookups.

My first step was to acquire an image of the employee's desktop hard drive. While this was going on, I attempted to collect information about any logs that may be available from the network. I had been told that a management report illustrating the most frequent DNS lookups had alerted them to the situation, and that there were some logs from a botnet detection appliance that illustrated some of the DNS lookups; however, noticeably absent was any reference to the Chinese domain name that had been the customer's primary concern during the call for help. I noticed that the network logs showed DNS lookups in alphabetical order, along with time stamps.

Once the acquisition of the hard drive image had completed and been verified, and I had ensured that all of my documentation was in order, I opened my case notes, mounted the acquired image as a read-only file system on my analysis laptop, and initiated a scan with an antivirus scanning application. As part of my process for data reduction and attempting to locate what amounted to an amorphous description of "something suspicious," I scanned the mounted image with several antivirus applications, including targeted microscanners to look for specific malware. My scans did reveal a number of files that may have been malware or remnants of malware, but the file metadata (MAC times) and contents seemed to indicate that these were false positives. My next step was to examine logs from the system, including the installed antivirus application logs and the MS Malicious Software Removal Tool logs (mrt.log, as discussed in Chapter 5). Neither indicated anything that would appear to be related to the issue at hand.

I then moved on to parsing the Windows Event Log. All three Event Logs from the system were 512 kilobytes in size, and the Security Event Log contained no records (I found through analysis of the Security Registry hive file that auditing had not been enabled). The Application Event Log revealed a number of event records generated by the antivirus application, but most important, the System Event Log showed that the system had been rebooted several times during the past two weeks. In each case, following the event record that stated that the Event Log service had started, there was another record stating that a specific antispyware application had started. I made a note of this and created a map illustrating approximate system start times based on these event records. I was able to correlate the system start times with several of the botnet appliance logs that the customer had provided; the three most complete logs (they were actually extracts from the appliance logs, illustrating activity associated only with the system in question) showed DNS lookups starting in almost direct correlation with the system starting up. In fact, the first entry in each log correlated very closely with the time that the antispyware application started. Again, however, the botnet appliance logs contained no reference to the suspicious Chinese domain.

I then ran a search across the entire image for the suspicious Chinese domain name, casting a wide net and fully expecting to see the only results in the pagefile. However, much to my surprise, I found several references to the domain name (as well as others) in several Registry hive files (most notably the NTUSER.DAT file for all users, as well as those that were found in the Windows XP System Restore Points), as well as in the hosts file (the importance of the hosts file with respect to name resolution is discussed at http://support.microsoft.com/kb/172218). Examination of the hosts file revealed that a separate antispyware tool that had been installed on the system had added a number of entries to the file (comments in the hosts file stated that the entries were added by the application), redirecting all of them to the localhost (i.e., 127.0.0.1), effectively "blackholing" attempts to connect to these domains. Examination of the Registry hive files revealed that on the same date (based on key *LastWrite* times) all of the same domain names, in the same order, had also been added to Registry keys, forcing the domains into the Internet Explorer (IE) "Restricted Zone." This effectively set restrictions on what users could do via Internet Explorer, if they were able to connect to hosts within those domains.

At this point, I was relatively sure that, based on all of the information I had obtained as well as some searching on the Internet, the suspicious activity was not the result of malware (virus, worm, or spyware) on the system but rather the interaction of two antispyware applications; that is, one had modified the Registry and the hosts file to protect the system, and the other performed DNS queries for each domain name found listed in the hosts file. A posting on an Internet forum indicated that this might be the case, and I worked with the customer to perform live testing of the system on the network to verify this information. We booted the system, disabled the antispyware application services and rebooted, reenabled the services and rebooted, and even modified the hosts file to contain specific entries and rebooted. Each time, we saw DNS traffic on the network (via a sniffer on a separate system on the same subnet), as we expected; in the case of rebooting the system with the antispyware application services disabled, we saw no DNS domain name queries at all.

Finally, neither Registry analysis nor analysis of the contents of the Prefetch folder provided any indication that the employee had installed a secure file wiping utility on the system, let alone run one from removable media.

Using a comprehensive investigative methodology and correlating multiple, corroborating sources of data allowed us to determine the source of suspicious and potentially malicious activity. During initial response, the customer had collected only a limited amount of data and then based the assumption of malicious activity on nothing more than a Google search for a single domain name. The lack of appropriate data (i.e., full network captures, more comprehensive network log data, physical memory or portions of volatile data from the suspect system, etc.) resulted in the examination taking considerably more time, in turn resulting in higher cost to the customer. Ultimately, live testing of the system, booted on the network, allowed us to confirm that the activity was the result of a legitimate application (two, actually, interacting) and that the DNS domain name queries were not followed by attempts to connect to hosts in those domains via either UDP or TCP.

# Getting Started

One question I see in public forums quite often is, How do you start your examination? Given a set of data—images acquired from multiple systems, packet captures, log files, and so on—where does an examiner start his or her examination? How do you get started?

The catchall, silver-bullet answer that I learned in six months of training at The Basic School in Quantico, Virginia (where all Marine officers receive their initial training), is, "it depends." It applied then and it applies now just as well because it's true. Let's say that you have an image acquired from a single system. What was the operating system running or available at the time the image was acquired? What was the platform? Was it documented? You're probably asking why this matters—but take a look around at your tools and see which ones are capable of handling which file systems. Is the image of a Linux system? If so, is the file system within the image ext2, ext3, or ReiserFS?

Okay, okay … I know that this is a book about Windows forensic analysis. But I hope you see my point. When starting an examination, there are a number of things that the examiner may need to take into account. One of those "things" is the file system: Do you have the right tools for opening and reviewing the acquired image? However, more important, the examiner has to consider her goals: What does she hope to obtain from the examination? What needs to be achieved through the examination of the available data? See how easy it was for me to circle back around to "it depends"?

The most important step to getting started on an examination is to understand the goals of that examination. Regardless of the environment you're in, any examination is going to have a reason, or a purpose. If you're law enforcement, what are you looking for? Are you attempting to locate information about a missing child or determine if the system owner was trafficking in illicit images? If you're a consultant, before beginning your examination, you should have already met with the customer and thoroughly discussed what they hope to obtain or achieve through your examination. Even if you're an incident responder, on the move responding to an incident, you need to understand what you're supposed to achieve as a result of your actions *prior* to actually performing them. If you're responding to a malware infection, are you attempting to determine the malware artifacts and possibly obtain a copy of the malware code to provide to your antivirus vendor? Are you responding to unusual traffic terminating at a system on your internal infrastructure? The goals of your examination or response drive your actions.

## Tools & Traps…

### The Goals of Incident Response

As an incident responder, one of the things I've noticed is that many times—in fact, increasingly more often—the initial response by the first responders on-site can expose the organization to greater risk than the incident itself.

Now, I realize that you're probably reading and re-reading that last sentence and trying to make sense of it. After all, that's not exactly intuitive, is it? Well, what I've seen is that in many cases, the first responders are IT staff, and their response activities and procedures are very IT-centric. Very often, IT staffs are tasked (by senior management) with keeping systems—e-mail servers, Internet access, and so on—up and running as their primary duties. So, if malware is discovered on a system, the IT staff's goals are to remove it and get the affected system back into service as quickly as possible. This may mean "cleaning" the system by removing the malware, or wiping all data from the system and reinstalling everything (operating system, data, etc.) from clean media or backup, or it may mean replacing the system altogether.

The most important factor that plays into all this comes from regulatory bodies. The state of California started with SB-1386, a law requiring notification of any California resident if their personally identifiable information (thoroughly defined

**Continued**

and documented in the text of the law) were exposed as a result of a breach or intrusion. As of this writing, several other states have similar laws, and a federal law may be on the way. Add to that the Visa PCI compliance standards, as well as HIPAA, the SEC, and other regulatory bodies, and you've got quite a bit of external stimulus for having a good, solid response plan. In many cases, the regulatory bodies require a response plan to be documented and reviewed in order to be compliant. On the flip side of the coin, the cost of *not* having that good, solid response plan can include fines as well as both the hard and soft costs of notification and public exposure of a breach and exposure of sensitive data.

The best way to explain how these two pieces of information fit together is with an example. A company gets hit with malware through a browser-borne vector and spends some time cleaning approximately two dozen infected systems. During the course of their response, they find some indications that the malware *may* include a keystroke logger component or a networking component, although nothing definitive is ever determined (remember, the systems were cleaned, with no root-cause analysis being performed or documented). When corporate legal counsel hears about this—after all of the systems have been cleaned and put back into service—the question then becomes, Was any sensitive data on any of the infected systems exposed? How does the IT staff answer that question? After all, their goal was to clean the systems and get them back into service to keep the business running. No data was collected in order to determine if any sensitive data—personally identifiable information such as names, addresses, and Social Security numbers, or other data such as credit card numbers—was on those systems or had been compromised as a result of the malware infection.

Where the issue of risk comes into play is that some regulatory bodies state that if you are unable to determine definitively that the data was not exposed in any way, then you must notify across the entire range of the data that was on or accessible by that system. Stated simply, if you cannot prove that the sensitive data was *not* exposed, then you must notify everyone that their data may have been exposed. This makes it absolutely clear that incident response is no longer an IT process: It is an overall business process involving legal counsel, human resources, public relations and communications, and even executive management.

# Documentation

The key to any examination or analysis you perform will be your documentation. Documentation must be kept in a manner that will allow you, or someone else, to return to the materials at a later date (e.g., six months, one year, or longer) and understand or even verify the findings of the examination. This means that your documentation should be clear and concise, and it should be detailed enough to provide a clear indication of what you did, what you found, and how you interpreted your findings.

Documentation can be kept in any means that is readily available. There is no need to locate or purchase a special application that saves your documentation in a proprietary format.

In fact, you probably don't want to do this because you may not be using the application in a year, or someone who needs to review your documentation may not have that application. Something as simple as a text document would suffice, but having access to formatting capabilities in a word processor such as Microsoft Word might be more desirable. For example, with a word processor, you can embed links and images into the document, including such things as hard drive pin-out diagrams, screen captures, and even links to laptop disassembly guides (very useful when provided a laptop that you need to disassemble to gain access to the hard drive). In addition, many word processor document formats (i.e., MS Word and Adobe PDF) can be viewed and accessed from a number of platforms, so the format is somewhat ubiquitous. Even on Linux (and Windows) systems, OpenOffice (www.openoffice.org/) provides access to MS Word format documents and is freely available. Another very useful thing to keep in mind about your documentation format is your reporting format. Using the same word processor for both allows you to keep your case notes and then, when you're ready, cut and paste items directly into your report. After all, when reporting, you may not need the level of detail found in your case notes, but that information may be easily transferred to your report and modified appropriately.

So, what should you document? As a consultant, one of the items I need to keep track of is hours that will be billed to a customer for the work performed during an examination. In some instances, I may be the senior analyst on an engagement and will track not only the hours of other analysts but also tasks provided to them and their responses, findings, and input. This can be extremely simple, using a table format, and at the same time very effective and easy to understand. Recording this information in my case notes, along with my analysis, allows me to show how the time was spent should I need to justify this information at a later date. At the same time, that same information is entered into the billing application directly from my case notes—there should be no discrepancy between the two. This allows me to minimize mistakes, particularly in this extremely important area of an examination.

Another item I tend to track in my documentation is the data that I have access to in order to examine and also the media that this data is on—that is, USB external hard drives, internal hard drives, CDs or DVDs, and so on. I track this information according to an item's serial number so that I can easily refer back to the appropriate item throughout the course of the examination.

A useful tool for tracking my case notes is the Forensic CaseNotes application from QCC Information Security (www.qccis.com/?section=casenotes). Figure 8.1 illustrates the tabs I have set up to capture all of the previously discussed information.

**Figure 8.1** QCCIS Forensic CaseNotes tabs

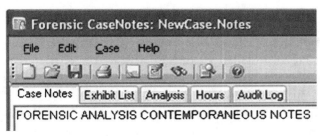

Regardless of the application you choose to use for maintaining your case notes, they should be accessible and concise, and they should clearly illustrate your analysis activities and results, to the point where those activities can be verified and validated, if necessary.

## Tools & Traps …

### Supporting Your Analysis

One thing I like to include in my case notes during an examination is any documentation that supports my line of reasoning. There are times when I may add notes based on testing a theory, but I also have an academic background, and one of the things I learned while writing my master's thesis was that I had to support what I was saying in the thesis. It's a simple matter to make a statement because you know something, but including similar statements made by others adds credibility to your analysis. An excellent source for this kind of supporting documentation when analyzing Windows systems is the Microsoft Knowledge Base. Many times searching either the Microsoft Knowledge Base itself, or even Google, will provide you with links to valuable information that can answer your questions and support your analysis. In other instances, you may get to the Microsoft Knowledge Base articles by way of another site, such as Eventid.net.

One of the Knowledge Base articles I use quite often for this purpose is http://support.microsoft.com/?kbid=299648, titled "Description of Ntfs date and time stamps for files and folders." This article describes how file Mac times are affected by copy and move operations between and within file systems (specifically, FAT and NTFS). Other Knowledge Base articles describe the MS Internet Information Server (IIS) Web server status codes visible in the Web server logs, how files are stored in the Recycle Bin on Windows XP and 2003, and so on. There are a number of Knowledge Base articles that can provide support and credibility to your analysis, and can be easily referenced in your case notes as well as your reports.

# Goals

A long time ago, I was discussing an examination performed by another analyst from another organization with a member of the security staff in our company. The consultant analyst had located the SubSeven Trojan installed within the acquired image, which was part of the contracted services (i.e., to determine if malware was installed on the system); however, as my colleague pointed out, the consultant did not identify the hidden DOS partition. Why? Because that wasn't the goal of the examination. When I spoke with the consultant, she stated that she did indeed notice the hidden partition when preparing to examine the image, and she even noted it in her examination notes. However, it was not one of the questions that needed to be answered with respect to the contract, was not pertinent to the examination, and therefore was not presented in the final report.

This is very important for all examiners to remember, regardless of whether you're a consultant or working for law enforcement. It is possible to go down a never-ending rabbit hole of analysis, looking for "suspicious activity" and never actually finishing, if you don't have (and adhere to) clearly defined goals for your examination.

Knowing what you should be or need to be looking for also gives you a starting point in your analysis. Is the issue one of a malware infection, or an intrusion? Are the goals of the examination to determine fraud or violations of acceptable use policies by a user? Understanding what you should be looking for helps determine where to start looking.

A friend of mine once told me about a report that he'd reviewed with respect to a malware incident. After collecting data and completing the examination, the examiner wrote up a report, including a thorough dissertation on the capabilities of the malware that went on for about two dozen pages. At the end of the report, my friend said that he had to ask the examiner whether this malware was actually found within the acquired system? After all, that's the question that the customer was paying them to answer, and in a report that spanned almost three dozen pages, there was no clear statement as to whether the malware had been found within the acquired image or not.

Digital forensic analysis can be an expensive proposition, and goals need to be clearly defined at the starting point. An analyst can spend a great deal of time examining an acquired image for malicious activity, and a team of responders can spend even longer combing through a multitude of systems within an infrastructure if their only guidance is to "find all of the bad stuff". Clearly defined goals help focus the analysis approach, guide the development of a response or analysis plan, as well as define the endpoint of the examination. Analysis goals need to be developed, understood, and clearly documented.

# Checklists

A great way to get started with analysis is with checklists. Checklists outline those things that we need to do, and a good checklist will often contain more items than we need, as it is intended to be comprehensive, and require us to justify and validate, through a logical thought process, our reasons for skipping items on the checklist, or not performing certain steps.

Checklists should be simple and straightforward. Your checklist can be something you do for every examination, such as mount the image as a read-only drive letter on your analysis system and scan the file system with antivirus (see Chapter 5) and antispyware applications. You may also include booting the image and scanning the "live" system with rootkit detection tools (see Chapter 7). You may include a search for credit card numbers, Social Security numbers, or other sensitive data as part of your checklist, or searches for e-mail (Web-based and otherwise) and chat logs based on the type of examination you're conducting.

One example of a checklist would be to document information about each image you're analyzing. For example, you may want to document the system name, last shutdown time, and other basic information extracted from the image that may be pertinent to your examination. Some settings, such as whether updating of last access times was disabled, or if the system was set to bypass the Recycle Bin when files are deleted, or if the pagefile was set to be cleared at shutdown, might have a significant impact on the rest of your analysis.

Another example of a checklist might include steps you would follow if malware was suspected to be on the system. This might be as simple as mounting the image with SmartMount and scanning the file system with a single antivirus application, or it might be more comprehensive, including several antivirus and antispyware applications (with their versions documented) as well as a number of other steps (see Chapter 5) included in order to be as thorough as possible. This might also include booting the image with LiveView and performing scans for rootkits. Generally, when I perform antivirus scans of an acquired image, the first thing I do is look within the image to determine if there was already an antivirus product installed, and if so, the application's vendor and version. From there, I can review the application logs to see if (or when) malware may have been detected, and if so, what actions were taken by the application (quarantined, attempted to quarantine but failed, etc.). Also, I usually check the Event Logs to determine if there were any notifications posted there, such as malware being detected or the antivirus application being abnormally stopped (a well-documented tactic of some malware). There's also the mrt.log file (see Chapter 5), which will provide me with some indication of protection mechanisms put in place on the system during Windows Updates.

However concise or expansive the checklist, it should include enough documentation to allow another analyst to replicate and verify your steps, should the need arise.

Checklists are not intended to be a step-by-step, check-the-box way of performing analysis. Checklist should be considered the beginning of an examination, a way of ensuring that specific tasks are completed (or at least documented as to why they weren't completed), rather than being considered the entire examination. What checklists allow you to do is ensure that you've covered all or most of your bases, and allow you to replicate those steps that need to be replicated across every examination, without having to worry about forgetting a step. Like your analysis applications and utilities, checklists are tools that you can use to your advantage. Checklists are a process, and by having a process, you also have something you can improve upon (conversely, if you don't remember what you did on your last examination, how can you improve?).

A sample checklist titled Incident Analysis Checklist.doc can be found on the media accompanying this book. The sample checklist is simply a Word document that contains some of the same fields identified by the tabs visible in Figure 8.1. The checklist provides some basic fields for identifying the incident and examiner, as well as the start and end dates for which the analysis occurs. There are also tables for identifying the items to be analyzed (acquired images, network traffic captures, log files, etc.), as well as checkboxes that identify some basic goals and analysis steps that may be used. This section can include items that are part of your organization's standard in-processing procedures, such as identification of an acquired image's operating system, any user accounts on the system, extraction of data from the Registry, scans for malware, and so on. While the checklist itself is only one page, additional pages may be added as the examiner conducts his analysis, and results may be recorded directly into the checklist. Again, this checklist serves only as a sample and an example, and may be expanded or modified to meet your specific needs.

## Tools & Traps…

### Which Version of Windows?

Often when working on live incident response, or even examining an acquired image, I will want to know which version of Windows I am working with. From what I see in public forums, often this isn't a concern for responders or examiners, but having conducted or assisted with a fair number of live response and forensic analysis engagements, what some people consider to be subtle nuances between the versions of Windows can actually be pretty significant differences. From Chapter 3, we know that key kernel structures (i.e., EProcess and EThread structures) found in memory not only change between Windows versions but also can change between service packs within the same version! From a forensic analysis perspective, there are artifacts available on some versions of Windows that are not available on others; one notable example is that System Restore Points are found on Windows XP but not on Windows 2000 or Windows 2003.

**Continued**

Perhaps the most well-known method for determining which operating system (OS) version of Windows you're working with is to check the contents of several Registry keys. Under the Microsoft\Windows NT\CurrentVersion key within the Software hive, you will find values such as CSDVersion, BuildLab, and ProductID that can be used to determine the Windows version. Microsoft Knowledge Base article 189249 (http://support.microsoft.com/kb/189249) provides information for programmatically determining the version for a live system, and it also provides indications for how to do the same during an examination.

Another way to determine the OS version is to locate the ntoskrnl.exe file in the system32 directory and parse the file version information from that executable file. This will also work with files such as cmd.exe and winver.exe (note that on a live system, running winver.exe at the command prompt opens an About Windows dialog box that displays some basic information about the OS, including the version and amount of physical memory).

Finally, if you're working with a version of Windows XP and need to determine whether it is the Home or Professional edition, locate the prodspec.ini in the system32 directory and look for (you may have to scroll down) the "[Product Specification]" entry. On my system, I see "Product=Windows XP Professional".

When it comes down to it, knowing the version of Windows that you're examining can guide you in what artifacts to look for, where to look, and also what should be there that may not be. All of these can have a significant impact on your findings.

# Now What?

Now that you have your documentation started, you understand your goals, and you have a checklist—then what? What happens next? Well, this is where you start your actual analysis. Let's say that you're analyzing an image acquired from a Windows system, and after documenting the acquisition, the operating system, and any user accounts on the system, you have several other analysis activities that you need to perform as part of your standard case processing, such as a keyword search and a malware scan. If the keyword list is relatively short, include at list of keywords directly in your analysis documentation and run the search. Or, identify why the search was not run, if you opted not to do so. Similarly, identify the application (or applications) used in your malware scan, or clearly state why the scan was not conducted.

Searching Google for "digital forensic analysis checklists" identifies a wide range of approaches used for these checklists. Some include file signature analysis, identification of graphics images (including movies and still images), parsing of Web browser activity, parsing of Recycle Bin and Windows shortcut (.lnk) files, and so on. All of these may be important to your examination or simply part of your organization's standard case processing procedures. Either way, your analysis activities should be thoroughly and concisely documented, particularly if you're going "off script" and pursuing a line of analysis that is outside the norm (some might call this a "hunch"). Documenting your hunches will expand your knowledge as well as your ability to go back at a later date and see what it was you did so that you can replicate those activities, as necessary.

# Extending Timeline Analysis

As discussed in Chapter 5, the timeline information that an analyst obtains as a result of using *fls* and mactime.pl is isolated to just the files and directories within the acquired image and does not take into consideration other events or artifacts within the acquired image that also contain time-stamped information. In part to address this issue, Michael Cloppert wrote a tool called Ex-Tip, which is available on Sourceforge (http://sourceforge.net/projects/ex-tip/). In addition, Michael's paper on the development and usage of Ex-Tip is available from SANS (https://www2.sans.org/reading_room/whitepapers/forensics/32767.php). Ex-Tip takes additional sources of time-stamped data, such as Registry keys and the contents of antivirus application scanning logs, into consideration, parses and normalizes them into a common time (Unix epoch time) format, and presents them in a slightly different, albeit text-based format.

Tools and utilities such as RegRipper (discussed at length in Chapter 4) can provide additional functionality for extracting time-stamped values from Registry hive files. Whereas the module provided with Ex-Tip extracts all keys and their *LastWrite* times from a hive file, RegRipper takes more of a surgical approach and can provide only the keys of interest, providing a modicum of data reduction (so as to not overwhelm the analyst with data points), as well as providing context to the data that is retrieved. For example, as discussed in Chapter 4, the RecentDocs key and its subkeys all contain MRU lists, and the most recently accessed file is relatively easily identified in the MRUList (or MRUListEx) value. Therefore, RegRipper plugins can provide not only the *LastWrite* time from the key but also the name of the most recently accessed file. Furthermore, Registry values such as those within the UserAssist keys contain time-stamped data and can be extracted by the appropriate plugin and then incorporated into a body file in the appropriate format.

Other files can be parsed for time-stamped data as well. For example, as discussed in Chapter 5, Windows Event Logs contain time stamps for when each event record was generated and written. Rp.log files from within Windows XP System Restore Points contain information about not only when the restore point was created but also the reason (system checkpoint, installation of a driver, etc.) for the restore point creation. This information adds context to the available data and can then be correlated to information derived from the output of fls.exe. There are also antivirus log files and a number of other files available that contain information that can (and perhaps should) be included in timeline analysis. An additional source of information can include events that are manually entered, such as the creation of crash dump files, and so on.

As discussed in Michael's paper, a number of facilities exist for parsing the available time-stamped data (once that data has undergone some form of normalization to a common data format, data reduction, etc.) and presenting that data in an understandable visual format. For example, Zeitline (http://projects.cerias.purdue.edu/forensics/timeline.php) and EasyTimeline (http://en.wikipedia.org/wiki/Wikipedia:EasyTimeline) are two such options. Zeitline is based on Java Swing, and it has apparently not been updated or seen any significant activity since 2006. EasyTimeline presents a graphical approach to representing time-stamped data. Another such tool that presents a great deal of potential is Simile Timeline, originally available from MIT and now available as a Google widget (http://code.google.com/p/simile-widgets/). Simile Timeline provides the capability not only for representing both point (an event that occurred at a single point in time, such as file last access date) and duration (an event that occurred over a span of time, such as an antivirus scan) events but also for presenting time-based data on separate, adjacent bands so that the information can be distinctly separate but viewed in correlation with other data.

One aspect to using a text-based output format or one of the graphically based output formats mentioned previously may include changing how analysts identify events, such as the output of the fls.exe utility.

# Summary

Most analysts will find that they won't be using one single area of an acquired image, such as the file system, to piece together their exams, and their cases. They'll end up using data from the Registry, files found in the file system, and even memory dumps and network packet captures to build a complete picture of their cases. After all, why hinge your conclusions on one piece of data when you can seal everything up airtight with multiple pieces of data to support your findings? Regardless of how much data you use, however, the key to everything is going to be your documentation.

# Solutions Fast Track

## Case Studies

☑ Case studies have always been a great way of illustrating how seemingly disparate bits of information and analysis techniques can be brought together into a cohesive framework to obtain far greater insight into analysis. Many people like to see what others have done, and in many cases this will get readers to consider what they've seen, try their own techniques, and even extend the technique.

## Getting Started

☑ Key items to keep in mind throughout your analysis are to stick to your analysis goals (getting off track or off focus can easily stall or delay your analysis) and to concisely and completely document your analysis.

## Extending Timeline Analysis

☑ Representing available data in a timeline format can be an extremely powerful tool for an analyst.

☑ Multiple sources of data within an acquired image can contain valuable time-based information, including the contents of log files, Registry keys and values, and the contents of the Recycle Bin.

# Frequently Asked Questions

**Q:** I have an examination in which I need to determine when a user was logged into the system; however, my initial work shows that auditing of logon events was not enabled, and I do not see any indications of those events in the Security Event Logs. How do I determine when the user was logged in?

**A:** There are several sources of information within the Windows operating system to determine when a user account was used to log into a system. Parsing the SAM hive file will give you the last logon date for the user, and that can be correlated to the last modification time on the NTUSER.DAT file within the user's profile to get the last time the user logged off of the system. Parsing the user's NTUSER.DAT file will provide a considerable amount of information about the user's activity, particularly from the UserAssist and RecentDocs keys. Also, the *LastWrite* times on keys used to maintain MRU lists can be very helpful. Because the NTUSER.DAT file maintains a great deal of information about the user's interaction with the Windows shell, a considerable amount of time-based information can be found in that file. In addition, parsing the same information from corresponding hive files in the System Restore Points in Windows XP will show you a historical progression of the data as well. This analysis technique uses a combination of file system and Registry analysis to develop a more comprehensive picture of the user's activity on the system.

**Q:** During incident response activities, I collected network traffic captures as well as volatile data from the system I thought was infected. How do I correlate these two pieces of data and tie them together?

**A:** Network traffic captures contain two important pieces of information that can be used to tie that data to a particular system—the source or destination IP address and port. The IP address will allow you to tie the traffic to a particular system (the MAC address in the Ethernet frames can also be used).

# Chapter 9

# Performing Analysis on a Budget

## Solutions in this chapter:

- **Documenting Your Analysis**
- **Tools**

☑ **Summary**

☑ **Solutions Fast Track**

☑ **Frequently Asked Questions**

# Introduction

To a number of folks, performing incident response and computer forensic analysis appears to be simply out of reach due to the cost associated with the various commercially available tools. This affects more than just hobbyists and those interested in delving into this fascinating (to me, anyway) realm, however. This affects schools: Computer forensic courses are offered not only at major universities but also at community colleges. The cost of commercial tools affects law enforcement officers and even consultants (such as myself—hey, we all have budgets we have to adhere to). Would it be nice to have access to all of the commercial tools? Sure, it would be, but from a budgetary perspective it just isn't practical.

It isn't particularly necessary, either. Commercial applications (EnCase, FTK, ProDiscover, etc.) are just that—tools. Every tool or application has its strengths and its weaknesses, and trained, knowledgeable analysts understand what they need to do before selecting the tool or application to assist them in their analysis. The key to forensic analysis isn't pushing the button on an application user interface. After all, as I've said time and time again, *the age of Nintendo forensics is over*! The key to forensic analysis is understanding what artifacts are available to you and having a logical, reasoned, and comprehensive plan or process for collecting and interpreting the data. From that perspective, you're not tied to a particular commercial application (in the absence of some specific requirement that forces you to use it) and can instead explore the use of low-cost or freely available tools and applications that your analysis needs.

## Tip

Now is a good time to discuss the topic of anti-forensic tools. Anti-forensic tools are those tools (and in some cases, techniques) that a bad guy will use to make our jobs more difficult, such as modifying file MAC times or wiping data (or "evidence") from the system. Many people think that anti-forensic tools target a particular commercial application; this simply is *not* the case. Sure, there have been public presentations at popular computer security conferences discussing how to subvert an analyst who uses EnCase, but the fact is that anti-forensic tools and techniques target the analyst, not the tools. An analyst who realizes this is one step ahead of, not behind, the bad guy.

Throughout this book, each chapter has presented, described, and/or demonstrated tools used for particular purposes, but in each case that presentation was simply, "hey, look at what this tool does and see how it's useful." My goal in this chapter is to fill in the gaps for many readers with a number of other tools that will get them started—tools such as hex editors, packet capture and analysis tools, etc. There are many tools that you can use, and many of them simply weren't designed with analysis in mind. However, someone has found these tools useful due to some functionality they provide. You should not consider this chapter, or even this book, a comprehensive and complete guide to everything and every tool you could possibly want. At best, this book serves to open that door a bit—to show you that there are options beyond those that are out of reach due to the cost of the product or cost of the training associated with that product.

Finally, if you know me or have read any of my previous books, you know I'm a fan of Perl. Some might even say that Perl is my hammer, and everything I see is a nail. And they'd be right. All humor aside, however, Perl can be an extremely powerful tool, such as when you have to parse several hundred megabytes of Web server logs for indications of a SQL injection attack *and* decode the hexadecimal or character encoding to decipher the actual injected commands to locate other affected systems. What might have taken you days now takes just minutes. I have seen and demonstrated this through scripts I've written, not the least of which ended up as RegRipper (www.regripper.net). I've heard others say the same thing—how a coworker's abilities with Perl reduced days of data manipulation by hand to a couple of hours using a Perl script. This not to say that Perl is the *only* programming language available, because any programming language you're comfortable with, such as Python, will work for you. Thanks to Dave Roth, I prefer Perl.

# Documenting Your Analysis

I begin this section by saying that I know I have discussed documentation in other chapters in this book, and here the subject is again. This is because the subject of documentation is extremely important, particularly because it is something extremely technical people do not like to do. From my perspective, I never liked documenting anything, until I started to see what happens when I didn't document my analysis. For example, I'd come across a great idea or find some great tool or technique for analysis, and three months later I wouldn't remember what it was. And I hadn't documented it! Documentation is a recurring theme throughout this book for the simple fact that it is so vital.

Another important theme throughout this book is the need for repeatability in work, be it data collection or analysis, which is achieved through documentation. Repeatability, which is essentially being able to take the same data, follow the same process, using the same tools, and achieving the same results, is a fundamental principle of forensic science. One reason that documentation needs to lead to repeatability is that analysts are not always around. One analyst or examiner may perform work, and then several months later when that analyst is on vacation or assigned to another task, someone may have a question about the results. Another analyst should be able to step in and, with original data and the previous analyst's notes, be able to repeat the same process and (it is hoped) achieve the same results. The same thing applies to work that an analyst may need to revisit a year later; without proper documentation, it is unlikely that the analyst will be able to remember exactly what he or she did.

The first step in performing any forensic analysis is to have a method for documenting what you do. After all, if you perform some analysis but fail to document it, *it didn't happen*. As much as technically oriented folks seem to hate to do this, documenting your analysis is paramount to what you do. Documentation must (not *should*) be detailed and clear enough to allow another analyst or examiner to understand what you did, as well as verify it. In addition, the documentation should be detailed and clear enough for *you* to pick up your own analysis notes from a year ago (or more) and be able to verify what you did. By *verify*, I mean using the same data and the same tools (because in your analysis notes, you listed the tools and versions used … right?), you or someone else should get the same results.

Think about that for a moment. Let's say you perform an analysis, and when the examination is complete and the final report has been delivered, you lock the drive in your safe awaiting final disposition. Then, a month later, a question about something in your report arises, and you need to go back to that data and verify some aspect of your analysis. But it's been a month (or six months or one year), and your operational tempo is such that not only have you performed several exams since then but also you've been assigned another examination, and your original data needs to be provided to another examiner. How embarrassing and difficult would it be if another examiner could not take the same data and, using the same tools, replicate your findings? How would you explain that? Most of us would probably say something like "You didn't do it right" or "You didn't use the right version of the tool", right? Well, what would it look like if *you* couldn't replicate your own results?

Documenting what you do is important, but documenting what you do to the point where someone else can replicate your findings is even more important. So, how do you do that? I've always found being concise to be the best approach. I've seen many folks who have been way too verbose in their notes, and what they actually did simply got lost in the prose. Let's say that you suspect that you may have a Web server that was subject to a SQL injection attack. The most logical place to look for indications of such an attack would be in the Web server logs. If the Web server is Microsoft's Internet Information Server (IIS) and the back-end database is MS SQL Server, then a logical place to start would be to look for the use of the SQL extended stored procedure *xp_cmdshell* in the Web server logs because that would not be something that you would normally see in the Web server logs. So let's say that you created a new ProDiscover project, added the image of the Web server to it, and then ran a search across the Web server logs for "xp_cmdshell". Your case notes might look as follows:

- *Created ProDiscover 5.0 project "intrusion_20081030". Added Web server image, saved project.*
- *Searched Web server logs (note full path) for "xp_cmdshell" using PD Search function; several hits found ex081002.log and ex081003.log.*

There you go. Simple, to the point, concise, yet clear and thorough. In the case of this search, you've listed what you searched for (xp_cmdshell), what you used to perform the search (ProDiscover 5.0 Search function), and what you found (hits in two log files). For example, "analyzed log files" or "searched log files" says nothing about what you did. Which log files did you search? What did you search for? If you did a keyword search, what were your keywords? How did you conduct the search? Using grep, or using the Windows Search tool (which I've done: Export the log files from an image using FTK Imager and then click **Start | Search | For Files and Folders**)? What were your results? See how incomplete documentation generates rather than answers questions? Also be sure to avoid being overly verbose; as I said, I've seen notes so verbose that the actual work done and the results were completely lost. Providing dates on each page or with each entry adds to the veracity of the notes, and if multiple team members are working on a major analysis, having each member initial or sign his or her own work can be a real advantage further down the road.

Including the tools you used and their versions in your documentation makes it easier to re-create and verify the results. The version of the tool you use may make a difference, particularly if there are major updates between versions of the tool. This can be particularly important if you're using an antivirus scanning application to scan either a mounted image or just a few exported files. Noting the version of the scanning engine as well as the virus definitions file(s) can make a world of difference, particularly when the files you scanned are found two weeks later to be malware.

Another important aspect of documenting your analysis includes substantiating your determinations. Analysts very rarely make a determination of something based on one piece of data alone; in most cases, there are multiple supporting pieces of data that are correlated to develop a determination. For example, if I need to determine when a user was logged into a Windows system, one of the first places I would look is the Security hive file. Parsing a key in this hive file will tell me whether auditing for logins was enabled or not. If it was, I will then look for the appropriate event records in the Security Event Log. I would also check the SAM hive file for indications of the last time the user logged in, as well as the NTUSER.DAT hive file in the user's profile directory for indications of activity during the time frame in question. All of these can be used to make a determination of when the user was logged in. Furthermore, referencing outside sources, such as Microsoft Knowledge Base articles, is a great way to substantiate the findings of your analysis.

One tool I've found to be extremely useful for documentation is Forensic CaseNotes from QCC Information Security in the United Kingdom (www.qccis.com/?section=casenotes). Forensic CaseNotes is a great tool for keeping examination case notes. It's free, configurable, and pretty versatile. Generally, the first thing I do after downloading and installing Case Notes to a new system is to set up the configurable tabs to suit my needs, as illustrated in Figure 9.1.

**Figure 9.1** Excerpt from Forensic CaseNotes GUI, after Configuration

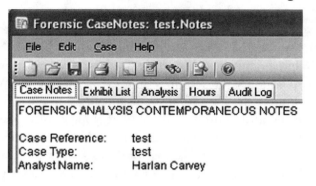

As you can see from Figure 9.1, there are a number of tabs available. I keep one for Exhibits: This is all of the media I have, along with any notes with respect to acquisitions. The information for this tab comes from my acquisition worksheets. I also have one for Hours: I use this to record hours spent on work that is directly attributable to the engagement and billed to the customer. This is extremely important for consultants. Perhaps the most important tab is Analysis: This is where I keep track of the actual work I do on a daily basis. Sometimes I'm working analysis on my own, whereas other times I'm working as a team lead and managing work performed not only by me but also by other team members, or perhaps another organization internal to the company. Having everything visible in one place lets me see what's been done and if additional hours need to be requested.

One beneficial aspect of CaseNotes is that you can add images (screen captures, digital pictures, etc.) into the text fields beneath each tab. When performing analysis, I will often cut and paste command lines used with various command-line interface (CLI) tools as well as excerpts from the output of various CLI tools directly into the contents of the tabs; if I have something special to add, such as pin-out diagrams for adapters, I can add those as well. Having these available for another analyst to review can be beneficial for future reference and can be extremely valuable when it comes to report writing. Often, adding a picture or diagram to a report can save a great deal of explanation and confusion.

What else goes into my case notes? Everything. Seriously. This includes URLs or links to information from the Internet that I used as part of my analysis, such as MS TechNet Knowledge Base articles, and even links to "hacking" sites if they were appropriate to the examination (and supported by corroborating data); screen captures, images of anything pertinent to the examination, etc.; and specific versions of tools used, as well as mention of and references to specific tools/scripts I've created to assist me in managing the available data. In some cases, if a number of tools or scripts are used, I will archive them in another location for later reference.

One caveat about the use of CaseNotes is that I know cases in which analysts have been unable to access their CaseNotes file after putting a password on it and closing it. Also, keep in mind that CaseNotes does not keep the contents of your notes in a file that can be necessarily opened in a variety of other formats; that is, if you use CaseNotes, don't expect to open the file in Notepad and get something that's easy to read.

Another tool that is available is NoteCase note manager (http://notecase.sourceforge.net/). I have not tried using NoteCase or, for that matter, other tools for maintaining my case notes. However, if you're looking for something that allows your case notes to be more accessible, one simple way to do this is to set up a format or checklist in MS Word. Most commercial organizations have MS Word, you can save the files in a number of formats, and a variety of commercial (Adobe) and freeware (PDFCreator) tools will allow you to print the files to a PDF format. The tabs I used in CaseNotes can easily be redone as headers in an MS Word document, and you can even use tables or an embedded Excel spreadsheet to manage and record your hours.

The overall idea here is that you do have *something*, some method for documenting your work in a consistent, verifiable manner. I have not yet mentioned another very good reason for doing this: What happens if you are called to testify about any of your work? Are you going to remember the specifics and the nuances of an examination or engagement six months or one year after the fact? There have been a number of occasions when I've been asked a question (not questioned in court or during a deposition) about some work I did awhile ago (four, six, or nine months) and I have needed to refer to my case notes to make sure I got the correct examination and the correct information.

# Tools

When performing incident response or forensic analysis, there are a wide variety of activities that either entails. As such, you'll need the right tool for the right job—but which tool works best for you? The purpose of this section is to present a range of tools that are useful for a variety of purposes so that you can get started on your road to discovery.

The tools listed in this chapter are freely available tools, and most are free for your use within the terms of the license agreement (of course). Some tools are evaluation versions, and the full version may require a nominal fee if you want to continue using the program.

## Acquiring Images

Acquiring data is a major part of what any incident response analyst does, and acquiring images of systems is just part of that.

### dd

dd is the utility most folks think of when it comes to acquiring images. dd, or "data definition," is a native Linux/UNIX command that allows the user to "convert or copy a file" (according to man pages such as http://linuxreviews.org/man/dd/), and it is very often seen as the "standard" or "granddaddy" utility for this purpose. There are a number of variations of this utility available, some with slightly different capabilities; however, they all perform essentially the same basic function—they allow you to acquire images of drives or volumes.

One version of dd that is available for Windows is from George M. Garner, Jr., and is part of the Forensic Acquisition Utilities he makes available (http://gmgsystemsinc.com/fau/). This package of utilities allows you to acquire images of systems, pipe them over the network (if you do not have local storage available), use compression, and generate and verify computational hashes to ensure the integrity of the acquired data.

### Tools & Traps …

### Using dd for Live Images

Most folks think that tools such as dd are meant only for acquiring images of drives removed from systems—hook the drive up to a write-blocker and use dd to acquire your image. This is, of course, the preferred methodology, but in a number of cases this may not be possible. Due to the nature of a customer's network infrastructure and the impact that taking a system down and offline in order to acquire an image of the hard drive would have had, we opted to use the native dd command (SUSE Linux 9) to acquire a live image of the physical hard drive. We made sure that we thoroughly documented the reason and process for this approach, including documenting the versions of the utilities used (dd, split, etc.) in our case notes and report.

Dcfldd (http://dcfldd.sourceforge.net/) is another freely available version of the dd tool that also runs on Windows. Dcfldd was written by Nick Harbour. The Sourceforge Web page for dcfldd describes it as an "enhanced version of the GNU dd," with additional features such as imaging/wiping verification, hashing, piping of logs, etc. All of these functions are extremely useful not only for ensuring the integrity of the image and allowing you to pipe the image off of the system (when acquiring an image of a live system, you do not want to write that file to the actual hard drive you are acquiring) but also for removing or wiping the image file when you've completed your analysis.

## Tools & Traps …

### dd Format Images

Increasingly more often, forensic examiners are seeing the need for some kind of standardization in all aspects of what we do. This applies to image acquisition as well. A responder's toolkit or "fly-away" kit should include a number of methods for acquiring images, such as hardware write-blockers (i.e., those that provide for straight drive-to-drive imaging as well as those that allow the responder to connect the drive to be imaged to a write-blocker and acquire the image using software, etc.), as well as means (tools and processes) for acquiring live images. In addition, response teams should include in their standard operating procedures a standardized format to which images should be (if possible) acquired.

Why is this important? Prior to the recent release of updated versions of forensic analysis applications, I had an opportunity to assist with an examination in which one drive from a system was acquired using the dd format and the other drive from the same system was acquired using a proprietary format specific to one forensic analysis application. At the time, this situation could have restricted me to using one specific forensic analysis application in my analysis.

Using a consistent format for acquiring images is important for other reasons as well. First, it adds an air of professionalism in the eyes of the customer, as well as your peers. Believe me, when I first sat down to look at the specifics of the examination I was going to assist with and saw two hard drives from the same system acquired in different formats, my first thought was "did these guys even *have* a process?"

Also, don't think for a minute that you're the only one who's ever going to see these images. I've performed a number of examinations where after everything was complete and the final report was delivered, the customer wanted the images rather than just having me wipe the drives and ship them back. Always be prepared to return the images to the customer or to turn the images over to someone else for analysis; having consistent image formats (along with your documentation) is simply more professional.

Second, requiring a consistent image format naturally leads to documentation that will address the issues not only of the process used to acquire the image but also justification as to why you needed to deviate from the standard. Overall, this is simply more professional and thorough.

# FTK Imager

Both FTK Imager and FTK Imager Lite are available for free from AccessData.com (www.accessdata.com/downloads.html). FTK Imager Lite is a "light" version of the FTK Imager tool that can be unzipped and burned to CD or copied to a thumb drive for use. There is a support article on the AccessData.com Web site that also lists which files you will need from the FTK Imager archive if you want to run that tool from a CD or thumb drive, in order to have one consistent tool and version at your disposal.

I've found FTK Imager to be extremely valuable for a number of uses. When I've had to perform examinations of images acquired using EnCase and not had EnCase readily available (or simply not wanted to use it), I've opened the .E0x files in FTK Imager and either extracted specific files or acquired an image to dd format. I've also used FTK Imager to verify file systems of acquired images, including an image of a SUSE Linux 9 system running the ReiserFS. Of course, I've also used FTK Imager as an image acquisition tool, either running it in conjunction with a properly employed write-blocker or running it from a CD and acquiring a live image of a Windows system to an external USB-connected hard drive (or some other media/location).

FTK Imager can also be used to open VMware .vmdk files. I have responded to engagements where systems running within the VMware virtual environment were part of the network infrastructure and even systems that we needed to acquire and analyze. As such, perhaps the easiest way to "acquire" such systems is to simply copy the .vmdk (and .vmem, if available) files off of the host system. With FTK Imager, you can choose to Add an Evidence Item to view the file system and extract specific files or choose Create Disk Image to acquire the .vmdk (or .E0x image) file to raw dd, SMART, or .E0x format. This can be extremely useful when using commercial analysis tools that may not recognize the .vmdk format or that may be more cumbersome than is necessary for the work you intend to perform.

If you don't want to or simply don't have the facilities to acquire your own images, there are places you can go on the Internet to download images provided for tool testing or as part of challenges. This is a great thing that some very smart folks have been providing. After all, how better to communicate an idea or concept or process of analysis than to describe it and then provide some facility for folks to try the "hands-on" approach to learning? Most of the images are posted with some kind of challenge or series of questions involved to guide the participant's examination. As a consultant, I am acutely aware of where direction such as "find all suspicious/malicious activity" can lead—to lots of billable hours that you can't recover. The posted challenges provide not only an excellent resource for honing your analysis skills but also a great example for what an examination should look like from the beginning.

One of the first locations I found for freely available image files was the CFReDS (Computer Forensics Reference Data Sets) Project at NIST. The "Hacking Case" (www.cfreds.

nist.gov/Hacking_Case.html) image files include not only a dd format split image but also an EnCase or EWF (Expert Witness Format; Expert Witness was the precursor to EnCase) for those who want to practice with other tools.

Another site that includes some specific images and test scenarios is the Digital Forensics Tool Testing (http://dftt.sourceforge.net/) site, set up by Dr. Brian Carrier. This site provides some very specific test images for testing forensic analysis tools, but as with other sites, the provided images can also be used as a basis for developing and honing analysis skills, as well as providing familiarization with various forensic analysis applications.

Lance Mueller provides two interesting practical application challenges via his ForensicKB. com blog site (www.forensickb.com/search?q=practical). Lance has graciously provided the practical scenarios, along with small (~400 MB) images acquired from a Windows XP system in compressed .E0x/EWF format. If you do not have a valid EnCase dongle, not to worry: FTK Imager will open these files easily, allowing you to export files from the image or simply generate a dd format image from the EWF format file. Some of the comments to Lance's blog, for those posts, also provide insight into what other examiners are looking for and have found.

# Image Analysis

Once you have an acquired image, have verified your image hashes and the file system, and have documented your entire process, you will need some means of opening the image and performing the basic analysis functions necessary as part of the work you're doing. Throughout this book, we've discussed various tools for doing this—for opening the entire image file and viewing the file system structure as a whole, running searches, etc., or simply extracting specific files for analysis (Registry hive files, Event Log files, etc.).

## The SleuthKit

The SleuthKit (TSK; www.sleuthkit.org/) tools were written by Dr. Brian Carrier and provide the backend components for the Autopsy Forensic Browser. TSK is a set of command-line tools that allow you to examine and analyze file and volume systems within image files. The TSK tools are also available for Windows systems; however, at the time of this writing, the Autopsy Forensic Browser has not been ported to a native Windows format (although all of the tools can be compiled on Windows using the Cygwin subsystem).

The TSK tools can be used on a Windows system in much the same manner as they are on Linux systems; however, there are a couple of caveats. First, according to Dr. Carrier, there is an issue with "globbing" at the command line, requiring you to list all of the component files to a split image file in order. This means that if you are analyzing a split image file that contains multiple files, you will need to list each of them as follows:

*command [options] image1 image2 image3…*

This is where tools such as FTK Imager come in handy, in that you can reassemble the split image files into a single unified image file. FTK Imager is adept at reassembling some split image file formats, such as its own as well as those produced by tools such as Guidance Software's EnCase. You can also use the native Windows *type* command to reassemble split image files that were acquired in the raw format:

```
D:\images>type image.001 >  image_all.img
D:\images>type image.002 >> image_all.img
D:\images>type image.003 >> image_all.img
...
```

TSK can open raw (i.e., dd), Expert Witness (i.e., EnCase, referred to as EWF), and AFF file system and disk images (www.sleuthkit.org/sleuthkit/desc.php). The TSK tool fls.exe (Version 3) for the Windows platform reports at the command line that it can parse raw (dd) image files, EWF image files, and split raw image files:

```
D:\tools\tsk>fls -i list
Supported image format types:
  raw (Single raw file (dd))
  ewf (Expert Witness format (encase))
  split (Split raw files)
```

There are a number of documents available at the SleuthKit Web site, as well as other locations online, that describe how to use the various command-line tools in combination to perform analysis of an image. For example, the File System Analysis Techniques (http://wiki.sleuthkit.org/index.php?title=FS_Analysis) and File Activity Timelines (http://wiki.sleuthkit.org/index.php?title=Timeline) references provide a great deal of extremely useful information about the TSK tools. Perhaps the best source of information about the tools is the TSK Wiki (http://wiki.sleuthkit.org/index.php?title=Main_Page).

Some straightforward usage examples of the TSK tools include using *dls* to collect unallocated space from an image file. The following command can be used to extract the unallocated space from an acquired image file:

```
dls -A image.dd > unalloc.dls
```

Removing unallocated space from the acquired image file can be useful in performing string/grep searches or file carving on just that unallocated space, such as when searching for credit card numbers, IP or email addresses, or just performing file carving.

The following command will give you information about the file system within the image file:

```
fsstat -f ntfs image.dd
```

The *fsstat* command provides file system, metadata, and content information about the image file. For example, running the command against an acquired image of a Windows XP system returns the following file system information:

```
FILE SYSTEM INFORMATION
--------------------------------------------
File System Type: NTFS
Volume Serial Number: 98B0A679B0A65D8E
OEM Name: NTFS
Version: Windows XP
```

On a live system, you can obtain much of this same information using fsutil.exe. For example, the following commands return similar information as fsstat.exe, albeit from a live system (including the volume serial number):

```
C:\>fsutil fsinfo volumeinfo C:\
C:\>fsutil fsinfo ntfsinfo C:
```

The volume serial number is created at and determined by the time that the drive was formatted and can be used in part to identify the acquired image when used in association with other documentation.

Perhaps the most useful tool for analysts that is part of the TSK tools is fls.exe (http://wiki. sleuthkit.org/index.php?title=Fls), which lists the file and directory names in a file system in a pipe-separated format that allows timeline information to be generated using mactime.pl. For example, the following command will run through the entire image file, recursing through directories and subdirectories:

```
D:\tools\tsk>fls -m c: -r d:\cases\xp\xp.001
```

The *-m* option allows you to prepend the file and directory listings with the name of the mount point used (in this case, C:\). Most often, the output of the command will be redirected to an output file and then run through a tool such as mactime.pl or ex-tip (timeline creation tool created by Mike Cloppert; https://www2.sans.org/reading_room/whitepapers/forensics/32767.php) to sort the file system information into a more readable and understandable timeline format.

## Tools & Traps …

### Timelines

Tools such as TSK's fls.exe, mactime.pl, and Mike Cloppert's ex-tip provide extremely useful open source functionality for creating timelines of file system activity. However, because they are open source, they are easily extensible. For example, any other time-stamped source of information from a Windows system can be included in the timeline as well; all that needs to occur is that the proper format (as illustrated on the TSK Wiki page for fls.exe) be followed, and Registry keys (as well as values whose data includes time stamps), Event Log entries, and even the contents of other files (ex-tip includes a filter for McAfee OnAccessScan log files, and filters can be written for other AV log files, the setupapi.log file, etc.). In addition, data can be manually added to the "body file" prior to filtering and sorting with a tool such as ex-tip, allowing for the entry of additional data that the analyst may wish to include in the timeline. Normalizing entries to a common format allows for them to be imported into other tools such as Zeitline (http://projects.cerias.purdue.edu/forensics/timeline.php).

For other useful TSK tool commands, CyberGuardians has a two–page PDF "cheat sheet" available (www.cyberguardians.org/docs/ForensicsSheet.pdf).

There is also a Windows version of the Selective File Dumper tool called FUNDL (for "File Undeleter") that uses the TSK tools available on Sourceforge (http://sfdumper.sourceforge.net/fundl.htm).

## Tools & Traps …

### Image Formats

Previously in this chapter, I mentioned the need for standardization in image formats. The purpose of this is to achieve consistency and professionalism through a standardized process. Some organizations may rely solely on one commercial forensic analysis application and may have an excellent reason for standardizing on a proprietary image format. Other organizations, such as consulting firms, may opt to standardize on a more accessible format (i.e., the dd format) to allow a wider range of access to

**Continued**

forensic analysis applications, which in turn allows for verification, etc. In 2008, Technology Pathways released ProDiscover Version 5.0, which included the ability to open EWF format images. Following the DFRWS 2008 conference, Dr. Michael Cohen released a version of his PyFlag application that runs natively on Windows systems. In April 2008, Dr. Brian Carrier released versions of the Sleuthkit tools that were compiled to run natively on Windows. These tools, although (at the time of this writing) they cannot be used with the Autopsy Forensic Browser (Cygwin versions of the tools must be used), provide command-line access to dd, EWF (via libewf), and Advanced Forensic Format AFF (via afflib; www.afflib.org/) format images.

# PyFlag

Following the DFRWS 2008 conference, Dr. Michael Cohen released a version of his PyFlag forensic and log analysis graphical user interface (GUI) that runs natively on Windows (www.pyflag.net/cgi–bin/moin.cgi/PyFlagWindows). This version of PyFlag goes by the name PyFlagWindows or WinPyFlag. Whatever you decide to call it, please be sure to thank Dr. Cohen profusely and repeatedly for his free (as in "beer") contribution to the community. PyFlag has been available for Linux systems for some time, and now the range of capabilities of PyFlag are available to those analysts who are more comfortable operating in a Windows environment. Once you download and install PyFlag for Windows per the instructions on the PyFlagWiki, all you need to do is launch the FlagHTTPServer.py file by double-clicking it, and then direct your Web browser to http://127.0.0.1:8000. Figure 9.2 shows a portion of PyFlag running through Firefox on Windows.

**Figure 9.2** Excerpt of PyFlag UI on Windows, in Firefox

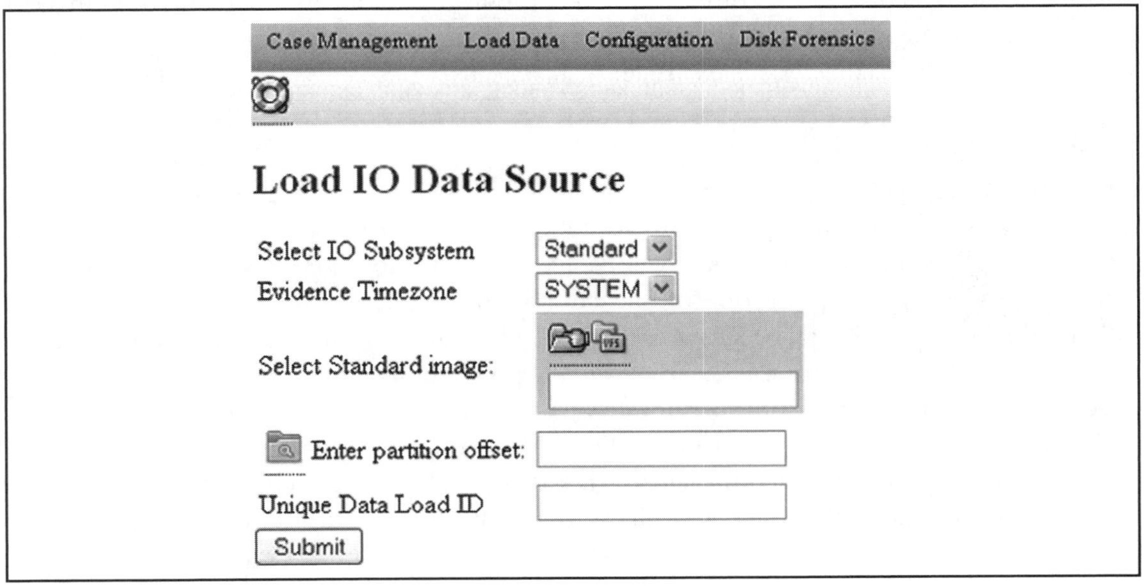

Once PyFlag is installed, you can use it normally, just as you would if it were running on Linux. PyFlag incorporates the use of the TSK tools and allows an analyst to incorporate acquired image files, log data, and packet captures all in one "case." Dr. Cohen has also incorporated Volatility's functionality within PyFlag, allowing an analyst to include memory dumps.

During the DFRWS 2008 Forensic Rodeo (www.dfrws.org/2008/rodeo.shtml), Dr. Cohen used PyFlag to perform his analysis, searching the provided data (a memory dump and an image acquired from a thumb drive) for clues to answer the questions posed in the challenge.

# ProDiscover Basic

ProDiscover is an excellent analysis application that I have had the privilege of having access to since Version 3; Version 5 was released in summer 2008. I have enjoyed using the rather intuitive GUI for analyzing images acquired from Windows systems because it allows me to see a good deal of information in a single, unified, albeit uncluttered interface. Whether I am performing file system verification of an image, some sort of quick analysis, or some detailed analysis, in many cases I have opted to start with ProDiscover.

Chris Brown (owner of Technology Pathways and author of *Computer Evidence: Collection and Preservation*) provides a basic version of ProDiscover for free download and use. Although the basic version of the application does not have anywhere near the capabilities of the full version, it is still a very useful tool.

One caveat to using ProDiscover is how it handles split image files. Acquired images that are full image files can be added to a ProDiscover project file, but to add an image that consists of split image files, you must create a .pds file. The .pds file consists of some header information and a complete, in-order listing of all split image files. When adding the image to a project, you need to choose the .pds file rather than the first split image file (the way you would with FTK Imager, for example).

# Mounting an Image File

An alternative to opening an acquired image file in an analysis application is to mount the image file as a read-only file system so that the image file appears on your analysis system as a drive letter. When done with proper care (software application used sets the mounted file system to read-only) and protection of the acquired image file (i.e., use a copy of the data rather than the original data, be sure to set NTFS file system permissions to prevent writing to the image file(s), etc.), this can be an extremely powerful tool for a wide spectrum of analysis. Aside from the programs previously mentioned in this book (SmartMount from ASRData and Mount Image Pro from GetData), there is a freeware tool that will allow you to do the same thing; it is called the virtual disk driver (VDK; http://chitchat.at.infoseek.co. jp/vmware/vdk.html). VDK is a device driver that will allow you to mount an acquired image file as a drive letter on your system. When used with the VDKWin GUI (http://petruska. stardock.net/Software/VMware.html), illustrated in Figure 9.3, you simply need to click a few buttons and you'll have your file system mounted and accessible from your analysis system.

**Figure 9.3** VDKWin GUI

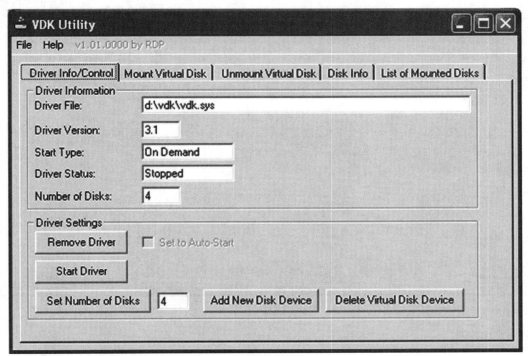

VDKWin obviously removes some of the complexity (and chance for making mistakes) from the use of the vdk.sys driver, but how is something like this useful? It is hoped that by now you've seen how an examiner does not have to be restricted to just one way of doing things; as long as the appropriate level of care is taken, and as long as you're documenting what you do (and why), the process you use to analyze acquired images is up to you (or your organization's standard operating procedures, as the case may be). However, there may simply be some analysis methodologies that are not accessible due to the fact that they are not built into the commercial analysis application you're using, or they are but, in having done so, the vendor has priced the application out of an affordable range.

Another freely available tool for mounting images is IMDisk (Version 1.1.3 was released on December 5, 2008, from www.ltr-data.se/opencode.html), a virtual disk driver that installs as CLI utility and has a Control Panel applet, which provides a GUI interface to the driver. Figure 9.4 illustrates the IMDisk UI with an image mounted as a read-only drive letter (H:\).

**Figure 9.4** IMDisk User Interface with an Image Mounted as H:\

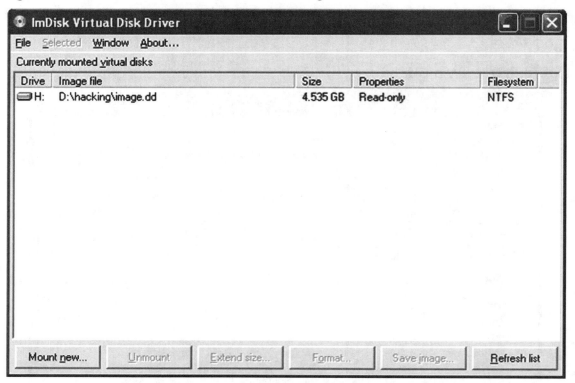

**TIP**

Microsoft has a free tool available (albeit unsupported and not advertised) called the "Virtual CD-ROM Control Panel for XP." This tool provides a virtual CD-ROM within the Windows XP Control Panel that you can use to mount .iso files (usually from a CD or DVD) as file systems.

The direct link to the tool is rather long, but a link can be found at the Microsoft Web site (http://msdn.microsoft.com/en-us/subscriptions/aa948864.aspx; scroll approximately two-thirds of the way down), as well as on such blogs as RaDaJo (http://radajo.blogspot.com/2006/09/mounting-cddvd-iso-images-in-windows.html) and help.net (http://weblogs.asp.net/pleloup/archive/2004/01/15/58918.aspx).

# File Analysis

Often, you will need to examine individual files rather than entire file or volume systems. Many times, these files will have proprietary formats (remember the Windows Recycle Bin INFO2 files from Chapter 5?) and may not have a suitable viewer available.

## Hashing Utilities

When extracting files from an acquired image, you may want to compute cryptographic hashes for the files to verify their integrity later. Hashing algorithms are cryptographic computations that generally take a variable length input and return a unique, fixed length output. If so much as a single bit within the file changes, the hash will change as well, demonstrating the usefulness of file hashes. Jesse Kornblum wrote a hashing program called MD5Deep (http://md5deep.sourceforge.net/) that will not only generate and compare MD5 hashes for files but also generate and compare SHA-1, SHA-256, Tiger, and Whirlpool hashes. These programs are all CLI programs, making them suitable for use in batch files in order to automate their deployment.

Besides identification and integrity checking, another way you can use file hashes is for a quick determination of whether the file you're working with has already been identified as malware. The VirusTotal Web site (www.virustotal.com/) will allow you to upload a file hash for comparison in its database, rather than uploading the entire file. So if the file you're interested in is very large, or you don't want to send copies of malware files out over the Internet, you might consider using the capability of this Web site to do a quick verification. After all, it doesn't take a great deal of effort, and it adds to the completeness of your case notes and your final report, regardless of whether you're a consultant or law enforcement.

Another hashing tool from Jesse Kornblum is ssdeep (http://ssdeep.sourceforge.net/), an excellent tool for performing piecewise fuzzy hashing. This hashing technique allows you to compare similar but not identical files by identifying the likelihood of similarity between the files. I used this hashing tool when comparing two files of similar size and the same name that were collected as a result of two different incident response engagements, and I found the files to be 98 percent to 99 percent similar.

## Hex Editors

A good hex editor that you're comfortable with using can be an indispensable tool for forensic analysis. Often, you will run across binary files that you need to open and view, and word processor applications simply will not render the data in a suitable format. There have been a number of times when I have received unusual responses from analysis tools, or when a Perl script I was writing to dissect the binary contents of a file simply wasn't working, and I had to open that file in a hex editor to review the binary/hexadecimal contents and see what the issue might be. One example of how I've used this was to explore the differences between Windows XP and Vista Prefetch files (see Chapter 5).

I prefer UltraEdit (www.ultraedit.com/) because I use it as a programming environment as well as a hex editor. I like many of the capabilities of this application (line numbers are visible so when a Perl script bombs, I can quickly find my error), so I'm willing to pay the nominal fee for it. Some of its other capabilities include syntax highlighting for Perl, auto-indent, the ability to open *really* large log or binary files, and hexadecimal content of a file side by side with the binary version. However, before I settled on UltraEdit, I looked at a number of freeware applications to find out what was available and what functionality I preferred. During this exploration, I ran across a number of other applications, such as the following:

- Cygnus Hex Editor Free Edition (www.softcircuits.com/cygnus/fe/)

- XVI32 (www.chmaas.handshake.de/delphi/freeware/xvi32/xvi32.htm)

- HDD Software's Free Hex Editor Neo (www.hhdsoftware.com/Products/home/hex-editor-free.html)

- HexEdit (www.physics.ohio-state.edu/~prewett/hexedit/)

Keep in mind that these are all just examples of hex editors, and as an analyst, you need to find what works for you. If you're interested in exploring other options, Wikipedia maintains a comparison of hex editors (http://en.wikipedia.org/wiki/Comparison_of_hex_editors) on various platforms that you may want to take a look at and perhaps even use as a basis for your own exploration into tools to use.

# Network Tools

I hope that throughout this book you've seen that analysis of systems, particularly during incident response, is not restricted to simply the host systems (although that is the primary focus of this book). Often, indications of a compromise, intrusion, or malware infection will start with an IDS alert, something unusual in the firewall logs, or simply some unusual network traffic. In other cases, subsequent information about an intrusion, such as communications between systems, where network connections originate from, and where outbound communications are destined (in the case of data exfiltration), will only be able to be determined through the collection and analysis of network-based data. As a subject unto itself, network-based data collection and analysis is beyond the scope of this book, but it is an important enough subject to provide you with some of the necessary tools that can be used in these activities.

## Scanning

One of the major issues faced by the incident response and forensic analysis community (in my humble opinion) is the gap that exists between this community and the vulnerability community. Vulnerabilities are discovered and verified on an almost daily basis, and soon after, a working exploit that takes advantage of that vulnerability may be posted on the Internet or discovered during incident response activities. Also, there are companies whose business model is to look for, find, and verify vulnerabilities in software products and then provide protection against these vulnerabilities to their customers.

The disparity comes into play by way of the fact that when a vulnerability is discovered, there is very often little to no research that goes into determining the artifacts left on a compromised system by the use of the exploit. For a vulnerability to be successfully exploited, there is very often a service or application that is listening on a network port (i.e., MS SQL Server listens for connections on TCP port 1433) and is subject to the exploit, and as a result, the researcher must have some means of verifying that the exploit succeeded. Once the exploit has succeeded, the result is a successfully compromised system that can then be analyzed for artifacts associated with the exploit.

Scanning applications are used in vulnerability assessments to identify potential holes in an infrastructure so that a prioritized, comprehensive plan can then be developed to reduce the "attack surface" of that infrastructure. This means that by identifying where weaknesses exist, and then working to address those weaknesses (patch systems, upgrade and securely configure applications, etc.), the opportunities available for an attacker to gain access to a network infrastructure are greatly reduced. These same scanning applications can be used as a part of your analysis to identify the attack surface of the system or systems involved so that you have a way of determining how the system may have been compromised. For example, in October 2008, Microsoft released an "out-of-cycle" patch for a vulnerability identified as MS08-067 (http://blogs.technet.com/msrc/archive/2008/10/23/ms08-067-released.aspx), which pertained to a critical vulnerability to the Windows Server service. Had you examined a compromised Windows XP system two months later and found that the critically important patch for that vulnerability had not been installed, this might provide you some indication of where to direct your analysis, particularly if the malware used on the system after a successful exploit was so new that it wasn't detected by antivirus applications.

There are several freely available tools that you can use to assist in your analysis, particularly when you are attempting to determine what vulnerability or "attack vector" *may* have been used in an incident. Not only will these tools work on live systems but also you can boot an acquired image with LiveView (http://liveview.sourceforge.net/) and then scan the system (by default, systems booted with LiveView do not have networking capabilities) to get an idea as to what vulnerabilities may have existed on the system. For example, Microsoft's own Baseline Security Analyzer (http://technet.microsoft.com/en-us/security/cc184924.aspx) can be used to scan a system and determine if there are updates or patches that apply to specific security alerts that are missing from the system.

Network-based scanning can provide very useful information during incident response activities or while performing analysis of an acquired image. Keep in mind, however, that for this type of scanning to be useful when analyzing an acquired image, the image needs to be "booted" into an environment with networking capabilities. Perhaps the most popular network-based scanner is the veritable Nmap scanner (www.Nmap.org). Besides simple port scanning, Nmap is capable of performing host operating systems (OS) and service identification scans, and with the advent of the Zenmap GUI, Nmap also has the ability to perform a modicum of network topology mapping.

---

### Tools & Traps …

### Tools Supporting Nmap

A number of freely available tools will help you in parsing through the results of Nmap scans. One such tool that may be particularly useful for large-scale scans is fe3d (http://projects.icapsid.net/fe3d/), a data visualization tool that you can use to display the output of an Nmap scan in a graphical format. In addition, several Perl modules are designed specifically for working with Nmap, including Nmap::Scanner, Nmap::Parser, and Nmap::Parser::XML. These last two modules allow you to parse through the output of an Nmap scan, organizing it and performing data reduction (i.e., searching for specific systems or services, etc.), as necessary.

---

Scanning a system most often goes beyond simply scanning for open ports and identifying the host OS and any available services. Vulnerability scanning, for example, can be a useful part of your analysis and take that analysis a step further. Some excellent tools to use for this purpose are Nessus (www.nessus.org/nessus/) and Sara (www-arc.com/sara/), with Nessus being the more popular and well known of the two. Both tools are listed within the top 100 network security tools (http://sectools.org/), along with several other application scanners.

## Packet Capture and Analysis

Another incident response activity that you may encounter is capturing and analyzing network traffic captures. Regardless of whether you capture network traffic yourself, work with on-site IT staff to ensure that network traffic is captured, or receive network traffic captures as data from someone else, you may be faced with the opportunity to capture and analyze network traffic.

Two popular network packet capture and analysis tools for Windows are Wireshark (www.wireshark.org) and NetworkMiner (http://sourceforge.net/projects/networkminer/). Both tools are freely available and extremely valuable to the responder's toolkit.

At the time of this writing, Wireshark Version 1.0.3 was available for the Windows platform. Wireshark will not only allow you to capture network traffic (based on the network interface you choose) but also allow you to analyze network traffic captures. Figure 9.5 illustrates an excerpt of the GUI for Wireshark.

**Figure 9.5** Excerpt of Wireshark v1.0.3 GUI

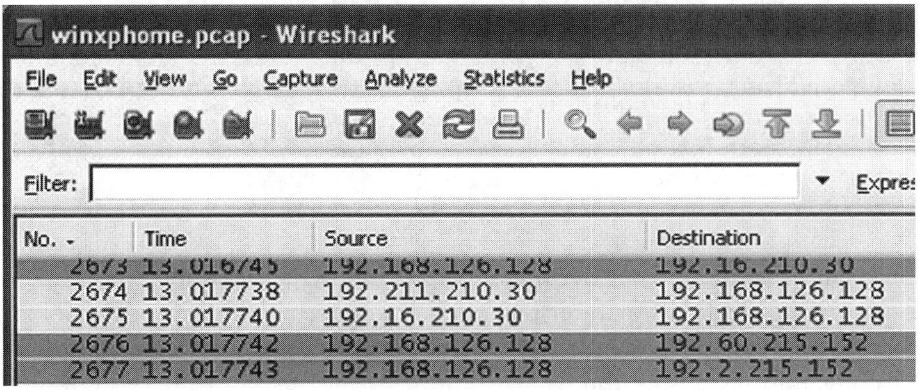

One of the capabilities of Wireshark that I have found to be extremely useful is its ability to completely reassemble TCP streams. To do this, with a network capture loaded into Wireshark, click **Analyze** in the menu bar and choose **Follow TCP Stream** from the drop-down menu. Wireshark will follow the stream and completely reassemble the contents of the TCP communications. This can be very useful in isolating a single communication, as well as in reconstructing a conversation. For example, you can reconstruct Web pages seen by a user, emails, botnet command-and-control communications, or unencrypted instant messaging exchanges. Wireshark provides the capability to do similar analysis with UDP and SSL packets.

## Tools & Traps …

### Network Traffic Captures

While we're discussing network traffic captures, I'll mention here where these captures fit into the overall incident response picture. Many incidents will involve a network component of some kind—a system gets infected by something downloaded from the Internet and then the infection spreads to other systems on the network, an intruder gains access to a system and controls it, or a bot gets onto a system and reaches out to a command-and-control server to await commands. Regardless of the type of incident, many incidents will involve a network component to some degree. That's where network traffic captures can be extremely valuable sources of data. First, you will find information about the packets themselves, including source and destination IP addresses and ports. This information allows you to identify (1) the hosts

**Continued**

> involved (based on the IP address) and (2) which programs may be involved, if you are able to correlate the port information with volatile data (output of tcpvcon.exe, netstat.exe, or data parsed from a memory dump) that was collected from at least one of the hosts involved. Second, information within the packets often reassembled from the TCP "conversations" can show a great deal about what data was exchanged. This is valuable information should the question of data exfiltration (i.e., what data was taken off of a system) arise.

Wireshark also includes a Statistics menu bar option, which provides you with some tools to help you narrow your focus or filter through a vast amount of data to find that literal needle in a haystack. You can look at overall statistics of the packet capture, a detailed listing of network conversations within the packet capture, or just get a listing of endpoints. All of this can be very useful in helping you dig through kilobytes or even megabytes of data.

Sometimes a GUI may be a bit more than you're interested in working with, and a CLI tool may be more preferable. If that's the case, Wireshark ships with several CLI tools, including tshark, tcpdump, and dumpcap. According to the information available on the Wireshark Web site, like any tool, each of these has its strengths and weaknesses. Although the CLI tools are great for loading onto remote systems and launching to capture network traffic from an alternate location within the network, tcpdump by default will only capture the first 68 bytes of a packet, truncating the information. Another CLI tool is windump (www.winpcap.org/windump/), which not only captures network traffic in a manner similar to tshark and dumpcap but also can be used with the appropriate drivers to capture network traffic via wireless access points.

NetworkMiner Version 0.85 (beta) is available for Windows. NetworkMiner is described on the Sourceforge project Web site as "a Network Forensic Analysis Tool (NFAT) for Windows that can detect the OS, hostname and open ports of network hosts through packet sniffing or by parsing a PCAP file." In addition, "NetworkMiner can also extract transmitted files from network traffic." These capabilities make NetworkMiner extremely valuable to an incident responder. As illustrated in Figure 9.6, NetworkMiner's GUI has a number of tabs for displaying automatically parsed information from within network packet captures, including files, user credentials, images, etc.

**Figure 9.6** Excerpt of NetworkMiner 0.85 (Beta) UI

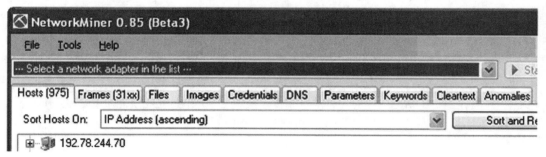

There is a tool available for Linux systems called tcpxtract (http://tcpxtract.sourceforge. net/; by Nick Harbour) that is a file carving utility intended for network traffic captures. Tcpxtract allows you to scan through a network traffic capture looking for files based on a library of file signatures. Although tcpxtract is not available for Windows systems, NetworkMiner provides similar functionality.

The screenshot from the NetworkMiner project page on Sourceforge illustrates the tool's capability to identify the host OS by analyzing the captured packets. NetworkMiner uses functionality derived from p0f (http://lcamtuf.coredump.cx/p0f.shtml) to determine the host OS passively from a network packet capture rather than by actively scanning the system (Nmap). Figure 9.7 illustrates NetworkMiner's ability to identify the OS of a host from a packet capture provided as part of one of Lance Mueller's forensic practical exercises.

**Figure 9.7** Excerpt from NetworkMiner Showing Host OS Identification

Yet another graphical tool for capturing and analyzing network traffic is PacketMon (www.analogx.com/contents/download/network/pmon.htm). PacketMon did not appear to have been updated at the time of this writing, nor does it appear to be as feature rich as Wireshark or NetworkMiner, but it is a useful tool to get you started down the road to analyzing network traffic captures.

A command-line tool (for those who enjoy that sort of thing) that may be helpful with network traffic analysis is ngrep (http://ngrep.sourceforge.net/download.html), a version of the GNU grep utility applied to the network layer allowing you to use extended regular or hexadecimal expressions to search for patterns within a network traffic capture.

All four of these tools allow you to access network traffic captures; the first three are GUIs that allow you to capture network traffic, in addition to parsing and analyzing it. These tools allow you to not only capture the network traffic but also work with network traffic captures provided by another source. This means that if you're responding to an incident and on-site staff or first responders have already captured network traffic, you can use these tools to analyze that data, provided that the capture is in an acceptable format. Most tools readily provide access to tcpdump format captures, which, much like dd format for image acquisition, can be considered a de facto standard for network traffic captures.

## TIP

In fall 2008, NetWitness released its Investigator product available for free at http://download.netwitness.com/download.php?src=DIRECT. Investigator allows an analyst to quickly import a .pcap file containing a network traffic capture or simply to capture the network traffic through the application. Investigator is described as an "interactive threat analysis application of the NetWitness NextGen product suite," allowing the analyst to perform "free-form contextual analysis of raw network data." This is an extremely powerful tool for the analyst, but be sure to read the end user license agreement carefully before downloading and using the tool.

## Tools & Traps …

### Snort

One freeware tool that is often overlooked for use in forensic analysis of network traffic captures is Snort (www.snort.org). This application is widely known as a freely available intrusion detection system (IDS). When I first became familiar with Snort many years ago, it was a straight IDS, and in the ensuing years, there has been a great deal of development effort put into the tool that has resulted in it also being referred to as an intrusion prevention system. One of the capabilities of Snort is to not only work by listening on a network interface (placed in promiscuous mode) capturing and filtering traffic from a live network but also work equally well when using just network traffic capture files. By directing Snort to read the network traffic from the .pcap file and process the captured network traffic through the rule-sets, you've achieved a capability similar to using ngrep with a prepackaged set of filters, some of which are much more complex than a regular expression. This capability can provide a great deal of data reduction. Consider an instance in which there is a network worm proliferating within a network infrastructure. Network traffic captures can be used to determine which systems are communicating on the network, and in large networks there can be a great deal of "normal" network communications that can easily overwhelm the analyst. Using Snort (and assuming that there is a signature for the worm's network communications), you can quickly sort the needle from the haystack, performing a great deal of data reduction with a level of granularity that exceeds that of other tools.

# Search Utilities

Whenever I talk to fellow analysts about core capabilities of forensic analysis and applications that support such activity, one of the primary capabilities I hear as a requirement for any such application is the ability to run searches, to include keyword searches and grep–style searches using regular expressions. Searches are generally used as a data reduction technique; using keywords or regular expressions, an analyst can comb through megabytes or even gigabytes of data, looking for items (files, log file entries, etc.) that are specific to his analysis goals.

## Tools & Traps …

### Searching the Registry

Searching most files on Windows systems for ASCII- or Unicode-formatted data is generally a straightforward process. However, Registry hive files can pose some interesting issues. For instance, you as an analyst need to pay very close attention to paths within the Registry. The path "SessionManager" is very different from "Session Manager". Similarly, if a key or value is in the path that includes "Windows NT", do not make the mistake of looking for "WindowsNT". As with most searches, spelling is very important. Aside from that, however, not all information is maintained in the Registry in a tidy ASCII or Unicode format. Some information is encoded in a DWORD (4 byte) value, and the value must be mapped to a key to be interpreted. In some cases, a DWORD value of '0' may mean that the functionality is enabled, whereas for other values, a value of '1' may mean "enabled." In still other cases, certain functionality will be encoded in a binary value in some manner. So do not be surprised if a keyword or regular expression search does not provide indications of what you're looking for within the hive files. The key to searching the Registry sometimes is to know what you're looking for and to focus the search with a manual process.

The search utilities listed in this section are meant to be utilized against live files, meaning that they can be used in a live response situation, or after you've mounted an acquired image as a live file system. Most commercial forensic analysis applications provide a built-in search capability (several, such as FTK and X-Ways Forensics, also provide indexing capabilities), as well as some preconfigured regular expression search strings.

An excellent source of utilities for searching files and file systems is the GNU utilities for Win32 Web site (http://unxutils.sourceforge.net/). This site provides access to an archive of UNIX-style utilities that provide a great deal of functionality through utilities that many UNIX administrators are familiar with, albeit the fact that these are all native Windows versions of the tools. These tools can be easily added to batch files and scripts for use in performing searches and other data reduction activities.

In addition to these tools, there are several versions of the grep utility available for the Windows platform. In fact, there are two such versions of this utility, both called "grep for Windows"; one is available from Sourceforge (http://gnuwin32.sourceforge.net/packages/grep.htm), and the other is available from InterLog (http://pages.interlog.com/~tcharron/grep.html). Both provide similar functionality.

There are instances in which you may want to search for specific items or terms, such as Social Security numbers (SSNs) or credit card numbers (CCNs). These items fall within the definition of "sensitive data," as defined by such things as California's state law SB-1386 and the Payment Card Industry's (PCI) data security standard (DSS), respectively. As such, there may be times when you will need to search for this kind of data as a specific function of your analysis. Fortunately, there are several tools available that can be used to meet these needs. One such tool is the Cornell Spider (www.cit.cornell.edu/security/tools/), which was designed to scan collections of files (files on a hard drive, Web sites, etc.) for sensitive data such as SSNs and CCNs. Running Spider results in a log file of all files containing sensitive data.

Another useful tool for searching for CCNs is ccsrch (http://sourceforge.net/projects/ccsrch). Ccsrch is a Windows-based command-line utility that can search for contiguous and unencrypted CCNs, as well as track data. Formatting specifications for credit card track 1 and 2 data include the CCN or primary account number (PAN) as contiguous data; that is, a sequence of numbers with no breaks, spaces, or dashes. Ccsrch results include the file name as well as the number found, send to standard output (STDOUT), which allows the results to be easily redirected to a file.

The following are useful resources for assisting you in your searches:

- Regular expression reference (www.regular-expressions.info/)

- Credit card number formats (http://en.wikipedia.org/wiki/Credit_card_number)

- Regular expressions for credit card numbers (www.regular-expressions.info/creditcard.html)

## Tools & Traps ...

### Searching for Sensitive Data

When searching for sensitive data of any kind, you need to ensure that you fully understand the nature and format of that data, as well as what the results of your search really mean. Specifically, SSNs and CCNs pose some interesting challenges with regard to formatting. Most analysts recognize the formats of these numbers, but we need to ensure that 16-digit CCN searches (for example) include searches that meet the necessary criteria not only for a CCN (i.e., length, starting digits, and the Luhn formula/Modulus-10 check) but also for a straight sequence of numbers with no breaks, as well as sequences of numbers with either spaces or dashes in the appropriate locations within the sequence.

Another issue of searching for sensitive data is testing your tools and determining what formats of the data they search for. Some tools may search only for contiguous sequences of numbers (as with CCNs or SSNs), whereas others may include searching for those numbers formatted with spaces or dashes.

# Summary

The cornerstone to an examination is not the tool you're using; it's your methodology. A good methodology is independent of the tool used, whether it be a commercial forensic analysis suite, a freeware open-source tool, or a custom-crafted Perl script. The keys are to know what questions you need to answer, where to go to get your data, and then how to correctly extract and interpret that data in a report. Keeping that and your core principles in mind will lead you to reach for the right tool, whether it is to extract the data for analysis or to corroborate other findings.

# Solutions Fast Track

## Documenting Your Analysis

☑ Documentation is an extremely important part of any examination. Documentation should be clear, concise, and thorough enough to allow for later replication and verification, particularly by another analyst.

☑ Many IT folks and responders must take the data or "evidence" they acquire to court and must be concerned with the standards that need to be met in order to do so. The key differentiator between running around with a CD full of tools and taking your data to court is the documentation you maintain: Do you have a documented process, and did you document your actions to the point that they are understandable and repeatable?

## Tools

☑ A number of free or low-cost tools are available that can more than adequately replace or even extend the functionality inherent to many of the commercial application bundles. With some knowledge and forethought, you can augment, replace, or even surpass what's available in those applications.

☑ As with other aspects of incident response and computer forensics, the various available commercial applications have their strengths and weaknesses. There are times when it is important to use a commercial application for data analysis and presentation. However, there may also be times when a freely available tool provides a greater degree of depth or visibility into the data and provides answers much faster.

# Frequently Asked Questions

**Q:** I need to perform analysis of the data I've collected; what tools do I use?

**A:** As with everything else, "it depends." Seriously. Before deciding which tool to use, you need to take a close look at and document the goals of your analysis because that's where everything starts and ends for an examination. Are you looking for illicit images? Are you concerned about who (i.e., which user account) may have downloaded, accessed, or viewed those images? Do you have several megabytes or even gigabytes of IIS logs and you're interested in determining whether or not a SQL injection attack occurred? There is no one tool that fits every situation, and in many cases, the tool used depends on the personal preference of the analyst; I've performed analysis on log files using Perl, whereas others have preferred to use Microsoft's Log Parser.

**Q:** How is a network traffic capture useful to an examination?

**A:** The network traffic capture contains a good deal of useful information that you can tie to a system (IP address) as well as to a process running on that system by correlating the port information in the packet headers to volatile data (network connections, process, process-to-port mapping) from the system. The contents of the packets may tell you what data or information was transmitted to or from the system.

**Q:** During an examination, I have multiple sources of data that I need to correlate, and I need to maintain the association between them (i.e., network packet captures, network device logs, server logs, and system images). What's the best way to do this?

**A:** At this point, documentation. I am not aware of any complete analysis suites that allow you to pull in, analyze, and correlate multiple sources of data, aside from PyFlag.

# Index